Oracle Database 12c Security

Scott Gaetjen
David Knox
William Maroulis

Mc
Graw
Hill
Education

New York   Chicago   San Francisco
Athens   London   Madrid   Mexico City
Milan   New Delhi   Singapore   Sydney   Toronto

Cataloging-in-Publication Data is on file with the Library of Congress

Oracle Database 12c Security

1234567890   DOC DOC   10987654

ISBN   978-0-07-182428-6
MHID   0-07-182428-6

Sponsoring Editor	**Copy Editor**	**Composition**
Paul Carlstroem	Lisa Theobald	Cenveo Publisher Services
Editorial Supervisor	**Proofreader**	**Illustration**
Patty Mon	Paul Tyler	Cenveo Publisher Services
Project Manager	**Indexer**	**Art Director, Cover**
Anubhooti Saxena,	Ted Laux	Jeff Weeks
Cenveo® Publisher Services	**Production Supervisor**	
Acquisitions Coordinator	Jean Bodeaux	
Amanda Russell		

About the Author

Scott Gaetjen is a Senior Technical Director for Oracle's National Security Group. He conducts research and design on new security solutions, leveraging his 20-plus years of experience with Oracle-based technologies to provide advanced information processing and security capabilities to Oracle customers. He has served as the technical lead and mentor on many projects for customers in the defense, finance, healthcare, intelligence, and telecommunications industries. In the process of helping these customers meet their organizational objectives, he has developed a keen technical understanding of operating system security, Oracle database security, J2EE application security, and identity management. He is the co-inventor of a handful of patents that led to the development of the Oracle Database Vault product. He co-authored the book *Applied Oracle Security* (Oracle Press, 2010). Scott holds a bachelor's degree in mathematics from James Madison University and a master's degree in computer systems management from the University of Maryland University College.

David Knox is recognizable as one of the top Oracle security experts working today. He regularly speaks on computer security and Oracle Database Security at conferences around the world. He is currently serving as Technology Vice President in Oracle's National Security Group.

David has authored several publications including *Effective Oracle Database 10g Security by Design* (Oracle Press, 2004) and was lead author for *Applied Oracle Security* (Oracle Press, 2009). His other published works include security contributions to *Expert One on One Oracle*, by Thomas Kyte (Wrox Press, 2001) and *Mastering Oracle PL/SQL: Practical Solutions* (Apress, 2003). David earned a bachelor's degree in computer science from the University of Maryland and a master's degree in computer science from Johns Hopkins University.

William Maroulis is a Senior Technical Director with Oracle's National Security Group. William has more than 20 years of IT experience, working mostly with Oracle-related products, and more than 8 years of experience teaching Oracle at the university level. He consults on security- and performance-related issues, including issues regarding hardware, operating systems, applications, and databases. William has led several efforts obtaining security-related approval to operate (ATO). He has a thorough technical and security understanding of software development, Oracle Database security products, and protecting operating systems. William earned a bachelor of science degree in computer science from the North Carolina State University and a masters of software engineering from the University of Maryland University College. William also holds current CISSP and GREM certifications.

Contents

PART I
Essential Database Security

PART II
Advanced Database Security

PART III
Security and Auditing for the Cloud

Foreword

When I first started in security many moons ago at Oracle, it was like being the Maytag repairman in those old TV commercials, who was constantly lonely because nobody ever called him. Security used to be something only a few customers—like those in the defense department—asked about. Now, cybersecurity is not merely "front and center" but front page news. Almost every business has an IT backbone and "security critical assets": data that is stored, retained, and analyzed by organizations because it is central to their mission.

Fortunately, there are not merely a lot of (technical term follows) way cool security technologies in the Oracle database that customers can use for digital defense, but there are lots of excellent security *kahunas*—like Scott Gaetjen, Bill Maroulis, and David Knox—who have implemented security successfully for many, many customers over more projects than they can count. Who better to provide DIY instructions on making your data heavily armored, if not bulletproof? As Benjamin Franklin said, "Either write something worth reading or do something worth writing." These guys have done both. So, prepare to be amazed at the ways you can secure your data in Oracle, and read on.

—Mary Ann Davidson
Chief Security Officer, Oracle Corporation

Acknowledgments

The authors would like to acknowledge both Paul Carlstroem and Amanda Russell for their patience and support. We could not have completed this book without you both!

We would also like to acknowledge the tremendous efforts of the Oracle Database Security Development group, led by Vipin Samar. This team has spent many years designing and developing a collection of advanced security features and options that simply do not exist in any other database available on the market.

We would also like to recognize the core Oracle Database Development group for collaborating as a (very large) team to bring Oracle Database 12c to the market.

Finally, we want to acknowledge both the Oracle Enterprise Manager Development and the Oracle Fusion Middleware Development groups for creating a complete security stack for the enterprise to support the effective use of Oracle Database 12c.

Bill, thank you for your sage advice and support, as well as your constant efforts to break bad software and build great software. Dave, I am also impressed by your ability to make security and technology accessible and understandable to everyone you meet. To Patrick Sack, thank you for constantly challenging me to excel. To the entire Oracle National Security Group team, thank you for all of your daily efforts to help secure our borders.

—Scott Gaetjen

Above all else, this book is the result of the enormous efforts of Bill and Scott. Their dedication to this book and perseverance is why this book exists, and for that, I am grateful and privileged to be a part of it. I'd like to thank Pat Sack for continuing to be a passionate and brilliant database security expert and providing thoughts and insights into this field over many years.

—David Knox

To David—thanks for the opportunity. To Scott—thanks for all of the help and support. To Pat Sack—thanks for continuing to push the envelope on security technology and for finding new and interesting technical challenges for us to tackle.

—William Maroulis

Introduction

Computer security is a vast and complex subject. With attacks on information systems continuing to grow in number and sophistication, operating in a secure information environment can be overwhelming. The good news is that there are pragmatic approaches to implementing security that will allow you to move forward with an effective security plan.

In this book, you'll learn how to apply Oracle Database 12c security features and options to your business problems, and you'll find a wealth of practical examples. You can also retrieve online all the scripts used in this book (see the section, "Retrieving the Examples," a bit later, for details).

With this book, you will learn about the following topics and technologies:

- The latest Oracle Database 12c security features
- The best ways to apply security in today's ever-changing environment
- Essential elements of user security
- The secure way to create connection pools and maintain user identity to the database
- Best practices for creating enterprise users and centralized privilege management
- Foundational elements for a secure database using discretionary access control (DAC)
- Many examples covering fundamental elements of database application security
- In-depth coverage of Oracle Real Application Security (RAS)
- Information on Oracle Virtual Private Database (VPD) for both row- and column-level access control
- Essential elements of sensitive data control using Data Redaction and Transparent Sensitive Data Protection (TSDP)

- Oracle Label Security (OLS)
- Oracle Database Vault (DBV)
- Oracle Transparent Data Encryption (TDE)
- Oracle Unified Auditing (OUA) and Oracle Traditional Auditing for accountability
- Security management for multitenancy
- Security monitoring for cybersecurity

Part I: Essential Database Security

Part I covers the basics of Oracle Database 12c security. We lay the foundation by defining security terminology and introduce a pragmatic approach to applying best practices to secure your database systems.

Chapter 1: Security for Today's World

This chapter establishes the security groundwork for the rest of the book. We cover the basic principles, definitions, and topics concerning computer security. We also cover the basic principles used throughout the rest of the book.

Chapter 2: Essential Elements of User Security

We review the first steps in the security process and possibly the most important decision you will make regarding your database security: user database account mapping. We say "most important" because the decisions you make here will allow or possibly disallow other security controls to be implemented in an effective manner. You will be deciding how to connect users to the databases in a secure manner so that users can fulfill their duties or interact with the data.

Chapter 3: Connection Pools and Enterprise Users

We find that the most universal client interface to enterprise business applications is an Internet browser or, more generally, as in the case with Web Services and REST APIs, an HTTP client. The browser uses HTTP to connect end users to applications rather than directly to databases. This has important implications for application security, because the connection from the application to the database does not usually include the end user's identity. This chapter demonstrates ways to maintain end user identity from the end user to the backend database.

Chapter 4: Foundational Elements for a Secure Database

We begin by reviewing the terms *access control*, *authorizations*, and *privileges*. You find these terms littered throughout security policies, and although they are often used interchangeably, they are, in fact, different in meaning. We cover the basics of users, roles, and privileges. How best to use and administer these security primitives, known as discretionary access control, is vital to having a robust and secure database system.

Chapter 5: Foundational Elements of Database Application Security

In this chapter, we discuss the fundamentals of database application security. It is common to find application security built into and throughout different architecture layers of an enterprise system. We cover application context, views, and PL/SQL stored procedures to implement security requirements using Oracle's intrinsic security capabilities.

We also cover entitlement analytics, which will give you a perspective of which privileges are being used by whom and, equally important, how the user acquired the privilege. We discuss how to share application code securely among multitenant databases.

Chapter 6: Real Application Security

We examine a new and powerful feature in Oracle Database 12c called *Oracle Real Application Security* (RAS). Oracle RAS provides a comprehensive and declarative security model that can be shared among enterprise applications. It provides the performance you expect for enterprise applications.

Part II: Advanced Database Security

Part II addresses the advanced security features and options that Oracle Database 12c offers.

Chapter 7: Controlled Data Access with Virtual Private Database

In this chapter, we cover Oracle Virtual Private Database (VPD), a database security feature that is implemented using Oracle's row-level security (RLS) package, DBMS_RLS. The feature restricts rows as well as individual columns of data from objects accessible via SQL SELECT or DML statements. We also discuss VPD performance, debugging, and exemptions.

Chapter 8: Essential Elements of Sensitive Data Control

We cover a new feature of the Oracle Database 12c called data redaction (DR). You can now implement full or partial redaction on result sets that are generated from database queries using the DR technology. DR is available as a feature of the Oracle Advanced Security Option (ASO) and has been back-ported to the 11gR2 version of Oracle Database.

Oracle Database 12c also includes a new feature called Transparent Sensitive Data Protection (TSDP) that allows you to discover sensitive data in your databases, define categories of sensitive information types, and define policies that will automatically apply DR or VPD policies. The Quality Management Data Discovery (QMDD) feature of Oracle Enterprise Manager Cloud Control (OEMCC) will analyze databases to detect sensitive information that can help you decide whether other policies are needed for access control, encryption, and auditing.

Chapter 9: Access Controls with Oracle Label Security

This chapter thoroughly covers Oracle Label Security (OLS), which controls row-level access to data in a protected table. The foundation of OLS is Virtual Private Database (VPD), implemented using the row-level security package DBMS_RLS. We demonstrate how to install, enable, and configure OLS in a standalone as well as multitenant database.

Chapter 10: Oracle Database Vault: Securing for the Compliance Regulations, Cybersecurity, and Insider Threats

In this chapter we cover Oracle Database Vault (DBV), which was introduced in 2005 to address separation of duties and cybersecurity challenges. DBV includes additional layers of security, which resulted in a fundamental change in how security is enforced. Unlike many features of the database, DBV radically changes what you do as a DBA and how you do it.

We discuss the reasons why DBV came into existence. Your understanding of the design and intent of a product is important to having a complete understanding of why you should use it, when you should use it, and how you should use it.

Chapter 11: Oracle Transparent Data Encryption: Securing for the Compliance Regulations, Cybersecurity, and Insider Threats

In this chapter, we cover Transparent Data Encryption (TDE), a transparent way to encrypt data in a database. The encryption is transparent because it occurs below the Structured Query Language (SQL) layer. The database engine automatically encrypts and decrypts data as it reads and writes it from the file system using encryption keys you can manage with key management tools provided with TDE. Here we explore how to use TDE and discuss some of the advantages of using it.

Part III: Security and Auditing for the Cloud

Part III covers security and auditing for the cloud. The term "cloud" has multiple meanings, depending on whom you ask—in the context of this book, we are referring to a multitenant consolidation model that requires each tenant to be confined to its resources and data.

Chapter 12: Audit for Accountability

In this chapter, you will see why auditing is not only possible, but also invaluable in the modern IT era, where meeting compliance regulations and defending cybersecurity attacks are at the forefront of corporate agendas. We will explore manual ways to audit and look at traditional auditing, fine-grained auditing, and the new Oracle unified audit trail technology available in Oracle Database 12c.

Chapter 13: An Applied Approach to Multitenancy and Cloud Security

This chapter pulls together all of the concepts and approaches from the book. We give you a pragmatic approach to identifying, designing, and implementing database security and monitoring for your enterprise database systems in a multitenant architecture. This approach can also be used for a standalone database system storing your company's important information.

Intended Audience

This book is suitable for the following readers:

- Security practitioners who need a pragmatic approach to Oracle Database security
- Database administrators who need in-depth knowledge of Oracle Database 12c security features and options
- Security architects who need a practical understanding of how to connect Oracle security features into an overall enterprise solution
- Technical managers or consultants who need step-by-step examples of how to apply Oracle Database 12c security features

Retrieving the Examples

All the SQL scripts and programs used in this book can be downloaded from the Oracle Press web site at http://community.oraclepressbooks.com. The files are contained in a Zip file. Once you've downloaded the Zip file, you need to extract its contents. This will create a directory named security_book that contains examples relevant to each chapter.

PART
I

Essential Database Security

CHAPTER
1

Security for Today's World

Computer security is a vast and complex subject. With attacks on information systems continuing to grow in number and sophistication, ensuring that your database system is operating in a secure information environment can be an overwhelming task. The good news is there are pragmatic approaches to implementing security that will allow you to move forward with an effective security plan.

This book brings a practical approach to Oracle Database security. We have gathered the most effective techniques from our collective experiences in designing, implementing, and certifying secure database systems. In this book, we discuss what we believe are the most relevant technologies, designs, and practices for securing the Oracle Database. We also include new security technologies developed for Oracle Database 12*c*.

Our objective is to cover the most relevant pieces and parts with enough depth to convey how the technologies can be used. This book is not intended to be a comprehensive discussion on every possible aspect of every possible security technology available. Instead, we hope you will find it to be concise, direct, and practical with respect to database security.

The Security Landscape

Oracle Database 12*c* offers numerous security technologies. To implement database security effectively, you need to apply the security technologies in a logical manner in accordance with an approach that allows you to identify your critical data assets, understand the risks and vulnerabilities to those assets, and then mitigate the risks to those assets. To be effective in creating a secure environment, you must understand what you need to secure and why. Your job is to ensure that the security measures you plan to enact accomplish the goals you want them to achieve. If you miss these goals, you may have underutilized your investments and may have inadvertently left your systems or databases vulnerable.

To create an effective security plan, you must focus on exactly *why* you are doing *what* you are doing. To increase a system's security posture, you can do a number of things, but your best success will occur when you think holistically about the entire technology landscape. In an effective security environment, components work together as a system. Although this book focuses on what you can do inside the Oracle Database, you'll also find it important to think about security from an overall system perspective versus an individual component perspective.

Before we get too far in discussing the security approach, you should consider the various elements that will impact your design.

Base Assumptions

Before you start rationalizing what to do first and how to do it, you need to establish some base assumptions about your environment. Too often, money, time, and effort are wasted securing parts of the system that pose low risk to or that have little impact on the overall security posture, while the high risk and high impact areas are often overlooked. This isn't always done out of ignorance as much out of comfort—that is, you might be more comfortable setting up Secure Sockets Layer (SSL) from the browser to the application server than protecting the Oracle Database from an over-privileged administrator account.

Following are general guidelines that you should employ to form a baseline perspective when considering how to approach database security.

Assume Compromise

The IT Security team generally spends most of its time on network and infrastructure security. Intrusion detection systems, firewalls, network flow analysis, and various other tools and detection mechanisms are dedicated to ensuring that bad things stay outside of the IT systems.

Infrastructure security is a good thing; however, assuming that nothing bad will ever get inside your network/system is probably the worst baseline mistake you can make. Instead, start with the assumption that malicious people can penetrate your networks and get to your databases. This should force you to be more rigorous in deciding what you need to do to ensure that your information is protected.

It's About the Data

There's an old saying that suggests that the reason people rob banks is because that is where the money is kept. Databases often hold much of your company's digital currency, proprietary financial information, and intellectual property. Making database security a priority is the prudent action.

You should assume that your network and perimeter security cannot hold off 100 percent of the bad things attempting to enter your network, and that when bad things enter your network, they will come looking for your databases. This perspective will assist you in justifying the time, money, and effort spent securing the database systems to your organization's executive management team.

The Insider Threat Is Always Present

Another problem with relying on perimeter security is that it does nothing to protect the system from authorized users who have decided to do something nefarious. Insider threats are serious problems. These threats include everything from a privileged administrator accessing a customer's sensitive data without cause to an admin purposefully not patching a system with a known vulnerability.

Fortunately, we have already assumed that our systems are vulnerable, and, therefore, the actions we take to fortify them will also protect them against insider threats.

Database Security Today

Database security has changed radically over the years. In some ways, it has outpaced the growth of the general security market. The creation of record- or column-level access controls via transparent query modifications—aka *virtual private database*—and the ability to perform conditional auditing—aka *fine-grained auditing*—are two examples of these changes. However, there is another side to this discussion: we have to recognize that many of the security design patterns are focused on the security needs of about 15 years ago. The good news is that Oracle Database 12c has incorporated significant advances in allowing these outdated architectures to be retired. We'll articulate these advances in the following sections.

To achieve the security designs required for today's environment, you must understand not only how things work but why they work. The intent of a product or technology is the first clue in understanding its usefulness and applicability to your systems. This book applies security technologies to the problems and architectures used today. Before we get into that, though, you need to understand how security technology has evolved.

Evolving Security Technologies

Simple technology models have always been used to explain complex systems, and a model can be used to explain security as well. There are many useful ways to think about the elements and dimensions of security. Ensuring the integrity of the data and the system is one dimension. Ensuring the availability of the system is another dimension. Ensuring the confidentiality of the data stored is yet another. For the majority of this book, we found it helpful to frame the security discussion around users interacting with the database. In this case, security can be described as an understanding of *who* gets access to *what*, from *where*, *when*, and *how*. Physical security and digital security are largely focused on the ability to control all aspects of people interacting with objects. With this in mind, consider how security has evolved as technology has matured.

The Evolving Four A's: Authentication, Authorizations, Access, and Auditing

It's helpful to think about security as a sequential set of things we need to do. We first need to figure out *who* is trying to perform *what* action. We present an identity, and we next want to verify that the identity presented is *authentic*. Authentication is the technique used to prove a user is who he says he is. Passwords are the most popular technique but are considered weak authentication, because they can be easily discovered. Strong authentication techniques such as *multi-factor authentication* are essential in today's environment, especially for critical data, systems, and users.

Authentication is an essential first step to security, but it is only the first step. It is not a best practice to think that simply employing strong authentication gives you strong security. You also need to consider separation of duties, a least privileged model, auditing, and monitoring. We will explain each of these topics in later chapters.

Authorization enforcement determines whether the system should allow or prevent users from performing specific actions or accessing specific data. In essence, the authorizations are telling you *who* gets access to *what*. After authentication establishes that the system can trust who is connected to the system, in the authorization stage, you have to map that user to a specific set of actions he or she can perform in the system.

Authorizations do not actually control who gets access to what. Database security controls (such as Oracle Label Security [OLS], Oracle Database Vault [DBV], and so on) enforce access between user and data. The enforcement controls are supposed to align with the authorizations. It is a common misunderstanding among IT professionals, however, to assume that authorizations and the controls that ensure the enforcement of the authorizations are the same, but this is not the case. In fact, it is possible to be authorized to do something and yet be prevented from doing it. In such a case, we might attribute this to a bug or a procedural error. It is also possible not to be authorized to do something, yet be able to do it, because either improper controls are in place or no controls are in place.

Finally, we want to capture the entire sequence of *who* can do *what* so we can prove, validate, and test that our security enforcements are all functioning as desired. Auditing captures action successes and failures for accountability purposes. Auditing should not be overlooked, because most systems are not authorized to operate without an extensive auditing and monitoring capability built in.

Let's translate the preceding concepts into how Oracle's technology has evolved over time. In the early years, much of Oracle's security was based on the concept of a database user, who logs in directly to the database using a dedicated account. Many IT professionals consider a user and a schema as one in the same, but this misunderstanding poses a few problems. Access controls and auditing in the Oracle database are optimized around the notion of users connecting directly to database schemas. The problem is, however, that building an application today is different from what it was when many of the security design patterns were developed.

Although appropriate at the time, direct database logins have given way to connection pools or lightweight sessions being used by middle-tier applications running on application servers. In this new pattern, it is typical for the application to log in to an application account, which breaks the direct association of an end user to a database user.

Proxy Authentication and Connection Pools for Fast DB Connections with Security

Oracle adopted the proxy authentication security pattern several years ago to avoid losing the end user's identity in the database. As you will read in later chapters, *proxy authentication* and more recently Real Application Security (RAS) allow applications to use connection pools and pre-create database connections. This solves the performance challenge of quickly connecting users to a database while maintaining the ability to support user-based access control and an accurate audit trail of the end user's actions.

An administration problem still exists, however, because proxy authentication still requires an end user to have a database account. Proxy authentication did not address user administration and management issues, which was addressed by Enterprise User Security (EUS). Proxy authentication supported that architecture as well. Manageability is an important principle in achieving an effective security implementation.

Enterprise User Security Addresses Manageability

To adapt the technology to meet the challenges of managing large-scale user populations, Oracle created the *enterprise user architecture*. In this architecture, the end users (or application users) are managed in a central Lightweight Directory Access Protocol (LDAP) repository. The directory includes an entry for each user, and each directory user maps to a shared database schema. Also included in the user's directory entry are *role mappings*, which provide for centralized administration of authorizations.

Enterprise User Security (EUS) provides a way to centralize end user management, which helps to reduce errors made during account creation and authorization. Centralization is a remedy for many manageability challenges that make EUS a very useful architecture.

Security Cannot Work with Anonymity

If security starts with understanding who gets access to what, then we need to ensure that the *who* makes its way to the enforcement points, or else the enforcement points will not be able to enforce security specific to the *who*. We call the process of maintaining the end user's identity from the end user's mobile or wired web browser to the database *identity preservation*. In today's multitier environments, it is common for the actual end user identity to be lost in the application tier. However, identity preservation is important for authorizations, access control, and auditing.

The most common security misstep is an assumption that database security and auditing work at the schema level—that is, the identity of the end user is the schema name. Security is sometimes implemented with a reliance on the Oracle function **USER**, as in the following query:

```
SH@db12cr[sales]> SELECT user,
  2      SYS_CONTEXT('USERENV','CLIENT_IDENTIFIER') ACTUAL_USER
  3  FROM dual;

USER                    ACTUAL_USER
--------------------    --------------------
SH                      WMAROULIS
```

In reality, "user" SH is the schema name and WMAROULIS is the connected end user. To solve these issues, you must write your own fine-grained security via Virtual Private Database (VPD), OLS, views, triggers, and so forth, which leverages the identity exposed via EUS or proxy authentication. Otherwise, you have no way of applying different security enforcements for users sharing the same database schema.

Another issue concerning identity preservation is that security architectures do not rely on end user identity as the sole mechanism for access enforcement. These security and control mechanisms are based on many factors, of which the user's identity may or may not be the most relevant piece.

Multifactor Identity

Security and access controls for systems are largely based on authorization models that use roles, group memberships, and data attributes such as the end user device type, the network from which the end user connection originates, whether the mobile device has been "jail broken" (the device's limitations have been modified), and so on. This is because the users in many situations are unknown not only to the database, but sometimes even to the application! Therefore, no user entry exists in an application's "users" table, in the Oracle Database USER$ table, and perhaps not even in the LDAP directory. With no user identity, you have no way to differentiate security controls from one user to the next. Without a way to create and provision users ahead of time, identity is meaningless for security enforcement purposes.

To understand this concept better, consider an example that consists of a web services architecture that is federated or that makes many calls as part of a single business transaction. Each of these services may be on a separate server that uses a different database. As such, the ability to execute a distributed transaction requires a way of conveying and preserving what actions the user is authorized to perform to the separated systems. Ideally, this model needs to support an infinite number of users and must be easily adaptable over time. User identities will therefore not be stored locally. Authorization information and aspects about how the information is being accessed or used will be employed to ensure that proper access is controlled. User identities, if properly propagated, may be used only for auditing and accountability reasons.

These highly distributed architectures supporting vast numbers of unknown users are forcing radical changes in architectures and implementations. In addition, another paradigm shift focuses on how security concerns are addressed: What are these concerns? How do you know if your data is secure? What are you protecting and why? You can address all these questions by looking at what motivates the use of security in businesses today.

Security Motivators

Many organizations still view security as a nice-to-have option that might get implemented at the end of a development cycle if time and money are available. Too many applications are focused on delivering the functions of the application, and consideration for creating a security design in the overall architecture simply does not occur. This is unfortunate for several reasons. First, security may not make it into the first version of the application. It is not uncommon to find applications that have no security. Another downside is that adding security after the first version can be more costly than it would be if it were designed from the start and may require that the application be redesigned.

Today, however, many people believe that security is more important than ever for two major reasons. First, there is significant oversight in the form of regulatory compliance. Compliance policies are intended to protect information that was once not considered sensitive but that is now considered highly sensitive. Personally identifiable information (PII) is a prime example of such data. PII is discussed in detail in the following section. The second reason for an increase in the importance of security centers around the negative impacts that a compromise or data breach can have on an organization. A compromise can affect an organization's reputation, the future employability of those considered accountable, financial penalties, monetary loss, and possibly incarceration.

Organizations have tremendous amounts of data that requires proper protection. This data is shared, transmitted, transferred, and analyzed, and each action represents an increased risk of compromise. With compromise comes demise. With corporate brands and public perception influencing stock prices and future viability, security is more important now than ever. Let's explore a little more deeply this sensitive information and consider how we should protect it.

Sensitive Data Categorization

To satisfy a security requirement properly, you must identify what you are protecting, from whom, and why. By understanding the characteristics and use of the data, you can then understand its importance and subsequently derive a protection plan.

Categorizing data helps us dictate how to protect the data. Categories also provide guidance for which database technologies and techniques to use. We define three categories of data:

- Personally identifiable information (PII)
- Protected health information (PHI)
- Proprietary information and intellectual property

Personally Identifiable Information

PII includes any information that can be used to obtain or create a false identity, such as names, addresses, Social Security numbers, and other personal information that can be used for nefarious purposes. The alarming thing about PII is that it is data about regular people—not just special people such as celebrities and politicians; it is data about everyone. Furthermore, this data is used many times a day to perform the most mundane tasks, such as paying bills, registering for a license, applying for a loan, and applying for a job.

There are two main reasons PII is increasing in its sensitivity and importance. The first is simply the basic protection of people's privacy. Many people are reluctant to have their personal information on the Internet for unknown people to access and use for malevolent proposes. This leads to the second reason for PII protections: Identity theft. Identity theft can not only be very costly to an individual in terms of finances, but it can take time to recover from these losses, which can be very debilitating. Organizations are struggling with ways to protect their customers', employees', and partners' sensitive information. Fortunately, there are some best practices for how to protect PII, and these will be discussed in later chapters.

Protected Health Information

PHI is private information that deals with a person's health or medical history. PHI is more formally described and governed in the U.S. Health Insurance Portability and Accountability Act (HIPAA).

PHI pertains to more than healthcare providers (such as hospitals) and healthcare payers (such as health insurance companies). Other organizations also collect PHI information, and have the data scattered throughout their IT systems in employee benefit submissions, paid time off, disability insurance, and so forth.

Both PII and PHI represent a challenge, because the regulatory compliance requires organizations to maintain this information for multiple years. Our challenge is in deciding how to employ the correct amount of security to protect the individuals' privacy without hampering business flows necessary to operate an organization efficiently.

Proprietary Information and Intellectual Property

Safeguarding proprietary information in a growing and global economy is more important today than ever. Trade secrets (such as research initiatives, intellectual property, patents, and so on), business transactions, costing/pricing, mergers, and acquisition strategies are among the top information categories that organizations are struggling to secure.

What makes this information difficult to secure is that large amounts of an organization's information in many forms is distributed to many people. As it flows through different media to different people, it becomes increasingly more difficult to control and thus secure. This category of information is as important as it is large, and thus is a main focus of this book.

Principles

Regardless of the sensitivity of data and the need to protect it, you should adhere to a few principles when considering a solution to your security challenges. These principles will guide you in implementing the correct level of security and are echoed throughout the book. Understanding why they are important is essential to your understanding of the complementary technologies, architectures, and best practices presented herein.

Principles can serve to prove due diligence or, in some cases, negligence. Incorporating the right amount of security is a delicate balance of preserving ease of use, performance, and manageability, while securing what is important. Because these factors often compete with security, it is important that you are able to justify and implement a balanced, prudent, and rational solution. The point is for you to be able to prove that the correct level of security is being implemented in the correct way. Doing so may assist you in preserving company brand, reputation, and viability and also in protecting your reputation and employability.

Layers of Common Security Policies

You probably know that dressing in layers of clothing is a prudent approach to staying warm in a cold climate. Security in layers provides an analogous benefit. It is important to design your system with multiple layers of security wherever possible, so that the removal of one layer by compromise or misconfiguration does not expose the entire system. There is no such thing as being too secure (which should not be confused with an overly cumbersome security implementation).

Security technologies such as Transparent Data Encryption (TDE) can add a layer of security (encryption at rest) and thereby increase the security posture of the system while keeping performance degradation at a minimum. Adding a second layer of security by encrypting network packets to and from the Oracle Database (encryption in motion) increases the security posture of the system even more.

Another security best practice is to apply a security layer as close to the data as possible. This is an optimization technique that allows for the biggest return for the effort. Securing the data in the database adds a layer of security regardless of how a user accesses the data (for example, SQL*Plus on the database server or the web application on a middle-tier application server). This concept of using common, shared security policies is more cost-effective than using different approaches for each application or database access path.

Manageable Security

As we have alluded to, being able to set up, develop, deploy, control, and adapt security is critical to any successful security strategy. You might look at these qualities and think that they are impossible to achieve. However, as you will see in the following chapters, there are ways to move toward effective security management. In fact, common ways for achieving manageable security have already been realized. Centralization of identities and authorizations personifies this security principle. Centralization of security is a major facilitator in managing security efficiently.

Business Congruency

The next principle to achieving security success is aligning it with existing business policies and technology architectures. If the business needs analytical tools to investigate the deep meaning and relationships of its data, then the security needs to align with how those tools function and how the users are accustomed to accessing the data.

An example of this comes from service-based architectures, also known as *service-oriented architectures (SOA)*. Although this book is not about SOA, we simply point out that the essence of SOA lies in its ability to allow anyone to link to any service from anywhere at any time. The security challenge lies in protecting anyone from linking to any service from anywhere at any time. The point here is that SOA exists and will continue to exist, and to work with it securely requires an implementation that is congruent with how the security architecture is employed.

Transparency

It should be commonly accepted that changing end user behavior is more difficult than adapting security technology. A simple way to employ a new security technology is to make it transparent, which ensures a successful implementation that exposes issues in manageability and performance. Transparency helps to eliminate the usability issues often associated with an unsuccessful security implementation. Transparency allows users to continue to access the system without being burdened with enhanced security controls and auditing.

Throughout this book, you will read how many of the technologies have incorporated these principles in their design and implementation. You should apply these concepts to your designs and implementations.

Summary

Threats to computer systems are continually changing, so security technologies must adapt accordingly. New thinking regarding architectural design, risks, and requirements has radically changed the security landscape in a short period of time. Understanding what you are trying to accomplish with an effective security posture is essential to creating a good plan that will be successful.

Common security motivators serve as good reference markers for what people are trying to protect and why. Personally identifiable information, protected health information, intellectual property, and an abundance of government regulations require developers and administrators to think about the pervasiveness of sensitive data and the things they can do to protect this valuable information.

A few guiding principles serve as a practical way to deal with the current security challenges. We addressed layers of security, manageability, and transparency as key areas to an effective security stance. With all technology—especially security—you also need to take a practical approach to design and implementation. Manageability is as much an issue for administrators as security practitioners and therefore must abide by this tenet as well. In this chapter we established a baseline to which the rest of the book can refer and that you can use to simplify the real issues around building and deploying a secure database system.

CHAPTER
2

Essential Elements
of User Security

I n Chapter 1, we reviewed the importance of having an appropriate approach to security. Only after understanding why you are protecting what you are protecting can you develop an effective security plan. We also discussed identity preservation and reviewed how the database technology has evolved over the years to support the basic tenets of security.

In this chapter, we shift our focus to the importance of database accounts and how to perform account management efficiently in Oracle Database 12*c*. Much of what we are about to cover, however, is relevant to all recent supported versions of the database. Oracle Database 12*c* introduces a new database option called *Oracle Multitenant*. This new option provides a new architecture that allows you to create a container database onto which you can then "plug in" other standard Oracle databases. This is important from a security perspective, and consequently we will study the ramifications of the fact that multiple users, accounts, and schemas will be attached to the same shared set of memory and processes, as well as database users and objects.

The multitenant architecture of Oracle Database 12*c* offers many benefits-related cost reductions in hardware, storage, and labor due to the database's ability to consolidate disparate databases into a centralized database environment. The administration and monitoring of the consolidated environment is also much easier compared to administering each database on separate servers or from separate software homes on the same server. Although these benefits are desirable, it does not remove the need to secure each database in the consolidated environment in the same manner and for the same reasons you would secure them if they were separate—that is, the tenets of security by design, defense in depth, separation of duties, and enforcing a least privilege environment still apply.

One might argue that these security tenets are even more applicable and important in a consolidated environment than in a separated environment because of the higher concentration of critical information and assets housed in a single location. Those who desire to steal or destroy these assets have fewer targets to focus on. In this chapter, we will examine how you can be prepared to meet the security requirements for account management of privileged administrators, application schemas, and database end users.

In this chapter, we will review the first steps in the security process and possibly the most important decision you will make regarding your database security: User-Database Account Mapping. We say most important because the decisions you make here will allow or possibly disallow other security controls to be implemented. You will be deciding how to connect users to the databases in a secure manner such that they can fulfill their duties or interact with the data.

To do this effectively, you must understand the types of database accounts and their intended use. In this chapter, we will start with a review of the first steps of connecting users to the database: identification and authentication. We will then outline the high-level security aspects of the types of database accounts that we typically encounter. We will then explore how these account types should be created and managed using the native database support for database accounts.

Understanding Identification and Authentication

Let's expand on the introductory concepts of identification and authentication (I&A) introduced in Chapter 1. To review, the database security flow can be summarized by the following three steps:

1. A user presents an identity to the database.

2. The user proves that he or she is authorized to use the identity presented by providing the password. The password is checked by the database to determine if it is the correct password for the identity presented.

3. Assuming the password is correct, the database assumes the user can be trusted with the identity presented. The database will then determine what privileges and authorizations the user has. Data security is implemented based on the user's privileges and authorizations.

Typically, people spend the majority of their time and security efforts implementing the processes and controls needed in step three. Step one is identification. Step two is authentication. The first two steps are equally important because they form the foundation of security you need for step three authorizations.

Identification Methods

Identification is the process of specifically and distinctly recognizing an individual. Identification is a part of everyday life. You identify yourself at work, on the telephone, through e-mail; you identify yourself so much that you probably don't even realize when you are doing it. Identification comes in many forms: your photo, your fingerprints, your employee number, and, of course, your username all represent you in the identification process.

Today, there are many forms of identification and many ways to identify you. Why you need to identify yourself and what or who you're identifying will help to determine what you use as the identification method. The methods for identification fall into two categories: user-supplied identity and technological identification.

User-Supplied Identification

Asking the user to supply his or her identity is the most prevalent method for identification today. In most computer applications, identification is based on the username. Your bank probably likes to identify you by your account number(s), and your favorite airline has transformed you into a series of alphanumeric characters. All of these names and numbers serve the single purpose of identifying who you are.

In all cases, the user is responsible for providing the correct identifying information. This is important because knowledge of a valid identity provides some security. For example, you can't log in to an application with an identity that does not exist or is unknown to the application. You are unlikely to log on to the database or application if you cannot provide a valid username. For hackers trying to penetrate a system, a good starting point is to obtain a list of valid identities on the system.

Obfuscating the user's name or choosing identifiers that don't indicate the privileges of the person is valuable, too. So, for example, the username "Administrator" indicates high privileges and thus a more valuable attack target for a hacker than does a more neutral name such as "user125." However, designing a security implementation exclusively based on the knowledge of the identifier—for example, a username or account number—is a risky proposition, because it may be relatively easy for someone to guess, predict, or obtain a valid identity from another source.

The benefit to using user-provided identification is that the identifier (such as username) is generally flexible. This allows administrators to create intuitive identifiers that are easy for users to remember. For example, a username may be created based on the person's first initial and last name, such as "jdoe." As discussed in the previous paragraph, the benefit is also the weakness. Identifiers that can be easily guessed or predicted may weaken the overall security. In the Authentication section a bit later in the chapter, you will see how verifying the user's identity provides the ability to maintain the security while simultaneously allowing flexibility in the choice of identifiers.

Oracle Database 12*c* provides support for storing usernames in the local database's native identity store, as we shall discuss later in this chapter. In a later chapter, we will discuss how Oracle Database 12*c* also supports usernames defined external to the database, such as those defined in an organization's enterprise directory server.

Technological Identification

Technology also offers a choice of ways to identify ourselves, including biometrics, computer identities, and digital identities.

Biometrics   *Biometrics* refers to the biological characteristics of people that can be measured to distinguish the differences among them. You use biometrics constantly to identify people. Your brain uses facial recognition when you see familiar people and voice recognition when you answer a phone call from someone you know.

Biometric technologies have come a long ways in recent years. Facial and voice recognition, iris scanners, hand geometry, and fingerprints are among the most popular biometrics used in identifying people.

Biometrics are ideal in many ways. Users cannot forget them, and they can be nearly impossible to guess. Spoofing or guessing another person's biometric is difficult. Theft of the biometric part is also unlikely, but there is a risk associated with having the digital biometric representation stolen. If this occurs, there is a chance that someone could pretend to be someone else by copying and replaying the biometric signature or altering the metadata that indicates whose biometric it is.

Biometrics are unique in that the same biometric can be used for both the identification and the authentication processes. With biometric identification, the biometric information is considered unique and can be used to accurately identify the person presenting the biometric. This differs from user-provided identification because with biometric identification, the user is not telling the system who they are; instead, the system identifies them automatically. Note that this is not authentication; this is identification only. Biometric authentication is the process of comparing the biometric signature with a reference to prove or disprove an identity—that is, the identity is already known.

Digital Identities   Another prevalent form of identification is by way of digital representation or digital identities. An example seen today is the digital certificates used as part of Public Key Infrastructures (PKIs). PKIs provide many security capabilities, including identification, authentication, encryption, and nonrepudiation.

For identification, the PKI uses digital certificates based on a standard format known as X.509 Version 3. Entities, typically users or computer servers, are given unique digital certificates that represent their identity. The certificates include descriptive information about the entity such as their name, employee number, organization, and location. Think of a certificate as a digitized passport. The digital identities are well defined both structurally and semantically and are consistent across all applications and platforms that support the certificate standards. This last point is critical to providing interoperability between applications and products provided by different vendors.

Digital certificates are popular not only because the certificates are standards based, but also because the certificates contain additional information that can be used in implementing effective security controls. For example, access to data can be based not only on the user's name, but also the user's organizational affiliation and location due to the fact that the distinguished name (DN) in a digital certificate can be in a format such as cn = *<username>*, ou = *<Organizational Unit>*, dc = *<Company>*, dc = *<Country>*.

For user identification, digital certificates are usually installed in the user's web browsers. They can also be embedded into physical devices such as smart cards. To secure the digital identity, the user may be forced to supply a PIN or password to unlock the certificate.

Many single sign-on (SSO) technologies, including Oracle Database and the SSO features of Oracle Access Manager (OAM), support digital certificates as an I&A method for users.

Computer Identities and Non-person Entities   In the computing environment, identity may be based on other nonstandard elements such as the computer's name, a web browser cookie, a physical network address (that is, a MAC address, the unique identifier on the network card for the computer), logical network address (IP address), or some other device that may be affixed to a computer.

It has also become common to refer to an abstract notion of a *person*. The word to replace person in this instance is *entity*. The abstraction exists to help discuss how to create security with "non-person entities" (NPEs). NPEs represent things that are interacting with the system that may not be an actual person. Batch jobs and web services are just a few examples of NPEs. NPEs still interact with your system and data, however. It is important, then, that you understand how to represent identities no matter whether or not they represent actual people. Computers, applications, batch jobs, services, and so forth need to interact with the database in a secure and verifiable way. The concept of multifactor identification, or using multiple factors from the session context, helps to establish trust for NPEs.

Authentication

Presenting an identity to a system is technically all that is needed for the system to apply authorizations, enforce access control, and audit. Unfortunately, our world is in fact inhabited by dishonest people. Therefore, an identity generally has to be accompanied by something else, such as a password that proves that the person's identity is legitimate.

For identification to work successfully, there has to be a process for proving that a person is who they claim to be: *authentication* is that process.

Authentication Methods

Authentication methods fall into the following three categories:

- *Something you know, such as a password or personal identification number (PIN)*. Passwords are the most common authentication method for computer systems because they are generally cheap to implement and maintain.

- *Something you possess, such as a token card, X.509 V3 certificate, smart card, car key, credit card, or software license key*. These last examples vary on their ability to support an individual's identity. Sometimes the authentication is just to prove that you are a legitimate entity, such as a building access card that proves you are an employee or a license key that proves you are a paying software subscriber.

- *Something you are, or biometrics*. Fingerprints, facial and voice recognition, and iris scans are prime examples used to authenticate people.

Strong and Weak Authentication   *Strong authentication* usually implies that the authentication cannot be easily guessed or compromised. Authentication technologies have varying abilities to perform their authenticating task. One of the metrics for determining the authentication strength is how hard it is to guess or otherwise fool a system into accepting the authentication method.

"Something you are" and "something you have" are considered stronger forms of authentication than "something you know." Passwords can be guessed, stolen, or just plain brute-force attacked and are therefore considered weaker authentication. Forging an X.509 V3 certificate (something you have) or duplicating a biometric (something you are) is not as easy. Consequently, digital certificates, token, and biometric authentications are considered strong authentication.

This is not meant to imply that passwords should not be used for authentication. Later in this chapter we discuss how you can ensure that your locally defined database users are using strong passwords by employing a password complexity routine and a database password profile.

Authentication Best Practices   As you might guess, authentication is the lynchpin to your overall security strength. After all, it doesn't matter what else you do to secure your system if the authentication method can be easily subverted. Therefore, the best practice is clearly to use strong authentication, but which strong authentication technique to use depends largely on the exposure of the system to potential hackers, how people are connecting to it, and the risk to the enterprise from regulatory compliance perspective if the system is compromised.

Today, the best practice for high-exposure or high-risk applications and databases is to use multifactor authentication to create a strong authentication environment. The individual factors don't have to be strong, but the combination of several key factors can make for strong authentication. Note the reference to "high-exposure" is a subjective term used to indicate an application (or database) that can be directly connected to by a large number of people. Alternatively, this is referred to as a *high-risk environment* and may have less to do with the number of people who can connect and more to do with the potential threat they may represent and/or how critical is the application and data contained within.

Although your databases are usually not directly accessible from the Internet, they will still require strong authentication for administrators, privileged users, and developers. The authentication strength of applications that are connected to your database has a transitive (weakest link in the chain) effect on the security of your database. Application hijacking and compromise are popular ways to get to the databases that are "safely" behind firewalls. Also recall from Chapter 1 that it is good to assume that you are working in a compromised environment, so that the protections you would therefore enact will help protect you from mishaps that may occur at other places in the IT infrastructure.

Understanding Database Account Types

Now that you understand the importance and methods of identification and authentication, you need to understand the types of accounts that will access your database. You need this understanding to determine which of the identification and authentication methods you can employ for each account type. Although we describe the following accounts by "account type," the database does not have a one-to-one support for the types or necessarily any specific syntax for creating different types (that is, they can all be created with the **CREATE USER** command). Types are used to categorize the common patterns we see people use when architecting their database and applications. The types are actually derived by the permissions the accounts possess and how they are used.

Let's first examine the account type categories that are typically found in an Oracle Database prior to Oracle Database 12*c*, as shown in Figure 2-1.

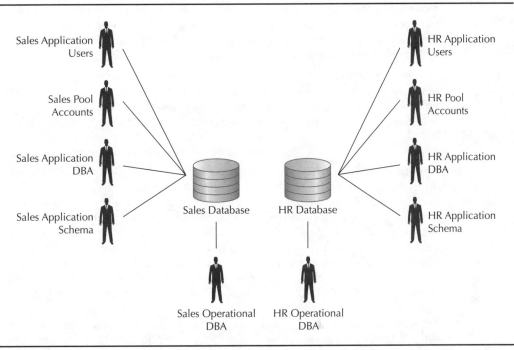

FIGURE 2-1.   *Database accounts before Oracle Database12c*

A typical Oracle Database has the following types of accounts:

■ **End user**   This account type is used to describe an account to be used by a specific person (and generally only that person). A user logging in directly to the database with SQL*Plus is a typical example of an end-user account. The account names are typically some representation of the user's first and last names (such as jdoe for user John Doe). This information is useful in auditing an existing database because it may indicate the existence of user accounts for individuals, at which point it is a best practice to verify that those people should still have database access and have not moved on to other opportunities. Also, from a security perspective, after the initial account setup, the end user manages the account passwords. Figure 2-1 illustrates these types of accounts in the categories of Sales Application Users or HR Application Users. These types of accounts typically have a limited number of database privileges that allow them to perform data operations such as read (**SELECT**), Data Manipulation Language or DML (**INSERT**, **UPDATE**, **DELETE**) on database tables, and **EXECUTE** privileges on stored programs.

■ **Connection pool**   This account type is typically used as part of a Java Database Connectivity (JDBC) Data Source in an application server, such as Oracle WebLogic Server, to support web applications or web services. Figure 2-1 illustrates these types of accounts with the names Sales Pool Accounts and HR Pool Accounts. These account types are not typically associated with specific end users, and their passwords are typically managed by a database or directory administrator. From an access perspective, these accounts are similar to end-user accounts with respect to having direct read and write privileges on an application's objects. As you will see in Chapter 3, these accounts are often used in web applications in support of real end users accessing database content, which introduces a whole new set of concerns from an identification perspective.

- **Non-person entities** This account type is similar to pool account types in that it is not associated with specific end users and has direct read and write privileges on an application's objects. NPE accounts support programs that run on an automated scheduled or ad-hoc basis in support of some application need or system maintenance function. However, they often have elevated privileges, allowing the account to perform system or application maintenance functions that require access to all data.

- **Application schema** This account type owns the database objects, such as tables, views, sequences, PL/SQL code, and so forth, all of which are used as part of an application. The account's password is typically managed by either an application database administrator or an operational database administrator. The application schema is called a *schema* and not an *account* to emphasize that this database user is not supposed to be an end user at all. This schema is only a container for data and data objects and is very important from a security perspective, because it has ownership rights on the data and database objects. As such, a direct connection to this account by a nefarious user could result in complete compromise or denial-of-service (DoS) attack. As a best practice, after you have installed the application, it is a best practice to lock the account and therefore prevent direct logins. The account should only have a limited set of database privileges such as Oracle CREATE TABLE, CREATE VIEW, and CREATE PROCEDURE. This account type will often have direct read and write privileges on other application schema objects in the database.

- **Operational database administrator (DBA)** This account type is the most privileged account in a database. The DBA performs a number of duties such as storage management, account management, privilege management, and audit management. The DBA will typically manage database scheduler/jobs, govern database resources, and identify and fix performance issues. The DBA can also perform patching functions and therefore requires constant privileged access to the database. The DBA may manage not only administrator passwords, but the passwords of other local database accounts such as those used in the technologies mentioned previously. From a security perspective, the DBA accounts are sometimes shared but should not be. Also of note, the DBA traditionally has the privileges to create and delete not only database objects but also database accounts. Many of the security privileges and ability to grant and disable security controls may reside with a traditional DBA.

- **Application database administrator** This account type is an end-user account that is responsible for maintaining database objects for a specific application and set of interrelated applications. The application DBA will typically manage not only his or her password but may also manage the passwords of other database accounts that interact and use the application. Note that this account may have powerful system privileges such as read all and write all privileges (Oracle SELECT ANY, UPDATE ANY, or DELETE ANY) such that he or she can maintain data in one or more application schema accounts.

As you can see, a number of different account types are found in an Oracle database. As a general rule, if you maintain the databases for large organization, a large number of end users will need to be maintained. There will often be a large number of applications and therefore application schema accounts in this environment. In this environment, we recommended you leverage a centralized identity store and integrate this for identification and authentication to your databases. In a later chapter, we will cover options such as proxy authentication and Enterprise User Security for this type of environment.

Database Account Types in Oracle Database 12*c* Multitenant Architecture

In this section we briefly introduce the Oracle Database 12*c* multitenant architecture. Your understanding of what this new architecture is and how it works is extremely important to understanding security topics such as account management in Oracle Database 12*c*.

The best and most concise description on the multitenant architecture can be found in Chapter 17, "Introduction to the Multitenant Architecture," of the *Oracle Database Concepts* documentation (http://docs.oracle.com/database/121/CNCPT/cdbovrvw.htm):

> The multitenant architecture enables an Oracle database to function as a multitenant container database (CDB) that includes zero, one, or many customer-created pluggable databases (PDBs). A PDB is a portable collection of schemas, schema objects, and nonschema objects that appears to an Oracle Net client as a non-CDB. All Oracle databases before Oracle Database 12*c* were non-CDBs....A container is either a PDB or the root container (also called the root). The root is a collection of schemas, schema objects, and nonschema objects to which all PDBs belong.

The documentation goes on to say that every multitenant container database will have exactly one root container, named CDB$ROOT, for common users and the standard data dictionary provided by Oracle. Each CDB will also contain exactly one immutable (read-only) PDB seed database, named PDB$SEED, used to create custom PDBs. Finally, the CDB can have zero or more customer-defined PDBs that will contain objects that support business applications.

Figure 2-2 illustrates how the account types we've discussed so far would map to an environment using the Oracle Database 12*c* multitenant architecture. As the figure shows, of two pluggable databases, one contains the schemas used for the Sales application, and the other contains the schemas for the Human Resources (HR) application. Both databases are plugged into a single 12*c* container database. The figure also demonstrates that the types of accounts we have do not really change in Oracle Database 12*c*.

At first glance, you might think this consolidation has only reduced the need for multiple operational DBAs. This is certainly desirable as it reduces that cost associated with managing these accounts on multiple database servers. There are also labor costs savings in the work that these operational DBAs perform. We will have fewer servers that we need to apply software patches to, so the cost to ensure our databases are running the latest functional or security patches is reduced. When one applies patches to the Oracle Database 12*c* installation home and container root, all of these pluggable databases that are attached will automatically have these patches activated. Finally, we find a cost savings related to the time it takes create and manage a database's secure initialization parameters, network security parameters, and shared encryption/credential stores (Oracle Wallets). We can share these security configurations between the root container and all attached pluggable databases to reduce the number of instances of these configurations we have to maintain.

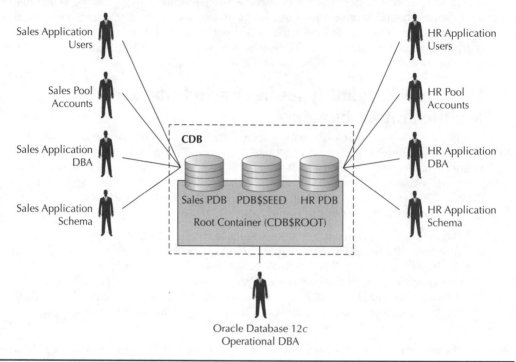

FIGURE 2-2. *Database accounts types on Oracle Database 12c*

Privileged Database Account Management in Oracle Database 12c

Oracle Database 12c supports all of the local identification and authentication mechanisms that existed in previous releases of the Oracle Database. In this section, we will review some of the important changes to these identification and authentication mechanisms that support the database's multitenant architecture. We begin by discussing the new Administrative Accounts that were introduced in Oracle Database 12c to support the separation of duties principle more fully.

Administrative Privileges for Separation of Duty

In a manner consistent with prior releases, Oracle Database 12c creates the SYS and SYSTEM schemas when you create a new database. The database also includes the traditional SYSDBA and SYSOPER administrative privileges that enable access and control of a database even when the database is not started or open.

The SYSDBA privilege is analogous to the "root" account on a UNIX operating system, as SYSDBA provides access to all objects and all privileges in the database. When the SYSDBA privilege is used to connect to an open database, the session assumes the SYS schema. The SYS schema also owns a large number database objects, referred to as the *data dictionary*.

When the SYSOPER privilege is used to connect to a database, it assumes the special PUBLIC database role and has a limited set of system privileges to perform database operations such as startup, shutdown, backup, and recovery.

The SYSTEM schema is an Oracle account that has the DBA role granted to it by default. The SYSTEM account also owns a number of database objects that are used by some Oracle options and features.

NOTE
It is considered a best practice to avoid creating database objects for custom applications under the SYS or SYSTEM schema.

Following is a description of the administrative privileges that are available in the Oracle Database 12*c*:

- **SYSDBA**   This privilege provides full control over all database objects in the database.

- **SYSOPER**   This privilege provides delegated administration of database startup, shutdown, initialization file management, database open, database mount, and database backup and recovery.

- **SYSBACKUP**   This privilege provides delegated administration of database backup and recovery capabilities using Oracle Recovery Manager (RMAN) and/or SQL*Plus.

- **SYSDG**   This privilege provides delegated administration of database offsite fail-over with the Oracle Data Guard (DG) using the DG Broker or DG Manager command line interface (dgmgrl).

- **SYSKM**   This privilege provides key management (KM) and delegated administration of Oracle Wallets (encryption keystores) used by Oracle Transparent Data Encryption (TDE).

- **SYSASM**   This privilege provides for separation of duty in the administration of the Oracle Grid Infrastructure (GI) installation and Automated Storage Management (ASM) instance. With this privilege one can separate the administration of GI and ASM (storage) from accounts that have the SYSDBA privilege. This privilege is not associated to an account in the standard Oracle database instance and is only applicable in an Oracle ASM instance. Oracle ASM is a special database used for managing disk storage that is shared across multiple, standard Oracle databases.

This new privilege model applies both to the root container and to each pluggable database that is attached to it. In other words, you can define separate accounts that are granted these special administrative privileges in each database as your requirements dictate. The separation of duty that is created by this new privilege model allows you to define separate administrators who are responsible for managing disk storage (SYSASM) from those who are responsible for how that disk storage is used in your databases (SYSDBA). Another set of administrators can be responsible for backup and recovery operations or continuity of operations (COOP) without having access to encrypted, sensitive data whose encryption keys are controlled by a security administrator (SYSKM). These examples illustrate how Oracle Database 12*c* can support the separation of duty requirements of a cloud-based provider environment or an environment subject to the regulatory requirements that were introduced in Chapter 1. To illustrate this point, consider Figure 2-3, which shows ABC Cloud Services providing database services to the companies XYZ Sales and People Pleasers.

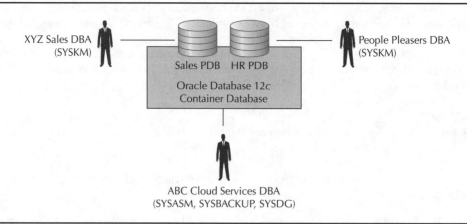

FIGURE 2-3.   *Separation of duties in a cloud services provider*

   The DBA accounts for XYZ Sales and People Pleasers have been granted the SYSKM privilege to manage the encryption keys and wallets for the Oracle TDE policies used in the Sales and HR pluggable databases, respectively. The XYZ Sales DBA does not have access to the TDE wallets that are maintained by the People Pleasers DBA for the HR pluggable database. Conversely, the People Pleasers DBA does not have access to the TDE wallets that are managed by the XYZ Sales DBA for the Sales pluggable database. The Cloud Services DBA can perform storage management, backup, recovery, and COOP operations for all of the databases (root container and pluggable) in this environment. The Cloud Services DBA cannot access the TDE wallets for either the Sales or HR pluggable databases. In essence, the Cloud Services DBA can support XYZ Sales and People Pleasers in the service provider role without the need to access the data these companies store in the cloud.

NOTE
For the examples in this book, we will follow a scenario that supports a Cloud Services provider that is maintaining SALES and HR applications using a separate pluggable database for each application. We will use a C##SEC_MGR account in the root container and a separate SEC_MGR account in each pluggable database for security-related configurations. The detailed setup for these pluggable databases and these accounts can be found in the Appendix of this book.

Methods for Privileged Database Account Management
Oracle Database 12c also introduces a number of new system accounts that are associated with the new administrative privileges. These new system accounts are the "landing" accounts when operating system (OS) Authentication is used with one of the new administrative privileges. These new accounts are displayed in the following query.

```
c##sec_mgr@db12cr[cdb$root]> SELECT username, account_status, common
  2   FROM dba_users WHERE username LIKE 'SYS%'
  3   AND username != 'SYSTEM'
  4   ORDER BY username;
```

```
USERNAME                                ACCOUNT_STATUS         COM
------------------------------ -------------------- ---
SYS                                     OPEN                   YES
SYSBACKUP                               EXPIRED & LOCKED       YES
SYSDG                                   EXPIRED & LOCKED       YES
SYSKM                                   EXPIRED & LOCKED       YES

4 rows selected.
```

Each system account listed in the example is granted one of the administrative privileges discussed earlier for delegating general database administration, database operation, database backup, database fail-over site operations, and key management. Notice that Oracle Database 12*c* added a "common" column for accounts to indicate the account is shared between the root container and all pluggable databases. The internal table V$PWFILE_USERS can be used to view the administrative privileges that are associated with these accounts.

```
c##sec_mgr@db12cr[cdb$root]> SELECT *
  2  FROM v$pwfile_users;

USERNAME    SYSDB SYSOP SYSAS SYSBA SYSDG SYSKM    CON_ID
---------- ----- ----- ----- ----- ----- ----- ----------
SYS         TRUE  TRUE  FALSE FALSE FALSE FALSE          0
SYSBACKUP   FALSE FALSE FALSE TRUE  FALSE FALSE          1
SYSDG       FALSE FALSE FALSE FALSE TRUE  FALSE          1
SYSKM       FALSE FALSE FALSE FALSE FALSE TRUE           1

4 rows selected.
```

Notice in the ACCOUNT_STATUS column that the new system accounts SYSBACKUP, SYSDG, and SYSKM are locked and expired.

NOTE
Security best practices dictate that these system accounts remain locked and their passwords expired. These same best practices dictate that you create separate named accounts that are granted only the necessary system privileges, because this enables not only a more complete audit trail but creates opportunities to build in additional authorization and access control policies.

Oracle Database 12*c* has two ways of creating accounts that can use the duty-specific privileges. Option one is to create a mapping from an OS account to the database administrative account and then use OS Authentication to connect the user to the database. The second option is to create a standard database account and grant the role/privileges to that user.

Let's first look at how to leverage OS Authentication with Oracle's built-in support for OS groups that map to the database privilege, as shown in the following example. This approach is considered secure because the database delegates the process of authentication and group membership to the operating system, and it is assumed that the OS on which the database runs is secure. If the OS is not secure, the database is already in jeopardy.

Privileged Database Account Management Based on Oracle OS Authentication

The Oracle OS Authentication feature allows you to define a set of separate OS groups that map to the Oracle administration privileges just described. You will typically define this mapping during the database installation. The mapping can also be changed after installation by editing the file $ORACLE_HOME/rdbms/lib/config.c, recompiling this file, and then relinking the Oracle Database binary. It is highly recommended that you create separate OS groups for each database administrative privilege before you install Oracle Database 12c and use those groups in the installation. You can include the software owner, e.g. oracle, as a member of this group. This approach allows you to use this native Separation of Duty (SoD) capability should you need it in the future.

The way in which Oracle OS Authentication works is intuitive. A system administrator creates a set of separate OS groups for each Oracle administrative privilege defined—for example, dba for SYSDBA, backupdba for SYSBACKUP, kmdba for SYSKM, and so on. These OS groups are identified during the Oracle Database installation process, as shown in Figure 2-4.

The system administrator creates separate named OS accounts for each real person who needs to serve as an Oracle DBA. The system administrator adds the OS account to one or more appropriate OS groups based on their job function and the separation of duty requirements.

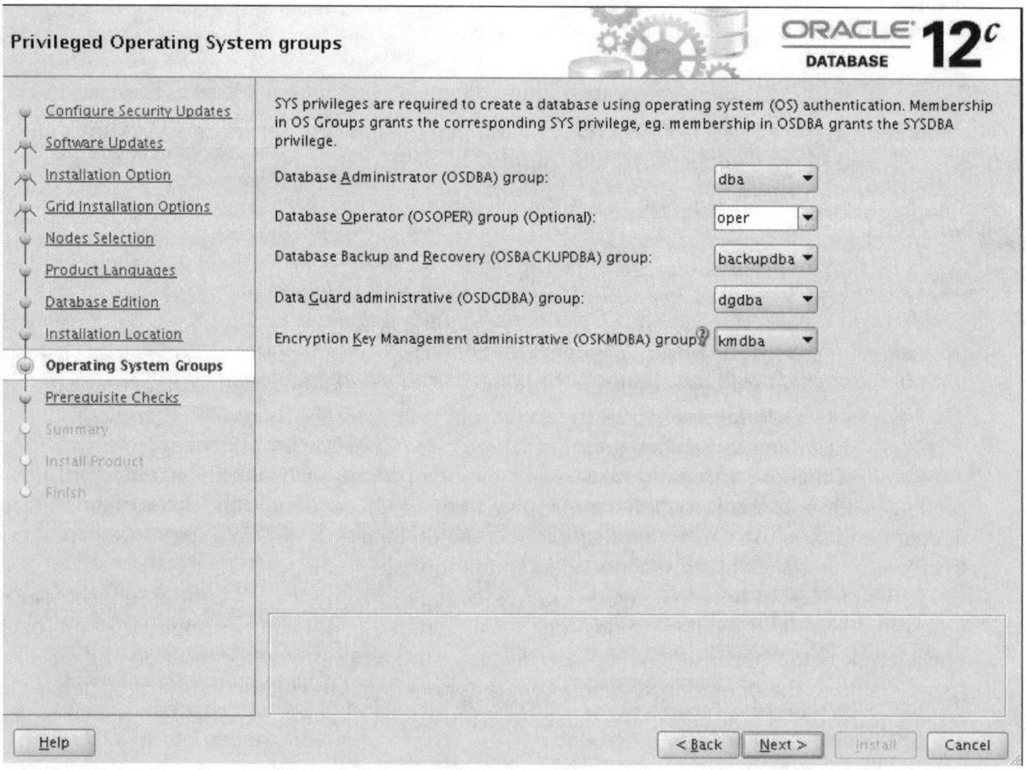

FIGURE 2-4. OS groups to privilege mapping in the Oracle Database 12c installation process

When the user logs in to the database from the OS account, he or she uses the following syntax, which purposefully omits any database username and password:

```
sqlplus / AS <privilege>
```

The Oracle Database will invoke operating system calls to determine the login identifier of the OS account issuing the **sqlplus** command and of which OS groups the OS account is a member. If the OS account is a member of the OS group that maps to the privilege requested, then the Oracle Database will not prompt for a password and will allow the logon to the database. Note that OS Authentication is not limited only to the Oracle SQL*Plus client, but is supported by all Oracle administration tools and low-level database connectivity APIs in C (OCI), Java (JDBC), and C# (ODP.NET).

The following example shows the details of creating and enabling an account to use OS Authentication for the administrative privilege SYSBACKUP. Assume that prior to database installation, we had created an OS Group called *backupdba*. During the installation process, we then associated that OS group to the SYSBACKUP database privilege as shown in Figure 2-4. We'll next create an OS account called *bill* and add the account to the OS group *backupdba*.

```
# useradd -u 602 -g backupdba bill

# id -a bill
uid=602(bill) gid=514(backupdba) groups=514(backupdba)

# passwd bill
Changing password for user bill.
New UNIX password:
Retype new UNIX password:
passwd: all authentication tokens updated successfully.
```

Next, we establish an OS session using the OS account for bill, and we set Oracle database environment variables ORACLE_SID and ORACLE_HOME accordingly. To illustrate how this is typically used, we will launch a secure shell session (**ssh**). In this example, we are doing a loopback to the same machine, but this is typically done across two separate machines or virtual machines.

```
# ssh bill@localhost
bill@localhost's password:

$ source /usr/local/bin/oraenv
ORACLE_SID = [bill] ? db12cr_1
ORACLE_HOME = [/home/oracle] ? /u01/app/oracle/product/12.1.0/dbhome_1
```

Now we can log on to the database without a password, leveraging Oracle's OS Authentication. As you can see from the following queries, the database session has been granted a limited set of system roles and privileges that are required to perform database backup and recovery operations. Specifying the **AS SYSBACKUP** parameter to the sqlplus utility or with the **CONNECT** command directs Oracle to use these administrative privileges for the connection.

```
$ sqlplus / as sysbackup
SQL*Plus: Release 12.1.0.1.0 Production on Tue Aug 20 12:20:50 2013
Copyright (c) 1982, 2013, Oracle.  All rights reserved.
Connected to:
Oracle Database 12c Enterprise Edition Release 12.1.0.1.0 - 64bit Production
```

```
With the Partitioning, Real Application Clusters, Automatic
Storage Management, Oracle Label Security,
 OLAP, Advanced Analytics, Oracle
Database Vault and Real Application Testing options
sysbackup@db12cr[cdb$root]> SELECT *
  2   FROM session_privs
  3   ORDER BY 1;

PRIVILEGE
----------------------------------------
ALTER DATABASE
ALTER SESSION
ALTER SYSTEM
ALTER TABLESPACE
AUDIT ANY
CREATE ANY CLUSTER
CREATE ANY DIRECTORY
CREATE ANY TABLE
DROP TABLESPACE
RESUMABLE
SELECT ANY DICTIONARY
SELECT ANY TRANSACTION
SYSBACKUP
UNLIMITED TABLESPACE

14 rows selected.
sysbackup@db12cr[cdb$root]> SELECT *
  2   FROM session_roles
  3   ORDER BY 1;

ROLE
--------------------
HS_ADMIN_SELECT_ROLE
SELECT_CATALOG_ROLE

2 rows selected.
```

In the following query, a number of session context variables are available, such as the OS account name, the hostname of the database client, and the user the session is connected to. You can use these types of session context variables in our audit and security policies, as you will discover in subsequent chapters of this book.

```
sysbackup@db12cr[cdb$root]> SELECT SYS_CONTEXT('USERENV','OS_USER') os_user
  2   ,SYS_CONTEXT('USERENV','HOST') host
  3   ,SYS_CONTEXT('USERENV','SESSION_USER') session_user
  4   FROM dual;

OS_USER      HOST         SESSION_USER
----------   ----------   --------------------
bill         nsgdc2       SYSBACKUP

1 row selected.
```

Accessing Pluggable Databases with Oracle OS Authentication   Using OS Authentication directly to a pluggable database (PDB) in Oracle Database 12*c* does not work the same way as it does in a standard (non-PDB) database. Using OS Authentication for privileged administrators in PDBs requires a different access method. In the following example, we are trying to connect to the PDB SALES using OS Authentication. Notice that the system does not allow the connection.

```
$ sqlplus /@sales as sysbackup

SQL*Plus: Release 12.1.0.1.0 Production on Tue Sep 17 11:51:38 2013

Copyright (c) 1982, 2013, Oracle.  All rights reserved.

ERROR:
ORA-01017: invalid username/password; logon denied
```

To access a PDB using OS Authentication, we must first log on to the root container and then alter our session to set the container to the name of the PDB we want to access. The following example demonstrates how this is done:

```
$ sqlplus / as sysbackup
SQL*Plus: Release 12.1.0.1.0 Production on Tue Aug 20 12:20:50 2013
Copyright (c) 1982, 2013, Oracle.  All rights reserved.
Connected to:
Oracle Database 12c Enterprise Edition Release 12.1.0.1.0 - 64bit Production
With the Partitioning, Real Application Clusters, Automatic
Storage Management, Oracle Label Security, OLAP, Advanced Analytics, Oracle
Database Vault and Real Application Testing options

sysbackup@db12cr[cdb$root]> SHOW con_name
CON_NAME
------------------------------
CDB$ROOT

sysbackup@db12cr[cdb$root]> ALTER SESSION SET CONTAINER = SALES;
Session altered.

-- display the name of the current container, e.g. SALES
-- also note that SHOW con_id will display the id of the current container
sysbackup@db12cr[cdb$root]> SHOW con_name
CON_NAME
------------------------------
SALES
```

Privileged Database Account Management Based on Named Accounts

The second option available to use these new administrative privileges uses locally defined, named database accounts that are granted the administrative privilege. We demonstrate this option in the following example. First we create the named user account in the root container.

```
c##sec_mgr@db12cr[cdb$root]> CREATE USER c##bill
  2  IDENTIFIED BY change_on_install
  3  CONTAINER = ALL;
User created.
```

With the multitenant option of Oracle Database 12c, the **CONTAINER = ALL** clause indicates that the account is "common to," or defined in, the root container and all pluggable databases that exist or that are ever created. The account name for all common accounts created in the root container must be prefixed with *C##*.

NOTE
*If you are not using the multitenant architecture of Oracle Database 12c, you would simply omit the **CONTAINER = ALL** clause from the **CREATE USER** command.*

We expire the password for the account so that C##BILL (user bill) is required to set the password during his first login to something only C##BILL will know.

```
c##sec_mgr@db12cr[cdb$root]> ALTER USER c##bill PASSWORD EXPIRE;
User altered.
```

Next we grant this account the SYSBACKUP privilege, which is required to perform backup and recovery operations, and we grant the CREATE SESSION privilege so that the account can log in to the database. A grant of SYSBACKUP must be done as SYS and cannot be done as C##SEC_MGR, because the administrative privileges cannot be granted by named accounts, even with the ADMIN OPTION.

```
sys@db12cr[cdb$root]> GRANT SYSBACKUP, CREATE SESSION TO c##bill;
Grant succeeded.
```

The Oracle SQL syntax supports combining the **CREATE USER** and **GRANT** commands into just a single **GRANT** command, as shown in the following example:

```
sys@db12cr[cdb$root]> GRANT SYSBACKUP, CREATE SESSION TO c##bill
  2  IDENTIFIED BY welcome1;
Grant succeeded.
```

The association of the administrative privilege to the named account and the password for the accounts is stored in the standard Oracle Database password file. The file is located in the directory $ORACLE_HOME/dbs for file-based database storage—for example, $ORACLE_HOME/dbs /orapwdb21cr. The file will be located in a file similar to +DATA/DB12CR/ orapwdb21cr for ASM-based database storage. The Oracle Database password file controls remote access to the database for privileged accounts. This password file can be viewed using an internal view named **V$PWFILE_USERS**, as shown in the following query.

```
sys@db12cr[cdb$root]> SELECT *
  2  FROM v$pwfile_users
  3  ORDER BY 1;
USERNAME               SYSDB SYSOP SYSAS SYSBA SYSDG SYSKM   CON_ID
---------------------- ----- ----- ----- ----- ----- ----- --------
C##BILL                FALSE FALSE FALSE TRUE  FALSE FALSE         1
SYS                    TRUE  TRUE  FALSE FALSE FALSE FALSE         0
SYSBACKUP              FALSE FALSE FALSE TRUE  FALSE FALSE         1
SYSDG                  FALSE FALSE FALSE FALSE TRUE  FALSE         1
SYSKM                  FALSE FALSE FALSE FALSE FALSE TRUE          1

5 rows selected.
```

Now we can log on to the database using the common account, C##BILL, that has been granted the SYSBACKUP administrative privilege on the local database server. Notice that we are required to set the account password the first time we log in because we created the account with an expired password. This allows C##BILL to define a password that is personal and not known to other accounts in the database.

```
sys@db12cr[cdb$root]> CONNECT c##bill/change_on_install as sysbackup

 ERROR:
ORA-28001: the password has expired
Changing password for c##bill
New password:
Retype new password:
Password changed
Connected.
```

Controlling Remote Access for Privileged Named Accounts   You can also control the use of these administrative privileges from remote systems using the initialization parameter **REMOTE_LOGIN_PASSWORDFILE**. This parameter is set to **EXCLUSIVE** by default, which indicates that remote connections for accounts that exist in the Oracle Password file are allowed. If we try to log on to the database remotely, using the C##BILL account from a remote server named appserver, the database will allow the remote logon, as shown here:

```
[bill@appserver]$ hostname
appserver

[bill@appserver$ sqlplus c##bill/welcome1@db12cr as sysbackup

SQL*Plus: Release 12.1.0.1.0 Production on Wed Sep 18 11:04:01 2013

Copyright (c) 1982, 2013, Oracle.  All rights reserved.
Connected to:
Oracle Database 12c Enterprise Edition Release 12.1.0.1.0 - 64bit Production
With the Partitioning, Real Application Clusters, Automatic Storage Management, Oracle
Label Security,
OLAP, Advanced Analytics, Oracle Database Vault and Real Application Testing options

SQL>
```

You can set the **REMOTE_LOGIN_PASSWORDFILE** value to **NONE**, which will prevent remote connections for the accounts, even if the account is defined in the Oracle Password file. The ability to prevent these remote connections would be desirable if your organization's security policy required that all privileged accounts access the database directly from an OS session on the database server.

```
sys@db12cr[cdb$root]> SHOW PARAMETER remote_login_passwordfile
NAME                            TYPE          VALUE
------------------------------- ------------- ------------------------------
remote_login_passwordfile       string        NONE

sys@db12cr[cdb$root]> ALTER SYSTEM SET remote_login_passwordfile = 'NONE'
  2  SCOPE=SPFILE;
System altered.
```

We restart the database for the parameter change to take effect:

```
sys@db12cr[cdb$root]> SHUTDOWN IMMEDIATE
Database closed.
Database dismounted.
ORACLE instance shut down.

sys@db12cr[cdb$root]> STARTUP
ORACLE instance started.
Total System Global Area    1068937216 bytes
Fixed Size                  2296576 bytes
Variable Size               729810176 bytes
Database Buffers            331350016 bytes
Redo Buffers                5480448 bytes
Database mounted.
Database opened.
```

If we try to log on to the database remotely, using the C##BILL account from a remote server named appserver, the database will deny the logon, as shown next:

```
[bill@appserver$ sqlplus c##bill/welcome1@db12cr as sysbackup

SQL*Plus: Release 12.1.0.1.0 Production on Wed Sep 18 11:04:01 2013

Copyright (c) 1982, 2013, Oracle.  All rights reserved.
ERROR:
ORA-01017: invalid username/password; logon denied
```

The database initialization parameter **REMOTE_LOGIN_PASSWORDFILE** gives you the control to restrict logons for privileged users to OS accounts that exist on the local database server(s), thus preventing access from any remote systems. The C##BILL account can log in locally only from the database server host nsgdc2, as shown next:

```
[oracle@nsgdc2 ~]$ sqlplus c##/welcome1 as sysbackup
SQL*Plus: Release 12.1.0.1.0 Production on Mon Nov 11 11:06:30 2013
Copyright (c) 1982, 2013, Oracle.  All rights reserved.

Connected to:
Oracle Database 12c Enterprise Edition Release 12.1.0.1.0 - 64bit Production
With the Partitioning, Real Application Clusters, Automatic Storage Management, Oracle
Label Security,
OLAP, Advanced Analytics, Oracle Database Vault and Real Application Testing options

sysbackup@db12cr[cdb$root]> SELECT *
  2  FROM session_privs
  3  WHERE privilege like 'SYS%';

PRIVILEGE
--------------------
SYSBACKUP

1 row selected.
```

Your decision to implement privilege administrator access using Oracle OS Authentication versus using remotely accessible named database accounts will be largely driven by organizational security policy and the environment in which your database(s) operate. The details of your corporate provisioning process and its support for provisioning accounts to servers and/or databases will also help drive this decision. If your organization does not maintain a large number of servers or databases, or if your organization is concerned about remote exploits over network channels, local-only access may be your best option from a cost and security perspective. Oracle OS Authentication helps reduce the cost to maintain named accounts in the database but may not work in a cloud environment or an environment that requires fine-grained control over the accounts that have administrative privileges such as SYSBACKUP and SYSKM in the root container and pluggable databases. Using named accounts for administrative privileges such as SYSBACKUP and SYSKM does offer this type of control, because you can choose which named database accounts are granted the privilege within each pluggable database. We have demonstrated how the Oracle Database 12c can be easily set up to prevent remote logins of privileged administrators using named accounts, while at the same time supporting a separation of duty model.

If your organization wants to reduce the number of privileged administrators to help reduce the cost of managing a large deployment footprint, then using OS Authentication or locally defined named database accounts may not be the best approaches available to you. Having more systems to keep up to date with local accounts (OS or database) and related policies can certainly lead to an increase in maintenance costs if not properly automated. In the next chapter, we will discuss how technologies such as Enterprise User Security (EUS) can support centralized identification and authentication for these privileged administrators, which will help to reduce maintenance costs. You can leverage Oracle Enterprise Manager Cloud Control to reduce costs further while offering remote access to general database monitoring and maintenance by accounts that do not require the special administrative privileges presented in this section.

Account Management in Multitenant Oracle Database 12c

Database accounts in Oracle Database 12c can be created with new security considerations to support the multitenant environment. In Oracle Database 12c, you can create accounts that exist in the root container and all current and future pluggable databases. These are called *common* database accounts. You can also create database accounts that have access to one or more pluggable databases, but not the root container. Considering the discussion on account types from earlier in this chapter, we can make the following recommendations when creating database accounts:

- Create common database accounts in the root container for privilege administrators or for other accounts with common database access requirements among one or more pluggable databases.

- Create local database accounts for application schema accounts, whose code or objects will be shared among one or more pluggable databases. You can use Oracle standard database roles and privileges to provide the first level of protection for any pluggable databases that will not utilize the code or objects from these schema accounts. We will demonstrate how you can use the Oracle pluggable database clone feature or Oracle database links to share common application code among pluggable databases.

- Create local database accounts for named users in each pluggable database to which the user is required to connect. It is suggested that you use EUS if possible for large-scale enterprise systems, because EUS helps reduce the costs associated with provisioning, deprovisioning, and password management for these types of accounts. We will discuss EUS in detail in the next chapter.

Creating Common Database Accounts

We demonstrated creating a common database account for a privileged administrator with the following statement:

```
sys@db12cr[cdb$root]> CREATE USER c##bill
  2  IDENTIFIED BY change_on_install
  3  CONTAINER = ALL;
User created.
```

The **CONTAINER = ALL** clause indicates that the account will exist in the container database and all pluggable databases (current and future). This clause is required in the root container. It is important to note that all customer-defined common database accounts must be prefixed with the letters C##. Several common accounts are supported by Oracle Database 12c, such as MDSYS for Oracle Spatial, CTXSYS for Oracle Text, and so on, which are created when you issue a **CREATE DATABASE** or **CREATE PLUGGABLE DATABASE** command. These accounts do not include the C## prefix. If you try to create a customer-defined common database account without this prefix, the command will fail, as shown in this example:

```
sys@db12cr[cdb$root]> CREATE USER bill IDENTIFIED BY welcome1;
CREATE USER bill IDENTIFIED BY welcome1
            *
ERROR at line 1:
ORA-65096: invalid common user or role name
```

Managing Accounts in a Pluggable Database

To create a local account in a pluggable database, we first need to decide which PDBs the account will be created in. The command **SHOW PDBS** lists the PDBs that are attached to the root container as well as the status of the PDBs.

```
sys@db12cr[cdb$root]> SHOW PDBS

    CON_ID CON_NAME                       OPEN MODE  RESTRICTED
---------- ------------------------------ ---------- ----------
         2 PDB$SEED                       READ ONLY  NO
         5 SALES                          READ WRITE NO
         7 HR                             READ WRITE NO
```

As discussed previously, the pluggable database PDB$SEED is an immutable, system-defined PDB that can be used to create other PDBs, and, therefore, our accounts cannot be created in that container. The SALES PDB was created from PDB$SEED with the following command:

```
CREATE PLUGGABLE DATABASE sales
  ADMIN USER pdbadmin IDENTIFIED BY welcome1
  ROLES = (DBA)
  DEFAULT TABLESPACE sales;
```

You will notice that this command creates a local database administrator account, PDBADMIN, without the C## prefix, and grants the account the role DBA. You will also notice that a tablespace named SALES is created as part of this command. The role and tablespace exist only in the PDB

(SALES) and neither the administrator account nor the tablespace is listed as belonging to the container database.

```
c##sec_mgr@db12cr[cdb$root]> SELECT username
  2  FROM dba_users
  3  WHERE username = 'PDBADMIN';

no rows selected

c##sec_mgr@db12cr[cdb$root]> SELECT tablespace_name
  2  FROM dba_tablespaces
  3  WHERE tablespace_name = 'SALES';

no rows selected
```

Identifying Local Accounts in a Container

We can identify the accounts (privileged or otherwise) that are defined in the container root or PDBs using the following query on the CDB_USERS and CDB_PDBS views:

```
c##sec_mgr@db12cr[cdb$root]> SELECT u.con_id
  2  , NVL(p.pdb_name,'CDB$ROOT') con_name
  3  , u.username
  4  , u.oracle_maintained
  5  FROM cdb_users u
  6  LEFT OUTER JOIN (SELECT pdb_id, pdb_name FROM cdb_pdbs) p
  7    ON u.con_id = p.pdb_id
  8  WHERE u.username IN ('SYS','PDBADMIN','C##BILL')
  9  ORDER BY u.con_id, u.username;

    CON_ID CON_NAME              USERNAME                         O
---------- -------------------- ------------------------------- -
         1 CDB$ROOT             C##BILL                          N
         1 CDB$ROOT             SYS                              Y
         2 PDB$SEED             SYS                              Y
         5 SALES                C##BILL                          N
         5 SALES                PDBADMIN                         N
         5 SALES                SYS                              Y
         7 HR                   C##BILL                          N
         7 HR                   PDBADMIN                         N
         7 HR                   SYS                              Y
9 rows selected.
```

The Oracle-supplied, common account SYS exists in all containers of our CDB. The account C##BILL was created as a common account for all containers, using the **CONTAINER = ALL** clause, so you will notice that it exists in both the root container, CDB$ROOT, and the custom-defined PDBs SALES and HR. Account C##BILL does not exist in PDB$SEED, as this is the read-only PDB seed. The account PDBADMIN exists only in the PDBs SALES and HR because the account was created at as part of the PDBs' creation process.

A brief explanation of the data dictionary views we are using up to this point is in order. You will notice that we used the views CDB_USERS and CDB_PDBS in the preceding query. Oracle Database 12c introduced several hundred new views that prefixed with *CDB_* for administrators to query the data dictionary for all containers within a CDB. These views are mostly a superset of the views that are prefixed with *DBA_*, such as DBA_USERS or DBA_TAB_PRIVS, which were included in previous releases of Oracle Database. The views that are prefixed with *DBA_*, *ALL_*, or *USER_* still exist within Oracle Database 12*c*, but they will return only those records that apply to the current container for the session in which they are used. That is, querying DBA_USERS from the root container will return different results than querying DBA_USERS from a pluggable database such as SALES. When the CDB_ views are queried from the root container, the view will return all records across all containers and include the CON_ID column for which the record applies. One exception is, interestingly enough, the CDB_PDBS view, where PDB_ID is the ID of the container that identifies the PDB. In general, however, the CON_ID column of these CDB views indicates the container ID of the root container or PDB to which the records is associated. The container ID can have one of the following values:

- A value of 1 indicates that the record is associated to root container, CDB$ROOT.
- A value of 2 indicates that the record is associated to the seed database, PDB$SEED.
- A value of 3–254 denotes the container ID of the PDB with which the record is associated.

Creating Named Accounts in a PDB

In this section we will demonstrate how to create a local, named account in a PDB using an application schema account for sales history (SH) as an example. As you will see, the steps in this PDB are no different from those in previous releases of Oracle Database. The difference is that we need to log on directly to the PDB to create the account. We cannot create the account for the PDB from the root container using **CONTAINER = <*pdb_name*>** as the following example demonstrates:

```
c##sec_mgr@db12cr[cdb$root]> CREATE USER SH
  2   IDENTIFIED BY welcome1
  3   CONTAINER = SALES;
CONTAINER = SALES
            *
ERROR at line 3:
ORA-65013: invalid CONTAINER clause
```

If we log on directly to the PDB SALES using the local administrator, PDBADMIN, we can successfully create local, named database accounts using the **CONTAINER = CURRENT** clause as shown in the following example:

```
c##sec_mgr @db12cr[cdb$root]> CONNECT sec_mgr/welcome1@sales
Connected.

-- create the local application schema account for sales history(SH)
-- the CONTAINER = CURRENT clause denotes that the account will be
-- created for the currently connected pluggable database.
-- the clause CONTAINER = CURRENT is optional and defaults to CURRENT
-- but including the clause improves the readability of your scripts
sec_mgr@db12cr[sales]> CREATE USER sh
  2   IDENTIFIED BY welcome1
  3   DEFAULT TABLESPACE sales
  4   CONTAINER = CURRENT;

User created.

-- establish a quota for the SH account on the SALES tablespace
```

```
sec_mgr@db12cr[sales]> ALTER USER sh QUOTA 10G ON SALES;

User altered.

-- grant the session and create object privileges the SH account will need
sec_mgr@db12cr[sales]> GRANT CREATE SESSION, CREATE TABLE TO sh;

Grant succeeded.

sec_mgr@db12cr[sales]> CONNECT sh/welcome1@sales
Connected.

sh@db12cr[sales]> CREATE TABLE sales_history (
  2    product VARCHAR2(30)
  3    , sales_date DATE
  4    , quantity NUMBER
  5    , total_cost NUMBER(10,2));

Table created.

sh@db12cr[sales]> INSERT INTO sh.sales_history
  2    VALUES ( 'Stereo' , SYSDATE-10 , 1 , 100.00 );

1 row created.

sh@db12cr[sales]> INSERT INTO sh.sales_history
  2    VALUES ( 'Walkman' , SYSDATE    , 5 , 250.00 );

1 row created.
sh@db12cr[sales]> COMMIT;

Commit complete.
```

The PDB administrator can create named, end user accounts in the same manner as the SH account was created in the preceding example. Object privileges such as SELECT, INSERT, and so forth can be granted to roles. These roles can then be granted to additional end user accounts.

The administrator account (C##BILL) we created previously cannot log in to the SALES PDB, because we granted the C##BILL account the CREATE SESSION privilege in the root container and not from within the SALES PDB. The following example demonstrates this important fact:

```
sec_mgr@db12cr[sales]> CONNECT c##bill@sales
Enter password:
ERROR:
ORA-01045: user C##BILL lacks CREATE SESSION privilege; logon denied
Warning: You are no longer connected to ORACLE.
```

The database will look up the account C##BILL in a view similar to the CDB_USERS view we examined earlier to discover that C##BILL is a common account identified in the context of the SALES container. However, when the database examines a view such as CDB_SYS_PRIVS, the privilege to create a session within the context of the PDB is not found, as shown in the following query:

```
c##sec_mgr@db12cr[cdb$root]> SELECT grantee, privilege, common, con_id
  2    FROM cdb_sys_privs
  3    WHERE grantee = 'C##BILL';
```

```
GRANTEE                         PRIVILEGE              COM    CON_ID
------------------------------- ---------------------- ---    ----------
C##BILL                         CREATE SESSION         NO              1
1 row selected.
```

As you can see, the privilege grant applies only to CON_ID #1 or CDB$ROOT and the privilege is not listed as common in the query results.

NOTE
*You must grant system privileges to common database accounts from each PDB in which the account requires the system privilege or perform the grant with the **CONTAINER = ALL** clause from the root container.*

To resolve the issue, you can perform the grant for the CREATE SESSION system privilege from within the context of the SALES PDB, as follows:

```
sec_mgr@db12cr[sales]> GRANT CREATE SESSION TO c##bill;

Grant succeeded
```

You could also perform the grant for the CREATE SESSION system privilege from within the root container and use the ***CONTAINER = ALL*** clause as follows:

```
c##sec_mgr@db12cr[cdb$root]> GRANT CREATE SESSION TO c##bill
  2   CONTAINER = ALL;

Grant succeeded.
```

If the preceding syntax was used initially, a query on the CDB_SYS_PRIVS view would display the following results:

```
c##sec_mgr@db12cr[cdb$root]> SELECT grantee, privilege, common, con_id
  2   FROM cdb_sys_privs
  3   WHERE grantee = 'C##BILL'
  4   ORDER BY common, con_id;
```

```
GRANTEE                         PRIVILEGE              COM    CON_ID
------------------------------- ---------------------- ---    ----------
C##BILL                         CREATE SESSION         NO              1
C##BILL                         CREATE SESSION         NO              5
C##BILL                         CREATE SESSION         YES             1
C##BILL                         CREATE SESSION         YES             5
C##BILL                         CREATE SESSION         YES             7

5 rows selected.
```

As you can see, the CREATE SESSION privilege is granted as a container-specific privilege (COMMON = NO) for both the root container (CON_ID = 1) and the SALES PDB (CON_ID = 5). You can also see the CREATE SESSION privilege is listed as a common privilege (COMMON = YES) for the root container and all of our PDBs. Once either form of the **GRANT** command has been completed, the account C##BILL can log on to the SALES PDB:

```
c##sec_mgr@db12cr[cdb$root]> CONNECT c##bill@sales
Enter password:
Connected.
```

Similarly, the **REVOKE** command also includes an optional **CONTAINER = ALL** clause to control system privilege revocation from common accounts across the CDB's containers, while **CONTAINER = CURRENT** (the default) would affect only the current session's container. The granting or revoking of object privileges (tables, views, procedures) also supports the **CONTAINER = ALL** syntax, but there are some interesting points to consider with object privileges. Each PDB will have a unique set of application objects defined by customers. We might load a sales history application under the SH schema into two PDBs named DEV and TEST. We could not use the following **GRANT** command syntax from the root container to allow an account such as C##BILL to query an SH table and expect it to work as desired:

```
c##sec_mgr@db12cr[cdb$root]> GRANT SELECT ON sh.sales_history
  2  TO C##BILL CONTAINER = ALL;
GRANT SELECT ON sh.sales_history TO C##BILL CONTAINER = ALL
                *
ERROR at line 1:
ORA-00942: table or view does not exist
```

One reason for this is the SH.SALES_HISTORY object is not an Oracle-supplied, common object across all PDBs or even in the current container. Further, the SH schema is not an Oracle-supplied common account across all PDBs. If the SH account were created in more than one PDB, it would be a unique account with uniquely identified objects in each PDB. With Oracle-supplied common objects, such as the Oracle Virtual Private Database (VPD) PL/SQL package DBMS_RLS, we can use the **GRANT** command syntax shown next:

```
c##sec_mgr @db12cr[cdb$root]> GRANT EXECUTE ON SYS.DBMS_RLS
  2  TO C##BILL CONTAINER = ALL;

Grant succeeded.
```

This grant authorizes the account C##BILL to execute the DBMS_RLS in all containers.

It's easy to see that the **CONTAINER** clause allows you to create and control privileged administrators and common accounts easily in all of a CDB's containers with the **CONTAINER = ALL** clause. Using **CONTAINER = CURRENT** also allows for fine-grained control of privilege management within all containers, so that the least privilege security tenant can be achieved. Finally, we have demonstrated that we can easily create and manage application schema accounts, or other named end user accounts, in each PDB in the same manner that was possible in previous releases of Oracle Database.

Managing Database Account Passwords and Profiles

Passwords are the most prevalent form of authentication to Oracle Databases. Oracle enabled you to enforce the choice of strong passwords through the use of password complexity routines. Passwords are often the weak link in the security chain. A poorly chosen password or well-known default password that has not been changed are the greatest security risks to a database.

Additionally, Oracle has profiles, which provide a way to ensure that good password management practices, such as password aging and password reuse controls, are also being followed.

The following section describes how you can enforce secure password policies in Oracle Database 12c and the associated methods to manage local database accounts and their associated passwords.

Managing Passwords for Local Database Accounts

Oracle Database stores user passwords in the data dictionary. However, passwords aren't stored in plain text, but in an encrypted form known as a *password verifier*. Password verifiers are encrypted representations of plain-text passwords. The value is stored in a hexadecimal representation (numbers 0–9 and letters A–F). Oracle authenticates a connection to the database by computing a password verifier for the plain-text password presented by the user and comparing it to the value stored in the data dictionary. The user is authenticated if the two password verifiers match. Oracle Database 12c supports case-sensitive passwords. In Oracle Database 11g, the database initialization parameter **SEC_CASE_SENSITIVE_LOGON** could be used to control this case sensitivity.

Maintaining Database Passwords

In previous examples, we demonstrated the ways that you can create new accounts and passwords using the **CREATE USER** and **GRANT** commands with the following syntax:

```
CREATE USER <account> IDENTIFIED BY <new password>
GRANT CREATE SESSION TO <account> IDENTIFIED BY <new password>
```

NOTE
*For named accounts, used by real end users (people), it is a best practice to expire the password using the **ALTER USER <account> PASSWORD EXPIRE** command. For application schema accounts, once the application is successfully deployed and configured, it is a best practice to expire the password and lock the account using the **ALTER USER <account> PASSWORD EXPIRE ACCOUNT LOCK** command.*

To change an account's password, you must have the ALTER USER system privilege and issue the following command in SQL*Plus:

```
ALTER USER <account> IDENTIFIED BY <new password>
```

This command applies to most accounts in both PDBs and the root container. If you do not have the ALTER USER system privilege, you can issue this command only for the account you have currently logged on to. You use the following command to change the password for all common accounts in the container database root container as well as all of the PDBs:

```
ALTER USER C##<account> IDENTIFIED BY <new password> CONTAINER = ALL;
```

You can also change a database account password by using SQL*Plus to connect to database and issuing the SQL*Plus **PASSWORD** command. The **PASSWORD** command has the following syntax:

```
PASSWORD [<account_name>];
```

If the *<account_name>* parameter is omitted, the password will be changed for the currently logged-in database account.

In the next section, we describe how to ensure that strong passwords and secure password policy management requirements can be met using Oracle Database profiles.

Authenticating Remote Database Clients

When remote clients or other remote databases connect to a database over a network, the plain-text password supplied by the client is never sent over the network. The challenge and response data during this authentication phase is encrypted using the Advanced Encryption Standard (AES) algorithm before it's sent across the network. The database initialization parameter **SEC_MAX_ FAILED_LOGIN_ATTEMPTS** should be used to control the number of times a remote client can fail login attempts before Oracle Database 12*c* drops the physical network connection between the client and server.

You should further encrypt the details of all client and server interaction using the Oracle Database network encryption feature. This feature supports an Oracle-supplied symmetric approach (native) and an asymmetric approach based on PKI/SSL. Further, the feature is no longer a separately priced option for any Oracle Database release, including those prior to Oracle Database 12*c*.

Secure External Password Store

One particularly difficult security problem that faced system and database administrators was how to protect database account passwords that were used by batch programs or third-party products (such as open source application servers). For years, administrators would store the account passwords unencrypted in a script or configuration file. Oracle created Secure External Password Store to address this security problem.

Many Oracle users are still unaware of this feature, so it is important that we introduce the feature here and describe how it works. The Secure External Password Store feature allows you to create a password-protected and encrypted Oracle wallet file where you can securely store database credentials. You can use the mkstore utility to create the wallet and then use the same tool to create and store database credentials. You can then configure Oracle SQL*Net file sqlnet.ora to identify the location of the wallet and add an alias to the tnsnames.ora file for each credential in the wallet. Using this approach, you can connect to the database using the alias stored in the wallet following this format:

```
sqlplus /@<wallet_tns_alias>
```

The Oracle client software will look for an entry in tnsnames.ora with the alias shown in the example to determine the connection parameters for the database to connect to. The Oracle client software will then look in the sqlnet.ora for the location of the Oracle wallet file. Finally, the Oracle client software will locate the secret store entry in the Oracle wallet with the alias shown in the preceding example and decrypt the username and password for that alias. The Oracle wallet is configured as an auto-login wallet, but auto-login will work only if the wallet is owned by the current OS account.

NOTE
For more information on the Secure External Password Store feature, refer to Chapter 3 of the Oracle Database Security Guide.

Managing Database Account Profiles

Oracle Database profiles have been used in the past to control resource consumption and to enforce secure password management policy controls such as password complexity checking functions, password aging, and password reuse. Secure password management policy controls are important to achieving strong authentication for local database accounts and avoiding lost or stolen passwords that result in unauthorized access to your databases. Controlling resource usage is an important security-related topic, because it helps to improve the availability of your database. If you do not take steps to control resource consumption in your database, you could be subject to a DoS attack.

Secure Password Management Policies

Oracle Database profiles are used to define the password constraints that make up your password management policies for database accounts. The **CREATE PROFILE** and **ALTER PROFILE** commands are used to create custom collections of password constraints controls. Oracle Database profiles include support for the following password constraints controls:

- **Failed logon attempts**   The number of times an incorrect password can be used before the account is locked.

- **Account lockout**   The amount of time that an account will remain locked after repeated incorrect password login attempts.

- **Password lifetime or age**   The number of days that a password can be used before it must be changed.

- **Password grace time**   The amount of time that an account can use an expiring password before it must be changed.

- **Password reuse time/max**   The number of times different passwords must be used before a password can be reused or the number of days before a password can be reused.

- **Password verification**   The ability to specify a custom PL/SQL function to verify that a password meets your organization's password complexity rules (that is, the custom PL/SQL function could check for total length of the password, types of characters used, character sequences used, dictionary-based passwords, and so on).

Oracle Database 12*c* includes a single profile named DEFAULT that serves as the default profile for database accounts that are created using the **CREATE USER** command without the PROFILE clause. Custom profiles can also be created with limit values that fallback to the DEFAULT profile for one or more of the controls. You can modify the profile used by one or more of your database accounts with the following command syntax:

```
ALTER USER <account_name> PROFILE <profile_name>
```

Normally, after creating a password profile, you will force your users to change their passwords to ensure all passwords being used comply with the profile. To do this, you expire the user's existing password. Upon the next login, the database prompts the user to reset the password. The new password is checked against the complexity routine and the other password profile values will also be enforced.

Let's look at the DEFAULT profile. The settings in this profile can be displayed as follows:

```
c##sec_mgr@db12c2[cdb$root]> SELECT resource_name, limit, common
  2   FROM dba_profiles
  3   WHERE profile = 'DEFAULT' AND resource_type = 'PASSWORD'
  4   ORDER BY resource_name;

RESOURCE_NAME              LIMIT            COM
------------------------   --------------   ---
FAILED_LOGIN_ATTEMPTS      10               NO
PASSWORD_GRACE_TIME        7                NO
PASSWORD_LIFE_TIME         180              NO
PASSWORD_LOCK_TIME         1                NO
PASSWORD_REUSE_MAX         UNLIMITED        NO
PASSWORD_REUSE_TIME        UNLIMITED        NO
PASSWORD_VERIFY_FUNCTION   NULL             NO

7 rows selected.
```

As you can see, the password age, password grace time, and account lock time for this profile are set, which is a good start. However, there is no password verification function set. You will also notice that there are no resource control limits in place. To enforce strong authentication, we must first implement a password verification function.

Password Complexity Verification   Oracle supports user-defined password complexity routines that allow you to validate the strength of passwords when they are set. Password complexity routines are critical to ensuring that password best practices are obeyed. The complexity routine technically implements the official password policy in your organization (assuming you have such a policy, and you should). You can check for many things within the routine. Here are a few common best practice checks you can implement within the complexity routine:

- Password is greater than some specified length.
- Password contains at a certain number of characters (upper or lower case), digits, and special characters.
- Password is not the same as or similar to the old password.
- Password is not easily guessable by using some form of the username, database hostname, or common words (think a dictionary).

Three template password verification PL/SQL functions are provided by Oracle Database 12c: verify_function_11g, ora12c_verify_function, and ora12c_strong_verify_function. The code for these functions is located in the file $ORACLE_HOME/rdbms/admin/utlpwdmg.sql. These functions are well documented in the *Oracle Database Security Guide*, but it is important that you know how to deploy these functions and create your own verification functions or customize those supplied by Oracle. The function that implements the password check has to be implemented in the SYS schema, and you will need to grant EXECUTE on the function to PUBLIC. The function declaration must remain the same, having three VARCHAR2 parameters:

```
CREATE OR REPLACE FUNCTION verify_function_custom
(username varchar2, password varchar2, old_password varchar2)
RETURN BOOLEAN
```

The password complexity function returns a Boolean value. The value TRUE means the password is okay. However, a good trick is to raise an exception in the function to notify the user of exactly what condition failed during the password complexity validation. Otherwise, password validation errors will result in a generic error. Some customers may consider this obscurity more desirable from a security standpoint!

To illustrate, we will first deploy the password complexity routines provided with Oracle Database 12c as follows:

```
sqlplus / as sysdba @$ORACLE_HOME/rdbms/admin/utlpwdmg.sql
```

We will not show the entire output listing for the sake of brevity, but focus on important points of the script. First, the script provides a very useful generic PL/SQL function named **complexity_check** that can be used across multiple verification functions for checking the password length and the minimums for the number of letters (upper or lower), digits, or special characters. This functions signature is as follows:

```
CREATE OR REPLACE FUNCTION complexity_check
    (password varchar2,
     chars integer := NULL,
     letter integer := NULL,
     upper integer := NULL,
     lower integer := NULL,
     digit integer := NULL,
     special integer := NULL)
    RETURN BOOLEAN ;
```

The script also includes a PL/SQL function named **string_distance** that is an implementation of the Levenshtein distance mathematical formula used for measuring the difference between two sequences. This function should be used if you want to enforce that new and old passwords are not the same or even similar.

Let's take a look at the code in $ORACLE_HOME/rdbms/admin/utlpwdmg.sql that implements the Oracle-supplied password verification function **ora12c_strong_verify_function**. We think that **ora12c_strong_verify_function** is the best function to start with either as it exists or as a basis for customization.

```
sys@db12cr[cdb$root] > CREATE OR REPLACE FUNCTION ora12c_strong_verify_function
  2 (username varchar2,
  3   password varchar2,
  4   old_password varchar2)
  5 RETURN BOOLEAN IS
  6     differ integer;
  7 BEGIN
  8     IF NOT complexity_check(password, chars => 9, upper => 2, lower => 2,
  9                             digit => 2, special => 2) THEN
 10         RETURN(FALSE);
 11     END IF;
 12
 13     -- Check if the password differs from the previous password by at least
 14     -- 4 characters
 15     IF old_password IS NOT NULL THEN
 16       differ := string_distance(old_password, password);
 17       IF differ < 4 THEN
 18         raise_application_error(-20032, 'Password should differ from previous '
```

```
19                                    || 'password by at least 4 characters');
20        END IF;
21      END IF ;
22
23      RETURN(TRUE);
24   END;
25   /
```

```
Function created.
```

```
sys@db12cr[cdb$root]> GRANT EXECUTE ON ora12c_strong_verify_function
 2 TO PUBLIC;
```

```
Grant succeeded.
```

In this function, we can see that the password verification function uses the **complexity_check** function to enforce passwords have a minimum length of nine characters and include two uppercase characters, two lowercase characters, two digits, and two special characters. The function then uses the **string_distance** function to ensure that any new passwords differ by at least four characters. Using these two controls, you can handle the recommendations of avoiding easily guessable passwords, such as "secret," "oracle," or the username itself (unless you use complex account names!), as well as the same or similar new and old passwords.

Database Profiles in Action

After running $ORACLE_HOME/rdbms/admin/utlpwdmg.sql, you will notice that the Oracle Database profile DEFAULT has been modified to include the password function **ora12c_verify_function**, as follows:

```
c##sec_mgr@db12cr[cdb$root]> ALTER PROFILE DEFAULT LIMIT
  2    PASSWORD_LIFE_TIME 180
  3    PASSWORD_GRACE_TIME 7
  4    PASSWORD_REUSE_TIME UNLIMITED
  5    PASSWORD_REUSE_MAX  UNLIMITED
  6    FAILED_LOGIN_ATTEMPTS 10
  7    PASSWORD_LOCK_TIME 1
  8    PASSWORD_VERIFY_FUNCTION ora12c_verify_function;
```

```
Profile altered.
```

We will modify the DEFAULT profile to leverage the **ora12c_strong_verify_function** for the **PASSWORD_VERIFY_FUNCTION** and to enforce more stringent password controls as follows:

```
c##sec_mgr@db12cr[cdb$root]> ALTER PROFILE DEFAULT LIMIT
  2        PASSWORD_LIFE_TIME 90
  3        PASSWORD_GRACE_TIME 7
  4        PASSWORD_REUSE_TIME 365
  5        PASSWORD_REUSE_MAX UNLIMITED
  6        FAILED_LOGIN_ATTEMPTS 5
  7        PASSWORD_LOCK_TIME 0.5
  8        PASSWORD_VERIFY_FUNCTION ora12c_strong_verify_function;
```

```
Profile altered.
```

Setting **PASSWORD_LIFE_TIME** to 90 days forces the user to change their password once every three months. A value of 365 for **PASSWORD_REUSE_TIME** means they must not reuse the same password for the next 365 days. Setting the **PASSWORD_GRACE_TIME** to 7 means the user will be notified seven days before they are required to change their password. If the user successfully changes their password, then the day counter behind the **PASSWORD_LIFE_TIME** setting is reset. A value of 5 for **FAILED_LOGIN_ATTEMPTS** means that if the user mistypes the password five times, the account will be locked. A **PASSWORD_LOCK_TIME** of 0.5 will keep the account locked for a half a day or 12 hours if the account was locked as a result of the **FAILED_LOGIN_ATTEMPTS** value being reached.

We now test the **ora12c_strong_verify_function** to see how it behaves with password policy violations as well as with valid passwords:

```
-- force a length violation
c##sec_mgr@db12cr[cdb$root] > CREATE USER c##user1
  2  IDENTIFIED BY welcome1;
CREATE USER c##user1
*
ERROR at line 1:
ORA-28003: password verification for the specified password failed
ORA-20001: Password length less than 9

-- force a minimum character type missing violation
c##sec_mgr@db12cr[cdb$root] > CREATE USER c##user1
  2  IDENTIFIED BY welcome123;
 CREATE USER c##user1
*
ERROR at line 1:
ORA-28003: password verification for the specified password failed
ORA-20023: Password must contain at least 2 uppercase character(s)
-- attempt a valid password

c##sec_mgr@db12cr[cdb$root] > CREATE USER C##user1
  2  IDENTIFIED BY "1qa@WS3#ed";

User created.

-- attempt to reuse the password
c##sec_mgr@db12cr[cdb$root] > ALTER USER C##user1
  2  IDENTIFIED BY "1qa@WS3#ed";
ALTER USER C##user1
*
ERROR at line 1:
ORA-28007: the password cannot be reused

-- note the Levenshtein distance algorithm will fire
-- for the real end user changing the password
-- not an administrator like SYSDBA
-- so let's login as the account to test this
c##sec_mgr@db12cr[cdb$root] > GRANT CREATE SESSION TO c##user1;

Grant succeeded.

-- login as c##user1
```

```
c##sec_mgr@db12cr[cdb$root]> CONNECT c##user1/"1qa@WS3#ed"
Connected.

-- SQL*Plus really does not echo the password below
-- they are just shown for readability
c##user1@db12cr[cdb$root]> PASSWORD
Changing password for C##USER1
Old password: 1qa@WS3#ed
New password: 2qa@WS3#ed
Retype new password: 2qa@WS3#ed
ERROR:
ORA-28003: password verification for the specified password failed
ORA-20032: Password should differ from previous password by at least 4 characters

Password unchanged
```

Keep the Password Policies Practical

A password profile is a great way to ensure that good password management practices are being used; however, you have to balance need for good security with usability. For example, forcing users to choose a new password each week (that is, expiring passwords too frequently) or requiring extremely long password with complex validation rules may result in users writing down their passwords and storing them in view of their coworkers.

As another example, you may decide that after three failed logins, the account will be locked for a day, which can have unintended consequences. The failed login and account locking can aid someone launching a DoS attack. The attack is made easy because a malicious person can intentionally lock *all* the database accounts by simply providing an incorrect password for each database user.

Limiting Database Resources with Database Profiles

Whether issues occur intentionally or maliciously, a computer's resources can be monopolized without much effort. Generally, when this is done maliciously, it is known as a denial-of-service (DoS) attack.

DoS attacks are easy to implement and hard to defend against. The defense challenge arises from the fact that there are an enormous number of ways to trigger such an attack. The result is simple: exhaust computing resources to the point that the database can no longer provide adequate service. Fortunately, you can mitigate the risk of DoS attacks in your database.

In addition to the password profile capabilities, Oracle also supports the use of resource profiles to limit the use of database resources. Resource limits help ensure that the application or user does not intentionally or inadvertently take over the database and system resources. You can view the various resources that can be managed as well as their current settings by querying the DBA_PROFILES view:

```
c##sec_mgr@db12cr[cdb$root]> SELECT resource_name, limit, common
  2   FROM dba_profiles
  3   WHERE profile = 'DEFAULT' AND resource_type = 'KERNEL'
  4   ORDER BY resource_name;

RESOURCE_NAME                      LIMIT                             COM
---------------------------------  --------------------------------  ---
COMPOSITE_LIMIT                    UNLIMITED                         NO
CONNECT_TIME                       UNLIMITED                         NO
```

```
CPU_PER_CALL                    UNLIMITED               NO
CPU_PER_SESSION                 UNLIMITED               NO
IDLE_TIME                       UNLIMITED               NO
LOGICAL_READS_PER_CALL          UNLIMITED               NO
LOGICAL_READS_PER_SESSION       UNLIMITED               NO
PRIVATE_SGA                     UNLIMITED               NO
SESSIONS_PER_USER               UNLIMITED               NO

9 rows selected.
```

You can see that the default values are all set to UNLIMITED. A best practice is to define specific values for as many of these values as possible. Some general guidelines on the parameters are as follows:

- **SESSIONS_PER_USER** should be set to the size of your application server connection pool. If you are not using a connection pool (or have no idea what that means), then set the value to something reasonable, large for applications and small for end user accounts. You should consider that an application may lock or a computer may freeze with the connection open, so a value of 1 may be too restrictive. Note that it is possible to create a DoS attack by utilizing the CREATE SESSION privilege and connecting to the database over and over until the database server exhausts all memory. Setting this parameter helps to ensure this will not happen.

- **IDLE_TIME** can be set to help ensure that users don't leave a connected terminal in the database while they step out for a lunch break. If their machine is left unlocked, then someone can simply walk up and start accessing the user's data without having to worry about breaking passwords or subverting privileges. This value is more applicable to client-server applications than to web applications; if the latter is using a connection pool, the server should not disconnect the pooled connections

- **CPU_PER_CALL** is a difficult parameter to guess, but it helps to ensure the availability of the database. Often CPU monopolization occurs not by a malicious user, but by insufficiently tested application code.

Refer to the CREATE PROFILE section in the *Oracle Database 12c SQL Reference* document for specific definitions on all the settings. Setting the profile parameters to the logical and correct values may take a few tries before you find the best values. Start with a least privilege mentality by setting the values very conservatively. If you find that you need to relax a few privileges for legitimate reasons, do so only after you have determined the values need to be relaxed as a result of sufficient application testing before release to production.

A best practice is to create a profile for each application or class of users in the database. This includes administrators at all levels.

Limiting Database Resources with Oracle Database Resource Manager

The Oracle Database Resource Manager's DBMS_RESOURCE_MANAGER PL/SQL package is the preferred way to control resource usage starting in Oracle Database 10g and remains so in Oracle Database 12c. The Oracle Database Resource Manager offers more features and flexibility for resource control when compared to the controls offered by Oracle Database profiles. Resource limits in Oracle Database profiles simply enforce cumulative usage of system resources such as CPU, logical reads, and memory usage to determine if a profile violation has occurred and have no proactive control that resource usage will not starve the system. The Oracle Database Resource Manager not only enforces limits on database usage, but works in tandem with the operating system to allocate resources to provide a guaranteed minimum level of service. It also prevents requests it knows might exceed limits from even starting. Oracle Database Resource Manager offers a delegated administration module that can control resources such as CPU, Idle Time Limit, Exadata I/O, Runaway Queries, Parallel Execution Servers, Active Session Pool with Queuing, and the Undo Pool. This flexibility makes the Oracle Database Resource Manager particularly useful in a cloud-computing environment where multiple tenants will be sharing server resources that are being used by Oracle Database 12*c*.

Database Resource Manager Policy Components   Oracle Database Resource Manager controls resource usage with the following policy components:

- **Resource Consumer Group**   A collection of database sessions that have common resource requirements. Resources are allocated to groups as opposed to database sessions.
- **Resource Plan**   A collection of directives that dictate resources allocation to resource consumer groups.
- **Resource Plan Directive**   The association of a resource consumer group with a resource plan.

Oracle Database Resource Manager includes the following default resource consumer groups. These groups represent a number of different types of database processing or transaction profiles you might encounter and should be used where applicable.

- **BATCH_GROUP**   Targeted batch operations that perform mixed read/write workloads
- **DSS_CRITICAL GROUP**   Targeted for high-priority Decision Support Systems (DSS) queries that perform heavy read or heavy analytical-based workloads used in DSS
- **DSS_GROUP**   Targeted for low-priority DSS queries that perform fewer read or fewer analytical-based workloads used in DSS systems
- **ETL_GROUP**   Targeted for Extract/Transformation and Loading (ETL) jobs
- **INTERACTIVE_GROUP**   Targeted Online Transaction Processing (OLTP) operations conducted in an interactive, ad-hoc manner that perform mixed read/write workloads
- **LOW_GROUP**   Targeted for low-priority sessions that are not known to consume a lot of resources
- **OTHER_GROUPS**   Default consumer group for all sessions that are not mapped to any consumer group at session startup; cannot be assigned through mapping rules
- **SYS_GROUP**   Initial consumer group for all sessions created by user accounts SYS or SYSTEM
- **Other System**   There are a few consumer groups prefixed with ORA$ that are used by Oracle Database for performance tuning and statistics collection jobs

Oracle Database Resource Manager includes the following default resource plans. These plans are configured to allocate resources for a number of different types of database processing or transaction profiles one might encounter. The default plans should be used where applicable.

- **DEFAULT_MAINTENANCE_PLAN**   Intended for maintenance windows defined within the Oracle Database or by customers
- **DEFAULT_PLAN**   A simple, default plan that prioritizes SYS_GROUP operations, allocating fewer resources to internal, automated database operations
- **DSS_PLAN**   Targeted to prioritize DSS operations over ETL operations
- **ETL_CRITICAL_PLAN**   Targeted for ETL operations typically used in a data warehouse loading environment
- **MIXED_WORKLOAD_PLAN**   Targeted for mixed read/write workload prioritizing interactive operations over batch operations

You can create your own resource consumer groups and resource plans using the DBMS_RESOURCE_MANAGER PL/SQL package. Refer to the script named 02.003000.sql that is included in the examples for this book. In this example, we create a SALES Application resource group for the SH account in the SALES PDB.

Assigning Resource Manager Policy Mappings   The finest granularity of resource control for Oracle Database profiles is at the account level. Achieving this granularity would be cumbersome due to the combined nature of the password controls and resources limits within Oracle Database profiles, as attempting this would result in significant increase in the number of profiles required. On the other hand, Oracle Database Resource Manager allows you to define resource consumer groups, using the DBMS_RESOURCE_MANAGER.SET_CONSUMER_GROUP_MAPPING procedure, based on the following criteria:

- Database Account Name
- Database Service Name
- OS Account Name for the Database Client
- OS Program Name for the Database Client
- OS Hostname for the Database Client
- Oracle Module Name set via DBMS_APPLICATION_INFO.SET_MODULE
- Oracle Action Name set via DBMS_APPLICATION_INFO.SET_ACTION
- Database Service Name and Oracle Module Name combination
- Database Service Name and Oracle Action Name combination
- Oracle Function Name when Oracle RMAN or Oracle Data Pump is used

The values for these criteria include support for wildcards as well. For example, we define a consumer group mapping rule to force all sessions from development workstations, whose hostnames begin with *devwks* to use the LOW_GROUP consumer group described previously.

```
BEGIN
    DBMS_RESOURCE_MANAGER.SET_CONSUMER_GROUP_MAPPING(
        ATTRIBUTE => DBMS_RESOURCE_MANAGER.CLIENT_MACHINE
```

```
        , VALUE => 'devwks%'
        , CONSUMER_GROUP => 'LOW_GROUP');
END;
/
```

There is an opportunity here to create flexible, dynamic, and fine-grained control of the specific resource consumer group that is active for any given SQL statement. You can combine one or more of these factors with other factors about your application's state to a resource consumer group. For example, you could modify an application to call a custom PL/SQL procedure before SQL is issued. The procedure would map combinations of contextual factors such as database user, service name, OS hostname, database module name, and the application's current transaction type to the name of the most desirable resource consumer group. In this procedure, you could simply switch to the mapped resource consumer group using the PL/SQL procedure DBMS_RESOURCE_MANAGER.SWITCH_CURRENT_CONSUMER_GROUP.

Chapter 27 of the *Oracle Database Administration Guide* is a great source of information on some of the concepts and features of Oracle Database Resource Manager we did not cover here, such as multilevel resource plans and instance caging. This document also discusses a number of views that exist to examine the configuration and run-time state of Oracle Database Resource Manager. The *Oracle Database PL/SQL Packages* and *Types Reference Guide* have details on the parameters for the functions and procedures defined in the DBMS_RESOURCE_MANAGER PL/SQL package. Consult these two sources to help you understand the flexibility of this feature to protect against runaway resource usage on your database servers and to understand the implementation options available to you.

Summary

In this chapter we discussed the native identification and authentication approaches that are available in Oracle Database 12*c*. We discussed how these approaches can be used for the variety of database accounts, from privileged administrator, to application schema account, to application end user. We demonstrated how to provide the two important security tenets, separation of duty and least privilege, for privileged system administrators. We also demonstrated how Oracle Database 12*c* provides a secure mechanism for local, named database account and password management to help you ensure secure propagation to the database. We briefly discussed how Oracle Database profiles and Oracle Database Resource Manager can be used to offer increased availability and resource sharing in a cloud-computing environment.

Identity propagation and the related session contextual factors are extremely important to maintaining a complete and accurate database audit trail and for enabling fine-grained security policies that govern access control to data. Local database account management is flexible enough to support small systems with just a few databases, but for large enterprises, we want to leverage identities stored in centralized directories. The next chapter explores how we can leverage identities stored in these centralized directories to provide identification, authentication, access control, and auditing in the database.

CHAPTER
3

Connection Pools and
Enterprise Users

In the modern computing world, we find that the most universal client interface to enterprise business applications is an Internet browser or more generally, as in the case with web services and representational state transfer (REST) APIs, an HTTP client. The browser uses HTTP to connect end users to applications rather than directly to databases. This has important implications on application security, because the connection from the application to the database does not usually include the end user's identity. The stateless nature of HTTP forces you to consider new ways of securing communications. In a stateless HTTP environment, potentially every mouse click is a new network call—it's like having to place a new phone call for every sentence in a conversation. This problem is exacerbated by the fact that the web server is conducting many conversations with end users simultaneously. Browser cookies, URL rewriting, and other techniques have addressed a stateful way to maintain end user identity and the ability of the application server to create and maintain transparent "sessions" and thus state for each client. However, this represents only half of the architecture, as we are missing information about the end user from the application to the database.

External Identification and Authentication Challenges

Web applications use databases to build dynamic and often personalized web pages. Connecting from the application server to the database is a challenge, because end users do not connect directly to the database. The application servers connect to the database on behalf of the end user. How this is done makes a difference in three critical areas: security, auditing, and performance.

Connection Challenges

To build dynamic, personalized, and secure web pages from database content, you would ultimately connect your users to the database using a 1:1 mapping model, in which each end user has his or her named database account. This is more secure, because the database knows who is connected and can employ its security capabilities for access control and auditing. In a web environment, the end user is rarely directly connected to the database; the user is connected to the application, and the application is connected to the database. Therefore, you might conclude that for a secure system, the application should connect each end user to a distinct database account.

However, many system administrators and designers dislike this authentication model because of password security. This design could require the application to keep track of end user passwords. Modern application servers have built-in authentication services that obviate the need for the applications to perform end user authentication. Moreover, for security reasons, the applications are prevented from acquiring and using end user passwords.

Resource limitations are another factor limiting the effectiveness of this design. Web applications typically support many end users, and to connect each end user to a database account, you would have to establish a dedicated database connection for each user. If you have many users, you could exhaust the computing resources on your application server, database, and administrative staff simply trying to create and maintain all the database accounts and connections. For applications with a small number of connections, dedicated accounts and connections may be possible. Also something to consider, there's no guarantee that a user will access the application, or once they have started accessing it, that they will continue to using it. For example, I use a web application to create expense reports and often realize, after logging in and looking at an enormous pile of receipts to be entered, that I am missing a receipt. So I click on the tab icon in my browser and spend the next couple hours trying to track down an electronic copy. The expense report application has no idea of what I am doing and expects me to complete and submit the expense report I started. If you are building a web application, you have to account for similar situations. Otherwise, the application may be wasting resources on open connections to the database for users who are not making use of the connections.

Performance

Suppose, for example, that user SCOTT wants to run a report. He connects to the application using his browser and requests the "YTD Report for Sales." The application converts this request—typically represented via a hyperlink in the form of a button—into SQL queries for the database. To fulfill SCOTT's request, the application has to connect to the database and issue the query or queries needed to satisfy the report. Note that SCOTT did not connected to the database; the application connected to the database on behalf of SCOTT. In a web application environment, many simultaneous end user requests must be supported. SCOTT is assumed to be one of many end users asking for a different database report. To present the report to the user, the system must connect to the database, issue queries, build web pages, and return the results as quickly as possible.

It is not optimal for stateless web applications to connect and disconnect constantly from the database. The establishment of a database connection adds significant time to the overall end user response time. In some cases, the database connection time limits the ability of the application to scale to meet the response time requirements placed upon it by a service level agreement (SLA). Think of the connection to the database as being similar to placing a phone call. You dial the phone number, some switching happens, the phone rings on the other end, someone answers, and you say who you are. All this has to happen before your conversation can begin. For a database connection, you have to figure out who you want to log in as, and then you call the database over a network connection; the database answers, asks who you are, and sets up the context of the database session. At this point, the database is ready for discourse.

The process of setting up a new database connection for each end user request consumes response time and is unnecessary. The problem is exacerbated as the number of users simultaneously accessing the database increases. Therefore, this design pattern of connecting to the database, issuing a query, and then disconnecting *is not scalable*.

Connection Pools

The performance shortcomings just described were recognized soon after applications connecting to a database came into existence. Today, the problem is commonly solved through the use of *connection pools*. When the system starts, the application or application server creates a pool of connections to the database using a shared database account such as PROD. The application or application server opens and keeps open several database connections. When an incoming end user request is made to the application, the application grabs a connection from the pool, issues a query (or queries), and then returns the connection back to the pool. A connection pool is similar to having the database predial all of the phone numbers it'll need to talk to the database. If someone needs to ask the database a question, the application simply hands them the equivalent of the telephone receiver and lets them talk (or query, as the case may be).

Connection pools are used to enhance performance in a multi-user environment. Concurrent requests can be handled by allowing each request to use one of the pre-established connections from the connection pool. Once the user's request has been satisfied, the connection is returned to the pool so it can be used in a future request. In this manner, the database connection overhead is minimized and effectively increases the overall performance and scalability of your application. Connection pool implementations vary widely, and early on the connection pools were created and managed by the application. Today, it's more common for the application server to provide the capabilities to make the connection pool management a service available to the applications. Releasing a connection from the application back to the connection pool doesn't close the physical database connection. Instead, the logical connection is returned to the pool where it's available for the next application request. The challenge is to ensure that residual identity or database privileges are removed from the last connection.

Security Risks

If all the connections are made to the same pool account, the database has no way of knowing the identity of the end user. Security can't be done on anonymity; therefore, more work is required to be able to use the database security features along with the connection pool. In most web-based applications, users have to authenticate to the application before using the application. The application will typically use this information to differentiate what the end user can see and mediate the actions they can perform. Application security is necessary, and applications should provide some level of security. However, application security shouldn't be the only layer of security in the system. Database security should exist to protect your company's important information. The security risks in not providing database security include inadvertent release or the malicious theft or destruction of information. If the application is the only place where security exists to protect the display of personally identifiable information (PII), such as Social Security numbers, a disgruntled employee might simply seek to obtain the name and password for the database connection pool account. With these credentials, the employee could connect directly to the database and use a number of SQL-based tools to retrieve PII.

The first step in the process of using a web-based application is application authentication. In many cases, the application server has been configured to perform end user authentication— that is, there is no code in the application to authenticate or to verify that an end user is authenticated. The application is configured to allow only authenticated users privilege to execute its functionality. The application isn't concerned with *how* the end user authenticated so much as that the end user *is* authenticated.

The application must work in concert with the database to ensure that effective system security is achieved. The application must ensure that the end user's identity isn't lost in the application server. Identity preservation is the security principle of securely passing the end user's identity from the application to the database for the purpose of access control and auditing. The process of performing access control and auditing in the database relies on the accuracy of the end user's identity and corresponding database security context. Identity preservation and the corresponding database security context help to ensure that the effective database privileges for the database connection are reset or re-established in a consistent manner.

External Identification and Authentication in Oracle Database 12c

The preferred approach for accomplishing identity preservation is to use one of Oracle's external authentication mechanisms. This includes Oracle Proxy Authentication, Oracle Enterprise User Security (EUS), Oracle Kerberos Authentication, or Oracle Real Application Security (RAS).

We discuss Proxy Authentication, Oracle EUS, and Kerberos Authentication in this chapter and will cover Oracle RAS in its entirety in Chapter 6.

Oracle Proxy Authentication

Oracle Proxy Authentication is an authentication API that is available in the Oracle Call Interface (OCI) connection pool technology. OCI is available in Oracle client software and can be used by any database client that uses the C or Java programming language that uses the Java Database Connectivity (JDBC) API to connect to the database. JDBC Data Source support can also be found in all of the most widely used Java-based application servers. The proxy authentication API can be configured not to require the end user's password and is secure because it requires special database privileges to implement.

Database Configuration for Proxy Authentication

The following example demonstrates how to configure Oracle Proxy Authentication. First we create two end user accounts, and then we create one application pool account. We create these accounts in one of our pluggable databases.

```
sec_mgr@db12cr[sales]> -- create two end user accounts
sec_mgr@db12cr[sales]> -- and grant CREATE SESSION
sec_mgr@db12cr[sales]> GRANT CREATE SESSION TO wendy
  2  IDENTIFIED BY VALUES 'impossible_password' ;
Grant succeeded.

sec_mgr@db12cr[sales]> GRANT CREATE SESSION TO pat
  2  IDENTIFIED BY VALUES 'impossible_password' ;
Grant succeeded.

sec_mgr@db12cr[sales]> -- create the application pool account
sec_mgr@db12cr[sales]> -- and grant CREATE SESSION
sec_mgr@db12cr[sales]> GRANT CREATE SESSION TO app_pool
  2  IDENTIFIED BY welcome1 ;
Grant succeeded.

sec_mgr@db12cr[sales]> -- authorize the application
sec_mgr@db12cr[sales]> -- end user accounts to connect over a physical
sec_mgr@db12cr[sales]> -- connection created by our application pool account
sec_mgr@db12cr[sales]> ALTER USER wendy GRANT CONNECT THROUGH app_pool;
User altered.

sec_mgr@db12cr[sales]> ALTER USER pat GRANT CONNECT THROUGH app_pool;
User altered.

sec_mgr@db12cr[sales]> -- validate that our end user account
sec_mgr@db12cr[sales]> -- can connect using the application
sec_mgr@db12cr[sales]> -- pool account's password.
sec_mgr@db12cr[sales]> -- the "[wendy]" syntax directs SQL*Plus
sec_mgr@db12cr[sales]> -- to perform proxy authentication
sec_mgr@db12cr[sales]> CONNECT app_pool[wendy]/welcome1@sales
Connected.
wendy@db12cr[sales]> SHOW USER

USER is "WENDY"
```

This example demonstrates that you can maintain end user accounts in the Oracle Database without having to maintain passwords for these end user accounts. With this approach, you can use a variety of mechanisms to identify and authenticate the end user in the application tier, and then at the point where an application needs a database connection from a connection pool, you can simply assert the end user being proxied. SQL*Plus connects to the database as the account APP_POOL with password welcome1, and then, because the end user account WENDY was given permission to "connect through" the database account APP_POOL, the database changes the connection to WENDY.

This example also demonstrates the identity preservation. That is, we connected to the database using APP_POOL as the connection pool account, but as you can see from the **SHOW USER** command, the database knows the identity of the connected session as WENDY.

Oracle Impossible Passwords

It is important to point out that for the two end user accounts we created (WENDY and PAT), we used an undocumented Oracle feature called *impossible passwords*, denoted by the **IDENTIFIED BY VALUES** clause in the preceding example. These accounts cannot directly connect to the database because no password hashes to the value **impossible_password**. Instead, they are required to connect through the proxy account APP_POOL. That is, end users WENDY and PAT will never know the password for APP_POOL and don't have usable passwords for their database accounts. Impossible passwords are similar to very strong passwords, but the former are better, because you can't use these passwords to connect to the database. Remember the discussion earlier regarding how end user passwords are hashed and the hash values are stored in the database? They are stored as password verifiers in HEX format using a complex encryption algorithm and not as actual plain-text passwords. The APP_POOL account requires only one privilege (CREATE SESSION), and no other privileges are required—nor should they be granted. This is in contrast to the way most connection pool accounts are configured today, where the account typically has more privileges than needed. The proxy account should have the ability only to connect to the database and it shouldn't have all privileges of all users!

NOTE
Providing the connect pool account with the minimal privilege needed to perform its job conforms to the least-privilege security principle.

End User Privileges Under Proxy Authentication

End user accounts that proxy through a connection pool account require the CREATE SESSION privilege as well as a set of privileges required to perform application-specific functions. The **ALTER USER** command offers a set of clauses (that is, **GRANT CONNECT THROUGH** and **DEFAULT ROLE ALL EXCEPT**) to define role-based access controls for the proxied end user account.

For example, let's assume our application requires the role APP_A_ROLE. We can prevent the application from enabling other database roles by altering the end user account to restrict the account to use only the role APP_A_ROLE—that is, the end user account is restricted from using the **SET ROLE** command. This is especially important for the DBA role and roles for other applications; this capability supports the security principle of least-privilege and assists in preventing privilege escalation. The following example statements demonstrate the role-based access control.

```
sec_mgr@db12cr[sales]> -- create a test application role
sec_mgr@db12cr[sales]> CREATE ROLE app_a_role;

Role created.

sec_mgr@db12cr[sales]> -- You would grant application
sec_mgr@db12cr[sales]> -- specific privileges to the role here
sec_mgr@db12cr[sales]> -- but we are omitting
sec_mgr@db12cr[sales]> -- this step in the example
sec_mgr@db12cr[sales]> -- Grant the role and others roles
sec_mgr@db12cr[sales]> -- to end user accounts
sec_mgr@db12cr[sales]> GRANT app_a_role TO wendy;

Grant succeeded.

sec_mgr@db12cr[sales]> GRANT app_a_role, dba, resource TO pat;

Grant succeeded.

sec_mgr@db12cr[sales]> -- disable role by default so it can
sec_mgr@db12cr[sales]> -- be enabled only when it is needed
sec_mgr@db12cr[sales]> ALTER USER wendy DEFAULT ROLE
  2  ALL EXCEPT app_a_role;

User altered.

sec_mgr@db12cr[sales]> ALTER USER pat DEFAULT ROLE
  2  ALL EXCEPT app_a_role;

User altered.

sec_mgr@db12cr[sales]> -- grant proxy privileges along with
sec_mgr@db12cr[sales]> -- ability to enable the app_a_role
sec_mgr@db12cr[sales]> ALTER USER wendy GRANT CONNECT THROUGH app_pool
  2  WITH ROLE app_a_role;

User altered.

sec_mgr@db12cr[sales]> ALTER USER pat GRANT CONNECT THROUGH app_pool
  2  WITH ROLE app_a_role;

User altered.
```

In this example, we use the **ALTER USER** command **GRANT CONNECT THROUGH** clause to restrict the end user accounts to just the APP_A_ROLE role. A few variations on this command are worth mentioning and disallow other roles from being used:

```
sec_mgr@db12cr[sales]> ALTER USER pat GRANT CONNECT THROUGH app_pool
  2  WITH NO ROLES;

User altered.
```

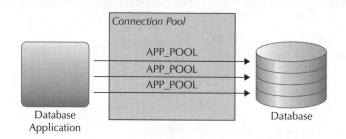

FIGURE 3-1. *Initial connection pool*

We can allow all roles except one or more roles granted to the account with the following syntax:

```
sec_mgr@db12cr[sales]> ALTER USER pat GRANT CONNECT THROUGH app_pool
  2  WITH ROLE ALL EXCEPT DBA, RESOURCE;

User altered.
```

With the use of this clause, the database session for this end user account is also restricted from issuing the **SET ROLE** command or executing the PL/SQL procedure **DBMS_SESSION.SET_ROLE**.

Proxy Authentication for Application Servers

The proxy authentication process is simple for application servers. The application server first establishes a pool of database connections using the proxy account. The proxy account (APP_POOL) is configured to allow for physical database connections. Figure 3-1 illustrates the connection pool for the database account APP_POOL.

Now, using the Oracle Java/JDBC APIs for proxy authentication on an application server, we implement the code in a manner similar to the following:

```java
package ESBD;
import java.sql.*;
import oracle.jdbc.*;
import oracle.jdbc.pool.OracleOCIConnectionPool;
import oracle.jdbc.oci.OracleOCIConnection;
public class TestProxyAuth {
  public static void main ( String args[] ) throws Exception {
    String tnsAlias = "(DESCRIPTION = (ADDRESS_LIST = (ADDRESS = " +
       " (PROTOCOL = TCP)(HOST = nsgdc2)(PORT = 1521)) )" +
       " (CONNECT_DATA = (SERVICE_NAME = sales) ) )";
    // Set the application pool connection information to a data source.
    // Most Java application servers hide the pool account's
    // credentials in encrypted configuration files.
    // We show this TNS alias, username and password
    // for brevity of the example and understanding
    // of how the JDBC are being used by the application server.
    // For standalone Java/JDBC programs you can leverage the Oracle
    // Secure External Password store to securely store
    // and use the username and password, without specifying a
    // password in your code
```

```
        OracleOCIConnectionPool ods = new OracleOCIConnectionPool();
        ods.setURL("jdbc:oracle:oci:@" + tnsAlias);
        ods.setUser("app_pool");
        ods.setPassword("welcome1");
        // set the connection pool thresholds
        java.util.Properties prop = new java.util.Properties();
        prop.setProperty(OracleOCIConnectionPool.CONNPOOL_MIN_LIMIT, "3");
        prop.setProperty(OracleOCIConnectionPool.CONNPOOL_MAX_LIMIT, "20");
        prop.setProperty(OracleOCIConnectionPool.CONNPOOL_INCREMENT, "1");
        ods.setPoolConfig(prop);
        // set up proxy authentication properties
        // and get a connection for wendy
        System.out.println ( "Connecting as wendy ...");
        java.util.Properties userNameProp = new java.util.Properties();
        userNameProp.setProperty(
                OracleOCIConnectionPool.PROXY_USER_NAME
                ,"wendy");
        Connection connWendy = ods.getProxyConnection(
                OracleOCIConnectionPool.PROXYTYPE_USER_NAME, userNameProp);
        System.out.println ( "Connected as "
+ connWendy.getMetaData().getUserName());
        connWendy.close();
        System.out.println ( "Connecting as pat ...");
        userNameProp = new java.util.Properties();
        userNameProp.setProperty(
                OracleOCIConnectionPool.PROXY_USER_NAME,"pat");
        Connection connPat = ods.getProxyConnection(
                OracleOCIConnectionPool.PROXYTYPE_USER_NAME
                , userNameProp);

System.out.println ( "Connected as " +
connWendy.getMetaData().getUserName() );
        connPat.close();
        ods.close();
    }
}
```

When this code is run, the output is as follows:

```
Connecting as wendy ...
Connected as WENDY
Connecting as pat ...
Connected as PAT
```

Oracle provides the JDBC class oracle.jdbc.pool.OracleOCIConnectionPool, and this class has the method getProxyConnection, which we are using in this example. We are required to populate only the name of the end user in the java.util.Properties object as follows:

```
        userNameProp.setProperty(
                OracleOCIConnectionPool.PROXY_USER_NAME,"<end user name>");
```

This JDBC class's **getProxyConnection()** method also supports proxy by certificate using the proxy type value PROXYTYPE_CERTIFICATE and proxy by distinguished name (DN) using the proxy type value PROXYTYPE_DISTINGUISHED_NAME.

In a typical web application where authentication is provide by the application server or a single sign-on (SSO) technology, such as Oracle Access Manager, the end user name is typically populated in a header attribute of an HTTP request. When using HTTPS for web applications, the certificate or DN can also be retrieved from the HTTP request attributes. The most common way to retrieve the user's name populated is by calling a standard J2EE method **getUserPrincipal()**, which is available from the HTTPServletRequest object, or by retrieving the REMOTE_USER header attribute from this object, as shown in the following examples:

```
String currentUser = request.getUserPrincipal().getName();
```

or

```
String currentUser = request.getRemoteUser();
```

Oracle WebLogic Server (WLS) includes built-in support for the Oracle JDBC Driver's proxy authentication by username feature. The configuration of a WLS JDBC data source can leverage WLS credential mapping so that WLS can transparently (to your code) create the proxy properties objects and call the OracleOCIConnectionPool methods, as shown in the preceding example. Refer to the documentation *Oracle Fusion Middleware Configuring and Managing JDBC Data Sources for Oracle WebLogic Server* for details on this feature.

In our example code, end user accounts PAT and WENDY proxy through the APP_POOL account. Figure 3-2 illustrates how the connections are established by the application and how they operate under the context and privilege model of the proxied accounts (PAT or WENDY).

When we issue the call to the JDBC function **getProxyConnection**, the Oracle Database reinitializes the session. This has the effect of resetting identity-related attributes, the session privilege model, and audit identification. This is important, because we do not want previous end user information in the session. If Oracle did not reinitialize the session, this could lead to privilege escalation, session stealing, or other unwanted effects.

Advantages and Disadvantages of Proxy Authentication

Oracle Proxy Authentication offers a number of advantages that we demonstrated earlier, such as ensuring identity preservation through the application tier and role-based access control enforcement. In addition, we demonstrated that neither the application nor database needs to be concerned with handling passwords. SSO technology handles end user authentication and application servers provide JDBC data sources that securely manage the storage and retrieval of credentials for pool accounts. Oracle WLS extends proxy authentication support to define mappings of end user accounts to database accounts. This significantly reduces the amount of labor required to maintain your application.

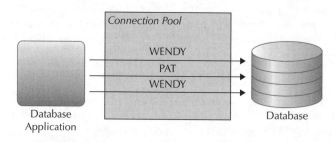

FIGURE 3-2. *Proxied physical database connections in connection pool*

From an enterprise perspective, one disadvantage of Proxy Authentication is that you still have to create and provision end user accounts in the database. This process can be quite cumbersome and imposes increased maintenance and operational costs for large organizations. The good news is that Proxy Authentication can be combined with native Oracle database support for external users stored in an enterprise's Lightweight Directory Access Protocol (LDAP) servers using EUS. EUS supports more than just using username and password as credentials. EUS supports proxy authentication by distinguished name (DN) and Public Key Infrastructure (PKI) certificates in X.509 V3 format that are maintained in LDAP-compliant directories.

Oracle Enterprise User Security

Oracle EUS enables users of the Oracle Database to be authenticated by and authorized from an LDAP directory. That is, EUS provides a mechanism whereby an administrator creates and provisions users in LDAP and not in the database. The goal of EUS is simple: centralize the administration of users accessing the database, thereby facilitating SSO, centralized usernames and passwords management, and increase overall system security by managing users more efficiently. In this section you'll see how EUS supports each of these objectives. EUS fits into a broader security area known as *identity management*.

Identity Management

With the expansion of applications and users, the computing industry has recognized the need for a better way to manage the relationship of user to application. Creating user accounts, resetting passwords, and assigning application privileges consumes an enormous amount of administrative cycles. Furthermore, the task of trying to keep privileges synchronized for user accounts in multiples of databases is prone to administrative error.

Identity management (IM) solutions are being developed and deployed to address these administrative challenges. IM provides complete user account management and offers the ability to create user accounts and manage their authentication credentials (passwords and digital certificates), assign privileges and authorizations, and suspend or delete accounts. IM provides the single source of truth for enterprise applications that need access to user authorizations and credentials. Centralized account management is the critical factor to providing reduced administration costs to your company.

Directory Services

In efforts to solve the IM challenges, the industry has gravitated to the use of LDAP directories as the single point of storage and access for information about their employees and application users. This concept is referred to as *directory services*. The first directories were built to handle the management of e-mail addresses. The computer industry quickly realized the value of a directory and a standard—ISO X.500—was developed to allow applications access to the directory in a standards-based way. The ISO X.500 standard represents a series of protocols and hierarchical categorization of data that gives applications a consistent and well-defined method for accessing information. ISO X.500 was comprehensive but it also was considered too complex to be practical for many implementations.

The LDAP standard was subsequently developed by the University of Michigan as a practical alternative to X.500. LDAP provides much of the same functionality as X.500 but without all the complexity and overhead. LDAP Version 3 is the current industry directory standard.

LDAP provides centralized storage and management of user information that can be accessed by enterprise applications. LDAP directories can also store authorizations for physical devices such as servers, network routers, and printers. A common use of LDAP directories is to provide publicly available user information, such as office phone numbers and e-mail addresses. Many commercially available e-mail programs allow you to connect to a LDAP directory to look up user e-mail addresses. The e-mail program can log on to the LDAP directory anonymously and conduct searches, which happens transparently to the end user. This works because the LDAP directory is built on a standard protocol. From a security perspective, directories are becoming the de-facto authentication mechanisms for the enterprise applications.

IM Components

The LDAP directory is one piece of the IM infrastructure. IM comprises other components that provide services and capabilities needed to manage IM. The Oracle IM infrastructure consists of these components:

- **Oracle Unified Directory (OUD)**   OUD is a lightweight LDAP-compliant directory that allows storage and retrieval of information about various directory entities (schemas, naming contexts, security, groups, and users). OUD uses file-based storage of these entities and offers replication and proxy services between OUD instances.

- **Oracle Internet Directory (OID)**   OID is also an LDAP-compliant directory that allows storage and retrieval of information about various directory entities. OID uses an Oracle Database for the storage of these entities.

- **Oracle Directory Integration Platform (DIP)**   DIP provides APIs for integrating and synchronizing directory information in OUD or OID from information stored in other directories in the enterprise. These services are generally centered on user management such that changes to user accounts are automatically synchronized. The Oracle Virtual Directory (OVD) product can be used in conjunction with DIP to expose federated directories or non-LDAP identity source as a centralized directory source.

As previously mentioned, Oracle Access Manager is a product that provides SSO capabilities and coarse-grained authorizations for web applications. This product is part of the Oracle Identity and Access Management Suite.

Oracle Directory Server Products

Oracle recognizes the value of centralizing information as well as the value of the LDAP standard. Consequently, Oracle built two LDAP V3–compliant directory products, OUD and OID, which serve as the "heart" of Oracle's IM solution.

The Oracle IM components—like Oracle Access Manager—can use OUD or OID as the centralized directory. The Oracle Database can also operate as an LDAP client—that is, the Oracle Database can be connected to an LDAP-compliant directory to centralize user authentication and authorization functions.

Enterprise User Security

Oracle EUS is a capability within the Oracle Database to allow a registered LDAP-compliant directory to authenticate users and provide user authorization data along with other user attributes. The IM benefits provided to applications and end users are precisely the same benefits that EUS provides to Oracle database administrators and database users, which could also be end users.

For database administrators, the directory becomes a centralized place for creating, updating, and deleting users; assigning database roles; and defining schema mappings. You will see in the upcoming "User-Schema Mappings" section how mapping combinations allow you to create unique or shared schemas for the end user access.

The LDAP directory stores database user I&A credentials, allowing them consistent access to registered Oracle databases. EUS can authenticate users by password, Kerberos, or X.509 V3 certificates. Also, OVD can use EUS with additional LDAP products, such as Oracle Directory Server Enterprise Edition and Microsoft Active Directory. Refer to the *Fusion Middleware Administrator's Guide for Oracle Virtual Directory* to configure OVD for EUS support.

Setting Up EUS

In this section, you will see how to configure your Oracle databases to use EUS. Note that the actual steps for this setup vary depending on database and LDAP versions. The following description is for the Oracle Database 12c and OUD 11g R2, specifically OUD version 11.1.2.1. See the *Oracle Database Enterprise User Security Administrator's Guide* for more details on setting up EUS for Oracle12c Database and OID 11g.

Directory Setup   The first step for EUS is to install the LDAP directory. Installing OUD to support EUS involves five steps:

1. Install Oracle WebLogic Server. Oracle WLS is required to run the Oracle Directory Services Manager (ODSM) web application that is used to maintain directory schemas, naming contexts, security (ACLs, password policies, and so on), directory groups, and directory users.

2. Install the Oracle Application Development Framework (ADF) run-time binaries that are required for ODSM.

3. Install the Oracle OUD software binaries into the Oracle WLS installation home.

4. Configure an Oracle OUD directory instance. Define the ports that the directory will listen on and identify SSL certificates used for secure communications. If you plan to use Oracle EUS with SSL authentication, make sure to use valid server certificates from your organization's certificate authority. Define the initial naming context for the directory, such as *dc=nsg,dc=net*. You can create additional naming context with ODSM later if you need to separate users into different directory trees. Finally, select the Enable For EUS radio button on the Oracle Components Integration dialog in this step, as this will deploy the directory schema required for EUS into the directory. When you have completed this step, start the OUD directory instance using *<**install_dir**>*/*<**OUD_instance**>*/**bin/start-ds**.

5. Create an Oracle WLS domain that will deploy the ODSM web application into the WLS admin server of the domain. When you have completed this step, start the WLS admin server using *<**install_dir**>*/**user_projects/domains/***<**DOMAIN_NAME**>*/**startWebLogic.sh**.

At this point you can access the ODSM web application with a URL similar to http://host:port/odsm. Create saved connection profiles as shown in Figure 3-3 to connect to a specific directory instance and manage its configuration.

Refer to the documentation entitled *Oracle Fusion Middleware Installation Guide for Oracle Unified Directory* for details on how to install OUD and the documentation entitled *Oracle Fusion Middleware Administrator's Guide for Oracle Unified Directory* for details on how to configure OUD.

Database Setup: Creating ldap.ora   Next you need to tell the database the location of the directory server to use and how to communicate with it (that is, the host, port, protocol, naming context). You do this by creating an ldap.ora file. It is good practice to use the Network Configuration

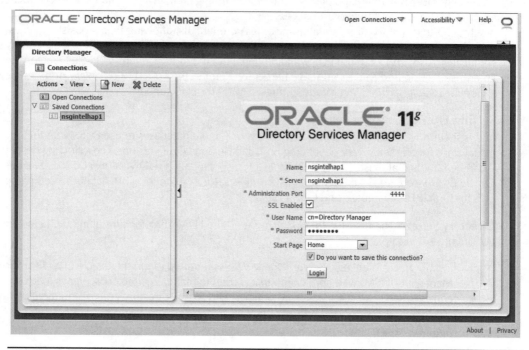

FIGURE 3-3. ODSM Connections screen

Assistant tool (command line utility name is netca) to create the ldap.ora file. When netca starts, do the following:

1. Click the Directory Usage Configuration button.

2. The next screen prompts you for a directory type. For configuring EUS with OUD, select the Oracle Internet Directory as the directory type.

3. In the next screen, enter the hostname, non-SSL port, and SSL port of the directory.

4. In the final screen, choose the naming context in which the user information will be placed. A default naming context is created when the IM schema is installed, and you can add naming contexts later to support different directories from different databases.

After you create the ldap.ora file, it resides in the $ORACLE_HOME/network/admin directory and tells the Oracle Database how to connect to the LDAP directory and where in the directory to look when authenticating users. The following is an example ldap.ora file:

```
DIRECTORY_SERVERS= (nsgintelhap1:1389:1636)
DEFAULT_ADMIN_CONTEXT = "dc=nsg,dc=net"
DIRECTORY_SERVER_TYPE = OID
```

This file must exist in the default location and contain accurate information before moving forward.

Database Setup: Registering Databases with DBCA   The second task required to complete the database setup is to register the root container and pluggable databases with the directory. Registering the database will write entries into the directory regarding the connection descriptor for the database and create credentials for the database to authenticate to the directory. As will we will see later, the registration entry for each database will be used to store the database accounts and database roles that will be used to map directory users to during the authentication process.

This registration process will leverage the standard Oracle Database Configuration Assistant (DBCA) tool. Run DBCA program in interactive mode by typing **dbca** at the command line. Make sure to run the DBCA with an OS account that has the SYSDBA privilege in the database.

NOTE
DBCA registration must proceed without Database Vault enabled if you have already configured these options. You can use the PLSQL package procedure DBMS_MACADM.DISABLE_DV to disable Database Vault if this option was already configured. You will have to restart the database instance for this change to have the desired effect in DBCA.

If you will be registering a pluggable database, register the root container and then register each pluggable database.

- To register the root container or a non-CDB, choose Configure Database Options and select the root container or the non-CDB you want to register.

- To register a pluggable database, choose Manage Pluggable Databases. DBCA will then prompt you for the name of the root container and then the name of the pluggable database you want to register.

DBCA will then prompt you for confirmation that you want to register the database.

NOTE
If the ldap.ora file does not exist, the option to register the database in a directory will not be available.

After clicking the Yes, Register The Database button, you will be prompted for the directory administrator's distinguished name, such as *cn=Directory Manager*, and password. Access to this directory account is required in the registration, because DBCA must access the entities described earlier. Subsequent access will use the registration credentials created for this database during this registration process.

DBCA also prompts you to enter an Oracle wallet password. The Oracle Database stores security credentials in the Oracle wallet. The Oracle wallet can store credentials needed by users or the database. The DBCA will generate a random strong password and securely store it in the wallet. Storing the directory credentials in the wallet is how the database authenticates to the directory when it needs to perform user authentication. The password the database uses to authenticate to the directory is not the same as the one you provide for the wallet. Figure 3-4 depicts this registration screen for the pluggable database named SALES.

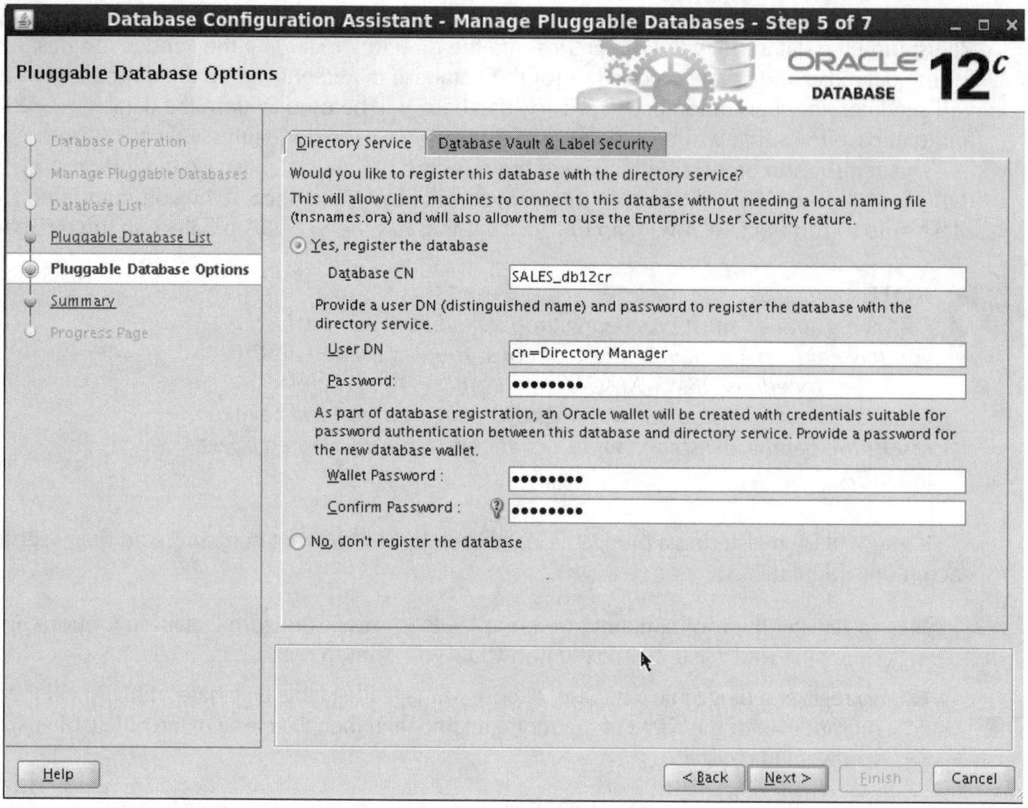

FIGURE 3-4. *DBCA database registration screen for EUS*

If you are registering a pluggable database, click the Database Vault & Label Security tab and uncheck the checkboxes that will configure these database options. DBCA will write information regarding the database to the directory and it will create the Oracle wallet. Oracle database will use the wallet to validate end user credentials (via an ldapbind operation) from this point on.

The DBCA also supports command-line, or silent, configuration options to register the root container and pluggable databases with the directory. Type the following command to view the command-line parameters for the registration root container or a non-container database (CDB):

```
dbca -configureDatabase -help
```

Type the following command to view the command-line parameters for the registration of a pluggable database:

```
dbca -configurePluggableDatabase -help
```

Database Setup: Set the Database Parameter LDAP_DIRECTORY_ACCESS   The final part of setting up EUS is to modify an initialization parameter LDAP_DIRECTORY_ACCESS. In Oracle Database 12c, the LDAP_DIRECTORY_ACCESS parameter serves as the indicator of the type of directory access. It supports the use of nondirectory SSL-authenticated users and can be used to disable directory use quickly. To disable directory access, a DBA simply issues the following in the root container database:

```
ALTER SYSTEM SET LDAP_DIRECTORY_ACCESS= NONE SCOPE=MEMORY;
```

This change alters the setting for the entire container database (that is, the root container and all pluggable databases). If you specify **SCOPE=BOTH**, the change is immediate and permanent after the next database restart.

The possible values for this parameter are NONE, SSL, and PASSWORD, with NONE set as the default. DBCA will change this value to PASSWORD and EUS security is activated immediately. The final parameter (SSL) instructs the database to use the end user's X.509 V3 certificate to authenticate to the directory.

SSL is a strong authentication option that enables database administrators to use X.509 V3 certificates and your PKI to authenticate users to the database. SSL with EUS is a more advanced configuration that requires each end user to have a certificate located on their workstation, and the user's certificate must also be loaded into the OUD or OID directory. The database must also have a valid certificate loaded in the same Oracle wallet created during the DBCA registration process. SSL with EUS offers a very secure approach to authentication because it encrypts communications from the end user's workstation to the database and from the database to LDAP.

NOTE
If you are interested in using SSL, we recommend you set up EUS with the PASSWORD authentication first, and then follow the steps in Chapter 4 of the Oracle Enterprise User Security Administrator's Guide *for setting up SSL authentication. This two-step approach is easier to troubleshoot in the event something isn't working properly. The Oracle Database software that supports SSL processing between the client and the database server can be configured to offload SSL to a third-party HSM vendor for performance reasons. Refer Chapter 18 of the* Oracle Security Guide *for details on how HSM integration can be achieved.*

Verifying the Database Setup   You should do three things to verify the database setup to support integration with the directory. First, the database parameter LDAP_DIRECTORY_ACCESS should be set to the value PASSWORD:

```
sys@db12cr[cdb$root]> show parameter LDAP_DIRECTORY_ACCESS

NAME                                 TYPE        VALUE
------------------------------------ ----------- ---------
LDAP_DIRECTORY_ACCESS                string      PASSWORD
```

Second, verify the existence of the database wallet. The wallet stores the distinguished name and password the database uses to connect securely to the directory. The actual values can be extracted by running the command **mkstore -viewEntry** and supplying the wallet's password.

For a container databases on UNIX, the wallet is located in the folder $ORACLE_BASE/admin/<*dbname*>/wallet. For a pluggable databases on UNIX, this wallet is located in the folder $ORACLE_BASE/admin/<*dbname*>/<*pdb_GUID*>/wallet.

Figure 3-5 illustrates the contents of the wallet Oracle Wallet Manager, which is invoked on UNIX by typing **owm** from the command line or running the Wallet Manager program in Microsoft Windows. You can see the Secret Store section of the Oracle wallet contains the distinguished name and password.

Now that the database is set for EUS security, you can verify that the database is registered in the directory. The best way to verify this is to perform the following steps:

1. Launch the Oracle Enterprise Manager Cloud Control

2. Select your container database target

3. Navigate to Administration

4. Navigate to Security

5. Navigate to Enterprise Security

6. Log in to LDAP directory as a directory administrator

7. Select Manage Databases

8. Click on OracleDefaultDomain

You should see the name of the database you just registered. Figure 3-6 shows the results of registering our pluggable database.

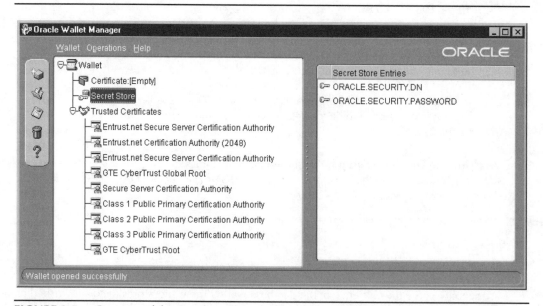

FIGURE 3-5. *Contents of the Oracle wallet*

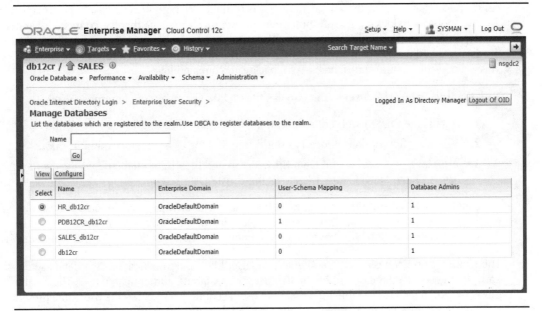

ORACLE **Enterprise Manager** Cloud Control 12c   Setup ▾   Help ▾   SYSMAN ▾   Log Out

Enterprise ▾   Targets ▾   Favorites ▾   History ▾   Search Target Name ▾

db12cr / SALES ⓘ   nsgdc2
Oracle Database ▾ Performance ▾ Availability ▾ Schema ▾ Administration ▾

Oracle Internet Directory Login > Enterprise User Security >   Logged In As Directory Manager Logout Of OID
Manage Databases
List the databases which are registered to the realm.Use DBCA to register databases to the realm.

Name [   ]

Go

View Configure

Select	Name	Enterprise Domain	User-Schema Mapping	Database Admins
◉	HR_db12cr	OracleDefaultDomain	0	1
○	PDB12CR_db12cr	OracleDefaultDomain	1	1
○	SALES_db12cr	OracleDefaultDomain	0	1
○	db12cr	OracleDefaultDomain	0	1

FIGURE 3-6.   *Cloud Control shows registered databases participating in EUS*

SSL Identification and Authentication

The database can be configured to authenticate to the directory using SSL. Doing so provides strong encryption and stronger nonrepudiation for both the database and the directory.

SSL authentication was the default security interface between the Oracle directory and the Oracle Database prior to version 10g. SSL authentication is no longer the default, however, because it is much more difficult to set up the PKI needed to support SSL certificates, and SSL encryption operates slower than without encryption. For some systems, the database and the directory may reside in the same network or private network, and the additional security of SSL is not necessary. Oracle recommends using SSL security for database-to-directory communications.

NOTE
Configuring SSL is unnecessary for the examples in this chapter. We suggest that you use password authentication first, because it is trivial to configure and it allows you to begin using EUS quickly. After you are comfortable using EUS, you can switch the database authentication to SSL. We recommend using SSL on your production systems unless the network can be protected through some other mechanism. Details for configuring your networks for SSL are given in the Oracle Enterprise Security Administrator's Guide.

Applying EUS

EUS is easy to integrate into an application from the application building perspective. EUS does not require that special code be written. EUS users are transparent to the application's client connection—that is, when the application connects to the database using a username and password and the application does not specify, hint, or in any other way indicate that the connecting user is a named database user or an enterprise user. It does not matter whether the user is connecting directly to the database or the application is connecting to the database on the user's behalf (proxy or otherwise). This is a powerful feature and is the basis for backward compatibility.

Creating the Enterprise User   You can use the ODSM to create new enterprise users.

1. Access the ODSM web console with a URL similar to *http://host:port/odsm*.
2. Select the appropriate directory connection and log as a directory administrator.
3. After logging in, select the Data Browser tab and then right-click an existing user and select Create New. Figure 3-7 shows the Create User screen.

Unfortunately, ODSM does not allow you to administer anything else in the database-directory relationship. For example, you cannot see any mapping or authorization information for the users. To access this information, you have to use the Enterprise Manager Cloud Control web console.

The Connection Process   When an enterprise user logs in to the database, the database does not know if the user is a directory authenticated user or a database authenticated user. The database must first search the USER$ table for a database user account that matches the username presented. If the database does not find an entry in the USER$ table, the database checks the value of the

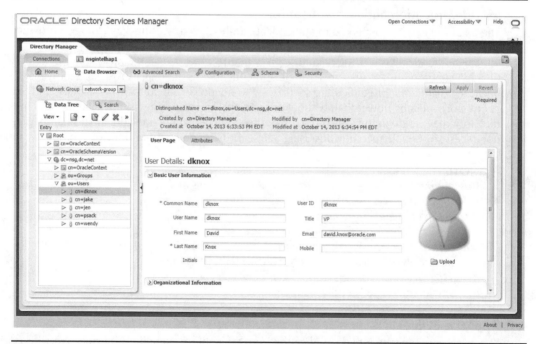

FIGURE 3-7.   *Directory Services Manager can be used to manage Enterprise Users*

LDAP_DIRECTORY_ACCESS parameter. If it is set to NONE, the database returns an error "ORA-1017: invalid username/password" message:

```
sys@db12cr[cdb$root]> -- disable directory access
sys@db12cr[cdb$root]> ALTER SYSTEM SET LDAP_DIRECTORY_ACCESS=NONE
  2  SCOPE=MEMORY;

System altered.

sys@db12cr[cdb$root]> -- connect as an enterprise user
sys@db12cr[cdb$root]> CONNECT dknox/welcome1@sales

ERROR:
ORA-01017: invalid username/password; logon denied
```

NOTE
*The **ALTER SYSTEM** command is a memory-only change and is a quick way a DBA can disable directory access if he or she thinks there is a security risk.*

If the LDAP_DIRECTORY_ACCESS parameter is set to either PASSWORD or SSL, the database assumes (after not finding the account in USER$) that the account is a directory-authenticated user. The database uses the values stored in the ldap.ora and wallet files to connect to the directory and query for the user entry matching this username. The username is a specific subcomponent of the user's distinguished name, referred to as the *nickname*. The default value for the nickname is the common name (cn), and is configurable during the initial directory setup. If the user is not a database user or a directory user, then Oracle returns a different error message:

```
sys@db12cr[cdb$root]> -- enable directory access
sys@db12cr[cdb$root]> ALTER SYSTEM SET ldap_directory_access=PASSWORD
  2  SCOPE=MEMORY;

System altered.

sys@db12cr[cdb$root]> -- connect as a user that does not exist in DB or directory
sys@db12cr[cdb$root]> CONNECT aldfjaslkjd/aslkd@sales
ERROR:
ORA-28273: No mapping for user nickname to LDAP distinguished name exists.
```

In this final example, we provide the correct directory name an associated password. The password presented for logon will be authenticated against the password stored in the LDAP server:

```
$ sqlplus dknox/welcome1@sales

SQL*Plus: Release 12.1.0.2.0 Production on Thu Aug 29 03:06:19 2013

Copyright (c) 1982, 2013, Oracle.  All rights reserved.


Connected to:
Oracle Database 12c Enterprise Edition Release 12.1.0.2.0 - 64bit Production
With the Partitioning, OLAP, Advanced Analytics and Real Application Testing options

app_public@db12cr[sales]> SHOW USER
USER is "APP_PUBLIC"
```

The user (DKNOX) was able to log on, and it appears that the user was mapped to the wrong schema (APP_PUBLIC). Actually, this mapping is correct, because DKNOX is not an account in the database. If there were a DKNOX database user, then the initial attempt to log in would have worked (assuming the password was correct) and the SQL*Plus prompt would have been

```
dknox@db12cr[sales]>
```

Creating a EUS user requires you to map the user to a database schema. This mapping determines the schema the end user will be attached to. In the preceding example, there is a mapping for the EUS user DKNOX to the APP_PUBLIC database schema. Setting up the user-schema mapping is a three-step process: create the database schema, create the EUS user, and define the mapping between the EUS user and the database schema.

User-Schema Mappings The directory maintains the mapping of EUS users to specific database schemas. Before EUS, if you wanted to create database users that had separate usernames and passwords, you had to create database schemas for each user. EUS allows for both the 1:1 mapping model and the shared schema model.

The decoupling of user from schema allows administrators to provision the end user once in the directory and then create a mapping or mappings to the databases that participate in EUS. The user will then be able to log on to any participating database within the domain as long as a mapping for the user exists.

Creating the Shared Schemas

The most common use of mapping is a shared schema to multiple enterprise users which is the one-to-many (1:M) mapping model. The first step is to create a database schema that will be shared by enterprise users. For the enterprise user DKNOX, we first have to create a shared schema account (APP_PUBLIC) and grant it CREATE SESSION privilege to connect to the database:

```
sec_mgr@db12cr[sales]> CREATE USER app_public
  2  IDENTIFIED GLOBALLY AS '';

User created.

sec_mgr@db12cr[sales]> GRANT CREATE SESSION TO app_public;

Grant succeeded.
```

The CREATE USER syntax used to create the schema APP_PUBLIC is what makes it sharable. Notice that no password is associated with the APP_PUBLIC account and the empty single quotes indicate that the account is not permitted to authenticate to the database directly. The directory will be able to map users to this schema because the password is IDENTIFIED GLOBALLY. There is no way to log in to the database using this schema/account, because there is no password. If you check the password value stored in the database, you will see a non-null value:

```
sec_mgr@db12cr[sales]> SELECT username, password
  2  FROM dba_users
  3  WHERE username = 'APP_PUBLIC';

USERNAME                        PASSWORD
------------------------------- --------------------
APP_PUBLIC                      GLOBAL
```

It appears as though behind the scenes Oracle created the database schema APP_PUBLIC using the IDENTIFIED BY VALUES 'GLOBAL' syntax even though we entered IDENTIFIED GLOBALLY AS ' ' syntax. These two creation statements have the same effect on the creation of the schema. To verify this point, in the following example the APP_PUBLIC user is first dropped and then re-created using the IDENTIFIED BY VALUES clause. We then verify that the enterprise user is able to connect to this schema.

NOTE
The following example is for illustrative purposes only and is not the Oracle-supported way to create shared schemas.

```
sec_mgr @db12cr[sales]> DROP USER app_public;

User dropped.

sec_mgr@db12cr[sales]> -- create user with password of GLOBAL
sec_mgr@db12cr[sales]> -- Note this is NOT the officially supported
sec_mgr@db12cr[sales]> -- way to create shared schemas
sec_mgr@db12cr[sales]> CREATE USER app_public IDENTIFIED BY VALUES 'GLOBAL';

User created.

sec_mgr@db12cr[sales]> GRANT CREATE SESSION TO app_public;

Grant succeeded.

sec_mgr@db12cr[sales]> CONNECT dknox/welcome1@sales
Connected.
app_public@db12cr[sales]>
```

You cannot map an enterprise user to a schema that has does not have the value GLOBAL as the password. If you map an enterprise user to a database-authenticated schema, then the enterprise user will receive an "ORA-01017: invalid username/password" error when trying to log in.

Directory Mappings　You must now map enterprise users to the previously created shared schemas. The mappings can be done at two different levels within the directory: at the domain level and at the individual database level. The domain-level mapping defines the user-schema relationship across all databases in a domain. You register your databases in specific domains when you set up EUS. The domain-level mapping is convenient, because you have to create only one mapping for all your databases. This also provides the consistency across all databases in your domain. You can be assured that users defined in the directory are always mapped to the same schemas for any database in your enterprise. Consequently, this requires that every database in the domain participating in EUS contain the same shared schemas.

The second mapping choice is to provide a user-schema mapping for each individual database. This provides flexibility in allowing the same user to attach to different schemas in different databases. This mapping model would be used in a system design where a schema already exists in the database for the user and differs across databases. For example, a user might have a schema named DKNOX in one database and one named DKNOX_US in a different database. These schemas can be preserved by specifying a different user-schema mapping for each database in the directory.

The benefit to the user is that he or she can log in to both databases using the same username and password.

Directory Entry Mappings and Subtree Mappings There are two additional ways to define the user-schema mapping for both the domain-level mapping and the individual database mapping. First, the user-schema mapping is from the individual directory user to a database schema. This is called an *entry mapping*, because it maps a specific user entry to a specific database schema. Second, the user-schema mapping is defined for a group of directory users. That is, all the users located in a certain part of the directory tree can share a mapping to a database schema. This is called *subtree mapping*.

Mapping Permutations Example

An enterprise user can be mapped to a schema in four ways. The database will follow the path of most specific to least specific in trying to determine which schema a user should be mapped to. The following example illustrates various mappings combinations as well as how the user's schema is resolved.

Creating the Schemas We create four database schemas for this example. Each schema will represent a different type of user-schema mapping.

```
sec_mgr@db12cr[sales]> -- create the application pool account for the
sec_mgr@db12cr[sales]> -- entire domain and grant CREATE SESSION
sec_mgr@db12cr[sales]> CREATE USER domain_entry IDENTIFIED GLOBALLY AS '';

User created.

sec_mgr@db12cr[sales]> GRANT CREATE SESSION TO domain_entry;

Grant succeeded.

sec_mgr@db12cr[sales]> -- create the application pool account for the
sec_mgr@db12cr[sales]> -- a domain subtree and grant CREATE SESSION
sec_mgr@db12cr[sales]> CREATE USER domain_subtree IDENTIFIED GLOBALLY AS '';

User created.

sec_mgr@db12cr[sales]> GRANT CREATE SESSION TO domain_subtree;

Grant succeeded.

sec_mgr@db12cr[sales]> -- create the application pool account for an
sec_mgr@db12cr[sales]> -- specific database and grant CREATE SESSION
sec_mgr@db12cr[sales]> CREATE USER db_entry IDENTIFIED GLOBALLY AS '';

User created.

sec_mgr@db12cr[sales]> GRANT CREATE SESSION TO db_entry;

Grant succeeded.

sec_mgr@db12cr[sales]> -- create the application pool account for an
sec_mgr@db12cr[sales]> -- a subtree and specific database and grant CREATE SESSION
```

```
sec_mgr@db12cr[sales]> CREATE USER db_subtree IDENTIFIED GLOBALLY AS '';

User created.

sec_mgr@db12cr[sales]> GRANT CREATE SESSION TO db_subtree;

Grant succeeded.
```

The shared schemas require the CREATE SESSION privilege to log on to the database. You can either grant this privilege to the shared schemas directly or use enterprise roles (discussed in Chapter 4). There is no security issue in granting the CREATE SESSION privilege to the shared schemas, because these are a special type of schema that cannot directly log in to the database.

NOTE
You should grant object and system privileges to shared database schemas only when all users that share the schema require those privileges.

Creating the User-Schema Mappings   We use the Oracle Cloud Control 12c web console to create user-schema mappings in the directory. For this example, we will create four user-schema mappings—one to each database schema. We will then log on to the database as the user DKNOX and show which schema mapping was used.

For clarity, the schema names created earlier indicate the location in the directory that the user-schema mapping occurs. For example, the DOMAIN_SUBTREE schema maps to all users in the directory subtree across all databases in the domain. Figure 3-8 depicts a domain mapping with one entry mapping and one subtree mapping. The first entry in the subtree indicates that all users that exist in the subtree will be mapped to the DOMAIN_SUBTREE schema. The second entry in the subtree indicates the user named DKNOX will be mapped to the DOMAIN_ENTRY schema. As you can see from the figure, four databases are defined in this domain. This means that user DKNOX is capable of connecting to all four databases. This also means that the schema DOMAIN_ENTRY must exist in all four databases for DKNOX to connect.

The directory does not verify that the database schema exists in each registered database. This is done at user logon time. If a user is mapped to a schema that does not exist in the database to which the user is attempting to connect, Oracle will return the error message "ORA-01017: invalid username/password." This is a great technique for quickly disabling a EUS user's ability to connect to a database—that is, an administrator could provide a mapping to a schema that does not exist and thus the user will not be able to log on.

TIP
To prevent a user from accessing your database and at the same time allowing general user access, create a user-schema mapping to a schema that does not exist.

The same type of user-schema mapping can be defined at the database level. You can specify a subtree mapping for each database in a domain. Figure 3-9 illustrates two entries for the SALES pluggable database. The first entry maps all users in the directory subtree to the DB_SUBTREE schema. The second entry maps the user DKNOX to the DB_ENTRY schema. Note that database-level mappings supersede the domain-level mappings.

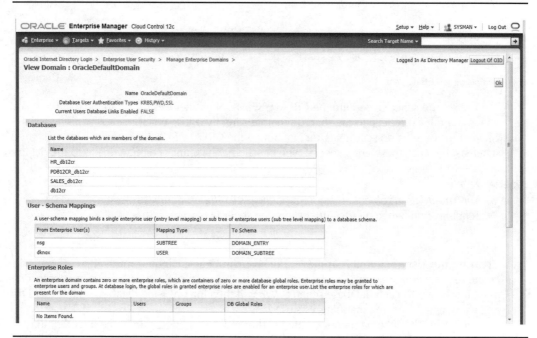

FIGURE 3-8. *Domain mappings apply to all databases registered in the domain*

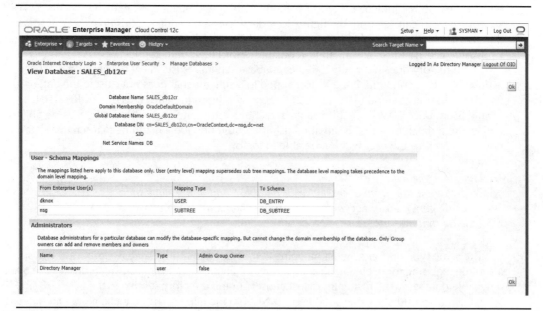

FIGURE 3-9. *Database mappings supersede domain mappings*

Testing the Mappings   We will now demonstrate user-schema mapping resolution using the four previously defined mappings. Taking the time to test this implementation is important, because these mapping combinations ultimately determine which schema the user will be mapped to and ensures the users have the correct database privileges.

The user-schema mapping resolution algorithm goes from the most specific mapping definition to the least specific. The directory will search in the following order:

1. Specific user entry for the specific database

2. Directory subtree entry for the specific database

3. Specific user entry for the domain

4. Directory subtree entry for the domain

For the pluggable database SALES, a database-specific mapping for the user DKNOX exists for the DB_ENTRY schema. When this user connects to the DAGGER database, there is no database-specific mapping, but there is an entry-level mapping to the DOMAIN_ENTRY schema.

To illustrate EUS identity preservation, user DKNOX connects to the database and then queries the database for schema and effective user information. The database name is also displayed.

```
sec_mgr@db12cr[sales]> -- test DB specific mappings
sec_mgr@db12cr[sales]> -- CONNECT to sales PDB which has database specific mapping
sec_mgr@db12cr[sales]> CONNECT dknox/welcome1@sales
Connected.
db_entry@db12cr[sales]> COL "Directory User" format a40
db_entry@db12cr[sales]> COL schema format a15
db_entry@db12cr[sales]> COL database format a10
db_entry@db12cr[sales]> SELECT SYS_CONTEXT ('userenv', 'external_name')
  2   "Directory User",
  3   USER SCHEMA,
  4   SYS_CONTEXT ('userenv', 'db_name') ||
  5   '[' || SYS_CONTEXT ('userenv', 'con_name') ||']' DATABASE
  6   FROM DUAL;

Directory User                           SCHEMA          DATABASE
---------------------------------------- --------------- ------------------
cn=dknox,ou=users,dc=nsg,dc=net          DB_ENTRY        db12cr[SALES]


db_entry@db12cr[sales]> -- test domain mapping by connecting to different
db_entry@db12cr[sales]> -- database. Note, we must create the database
db_entry@db12cr[sales]> -- schema on HR for this to work
db_entry@db12cr[sales]> CONNECT dknox/welcome1@hr
Connected.
domain_entry@db12cr[hr]> SELECT SYS_CONTEXT ('userenv', 'external_name')
  2   "Directory User",
  3   USER SCHEMA,
  4   SYS_CONTEXT ('userenv', 'db_name') ||
  5   '[' || SYS_CONTEXT ('userenv', 'con_name') ||']' DATABASE
  6   FROM DUAL;

Directory User                           SCHEMA          DATABASE
---------------------------------------- --------------- ------------------
cn=dknox,ou=users,dc=nsg,dc=net          DOMAIN_ENTRY    db12cr[HR]
```

Removing the user-specific mappings for the user DKNOX at both the database and the domain level forces the system to resolve the mappings at the subtree level. After the modifications have been made, running the connection test again validates the resolution order:

```
sec_mgr@db12cr[sales]> -- CONNECT to sales PDB with database specific entry
sec_mgr@db12cr[sales]> CONNECT dknox/welcome1@sales
Connected.
db_subtree@db12cr[sales]> SELECT SYS_CONTEXT ('userenv', 'external_name')
  2  "Directory User",
  3  USER SCHEMA,
  4  SYS_CONTEXT ('userenv', 'db_name') ||
  5  '[' || SYS_CONTEXT ('userenv', 'con_name') ||']' DATABASE
  6  FROM DUAL;

Directory User                            SCHEMA            DATABASE
----------------------------------------  ---------------   ------------------
cn=dknox,ou=users,dc=nsg,dc=net           DB_SUBTREE        db12cr[SALES]

db_subtree@db12cr[sales]> -- test mapping by connecting to different
db_subtree@db12cr[sales]> -- database Note, we must create
db_subtree@db12cr[sales]> -- database schemas on DAGGER for this to work

db_subtree@db12cr[sales]> CONNECT dknox/welcome1@hr
Connected.
domain_subtree@db12cr[hr]> SELECT SYS_CONTEXT('userenv','external_name')
  2  "Directory User",
  3  USER SCHEMA,
  4  SYS_CONTEXT ('userenv', 'db_name') ||
  5  '[' || SYS_CONTEXT ('userenv', 'con_name') ||']' DATABASE
  6  FROM DUAL;

Directory User                            SCHEMA            DATABASE
----------------------------------------  ---------------   ------------------
cn=dknox,ou=users,dc=nsg,dc=net           DOMAIN_SUBTREE    db12cr[HR]
```

Exclusive Schemas

The enterprise users do not have to share database schemas. You can create distinct user-schema (1:1) mappings. The benefit of this approach is that the database security can be based on database schemas. It is often desirable to have exclusive mappings for privileged users, because the accountability of their actions is higher than in a shared schema approach. Access controls and auditing operate at a schema level and can be easily and more intuitively implemented. (For two users sharing a database schema, there is no way to audit one of the users and not the other.) The obvious administration drawback with user-schema (1:1) mapping is that a database administrator has to create a database account and a directory administrator has to create a directory tree entry for each end user.

There are two ways to implement exclusive schemas. First, you can use Oracle Enterprise Manager Cloud Control to create an entry-level mapping for the directory user to a database schema. The exclusivity is implied because the administrator doesn't assign other directory users to the database schema. However, there is no way to enforce the exclusive mapping in the directory.

The alternative implementation is to have the database create the user-schema mapping. This does ensure that the schema exclusivity is maintained. You create the user-schema mapping at the time you create the database schema by providing the user's DN in the CREATE USER statement.

For example, to create an exclusive schema mapping for the directory user DKNOX to the database schema DKNOX_DB, you would issue the following commands:

```
sec_mgr@db12cr[sales]> -- Create a database mapped Enterprise User
sec_mgr@db12cr[sales]> CREATE USER dknox_db IDENTIFIED
  2  GLOBALLY AS 'cn=dknox,ou=users,dc=nsg,dc=net';

User created.

sec_mgr@db12cr[sales]> GRANT CREATE SESSION TO dknox_db;

Grant succeeded.

sec_mgr@db12cr[sales]> CONNECT dknox/welcome1@sales
Connected.

dknox_db@db12cr[sales]> COL "Directory User" format a40
dknox_db@db12cr[sales]> SELECT SYS_CONTEXT ('userenv', 'external_name')
  2  "Directory User"
  3  FROM DUAL;

Directory User
----------------------------------------
cn=dknox,ou=users,dc=nsg,dc=net
```

Notice the user provides DKNOX as the username during database logon. The directory is doing the authentication, however the database is providing the schema mapping. A database schema mapping supersedes directory mappings for the user. Unlike OS authenticated users (that is, OPS$_*), there is no dependency on the database schema name and the directory user name. The database schema name in the preceding example could have been named anything and it would have worked.

When you view the exclusive schema name in the DBA_USERS view, you can identify the mapped directory user by looking at the EXTERNAL_NAME column. Notice that both the exclusive schema DKNOX_DB and the shared schema APP_PUBLIC have the password GLOBAL and that the DKNOX_DB schema also has a value for EXTERNAL_NAME. This indicates that both database schemas are used for EUS. Also notice that the APP_PUBLIC mappings are done by the directory and the DKNOX_DB mappings are provided by the local database:

```
sec_mgr@db12cr[sales]> COL password format a20
sec_mgr@db12cr[sales]> COL username format a10
sec_mgr@db12cr[sales]> COL external_name format a40
sec_mgr@db12cr[sales]> SELECT username, password, external_name
  2  FROM dba_users
  3  WHERE username IN ('DKNOX_DB', 'APP_PUBLIC');

USERNAME   PASSWORD             EXTERNAL_NAME
---------- -------------------- ----------------------------------------
APP_PUBLIC GLOBAL
DKNOX_DB   GLOBAL               cn=dknox,ou=users,dc=nsg,dc=net
```

Converting Existing Database Users to Directory Users   The exclusive schema design is often the first step in migrating existing applications to EUS. The user-schema (1:1) mapping is consistent with the existing security. Assuming that you have already configured your database for EUS support, you can migrate existing database users to enterprise users in three easy steps. The following example shows how this can be done for the database user SCOTT. First, you issue the **ALTER USER** command to change SCOTT's database authentication model to directory-based. Note that issuing this command does not affect previously granted schema objects or privileges.

```
sec_mgr@db12cr[sales]> ALTER USER scott IDENTIFIED GLOBALLY AS '';

User altered.
```

You next have to create the user in the directory. The DSM web console can be used to create the SCOTT in the directory. The final step is to create the exclusive mapping between the SCOTT directory user and the SCOTT database schema. After you complete this step, the database will authenticate the SCOTT user and password against the directory and not the database. Existing schema and object privileges are still available. The transparency to the application of making these changes makes them applicable to existing applications. Neither the user nor the application will realize that the user is now being authenticated by the directory.

```
sec_mgr@db12cr[sales]> CONNECT scott@sales
Enter password:

Connected.
scott@db12cr[sales]>
```

If you later decide you want to revert back to database authentication, you can simply issue the **ALTER USER** command and set the user's password:

```
sec_mgr@db12cr[sales]> ALTER USER scott IDENTIFIED BY tiger;

User altered.

sec_mgr@db12cr[sales]> CONNECT scott/tiger@sales
Connected.
scott@db12cr[sales]>
```

Recall the earlier section "The Connection Process" and the explanation of how the database processes user authentication. The database first checks locally for the account name. If the database finds it and the password has the value GLOBAL, then the database refers to the directory for user authentication. This fact allows you to switch database users from locally authenticated to directory authenticated by simply using the **ALTER USER** command as just illustrated.

A convenient tool for moving lots of database users to enterprise users is the Oracle User Migration Utility. You can configure this program for bulk migration of existing database users to directory users. Both exclusive and shared schemas mapping models are supported. See Appendix A of the *Oracle Enterprise User Security Administrator's Guide* for more information.

Extended EUS for Security

Most EUS implementations use the shared schema design pattern. As the name implies, users share a database schema but can have different privileges in the database. This differs from the single user connection pools where the application connects to the same schema and the end user's identity may not be preserved for auditing or authorization purposes.

As shown in the previous examples, the EUS shared schema design preserves the user's identity. The identity is automatically stored in the USERENV namespace and in attribute EXTERNAL_NAME.

This session context value (as well as others) is accessible to your database programs—triggers, secure application roles, VPD policies, and so on—and it can also be used in auditing. This allows you to use database security with a high level of assurance that the security controls are being accurately applied to the end users. We will demonstrate how to leverage session context information for auditing later in this section and how to expose additional information from the directory in the session context. We will conclude with a discussion of how to enable EUS for privileged administrators that required the SYS% administrative privileges using the Oracle EUS enterprise roles.

In Chapter 4 we will expand on the topic of enterprise roles for managing the database object and system privileges required for your EUS end users. Enterprise roles offer an efficient mechanism for grouping and managing the privileges that are common across applications and databases.

Auditing EUS Sessions   One of the interesting aspects of this example is that we can access an end user's DN via SQL. This is the case with many of the authentication methods that we cover. You can add the association of the end user's identity with any auditable database action in the Oracle audit trail by simply calling the PL/SQL procedure DBMS_SESSION.SET_IDENTIFIER as shown in the following example:

```
DBMS_SESSION.SET_IDENTIFIER(SYS_CONTEXT('userenv', 'external_name'));
```

This call to DBMS_SESSION can be included in an Oracle database logon trigger. Once this is done the CLIENT_ID column of the DBA_AUDIT_TRAIL view will be populated with the DN of the EUS user.

Extending EUS Session Context   EUS will automatically retrieve and populate a number of predefined LDAP attributes in the session context on login, if the attribute has a value defined in LDAP. These attributes include the following

- From the person LDAP schema object: userPassword, telephoneNumber, seeAlso, description

- From the organizationalPerson LDAP schema object: title, x121Address, registeredAddress, destinationIndicator, preferredDeliveryMethod, telexNumber, teletexTerminalIdentifier, internationaliSDNNumber, facsimileTelephoneNumber, street, postOfficeBox, postalCode, postalAddress, physicalDeliveryOfficeName, st, l

- From the inetOrgPerson LDAP schema object: audio, businessCategory, carLicense, departmentNumber, employeeNumber, employeeType, givenName, homePhone, homePostalAddress, initials, jpegPhoto, labeledURI, mail, manager, mobile, o, pager, photo, roomNumber, secretary, uid, userCertificate, x500uniqueIdentifier, preferredLanguage, userSMIMECertificate, userPKCS12

The following example demonstrates SQL statements that can be used to retrieve these attributes.

```
domain_subtree@db12cr[hr]> SELECT *
  2  FROM session_context
  3  WHERE namespace = 'SYS_LDAP_USER_DEFAULT'
  4  ORDER BY 1,2;
```

```
NAMESPACE              ATTRIBUTE        VALUE
---------------------  ---------------  ---------------------------
SYS_LDAP_USER_DEFAULT  GIVENNAME        David
SYS_LDAP_USER_DEFAULT  MAIL             david.knox@oracle.com
SYS_LDAP_USER_DEFAULT  TITLE            VP
SYS_LDAP_USER_DEFAULT  UID              dknox
SYS_LDAP_USER_DEFAULT  USERPASSWORD     {SSHA}bmTlPGEEEDjnM1MdB+UsPobl
                                        nTheH+GFwxT8PA==

5 rows selected.

domain_subtree@db12cr[hr]> SELECT SYS_CONTEXT('SYS_LDAP_USER_DEFAULT',
  2  'TITLE') TITLE
  3  FROM DUAL;


TITLE
-----------------------------------
VP
```

You may be wondering if you could extend your LDAP schema with custom LDAP attributes and whether these attributes would automatically appear in your session context. The unfortunate answer is no. However, the approach defined in Oracle Support note 242156.1, "An Example of Using Application Context's Initialized Globally," can also be used with EUS to extend this generic capability to include group membership information or to include custom attributes. To demonstrate this capability, consider the following scenario. We want to track the end users in our LDAP directory who are the primary sales contacts for different product types. We will configure the end user DKNOX as the primary sales contact for the Electronics product type. First we will create a standard Oracle application context that is initialized globally (meaning externally) with a nonexistent PL/SQL function as follows:

```
sec_mgr@db12cr[sales]> CREATE CONTEXT SALES_CONTEXT
  2  USING non_existent_plsql
  3  INITIALIZED GLOBALLY;

Context created.
```

If you are using OUD, you will need to use ODSM to add a new object class named orclDBApplicationContextValue, as shown in Figure 3-10.

Next we will create a special container within our OUD directory instance using the following LDAP Data Interchange Format (LDIF) file:

```
dn: cn=OracleDBAppContext,cn=OracleDefaultDomain,cn=OracleDBSecurity,cn=Products,cn=Orac
leContext,dc=nsg,dc=net
changetype: add
cn: OracleDBAppContext
objectclass: top
objectclass: orclContainer

dn: cn=SALES_CONTEXT,cn=OracleDBAppContext,cn=OracleDefaultDomain,cn=OracleDBSecurity,cn
=Products,cn=OracleContext,dc=nsg,dc=net
changetype: add
cn: SALES_CONTEXT
objectclass: top
objectclass: orclContainer
```

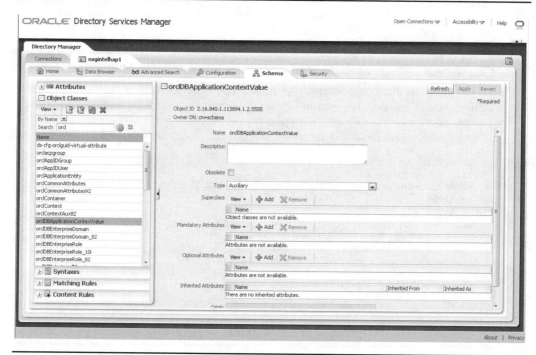

FIGURE 3-10. *Extending the OUD schema for additional EUS session context support*

```
dn: cn=PRODUCT_TYPE_CONTACT,cn=SALES_CONTEXT,cn=OracleDBAppContext,cn=OracleDefaultDomai
n,cn=OracleDBSecurity,cn=Products,cn=OracleContext,dc=nsg,dc=net
changetype: add
cn: PRODUCT_TYPE_CONTACT
objectclass: top
objectclass: orclContainer

dn: cn=Electronics,cn=PRODUCT_TYPE_CONTACT,cn=SALES_CONTEXT,cn=OracleDBAppContext,cn=Ora
cleDefaultDomain,cn=OracleDBSecurity,cn=Products,cn=OracleContext,dc=nsg,dc=net
changetype: add
cn: Electronics
objectclass: top
objectclass: groupofuniquenames
objectclass: orclDBApplicationContextValue
uniquemember: cn=dknox,ou=users,dc=nsg,dc=net
```

We will then load this LDIF file as shown next:

```
$ ldapmodify -D "cn=Directory Manager" -w "welcome1" -h "nsgintelhap1" -p 1389 -f sales_
context.ldif
adding new entry cn=OracleDBAppContext,cn=OracleDefaultDomain,cn=OracleDBSecurity,cn=Pro
ducts,cn=OracleContext,dc=nsg,dc=net

adding new entry cn=SALES_CONTEXT,cn=OracleDBAppContext,cn=OracleDefaultDomain,cn=Oracle
DBSecurity,cn=Products,cn=OracleContext,dc=nsg,dc=net
```

```
adding new entry cn=PRODUCT_TYPE_CONTACT,cn=SALES_CONTEXT,cn=OracleDBAppContext,cn=Oracl
eDefaultDomain,cn=OracleDBSecurity,cn=Products,cn=OracleContext,dc=nsg,dc=net

adding new entry cn=Electronics,cn=PRODUCT_TYPE_CONTACT,cn=SALES_CONTEXT,cn=OracleDBAppC
ontext,cn=OracleDefaultDomain,cn=OracleDBSecurity,cn=Products,cn=OracleContext,dc=nsg,dc
=net
```

You can create additional groups, such as Software or Appliances, using the last line in this
LDIF file and customizing it as your needs dictate. Another option is to manage these groups and
group membership in the ODSM web application as shown in Figure 3-11.

When we log in as DKNOX we can see that our custom attribute exists in the session context.

```
db_entry@db12cr[sales]> SELECT *
  2   FROM session_context
  3   WHERE namespace IN ('SYS_LDAP_USER_DEFAULT','SALES_CONTEXT')
  4   ORDER BY 1,2;

NAMESPACE              ATTRIBUTE             VALUE
---------------------  --------------------  ----------------------------
SALES_CONTEXT          PRODUCT_TYPE_CONTACT  Electronics
SYS_LDAP_USER_DEFAULT  GIVENNAME             David
SYS_LDAP_USER_DEFAULT  MAIL                  david.knox@oracle.com
SYS_LDAP_USER_DEFAULT  TITLE                 VP
```

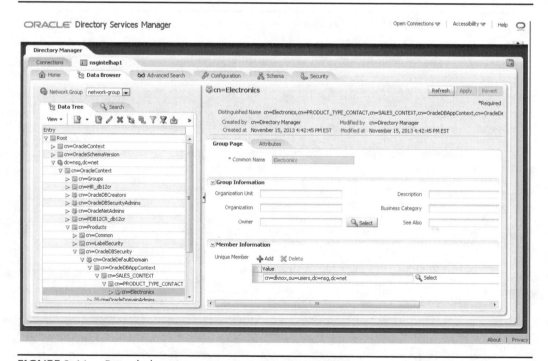

FIGURE 3-11. *Extended session context support entry in OUD*

```
SYS_LDAP_USER_DEFAULT UID              dknox
SYS_LDAP_USER_DEFAULT USERPASSWORD     {SSHA}bmTlPGEEEDjnM1MdB+UsPobl
                                       nTheH+GFwxT8PA==
```

```
6 rows selected.
```

In subsequent chapters we will demonstrate how you can use these LDAP attributes and custom attributes in your security policies.

Privileged Administrators as Enterprise Users

In the course of discussing EUS, we have gone to great lengths to demonstrate how to authenticate users defined in your centralized directories with the database. The examples we've shown have focused on creating database sessions that are not privileged administrators. We can also leverage EUS for privileged database administrators with the SYS% administrative privileges. The first step to configuring this support is to set the LDAP_DIRECTORY_SYSAUTH parameter to YES as shown here:

```
ALTER SYSTEM SET LDAP_DIRECTORY_SYSAUTH = YES SCOPE = SPFILE;
```

You must restart the database for this setting to take effect.

Next we will log in to the Oracle Enterprise Manager Cloud Control console and configure an Oracle EUS Enterprise Role named CLOUD_BACKUP, which we will use to support the SYSBACKUP administrative privilege. (The name you choose for the role is up to you.) Figure 3-12 shows a few roles we've created in Oracle Enterprise Manager Cloud Control.

After the roles are defined, we can edit the roles and add directory users to the roles in Oracle Enterprise Manager Cloud Control, as shown in Figure 3-13.

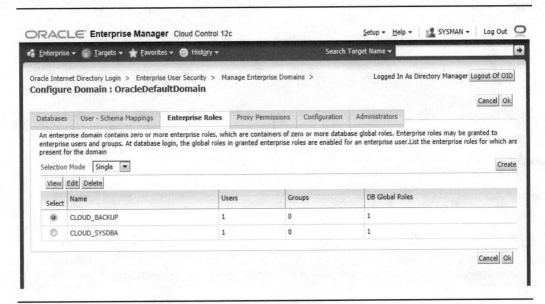

FIGURE 3-12. *EUS enterprise roles for privileged administrators*

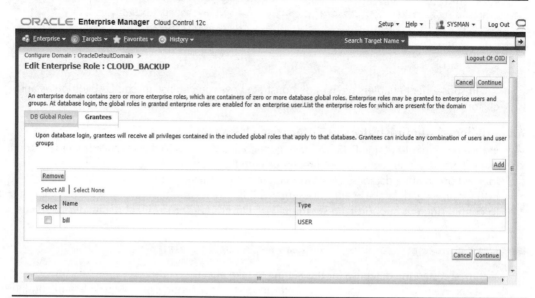

FIGURE 3-13. *EUS enterprise roles membership*

Next we must create a shared schema in the root container for these privileged administrators to leverage in the same manner as our previous examples:

```
c##sec_mgr@db12cr[cdb$root]> CREATE USER c##root_shared_schema
  2  IDENTIFIED GLOBALLY AS '';

User created.

c##sec_mgr@db12cr[cdb$root]> GRANT CREATE SESSION TO c##root_shared_schema;

Grant succeeded.
```

We will then use an LDIF file to map this shared schema to our directory's naming context "dc=nsg,dc=net" and the root container "db12cr".

```
$ cat sysauth.map.ldif
dn: cn=mapping0,cn=db12cr,cn=OracleContext,dc=nsg,dc=net
changetype: add
cn: mapping0
objectclass: top
objectclass: orclDBSubtreeLevelMapping
orcldbdistinguishedname: dc=nsg,dc=net
orcldbnativeuser: C##ROOT_SHARED_SCHEMA

$ ldapmodify -D "cn=Directory Manager" -w "welcome1" -h "nsgintelhap1" -p 1389 -f
sysauth.map.ldif
modifying entry cn=mapping0,cn=db12cr,cn=OracleContext,dc=nsg,dc=net
```

Finally, we create an entry in the directory that specifies that SYSBACK is granted to the Enterprise Role CLOUD_BACKUP we created earlier for the db12cr database:

```
$ cat sysauth.sysbackup.grant.ldif
dn: cn=CLOUD_BACKUP,cn=OracleDefaultDomain,cn=OracleDBSecurity,cn=Products,cn=OracleCont
ext,dc=nsg,dc=net
changetype: modify
add: orcldbserverrole
orcldbserverrole:cn=db12cr,cn=oraclecontext,dc=nsg,dc=net,GlobalRole=SYSBACKUP
$ ldapmodify -D "cn=Directory Manager" -w "welcome1" -h "nsgintelhap1" -p 1389 -f
sysauth.sysbackup.grant.ldif
modifying entry cn=CLOUD_BACKUP,cn=OracleDefaultDomain,cn=OracleDBSecurity,cn=Products,
cn=OracleContext,dc=nsg,dc=net
```

Once this configuration is completed we can log in to the root container as user bill, using the SYSBACKUP privilege:

```
c##sec_mgr@db12cr[cdb$root]> CONNECT bill/welcome1 as sysbackup
Connected.
sysbackup@db12cr[cdb$root]> SELECT privilege
  2  FROM session_privs
  3  WHERE privilege LIKE 'SYS%';

PRIVILEGE
-------------------
SYSBACKUP

1 row selected.
```

Considerations
The EUS capabilities are impressive, and many organizations have standardized on the EUS concept for their best practices. Before you begin converting your enterprise systems, however, you should be aware of a few caveats.

SSO Credentials and Performance   SSO is motivated by two important principles: ease of administration, which is accomplished by centralizing user information, and ease of use, meaning that the user does not have to remember or supply multiple account names and passwords for the different applications or databases. The primary goal with EUS is to support these two principles for database users. The user information is centrally stored in a directory. Oracle databases are also registered with the directory. When the user wants to access a database, the database defers authentication to the directory. The directory also provides authorization information by way of role mappings (discussed in more detail in Chapter 4).

Although often promoted as an SSO capability, the EUS implementation is actually a single-credential capability. The authentication occurs every time a user requests a connection to the Oracle Database. The username and password just happen to be the same for all Oracle databases participating in EUS. When using a certificate for logon, the user simply connects to a database by supplying the connection alias—no username or passwords are required. This is an important distinction to recognize when you are deciding on overall system performance, because every login will require an authentication call to LDAP.

A potential issue for deploying EUS centers on performance. For every enterprise user, the database has to look up the user's authentication, find their schema mapping, and determine which authorizations the user should receive. As such, the connection process can take substantially more time than if the user were database authenticated. It's not that the process is necessarily slow, but it is slower than if the database were performing authentication locally. Additionally, using SSL between the database and LDAP server will slow the time to connect and impact performance. This slowdown in the authentication process may not be an issue in your system. It is generally an issue only when the application scalability or system load characteristics are high.

Kerberos Authentication and EUS   In many UNIX and Microsoft Windows computing environments, Kerberos is used for operating system authentication. Oracle supports the use of Kerberos authentication with EUS. The configuration steps are for the most part the same as we have demonstrated for password-based authentication.

You must also identify the Kerberos principal attribute name in your LDAP schema attributes. The Kerberos authentication type in the EUS configuration within OEM Cloud Control must also be enabled. You can read about the Kerberos configuration setup in Chapter 4 of *Oracle Enterprise User Security Administrator's Guide*.

When using Kerberos and EUS, the end user must obtain a Kerberos ticket first. In Windows environments, this is often done automatically on end user logon. In UNIX environments, you can leverage the Oracle-supplied okinit tool to obtain this ticket. Once this ticket is obtained, the user can simply log on to the database using the SQL*NET TNS alias for a service:

```
sqlplus /@servicesys@db12cr[cdb$root]>
```

If your enterprise leverages Kerberos in a Windows or UNIX environment, then integrating this authentication infrastructure with EUS for database authentication will save operational costs and provide a secure and seamless end user experience.

Dependencies

With the implementation of a single authentication source comes the risk of a single point of failure. OUD is built to support replication and proxy services for high availability so you will need to use these services in your architecture to avoid a single point of failure. OID is built on top of the Oracle Database to ensure reliability, scalability, and availability. However, if you do not use Oracle's features (such as Real Application Clusters for OID's database), you won't have a high availability solution.

Other bad things can happen, too. Network failures or other hardware failures can make the LDAP server unreachable or unavailable. It is important that you consider this when deciding on how and when to use EUS. Network redundancy and data mirroring are two critical elements for ensuring that the enterprise directory is always available and accessible.

Oracle Kerberos Authentication

As we described earlier, many UNIX and Windows computing environments use Kerberos for operating system authentication. The Oracle Database and Oracle Database client support Kerberos as an external authentication method. The details of setting up Kerberos to support external authentication are quite lengthy and are clearly documented in Chapter 17 of the *Oracle Database Security Guide*.

The basic approach involves creating a service principal for the database server in your key distribution center (KDC) and extracting the service key table for use on the database server. On the Oracle Database server, you configure the sqlnet.ora file for Kerberos authentication using this service key table. On the Oracle Database you must configure the initialization parameter OS_AUTHENT_PREFIX as follows:

```
sys@db12cr[cdb$root]> ALTER SYSTEM SET OS_AUTHENT_PREFIX='' SCOPE=SPFILE;
```

Without EUS, you must create an externally identified user and grant the required privileges to this user, as shown in the following example:

```
sec_mgr@db12cr[sales]> CREATE USER "david.knox@oracle.com"
  2  IDENTIFIED EXTERNALLY;

User created.

sec_mgr@db12cr[sales]> GRANT CREATE SESSION TO "david.knox@oracle.com";

Grant succeeded.
```

The end user must obtain a ticket from the KDC first. The end user can use the Oracle-supplied tool, okinit, to obtain the KDC ticket. Once this ticket is obtained, the user can also log on to the database using just the SQL*NET TNS alias for a service as follows:

```
sqlplus /@sales
```

If your enterprise uses Kerberos, then integrating this authentication infrastructure with standard database authentication has the potential to save operational costs related to password management and provide a secure and seamless end user experience. The cost savings are not as great as when Kerberos is integrated with EUS, because you will still need to provision and deprovision the external accounts within each of your databases. Identity provision tools such as Oracle Identity Manager can help offset these costs by provisioning these database accounts as part of an employee onboarding workflow.

Oracle RADIUS Authentication

If your enterprise uses RADIUS authentication and the related smart cards, you can integrate this authentication infrastructure with the Oracle Database. The details of this configuration to support RADIUS as an external authentication method are also quite lengthy and are clearly documented in Chapter 19 of the *Oracle Database Security Guide*. You still create externally identified database accounts as is done with standard Kerberos authentication support. If your enterprise leverages RADIUS, integrating this authentication infrastructure with standard database authentication will save operational costs related to password management.

Summary

In this chapter we discussed some of the technical and performance challenges in supporting identity propagation from web applications to the database. We demonstrated how Oracle Proxy Authentication can overcome these technical challenges and provide a performance profile that is acceptable for production use.

We also discussed a number of external identification and authentication approaches that are available in Oracle Database 12c for large enterprises that maintain centralized directory and authentication services. We also demonstrated how Oracle Enterprise User Security in Oracle Database 12c supports end user identity propagation as well as the ability to retrieve a number of end user attributes from directory services. These end user attributes can be used to help create fine-grained security policies for database access control and to maintain accurate audit trail entries.

In the next chapter, we will begin to discuss how to create and manage the database roles and privileges that take part in fine-grained security policies for database access control.

CHAPTER
4

Foundational Elements
for a Secure Database

I n this chapter we discuss the fundamentals of database security. Topics covered here provide the foundation for a secure operating environment. The intent of this chapter is not to duplicate the Oracle product documentation, which extensively discusses both privileges and roles, but to point out some of the important and subtle aspects that are associated with privileges and roles and their management.

Access Control, Authorization, and Privilege

We begin by reviewing the terms *access control, authorization,* and *privilege.* You'll find these terms littered throughout security policies, and although these terms are often used interchangeably, they are, in fact, different. A good understanding of these terms is necessary to better understand security policies and implementations.

Access Control

Access control is the process of allowing or preventing a user access to a resource. A simple way to describe access control is to associate it with a commonly understood implementation called access control lists (ACLs). Security administrators use ACLs to describe a security policy.

An ACL describes who can access what resource and how they get access to the resource. ACLs are typically derived from the organization's security policies. For example, if a user is the manager for a department, the user gets access to the salaries for the department's employees. ACLs are not enforcement mechanisms. Enforcement mechanisms are the security features inside the database that use the ACL to determine whether access should or shouldn't be granted.

Authorization

Authorization is an abstraction that represent a binding between a security policy and the actual privileges a user has in a given context. A person is considered "authorized" when he or she is allowed to perform an action as described by a security policy. For example, a boarding pass may authorize a person to board an airplane, or a special badge may authorize a person to enter a secure area. You will see later that authorizations translate into one or more privileges.

Privilege

Permission to perform an action in the database is known as a privilege. When a user performs any action (**SELECT**, **INSERT**, **UPDATE**, and so on) in the database, the database verifies that the user has the privilege needed to execute the action. Enforcement mechanisms are executed in the database to check the user's privileges against the required privilege(s) needed to perform the action. If the user possesses the required privilege(s), then the action is performed.

Oracle Database 12*c* offers two types of system and object privileges, which are discussed in this chapter. A third type, the intra-object privilege, will be discussed in Chapter 5. As we have discussed in previous chapters, Oracle Database 12*c* includes a multitenant capability that adds yet another security dimension during security policy establishment—that is, the database administrator has to determine who gets what privilege and for which container(s). The privilege management commands **GRANT/REVOKE** now has a CONTAINER clause that must be correctly used when granting privileges; otherwise, an administrator can easily over- or incorrectly privilege a user. **GRANT** and **REVOKE** commands are used by a database administrator to implement a security policy in the database.

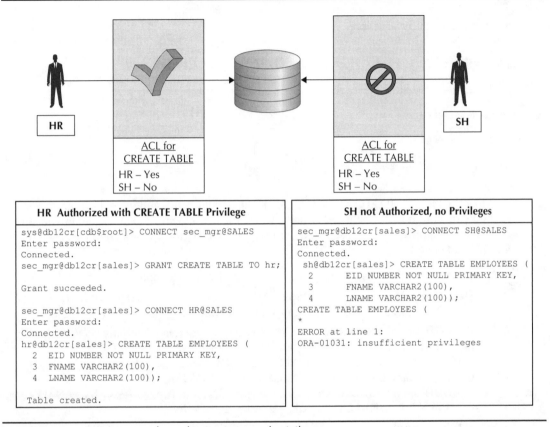

FIGURE 4-1.   *Access controls, authorizations, and privileges*

Figure 4-1 illustrates how access control, authorization, and privileges work and interact in a security policy.

System Privileges

A system privilege permits a user to perform an action in the database or specific to a pluggable database. Oracle Database 12*c* supports a number of system privileges. System privileges can be split into two types: ANY and ADMINISTRATIVE.

ANY System Privileges   ANY system privileges are not limited to a specific schema, but rather to any object of a specific type regardless of schema. ANY system privileges are extremely powerful and should be thoroughly reviewed as to their need and use. There are 142 ANY privileges in Oracle Database 12*c*. The following query illustrates a few ANY privileges:

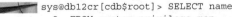

```
sys@db12cr[cdb$root]> SELECT name
  2  FROM system_privilege_map
  3  WHERE name LIKE '%ANY%'
  4  ORDER BY name;
```

```
NAME
-----------------------------
ADMINISTER ANY SQL TUNING SET
ALTER ANY ASSEMBLY
...
DELETE ANY TABLE
...
EXECUTE ANY PROCEDURE
...
INSERT ANY TABLE
...
SELECT ANY TABLE
...
UPDATE ANY TABLE
...
```

INSERT, **UPDATE**, **DELETE**, and **SELECT ANY TABLE** commands authorize the granted user the ability to perform DML against ANY non-SYS table without being granted explicit permission to do so from the object owner. A quick description of the categorization of commands within the Oracle Database follows:

- **SELECT**   A read-only query against a table or view, for example
- **Data Manipulation Language (DML)**   Write actions such as **INSERT**, **UPDATE**, or **DELETE** against a table or view for example, or **EXECUTE** actions on PL/SQL code.
- **Data Definition Language (DDL)**   Database structure related commands that typically have the form **CREATE** <object type>, **ALTER** <object type> and **DROP** <object type>, such as **CREATE TABLE**, **ALTER TABLE**, and **DROP TABLE**. This category also includes privilege-related commands such as **GRANT** and **REVOKE**, auditing commands such as **AUDIT** and **NOAUDIT**, and data table administration commands such as **ANALYZE**, **COMMENT**, **FLASHBACK**, **PURGE**, **RENAME**, and **TRUNCATE**.
- **System Control**   Commands such as **ALTER SYSTEM** and **ALTER DATABASE**
- **Session Control**   Commands such as **ALTER SESSION** and **SET ROLE**
- **Transaction Control**   Commands such as **COMMIT** and **ROLLBACK**

Now let's consider the EXECUTE ANY PROCEDURE system privilege, which authorizes the user to execute any procedure defined in any non-SYS schema in the database. It also allows the user to view the source code (DBA_SOURCE) for any non-SYS procedure in the database. It is important to note that if a non-SYS user is granted an ANY privilege, it cannot be used against certain SYS objects if the O7_DICTIONARY_ACCESSIBILITY initialization parameter is set to FALSE. If this parameter were set to TRUE, then a non-SYS user could access USER$, RLS$, and other values. Therefore, it is important to set this parameter to FALSE.

For example, if the O7_DICTIONARY_ACCESSIBILITY parameter was set to TRUE and a user was granted the INSERT ANY TABLE privilege, then the user could create users by adding a records to the SYS.USER$ table. Or if the parameter was set to TRUE and the user was given the DELETE ANY TABLE privilege, then the user could remove virtual private database (VPD) security policies by deleting records from SYS.RLS$. A re-caching of these new values into Oracle would need to take place, such as bouncing the Oracle instance. It is clear to see that the O7_DICTIONARY_ACCESSIBILITY parameter should always be set to FALSE.

ADMINISTRATIVE System Privileges   Administrative privileges affect the state of the database or pluggable database. For example, the ability to issue **ALTER DATABASE TRIGGER**, **ALTER SYSTEM**, **ALTER USER**, and other commands are examples of system privileges. Even the privilege to connect (CREATE SESSION) to the database is a system privilege.

The SET CONTAINER system privilege is the Oracle Database 12c privilege that permits the user to switch between pluggable databases. As was demonstrated in Chapter 2, the user must have the CREATE SESSION privilege granted in the container the user is switching to.

Viewing System Privileges

The SYSTEM_PRIVILEGE_MAP view lists many of the common system privileges and can be helpful when you forget the exact name of a privilege. For example, suppose you know there is a privilege to create application contexts, and you cannot remember the exact wording of the privilege; you could issue the following query:

```
sys@db12cr[cdb$root]> SELECT name
  2  FROM system_privilege_map
  3  WHERE name LIKE '%CONTEXT%'
  4  ORDER BY name;

NAME
---------------------------
ALTER ANY EVALUATION CONTEXT
CREATE ANY CONTEXT
...
```

This view is good for finding privileges, but it does not tell you who has been granted the privileges or what the privileges allow the user to do. Explaining what each privilege does is beyond the scope of this book. Refer to the listings of system and object privileges in the **GRANT** command section of the *Oracle Database SQL Language Reference*. You can determine which accounts or roles have been granted which system privileges by querying the view DBA_SYS_PRIVS while connected to a specific pluggable database or CDB_SYS_PRIVS for all databases. For example, if you want to see which accounts or roles have been granted the SELECT ANY TABLE privilege in the current database, you would issue the following query:

```
sys@db12cr[cdb$root]>  SELECT grantee
  2  FROM dba_sys_privs
  3  WHERE privilege = 'SELECT ANY TABLE'
  4  ORDER BY grantee;

GRANTEE
---------------------------
DATAPUMP_IMP_FULL_DATABASE
DBA
DV_REALM_OWNER
EXP_FULL_DATABASE
IMP_FULL_DATABASE
LBACSYS
MDSYS
OLAP_DBA
SYS
SYSTEM
WMSYS
```

The results from this query show both the accounts (SYS, SYSTEM, and so on) and database roles (DBA, EXP_FULL_DATABASE, and so on) that have the SELECT ANY TABLE privilege. Roles are collections of privileges and are described later in this chapter. Granting a database role to a user effectively grants the user all the privileges that were granted to that role.

You can determine who has SELECT ANY TABLE across all pluggable databases by issuing the following query:

```
sys@db12cr[cdb$root]> SELECT grantee, pdb_name
  2  FROM cdb_sys_privs csp JOIN cdb_pdbs cp
  3  ON (csp.con_id = cp.con_id)
  4  WHERE privilege = 'SELECT ANY TABLE'
  5  ORDER BY grantee;

GRANTEE                              PDB_NAME
------------------------------------ ---------------------------------
DATAPUMP_IMP_FULL_DATABASE           PDBORCL
DATAPUMP_IMP_FULL_DATABASE           SALES
DATAPUMP_IMP_FULL_DATABASE           PDB$SEED
DBA                                  SALES
DBA                                  PDBORCL
DBA                                  PDB$SEED
DV_REALM_OWNER                       PDB$SEED
DV_REALM_OWNER                       SALES
DV_REALM_OWNER                       PDBORCL
...
```

You can determine all privileges a connected user has by selecting from the view SESSION_PRIVS. The following query shows all privileges for the connected user:

```
sys@db12cr[cdb$root]>  SELECT *
  2  FROM session_privs
  3  ORDER BY privilege;

PRIVILEGE
----------------------------------------------------
ADMINISTER ANY SQL TUNING SET
ADMINISTER DATABASE TRIGGER
ADMINISTER RESOURCE MANAGER
ADMINISTER SQL MANAGEMENT OBJECT
ADMINISTER SQL TUNING SET
...
```

Likewise, you can determine all roles a connected user has by selecting from SESSION_ROLES. The following query shows all roles for the connected user:

```
sys@db12cr[cdb$root]>  SELECT *
  2 FROM session_roles
  3 ORDER BY role ;

ROLE
-----------------------------------------
AQ_ADMINISTRATOR_ROLE
CAPTURE_ADMIN
DATAPUMP_EXP_FULL_DATABASE
...
```

The previous two queries show the roles and privileges for the connected user. What remains to be determined is for which objects the non-administrative privileges pertain. We will demonstrate a query to determine this in the next section.

Object Privileges

Object privileges authorize a user to perform actions (INSERT, SELECT, EXECUTE, and so on) on database objects (table, view, PL/SQL function, and so on). Database users are authorized to perform actions against objects they own. For example, if the Sales History (SH) user has a table named CUSTOMERS, then the SH user can use SELECT, INSERT, UPDATE, and other commands against the table without being given explicit object privileges. However, if the SH user has a need to query a different schema's object, then the SELECT privilege for that object must be granted to SH before the action can be performed. For example, if SH needs to query from the user HR's EMPLOYEES table, then the HR user (or privileged DBA) must explicitly grant SELECT on the user HR's EMPLOYEES table to SH. As with system privileges, the object privileges can be granted in several ways—granted directly to a user, granted to a role, and so on. We call this type of access control *discretionary access control* (DAC), because the granting of access to an object is left to the discretion of the object owner or to someone with the GRANT ANY privilege.

Viewing Object Privileges

You can determine how your have received a privilege to an object by running the following query. This query illustrates the privilege that was granted to the role, the schema and object that it affects, and the type of object for roles in the pluggable database SALES.

```
sec_mgr@db12cr[sales]> SELECT grantee ROLE, privilege,
  2      table_schema||'.'||table_name OBJECT_NAME, type
  3  FROM all_tab_privs
  4  WHERE grantee IN (SELECT * FROM session_roles)
  5  UNION
  6  SELECT DECODE(grantee, UPPER(USER), 'DIRECT', grantee) ROLE, privilege,
  7    table_schema||'.'||table_name OBJECT_NAME, TYPE
  8  FROM all_tab_privs
  9  WHERE grantee = UPPER(USER)
 10  ORDER by role, privilege, object_name;


ROLE                     PRIVILEGE OBJECT_NAME                      TYPE
------------------------ --------- -------------------------------- -------
AQ_ADMINISTRATOR_ROLE    EXECUTE   SYS.DBMS_AQ                       PACKAGE
AQ_ADMINISTRATOR_ROLE    EXECUTE   SYS.DBMS_AQADM                   PACKAGE
AQ_ADMINISTRATOR_ROLE    EXECUTE   SYS.DBMS_AQELM                   PACKAGE
AQ_ADMINISTRATOR_ROLE    EXECUTE   SYS.DBMS_AQIN                    PACKAGE
AQ_ADMINISTRATOR_ROLE    EXECUTE   SYS.DBMS_AQJMS_INTERNAL          PACKAGE
AQ_ADMINISTRATOR_ROLE    EXECUTE   SYS.DBMS_AQ_IMPORT_INTERNAL      PACKAGE
AQ_ADMINISTRATOR_ROLE    EXECUTE   SYS.DBMS_RULE_EXIMP              PACKAGE
AQ_ADMINISTRATOR_ROLE    EXECUTE   SYS.DBMS_TRANSFORM               PACKAGE
AQ_ADMINISTRATOR_ROLE    SELECT    SYS.AQ$INTERNET_USERS            VIEW
AQ_ADMINISTRATOR_ROLE    SELECT    SYS.AQ$_PROPAGATION_STATUS       TABLE
AQ_ADMINISTRATOR_ROLE    SELECT    SYS.DBA_AQ_AGENTS                VIEW
AQ_ADMINISTRATOR_ROLE    SELECT    SYS.DBA_AQ_AGENT_PRIVS           VIEW
AQ_ADMINISTRATOR_ROLE    SELECT    SYS.DBA_QUEUES                   VIEW
...
```

This query is helpful because you can tailor it to determine which specific privileges have been granted to a specific schema.

The following query shows all object privileges that have been granted to the XDB schema objects for the pluggable database SALES:

```
sec_mgr@db12cr[sales]> SELECT grantee ROLE, privilege,
  2 table_schema||'.'||table_name OBJECT_NAME, type
  3 FROM all_tab_privs
  4 WHERE grantee IN (SELECT * FROM session_roles)
  5 UNION
  6 SELECT DECODE(grantee, UPPER(USER), 'DIRECT', grantee) ROLE, privilege,
  7 table_schema||'.'||table_name OBJECT_NAME, type
  8 FROM all_tab_privs
  9 WHERE grantee = UPPER(USER)
 10 ORDER by role, privilege, object_name;

ROLE                     PRIVILEGE OBJECT_NAME                          TYPE
------------------------ --------- ------------------------------------ -----
DBA                      ALTER     XDB.XDB$ACL                          TABLE
DBA                      ALTER     XDB.XDB$CHECKOUTS                    TABLE
DBA                      ALTER     XDB.XDB$CONFIG                       TABLE
DBA                      ALTER     XDB.XDB$D_LINK                       TABLE
DBA                      ALTER     XDB.XDB$H_INDEX                      TABLE
DBA                      ALTER     XDB.XDB$H_LINK                       TABLE
DBA                      ALTER     XDB.XDB$NLOCKS                       TABLE
DBA                      ALTER     XDB.XDB$RESCONFIG                    TABLE
...
```

Column Privileges

Oracle Database 12c enables you to grant privileges (INSERT, UPDATE, and so on) to the individual columns within a table. This feature can be very useful because it aids in meeting the least-privilege security objective. If a user or group of users (ROLE) need SELECT, INSERT, and UPDATE access to a column or set of columns, you can grant access directly on the table's columns and are not forced to create an elaborate view structure or partially duplicate the data to control access.

UPDATE Column Privileges

Updating an individual column's value aids in simplifying the security controls used in your system. Furthermore, this feature can be used with VPD or OLS to restrict rows or sets of rows from being updated and thus further controlling what/how data is changed in your system.

For example, consider a Human Resources (HR) pluggable database with a (HR) schema and a table to store information about employees (EMPLOYEES). We also have three departments (IT, SALES, MTG), each with a manager. Each employee reports to one of the three departments. In this scenario, we want to give managers access only to the employees who are in their department. Furthermore, we want to control what columns the managers are allowed to update. That is, we want them to update the SALARY column only for employees in their associated department. To accomplish this, we must first implement an OLS or VPD policy to restrict managers' access to employees they manage or who are in their department. We will explain how this is accomplished in Chapter 6 for VPD and in Chapter 8 for OLS.

To accomplish the second part of our scenario, we grant UPDATE privileges on the SALARY column of the EMPLOYEES table to the managers. OLS/VPD will control the rows that our managers have access to and the GRANT will control the column that our managers can update. The following example demonstrates this:

```
sec_mgr@db12cr[hr]> CONNECT hr@hr
Enter password:
Connected.
hr@db12cr[hr]> GRANT SELECT ON employees TO katherine;
Grant succeeded.

hr@db12cr[hr]> GRANT UPDATE (salary) ON employees TO katherine;
Grant succeeded.

hr@db12cr[hr]> CONNECT katherine@hr
Enter password:
Connected.
katherine@db12cr[hr]> -- Katherine is giving every employee (10 of them)
katherine@db12cr[hr]> -- she manages a 20% raise
katherine@db12cr[hr]> UPDATE hr.employees SET salary=salary*1.20;

10 rows updated.

katherine@db12cr[hr]> -- However Katherine is not authorized
katherine@db12cr[hr]> -- to set her employee's commission percent
katherine@db12cr[hr]> UPDATE hr.employees SET commission_pct=.90;
UPDATE hr.employees SET commission_pct=.90
                *
ERROR at line 1:
ORA-01031: insufficient privileges
```

INSERT Column Privileges

Granting INSERT on a specific column within a table doesn't imply that the INSERT statement will work—that is, when you are inserting data into a table, several conditions must be met for the statement to work (permission to insert, inserting data must match the column datatype, and so on). One condition that must be met is that you must provide all NOT NULL column values in the INSERT statement or have DEFAULT values for them for the INSERT statement to succeed.

In the following example, manager Katherine is trying to INSERT an evaluation of employee 101 with a score of 98. However, she has been given INSERT privilege only to two of the three required fields in the table:

```
sec_mgr@db12cr[hr]> CONNECT hr@hr
Enter password:
Connected.
hr@db12cr[hr]> DESCRIBE evaluations
 Name                       Null?    Type
 ----------------------- -------- ----------------
 EID                        NOT NULL NUMBER
 EVAL_DATE                  NOT NULL DATE
 EVAL_SCORE                 NOT NULL NUMBER

hr@db12cr[hr]> -- Only granted two of the three required columns
hr@db12cr[hr]> GRANT INSERT (eid, eval_scope) ON evaluations TO katherine;

Grant succeeded.

hr@db12cr[hr]> CONNECT katherine@hr
```

```
Enter password:
Connected.
katherine@db12cr[hr]> -- Katherine tries to insert into the table
katherine@db12cr[hr]> -- She want to give employee 101 a score of 98
katherine@db12cr[hr]> INSERT INTO hr.evaluations (eid, eval_scope)
  VALUES (101, 98);
INSERT INTO hr.evaluations (eid, eval_scope)
*
ERROR at line 1:
ORA-01400: cannot insert NULL into (???)

katherine@db12cr[hr]> -- Katherine can describe the table to determine
katherine@db12cr[hr]> -- which column(s) are missing
katherine@db12cr[hr]> DESCRIBE hr.evaluations
 Name                          Null?    Type
 ----------------------------- -------- ----------------
 EID                           NOT NULL NUMBER
 EVAL_DATE                     NOT NULL DATE
 EVAL_SCORE                    NOT NULL NUMBER

katherine@db12cr[hr]> -- Trying to access EVAL_DATE gives error as she
katherine@db12cr[hr]> -- has not been given INSERT privileges to that column
katherine@db12cr[hr]> INSERT INTO hr.evaluations (eid, eval_date, eval_scope)
VALUES (101, sysdate, 98);
INSERT INTO hr.evaluations (eid, eval_date, eval_scope)            *
ERROR at line 1:
ORA-01031: insufficient privileges
```

Synonyms

Oracle Database 12*c* enables you to create synonyms to give user-friendly names for objects. Synonyms are a good method for aliasing the owner and real name of the object to make it simpler to reference. However, this method does not hide the owner or real name of the object.

For example, in the following example, we create a table (SREGIONS) in the SH schema and load it with some data. We then create a public synonym named SALES_REGIONS for the table SREGIONS.

```
sh@db12cr[sales]> CREATE TABLE sregions (
  2  sr_id NUMBER NOT NULL PRIMARY KEY,
  3  region VARCHAR2(100));

Table created.

sh@db12cr[sales]> INSERT INTO sregions
  2  VALUES (1, 'NORTH');

1 row created.

sh@db12cr[sales]> INSERT INTO sregions
  2  VALUES (2, 'SOUTH');

1 row created.

sh@db12cr[sales]> INSERT INTO sregions
  2  VALUES (3, 'EAST');
```

```
1 row created.

sh@db12cr[sales]> INSERT INTO sregions
  2   VALUES (4, 'WEST');

1 row created.

sh@db12cr[sales]> COMMIT;

Commit complete.

sh@db12cr[sales]> CREATE PUBLIC SYNONYM sales_regions FOR sregions;

Synonym created.

sh@db12cr[sales]>
```

Authorized and privileged users can access the SREGIONS table directly by referencing SH .SREGIONS or by referencing the public synonym SALES_REGIONS. From a security perspective, the public synonym does not mask the identity of the underlying object—the synonym is merely an alias for the real object. Notice in the following example that HR can determine that the public synonym SALES_REGIONS is referencing SH.SREGIONS, even though HR does not have access to the table:

```
sh@db12cr[sales]> CONNECT hr@sales
Enter password:
Connected.
hr@db12cr[sales]> DESCRIBE sales_regions
ERROR:
ORA-04043: object "SH"."SREGIONS" does not exist
```

Privileges and Synonyms

Privileges granted to synonyms are actually granted to the base objects. It would be logical to assume that grants given by way of a public synonym would be revoked when the public synonym was dropped. However, that is not what happens. Dropping the public synonym does not remove privileges to the base tables, even though the grants to the base tables came through the public synonym.

To illustrate this point, we continue with our example and GRANT SELECT on the synonym SALES_REGIONS to HR.

```
sh@db12cr[sales]> GRANT SELECT ON sales_regions TO hr;

Grant succeeded.
```

You can see that HR can access the public synonym and base table:

```
sh@db12cr[sales]> CONNECT hr@sales
Enter password:
Connected.
hr@db12cr[sales]> SELECT *
  2   FROM sales_regions;
```

```
       SR_ID REGION
---------- ----------
         1 NORTH
         2 SOUTH
         3 EAST
         4 WEST

4 rows selected.

hr@db12cr[sales]> SELECT *
  2  FROM sh.sregions;

       SR_ID REGION    '
---------- ----------
         1 NORTH
         2 SOUTH
         3 EAST
         4 WEST

4 rows selected.
```

We then drop the public synonym.

```
sys@db12cr[sales]> CONNECT sh@sales
Enter password:
Connected.
sh@db12cr[sales]> DROP PUBLIC SYNONYM sales_regions;

Synonym dropped.
```

Notice that dropping the public synonym did not revoke the privileges on the base table. HR can still access the base table directly.

```
sh@db12cr[sales]> CONNECT hr@sales
Enter password:
Connected.
hr@db12cr[sales]> SELECT *
  2  FROM sh.sregions;

       SR_ID REGION
---------- ----------
         1 NORTH
         2 SOUTH
         3 EAST
         4 WEST

4 rows selected.

hr@db12cr[sales]> SELECT *
  2  FROM sales_regions;
FROM sales_regions
     *
ERROR at line 2:
ORA-00942: table or view does not exist
```

The point of this exercise is to illustrate that haphazard or random privilege grants, via public synonyms in some cases and direct object grants in others, can lead to confusion, misconfiguration, and ultimately unauthorized access.

System and Object Privileges Together

One challenging area associated with access control is determining what privileges a user has and how they were granted. Privileges can be granted in multiple ways. This is convenient from an administrative perspective, but it may also be a security risk, as oversight of this fact could allow an administrator to make inadvertent mistakes.

For example, the privilege to query the table SREGIONS could occur by a direct grant to the table or by possessing the system privilege SELECT ANY TABLE. The following example shows the database administrator granting HR the system privilege to query any table and the schema owner (SH) granting SELECT on the SREGIONS table:

```
sec_mgr@db12cr[sales]> GRANT SELECT ANY TABLE TO hr;

Grant succeeded.

sec_mgr@db12cr[sales]> CONNECT sh@sales
Enter password:
Connected.
sh@db12cr[sales]> GRANT SELECT ON SREGIONS TO hr;

Grant succeeded.
```

At some point in the future, we decide that we no longer want HR to access SREGIONS. So we revoke SELECT on SREGIONS from HR:

```
sh@db12cr[sales]> REVOKE SELECT ON sregions FROM hr;

Revoke succeeded.
```

You also verify that no one else has granted direct SELECT privilege to the table SREGIONS:

```
sh@db12cr[sales]> SELECT GRANTEE
  2  FROM all_tab_privs
  3  WHERE table_schema='SH' AND table_name='SREGIONS';

no rows selected
```

Unfortunately you are unaware that the SEC_MGR gave HR the system privilege SELECT ANY TABLE and that revoking the object privilege on SREGIONS does not affect the system privilege. That is, the system privilege is still available to HR, and revoking the object privilege does not prevent HR from querying the table.

```
sh@db12cr[sales]> CONNECT hr@sales
Enter password:
Connected.
hr@db12cr[sales]> SELECT *
  2  FROM sh.sregions;

    SR_ID REGION
---------- ----------
        1 NORTH
        2 SOUTH
        3 EAST
        4 WEST

4 rows selected.
```

You should have also asked SEC_MGR to check for users with the SELECT ANY TABLE privilege.

```
sec_mgr@db12cr[sales]> CONNECT sec_mgr@sales
Enter password:
Connected.
sec_mgr@db12cr[sales]> SELECT grantee
  2    FROM dba_sys_privs
  3    WHERE privilege = 'SELECT ANY TABLE'
  4    ORDER BY grantee;

GRANTEE
------------------------------
DATAPUMP_IMP_FULL_DATABASE
DBA
DV_REALM_OWNER
EXP_FULL_DATABASE
HR
IMP_FULL_DATABASE
LBACSYS
MDSYS
OLAP_DBA
SYS
SYSTEM
WMSYS

12 rows selected.
```

The solution to this problem is knowledge of how Oracle manages object and system privileges, which is paramount for ensuring a secure database. It is important to note that the Oracle Database 12c security option Database Vault (DBV) has a privilege analysis feature we will discuss in Chapter 10 that can capture privileges granted to users and used during database operations.

Privilege Conveyance and Retraction

Another important concept to understanding how privileges work in the database is how they are granted, authorized to be granted, and revoked. We have seen the GRANT statement earlier, which is the way to grant a privilege. However, if you GRANT an object privilege to a user and add the syntax WITH GRANT OPTION, then that user is authorized to GRANT the object privilege to other users. If you REVOKE the object privilege from the user, then all object privileges the user granted are also revoked. The WITH GRANT OPTION does not pertain to system privileges.

The following example illustrates these subtle but important points. First, we authorize HR to GRANT SELECT on SH.SREGIONS to other users. We then connect as the Order Entry (OE) user and verify that the GRANT has worked. Finally, we revoke the privilege to see the cascading effect.

```
sec_mgr@db12cr[sales]> CONNECT sh@sales
Enter password:
Connected.
sh@db12cr[sales]> -- SH grants SELECT to HR with the GRANT option
sh@db12cr[sales]> GRANT SELECT ON sregions TO hr WITH GRANT OPTION;

Grant succeeded.

sh@db12cr[sales]> CONNECT hr@sales
Enter password:
```

```
Connected.
hr@db12cr[sales]> -- HR has access to SREGIONS
hr@db12cr[sales]> SELECT *
  2  FROM sh.sregions;

     SR_ID REGION
---------- ----------
         1 NORTH
         2 SOUTH
         3 EAST
         4 WEST

4 rows selected.

hr@db12cr[sales]> -- HR is authorized to GRANT
hr@db12cr[sales]> -- notice "GRANTABLE" column
hr@db12cr[sales]> SELECT grantee ROLE, privilege,
  2     table_schema||'.'||table_name OBJECT_NAME,
  3     type, grantable
  4  FROM all_tab_privs
  5  WHERE grantee IN (SELECT * FROM session_roles)
  6  UNION
  7  SELECT DECODE(grantee, UPPER(user), 'DIRECT', grantee) ROLE,
  8     privilege,
  9     table_schema||'.'||table_name OBJECT_NAME,
 10     type, grantable
 11  FROM all_tab_privs
 12  WHERE grantee = UPPER(USER)
 13  ORDER by role, privilege, object_name;

ROLE       PRIVILEGE            OBJECT_NAME  TYPE   GRANTABLE
---------- -------------------- ------------ ------ ---------
DIRECT     SELECT               SH.SREGIONS  TABLE  YES

1 row selected.

hr@db12cr[sales]> GRANT SELECT ON sh.sregions TO oe;

Grant succeeded.

hr@db12cr[sales]> CONNECT oe@sales
Enter password:
Connected.
oe@db12cr[sales]> -- OE has access
oe@db12cr[sales]> SELECT *
  2  FROM sh.sregions;

     SR_ID REGION
---------- ----------
         1 NORTH
         2 SOUTH
         3 EAST
         4 WEST

4 rows selected.
```

```
oe@db12cr[sales]> -- However - OE can't GRANT
oe@db12cr[sales]> SELECT grantee ROLE, privilege,
  2      table_schema||'.'||table_name OBJECT_NAME,
  3      type, grantable
  4  FROM all_tab_privs
  5  WHERE grantee IN (SELECT * FROM session_roles)
  6  UNION
  7  SELECT DECODE(grantee, UPPER(user), 'DIRECT', grantee) ROLE,
  8      privilege,
  9      table_schema||'.'||table_name OBJECT_NAME,
 10      type, grantable
 11  FROM all_tab_privs
 12  WHERE grantee = UPPER(USER)
 13  ORDER by role, privilege, object_name;

ROLE        PRIVILEGE            OBJECT_NAME   TYPE   GRANTABLE
----------  --------------------  ------------  ------  ---------
DIRECT      SELECT               SH.SREGIONS   TABLE  NO

1 row selected.

oe@db12cr[sales]> CONNECT sh@sales
Enter password:
Connected.
sh@db12cr[sales]> -- Revokes SELECT from HR and OE
sh@db12cr[sales]> REVOKE SELECT ON sregions FROM hr;

Revoke succeeded.

sh@db12cr[sales]> CONNECT hr@sales
Enter password:
Connected.
hr@db12cr[sales]> SELECT *
  2 FROM sh.sregions;
FROM sh.sregions
        *
ERROR at line 2:
ORA-00942: table or view does not exist


hr@db12cr[sales]> SELECT grantee ROLE, privilege,
  2      table_schema||'.'||table_name OBJECT_NAME,
  3      type, grantable
  4  FROM all_tab_privs
  5  WHERE grantee IN (SELECT * FROM session_roles)
  6  UNION
  7  SELECT DECODE(grantee, UPPER(user), 'DIRECT', grantee) ROLE,
  8      privilege,
  9      table_schema||'.'||table_name OBJECT_NAME,
 10      type, grantable
 11  FROM all_tab_privs
 12  WHERE grantee = UPPER(USER)
 13  ORDER by role, privilege, object_name;

no rows selected
```

```
hr@db12cr[sales]> CONNECT oe@sales
Enter password:
Connected.
oe@db12cr[sales]> SELECT *
  2 FROM sh.sregions;
FROM sh.sregions
        *
ERROR at line 2:
ORA-00942: table or view does not exist


oe@db12cr[sales]> SELECT grantee ROLE, privilege,
  2     table_schema||'.'||table_name OBJECT_NAME,
  3     type, grantable
  4  FROM all_tab_privs
  5  WHERE grantee IN (SELECT * FROM session_roles)
  6  UNION
  7  SELECT DECODE(grantee, UPPER(user), 'DIRECT', grantee) ROLE,
  8     privilege,
  9     table_schema||'.'||table_name OBJECT_NAME,
 10     type, grantable
 11  FROM all_tab_privs
 12  WHERE grantee = UPPER(USER)
 13  ORDER by role, privilege, object_name;

no rows selected
```

Effective security management requires you to understand the principles and implications of GRANTing and REVOKEing Oracle privileges.

Roles

A database role is a database object used to group privileges. A database role is an easier way to administer granting many privileges to many users. For example, let's suppose we have 100 tables, each of which has four privileges (INSERT, UPDATE, DELETE, and, SELECT) that we want to grant to 100 users. Let's also suppose that every user gets read access (one object privilege – SELECT) to our 100 tables and that we have an additional privileged group of 50 users that get to manipulate the data (three object privileges – INSERT, UPDATE, and DELETE) in the 100 tables.

First we illustrate administering this example without using database roles. It requires 10,000 grants—(100 users) × (1 object privilege) × (100 tables)—just for read access. It requires 15,000 grants—(50 users) × (3 privileges) × (100 tables)—grants for INSERT, UPDATE, and DELETE privileges.

We have to issue 25,000 grants to administer the example. Not only is this an administrative nightmare to set up, it is prone to inadvertent errors and is extremely hard to manage. This example clearly shows that trying to manage a one-to-one relationship between object privileges and database users is effective only for a small number of users and a small number of objects.

A more efficient way to manage granting privileges to users is by using a database role. Database roles can be granted multiples of privileges (system or object) and be hierarchical in nature. For example, let's redo our example using database roles.

First, we create a role named PROD_READ and grant the 100 SELECT privileges to the role. Second, we create a role named PROD_WRITE and grant the 100 INSERT, UPDATE, and DELETE privileges to it. We also grant PROD_READ to PROD_WRITE because every use that can manipulate data can also read the data. To set up this example using roles it takes 401 grants, which is considerably less than the 25,000 grants required without roles.

Furthermore, if an administrator wants to add or subtract privileges, we can simply perform the grant or revoke action against the role and all users that have been granted the role will receive/revoke the privileges the next time they connect. Roles also provide a way to grant only the privileges needed to perform a person's job. Consequently, roles are a powerful way to provide a least-privileged environment, which is important to ensuring a sound and secure database. Figure 4-2 shows how privilege management can be simplified.

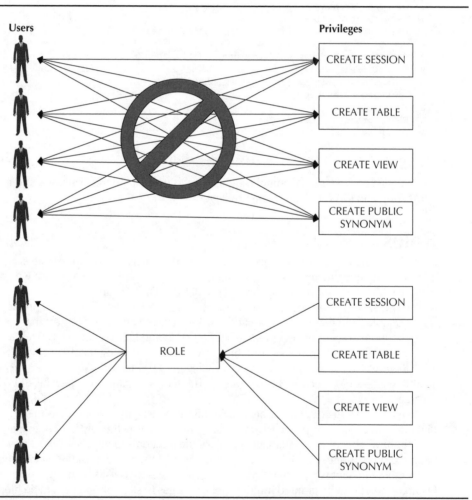

FIGURE 4-2. *Database roles simplify privilege management*

A few database parameters affect the use of database roles. For example, the following indicates that this pluggable database does not allow for OS roles and each user is capable of having 30 database roles enabled per session (this is a depreciated parameter retained for backward compatibility):

```
oe@db12cr[sales] > CONNECT sec_mgr@sales
Enter password:
Connected.
sec_mgr@db12cr[sales] > SHOW PARAMETER ROLES

NAME                                 TYPE       VALUE
------------------------------------ ---------- -------------
max_enabled_roles                    integer    30
os_roles                             boolean    FALSE
remote_os_roles                      boolean    FALSE
```

OS_ROLES and REMOTE_OS_ROLES can increase the attack surface of an unauthorized administrator attempting to gain access locally or remotely to the database. You could change the value of MAX_ENABLED_ROLES to add increased control over the number of roles enabled for the database session. However, we often see systems and customers more concerned about which roles (and associated privileges) are enabled simultaneously as opposed to how many roles are enabled. We will discuss how to enforce mutual exclusivity of privileges in Chapter 10.

Role and Privilege Immediacy

Roles are checked or introduced to a database session only during connection time. That is, if SEC_MGR granted HR the role RESOURCE, then HR would not realize or be able to use the role at the next logon. However, the same is not true about privileges. Privileges are realized or are accessible immediately upon issuing of the GRANT statement. The following are two concurrent sessions in the database, and they show the immediate and delayed effects of granting roles and privileges.

Time	SEC_MGR Session	HR Session
23:10:42	CONNECT sec_mgr@sales Enter password: Connected.	CONNECT hr@sales Enter password: Connected.
23:11:24		SELECT * FROM sh.sregions; FROM sh.sregions * ERROR at line 2: ORA-00942: table or view does not exist
23:12:56	GRANT SELECT ON sh.sregions TO HR;	

Time	SEC_MGR Session	HR Session
23:13:08		SELECT * FROM sh.sregions;

```
                                     SR_ID REGION
                                ---------- ----------
                                         1 NORTH
                                         2 SOUTH
                                         3 EAST
                                         4 WEST

                                4 rows selected.
```

Time	SEC_MGR Session	HR Session
23:13:22		SELECT * FROM session_roles;

```
                                no rows selected
```

Time	SEC_MGR Session	HR Session
23:13:49	GRANT RESOURCE TO hr;	
23:14:12		SELECT * FROM session_roles;

```
                                no rows selected
```

Time	SEC_MGR Session	HR Session
23:14:21		CONNECT hr@sales

```
                                Enter password:
                                Connected.
```

Time	SEC_MGR Session	HR Session
23:14:42		SELECT * FROM session_roles;

```
                                ROLE
                                ----------
                                RESOURCE

                                1 row selected.
```

You can see from the example that the GRANT for the database role does not take immediate effect, but the direct object grant to SH.SREGIONS does.

Roles and Container Databases

As with other object create statements, Oracle Database 12*c* allows for objects (ROLES in this case) to be created in the current container or all containers. Remember also that if you are creating a ROLE from the root container that you intend to use across all containers, you must use the common name format (that is, C##<*ROLE_NAME*>).

If you are in the root container and you create a role without using the CONTAINER clause, Oracle will default to using CONTAINER = ALL syntax. The ROLE name must conform to the common name format and start with C## or c##. Oracle Database 12*c* refers to this role as a common role. If you are not in the root container and you create a role using the CONTAINER = CURRENT syntax, you can name the role as you have in the past.

If you are in a pluggable container and you create a role without using the CONTAINER clause, Oracle will default to using CONTAINER = CURRENT syntax. The ROLE name does not have to conform to common role name format. That is, you can name the ROLE as you have in previous versions of Oracle. Oracle Database 12c refers to this role as a local role or local to the container database only.

The following example demonstrates these points:

```
sec_mgr@db12cr[sales]> -- Connect to the root container as SYSTEM
sec_mgr@db12cr[sales]> CONNECT system
Enter password:
Connected.
system@db12cr[cdb$root]> -- Fails because ALL_CONTAINERS_ROLE does not conform
system@db12cr[cdb$root]> -- to the common name format and CONTAINER=ALL
system@db12cr[cdb$root]> -- is implied
system@db12cr[cdb$root]> CREATE ROLE all_containers_role;
CREATE ROLE all_containers_role
            *
ERROR at line 1:
ORA-65096: invalid common user or role name


system@db12cr[cdb$root]> -- Same effect - explicitly stating CONTAINER=ALL
system@db12cr[cdb$root]> CREATE ROLE all_containers_role CONTAINER=ALL;
CREATE ROLE all_containers_role CONTAINER=ALL
            *
ERROR at line 1:
ORA-65096: invalid common user or role name


system@db12cr[cdb$root]> -- Can't create roles in the root container
system@db12cr[cdb$root]> CREATE ROLE root_container_role CONTAINER=CURRENT;
CREATE ROLE root_container_role CONTAINER=CURRENT
*
ERROR at line 1:
ORA-65049: creation of local user or role is not allowed in CDB$ROOT


system@db12cr[cdb$root]> -- Works - correct format and for all containers
system@db12cr[cdb$root]> CREATE ROLE  C##all_containers_role CONTAINER=ALL;

Role created.
```

Public and Default Database Roles

The role PUBLIC is created by Oracle Database 12c by default during the process of creating a database or by cloning the SEED or another pluggable database. Oracle creates or clones several default roles (DATAPUMP_EXP_FULL_DATABASE, DBA, RESOURCE, and so on) and grants the roles the corresponding privileges.

The PUBLIC role is a general purpose role to which every connected user can grant privileges. However, the PUBLIC role doesn't present in the user's session the same way other database roles do. Recall from our previous discussion that the SESSION_ROLES view displays roles that are active in the connected session. The following example demonstrates that the PUBLIC role does not show in the view SESSION_ROLES; however, the objects are accessible based on the privileges that were granted to PUBLIC.

```
system@db12cr[cdb$root]> CONNECT sec_mgr@sales
Enter password:
Connected.
sec_mgr@db12cr[sales]> CREATE USER test_user INDENTIFIED BY oracle;

User created.

sec_mgr@db12cr[sales]> GRANT CREATE SESSION TO test_user;

Grant succeeded.
sec_mgr@db12cr[sales]> -- Connect as test_user and determine
sec_mgr@db12cr[sales]> -- what privs the user has
sec_mgr@db12cr[sales]> CONNECT test_user@sales
Enter password:
Connected.
test_user@db12cr[sales]> -- PUBLIC is not a "granted" role
test_user@db12cr[sales]> SELECT *
  2  FROM session_roles;

no rows selected

test_user@db12cr[sales]> -- However, I still have access to DUAL
test_user@db12cr[sales]> SELECT *
  2  FROM dual;

D
-
X

1 row selected.

test_user@db12cr[sales]> -- I even know SYS owns DUAL
test_user@db12cr[sales]> SELECT *
  2  FROM sys.dual;

D
-
X

1 row selected.

test_user@db12cr[sales]> -- I can find what privs I have on DUAL
test_user@db12cr[sales]> -- and how I received the privs by querying
test_user@db12cr[sales]> SELECT grantor, grantee, table_name, privilege
  2  FROM all_tab_privs
  3  WHERE table_name = 'DUAL';

GRANTOR              GRANTEE              TABLE_NAME           PRIVILEGE
-------------------- -------------------- -------------------- ---------
SYS                  PUBLIC               DUAL                 SELECT

1 row selected.
```

Role Hierarchies

Roles can be granted object and system privileges and they can be granted other roles. As in the preceding example, PROD_WRITE was granted the role PROD_READ. The ability to nest roles adds flexibility in capturing real-world security policies. Unfortunately, this flexibility can also lead to complexity and confusion when you're trying to unravel which privileges are granted to what or whom.

The previous queries will help you determine which specific privileges a user has regardless of how the privileges were obtained. You should also consider the management burden when creating the role structure in your database; limiting the number of nested roles will help simplify the complexity of your privilege structures and make overall security management easier.

Object Privileges Through Roles and PL/SQL

There is a restriction on being able to use object privileges obtained through a grant to a role in PL/SQL program units. If you need to use an object privilege in PL/SQL program units, the PL/SQL program unit owner account must be granted the object privilege directly. The following example demonstrates this restriction and the way to achieve the desired effect of being able use an object privilege in the PL/SQL program unit.

```
sec_mgr@db12cr[sales]> -- create the PL/SQL program unit owner account
sec_mgr@db12cr[sales]> CREATE USER sales_app
  2  IDENTIFIED BY welcome1;

User created.

sec_mgr@db12cr[sales]> GRANT create session , create procedure
  2  TO sales_app;

Grant succeeded.

sec_mgr@db12cr[sales]> -- create a role
sec_mgr@db12cr[sales]> CREATE ROLE sales_read_role ;

Role created.

sec_mgr@db12cr[sales]> -- grant the role to the PL/SQL program
sec_mgr@db12cr[sales]> -- unit owner account
sec_mgr@db12cr[sales]> GRANT sales_read_role
  2  TO sales_app;

Grant succeeded.

sec_mgr@db12cr[sales]> -- grant an object privilege to the role
sec_mgr@db12cr[sales]> CONNECT sh@sales
Enter password:
Connected.
sh@db12cr[sales]> GRANT SELECT ON sh.sales_history
  2  TO sales_read_role;

Grant succeeded.

sh@db12cr[sales]> -- attempt to use the object privilege obtained
sh@db12cr[sales]> -- through the role
```

```
sh@db12cr[sales]> CONNECT sales_app@sales
Enter password:
Connected.
sales_app@db12cr[sales]> SELECT * FROM session_roles;

ROLE
-----------------------------------------------------------------------
SALES_READ_ROLE

1 row selected.

sales_app@db12cr[sales]> -- the privilege can be used in a SQL statement
sales_app@db12cr[sales]> SELECT count(*) FROM sh.sales_history;

  COUNT(*)
----------
         2

1 row selected.

sales_app@db12cr[sales]> -- the privilege cannot be used in PL/SQL
sales_app@db12cr[sales]> CREATE OR REPLACE FUNCTION sales_history_count
  2   RETURN NUMBER IS
  3          i NUMBER;
  4   BEGIN
  5     SELECT COUNT(*) INTO i
  6     FROM sh.sales_history;
  7     RETURN i;
  8   END;
  9   /

Warning: Function created with compilation errors.

sales_app@db12cr[sales]> SHOW ERRORS
Errors for FUNCTION SALES_HISTORY_COUNT:

LINE/COL ERROR
-------- ----------------------------------------------------------------
5/3      PL/SQL: SQL Statement ignored
6/11     PL/SQL: ORA-00942: table or view does not exist
sales_app@db12cr[sales]> -- grant the object privilege directly to
sales_app@db12cr[sales]> -- the PL/SQL program unit owner account
sales_app@db12cr[sales]> CONNECT sh@sales
Enter password:
Connected.
sh@db12cr[sales]> GRANT SELECT ON sh.sales_history
  2   TO sales_app;

Grant succeeded.

sh@db12cr[sales]> -- now we can use a direct object privilege
sh@db12cr[sales]> -- grant in the PL/SQL
sh@db12cr[sales]> CONNECT sales_app@sales
Enter password:
```

```
Connected.
sales_app@db12cr[sales]> CREATE OR REPLACE FUNCTION sales_history_count
  2  RETURN NUMBER IS
  3          i NUMBER;
  4  BEGIN
  5    SELECT COUNT(*) INTO i
  6    FROM sh.sales_history;
  7    RETURN i;
  8  END;
  9  /

Function created.
```

Selective Privilege Enablement

An advantage to using roles versus direct grants is that roles can be selectively enabled or disabled for the user. Direct grants are enabled (and thus "on") all the time; roles can be granted to a user but not enabled and the privileges for the user are not "on" until the role is enabled.

I have seen people try to mimic selective privileges by having their application dynamically grant and revoke object privileges. For example, they might create a procedure that the application will call to enable the privileges. Likewise, there will be a procedure to undo the user's privileges. Why would you want to introduce new application code into the system when Oracle has a built-in way to accomplish the same thing and it has been thoroughly tested?

In the following example, privileges to control access to SH's SREGIONS have been granted to the HR:

```
sec_mgr@db12cr[sales]> -- Delegate privs to HR
sec_mgr@db12cr[sales]> GRANT ALL ON sh.sregions TO hr
  2     WITH GRANT OPTION;

Grant succeeded.
```

To implement dynamic privilege enablement, we would then create a program similar to the following:

```
sec_mgr@db12cr[sales]> CONNECT sh@sales
Enter password:
Connected.
sh@db12cr[sales]> CREATE OR REPLACE PROCEDURE set_privs
  2  AS
  3  BEGIN
  4    EXECUTE IMMEDIATE  'GRANT SELECT ON sh.sregions TO '||USER;
  5  END;
  6  /

Procedure created.

sh@db12cr[sales]> CREATE OR REPLACE PROCEDURE unset_privs
  2  AS
  3  BEGIN
  4    EXECUTE IMMEDIATE  'REVOKE SELECT ONsh.regions FROM '||USER;
  6  END;
  7  /
```

```
Procedure created.

sh@db12cr[sales]> GRANT EXECUTE ON set_privs TO oe;

Grant succeeded.

sh@db12cr[sales]> GRANT EXECUTE ON unset_privs TO oe;

Grant succeeded.
```

For the user to enable their privileges selectively, the application simply calls the SET_PRIVS procedure while logged in as the appropriate user:

```
sh@db12cr[sales]> CONNECT oe@sales
Enter password:
Connected.
oe@db12cr[sales]> SELECT * FROM sh.sregions;
SELECT * FROM sh.sregions
                    *
ERROR at line 1:
ORA-00942: table or view does not exist


oe@db12cr[sales]> EXEC sh.set_privs;

PL/SQL procedure successfully completed.

oe@db12cr[sales]> SELECT * FROM sh.sregions;

     SR_ID REGION
---------- ----------
         1 NORTH
         2 SOUTH
         3 EAST
         4 WEST

4 rows selected.
```

This is a *bad* design for several reasons. A major security flaw exists, because privilege grants are not restricted to a specific user. We see design patterns like this used repeatedly in our customer systems. *Do not use this design!*

An alternative design for supporting selective privileges is based on assigning roles to a user and not enabling them by default. For example, suppose that you require a user to have the APP_USER role to access the application's data in the SALES pluggable database. A user is granted the role, *but the role is not enabled by default*. This is done such that if the user were to connect directly to the database and select from SESSION_ROLES view, the user would not see the granted role. However, when the user accesses the database via the application, the application knows it has to enable the role and does so transparently for the user. The following example illustrates this point:

```
oe@db12cr[sales]> CONNECT sec_mgr@sales
Enter password:
Connected.
sec_mgr@db12cr[sales]> CREATE ROLE app_user_role;
```

```
Role created.

sec_mgr@db12cr[sales]> -- Grant privileges to role
sec_mgr@db12cr[sales]> GRANT ALL ON sh.sregions TO app_user_role;

Grant succeeded.

sec_mgr@db12cr[sales]> -- Grant role to users
sec_mgr@db12cr[sales]> GRANT app_user_role TO oe, hr;

Grant succeeded.

sec_mgr@db12cr[sales]> -- Disable this role by default.
sec_mgr@db12cr[sales]> -- Privileges are not available
sec_mgr@db12cr[sales]> -- till role is enabled
sec_mgr@db12cr[sales]> ALTER USER hr DEFAULT ROLE ALL
  2      EXCEPT app_user_role;

User altered.
```

If the user logs in via SQL*Plus and tries to query the application's tables, the login will fail, because the privileges to do so are not available until the role is enabled:

```
sec_mgr@db12cr[sales]> CONNECT oe@sales
Enter password:
Connected.
oe@db12cr[sales]> SELECT * FROM sh.sregions;
SELECT * FROM sh.sregions
                  *
ERROR at line 1:
ORA-00942: table or view does not exist


oe@db12cr[sales]> SELECT * FROM session_roles;

no rows selected

oe@db12cr[sales]> SET ROLE app_user_role;

Role set.

oe@db12cr[sales]> SELECT * FROM sh.sregions;

     SR_ID REGION
---------- ----------
         1 NORTH
         2 SOUTH
         3 EAST
         4 WEST

4 rows selected.

oe@db12cr[sales]> SELECT * FROM session_roles;

ROLE
----------------------
APP_USER_ROLE
```

This solution does not appear to be more secure than the procedural based method. The only difference is the SET ROLE implementation enables the privileges only for the current OE database session, whereas the SET_PRIVS procedure enables privileges for all OE database sessions.

In the preceding examples, knowing or not knowing the existence of a procedure or role that has to be executed or enabled provides no security. Basing security on the simple knowledge of something that can be easily guessed or derived is called *security through obscurity*. This approach is not considered a security best practice. Forcing applications or users to enable roles and/or privileges explicitly does not provide adequate security, and believing it does fosters a false sense of security.

Selective Privilege Use Cases

The real power of selective privileges implemented via roles is magnified when using roles that require something other than just knowing the role's name. We will look at two ways to secure roles soon. Before we do that, let's look at several important use cases that frame the complexities and requirements for least privileges through roles.

Privileges Only when Accessed via an Application

One frequent requirement is to allow user database access only when the access is via an application. This is very popular with web applications. You might wonder why this is so difficult: the answer is standards and interoperability.

Normally, standards and interoperability are good things. In the security world, standards and interoperability for establishing database connections can be a challenge, as they may facilitate unwanted access into the database. Oracle Database 12*c* supports numerous applications and protocols—ODBC, JDBC, Oracle Net clients, Web Services, HTTP, FTP, and so on. These protocols and capabilities are important to ensuring interoperability with commercial applications as well as facilitating emerging ways to access data.

From a security standpoint, each one represents an expanded attack surface into the database that needs to be secured. The best mechanism for securing them and reducing the attack surface is to turn them off. That may not be a practical choice, however, if applications require that the protocols interact with the database.

Moreover, what we typically see are users accessing the database via a small set of known applications and protocols. The security requirement then is to ensure that these well-known and trusted protocols are the only way users can get access to the database. The applications may also be providing extra layers of security to prevent users from poking around in the database. It does not take much for a user to, intentionally or inadvertently, launch a denial-of-service (DoS) attack via some poorly formed SQL or for a malicious user to take advantage of a known issue in a protocol driver or a background service. So the more you can reduce your attack surface, the more secure your system will be.

As shown in Figure 4-3, you want to restrict direct user access to application tables and allow access to the tables only via the application.

Privileges Based on User and Application

Refining the issue is a more complex problem in which the security privileges are based not just on the user, but the user *and* the application. As shown in Figure 4-3, the user may have several applications accessing the same database. The difference between this issue and the one just described is that you are assuming the user has access to the same database through multiple applications. This is a popular model for two application types: a web-based application and an ad hoc reporting tool.

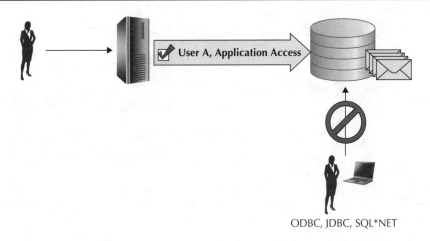

FIGURE 4-3. *Access application tables only via the application*

The security concern is that the user will point the ad hoc query tool at the web application data or the financial application data. Because the application data may not rely on database security alone (if at all), the user may have full access, or more access than you would like. This application data was not intended to be accessed in an ad hoc manner. To maintain least privilege, privileges should be based on the user *and the* application, not the user *and all* the applications.

Privileges Based on User, Application, Location, and Time

Another variation on privileges can be seen when the same user, using the same application, accesses a database in different ways, from different places, at different times. The point is that arbitrarily complex security policies may be required. Privileges for a user accessing the database via multiple applications should vary depending on which application the user is using, as shown in Figure 4-4.

As shown in Figure 4-5, the user may be accessing the application from within her office. Access to the office is physically controlled by the security guard at the entrance of the building and

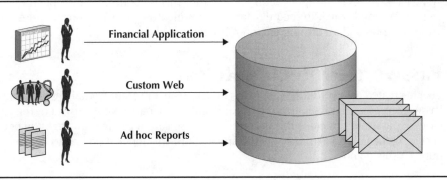

FIGURE 4-4. *A user may access the database via multiple applications*

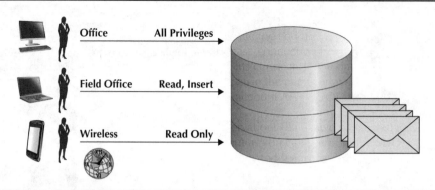

FIGURE 4-5. *User privileges may vary based on access method, location, and time of day*

a lock on the office door. Because of the physical security controls, a user accessing the application from within her office provides some sense of assurance that the person accessing the application is really the user. Therefore, the user is allowed all privileges necessary. When the user travels to a field office, the location may still be controlled, but there is less assurance that it really is the user. Therefore, she gets only read and insert privileges. Finally, access via a wireless device is least trusted because these devices are frequently lost or stolen. As such, the user has the ability to read data only, and no data manipulation would be allowed. Furthermore, all of these examples could be further constrained to certain hours of the day, as shown in Figure 4-5. If the user tries to gain access on Sunday at 3 A.M., for example, she is not allowed.

The common thread among all these use cases is that the privileges are not based solely on the user's identity. The security policy and resultant effective privileges should be based on everything you know—the application, how the user authenticated, the user's location, the time of day, and, of course, the user's identity. The trick to making this security approach work is the Oracle Database 12*c* support for *selective privileges*. Database roles and the database's ability to securely enable and disable them is critical to making selective privileges work.

Securing the roles is important because of a philosophical reason, too. If the roles are simply enabled whenever the application makes the SET ROLE call, then the application is in fact controlling the database privileges—that is, the database role has no say in the matter and follows along with whatever the application tells it to do. This is not defense in depth, however, and therefore is not optimal. To secure database roles involves two variations on roles: password-protected roles and secure application roles, discussed next.

Password-Protected Roles

Oracle created password-protected roles to help meet the security challenges just presented. Password-protected roles cannot be enabled unless the password is provided. The primary use case for password-protected roles is prohibiting users from gaining privileges unless they are accessing the database from a specific application. The application knows the role's password, but the users do not.

Password-Protected Role Example

The following example illustrates how easy these roles are to use. To create a password-protected role, you simply add the clause **IDENTIFIED BY <*password*>** to the **CREATE ROLE** command. For example, to create a role with a password of verysecretpass, you would use the following:

```
oe@db12cr[sales]> CONNECT sec_mgr@sales
Enter password:
Connected.
sec_mgr@db12cr[sales]> CREATE ROLE pass_protected_role_a
  2     IDENTIFIED BY verysecretpass;

Role created.
```

The syntax is similar to that of creating a user, as they both use **IDENTIFIED BY <*password*>**. The next step is to grant the role to a user. Note that you want to disable the role explicitly; otherwise, it defeats the purpose of having a password-protected role:

```
sec_mgr@db12cr[sales]> GRANT pass_protected_role_a TO OE;

Grant succeeded.

sec_mgr@db12cr[sales]> ALTER USER OE DEFAULT ROLE ALL
  2     EXCEPT pass_protected_role_a;

User altered.
```

To enable the role, the user or application has to supply the password via the **SET ROLE** command or by calling the DBMS_SESSION.SET_ROLE procedure. To enable the preceding role, the user or application could issue either of the following two statements:

```
sec_mgr@db12cr[sales]> CONNECT oe@sales
Enter password:
Connected.
oe@db12cr[sales]> SELECT * FROM session_roles;

ROLE
---------------------
APP_USER_ROLE

oe@db12cr[sales]> SET ROLE pass_protected_role_a
  2     IDENTIFIED BY verysecretpass;

Role set.

oe@db12cr[sales]> SELECT * FROM session_roles

ROLE
-----------------------------------------
PASS_PROTECTED_ROLE_A

oe@db12cr[sales]> -- Another way is call the DBMS_SESSION's
oe@db12cr[sales]> -- Set role by procedure call. This method
oe@db12cr[sales]> -- is typically done by applications.
oe@db12cr[sales]> BEGIN
  2     DBMS_SESSION.SET_ROLE
```

```
       3                       ('pass_protected_role_A'
       4                       || ' INDENTIFIED BY verysecretpass');
       5  END;
       6  /

PL/SQL procedure successfully completed.
```

Password-Protected Roles and Proxy Authentication

Password-protected roles work in a controlled environment; however, one limitation of a password-protected role is that Oracle doesn't allow for the restriction of their use during proxy authentication account setup. For example, let's say that you want to allow user SCOTT to be able to proxy a connection through APP_PUBLIC. However, you want to restrict SCOTT from using PASS_PROTECTED_ROLE_A. You cannot restrict assigning the password-protected role PASS_PROTECTED_ROLE_A to user SCOTT.

```
oe@db12cr[sales]> CONNECT sec_mgr@sales
Enter password:
Connected.
sec_mgr@db12cr[sales]> CREATE USER app_public IDENTIFIED BY app_public;

User created.

sec_mgr@db12cr[sales]> ALTER USER scott
  2      GRANT CONNECT THROUGH app_public
  3     WITH ROLE ALL EXCEPT pass_protected_role_a;
   WITH ROLE ALL EXCEPT pass_protected_role_a
                        *
ERROR at line 3:
ORA-28168: attempted to grant password-protected role
```

Even if you wanted to grant the password-protected role to SCOTT you are not permitted.

```
sec_mgr@db12cr[sales]> ALTER USER scott
  2      GRANT CONNECT THROUGH app_public
  3     WITH ROLE pass_protected_role_a;
   WITH ROLE pass_protected_role_a
             *
ERROR at line 3:
ORA-28168: attempted to grant password-protected role
```

Unlike standard roles, you cannot use password-protected roles with proxy authentication.

Challenges to Securing the Password

The fundamental challenge with password-protected roles is in keeping the password a secret. Keep in mind that passwords are considered by some to be "weak" authentication. Choosing a strong password is just as critical for roles as it is for users.

The real challenge with role passwords comes down to four fundamental issues. First, it is difficult to secure plain-text passwords. If passwords are stored in application code then they may be easily viewed by anyone who can get access to the code. If the application is a script, then the code is never compiled and the password is even more vulnerable to being detected. The compilation process can obfuscate the code more than scripting, but even doing this may not be adequate protection from programs such as strings found on most UNIX-based systems.

Having users supply the password may defeat the purpose of having a password-protected role in the first place. Recall that certain database privileges are enabled only when the user is accessing the database through the application. If the user knows the password, then the possibility exists that the user can use the role outside the application by directly connecting to the database (via SQL*Plus). One solution to this problem is not to distribute the password to users and to have the application obtain the password via some other method, such as reading it from an encrypted file or from a secure LDAP account.

Second, unlike user passwords that are encrypted or hashed prior to sending them over the network, which is a fundamental part of Oracle's SQL*Net protocol, role passwords may travel in the clear. This will happen if the application is communicating with the database and the network traffic is not being encrypted. Sniffing network packets is trivial, and many applications to do this can be found on the Internet.

Also setting the trace level to ADMIN (16) in the SQLNET.ORA file will capture all SQL*Net network packets. The user can then obtain the role password that has been carefully hidden in the application simply by looking in the SQL*Net trace files. Sending any sensitive traffic over the network is a bad idea and defeats the reason for using password-protected roles. The solution to this problem is to use Oracle Advanced Security Option (ASO) and to enable network encryption specifically.

Third, if multiple applications required the role, then the password would need to be shared among the applications. Sharing passwords only increases the chance for misuse or unintended exposure on the network. Sharing passwords among applications is not easy, practical, or secure.

Finally, the database has no say in whether the role is enabled or disabled. The application requests the database to enable the role with the appropriate password and the database complies. Consequently, the security resides only in the application, and once the password is exposed, even the application can't enforce the security policy.

Password-protected roles have their use in certain situations and circumstances; however, there is a more secure way to control the use of protected roles and privileges: secure application roles. Password-protected roles provide an extra layer of security, as they require having the password to enable the role. This feature can be useful if a database uses multiple roles controlling access to different application schema and data. Each application schema can have its own role and corresponding password, thus providing another security enforcement point to access application data.

Secure Application Roles

Secure application roles were introduced in Oracle9*i* and were designed to meet the same requirements of password-protected roles, but they can actually do more.

The requirement is to prevent users or rogue applications from enabling certain roles. To do this, Oracle ensures that the secure application role can be enabled only from within a PL/SQL program. There are two security aspects to this. First, the user or application has to have EXECUTE rights on the PL/SQL program to enable the role. Second, the PL/SQL program performs a series of verifications and validations to ensure that everything is as it should be *before* setting the role(s). In this way, the PL/SQL program acts as a enforcement point guarding the use of the role.

This proves invaluable and it solves the problem not resolved in the previous example—the database now has a say in whether or not the role should be enabled. The way secure application roles work is that the application executes a secure procedure, which can be considered a request from the application to turn on the privileges associated with the role. It is up to the database and the code you write to determine whether or not the role will be enabled.

For example, if a request to enable a role occurs at 3 A.M. on a Sunday, the database will execute your PL/SQL code, and it may determine that this request is not during normal business hours and therefore reject the request to enable the role.

Secure Application Role Example

Creating a secure application role requires you to start by determining your security requirements, creating a role with appropriate privileges to support your security requirements, then writing a PL/SQL subprogram to protect the use of the role.

The following example creates a role named SEC_APP_ROLE that will be enabled by the PL/SQL procedure PRIV_MGR_PROC in the SEC_MGR schema.

```
sec_mgr@db12cr[sales]> CREATE ROLE sec_app_role
  2    IDENTIFIED USING sec_mgr.priv_mgr_proc;

Role created.

sec_mgr@db12cr[sales]> GRANT sec_app_role TO scott;

Grant succeeded.

sec_mgr@db12cr[sales]> -- Disable the role by not listing as a default
sec_mgr@db12cr[sales]> ALTER USER scott DEFAULT ROLE CONNECT, RESOURCE;

User altered.
```

There are a couple of things worth noting in the code. First, notice the one-word difference between IDENTIFIED *BY* for password-based roles and IDENTIFIED *USING* for secure application roles. INDENTIFIED USING indicates the name of the secure program that controls access to the role. Also, the secure application role program PRIV_MGR_PROC does not have to exist before the role is created. In fact, the schema does not have to exist either. Furthermore, the syntax does not require the securing program to be a PL/SQL procedure or function. After you create the role, you have to grant appropriate users. Remember also to disable the role from the granted users (recall the discussion earlier regarding password-protected roles).

The program that protects the secure application role must be created with invoker rights, which is not the default invocation method in Oracle. When programs are created in the database and no invocation method is specified, then the creator or definer rights are used. As you will see in Chapter 5, database roles are disabled in definer rights invocations and enabled in invoker rights. For consistency reasons among users of the system, roles are enabled only from within invoker rights programs. This includes standard roles as well as password-protected roles.

To illustrate secure application roles, next we remove the previous grant on the SH.SREGIONS table from the standard APP_USER_ROLE and grant the privilege to the secure application role:

```
sec_mgr@db12cr[sales]> -- Revoke privilege from standard role
sec_mgr@db12cr[sales]> REVOKE ALL ON sh.sregions FROM app_user_role;

Revoke succeeded.

sec_mgr@db12cr[sales]> -- Grant select privilege on SH.SREGIONS
sec_mgr@db12cr[sales]> --    to the secure application role
sec_mgr@db12cr[sales]> GRANT SELECT ON sh.sregions TO sec_app_role;

Grant succeeded.
```

In this example, we only want to enable access to the table for users accessing the database directly from the database server. We do this by checking the value in the application context CONNECTION attribute name LOCAL_OR_REMOTE. A value of LOCAL indicates that the connection is directly connected to Oracle and not coming from a remote server.

The first security check happens before the code executes. The database verifies that the user has rights to execute the PL/SQL program. Therefore, we must grant EXECUTE on the PL/SQL program to SCOTT before starting.

```
sec_mgr@db12cr[sales]> CREATE OR REPLACE PROCEDURE PRIV_MGR_PROC
  2  AUTHID CURRENT_USER
  3  AS
  4  BEGIN
  5    IF (SYS_CONTEXT ('CONNECTION', 'LOCAL_OR_REMOTE') = 'LOCAL') THEN
  6      DBMS_SESSION.SET_ROLE ('sec_app_role');
  7    END IF;
  8  END;
  9  /

Procedure created.

sec_mgr@db12cr[sales]> GRANT EXECUTE ON priv_mgr_proc TO scott;

Grant succeeded.
```

Logging in from a remote server as SCOTT using SQL*Plus, we see that the role has not been enabled, even though the procedure executes successfully. We can view the value of the context from session to determine which roles are enabled.

```
sec_mgr@db12cr[sales]> CONNECT scott@sales
Enter password:
Connected.
scott@db12cr[sales]> -- Show current network protocol
scott@db12cr[sales]> SELECT SYS_CONTEXT ('CONNECTION', 'LOCAL_OR_REMOTE')
  2 FROM dual;

SYS_CONTEXT ('CONNECTION', 'LOCAL_OR_REMOTE')
--------------------------------------------------------------------
REMOTE

scott@db12cr[sales]> -- Show enabled roles
scott@db12cr[sales]> SELECT role FROM session_roles;

ROLE
------------------------------
CONNECT
RESOURCE
```

Even if SCOTT knows how to enable roles using the DBMS_SESSION package, as shown, he is not permitted to enable the SEC_APP_ROLE role directly; recall that calling program PRIV_MGR_PROC is the only way the role can be enabled. The call to DBMS_SESSION fails.

```
scott@db12cr[sales]> -- Show role cannot be enabled
scott@db12cr[sales]> EXEC dbms_session.set_role('sec_app_role');
BEGIN dbms_session.set_role('sec_app_role'); END;
```

```
        *
ERROR at line 1:
ORA-28201: Not enough privileges to enable application role 'SEC_APP_ROLE'
ORA-06512: at "SYS.DBMS_SESSION", line 164
ORA-06512: at line 1
```

Next SCOTT tries to execute the procedure to enable the role. The following procedure call (SEC_MGR.PRIV_MGR_PROC) executes successfully. He then tries to query the table with no success. Querying the SESSION_ROLES view indicates that the role was not set by the procedure.

```
scott@db12cr[sales]> -- Try to enable the secure application role
scott@db12cr[sales]> EXEC sec_mgr.priv_mgr_proc

PL/SQL procedure successfully completed.

scott@db12cr[sales]> -- Access object
scott@db12cr[sales]> SELECT * FROM sh.sregions;
SELECT * FROM sh.sregions
                *
ERROR at line 1:
ORA-00942: table or view does not exist


scott@db12cr[sales]> -- Show enabled roles
scott@db12cr[sales]> SELECT ROLE FROM session_roles;

ROLE
------------------------------
CONNECT
RESOURCE
```

SCOTT now connects to the database server and performs the same set of operations. As you can see, the program executes and grants SCOTT the role SEC_APP_ROLE.

```
scott@db12cr[sales]> SELECT SYS_CONTEXT ('CONNECTION', 'LOCAL_OR_REMOTE')
    2 from dual;

SYS_CONTEXT ('CONNECTION', 'LOCAL_OR_REMOTE')
---------------------------------------------------------------------
LOCAL

scott@db12cr[sales]> EXEC sec_mgr.priv_mgr

PL/SQL procedure successfully completed.

scott@db12cr[sales]> SELECT * FROM sh.sregions;

     SR_ID REGION
---------- ----------
         1 NORTH
         2 SOUTH
         3 EAST
         4 WEST
```

```
4 rows selected.

scott@db12cr[sales]> SELECT role FROM session_roles;

ROLE
----------------------------
SEC_APP_ROLE
```

The benefit of using a secure application role is that your PL/SQL program decides whether the role is enabled or not. This is advantageous because it will allow you to modify your security policy without needing to change your deployed applications. For example, if your security policy now requires that the role can be enabled only during normal business hours, you simply modify your PL/SQL program to reflect the security policy change and the new requirement takes effect immediately.

```
scott@db12cr[sales]> CONNECT sec_mgr@sales
Enter password:
Connected.
sec_mgr@db12cr[sales]> -- Modify security policy to only allow the role
sec_mgr@db12cr[sales]> -- during 8 a.m. to 5 p.m.
sec_mgr@db12cr[sales]> CREATE OR REPLACE PROCEDURE priv_mgr_proc
  2   AUTHID CURRENT_USER
  3   AS
  4   BEGIN
  5    IF (TO_NUMBER(TO_CHAR (SYSDATE, 'HH24')) BETWEEN 8 AND 17) THEN
  7      DBMS_SESSION.SET_ROLE ('sec_app_role');
  8    END IF;
  9   END;
 10   /

Procedure created.
```

Connect as SCOTT at 9 P.M. to see if you can gain access to the table:

```
sec_mgr@db12cr[sales]> CONNECT scott@sales
Enter password:
Connected.
scott@db12cr[sales]> SELECT TO_CHAR (SYSDATE, 'HH24') HOUR
  2     FROM dual;

HOUR
--------
21

scott@db12cr[sales]> EXEC sec_mgr.priv_mgr_proc

PL/SQL procedure successfully completed.

scott@db12cr[sales]> SELECT * FROM sh.sregions;
SELECT * FROM sh.sregions
                *
ERROR at line 1:
ORA-00942: table or view does not exist
```

Restrictions

As with password-protected roles, secure application roles cannot be used with proxy authentication. Recall the DDL restricts password-protected roles for a proxy account.

```
scott@db12cr[sales]> CONNECT sec_mgr@sales
Enter password:
Connected.
sec_mgr@db12cr[sales]> ALTER USER scott
  2      GRANT CONNECT THROUGH app_public
  3      WITH ROLE sec_app_role;
    WITH ROLE sec_app_role
              *
ERROR at line 3:
ORA-28168: attempted to grant password-protected role
```

Practical Uses

Secure application roles are a great solution when your architecture depends on the selective nature of enabling roles and privileges. For example, if you want to maintain separate privileges for different users, you can use secure application roles along with your PL/SQL program to decide when to enable the role.

Secure application roles are the preferred way to meet the requirements listed previously, in which privileges are to be granted only after the validation process occurs. The PL/SQL program can not only check environmental attributes, but the code can take parameters as well, which helps it enforce your security policy.

The best method for implementing the PL/SQL program is to use a combination of parameters and non-parameter checks. This is because the parameters can be faked or manipulated; the non-parameter information (time, authentication mode, and so on) is more controlled and harder to alter without causing other system auditing or intrusion detection/monitoring systems to be alerted. Also note that this security model is only as good as the code that is written. In the example, you check for local or remote connections. Although this is certainly better than nothing, it still represents a single check. Secure application roles are most effective when the supporting PL/SQL program checks a combination of properties, and while each check in itself may not be secure, the combination of multiple checks typically provides the necessary security.

Incorporating checks that are less prone to spoofing, such as Commercial Internet Protocol Security Option (CIPSO), Kerberos tickets, signed client JAR files, call stack/registration keys, and so on, aid in higher assurance and trustworthiness of the information being presented and can yield a more secure system.

Global Roles and Enterprise Roles

Oracle added another type of database role to support Enterprise User Security (EUS). Global roles allow administrators to use an LDAP directory server not only for centralized authentication, but also for centralized authorization. Global roles are created in the database and have privileges assigned to them from database objects in the same manner as "standard" database roles. However, global roles cannot be directly assigned to database users. Enterprise users must have the global roles assigned to them in their corresponding enterprise directory.

The LDAP directory servers refer to global roles as enterprise roles. Enterprise roles are unique to each registered database—that is, the LDAP directory server can store multiple global roles from multiple databases. The LDAP directory server maintains a mapping between the enterprise role and the global role for each database.

The database checks the LDAP directory server for global roles during enterprise user logon. If the user's enterprise role(s) have global roles for the database, the database will automatically enable the global roles.

Global roles do not restrict shared schemas from maintaining different object and system privileges. Privileges granted directly to the schema would typically be available to all users that are mapped to that schema. With global roles, two users with different enterprise roles that map to different global roles will have different privileges in the database, even if they map to the same shared schema.

Creating and Assigning Global and Enterprise Roles

Global roles are created in the database, and privileges are assigned to the role in the database. Global roles cannot be granted to other database users or roles. The following example illustrates creating a global role:

```
sec_mgr@db12cr[sales]> -- Create a global role
sec_mgr@db12cr[sales]> CREATE ROLE app_a_global IDENTIFIED GLOBALLY;

Role created.

sec_mgr@db12cr[sales]> -- Grant privileges to role
sec_mgr@db12cr[sales]> GRANT SELECT ON sh.sregions TO app_a_global;

Grant succeeded.
```

Note that you cannot assign the role to other database users or roles.

```
sec_mgr@db12cr[sales]> -- Cannot grant role to users
sec_mgr@db12cr[sales]> GRANT app_a_global TO scott;
GRANT app_a_global TO scott
*
ERROR at line 1:
ORA-28021: cannot grant global roles

sec_mgr@db12cr[sales]> -- Cannot grant global role to other roles
sec_mgr@db12cr[sales]> GRANT app_a_global TO DBA;
GRANT app_a_global TO DBA
*
ERROR at line 1:
ORA-28021: cannot grant global roles
```

To add the global role to a database user, you must use the Oracle Enterprise Manager Cloud Control (OEMCC). OEMCC is a web application tool that manages enterprise roles, global roles, and their mappings to enterprise users. First, you create an enterprise role, and then you map the global role from your databases to the enterprise role.

In Figure 4-6, you can see that the enterprise role APP_A_ENTERPRISE_ROLE is mapped to the global role in the databases. The APP_A_GLOBAL role is highlighted for the sales pluggable database.

You next grant the enterprise role to the LDAP directly server user. Clicking the Users tab in the OEMCC web application reveals the screen that allows the administrator to assign the enterprise role to users.

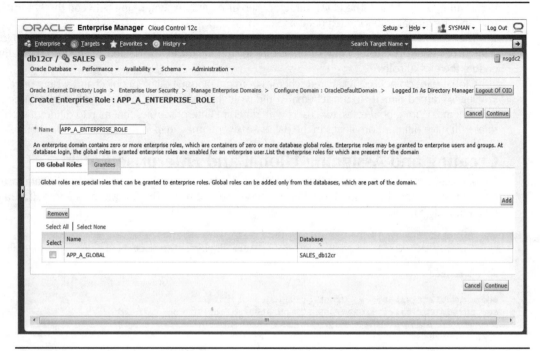

FIGURE 4-6. *Enterprise roles are created with Oracle Enterprise Manager*

Figure 4-7 shows that enterprise user dknox has been granted the enterprise role APP_A_ENTERPRISE_ROLE. The OEMCC web application created the enterprise role to global role mapping for the database and user.

When enterprise user dknox logs on to the database, the LDAP directory server maps dknox to the shared database schema DB_ENTRY. The enterprise role APP_A_ENTERPRISE_ROLE also maps to the database global role APP_A_GLOBAL and is enabled in his session, as shown next:

```
sec_mgr@db12cr[sales]> CONNECT dknox@sales
Enter password:
Connected.
db_entry@db12cr[sales]> -- Show identity for enterprise user
db_entry@db12cr[sales]> SELECT SYS_CONTEXT ('userenv', 'external_name') name
  2     FROM dual;

NAME
----------------------------------------
cn=dknox,ou=Users,dc=nsg,dc=net

db_entry@db12cr[sales]> -- Show roles.
db_entry@db12cr[sales]> SELECT role FROM session_roles;

ROLE
------------------------------
APP_A_GLOBAL
```

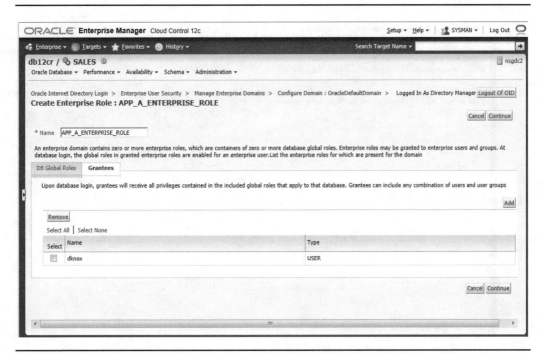

FIGURE 4-7. *Role authorizations are assigned by the Oracle Enterprise Manager*

One of the newer features of Oracle enterprise roles is the ability to map LDAP groups to enterprise roles. This feature is called Oracle enterprise groups. You can use the OEMCC to map an LDAP group to an enterprise role as shown in Figure 4-8. You can maintain the LDAP group membership versus mapping users to each enterprise role.

In the following example, psack is an LDAP user who is a member of the LDAP group cn=ApplicationA, ou=Groups, dc=nsg, dc=net. When psack logs in to the database, his LDAP membership implies the APP_A_GLOBAL database role is active for the database session.

```
db_subtree@db12cr[sales]> CONNECT psack@sales
Enter password:
Connected.
db_subtree@db12cr[sales]> SELECT ROLE role FROM session_roles;

ROLE
--------------------------------------------
APP_A_GLOBAL

1 row selected.
```

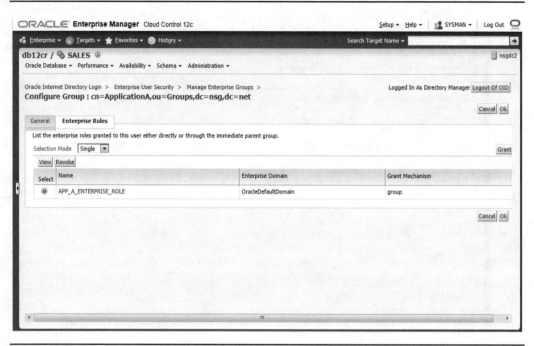

FIGURE 4-8. *Creating Oracle enterprise groups with OEMCC*

Combining Standard and Global Roles

One of the difficulties in using both enterprise and global roles is reconciling which end users
have which privileges. Database privileges granted to global roles cannot be seen from the LDAP
directory server. So the LDAP directory server has no visibility to the authorizations of the end
user in the database. Similarly, the database doesn't know the name of the end user because the
LDAP directory server manages the end user to shared schema mapping. So the database doesn't
have nonrepudiation with respect to the audit information collected during the user's session
connecting it to the actual end user.

You have to perform a two-step process to make these connections. First, you need to determine
the privileges that have been granted to the global roles. Next, you need to query the LDAP directory
server to determine which enterprise roles are mapped to which global roles and which enterprise
users are mapped to which enterprise roles.

Oracle provides a tool named ldapsearch, which makes querying LDAP directory servers easy.
We have added in some command-line kung-fu (http://blog.commandlinekungfu.com) to clean
up the output:

```
[oracle@oel5512c ~]$ ldapsearch -b "dc=nsg,dc=net" \
>     -D "cn=Directory Manager" -w "password" "uniquemember=cn=dknox*" | \
>     grep "^cn=.*net$" | cut -f1 -d\, | cut -f2 -d=

APP_A_GLOBAL
```

When you are using the shared schema design, it is a good idea also to use global and enterprise roles. However, not all privileges have to be granted to global roles. Common privileges can be granted to the shared schema either directly or using a regular database role. This will make the task of figuring out who has access to what easier.

Using Roles Wisely

Standard database roles are very powerful. There are a few important things that can affect your design with respect to roles, privileges, and the subsequent assignments to users.

Too Many Roles

The ability to create and assign roles to other roles repeatedly, coupled with the ability to grant privileges both to users and roles in a redundant way, can make absolute security management confusing and difficult. An almost endless hierarchy of roles can be created. The confusion is not from Oracle for allowing roles to be granted to roles or redundant privileges, but rather from administrators designing a security policy that uses this capability.

Also, keep in mind that every role enabled for a user takes up a small percentage of memory. Recall the MAX_ENABLED_ROLES init.ora parameter restricts the number of roles for this very reason. You should also take this into consideration when creating and assigning roles (again this is a depreciated parameter for backward compatibility).

Naming

Naming roles may seem trivial, you should consider at least two things when coming up with a naming convention. First, role names have to be unique not only from other roles, but from other usernames, too. This may seem obvious at first, but often developers create role names, forgetting that the name is global. If two applications create a role with the same name but require different privileges per role (such as PROD, DEVELOPER, TEST, and so on), it may not be possible to install both applications on the same database.

Second, there are often implied meanings associated with a role name. A role named Administrator implies powerful privileges. Unfortunately, the name is too vague. If you were conducting a security audit, the role name could be either helpful or a hindrance depending on how carefully the name is chosen. A user with this role is an Administrator of what?

A solution to both of these problems simply requires a bit of thought at the design stage. For example, inserting a prefix for the specific application name in front of the role name may prove to be descriptive as well as help ensure global uniqueness. You may want to create the APP_X_ DEVELOPER and APP_Y_ADMINISTRATOR roles instead of simply Developer and Administrator, for example, which do not convey their true meaning.

Dependencies

Database roles are schema objects owned by SYS. If user HR creates HR_MANAGERS, then dropping HR still leaves the HR_MANAGERS role. This is because Oracle stores roles in the data dictionary (SYS schema) rather than in the user's schema. Even if you issue the statement **DROP USER HR CASCADE**, Oracle does not delete the role or remove the privileges. Roles can be dropped only using the DROP ROLE statement, and the DROP ANY ROLE privilege is required or you must have been granted the role WITH ADMIN option.

Summary

Database access control is the fundamental security mechanism for data security. Oracle provides two types of privileges: system privileges, which apply across the database, and object privileges, which apply to specific database objects. Effective security implies a good understanding of the different types of privileges, their relationships and dependencies, and the ability to assign and verify these privileges database users.

Roles have many advantages, and when used effectively, they provide a flexible, secure, and easy way of ensuring least privileges and solid database security. Oracle supports different role types for different situations. Standard roles allow users' privileges to be easily aggregated and managed. Global and enterprise roles support Oracle's EUS strategy by allowing LDAP directory servers to maintain end user identities to shared schema mappings and enterprise roles to global role mappings. This is a powerful feature of enterprise security management as it centralizes authentication and authorization for users of multiple systems.

Another advantage to using roles can also be seen with the ability to support selective privilege enablement. Roles can be enabled or disabled by default. This can facilitate many real-world security policies. To do this effectively, enabling the roles must be done in a secure manner. Password-protected roles provide security for enabling roles. Although password-protected roles are good in many situations, they are vulnerable to several password management–related issues.

Secure application roles extend the ability of the database to protect the use of roles. Secure application roles allow the database (your PL/SQL program) to decide ultimately whether a role and its related privileges should be enabled. Security is often not based on the user's identity alone. Access must be controlled based on many things, such as how and when the user authenticated, the application the user is using, the user's location when accessing the database, and so on. Secure application roles provide a way to meet this complex and varying set of security requirements.

CHAPTER
5

Foundational Elements of Database Application Security

I n this chapter we discuss the fundamentals of database application security. It is common to find application security built into and throughout different architecture layers of an enterprise system. For example, there might be data input validation via JavaScript in the client tier (web browser), certainly there has been plenty of application security code (Java Servlets, Java Authentication and Authorization Service [JAAS], Java Authorization [JAZN], and so on) written in the middle tier (application server), and obviously Oracle Database 12*c* has several intrinsic security features plus several security options to protect the backend database.

So you might ask the question, "Where should I code security for my application?" We believe as a general rule-of-thumb that *security should be enforced closest to the data*. That is, it makes no security sense to write code for data security in your web application when a user can simply connect to the backend database using SQL*Plus, bypassing the middle-tier security altogether. Your security goal should be to enforce your security policy regardless of the way the user connects to the database. Security transparency is key to adoption. The essence of security transparency is that applications and users are not encumbered by the mechanics of security enforcement. If security enforcement becomes too cumbersome, then you are in danger of an administrator or a developer turning off security or finding ways to get around it.

As you build your database security policy(s), you will invariably find yourself needing to store information about the connected user or the operating context of the user's database session. For example, you may need to store security labels the user has access to, or special application groups the user is a member of, and so on. Your first thought might be to create a table, store the values in the table, and then query the values later during policy enforcement. Depending on how you intend to use the values, the number of values, and the frequency of access, this might be a perfectly acceptable solution. However, you might find that you need quicker access to the information than what can be afforded by querying a table. Or you might find that your security code is consuming too many database resources by constantly querying the security table.

There is a better, faster, and more secure way to store and retrieve information specific to a user, and Oracle calls it an *application context*.

Application Context

An application context allows for the storage and retrieval of name-value pairs that are held in memory and called a *namespace*. The names (known as *attributes*) and their associated values can be defined, set/updated, and retrieved by users or applications. Attributes and values are typically established during database logon. However, the attributes and values can be updated at any point during the session. Related attributes and values can be grouped together in a namespace. The namespace is simply the arbitrary name you give for the application context. We will use *namespace* and *application context* interchangeably throughout this chapter. Attributes and their associated values are stored in the database server's memory (User Global Area [UGA] for dedicated server processes and System Global Area [SGA] for shared server processes). Accessing the namespace's attributes and values in memory is quicker than querying them from a table.

Figure 5-1 illustrates the concept of application contexts for the two database connection modes. In dedicated server session mode, the application context is stored in UGA as part of the Program Global Area (PGA) memory. In shared server session mode, the application context is stored in the database's SGA as part of the LARGE_POOL.

Application contexts hold multiples of attribute-value pairs such as the name of the application, end user, organization, role, and so on, and are immutable/read-only to the end user if implemented

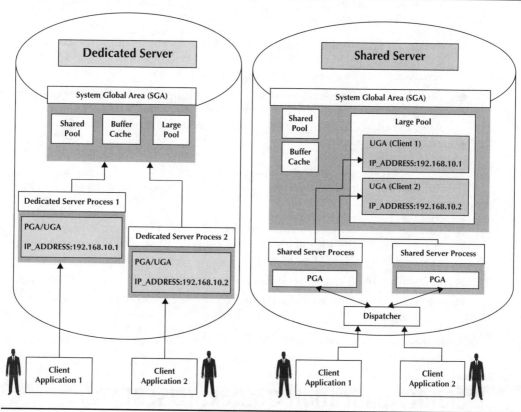

FIGURE 5-1. *Oracle application contexts*

correctly. Your security policies may reference these attributes in controlling user access. Storing the values in memory saves the time and resources that would be required to query tables repetitively to retrieve this information. Consequently, you will often see the application context descriptions in security documentation; however, there is no requirement to use an application context with a security implementation.

Oracle built application contexts to increase the performance of fine-grained access control (FGAC), which is a core component of a virtual private database (VPD). The material presented here will provide you with the foundation for using application context as part of your security implementations. Application context does not require VPD; instead, application contexts enable security controls in VPD, VIEW definitions, user queries, and so on, to enforce security.

You might be thinking, "If users and applications can change the application context values, then how are the attributes and values in a namespace secured?" As you will see, a "trusted" PL/SQL stored program (function, procedure, or package) is associated with the application context, and it is the only way attributes and values in the context can be added, updated, or cleared. As long as you do not mistakenly grant EXECUTE on the "trusted" PL/SQL stored program to an end user, the end user cannot change the application context. For simplicity, we will refer to the "trusted" PL/SQL stored program as the *namespace manager* throughout the rest of the chapter.

For the discussions in this chapter, application contexts are categorized into the following three types, which we discuss in detail in the following sections:

- **Database** Private application contexts that hold user- or application-specific data for the user's database session (values stored in the UGA). The database has a default database application context named USERENV.

- **Global** Sharable application contexts accessible by multiple database sessions used in connection pools, in complex multi-threaded applications as a way to maintain thread state or exclusive (semaphore) object access (values are stored in the SGA).

- **Client** Client-side Oracle Call Interface (OCI) functions set context values in the user's database session.

The attributes and values in the database session application contexts can be initialized in three ways:

- **Locally** The attributes and values are set using a package or procedure; this can be accomplished using a logon trigger or set in the database session using the DBMS_SESSION.SET_CONTEXT procedure.

- **Externally** The attributes and values are set via database link or OCI client application.

- **Globally** The attributes and values are set during the logon process via an external LDAP directory.

Application contexts are stored in the SYS schema. We will now examine the default application context, USERENV.

Default Application Context (USERENV)

The database provides a default application context for each database session. It has the namespace of USERENV and the attribute names are predefined by the Oracle database. The USERENV attributes give many important details about the database session: the client's IP address, the session identifier, the name of the proxy user if using proxy authentication, the protocol used to connect to the database, and even how the user authenticated are just a few examples.

All application context's attributes and values are accessible using the SYS_CONTEXT SQL function. The SYS_CONTEXT function takes the namespace as the first parameter and the attribute name as the second parameter. It also takes an optional length value as the third parameter, which truncates the returned value to the number provided. The length of the value being stored and retrieved is important. Secure programming practices would dictate that you verify the size of information being put into or taken out of the application context. A common malware attack is a buffer overflow. That is, malware developers look to exploit places in code where developers have been lazy or have missed validating input for length and content.

A useful technique for displaying the attributes you use most often is to create a view consisting of the results of the SYS_CONTEXT function on the standard USERENV namespace. Refer to the SYS_CONTEXT section of Chapter 7 in the *Oracle SQL Reference* for a complete list of attributes available in the USERENV namespace. This requires less typing when checking multiple values.

Refer to the script named 05.create.env.sql that is included with the examples for this book to create this type of view.

View the following attributes and the values they return on your database when connected through various applications. You will see that the USERENV application context provides useful information that can be used in implementing your security policies.

```
sec_mgr@db12cr[sales]> -- You can select the individual
sec_mgr@db12cr[sales]> -- attributes from the view
sec_mgr@db12cr[sales]> SELECT session_user, identification_type, ip_address
  2  FROM env;

SESSION_USER         IDENTIFICATION_TYPE   IP_ADDRESS
-------------------  -------------------   --------------------
SEC_MGR              LOCAL                 192.168.10.23

1 row selected.
```

Auditing with USERENV

We go into depth regarding auditing in Chapter 13, but we wanted to demonstrate quickly here how you can use the USERENV context with auditing. Most of the USERENV attributes are set by the database at connection time and are not updatable. However, Oracle does allow the CLIENT_ IDENTIFIER and CLIENT_INFO attributes to be set by the application. The CLIENT_IDENTIFIER is important, because it is part of the audit trail. As we demonstrated with EUS in Chapter 3, you can use the DBMS_SESSION.SET_IDENTIFIER procedure to set its value. When an auditable event happens in Oracle, Oracle collects information regarding the audit event (object, SQL statement, bind values, and so on) and the database session (username, time, and so on). Oracle collects the CLIENT_IDENTIFIER attribute from the USERENV context and stores the value in the CLIENT_ID column of the DBA_AUDIT_TRAIL view (values are actually stored in the SYS.AUD$ table).

```
sec_mgr@db12cr[sales]> DESCRIBE dba_audit_trail
 Name                      Null?     Type
 ----------------------  --------  ----------------
 OS_USERNAME                       VARCHAR2(255)
 USERNAME                          VARCHAR2(128)
 ...
 CLIENT_ID                         VARCHAR2(128)
 ...
```

Oracle also collects and stores the database session username in the USERNAME column. You might be thinking, "Aren't these values the same?" The USERNAME column will always contain a value, but the value of the CLIENT_ID column is dependent on the application developer. For example, if you are using EUS, then by default the end user's identity is not stored in the audit trail. In our examples, EUS connections map either to schema owner DB_ENTRY or DB_SUBTREE. If an auditable event occurs, the audit trail will indicate that DB_ENTRY or DB_SUBTREE originated the audit event. The identity of the end user (the user that actually caused the audit event) is not captured. However, if you create a logon trigger or if your application sets the CLIENT_IDENTIFIER to the end user, the identity of the end user is preserved in the audit trail for the audited event.

For example, let's say that we are auditing SELECT on the SH.SALES_HISTORY table. If we did not set the CLIENT_IDENTIFIER, then all audited events for SELECT on SALES_HISTORY would indicate that DB_ENTRY or DB_SUBTREE performed them.

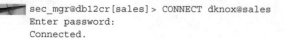

```
sec_mgr@db12cr[sales]> -- Set up auditing for SELECT on SALES_HISTORY
sec_mgr@db12cr[sales]> CONNECT sh@sales
Enter password:
Connected.
sh@db12cr[sales]> AUDIT select ON sales_history;

Audit succeeded.

sh@db12cr[sales]> GRANT select ON sales_history TO DB_ENTRY;

Grant succeeded.

sh@db12cr[sales]> -- Connect as an EUS user who maps to DB_ENTRY
sh@db12cr[sales]> CONNECT dknox@sales
Enter password:
Connected.
db_entry@db12cr[sales]> -- Create an AUDIT event
db_entry@db12cr[sales]> SELECT count(*)
  2  FROM sh.sales_history;

  COUNT(*)
----------
         6

1 row selected.

db_entry@db12cr[sales]> -- Review the AUDIT trail - it appears that DB_ENTRY
db_entry@db12cr[sales]> -- created the AUDIT event
db_entry@db12cr[sales]> CONNECT sec_mgr@sales
Enter password:
Connected.
sec_mgr@db12cr[sales]> SELECT username, client_id, owner, obj_name, action_name
  2  FROM dba_audit_trail
  3  WHERE owner = 'SH'
  4  ORDER BY timestamp;

USERNAME        CLIENT_ID       OWNER           OBJ_NAME        ACTION_NAME
--------------- --------------- --------------- --------------- -----------
DB_ENTRY                        SH              SALES_HISTORY   SELECT

1 row selected.
```

As you can see from the output, the USERNAME that originated the audit event was DB_ENTRY. We know that the end user DKNOX actually originated the audit event. If we use the DBMS_SESSION.SET_IDENTIFIER procedure, we can audit the name of the actual end user that created the AUDIT event. Typically, using the SET_IDENTIFIER procedure is performed transparently to the end user in a logon trigger or as part of the application code. We are showing it here in the database session for illustration purposes only.

```
sec_mgr@db12cr[sales]> CONNECT dknox@sales
Enter password:
Connected.
```

```
db_entry@db12cr[sales]> -- We set the CLIENT_IDENTIFIER value to
db_entry@db12cr[sales]> -- the value of the actual end-user (DKNOX)
db_entry@db12cr[sales]> EXECUTE DBMS_SESSION.SET_IDENTIFIER('DKNOX')

PL/SQL procedure successfully completed.

db_entry@db12cr[sales]> -- We can see it in database session
db_entry@db12cr[sales]> SELECT client_identifier
  2  FROM env;

CLIENT_IDENTIFIER
-----------------------------------------------
DKNOX

1 row selected.

db_entry@db12cr[sales]> -- Create an AUDIT event
db_entry@db12cr[sales]> SELECT count(*)
  2  FROM sh.sales_history;

  COUNT(*)
----------
         6

1 row selected.

db_entry@db12cr[sales]> -- Review the AUDIT trail - looks like DB_ENTRY
db_entry@db12cr[sales]> -- created the AUDIT event
db_entry@db12cr[sales]> CONNECT sec_mgr@sales
Enter password:
Connected.
sec_mgr@db12cr[sales]> SELECT username, client_id, owner, obj_name, action_name
  2  FROM dba_audit_trail
  3  WHERE owner = 'SH'
  4  ORDER BY timestamp;

USERNAME         CLIENT_ID        OWNER            OBJ_NAME         ACTION_NAME
---------------  ---------------  ---------------  ---------------  -----------
DB_ENTRY                          SH               SALES_HISTORY    SELECT
DB_ENTRY         DKNOX            SH               SALES_HISTORY    SELECT

2 rows selected.
```

The CLIENT_IDENTIFIER and CLIENT_INFO attributes within the default USERENV namespace can be set by the application or database login trigger. However, you might find that it is not sufficient for your security purposes to store all possible bits of information in either or both of these attributes. Conveniently, Oracle Database supports the ability to create your own application contexts to store additional attributes and values.

Database Session-Based Application Context

Database session-based application contexts have their attributes and values set by the namespace manager (PL/SQL package, function, and so on) that is specified when you create the context. The purpose of this type of context is to enable application developers to store application information in the database session. The attributes and values in the session context are accessible only in the user's session and cannot be accessed by other connected users.

Creating a Database Session-Based Application Context

You must have CREATE ANY CONTEXT system privilege to create a context. Application contexts are similar to database ROLES in that they are owned by SYS. The following SQL statement creates the SALES_CTX context assigning the trusted program SALES_CTX_MGR. Schema SH will implement the trusted program, which will manage the context.

```
sec_mgr@db12cr[sales] > CONNECT sh@sales
Enter password:
Connected.
sh@db12cr[sales] > CREATE CONTEXT sales_ctx USING sales_ctx_mgr;

Context created.
```

Oracle requires that you associate a trusted program or namespace manager to set, update, or clear values in the context. In the preceding example, the SALES_CTX_MGR trusted program resides in the SH schema, and it is the only way that values can be changed in the SALES_CTX context. Oracle assigns no special meaning to the name of the package or procedure that manages the application context.

You must be granted EXECUTE on SALES_CTX_MGR to set or clear attributes or values in the SALES_CTX context. Reading values from the SALES_CTX context is done through the SQL function SYS_CONTEXT. At this point, we don't know if the namespace manager (SALES_CTX_MGR) is a package or procedure, and we really don't care—all we need to know is that it is the only way attributes and values can be added or changed in the context. You typically don't grant end users the privilege to execute the namespace manager, so you should not grant EXECUTE privilege on the namespace manager to end users or PUBLIC. Restricting execute ability on the namespace manager provides an initial layer of security. Without the ability to manipulate the values, the values are considered secure.

A second layer of security comes from the implementation code itself. Namespace managers perform critical checks and validations on incoming attributes and values *prior* to setting them in the application context. Checks would include checking for minimum and maximum lengths of input values along with checking for NULL. Checks might also include checking the input value against a known list of values or using a regular expression function to validate input against a complex expression.

For example, in the following code snippet we check that the input parameter (P_STATUS) is NULL and check for one of two constant values (OPEN or CLOSED). We can be assured that the value being used in line 13˙ is valid.

```
     ...
   4        BEGIN
   5           IF (p_status IS NOT NULL AND
   6               p_status IN (
   7                   sales_status_pkg.OPEN,
   8                   sales_status_pkg.CLOSED)) THEN
   9
  10              DBMS_SESSION.SET_CONTEXT
  11                 (namespace => sales_status_pkg.CTX_NAME,
```

```
12                    attribute => sales_status_pkg.CTX_ATTR,
13                    value     => upper(p_status));
14           END IF;
...
```

Setting Context Attributes and Values

Attributes and values in the context are created and set by calling the DBMS_SESSION.SET_CONTEXT procedure from within the namespace manager. If you call SET_CONTEXT with an attribute name that doesn't exist, Oracle will create the attribute in the database session and set its value to the value that you provide. You can create attributes with names no longer than 30 bytes (30 characters if using a 7- or 8-bit character set). You can assign values no longer than 4000 bytes that are relevant to your application or security needs.

A common approach to using application contexts is to store values that are derived as the result of a function call, internal database query, or external query (a query to an LDAP directory). By executing the function or query once and storing the result in the context, subsequent references by your database security implementations will be much faster than if they had to be queried per access. That is, retrieving values stored in the application context proves extremely fast for values referenced in the WHERE clause of a SELECT statement, in expressions for Database Vault rules, in data redaction policies, and so on, as we will see in later chapters of this book.

To illustrate this point, let's also suppose we want to restrict SALES_HISTORY records for a sales associate only to those within his or her sales department. To accomplish this, we use an application context to store the user's sales department number. The department number value is looked up once, set in context, and then referenced many times. We will set the attribute and value transparently to the user via a logon trigger.

To set the values in the application context, we have to implement the SALES_CTX_MGR PL/SQL stored program (function, procedure, or package) in the SH schema. It is common to use a PL/SQL package to manage an application context. Packages group together related procedures, functions, constants, and so on, that are required to perform input verification, set attributes, and clear values within the application context. It is also often convenient to have a procedure to clear all attributes and values from the application context, for example, when an application is switching between users in a connection pool.

```
sh@db12cr[sales]> CONNECT hr@sales
Enter password:
Connected.
hr@db12cr[sales]> -- We create the EMPLOYEES table for HR
hr@db12cr[sales]> CREATE TABLE hr.employees (
  2     EMPLOYEE_ID     NUMBER NOT NULL,
  3     FIRST_NAME      VARCHAR2(20),
  4     LAST_NAME       VARCHAR2(25),
  5     EMAIL           VARCHAR2(20),
  6     PHONE_NUMBER    VARCHAR2(20),
  7     HIRE_DATE       DATE,
  8     JOB_ID          VARCHAR2(10),
  9     SALARY          NUMBER(8,2),
 10     COMMISSION_PCT  NUMBER(2,2),
 11     MANAGER_ID      NUMBER(6),
 12     DEPARTMENT_ID   NUMBER(4),
 13     ENAME           AS (UPPER(SUBSTR(FIRST_NAME,1,1))||UPPER(LAST_NAME)))
 14  /
```

```
Table created.

hr@db12cr[sales]> INSERT INTO employees (
  2      EMPLOYEE_ID,
  3      FIRST_NAME,
  4      LAST_NAME,
  5      PHONE_NUMBER,
  6      COMMISSION_PCT,
  7      MANAGER_ID,
  8      DEPARTMENT_ID)
  9  VALUES (
 10      100,
 11      'David',
 12      'Knox',
 13      '555-555-5555',
 14      .23,
 15      98,
 16      100);

1 row created.

hr@db12cr[sales]> INSERT INTO employees (
  2      EMPLOYEE_ID,
  3      FIRST_NAME,
  4      LAST_NAME,
  5      PHONE_NUMBER,
  6      COMMISSION_PCT,
  7      MANAGER_ID,
  8      DEPARTMENT_ID)
  9  VALUES (
 10      101,
 11      'Scott',
 12      'Gaetjen',
 13      '555-555-1111',
 14      .23,
 15      103,
 16      300);

1 row created.

hr@db12cr[sales]> INSERT INTO employees (
  2      EMPLOYEE_ID,
  3      FIRST_NAME,
  4      LAST_NAME,
  5      PHONE_NUMBER,
  6      COMMISSION_PCT,
  7      MANAGER_ID,
  8      DEPARTMENT_ID)
  9  VALUES (
 10      102,
 11      'William',
 12      'Maroulis',
 13      '555-555-2222',
 14      .23,
 15      101,
 16      300);
```

```
1 row created.

hr@db12cr[sales]> INSERT INTO employees (
  2       EMPLOYEE_ID,
  3       FIRST_NAME,
  4       LAST_NAME,
  5       PHONE_NUMBER,
  6       COMMISSION_PCT,
  7       MANAGER_ID,
  8       DEPARTMENT_ID)
  9   VALUES (
 10       103,
 11       'Pat',
 12       'Sack',
 13       '555-555-3333',
 14       .23,
 15       98,
 16       100);

1 row created.

hr@db12cr[sales]> COMMIT;

Commit complete.

hr@db12cr[sales]> GRANT SELECT ON employees TO sh;

Grant succeeded.

hr@db12cr[sales]> connect sh@sales
Enter password:
Connected.
sh@db12cr[sales]> CREATE OR REPLACE PACKAGE sales_ctx_mgr AS
  2       PROCEDURE set_department_id;
  3       PROCEDURE clear_department_id;
  4   END sales_ctx_mgr;

Package created.

sh@db12cr[sales]> SHOW ERRORS
No errors.
sh@db12cr[sales]> CREATE OR REPLACE PACKAGE BODY sales_ctx_mgr AS
  2         PROCEDURE set_department_id AS
  3           ldepartment_id  NUMBER;
  4         BEGIN
  5           SELECT department_id
  6           INTO ldepartment_id
  7           FROM hr.employees
  8           WHERE UPPER(ename) =
  9             UPPER(SYS_CONTEXT ('userenv', 'authenticated_identity'));
 10         DBMS_SESSION.SET_CONTEXT
 11           (namespace    => 'sales_ctx',
 12            attribute    => 'department_id',
 13            value        => ldepartment_id);
 14       END set_department_id;
```

```
15          PROCEDURE clear_department_id AS
16          BEGIN
17             DBMS_SESSION.CLEAR_CONTEXT
18                (namespace    => 'sales_ctx',
19                 attribute    => 'department_id');
20          END clear_department_id;
21       END sales_ctx_mgr;
22    /

Package body created.

sh@db12cr[sales]> SHOW ERRORS
No errors.
```

The security for this example is based on the data stored in the HR.EMPLOYEES table. Guarding access to and manipulation of this data is therefore critical for an effective security plan. We connect as our security policy account (SEC_POL) and create a database logon trigger to set the DEPARTMENT_ID and CLIENT_IDENTIFIER. We use SEC_POL because we are setting our security policy versus managing a security (that is, creating users, granting privileges, and so on), for which we use SEC_MGR.

```
sh@db12cr[sales]> GRANT EXECUTE ON sales_ctx_mgr TO sec_pol;

Grant succeeded.

sh@db12cr[sales]> CONNECT sec_pol@sales
Enter password:
Connected.
sec_pol@db12cr[sales]> CREATE OR REPLACE TRIGGER set_user_deptid
 2      AFTER LOGON ON DATABASE
 3      BEGIN
 4         -- Set the Department ID
 5         sh.sales_ctx_mgr.set_department_id;
 6         -- Set the CLIENT_IDENTIFIER
 7         DBMS_SESSION.SET_IDENTIFIER(
 8            UPPER(SYS_CONTEXT ('userenv', 'authenticated_identity')));
 9      EXCEPTION
10         WHEN NO_DATA_FOUND THEN
11            -- If no data is found, user is not in the table
12            -- so the value will not be set.
13            -- If this exception is not handled, then some users
14            -- may be unable to logon
15            -- To be safe - let's clear any residual data
16            sh.sales_ctx_mgr.clear_department_id;
17      END;
18    /

Trigger created.
```

You do not have to grant execute privileges on the package to call it from a database logon trigger. The ability to execute the namespace manager comes from the definer rights model used by the logon trigger, which fires automatically after the user has authenticated.

Test the design by logging in as DKNOX; the value is automatically set via the logon trigger. The value can be retrieved by querying the SYS_CONTEXT function:

```
sec_pol@db12cr[sales]> CONNECT dknox@sales
Enter password:
Connected.
db_entry@db12cr[sales]> SELECT SYS_CONTEXT ('sales_ctx',
  2      'department_id') department_id
  3   FROM dual;

DEPARTMENT_ID
-----------------------------
100

1 row selected.
```

Note that application context names and attributes are not case-sensitive. Setting or referencing them can be done in either upper- or lowercase.

Applying the Application Context to Security

You can now use this application context to implement your database security policy. We explain in detail how to use application contexts for security within views and for VPD in Chapter 10.

Application Context in a View

We present a simple security use case that creates a view to restrict user queries to return rows only within the department in which they work. We use the SALES_CTX context attributes and values in the view:

```
db_entry@db12cr[sales]> CONNECT hr@sales
Enter password:
Connected.
hr@db12cr[sales]> CREATE OR REPLACE VIEW sales_colleagues AS
  2      SELECT ename, last_name, department_id
  3      FROM hr.employees
  4      WHERE department_id = SYS_CONTEXT ('sales_ctx', 'department_id');

View created.

hr@db12cr[sales]> GRANT SELECT ON sales_colleagues TO PUBLIC;

Grant succeeded.

hr@db12cr[sales]> -- View restricts rows based on value of
hr@db12cr[sales]> -- department_id in the application context
hr@db12cr[sales]> CONNECT dknox@sales
Enter password:
Connected.
db_entry@db12cr[sales]> SELECT SELECT last_name, department_id
  2   FROM hr.sales_colleagues;

LAST_NAME    DEPARTMENT_ID
----------   ----------------
KNOX                      100
SACK                      100

2 rows selected.
```

Application Context in a Trigger

We now create a simple trigger-based security example. Suppose you want to create a trigger that prevents users from modifying data outside their department. You should consider using the application context for this implementation, because a trigger will execute for each row and consequently needs to perform quickly. The following example illustrates this point:

```
db_entry@db12cr[sales] > CONNECT sh@sales
Enter password:
Connected.
sh@db12cr[sales]>  -- We alter the SALES_HISTORY table created
sh@db12cr[sales]>  -- in Chapter 2 and added the DEPARTMENT_ID column
sh@db12cr[sales]>  -- The column was updated with the value
sh@db12cr[sales]>  -- for each sales associate.
sh@db12cr[sales]>  ALTER TABLE sales_history ADD (commission NUMBER);

Table altered.

sh@db12cr[sales]>  -- We arbitrarily update set the COMMISSION to 23%
sh@db12cr[sales]>  -- for our examples
sh@db12cr[sales]>  UPDATE sales_history
  2  SET commission = 23;

6 rows updated.

sh@db12cr[sales]> COMMIT;

Commit complete.

sh@db12cr[sales]> -- Create a trigger which prevents a user from
sh@db12cr[sales]> -- modifying data outside his or her department
sh@db12cr[sales]> CREATE OR REPLACE TRIGGER restrict_dml
  2      BEFORE delete OR update
  3      ON sales_history
  4      FOR EACH ROW
  5    BEGIN
  6      IF (:OLD.dept_id !=
  7                  SYS_CONTEXT ('sales_ctx', 'department_id')) THEN
  8        RAISE_APPLICATION_ERROR
  9          (-20001,
 10             CHR (10)
 11          || '** You can only update/delete records within your department.'
 12          || CHR (10)
 13          || '** Your department number is '
 14          || SYS_CONTEXT ('sales_ctx', 'department_id'));
 15      END IF;
 16    END;
 17  /

Trigger created.

sh@db12cr[sales]> GRANT update, delete ON sales_history TO public;

Grant succeeded.
```

Issuing an unqualified update or delete validates that the trigger is working:

```
sh@db12cr[sales]> CONNECT dknox@sales
Enter password:
Connected.
db_entry@db12cr[sales]> UPDATE sh.sales_history
  2    SET commission = commission*1.25
  3    WHERE dept_id = 20;
UPDATE sh.sales_history
         *
ERROR at line 1:
ORA-20001:
**  You can only update/delete records within your department.
**  Your department number is 100
ORA-06512: at "SH.RESTRICT_DML", line 5
ORA-04088: error during execution of trigger 'SH.RESTRICT_UPDATES'

db_entry@db12cr[sales]> DELETE sh.sales_history;
DELETE sh.sales_history
          *
ERROR at line 1:
ORA-20001:
**  You can only update/delete records within your department.
**  Your department number is 100
ORA-06512: at "SH.RESTRICT_DML", line 5
ORA-04088: error during execution of trigger 'SH.RESTRICT_DML'
```

You can check how this implementation compares with a SQL-based alternative to determine how much faster the application context version is compared to a SQL-based alternative. To illustrate this, you can time how long it takes to issue updates on the table. Each update causes the trigger to fire. You can run two tests—one using the application context and another that queries the department number from within the trigger itself:

```
db_entry@db12cr[sales]> SET timing on
db_entry@db12cr[sales]> -- Issue authorized updates.
db_entry@db12cr[sales]> -- Each update will cause trigger to fire
db_entry@db12cr[sales]> BEGIN
  2    FOR i IN 1 .. 100000 LOOP
  3      UPDATE hr.employees
  4        SET last_name = last_name
  5        WHERE department_id = 100;
  6    END LOOP;
  7  END;
  8  /

PL/SQL procedure successfully completed.

Elapsed: 00:00:46.71
```

It took nearly 47 seconds using the application context implementation. Changing the trigger code implementation, you have to fetch the department number from the lookup table. The trigger is based on the value returned from this table:

```
db_entry@db12cr[sales]> CONNECT hr@sales
Enter password:
Connected.
```

```
hr@db12cr[sales]> SET timing off
hr@db12cr[sales]> -- Modify trigger to use select instead of context
hr@db12cr[sales]> CREATE OR REPLACE TRIGGER restrict_updates
  2  BEFORE DELETE OR UPDATE
  2    ON hr.employees
  4      FOR EACH ROW
  5    DECLARE
  6      ldepartment_id  NUMBER;
  7    BEGIN
  8      SELECT department_id
  9      INTO ldepartment_id
 10      FROM hr.employees
 11      WHERE UPPER(ename) =
 12        UPPER(SYS_CONTEXT ('userenv', 'authenticated_identity'));
 13
 14    IF (:OLD.department_id != ldepartment_id) THEN
 15        RAISE_APPLICATION_ERROR
 16          (-20001,
 17              CHR (10)
 18          || '**  You can only update/delete records within your department.'
 19          || CHR (10)
 20          || '**  Your department number is '
 21          || ldepartment_id);
 22      END IF;
 23    END;
 24  /

Trigger created.

hr@db12cr[sales]> CONNECT dknox@sales
Enter password:
Connected.
db_entry@db12cr[sales]> SET timing on
db_entry@db12cr[sales]> -- Time new trigger implementation based on SQL query
db_entry@db12cr[sales]> BEGIN
  2    FOR i IN 1 .. 100000 LOOP
  3      UPDATE hr.employees
  4          SET last_name = last_name
  5        WHERE department_id = 100;
  6    END LOOP;
  7  END;
  8  /

PL/SQL procedure successfully completed.

Elapsed: 00:05:17.02
```

You can see that the test using the application context is clearly faster than querying from the table. The performance increase from using an application context comes from getting the department ID from memory versus querying from a table. Sometimes it makes sense to query from a table (when sets of information are needed, table contains dynamic data, and so on), but application contexts are secure and provide a clear speed advantage over querying a table.

Secure Use

An important point with regard to using an application context is that the values are private to the user's session. The values are stored in the database session's UGA for dedicated server sessions.

The only issue to consider is that if you are using application contexts and connection pools or are otherwise reusing the database connection for multiple end users, you are responsible for clearing the application context values between user access. You can use the DBMS_SESSION .CLEAR_CONTEXT procedure (recall the logon trigger from earlier) to clear individual attributes, or you can clear all attributes by invoking DBMS_SESSION.CLEAR_ALL_CONTEXT.

Common Mistakes

Although there is tremendous flexibility in using an application context, it can be a little difficult to debug. The following examples represent some of the popular mistakes encountered by developers new to using an application context.

Incorrect Namespace or Attribute

Debugging code that references application context values can be frustrating if the application has misspelled either the application context name or the attribute. Referencing an application context that does not exist or an attribute that does not exist within it does not cause an error—it simply returns a NULL value.

```
db_entry@db12cr[sales]> -- No errors for user's undefined attribute
db_entry@db12cr[sales]> SELECT SYS_CONTEXT ('sales_ctx', 'foo')
  2 FROM DUAL;

SYS_CONTEXT('SALES_CTX','FOO')
-------------------------------------------


1 row selected.
```

This is in contrast to accessing an undefined attribute in the USERENV namespace. In this case, the database does throw an error:

```
db_entry@db12cr[sales]> -- Database errors with undefined attribute
db_entry@db12cr[sales]>  SELECT SYS_CONTEXT ('userenv', 'foo')
  2 FROM DUAL;
FROM DUAL
     *
ERROR at line 2:
ORA-02003: invalid USERENV parameter
```

Good coding practices can resolve this by using package variable constants for the attribute names in the namespace manager:

```
db_entry@db12cr[sales]> CONNECT sh@sales
Enter password:
Connected.
sh@db12cr[sales]> CREATE OR REPLACE PACKAGE sales_ctx_mgr AS
  2     namespace      CONSTANT VARCHAR2 (9) := 'SALES_CTX';
  3     department_id  CONSTANT VARCHAR2 (6) := 'DEPARTMENT_ID';
  4
```

```
    5      PROCEDURE set_department_id;
    6      PROCEDURE clear_department_id;
    7  END sales_ctx_mgr;
    8  /

Package created.

sh@db12cr[sales]> CREATE OR REPLACE PACKAGE BODY sales_ctx_mgr AS
    2      PROCEDURE set_department_id AS
    3         ldepartment_id  NUMBER;
    4      BEGIN
    5         SELECT department_id
    6         INTO ldepartment_id
    7         FROM hr.employees
    8         WHERE upper(ename) =
    9           upper(SYS_CONTEXT ('userenv', 'authenticated_identity'));
   10
   11         DBMS_SESSION.SET_CONTEXT
   12                 (namespace     => sales_ctx_mgr.namespace,
   13                  attribute     => sales_ctx_mgr.department_id,
   14                  value         => ldepartment_id);
   15
   16   END set_department_id;
   17   PROCEDURE clear_department_id AS
   18      BEGIN
   19         DBMS_SESSION.CLEAR_CONTEXT
   20             (namespace     => sales_ctx_mgr.namespace,
   21              attribute     => sales_ctx_mgr.department_id);
   22
   23      END clear_department_id;
   24   END sales_ctx_mgr;
   25   /

Package body created.

sh@db12cr[sales]> SHOW ERRORS
No errors.
sh@db12cr[sales]> SELECT SYS_CONTEXT ('sales_ctx', 'department_id')
    2    FROM DUAL;

SYS_CONTEXT('SALES_CTX','DEPARTMENT_ID')
------------------------------------------------------------


1 row selected.

sh@db12cr[sales]> -- Manually execute the package to set the context
sh@db12cr[sales]> EXEC sales_ctx_mgr.set_department_id

PL/SQL procedure successfully completed.

sh@db12cr[sales]> SELECT SYS_CONTEXT ('sales_ctx', 'department_id')
    2    FROM DUAL;

SYS_CONTEXT('SALES_CTX','DEPARTMENT_ID')
```

```
-----------------------------------------------------------
50

1 row selected.
```

Incorrect Namespace Manager

Another frequent mistake occurs when you misname the namespace manager or store the namespace manager in an incorrect schema. The context creation DDL defines the name of the trusted program used to protect the namespace from unauthorized modification. However, during compilation of the namespace manager PL/SQL program, the database cannot determine how you're intending to use the program. That is, it cannot tell you that you are trying to use the program to protect a context namespace. Upon execution, the error message indicates "insufficient privileges," which is not particularly helpful.

In this example, the namespace manager is set to be the SALES_CTX program. Since the namespace manager is not qualified with a schema name, the database assumes the current user's schema (SYSTEM in this example):

```
sec_mgr@db12cr[sales]> CONNECT system@sales
Enter password:
Connected.
system@db12cr[sales]> CREATE CONTEXT sales_ctx_error USING sales_ctx_mgr;

Context created.
```

Accidentally implementing the SALES_CTX_MGR program in a different schema or using a program with a name other than SALES_CTX_MGR will cause an error. Notice that a correctly named program in the SH schema compiles but fails to execute:

```
system@db12cr[sales]> CONNECT sh@sales
Enter password:
Connected.
sh@db12cr[sales]> -- We are in the WRONG schema - to illustrate the issue
sh@db12cr[sales]> CREATE OR REPLACE PROCEDURE sales_ctx_mgr_error AS
  2  BEGIN
  3     DBMS_SESSION.SET_CONTEXT
  4             (namespace => 'SALES_CTX_ERROR',
  5              attribute => 'TITLE',
  6              value     => 'VICE_PRESIDENT');
  7  END;
  8  /

Procedure created.

sh@db12cr[sales]> SHOW ERRORS
No errors.
sh@db12cr[sales]> -- No compile errors, so assume everything is fine
sh@db12cr[sales]> EXEC sales_ctx_mgr_error
BEGIN sales_ctx_mgr_error; END;

*
ERROR at line 1:
ORA-01031: insufficient privileges
ORA-06512: at "SYS.DBMS_SESSION", line 122
ORA-06512: at "SH.SALES_CTX_MGR_ERROR", line 3
ORA-06512: at line 1
```

It's only upon checking the `DBA_CONTEXT` view that you see the mistake.

```
sh@db12cr[sales]> SELECT SCHEMA, PACKAGE, TYPE
  2  FROM dba_context
  3  WHERE namespace = 'SALES_CTX'
  4  /

SCHEMA              PACKAGE              TYPE
------------------- -------------------- --------------------
SH                  SALES_CTX_MGR        ACCESSED LOCALLY

1 row selected.
```

Global Application Context

Oracle introduced the *global application context* (GAC) in Oracle9i Database as an addition to the application contexts. As the name implies, these values are accessible by multiple database sessions and by separate users. Global contexts store their values in SGA (large pool) memory, unlike the local contexts, which store values in private UGA memory.

You can use multiple applications contexts in a database session. For example, if you want to store private data for the user's session, you would use a local application context, and if you also have data to share, you would create a second context of type Global to store those values.

Global contexts can store data specific to USERNAME/CLIENT_IDENTIFIER—that is, you can include user-specific data in the global context. However, keep in mind that the data is accessible by all connected users.

GAC Uses

GACs are typically used when you want to share values across database sessions. This implies that the values are not user-specific or private to a user's database session. With a GAC, a value can be set once, and each connected session has immediate access to the value. If you wanted to accomplish the same effect with local application contexts, the application would have to set the context in each session.

An example of the use for global contexts is to convey security situational awareness quickly between all database sessions (that is, is the IDS up and running, has the virus scanner detected malware, has a person from competitive company just walked into the office, and so on) and use this information to control the dissemination of data to the user's screen or across the network. The gist is that GACs are a quick way to pass information between the database sessions with little impact to the calling application.

GAC Example

The purpose of the following example is to protect the company's SALES_HISTORY records during the process of "closing the monthly books." The process of closing the monthly books happens once near the end of the month and involves calculating the sales volume for the month, sales commission per employee, excess inventory, and similar tasks. We use a global context so that at the moment the books are closed, no DML transactions can be performed on the SALES_ HISTORY table until the books are reopened.

We first create a global context to keep track of the sales status (OPEN or CLOSED). We add the clause ACCESSED GLOBALLY to the end of the CREATE CONTEXT statement to create a global context.

```
sh@db12cr[sales]> -- Create a global context
sh@db12cr[sales]> CREATE CONTEXT sales_status_ctx
  2  USING sh.sales_status_pkg ACCESSED GLOBALLY;

Context created.
```

Next, we create the namespace manager (PL/SQL package) to protect the context. The namespace manager has two procedures: one for setting the attribute and one that clears all attributes in the namespace:

```
sh@db12cr[sales]> CREATE OR REPLACE PACKAGE sales_status_pkg AS
  2      OPEN      CONSTANT VARCHAR2(4)  := 'OPEN';
  3      CLOSED    CONSTANT VARCHAR2(6)  := 'CLOSED';
  4      --
  5      CTX_NAME  CONSTANT VARCHAR2(17) := 'SALES_STATUS_CTX';
  6      CTX_ATTR  CONSTANT VARCHAR2(12) := 'SALES_STATUS';
  7      --
  8      PROCEDURE set_status (p_status IN VARCHAR2);
  9      PROCEDURE clear;
 10  END;
 11  /

Package created.

sh@db12cr[sales]> CREATE OR REPLACE PACKAGE BODY sales_status_pkg AS
  2      --
  3      PROCEDURE set_status (p_status IN VARCHAR2) AS
  4        BEGIN
  5          IF (p_status IS NOT NULL AND
  6              p_status IN (
  7                sales_status_pkg.OPEN,
  8                sales_status_pkg.CLOSED)) THEN
  9
 10            DBMS_SESSION.SET_CONTEXT
 11              (namespace => sales_status_pkg.CTX_NAME,
 12               attribute => sales_status_pkg.CTX_ATTR,
 13               value     => upper(p_status));
 14          END IF;
 15        END;
 16      --
 17      PROCEDURE clear AS
 18        BEGIN
 19          DBMS_SESSION..CLEAR_ALL_CONTEXT
 20            (namespace => sales_status_pkg.CTX_NAME);
 21        END;
 22  END;
 23  /

Package body created.

sh@db12cr[sales]> SHOW ERRORS
No errors.
```

Next, we set the sales status to OPEN:

```
sh@db12cr[sales]> BEGIN
  2      sales_status_pkg.set_status (
  3          sales_status_pkg.OPEN );
  4  END;
  5  /

PL/SQL procedure successfully completed.
```

We then verify that the values are set properly:

```
sh@db12cr[sales]> SELECT NAMESPACE, ATTRIBUTE, VALUE
  2  FROM global_context;

NAMESPACE           ATTRIBUTE      VALUE
------------------- -------------- -------
SALES_STATUS_CTX    SALES_STATUS   OPEN

1 row selected.
```

We can also verify the value using the SYS_CONTEXT function:

```
sh@db12cr[sales]> SELECT SYS_CONTEXT ('sales_status_ctx',
  2      'sales_status') sales_status
  3  FROM dual;

SALES_STATUS
------------
OPEN

1 row selected.
```

We now update the RESTRICT_DML trigger from the preceding code to include INSERTs and to take into consideration the sales status:

```
sh@db12cr[sales]> CREATE OR REPLACE TRIGGER restrict_dml
  2      BEFORE insert OR delete OR update
  3      ON sales_history
  4      FOR EACH ROW
  5      DECLARE
  6          v_sales_status VARCHAR2(6);
  7      BEGIN
  8          -- Retrieve the sales status
  9          v_sales_status := SYS_CONTEXT('sales_status_ctx', 'sales_status');
 10          -- Verify it is NOT NULL
 11          IF (v_sales_status IS NOT NULL) THEN
 12              -- Determine if sales are OPEN or CLOSED
 13              IF (v_sales_status = sales_status_pkg.CLOSED) THEN
 14                  RAISE_APPLICATION_ERROR (-20001,
 15                      'Sales Status is CLOSED - DML not permitted.');
 16              END IF;
 17          ELSE
 18              RAISE_APPLICATION_ERROR (-20002,
```

```
19                'SALES_STATUS_CTX not initialized properly.');
20        END IF;
21     END;
22  /

Trigger created.

sh@db12cr[sales]> -- Update the grant to include SELECT and INSERT
sh@db12cr[sales]> GRANT select, insert, update, delete
  2  ON sales_history TO PUBLIC;

Grant succeeded.
```

We now connect on as SGAETJEN and verify the SALES_STATUS_CTX:

```
sh@db12cr[sales]> CONNECT sgaetjen@sales
Enter password:
Connected.
sgaetjen@db12cr[sales]> -- Verify sales status
sgaetjen@db12cr[sales]>  SELECT SYS_CONTEXT ('sales_status_ctx',
  2  'sales_status') sales_status
  3  FROM dual;

SALES_STATUS
-------------------------------------------------
OPEN

1 row selected.
```

We now try to INSERT a sale and are successful because the sales status is OPEN:

```
sgaetjen@db12cr[sales]> INSERT INTO sh.sales_history (
  2      PRODUCT,
  3      SALES_DATE,
  4      QUANTITY,
  5      TOTAL_COST,
  6      DEPT_ID,
  7      COMMISSION,
  8      EMP_ID)
  9  VALUES (
 10      'Speakers',
 11      sysdate,
 12      4,
 13      521,
 14      300,
 15      23,
 16      101);

1 row created.
sgaetjen@db12cr[sales]> COMMIT;

Commit complete.
```

We now create a second connection to the database in a separate session. That is, we leave user SGAETJEN connected and connect as SH in a separate terminal window. We set the sales status to CLOSED, simulating the close of the month:

```
[oracle@nsgdc2 ~]$ sqlplus sh@sales

SQL*Plus: Release 12.1.0.1.0 Production on Wed Jan 22 17:15:13 2014

Copyright (c) 1982, 2013, Oracle.  All rights reserved.

Enter password:
Last Successful login time: Wed Jan 22 2014 17:12:45 -05:00

Connected to:
Oracle Database 12c Enterprise Edition Release 12.1.0.1.0 - 64bit Production
With the Partitioning, Real Application Clusters, Automatic Storage Management, Oracle
Label Security,
OLAP, Advanced Analytics, Oracle Database Vault and Real Application Testing options

sh@db12cr[sales]> -- Set sales status to CLOSED
sh@db12cr[sales]> BEGIN
  2      sales_status_pkg.set_status (
  3          sales_status_pkg.CLOSED );
  4   END;
  5   /

PL/SQL procedure successfully completed.
```

We verify that the values were set properly:

```
sh@db12cr[sales]> SELECT NAMESPACE, ATTRIBUTE, VALUE
  2  FROM global_context;

NAMESPACE           ATTRIBUTE       VALUE
------------------  -------------   -------
SALES_STATUS_CTX    SALES_STATUS    CLOSED

1 row selected.
```

We now go back to the SGAETJEN session and try to INSERT a new record. Again, we are not logging back in as SGAETJEN; we are simply switching back to the existing session:

```
sgaetjen@db12cr[sales]> INSERT INTO sh.sales_history (
  2      PRODUCT,
  3      SALES_DATE,
  4      QUANTITY,
  5      TOTAL_COST,
  6      DEPT_ID,
  7      COMMISSION,
  8      EMP_ID)
  9   VALUES (
 10      'Speakers Wires',
 11      sysdate,
 12      8,
 13      53,
 14      300,
```

```
 15     23,
 16     101);
INSERT INTO sh.sales_history (
              *
ERROR at line 1:
ORA-20001: Sales Status is CLOSED - DML not permitted.
ORA-06512: at "SH.RESTRICT_DML", line 10
ORA-04088: error during execution of trigger 'SH.RESTRICT_DML'

sgaetjen@db12cr[sales]> -- We verify that sales status is CLOSED
sgaetjen@db12cr[sales]> SELECT SYS_CONTEXT ('sales_status_ctx',
  2  'sales_status') sales_status
  3  FROM dual;

SALES_STATUS
-----------------------------------------------------------
CLOSED

1 row selected.
```

This example demonstrates the principle of GAC enforcement because DML is not permitted when the Sales department is CLOSED for end-of-month processing.

Global Context Memory Usage

Global context values are stored in the SGA (large pool). Oracle Database provides a way to monitor how much SGA memory is being used for the global contexts. For example, the following query indicates that 872 bytes are currently being used:

```
sgaetjen@db12cr[sales]> CONNECT sec_mgr@sales
Enter password:
Connected.
sec_mgr@db12cr[sales]> SELECT SYS_CONTEXT ('userenv', 'global_context_memory')
  2  FROM dual;

SYS_CONTEXT('USERENV','GLOBAL_CONTEXT_MEMORY')
-----------------------------------------------
872

1 row selected.
```

External and Initialized Globally

We covered contexts initialized globally in Chapter 3 with regard to Enterprise User Security (EUS); however, for completeness of this topic, here we illustrate how to incorporate contexts initialized globally into views. Oracle Database 12c also supports application contexts that have their values set from external sources. The motivation for external context is twofold: the values are automatically populated for the user, and setting the values for the users can be centrally managed outside the database. The external sources can be a job queue process, a database link, or a program using the OCI interface. Additionally, an LDAP directory server can also be used to set context values automatically. We use the departmentNumber attribute from the default LDAP application context SYS_LDAP_USER_DEFAULT.

We now update our view (SALES_COLLEAGUES) to restrict users' access to records that fall within their department. However, we use the departmentNumber attribute that is stored in the LDAP directory server, as the following example demonstrates.

```
sec_mgr@db12cr[sales]> CONNECT hr@sales
Enter password:
Connected.
hr@db12cr[sales]> CREATE OR REPLACE VIEW SALES_COLLEAGUES AS
  2      SELECT last_name, department_id
  3       FROM hr.employees
  4       WHERE department_id =
  5          SYS_CONTEXT('sys_ldap_user_default',' departmentnumber');

View created.
```

Now we grant access to the shared schema to which the EUS users will connect (in this case, the DB_ENTRY schema). First we revoke the GRANT on SALES_COLLEAGUES from PUBLIC that we used in a previous example:

```
hr@db12cr[sales]> REVOKE SELECT ON sales_colleagues FROM PUBLIC;

Revoke succeeded.

hr@db12cr[sales]> GRANT SELECT ON sales_colleagues TO db_entry;

Grant succeeded.
```

We now connect as a EUS user that has been mapped to the DB_ENTRY schema. During the connection process, Oracle will retrieve values from the directory and store them in the SYS_LDAP_USER_DEFAULT context.

```
hr@db12cr[sales]> CONNECT dknox@sales
Enter password:
Connected.
db_entry@db12cr[sales]> SELECT SYS_CONTEXT('sys_ldap_user_default',
  2                          'departmentNumber')
  3  FROM dual;

SYS_CONTEXT('SYS_LDAP_USER_DEFAULT','DEPARTMENTNUMBER')
-----------------------------------------------------------
100

1 row selected.

db_entry@db12cr[sales]> SELECT last_name, department_id
  2  FROM hr.sales_colleagues;

LAST_NAME                  DEPARTMENT_ID
------------------------   -------------
Knox                                 100
Sack                                 100

2 rows selected.
```

Using Views in Security

Views can be used to solve many security challenges, such as controlling access to rows, hiding columns, hiding the complexity join conditions, or masking data values. Views can preprocess data to remove personally identifiable information (PII) for maintaining privacy or to remove sensitive data from the results based on your company's security policy. The important part about most views (materialized views being the exception) is that no redundant data is stored in a view. In fact, most views are stored SQL SELECT statement(s) that are executed on access.

A security design usually involves using views for some or all of the reasons cited in the preceding paragraph. Object-level privileges are required to access a view. Privileges on views are separate from privileges on the underlying objects (typically tables) the view accesses. The user is not required to have privileges on the underlying objects to use the view. Allowing users access to a view and not to the underlying objects is an effective security technique.

Consider an example in which the user SH needs to allow certain users to determine the number of items sold in each department. To solve this problem without using views, SH would have to grant SELECT on SALES_HISTORY, and HR would have to grant SELECT on the DEPARTMENTS tables and show a developer how to construct valid JOIN syntax to connect the two tables. This type of a solution might introduce a new problem—what if the SALES_HISTORY table keeps track of the commission percentage each sales associate made on each sale? Sharing this type of information might not be appropriate.

Solving this problem using a view solves a couple issues presented here. First, the SH user creates the view syntax and can verify the JOIN syntax prior to the view being accessed. Second, the SH user chooses which columns to include in the view. As mentioned, it might not be appropriate to include all columns from both tables in the view. Furthermore, SH does not want to grant access to the underlying SALES_HISTORY table and likewise with HR and the DEPARTMENTS table.

SH simply creates a view, which performs the calculation on the user's behalf. SH then grants SELECT on the view and not the underlying tables, which allows users to retrieve the summary data while security is maintained for the underlying objects:

```
db_entry@db12cr[sales]> CONNECT hr@sales
Enter password:
Connected.
hr@db12cr[sales]> GRANT SELECT ON employees TO sh WITH GRANT OPTION;

Grant succeeded.

hr@db12cr[sales]> GRANT SELECT ON departments TO sh WITH GRANT OPTION;

Grant succeeded.

hr@db12cr[sales]> CONNECT sh@sales
Enter password:
Connected.
sh@db12cr[sales]> CREATE OR REPLACE VIEW sales_per_dept_view AS
  2  SELECT INITCAP (d.dept_name) "Department",
  3      sum (sh.total_cost) "Total_Sales"
  4  FROM  sales_history sh JOIN hr.departments d
  5  ON (d.dept_id = sh.depart_id)
  6  GROUP BY d.dept_name;
```

```
View created.

sh@db12cr[sales]> GRANT SELECT ON sales_per_dept_view TO wmaroulis;

Grant succeeded.

sh@db12cr[sales]> CONNECT wmaroulis@sales
Enter password:
Connected.
wmaroulis@db12cr[sales]> SELECT *
  2  FROM sales_per_dept_view;

Department          Total_Sales
------------------- -----------
Online                      350
Northwest                  3800
Southeast                 24500

3 rows selected.

wmaroulis@db12cr[sales]> SELECT *
  2  FROM sh.sales_history;
FROM sh.sales_history
        *
ERROR at line 2:
ORA-00942: table or view does not exist
```

The view could easily be showing a medical researcher, for example, the number of patients who have been diagnosed with a certain illness. Similarly, the view could show a bank manager the number of customers with a certain financial status. Because the actual names are hidden by the view, any sensitive information that can be derived by correlating the department, diagnosis, or financial status with an individual is prevented.

Views for Column- and Cell-Level Security

Views can provide column- and cell-level security (CCLS). CCLS has three definitions:

■ Preventing access to the column (restrict)

■ Masking values returned in a column (redaction)

■ Controlling access to values within a column (cell-level)

Column Removal

In the first definition of CCLS, preventing access to the column means that the column is not listed in the view syntax and consequently is inaccessible to users. For example, your security policy for the SALES_HISTORY table may require you to remove access to the COMMISSION column because it contains sensitive data.

The view solution for CCLS simply uses all columns except the COMMISSION column. By granting users access to the view and not to the underlying table, you have successfully removed user access to sensitive data. This example is largely a security by design solution—that is, the security was done prior to developing and deploying application code. This example may or may not be a possible solution for existing applications. Views typically can replace tables, because applications have no bias or make no distinction from querying directly against a table or view.

If the application does not care which type of object it is querying against, then you could rename the underlying table and create a view using the same name as the table. The application will continue working properly, and you will be able to implement security as necessary.

This trick may not work in all cases, however, because some applications depend on the existence of some or all the columns you are attempting to remove. Removing access to the column may break an already developed application. A challenge also exists if the application does make a distinction between tables and views. These cases are rare, but we have seen cases where older legacy applications check the Oracle data dictionary object definition, referential integrity constraints, use table hints, and so on. In this case, you might have to use VPD (row or column) and/or redaction to satisfy your security requirements.

Masking Column Values

The second CCLS definition indicates that some, but not all, of the column values are accessible. You can mask the values returned to the user. For example, you may elect to return the string "NOT AUTHORIZED" or "Contact your Manager for access to this record," or you might return the value 0 when a user queries a column whose real value must be hidden. Be careful, however: a value of 0 may imply one meaning (the actual value is 0) versus your intended meaning (the user does not have access).

Another masking option is to return a NULL value. Returning a NULL value is a good choice, because it is a standard value that does not exist and most applications can handle the absence of data. However, just as returning a 0 has a caveat, NULL values may incorrectly indicate the absence of a value, when in reality the value exists but the user is not authorized to see it. If the application needs to distinguish between actual NULL values and masked data, then NULL values should not be used.

Consider an example in which a sales associate can access only her commission and is prohibited from accessing other sales associates' commission data. Because the sales associate can access her commission, you cannot simply omit the COMMISSION column from the view definition. To meet this CCLS requirement, a view is used with a function that masks the values of the COMMISSION column. Views with functions are an effective column-level security technique. The functions return different values for different rows based on a policy decision that is implemented within the view.

The view will use the Oracle built-in DECODE function to implement the column masking. If the sales associate accessing (as indicated by the USER function) the record is the same as the person in the record (E.ENAME), then the COMMISSION is displayed. Otherwise, a NULL value is returned:

```
wmaroulis@db12cr[sales]> CONNECT sh@sales
Enter password:
Connected.
sh@db12cr[sales]> -- ENAME is a virtual column from EMPLOYEES
sh@db12cr[sales]> -- and is being included in this view
sh@db12cr[sales]> CREATE OR REPLACE VIEW sales_commission AS
  2         SELECT e.ename employee_name,
  3                DECODE (e.ename,
  4                    USER, sh.commission,
  5                    NULL) commission
  6         FROM sales_history sh JOIN hr.employees e
  7         ON (sh.emp_id = e.employee_id);
```

```
View created.

sh@db12cr[sales]> GRANT SELECT ON sales_commission to PUBLIC;

Grant succeeded.
```

You can allow all users to access all records because the DECODE function provides the CCLS to mask out other sales associates' commissions. Do not grant privileges on the underlying tables.

The column masking requirement is very popular in applications such as those used by reporting tools. The reports have a predefined structure that often requires the existence of a column value for all records. A challenge exists in producing the report and maintaining security, because you may not want users to see the actual values in all the columns for all the records. The view can be used as the source for the report generation:

```
sh@db12cr[sales]> CONNECT wmaroulis@sales
Enter password:
Connected.
wmaroulis@db12cr[sales]> SELECT *
  2  FROM sh.sales_commission;

EMPLOYEE_NAME    COMMISSION
--------------- ----------
PSACK
WMAROULIS                23
SGAETJEN
DKNOX
...
```

Note that even aggregate queries are subject to the security:

```
wmaroulis@db12cr[sales]> -- Computing commission for all sales
wmaroulis@db12cr[sales]> -- associates - only returns the connected
wmaroulis@db12cr[sales]> -- user's commission
wmaroulis@db12cr[sales]> SELECT SUM (commission)
  2  FROM sh.sales_commission;

SUM(COMMISSION)
---------------
             23
```

Updates to CCLS Views

The preceding view provides security for SELECT statements. Oracle does allow INSERT, UPDATE, and DELETE using simple views (versus complex views that have Group By clauses, JOINS, multivalve functions, and so on). However, Oracle does not allow updates on virtual columns used in tables or views, and because we are using the DECODE function in the view definition for the COMMISSION column, Oracle treats the COMMISSION column as a virtual column.

```
wmaroulis@db12cr[sales]> CONNECT sh@sales
Enter password:
Connected.
sh@db12cr[sales]> -- Give everyone a 20% raise
sh@db12cr[sales]> -- This will fail because of the virtual column
sh@db12cr[sales]> UPDATE sales_commission
```

```
  2  SET commission = commission*1.2;
set commission = commission*1.2
     *
ERROR at line 2:
ORA-01733: virtual column not allowed here
```

The simplest way to solve this problem is to use an instead-of trigger for performing DML operations on the view. You simply create an instead-of trigger for the view, and then Oracle will fire the trigger when a DML statement is issued against the view, instead-of issuing the DML statement directly against the table.

```
sh@db12cr[sales]> -- Create an instead-of trigger to perform updates on
sh@db12cr[sales]> -- base table. Trigger logic is similar to our view security.
sh@db12cr[sales]> -- The user's manager is the only user authorized
sh@db12cr[sales]> -- to update SALES_HISTORY records for his/her department
sh@db12cr[sales]> CREATE OR REPLACE TRIGGER sales_commission_update
  2  INSTEAD OF UPDATE ON sales_commission
  3  FOR EACH ROW
  4     DECLARE
  5        MANAGES_DEPARTMENT_ID NUMBER :=-1;
  6        BEGIN
  7
  8            -- Trap Errors (NO DATA FOUND, etc.)
  9            BEGIN
 10                -- Determine which department the
 11                -- connected EUS user manages
 12                SELECT department_id
 13                INTO manages_department_id
 14                FROM hr.employees m
 15                WHERE ENAME =
 16                    UPPER(SYS_CONTEXT('userenv',
 17                        'authenticated_identity'))
 18                CONNECT BY PRIOR employee_id = manager_id;
 19            EXCEPTION
 20                WHEN OTHERS THEN
 21                    NULL;
 22            END;
 23
 24            -- Only allow the manager to update records
 25            -- in his/her department
 26            IF MANAGES_DEPARTMENT_ID <> -1 THEN
 27                UPDATE sales_history
 28                    SET commission = :NEW.commission
 29                    WHERE department_id = manages_department_id;
 30            END IF;
 31        END;
 32  /
```

```
Trigger created.
```

```
sh@db12cr[sales]> SHOW ERRORS
No errors.
```

To demonstrate the effectiveness of this view, you can view the current values, issue an UPDATE statement, and then validate the effects of the update. Note that the intention of this view is to transparently provide the CCLS for the table. The base table should not be accessible to the application or users:

```
sh@db12cr[sales]> -- PSACK manages WMAROULIS
sh@db12cr[sales]> -- PSACK maps to DB_SUBTREE
sh@db12cr[sales]> GRANT UPDATE ON sales_commission TO db_subtree;

Grant succeeded.

sh@db12cr[sales]> -- Verify current commission
sh@db12cr[sales]> CONNECT wmaroulis@sales
Enter password:
Connected.
wmaroulis@db12cr[sales]> SELECT *
  2  FROM sh.sales_commission;

EMPLOYEE_NAME    COMMISSION
---------------  ----------
WMAROULIS                23
SGAETJEN
DKNOX
...
wmaroulis@db12cr[sales]> -- Connect as 'WMAROULIS' manager
wmaroulis@db12cr[sales]> -- PSACK and update his commission
wmaroulis@db12cr[sales]> CONNECT psack@sales
Enter password:
Connected.
db_subtree@db12cr[sales]>  -- Give a 20% commission increase
db_subtree@db12cr[sales]> UPDATE sh.sales_commission
  2  SET commission = commission*1.2;

6 rows updated.

db_subtree@db12cr[sales]> COMMIT;

Commit complete.

db_subtree@db12cr[sales]> CONNECT wmaroulis@sales
Enter password:
Connected.
wmaroulis@db12cr[sales]> SELECT *
  2  FROM sh.sales_commission;

EMPLOYEE_NAME    COMMISSION
---------------  ----------
WMAROULIS              27.6
SGAETJEN
DKNOX
...
```

The update statement succeeds and user WMAROULIS's commission is updated by 20 percent.

Performance of Views with CCLS Functions

Using functions such as DECODE in the view definition is a powerful and convenient way to mask column values. However, security often competes with performance. You should always conduct performance tests on your security design before using it.

To test the performance of this design, we create a PL/SQL function and test it by calling it multiple times. Oracle built-in functions generally perform better than user-created PL/SQL functions.

```
wmaroulis@db12cr[sales] > CONNECT sec_mgr@sales
Enter password:
Connected.
sec_mgr@db12cr[sales] > -- Create test function - it simply returns the value
sec_mgr@db12cr[sales] > -- it was passed
sec_mgr@db12cr[sales] > CREATE OR REPLACE FUNCTION view_filter (
  2    p_owner  IN  VARCHAR2) RETURN VARCHAR2 AS
  3  BEGIN
  4    RETURN p_owner;
  5  END;
  6  /

Function created.
```

The purpose of the test is to isolate the cost of calling the function for each record. This design is consistent with the previous implementation example, because the view uses a function's return value to generate column values.

This test will determine how long it takes to count records from a base table as compared to a function-computed column in the view. To ensure your time quantities are measurable (Oracle queries can be done very quickly), you'll need a large table. The following SQL first creates the large table:

```
sec_mgr@db12cr[sales] > CREATE TABLE big_tab AS
  2  SELECT * FROM all_objects;

Table created.

sec_mgr@db12cr[sales] > -- increase table size
sec_mgr@db12cr[sales] > BEGIN
  2    FOR i IN 1 .. 5 LOOP
  3      INSERT INTO sec_mgr.big_tab
  4        (SELECT *
  5          FROM sec_mgr.big_tab);
  6      COMMIT;
  7    END LOOP;
  8  END;
  9  /

PL/SQL procedure successfully completed.

sec_mgr@db12cr[sales] > ANALYZE TABLE big_tab COMPUTE STATISTICS;

Table analyzed.
```

We next create two views. The first view uses the previously created VIEW_FILTER function. The second view uses the Oracle built-in DECODE function:

```
sec_mgr@db12cr[sales] > -- Create view calling user-defined PL/SQL function
sec_mgr@db12cr[sales] > CREATE OR REPLACE VIEW big_ud_view AS
  2    SELECT owner, view_filter (owner) function_owner
  3    FROM big_tab;
```

```
View created.

sec_mgr@db12cr[sales]> -- Create view calling a built-in PL/SQL function
sec_mgr@db12cr[sales]> CREATE OR REPLACE VIEW big_bi_view AS
  2  SELECT owner, DECODE (owner, owner, owner) function_owner
  3  FROM big_tab;

View created.
```

The performance test consists of counting all the records from the base table and then counting the records from the two views:

```
sec_mgr@db12cr[sales]> SET timing on
sec_mgr@db12cr[sales]> -- time the query on the base table
sec_mgr@db12cr[sales]> SELECT COUNT (owner)
  2  FROM big_tab;

COUNT(OWNER)
------------
     2852864

1 row selected.

Elapsed: 00:00:04.97
sec_mgr@db12cr[sales]> -- Time the query on the PL/SQL function view
sec_mgr@db12cr[sales]> SELECT COUNT (function_owner)
  2  FROM big_ud_view;

COUNT(FUNCTION_OWNER)
---------------------
              2852864

1 row selected.

Elapsed: 00:01:01.75
sec_mgr@db12cr[sales]> -- We now time the query on the DECODE view
sec_mgr@db12cr[sales]> SELECT COUNT (function_owner)
  2  FROM big_bi_view;

COUNT(FUNCTION_OWNER)
---------------------
              2852864

1 row selected.

Elapsed: 00:00:05.17
```

The built-in functions add very little time (a couple tenths of a second) to the overall query time. The user-defined function added considerably more time to the overall query time. Also, note that this example is a best-case scenario. If we added security code to the user-defined function, the performance would have slowed even further.

When possible, consider using application contexts and built-in functions to increase performance. Performance tuning PL/SQL programs is beyond the scope of this book. You can find helpful tuning information in the chapter "Tuning PL/SQL Applications for Performance" in the *Oracle PL/SQL User's Guide and Reference*.

CCLS for Controlling Access to All Records Within a Column

This is the third definition of CCLS. Oracle controls whether a user is authorized to execute an INSERT or a DELETE statement against an object at the object level. However, Oracle does provide the flexibility to authorize a user to execute an UPDATE statement at either the object level or column level.

For example, to ensure that the user can update only his phone number, you can specifically restrict the update privileges to just this column:

```
sec_mgr@db12cr[sales]> CONNECT hr@sales
Enter password:
Connected.
hr@db12cr[sales]> -- This GRANT makes sense - SGAETJEN can only
hr@db12cr[sales]> -- update the PHONE_NUMBER column
hr@db12cr[sales]> GRANT UPDATE (phone_number) ON employees TO SGAETJEN;

Grant succeeded.

hr@db12cr[sales]> -- Column level GRANT for INSERT statement only
hr@db12cr[sales]> -- makes sense if you grant all NOT NULL columns
hr@db12cr[sales]> -- to SGAETJEN otherwise the INSERT will fail
hr@db12cr[sales]> GRANT INSERT (phone_number) ON employees TO SGAETJEN;

Grant succeeded.
```

The ability for the database to support column-level privileges allows the schema owner to restrict inserts or updates to specific columns in a table. However, column-level privileges affect values for all records in the table.

For example, in the following code, it may be unlikely that user SGAETJEN should have the ability to update other sales associates' phone numbers.

```
hr@db12cr[sales]> CONNECT sgaetjen@sales
Enter password:
Connected.
sgaetjen@db12cr[sales]> -- Set all phone numbers
sgaetjen@db12cr[sales]> UPDATE hr.employees
  2   SET phone_number = '555-555-5555';

25 rows updated.
```

The unqualified update just set everyone's phone number to 555-555-5555, regardless of their sales department or owner of the record. This is a critical and often overlooked point: the database column privileges do not provide security for the individual rows. The next section discusses a way to control row-level access.

Views for Row-Level Security

The previous example demonstrated column-level security by granting an INSERT or UPDATE privilege to specific columns. This capability might be useful in certain situations; however, if we wanted to refine our security policy further to only allow updates to a specific set of rows, then we need to implement row-level security. Views provide a great way to control column-level security either by hiding the column or masking the value. These controls are part of the projection of the table. If we want to control the rows, then we need to implement finer-grained access control in the predicate (WHERE clause) to restrict specific sets of rows that we authorize for update.

For example, in the previous example SGAETJEN was authorized to update the PHONE_
NUMBER column in the SALES_EMPS table using a GRANT statement with the column restriction
syntax. However, the GRANT statement does not provide grammar to restrict rows. Row-level
restriction is sometimes referred to as fine-grained access control (FGAC), which ensures that
security is applied to each row within the object.

Let's investigate how we can apply views as an implementation of row-level security. In this
example, we create a view to allow a sales associate to update his personal information record.
The view ensures that the record displayed is that of the sales associate and no one else. This is
done by adding a predicate or WHERE clause to the query on the base table.

```
sgaetjen@db12cr[sales]> CONNECT hr@sales
Enter password:
Connected.
hr@db12cr[sales]> -- The WITH CHECK OPTION restricts INSERTs
hr@db12cr[sales]> -- into the base table to records that satisfy
hr@db12cr[sales]> -- the WHERE clause and in our case -
hr@db12cr[sales]> -- there is only one record that can be updated -
hr@db12cr[sales]> -- the one for the connected user
hr@db12cr[sales]> CREATE OR REPLACE VIEW sales_emp_info AS
  2   SELECT ename, phone_number
  3   FROM employees
  4   WHERE ename =
  5        UPPER(SYS_CONTEXT ('userenv', 'session_user'))
  6   WITH CHECK OPTION;

View created.

hr@db12cr[sales]> GRANT select, insert, update, delete
  2   ON sales_emp_info TO sgaetjen;

Grant succeeded.

hr@db12cr[sales]> -- User WMAROULIS will verify that user SGAETJEN
hr@db12cr[sales]> -- did not change his phone_number
hr@db12cr[sales]> GRANT select
  2   ON sales_emp_info TO wmaroulis;

Grant succeeded.
```

This example assumes the users will be directly authenticated to the database. Furthermore,
each user has an exclusive schema in which the schema name matches the value stored in the
ENAME column. However, this view could be easily modified to support a user's identity based
on the client identifier, the enterprise user's external name, or some identifying value set in an
application context.

You can see that the queries are restricted to user records by querying from the view. Updates
behave in a similar manner. When SGAETJEN tries to update a record for which he is not
authorized, the update simply does not occur:

```
hr@db12cr[sales]> CONNECT sgaetjen@sales
Enter password:
Connected.
sgaetjen@db12cr[sales]>  SELECT ename, phone_number
  2   FROM sh.sales_emp_info;
```

```
ENAME                  PHONE_NUMBER
-------------------    --------------------
SGAETJEN               555-555-1111

1 row selected.

sgaetjen@db12cr[sales]> CONNECT wmaroulis@sales
Enter password:
Connected.
wmaroulis@db12cr[sales]> SELECT ename, phone_number
  2  FROM sh.sales_emp_info;

ENAME                  PHONE_NUMBER
-------------------    --------------------
WMAROULIS              555-555-2222

1 row selected.

wmaroulis@db12cr[sales]> CONNECT sgaetjen@sales
Enter password:
Connected.
sgaetjen@db12cr[sales]> -- Try to update WMAROULIS' phone number
sgaetjen@db12cr[sales]> UPDATE sh.sales_emp_info
  2    SET phone_number = '111-111-1111'
  3    WHERE ename = 'WMAROULIS';

0 rows updated.
```

Updating records outside of the view definition has no effect; deletes are also constrained to the view definition.

```
sgaetjen@db12cr[sales]> -- Try to delete all records.
sgaetjen@db12cr[sales]> DELETE sh.sales_emp_info;

1 row deleted.

sgaetjen@db12cr[sales]> INSERT INTO sh.sales_emp_info (ename, phone_number)
  2    VALUES ('PSACK', '111-1111-1111');
INSERT INTO sh.sales_emp_info (ename, phone_number)
                  *
ERROR at line 1:
ORA-01402: view WITH CHECK OPTION where-clause violation

sgaetjen@db12cr[sales]> -- Rollback the DELETE - Oracle automatically
sgaetjen@db12cr[sales]> -- rolled back the INSERT statement when it failed
sgaetjen@db12cr[sales]> ROLLBACK;

Rollback complete.
```

Functions in Views for Row-Level Security

A popular approach to creating security within views is to place a PL/SQL function inside the view definition to assist in restricting data returned to the end user. When the function is placed in the projection of the view (SELECT clause), the function performs as column-level security. When the function is placed in the predicate (WHERE clause), the function acts as row-level security. As we indicated earlier, view performance should be evaluated when considering using functions.

To illustrate the effect on performance, consider a view that calls a PL/SQL function in the WHERE clause to perform the security check. The security policy for this example, once again, says the connected user can see her records. We have updated this view to add an exception—a DBA gets to see all records.

```
sgaetjen@db12cr[sales]> CONNECT sec_mgr@sales
Enter password:
Connected.
sec_mgr@db12cr[sales]> CREATE OR REPLACE FUNCTION view_filter (
  2       p_owner IN VARCHAR2) RETURN NUMBER AS
  3  BEGIN
  4     IF ( p_owner = USER OR
  5          SYS_CONTEXT ('userenv', 'isdba') = 'TRUE') THEN
  6         RETURN 1;
  7     ELSE
  8         RETURN 0;
  9     END IF;
 10  END;
 11  /

Function created.
```

We create a view BIG_VIEW from the BIG_TAB table we previously created. The view places the security function in the WHERE clause. By doing so, the function acts as a row-level security enforcement mechanism.

```
sec_mgr@db12cr[sales]> -- Creating view over table with function to filter rows
sec_mgr@db12cr[sales]> CREATE OR REPLACE VIEW big_view AS
  2  SELECT *
  3  FROM big_tab
  4  WHERE 1 = view_filter (owner);

View created.
```

The point of this exercise is to show that although the results are technically correct, the performance of our PL/SQL function in the view may not be acceptable. For performance comparison, we first query by counting all records on the base table (BIG_TAB). We modify this query adding the security (that is, the security the function ultimately implements) into the WHERE clause. This will return the same number of records as the view, so our performance number should not be influenced by the number of records returned:

```
sec_mgr@db12cr[sales]> SET timing on
sec_mgr@db12cr[sales]> SELECT COUNT (*)
  2  FROM big_tab
  3  WHERE 1 = DECODE (owner, USER, 1, 0) OR
  4     SYS_CONTEXT ('userenv', 'isdba') = 'TRUE';

  COUNT(*)
----------
       352

1 row selected.

Elapsed: 00:00:13.78
```

Now we run the query against the view for comparison:

```
sec_mgr@db12cr[sales]> SELECT COUNT(*)
  2  FROM big_view;

 COUNT(*)
----------
     1184

Elapsed: 00:01:07.60
```

The difference in times is due to the overhead of invoking the PL/SQL function for every record in the table. The query results are the same, but the performance is not. This is because the security implementation is not an effective performance implementation.

We could have modified the view definition:

```
sec_mgr@db12cr[sales]> CREATE OR REPLACE VIEW big_view AS
  2     SELECT * FROM big_tab
  3     WHERE 1 = DECODE (owner, USER, 1, 0)
  4        OR SYS_CONTEXT ('userenv', 'isdba') = 'TRUE';

View created.
```

Making this change increases performance while maintaining the security. Calling built-in database functions such as DECODE and CASE statements is an effective way to implement security while maintaining performance.

There may be a point at which the security logic becomes so complex that a PL/SQL function call is desired or needed. Making the call to a PL/SQL function will reduce the performance, which may or may not make the security implementation an effective solution. Helping to solve this problem is the virtual private database (VPD) technology discussed in Chapter 7.

Definer's vs. Invoker's Privileges/Rights for PL/SQL

Oracle provides two security enforcement modes during PL/SQL and Java Stored Procedure execution. As an application developer, Oracle allows you to pick either the definer's rights (the rights/privileges of the user that created the PL/SQL or Java program) or the invoker's rights (the rights/privileges of the user that is calling or executing the PL/SQL or Java program) to be in effect during the execution of the PL/SQL or Java program. That is, Oracle allows you to set at creation time which privilege model to use during the execution of the PL/SQL or Java program. Oracle stores this value in the AUTHID property of the PL/SQL program, and you can view the AUTHID value per stored program by selecting from the USER_PROCEDURES view.

Oracle provides two options because in some cases it is more secure to grant privileges to one schema (definer), and in other cases it is more secure to grant specific privileges to the calling user (invoker). Let's explore both and you will see which is right for your security policy.

Definer's Rights Invocation on PL/SQL Programs

The default invocation security model for PL/SQL programs is definer's rights—that is, by default, when a PL/SQL program executes, the privileges that are in effect are from the schema that owns the PL/SQL program. This makes sense, because if the PL/SQL program used a CURSOR that queried a table, then not only would you have to grant EXECUTE on the PL/SQL program, but you would also have to grant SELECT on the table the PL/SQL program referenced. As you have seen in previous chapters, if you have the privilege to create a table (CREATE TABLE), then you inherently get the privilege to INSERT, UPDATE, DELETE, SELECT, and so on.

In some cases, this is a very good and secure policy as it limits the granting of direct object privileges to the underlying tables to all end users. In the next example, we create a very simple PL/SQL function to calculate the total sales in the SALES_HISTORY table. We then test the privilege model to demonstrate that the calling or invoking user does not have access to the underlying table.

```
sec_mgr@db12cr[sales]> CONNECT sh@sales
Enter password:
Connected.
sh@db12cr[sales]> CREATE OR REPLACE FUNCTION sales_total_fn RETURN number AS
  2     rtn_total_cost NUMBER;
  3  BEGIN
  4     SELECT SUM(total_cost)
  5     INTO rtn_total_cost
  6     FROM SALES_HISTORY;
  7     RETURN rtn_total_cost;
  8  END;
  9  /

Function created.

sh@db12cr[sales]> SHOW ERRORS
No errors.
sh@db12cr[sales]> -- Verify AUTHID setting - invoker or definer
sh@db12cr[sales]> SELECT object_name, authid
  2  FROM user_procedures;

OBJECT_NAME                      AUTHID
------------------------------   ------------
SALES_TOTAL_FN                   DEFINER

1 rows selected.

sh@db12cr[sales]> GRANT EXECUTE ON sales_total_fn to PUBLIC;

Grant succeeded.

sh@db12cr[sales]> -- Cleanup from previous examples
sh@db12cr[sales]> REVOKE SELECT ON sales_history FROM wmaroulis;

Revoke succeeded.

sh@db12cr[sales]> -- Now let's connect as WMAROULIS and use the new function
sh@db12cr[sales]> CONNECT wmaroulis@sales
Enter password:
Connected.
wmaroulis@db12cr[sales]> SELECT sh.sales_total_fn()
  2  FROM dual;
```

```
SH.SALES_TOTAL_FN()
------------------
               28650

1 row selected.

wmaroulis@db12cr[sales]> SELECT *
  2  FROM sh.sales_history;
FROM sh.sales_history
        *
ERROR at line 2:
ORA-00942: table or view does not exist
```

Definer's rights are useful when object privileges or DAC security is most important, but what about FGAC? If row-level or column-level security is important, then you would have to write code to determine who the invoking user is and what privileges to apply. Or you might think about using invoker's rights.

Invoker's Rights Invocation for PL/SQL

In this model, the invoking, or calling, user's rights/privileges are used. Let's reexamine the preceding example using this invoker's rights model. Notice that to change security models, we only have to change the definition of the PL/SQL program. By adding AUTHID CURRENT_USER, we change from the default invocation (DEFINER) to the invoker, or CURRENT_USER. We could have created the original function with AUTHID DEFINER or not included this clause (which is what we did); they would have had the same effect.

```
wmaroulis@db12cr[sales]> CONNECT sh@sales
Enter password:
Connected.
sh@db12cr[sales]>  CREATE OR REPLACE function SALES_TOTAL_FN
  2  RETURN number
  3  AUTHID CURRENT_USER AS
  4    rtn_total_cost number;
  5  BEGIN
  6     SELECT SUM(total_cost)
  7     INTO rtn_total_cost
  8     FROM SALES_HISTORY;
  9     RETURN rtn_total_cost;
 10  END;
 11  /

Function created.

sh@db12cr[sales]> -- Let's check the security invocation rights
sh@db12cr[sales]> -- The function is set to CURRENT_USER or INVOKER
sh@db12cr[sales]> -- rights
sh@db12cr[sales]> SELECT object_name, authid
  2  FROM user_procedures;

OBJECT_NAME                      AUTHID
-------------------------------- ------------
SALES_TOTAL_FN                   CURRENT_USER
```

```
1 row selected.

sh@db12cr[sales]> -- As SH I am able to execute the function
sh@db12cr[sales]> -- because I have access to the underlying table
sh@db12cr[sales]> -- the function queries
sh@db12cr[sales]> SELECT sh.sales_total_fn()
  2  FROM dual;


SH.SALES_TOTAL_FN()
-------------------
              28650

1 row selected.

sh@db12cr[sales]> -- Quick point about the dependency or underlying table auth
sh@db12cr[sales]> -- This is a query to determine the dependencies on the
sh@db12cr[sales]> -- SALES_TOTAL_FN function
sh@db12cr[sales]> SELECT name, type, referenced_name, referenced_type
  2  FROM user_dependencies
  3  WHERE name = 'SALES_TOTAL_FN';


NAME           TYPE     REFERENCED_NAME                 REFERENCED_TYPE
-------------- -------- ------------------------------- ---------------
SALES_TOTAL_FN FUNCTION STANDARD                        PACKAGE
SALES_TOTAL_FN FUNCTION SYS_STUB_FOR_PURITY_ANALYSIS    PACKAGE
SALES_TOTAL_FN FUNCTION SALES_HISTORY                   TABLE

3 rows selected.

sh@db12cr[sales]> -- The above results indicate a dependency on the
sh@db12cr[sales]> -- SALES_HISTORY table
sh@db12cr[sales]> -- Recall from above we have revoked SELECT from
sh@db12cr[sales]> -- user WMAROULIS on the SALES_HISTORY table
sh@db12cr[sales]> CONNECT wmaroulis@sales
Enter password:
Connected.
wmaroulis@db12cr[sales]> SELECT sh.sales_total_fn()
  2  FROM dual;
SELECT sh.sales_total_fn()
       *
ERROR at line 1:
ORA-00942: table or view does not exist
ORA-06512: at "SH.SALES_TOTAL_FN", line 6

wmaroulis@db12cr[sales]> -- Line 6 refers to the PL/SQL program
wmaroulis@db12cr[sales]> -- and from above we can see that is
wmaroulis@db12cr[sales]> -- SELECT statement's reference to the SALES_HISTORY
wmaroulis@db12cr[sales]> -- table
wmaroulis@db12cr[sales]> CONNECT sh@sales
Enter password:
Connected.
sh@db12cr[sales]> GRANT SELECT ON sales_history to WMAROULIS;

Grant succeeded.
```

```
sh@db12cr[sales]> CONNECT wmaroulis@sales
Enter password:
Connected.
wmaroulis@db12cr[sales]> SELECT sh.sales_total_fn()
  2  FROM dual;
SELECT sh.sales_total_fn()
        *
ERROR at line 1:
ORA-00942: table or view does not exist
ORA-06512: at "SH.SALES_TOTAL_FN", line 6
```

What happened? Why didn't it work? This is an issue that happens quite a bit with invoker's rights PL/SQL code. The developer made the assumption that during the execution of the PL/SQL code, all object references (table – SALES_HISTORY) were local to the user calling the code. User WMAROULIS does not have a SALES_HISTORY table, and there is no public synonym or private synonym for this object, so Oracle couldn't resolve the table reference and we got the above error. If we qualify the SALES_HISTORY table reference to SH.SALES_HISTORY, then the code will work.

Let's try it again and see what we get:

```
wmaroulis@db12cr[sales]> CONNECT sh@sales
Enter password:
Connected.
sh@db12cr[sales]> CREATE OR REPLACE function sales_total_fn
  2    RETURN number
  3    AUTHID CURRENT_USER AS
  4    rtn_total_cost number;
  5  BEGIN
  6     SELECT SUM(total_cost)
  7     INTO rtn_total_cost
  8     FROM SH.SALES_HISTORY;
  9     RETURN rtn_total_cost;
 10  END;
 11  /

Function created.

sh@db12cr[sales]> CONNECT wmaroulis@sales
Enter password:
Connected.
wmaroulis@db12cr[sales]> SELECT sh.sales_total_fn()
  2  FROM dual;

SH.SALES_TOTAL_FN()
-------------------
             28650

1 row selected.

wmaroulis@db12cr[sales]> -- NOTE: I am selecting from the underlying
wmaroulis@db12cr[sales]> -- table here to show that I have direct access
wmaroulis@db12cr[sales]> -- to the underlying table - it will become
wmaroulis@db12cr[sales]> -- clear that there is a more secure solution
wmaroulis@db12cr[sales]> -- in the next section
wmaroulis@db12cr[sales]> SELECT count(*)
```

```
  2  FROM sh.sales_history;

  COUNT(*)
----------
         6
```

1 row selected.

This example illustrates the importance of determining how you, as a developer or an administrator, are going to grant access to your PL/SQL programs and dependent objects (database table in our example). However, as stated in the notes of the last example, you might want an invoker's rights security model, but you might not want to grant users SELECT access on schema objects (tables, in this case). You will learn in the next section that Oracle Database 12*c* has a new capability to satisfy both.

Definer's vs. Invoker's Privileges/Rights on Java Stored Procedures

Oracle Database 12*c* supports the same invocation rights for Java stored procedures as it does for PL/SQL stored procedures. To illustrate this point, we create a simple Java stored procedure that performs the same function as the PL/SQL function in the preceding example.

Java Stored Procedure and Definer's Rights

We first create the SalesHistory.java file with the following content. Notice the SELECT statement is similar to the PL/SQL function we used earlier:

```java
import java.sql.*;
import java.io.*;
import oracle.jdbc.*;

public class SalesHistory {

  public static int totalCost () throws SQLException {

      // Connect to Oracle using JDBC driver
      Connection conn = DriverManager.getConnection("jdbc:default:connection:");
      String sql = "SELECT SUM(total_cost) FROM SALES_HISTORY";
      int rtn=-1;
      try {
          Statement stmt = conn.createStatement();
          ResultSet rset = stmt.executeQuery(sql);
          rset.next();
          rtn=rset.getInt(1);
      } catch (SQLException e) {
        System.err.println(e.getMessage());
      } finally {
        return rtn;
      }
  }
}
```

We compile the Java class into byte code (.class):

```
[oracle@nsgdc2 work]$ $ORACLE_HOME/jdk/bin/javac -cp \
$ORACLE_HOME/jdbc/lib/ojdbc6.jar SalesHistory.java
[oracle@nsgdc2 work]$ ls -l
total 8
-rw-r--r-- 1 oracle dba 1132 Jan 19 22:19 SalesHistory.class
-rw-r--r-- 1 oracle dba  621 Jan 19 22:06 SalesHistory.java
```

We now load it into the database. The loadjava works on definer's rights and it cannot be changed. However, this is just for loading the class, not executing the stored procedure, which can be either definer's or invoker's rights.

```
[oracle@nsgdc2 work]$ loadjava -u sh@sales SalesHistory.class

Password:
*********
```

We create a PL/SQL wrapper for the Java stored procedure. We do this so that we can call the Java stored procedure in SQL and PL/SQL:

```
oracle@nsgdc2 work]$ sqlplus /nolog

SQL*Plus: Release 12.1.0.1.0 Production on Sun Jan 19 22:20:19 2014

Copyright (c) 1982, 2013, Oracle.  All rights reserved.

SQL> connect sh@sales
Enter password:
Connected.
sh@db12cr[sales]> -- By default AUTHID is DEFINER for this statement
sh@db12cr[sales]> CREATE OR REPLACE function jTotalCost RETURN number AS
  2  LANGUAGE JAVA
  3  NAME 'SalesHistory.totalCost() return BigDecimal';
  4  /

Function created.

sh@db12cr[sales]> -- Verify the function is working properly
sh@db12cr[sales]> SELECT jTotalCost()
  2  FROM dual;

JTOTALCOST()
------------
       28650

1 row selected.

sh@db12cr[sales]> GRANT EXECUTE ON jTotalCost TO wmaroulis;

Grant succeeded.

sh@db12cr[sales]> CONNECT wmaroulis@sales
Enter password:
Connected.
wmaroulis@db12cr[sales]> -- Works as expected - because the function
```

```
wmaroulis@db12cr[sales]> -- is operating as the DEFINER
wmaroulis@db12cr[sales]> SELECT sh.jTotalCost()
  2  FROM dual;

SH.JTOTALCOST()
---------------
          28650

1 row selected.

wmaroulis@db12cr[sales]> -- Works as expected - wmaroulis should not
wmaroulis@db12cr[sales]> -- be able to access the underlying table
wmaroulis@db12cr[sales]> SELECT *
  2  FROM sh.sales_history;
FROM sh.sales_history
        *
ERROR at line 2:
ORA-00942: table or view does not exist
```

Java Stored Procedure and Invoker's Rights

We have to change only the way the PL/SQL wrapper is created for the Java stored procedure to change the rights invocation mode. Notice the AUTHID CURRENT USER syntax, which is similar to the PL/SQL example shown previously.

```
wmaroulis@db12cr[sales]> CONNECT sh@sales
Enter password:
Connected.
sh@db12cr[sales]> CREATE OR REPLACE function jTotalCost RETURN number
  2  AUTHID CURRENT_USER AS LANGUAGE JAVA
  3  NAME 'SalesHistory.totalCost() return BigDecimal';
  4  /

Function created.

sh@db12cr[sales]> CONNECT wmaroulis@sales
Enter password:
Connected.
wmaroulis@db12cr[sales]> -- WMAROULIS does not have access to the object
wmaroulis@db12cr[sales]> SELECT sh.jTotalCost()
  2  FROM dual;
FROM dual
     *
ERROR at line 2:
ORA-29540: class SalesHistory does not exist
```

We update the code to show that the error is not simply a schema reference error:

```
wmaroulis@db12cr[sales]> CONNECT sh@sales
Enter password:
Connected.
sh@db12cr[sales]> -- We add a schema reference (SH) to the Java Stored Procedure
sh@db12cr[sales]> CREATE OR REPLACE FUNCTION jTotalCost RETURN number
  2  AUTHID CURRENT_USER AS LANGUAGE JAVA
  3  NAME 'sh.SalesHistory.totalCost() return BigDecimal';
```

```
  4  /

Function created.

sh@db12cr[sales]>  CONNECT wmaroulis@sales
Enter password:
Connected.
wmaroulis@db12cr[sales]>  SELECT sh.jTotalCost()
  2  FROM dual;
FROM dual
      *
ERROR at line 2:
ORA-29540: class sh/SalesHistory does not exist
```

Code-Based Security

In the previous section's invoker's rights example, we had to grant EXECUTE privilege to the PL/SQL program and grant SELECT privilege on the dependent table (SALES_HISTORY) to use invoker's rights. If the calling user doesn't need to query the SALES_HISTORY table independent of calling the PL/SQL program, then it seems excessive to grant SELECT on the table without being able to define a context in which the calling user can issue a SELECT statement. That is, we would have a more secure solution if we could tell Oracle that we only want the calling user to use the SELECT privilege during the execution of the PL/SQL program. Otherwise, we either have to over-privilege or elevate the privileges of the connected user to run the PL/SQL program.

Oracle Database 12*c* added the capability to grant privileges, via roles, to PL/SQL procedures. Using this capability reduces the number of direct grants to end users and thus adheres to the least-privilege security model.

Granting Roles and Privileges to PL/SQL

Let's re-examine the preceding example using the new Oracle Database 12*c* code-based security feature. First, we remove the existing direct grant on SALES_HISTORY from WMAROULIS to illustrate how this new feature works. We then create the SALES_HISTORY_READ role, grant SELECT on the SALES_HISTORY table to the new role, and finally connect as WMAROULIS and test the solution.

```
wmaroulis@db12cr[sales]> CONNECT sh@sales
Enter password:
Connected.
sh@db12cr[sales]> -- Clean up from the previous example
sh@db12cr[sales]> REVOKE SELECT ON sales_history FROM wmaroulis;

Revoke succeeded.

sh@db12cr[sales]> -- Create a role to hold our privileges
sh@db12cr[sales]> CREATE ROLE sales_history_read;

Role created.

sh@db12cr[sales]> -- Grant SELECT privileges to the role
sh@db12cr[sales]> GRANT SELECT ON sales_history TO sales_history_read;

Grant succeeded.
```

```
sh@db12cr[sales]> -- Grant the ROLE to the PL/SQL program
sh@db12cr[sales]> GRANT sales_history_read TO FUNCTION sales_total_fn;

Grant succeeded.

sh@db12cr[sales]> -- Connect as WMAROULIS and verify that we
sh@db12cr[sales]> -- can execute the function and get results as before
sh@db12cr[sales]> CONNECT wmaroulis@sales
Enter password:
Connected.
wmaroulis@db12cr[sales]> SELECT sh.sales_total_fn()
  2  FROM dual;


SH.SALES_TOTAL_FN()
-------------------
              28650

1 row selected.

wmaroulis@db12cr[sales]> -- The difference from the previous example
wmaroulis@db12cr[sales]> -- is that now WMAROULIS does not have
wmaroulis@db12cr[sales]> -- direct object grants or access to the
wmaroulis@db12cr[sales]> -- underlying table
wmaroulis@db12cr[sales]> SELECT count(*)
  2  FROM sh.sales_history;
FROM sh.sales_history
         *
ERROR at line 2:
ORA-00942: table or view does not exist
```

Entitlement Analytics

In the process of evaluating a system for regulatory compliance or certification, you may be asked for a report that maps database user, roles, and privileges. This type of report typically lists which privileges and roles have been granted to which users and which privileges have been granted to which roles. This gives the personnel evaluating a system for regulatory compliance or certification an understanding of granted user/roles/privileges at the point-in-time the report was generated. This type of report is a snapshot of the system at a point-in-time and does not really help to answer some fundamental security questions: Could the SH schema operate properly without the system privilege CREATE TABLE? Are you sure that user SGAETJEN requires EXECUTE on package CTXSYS.CTX_QUERY? These questions are simple enough and could be answered with asking the DBA or digging through some source code. The point is that the people evaluating your system need to be assured that you have not inadvertently created an over-privileged database account.

Now consider a large-scale distributed enterprise system that consists of more than 19,000 tables and hundreds of users; how would you enforce a least privilege model in this type of system? Or what about a legacy multithreaded application with hundreds of tables using multiple connection pools—how would you determine which user is executing what SQL statement when and with what privilege? These problems are harder if not intractable.

The big question is simply this: How can we answer these questions so that we can pass our evaluation? Or maybe the question is—have we done an adequate job removing unused or unnecessary privileges from database users?

Fortunately, Oracle has a straightforward answer to these types of questions. Oracle Database Vault (a database security option) now contains a PL/SQL package named DBMS_PRIVILEGE_ CAPTURE that contains several procedures to answer these and other user-to-privilege mapping questions. The package enables privilege capture during the execution of specific PL/SQL procedures or during normal operating hours, or until you feel that you have exercised enough application code to have a representative. You then generate a report to display the captured information and can take action to reduce privileges as necessary.

Profile Application Use

The first thing you must do is determine the objective of profiling privileges used in the database. Is the objective to determine specific privileges used during a PL/SQL program call? Is the objective to determine system and object privileges used by a specific database user? Is the objective to determine all privileges used by a legacy application? For the purposes of our example, we pose a couple questions: What privilege does database user WMAROULIS use to query the SH.SALES_ HISTORY table? By what means did the user receive the privilege?

Create a Privilege Capture Policy

Next we create a privilege capture policy. You can perform several types of captures using the CREATE_CAPTURE procedure from the DBMS_PRIVILEGE_CAPTURE package:

- **G_DATABASE**   Captures all privileges used (except privileges used by SYS). This is the default capture type.

- **G_ROLE**   Captures privileges used by a specific role or roles.

- **G_CONTEXT**   Captures privileges when the CONDITION parameter evaluates to TRUE.

- **G_ROLE_AND_CONTEXT**   Captures privileges used by a specific role or list of roles, but only when the CONDITION parameter evaluates to TRUE.

We use G_DATABASE (the default) to get all privileges used on the system. We can then filter by WMAROULIS to determine how the user received privilege to query the SH.SALES_HISTORY table.

```
wmaroulis@db12cr[sales]> CONNECT sec_mgr@sales
Enter password:
Connected.
sec_mgr@db12cr[sales]> -- By default the CAPTURE is disabled.
sec_mgr@db12cr[sales]> -- This is done to allow you to better
sec_mgr@db12cr[sales]> -- control when you turn it on an off
sec_mgr@db12cr[sales]> BEGIN
  2     DBMS_PRIVILEGE_CAPTURE.CREATE_CAPTURE(
  3         name  => 'sales_history_capture',
  4         type  => DBMS_PRIVILEGE_CAPTURE.G_DATABASE);
  5     DBMS_PRIVILEGE_CAPTURE.ENABLE_CAPTURE(
  6         name  => 'sales_history_capture');
  7  END;
  8  /

PL/SQL procedure successfully completed.
```

Execute Your Application Code

At this point the system is capturing events in the database. So we now execute the code or SQL statements that we want to watch. In our case, we connect as user WMAROULIS and query the SH.SALES_HISTORY table.

```
sec_mgr@db12cr[sales]> CONNECT wmaroulis@sales
Enter password:
Connected.
wmaroulis@db12cr[sales]> SELECT COUNT(*)
  2  FROM sh.sales_history
  3  /

  COUNT(*)
----------
         6

1 row selected.
```

Generate the Report

We now connect as SEC_MGR and disable privilege capture. We then query the DBA_PRIV_USED view to determine which privilege was used to query the table.

```
wmaroulis@db12cr[sales]> CONNECT sec_mgr@sales
Enter password:
Connected.
sec_mgr@db12cr[sales]> BEGIN
  2  DBMS_PRIVILEGE_CAPTURE.DISABLE_CAPTURE(
  3     name => 'sales_history_capture');
  4  END;
  5  /

PL/SQL procedure successfully completed.

sec_mgr@db12cr[sales]> -- Generate the report
sec_mgr@db12cr[sales]> BEGIN
  2  DBMS_PRIVILEGE_CAPTURE.GENERATE_RESULT (
  3     name => 'sales_history_capture');
  4  END;
  5  /

PL/SQL procedure successfully completed.

sec_mgr@db12cr[sales]> -- We use the DBA_USED_PRIVS view to see the answer
sec_mgr@db12cr[sales]> DESCRIBE dba_used_privs
 Name                    Null?    Type
 ----------------------- -------- ----------------
 CAPTURE                 NOT NULL VARCHAR2(128)
 SEQUENCE                NOT NULL NUMBER
 OS_USER                          VARCHAR2(128)
 USERHOST                         VARCHAR2(128)
 MODULE                           VARCHAR2(64)
 USERNAME                NOT NULL VARCHAR2(128)
```

```
USED_ROLE                      VARCHAR2(128)
SYS_PRIV                       VARCHAR2(40)
OBJ_PRIV                       VARCHAR2(40)
USER_PRIV                      VARCHAR2(18)
OBJECT_OWNER                   VARCHAR2(128)
OBJECT_NAME                    VARCHAR2(128)
OBJECT_TYPE                    VARCHAR2(23)
COLUMN_NAME                    VARCHAR2(128)
OPTION$                        NUMBER
PATH                           SYS.GRANT_PATH


sec_mgr@db12cr[sales]> SELECT sys_priv, path, username,
  2      object_owner||'.'||object_name object
  3  FROM dba_used_privs
  4  WHERE username = 'WMAROULIS' and
  5      object_name = 'SALES_HISTORY';


SYS_PRIV          PATH                     USERNAME    OBJECT
----------------  -----------------------  ----------  ----------------
SELECT ANY TABLE  GRANT_PATH('WMAROULIS')  WMAROULIS   SH.SALES_HISTORY

1 row selected.
```

We are able to see that user WMAROULIS used the SELECT ANY TABLE privilege to query the SH.SALES_HISTORY table. The PATH column indicates how the user received the privilege. In this case, the privilege was directly granted to WMAROULIS. If the PATH column displayed GRANT_PATH('WMAROULIS','PUBLIC'), then this would indicate that the user received the privilege via the PUBLIC role.

Privilege Reduction

At this point we know how user WMAROULIS was able to query the SH.SALES_HISTORY table. Now we have to answer the question, Does user WMAROULIS need SELECT ANY TABLE to perform his job or is the user over-privileged?

Privilege reduction can be split into two areas for further analysis. In a *least privilege analysis*, each privilege is analyzed to determine whether an alternative privilege exists to accomplish the task. *Unused privilege analysis* is an analysis of which privileges the user didn't use.

Least Privilege Analysis

To answer this question, you need to enable the privilege capture routine and exercise the application code until you have performed all the duties for user WMAROULIS. You then stop the privilege capture and generate the privilege report. By reviewing the results, you can determine whether the system, object, or user privileges are required.

In our previous example, user WMAROULIS was directly granted the system privilege SELECT ANY TABLE, and for the sake of brevity, let's assume that we exercised the application code thoroughly enough and reviewed the generated report to determine that user WMAROULIS performed all required duties without the need of the system privilege. We would then conclude that user WMAORULIS does not require the system privilege SELECT ANY TABLE to complete his duties. He is indeed over-privileged. We would then revoke the system privilege SELECT ANY TABLE from user WMAROULIS and replace it with a SELECT grant on the object directly or through a database role.

Unused Privilege Analysis

Unused privilege analysis is somewhat easier to perform. You simply run a query against the DBA_UNUSED_PRIVS view to determine which privileges were not used during your privilege capture session. You would then REVOKE the privileges as necessary.

For example, let's see what privileges user WMAROULIS did not use during our privilege capture session.

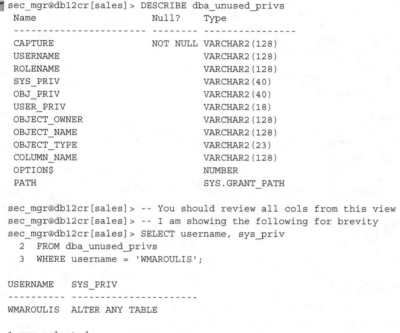

```
sec_mgr@db12cr[sales]> DESCRIBE dba_unused_privs
 Name                      Null?    Type
 ----------------------- -------- ----------------
 CAPTURE                 NOT NULL VARCHAR2(128)
 USERNAME                         VARCHAR2(128)
 ROLENAME                         VARCHAR2(128)
 SYS_PRIV                         VARCHAR2(40)
 OBJ_PRIV                         VARCHAR2(40)
 USER_PRIV                        VARCHAR2(18)
 OBJECT_OWNER                     VARCHAR2(128)
 OBJECT_NAME                      VARCHAR2(128)
 OBJECT_TYPE                      VARCHAR2(23)
 COLUMN_NAME                      VARCHAR2(128)
 OPTION$                          NUMBER
 PATH                             SYS.GRANT_PATH

sec_mgr@db12cr[sales]> -- You should review all cols from this view
sec_mgr@db12cr[sales]> -- I am showing the following for brevity
sec_mgr@db12cr[sales]> SELECT username, sys_priv
  2  FROM dba_unused_privs
  3  WHERE username = 'WMAROULIS';

USERNAME    SYS_PRIV
---------- ----------------------
WMAROULIS   ALTER ANY TABLE

1 row selected.
```

User WMAROULIS did not use the system privilege ALTER ANY TABLE during the privilege capture session, and therefore the system privilege can be removed without breaking the application or impacting the job user WMAROULIS performs.

Oracle Enterprise Manager Cloud Control (OEMCC) 12c

OEMCC provides a GUI-based approach to capturing privileges. OEMCC enables you to create and manage multiples of privilege capture configurations. You can easily enable or disable them as you are running or testing your application code. Privilege analysis has a nice feature that lets you create a configuration and click Show SQL, which enables you to copy the SQL statements used to create the capture policy.

To use the privilege analysis/capture feature of OEMCC, navigate to the target databases, and select Security | Privilege Analysis, as shown in Figure 5-2.

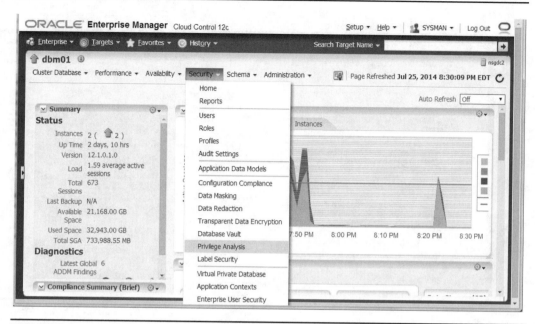

FIGURE 5-2. *Navigating to Privilege Analysis*

You can create multiple privilege capture policies. The following capture scopes are supported:

- **Database** Captures all privileges used (except privileges used by SYS). This is the default capture type.
- **Role** Captures privileges used by a specific role or roles.
- **Context** Captures privileges when the CONDITION parameter evaluates to TRUE.
- **Role and Context** Captures privileges used by a specific role or list of roles, but only when the CONDITION parameter evaluates to TRUE.

Figure 5-3 illustrates creating a privilege capture policy to capture privileges used during our monthly sales close processing. We give the policy a name, add in selected roles of interest, and click OK. We can then schedule a database job to have it run, or we can run and stop it at our discretion.

Another time-saving feature of OEMCC Privilege Analysis is that it allows you to create a database role from Privilege Analysis results. That is, you can turn on privilege capture, run your application, review the results, and then create a database role with privileges used. Figure 5-4 shows the screen for creating a database role for the Sales History Access capture.

OEMCC Privilege Analysis has extensive reporting capabilities. As with the DBMS_PRIVILEGE_CAPTURE package, you can capture used and unused privileges during Privilege Analysis. You can then run a report to display which privileges were used or not used. Figure 5-5 displays a summary of privileges used. You can drill down, for example, on system privileges used and determine exactly which were used.

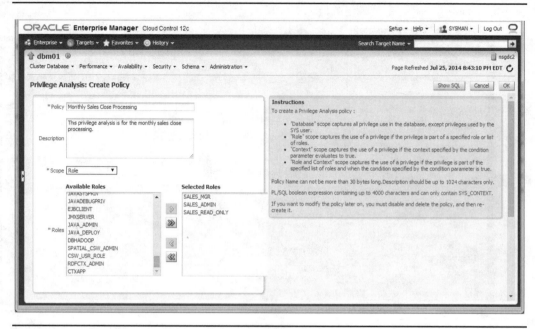

FIGURE 5-3. *Creating a monthly sales close analysis policy*

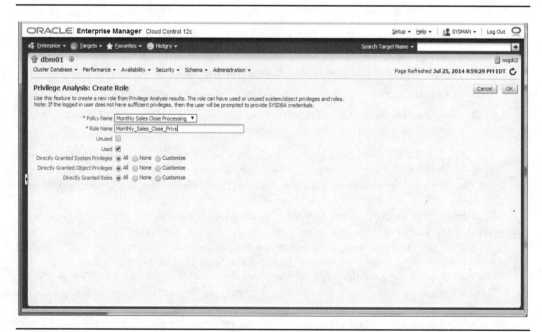

FIGURE 5-4. *Creating a database role from Privilege Analysis capture*

FIGURE 5-5. *OEMCC 12c Privilege Capture report*

Sharing Application Code

Prior to Oracle Database 12c, application code was shared by creating a schema, loading the application code (PL/SQL), and granting EXECUTE on the code. For example, if you had a set of currency conversion utilities, you would create a CURRENCY schema, load the code for the utilities, and grant EXECUTE on the code to schemas such as Sales History (SH). You might have also checked your code into a version control system to be checked out at a later date, updated, reapplied to the database, and checked back in. If you wanted to share your code with a new database, you would check out the latest version of the code, connect to the new system as SYS, and run your scripts.

In some sense, Oracle Database 12c using pluggable databases can be considered separate databases and the preceding model still works. However, Oracle Database 12c makes managing schemas, application code, and even the version of code simpler.

We cover two approaches to managing common code. The first way is to create a database template with the common code, and then create pluggable databases from the template. In this approach, each of the pluggable databases is guaranteed to have the same code. The second way is to create a database with the common code, and then have the pluggable or non-pluggable databases use database links to the common code repository. Figure 5-6 illustrates both approaches.

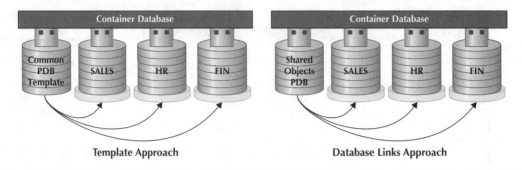

Template Approach   Database Links Approach

FIGURE 5-6. *Sharing common code approaches*

Managing Common Application Code with Pluggable Databases

In an enterprise system that has multiples of databases, configuration management is critically important to operation stability and to a large part maintaining a good security posture. It is therefore advantageous to be able create objects and application code that are created once, maintained centrally, and shared among all pluggable databases.

A good example would be a schema that contains custom PL/SQL code providing common business services, such as, for example, currency conversion or custom scientific calculations. One approach to solving this problem is to leverage the multitenant architecture of Oracle Database 12c and use the CREATE PLUGGABLE DATABASE statement to create a template pluggable database. We can then load our "shared" schema and objects into the template pluggable database. Finally we create new PDB from this template. This approach is similar to the concept of the PDB$SEED container, except that it contains application code we want to share among newly created PDBs.

NOTE
You can find an example that demonstrates this approach in the script named 05.code.share.template.sql in the example scripts available with this book.

When you create a new pluggable database from this template PDB, the new PDB will have the common application schema accounts, required storage, database objects, and security policies defined when you first open the new database. You will need to patch each clone of the template database for structural or code changes, but there is value in having a consistent database build process with common components.

Managing Common Application Code with Database Links

You can also leverage Oracle loopback database links for shared application schema accounts. For example, suppose we have a source database with tables, views, and PL/SQL code that we want to maintain in a single location. We can create a proxy database account on all pluggable databases that will connect to the source pluggable database, thus giving the pluggable database access to these shared objects. The proxy database accounts will have the minimal system and object privileges required to support connecting and retrieving data.

NOTE
You can find an example that demonstrates this approach in the script named 05.code.share.link.sql in the example scripts that are available with this book.

The following example builds on the previous example to demonstrate this approach. For brevity, this example will reuse TEMPLATE PDB as the shared code repository and access the currency conversion routine to SALES PDB using a database link.

In this example, the code for the currency conversion is actually executing on the TEMPLATE PDB versus the SALES PDB. This approach is consistent with the manner in which PL/SQL code accessed via a database link would execute in previous releases of Oracle Database.

Summary

In this chapter we discussed the fundamentals of database application security. The important takeaway from this chapter is that adding security closest to the data is integral for an overall effective security policy. It does not make sense to code data security rules in an application running on the middle tier when an administrator can simply connect to the database using SQL*Plus, bypassing middle-tier application security.

Application contexts are an efficient and flexible mechanism for storing security-related name-value pairs. Oracle Database 12c provides many default attributes in the USERENV namespace. These attributes are automatically populated and generally provide useful information about the user's environment—IP address, authentication method, and so on. The CLIENT_IDENTIFIER is also part of the USERENV namespace, and it can be set by a user or N application. It also has the added benefit of being recorded in the audit trails.

The ability to define your own application contexts allows for many creative security solutions. You can create and locally manage application context values. Each context is held in the user's private memory regions and is therefore secure for each database session. Local application contexts are ideal for performing security functions. They are secure because they can be manipulated only by the namespace manager. They are also fast, because the values are stored in memory. They are flexible as well, because they can be set to any user-defined string.

You can also define global application contexts. This allows the sharing of information, in a secure manner, across database schemas and database sessions. The database provides various ways in which global contexts can be defined and used. Global contexts are a great utility for sharing contextual information across multiple database sessions, as you might find with connection pooled applications or shared schema designs. Oracle Database 12c also supports contexts initialized by external sources. When the source is initialized by the directory, the design supports Oracle's centralized user management strategy, which is a critical component to the identity management functionality.

You can use views for various definitions of column security. They can remove entire columns from the user's access or mask a column's values. The database also provides column security through object privileges on insert and update operations. Views can be easily defined and managed and often implemented transparently for almost all simple security requirements. Use views with both Oracle built-in functions and user-defined functions to provide FGAC; they should always be one of the first security solutions you consider.

However, views are not always a perfect solution. The performance degradation of views with user-defined PL/SQL functions, especially when used with row-level security, may make them impractical in certain situations. Also keep in mind that built-in functions perform very well. A view-based security solution can be difficult to manage, as the number and complexity of the views increases. Many of the benefits can be diminished if the view solution requires copious numbers of instead-of triggers.

Database Vault's Privilege Capture provides a reporting mechanism that can aid in removing unnecessary or unused privileges. The reporting mechanism can also aid in the analysis of how a user received a privilege to perform an operation, but it can also help in the analysis, finding users that are over-privileged. This feature can help you improve the overall security posture of your database applications with a minor time investment and some thoughtful analysis about how your database applications operate.

Finally, we demonstrated two solutions, preloading pluggable databases and local database links, to share common code in the multitenant architecture of Oracle Database 12c. Depending on your security environment, the frequency of source code change, and other factors, you may find that either or a combination of both solutions works for you.

CHAPTER
6

Real Application Security

I n this chapter, we examine a new and powerful feature in Oracle Database 12c called *Oracle Real Application Security (RAS)*. Oracle RAS was built to provide a comprehensive, common, declarative security model that can be shared among enterprise applications and to provide the performance you expect for enterprise applications. The word "comprehensive" is a key descriptor. Oracle RAS provides security policy constructors for account management, role management, database session management with application contexts, fine-grained data security (privileges and authorizations), and auditing. The fact that Oracle RAS provides a common and declarative security model is in keeping with the existing Oracle Database security features that operate within the security paradigm of "transparency," wherein the policies are defined within the database and do not have to be coded into each database application.

Traditional database applications, such as those that run on web-based application servers, can perform poorly if not properly designed. The performance cost to switch database connections to an account or role that has the correct database privileges for a given web application module can be costly. The unfortunate solution to the performance problem has often been simply to grant all privileges an application may ever need to a single pool account and to use that pool account for all web application modules. This step to over-privilege a single pool account can lead to accidental data loss as well as malicious data theft.

Another frequent challenge in web-based application is knowing the end-user identity within the context of the database. As we have mentioned before, knowing the end-user identity is important for enforcing security policies and maintaining an accurate audit trail. Creating and managing database accounts for all end users for all of your applications can be cost-prohibitive. The unfortunate solution to this challenge has often been simply to ignore the end-user identity in the database and to code security policies repetitively in each application. This approach is not the most efficient use of your company's programming resources and is prone to errors or misconfigurations. Oracle RAS was built to help meet these challenges as well as the following objectives:

- Introduce the concepts of application users and application roles.
- Create a lightweight session model to improve performance for database applications.
- Create declarative and fine-grained data security policies for application users and application roles that can be shared among multiple database applications.
- Support the native Oracle database auditing facilities.

One of the most important features of Oracle RAS is its design to work in conjunction with Oracle Fusion Middleware (FMW) security and, more generally, any Java-based database application. FMW supports technologies such as Oracle Identity Management, Oracle SOA Suite, Oracle WebCenter, and the Oracle Application Development Framework (ADF). Each of these technologies leverages a J2EE standards–based set of security infrastructure services called Oracle Platform Security Services (OPSS) for authentication, role-based authorization, auditing, encryption, and more. OPSS can provide authentication services for web applications and delegate database authorization decisions to Oracle RAS using identity propagation and ensuring that the audit trail includes the end-user identity. Oracle RAS includes a component named the Application Session Service that can be deployed as a J2EE servlet filter to FMW. This servlet filter transparently performs application session synchronization with the database and supports externally defined application users, roles, and security contexts. If you are using Oracle FMW and OPSS, we encourage you to read this chapter to understand the features and capabilities of Oracle RAS. You can then use the detailed instructions in Chapter 8 of the *Oracle Database Real Application Security Administrator's and Developer's Guide* to set up the Application Session Service for your applications.

In the first two sections we introduce application users, application roles, and the lightweight session model from a RAS perspective. These examples will leverage the Java APIs to demonstrate how the Oracle RAS lightweight session framework differs from traditional Oracle Database sessions. You will begin to realize that the Oracle RAS lightweight session framework has similar features to Oracle Proxy Authentication that was covered in Chapter 3 and incorporates many of the same capabilities as session application context that was covered in Chapter 5. Oracle RAS offers more comprehensive, extensible, and mature technologies around these concepts. We will conclude the chapter with background and examples of Oracle RAS support for the fine-grained declarative security policies as well as a discussion of auditing within Oracle RAS. Data security policies within Oracle RAS leverage the Oracle Virtual Private Database (VPD) security feature that we will present in the next chapter.

Account Management in Oracle RAS

Oracle RAS security policies operate on a very simple grammar that is commonly used to define policies in security protection profiles. RAS security policies define the success criteria during the security certification process. The general security grammar is as follows:

<subject> <verb> <object> <conditions>

Oracle expands the grammar for the database and RAS as follows:

<Principal> perform <operation> on <data> subject to <privilege>

In Oracle RAS, a principal can be an application user or application role. Oracle RAS application users can be defined in two ways:

- **Direct Login Application User (DLAU) account**   This type of account has the ability to connect to the database and is typically used as a RAS pool account for applications or a RAS dispatcher account for session management. The account does not own database objects but can be associated with a traditional database account for the purpose of object name resolution. The account has no default privileges but does have the ability to connect to the database.

- **Simple Application User (SAU) account**   This type of user is intended to be a lightweight representation of a real end user in your organization—for example, user MARY or user ANTHONY. The account does not have the ability to connect to the database, has no database privileges, and does not own database objects.

Configuring DLAU Accounts

DLAU accounts are created using the XS_PRINCIPAL PL/SQL package. The XS in the name stands for "eXtended Security." In practice, you will want to create one or more Oracle RAS traditional administrator accounts to manage your Oracle RAS policies using the XS_PRINCIPAL package.

We use the SEC_MGR account we created in Chapter 2 in the following example to demonstrate how to authorize the SEC_MGR account to be a RAS administrator:

```
sys@db12cr[sales]> CONNECT sys@sales AS SYSDBA
Enter password:
Connected.
sys@db12cr[sales]> GRANT XS_SESSION_ADMIN TO sec_mgr;

Grant succeeded.
```

Once our RAS administrator has been authorized, we create a DLAU named SH_DIRECT that maps to the Sales History (SH) schema for name resolution:

```
sys@db12cr[sales]> CONNECT sec_mgr@sales
Enter password:
Connected.
sec_mgr@db12cr[sales]> BEGIN
  2      SYS.XS_PRINCIPAL.CREATE_USER(
  3             name=>'SH_DIRECT'
  4           , schema=>'SH');
  5   END;
  6   /

PL/SQL procedure successfully completed.

sec_mgr@db12cr[sales]> -- query the Oracle RAS view for application users
sec_mgr@db12cr[sales]> SELECT name,status,schema
  2   FROM dba_xs_users
  3   ORDER BY name;

NAME                            STATUS            SCHEMA
------------------------------- ----------------- ----------------------------
SH_DIRECT                       ACTIVE            SH
XSGUEST                         ACTIVE

2 rows selected.
```

The XSGUEST account is a predefined RAS user that can be used for anonymous lightweight RAS sessions. Note that new RAS accounts are not created using the traditional **CREATE USER** command but are created using the XS_PRINCIPAL.CREATE_USER procedure. This procedure supports the following parameters:

- **name** The name of the application user to be created.
- **status** The status of the user, one of ACTIVE, INACTIVE, PASSWORDEXPIRED, or LOCKED. The status of a user is ACTIVE by default.
- **schema** An optional database schema to associate with the user.
- **start_date** The first date the user is active.
- **end_date** The last date the user is active.
- **guid** A globally unique identifier of the user, which can be set only if the user is external.
- **external_source** An optional source system name for the user.
- **description** An optional description for the user.

The XS_PRINCIPAL package has SET procedures to set the individual attributes shown in this list. One common characteristic of the account and role management is the ability to set the effective start and end dates. Another common characteristic of the account and role management is the ability to set the name of an external system the account or role is associated with, which is usually the associated database application. You use the XS_PRINCIPAL.DELETE_PRINCIPAL procedure to remove a user.

We must set the password for the DLAU account SH_DIRECT prior to logging in to the database:

```
sec_mgr@db12cr[sales] > BEGIN
  2       SYS.XS_PRINCIPAL.SET_PASSWORD(
  3             user => 'SH_DIRECT'
  4           , password => 'welcome1'
  5           , type => XS_PRINCIPAL.XS_SALTED_SHA1);
  6  END;
  7  /

PL/SQL procedure successfully completed.
```

The type parameter indicates the password verifier, which can be SALTED_SHA1, XS_MD4, or XS_O3LOGON. The default is SALTED_SHA1 and is recommended. A database administrator can use the XS_PRINCIPAL.SET_VERIFIER procedure to migrate existing database accounts to RAS DLAU accounts, as shown in the following example:

```
sec_mgr@db12cr[sales] > -- create a standard database account to test
sec_mgr@db12cr[sales] > CREATE USER oracle11_user IDENTIFIED BY
  2  welcome1;

User created.

sec_mgr@db12cr[sales] > -- create a RAS DLAU account to "take over"
sec_mgr@db12cr[sales] > -- for this standard database account
sec_mgr@db12cr[sales] > BEGIN
  2       SYS.XS_PRINCIPAL.CREATE_USER(
  3             name=>'ORACLE11_USER'
  4           , schema=>'SH');
  5  END;
  6  /

PL/SQL procedure successfully completed.

sec_mgr@db12cr[sales] > -- set the standard database account
sec_mgr@db12cr[sales] > -- to the password for the DLAU account
sec_mgr@db12cr[sales] > DECLARE
  2       l_pwd SYS.USER$.PASSWORD%TYPE;
  3  BEGIN
  4         SELECT password
  5         INTO l_pwd
  6         FROM SYS.USER$
  7         WHERE name = 'ORACLE11_USER';
  8       SYS.XS_PRINCIPAL.SET_VERIFIER(
  9             user => 'ORACLE11_USER'
 10           , verifier => l_pwd
 11           , type => XS_PRINCIPAL.XS_O3LOGON);
```

```
 12  END;
 13  /

PL/SQL procedure successfully completed.

sec_mgr@db12cr[sales]> -- drop the standard database account
sec_mgr@db12cr[sales]> DROP USER oracle11_user CASCADE;

User dropped.

sec_mgr@db12cr[sales]> -- test the new RAS DLAU account
sec_mgr@db12cr[sales]> CONNECT oracle11_user/welcome1@sales
Connected.
```

The XS_PRINCIPAL.SET_PROFILE procedure can be used to associate a database profile (see Chapter 2) to the DLAU account. The database profile lists the required password complexity check function and enforces session resource limits on the account.

```
sec_mgr@db12cr[sales]> BEGIN
  2      XS_PRINCIPAL.SET_PROFILE('SH_DIRECT','DEFAULT');
  3  END;
  4  /

PL/SQL procedure successfully completed.
```

Once the password has been set for a DLAU account, we can then log in to the database:

```
sec_mgr@db12cr[sales]> CONNECT sh_direct/welcome1@sales
Connected.
xs$null@db12cr[sales]> -- notice that the database user is XS$NULL we can
xs$null@db12cr[sales]> -- use the XS_SYS_CONTEXT context to determine xs$null@
db12cr[sales]> -- which database account the DLAU is associated to
xs$null@db12cr[sales]> -- and SYS_CONTEXT to obtain the RAS session user
xs$null@db12cr[sales]> -- and default schema
xs$null@db12cr[sales]> SELECT SYS_CONTEXT('USERENV','SESSION_USER')
  2    SESSION_USER
  3  , XS_SYS_CONTEXT('XS$SESSION','USERNAME') RAS_SESSION_USER
  4  , SYS_CONTEXT('USERENV','CURRENT_SCHEMA') CURRENT_SCHEMA
  5  FROM DUAL;
SESSION_USER     RAS_SESSION_USE CURRENT_SCHEMA
-------------- --------------- ---------------
XS$NULL          SH_DIRECT        SH

1 row selected.xs$null@db12cr[sales]> -- notice that the session has no
xs$null@db12cr[sales]> -- privileges or roles by default
xs$null@db12cr[sales]> SELECT *
  2  FROM session_privs;

no rows selected

xs$null@db12cr[sales]> SELECT *
  2  FROM session_roles;

no rows selected
```

As you can see, information about both the database user, XS$NULL, and the Oracle RAS application user, SH_DIRECT, are available in session context as is the default schema, SH. The XS$NULL account is a special Oracle Database account that has no database privileges or roles. Further, no one can authenticate to the database using the XS$NULL account directly (similar to the EUS landing schemas we created in Chapter 2). The SQL functions ORA_INVOKING_USER, ORA_INVOKING_USERID, and ORA_INVOKING_XS_USER are also available as shortcuts to the XS$SESSION context names and attributes.

```
xs$null@db12cr[sales]> SELECT ora_invoking_user
  2   FROM dual;

ORA_INVOKING_USER
-------------------------------------------------------
XS$NULL

1 row selected.
```

Configuring Simple Application User Accounts

We will now create two SAU accounts named MARY and ANTHONY. We will use these accounts to demonstrate Oracle RAS support for lightweight sessions later in this section.

```
xs$null@db12cr[sales]> CONNECT sec_mgr@sales
Enter password:
Connected.
sec_mgr@db12cr[sales]> -- create two RAS SAU accounts
sec_mgr@db12cr[sales]> BEGIN
  2      SYS.XS_PRINCIPAL.CREATE_USER(
  3         name    => 'MARY');
  4      SYS.XS_PRINCIPAL.CREATE_USER(
  5         name    => 'ANTHONY');
  6   END;
  7   /

PL/SQL procedure successfully completed.

sec_mgr@db12cr[sales]> -- query the Oracle RAS view for SAU users
sec_mgr@db12cr[sales]> SELECT name, status, schema
  2   FROM dba_xs_users
  3   ORDER BY name;

NAME                            STATUS           SCHEMA
------------------------------- ---------------- -----------------
ANTHONY                         ACTIVE
MARY                            ACTIVE
ORACLE11_USER                   ACTIVE           SH
SH_DIRECT                       ACTIVE           SH
XSGUEST                         ACTIVE

5 rows selected.
```

As you can see, these accounts do not require a schema, because they are SAU accounts. We will not set a password for these accounts, because they will not be directly connecting to the database.

Oracle RAS Roles

Application roles in Oracle RAS manage a logical set of privileges that are defined using access control lists (ACLs) rather than traditional object grants. A standard database role can be granted to a RAS application role as well. A RAS application role can be granted only to a RAS application user or another RAS application role. We will examine the relationship of application roles and ACLs later in this chapter.

Integration of Standard Database Roles with Oracle RAS Roles

You can grant traditional database roles to Oracle RAS application roles and then control access to those roles via Oracle RAS privileges. In the following example, we will create two standard database roles named DB_SH_READ and DB_SH_WRITE, grant the appropriate privileges on the SH.SALES_HISTORY table to those standard roles, create two Oracle RAS application roles named XS_SH_READ and XS_SH_WRITE, grant DB_SH_READ to XS_SH_READ, grant DB_SH_WRITE to XS_SH_WRITE, and finally grant XS_SH_READ and XS_SH_WRITE to our Oracle RAS application accounts, ANTHONY and MARY.

```
sec_mgr@db12cr[sales]> -- create standard database role for
sec_mgr@db12cr[sales]> -- sales history for read and write
sec_mgr@db12cr[sales]> CREATE ROLE db_sh_read;

Role created.

sec_mgr@db12cr[sales]> CREATE ROLE db_sh_write;

Role created.

sec_mgr@db12cr[sales]> -- grant the object privileges
sec_mgr@db12cr[sales]> -- required for these roles
sec_mgr@db12cr[sales]> GRANT SELECT
  2  ON sh.sales_history
  3  TO db_sh_read;

Grant succeeded.

sec_mgr@db12cr[sales]> GRANT SELECT, INSERT, UPDATE, DELETE
  2  ON sh.sales_history
  3  TO db_sh_write;

Grant succeeded.

sec_mgr@db12cr[sales]> -- create two RAS application roles
sec_mgr@db12cr[sales]> -- that will map to these standard
sec_mgr@db12cr[sales]> -- database roles
sec_mgr@db12cr[sales]> BEGIN
  2  SYS.XS_PRINCIPAL.CREATE_ROLE(
  3     name   => 'XS_SH_READ'
  4   , enabled => TRUE );
  5  SYS.XS_PRINCIPAL.CREATE_ROLE(
  6     name   => 'XS_SH_WRITE'
  7   , enabled => TRUE );
  8  END;
  9  /
```

```
PL/SQL procedure successfully completed.

sec_mgr@db12cr[sales]> -- grant the standard database role to
sec_mgr@db12cr[sales]> -- the appropriate RAS application role
sec_mgr@db12cr[sales]> GRANT db_sh_read TO xs_sh_read;

Grant succeeded.

sec_mgr@db12cr[sales]> GRANT db_sh_write TO xs_sh_write;

Grant succeeded.

sec_mgr@db12cr[sales]> -- query the RAS dictionary views
sec_mgr@db12cr[sales]> -- to see the roles we created
sec_mgr@db12cr[sales]> SELECT name, default_enabled
  2  FROM dba_xs_roles
  3  ORDER BY name;

NAME                         DEF
---------------------------- ---
XSBYPASS                     NO
XSCACHEADMIN                 YES
XSDISPATCHER                 YES
XSNAMESPACEADMIN             YES
XSPROVISIONER                YES
XSPUBLIC                     YES
XSSESSIONADMIN               YES
XS_SH_READ                   YES
XS_SH_WRITE                  YES

9 rows selected.

sec_mgr@db12cr[sales]> -- now grant the read and write roles
sec_mgr@db12cr[sales]> -- to our SAU accounts
sec_mgr@db12cr[sales]> BEGIN
  2  SYS.XS_PRINCIPAL.GRANT_ROLES(
  3      grantee => 'ANTHONY'
  4    , role    => 'XS_SH_READ' );
  5  SYS.XS_PRINCIPAL.GRANT_ROLES(
  6      grantee => 'MARY'
  7    , role    => 'XS_SH_WRITE' );
  8  END;
  9  /

PL/SQL procedure successfully completed.
sec_mgr@db12cr[sales]> -- query the RAS dictionary views
sec_mgr@db12cr[sales]> -- to see these grants
sec_mgr@db12cr[sales]> SELECT grantee, granted_role
  2  FROM dba_xs_role_grants
  3  ORDER BY grantee, granted_role;

GRANTEE                      GRANTED_ROLE
---------------------------- ----------------------------
ANTHONY                      XSPUBLIC
ANTHONY                      XS_SH_READ
MARY                         XSPUBLIC
MARY                         XS_SH_WRITE
```

```
ORACLE11_USER              XSPUBLIC
SH_DIRECT                  XSPUBLIC

6 rows selected.
```

Figure 6-1 illustrates the relationship between Oracle RAS application roles and standard database roles, Oracle RAS application accounts and Oracle RAS ACLS.

In Figure 6-1, you can see that Oracle RAS roles XS_SH_READ and XS_SH_WRITE have been granted standard database roles, DB_SH_READ and DB_SH_WRITE, respectively. In order for Oracle RAS accounts such as ANTHONY and MARY to use the effective privileges of the standard database roles DB_SH_READ and DB_SH_WRITE, they must be granted the Oracle RAS roles XS_SH_READ or XS_SH_WRITE, because standard database roles cannot be granted to Oracle RAS accounts directly.

Role Management Procedures in Package XS_PRINCIPAL

The procedures XS_PRINCIPAL.CREATE_ROLE and XS_PRINCIPAL.GRANT_ROLE have parameters that allow you to set the start and end dates/times when the application role can be used to control application account usage. You can use the standard SQL command **DROP ROLE** to drop an application role; however, you must first use the procedure XS_PRINCIPAL.REVOKE_ROLES to revoke the application role from any application accounts or other application roles to which the application role is granted. The procedure XS_PRINCIPAL.ENABLE_ROLES_BY_DEFAULT is similar to the SQL command **ALTER USER DEFAULT ROLE** but it does not offer the same level of control over the roles enabled during database session establishment.

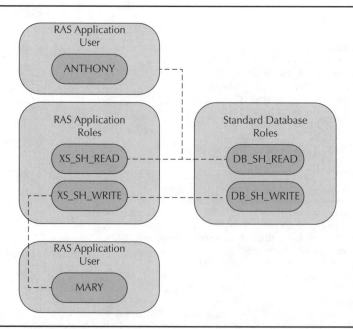

FIGURE 6-1. *Relationship of Oracle RAS application roles, application accounts, ACLs and standard database roles*

You can immediately migrate standard database accounts and even externally identified users to Oracle RAS application users, while maintaining your existing standard database roles. Then, when you have time, you can migrate from standard database roles to Oracle RAS ACLs and policies.

Oracle 12*c* RAS introduces a new role called *dynamic application role*. This type of role isn't granted to an application user or application role; instead, dynamic roles can be enabled by applications when attaching to RAS lightweight sessions, which we will describe later.

You will notice that our application user accounts (DLAU or SAU) were automatically granted the XSPUBLIC role, which is similar in intent as the PUBLIC role being automatically granted to standard database users. The difference between XSPUBLIC and PUBLIC is in the number of privileges available to XSPUBLIC. A quick review of the default Oracle RAS access control entries (ACE) view shows just two grants to Oracle RAS security classes. An ACE is the association of a privilege to a RAS principal such as an application user or role. ACEs can be assigned to RAS ACLs.

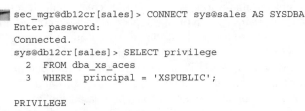

```
sec_mgr@db12cr[sales]> CONNECT sys@sales AS SYSDBA
Enter password:
Connected.
sys@db12cr[sales]> SELECT privilege
  2  FROM dba_xs_aces
  3  WHERE  principal = 'XSPUBLIC';

PRIVILEGE
--------------------
MODIFY_SESSION
ADMIN_NAMESPACE

2 rows selected.
```

The MODIFY_SESSION privilege allows the user to create, attach, and destroy Oracle RAS lightweight sessions. The MODIFY_SESSION privilege allows application users to set and get session context variables in the Oracle RAS lightweight session context. These are the minimum privileges required for lightweight session users with no access to read or write access to application data or ability to execute traditional PL/SQL routines. RAS sessions still inherit the numerous privileges exposed by the PUBLIC role but are limited by default with respect to objects protected by Oracle RAS policies.

Out-of-the-Box Roles in Oracle RAS

You will recall when we queried the view XS_ROLES that we saw a number of XS roles that we did not specifically grant to any accounts. Oracle provides three important roles for XS users:

- XSSESSIONADMIN is required to create and reattached to RAS lightweight sessions.
- XSNAMESPACEADMIN is required to manage RAS namespaces application context structures.
- XSCACHEADMIN is required to manage the caching of lightweight sessions in the middle tier.

In addition, XSDISPATCHER is a convenience role that has been granted XSSESSIONADMIN and XSNAMESPACEADMIN roles; however, as you will see later in this chapter, it is not advisable to grant XSDISPATCHER or XSNAMESPACEADMIN to Oracle RAS application accounts.

The XSPROVISIONER role has the privileges required to create database server-side event callbacks for lightweight sessions, which we will discuss shortly. The XSBYPASS role is a special role intended for bypassing ACLs and is disabled by default. You should strive to design applications without the need for this role.

At this point, we could introduce a set of PL/SQL-based examples that demonstrate the use of our DLAU and SAU application accounts and the application roles. However, the most frequent implementations of Oracle RAS use Java technology. Further, in order to demonstrate Oracle RAS application accounts and roles, we first need to introduce the topic of Oracle RAS lightweight sessions.

Lightweight Sessions in Oracle RAS

Oracle RAS provides a lightweight application session framework that can be used once a traditional database session has been established. Using this framework, you can quickly create multiple long-running application sessions, each of which contains its own private application session context and roles and privileges. This application session context is called a RAS namespace, and it is similar to a standard database session context. The RAS API to create application sessions is available in both PL/SQL and Java. We focus on the Java approach. The RAS APIs allow you to switch from one lightweight session, a process called *attaching*, to any other lightweight session, quickly and efficiently. If you consider this scenario of a web application running on a Java-based application server such as Oracle WebLogic Server, you could use the JSESSIONID HTTP cookie as the identifier for each lightweight session. Java guarantees the value to be unique across all HTTP sessions. In this scenario, Oracle RAS provides an efficient mechanism to change to or establish a database session quickly with both the appropriate end-user identity and session privileges for any database connection that supports the web application. Oracle RAS also provides both an application session cache component and an ACL cache component as part of its Java-based implementation to improve performance further.

Figure 6-2 depicts the relationship between Oracle RAS lightweight sessions in the application tier and standard database sessions in the database.

If we consider our web-based application server scenario, a named user such as MARY or ANTHONY accesses the web application using a desktop browser. Single sign-on (SSO) technologies such as Oracle Access Manager could be used to identify and authenticate each user. As a result of this I&A step, a standard HTTP-header attribute could be populated with the name of the user. We could then use the Oracle RAS Application Session Manager to create a lightweight application session for each user and assign a cookie for the session before the application uses or creates a database connection. The lightweight application session is automatically cached in the Oracle RAS Application Session Cache and a representative lightweight database session is also created on the database server. When the RAS Application Session Manager reattaches to a given session, such as one for ANTHONY, as depicted in Figure 6-2, Oracle RAS will automatically reestablish the session roles, privileges, and namespaces associated with that lightweight database session. For security reasons, it is important to use a separate database connection from the application, called a *dispatcher connection*, whose account has the XSSESSIONADMIN and XSCACHEADMIN roles. We do not want the connecting application to be able to directly modify the session cache or namespace values. We want to delegate this control to the dispatcher connection.

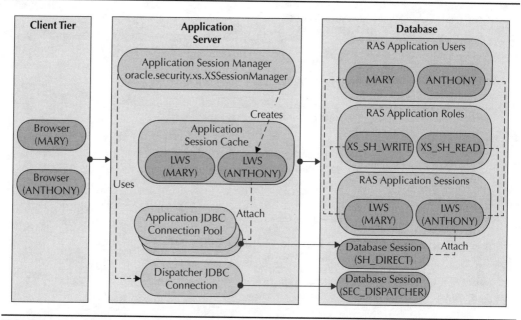

FIGURE 6-2. *Oracle RAS lightweight sessions in the application and database tiers*

Setting Privileges for Direct Login Application User Accounts

In order to create lightweight sessions on behalf of Oracle RAS application accounts, we need two DLAU accounts—one to serve as an application connection pool account and a second to serve as the RAS session manager. We will use the DLAU account SH_DIRECT as our application connection pool account. We will also create a new DLAU account named SEC_DISPATCHER to support the RAS session manager tasks and grant this account the database role; the XSDISPATCHER role. This account will manage RAS lightweight sessions, RAS namespaces, and the RAS middle-tier cache.

The following creates a manager account named SEC_DISPATCHER and grants the XSSESSIONADMIN and XSCACHEADMIN roles to the account.

```
sys@db12cr[sales]> CONNECT sec_mgr@sales
Enter password:
Connected.
sec_mgr@db12cr[sales]> -- create the DLAU manager account
sec_mgr@db12cr[sales]> BEGIN
  2       SYS.XS_PRINCIPAL.CREATE_USER(
  3              name=>'SEC_DISPATCHER'
  4            , schema=>'SEC_POL');
  5  END;
  6  /

PL/SQL procedure successfully completed.

sec_mgr@db12cr[sales]> -- set the password for the DLAU account
sec_mgr@db12cr[sales]> BEGIN
  2       SYS.XS_PRINCIPAL.SET_PASSWORD(
```

```
3                 user => 'SEC_DISPATCHER'
4               , password => 'welcome1'
5               , type => XS_PRINCIPAL.XS_SALTED_SHA1);
6  END;
7  /

PL/SQL procedure successfully completed.

sec_mgr@db12cr[sales]> -- grant roles for session
sec_mgr@db12cr[sales]> -- and cache administration
sec_mgr@db12cr[sales]> BEGIN
2      SYS.XS_PRINCIPAL.GRANT_ROLES(
3            grantee => 'SEC_DISPATCHER'
4          , role    => 'XSSESSIONADMIN' );
5  END;
6  /

PL/SQL procedure successfully completed.

sec_mgr@db12cr[sales]> BEGIN
2      SYS.XS_PRINCIPAL.GRANT_ROLES(
3            grantee => 'SEC_DISPATCHER'
4          , role    => 'XSCACHEADMIN' );
5  END;
6  /

PL/SQL procedure successfully completed.

sec_mgr@db12cr[sales]> -- verify the setup
sec_mgr@db12cr[sales]> SELECT grantee, granted_role
2  FROM dba_xs_role_grants
3  WHERE grantee = 'SEC_DISPATCHER'
4  ORDER BY grantee, granted_role;

GRANTEE                          GRANTED_ROLE
------------------------------   ------------------------------
SEC_DISPATCHER                   XSCACHEADMIN
SEC_DISPATCHER                   XSPUBLIC
SEC_DISPATCHER                   XSSESSIONADMIN

3 rows selected.
```

Note that the SEC_DISPATCHER account has no privileges on the objects in the SH schema and has not been granted the SH roles we created earlier. The SEC_DISPATCHER account can log in to the database and create lightweight sessions for MARY and ANTHONY. We use the SH_DIRECT DLAU for the application connection because this account has the ability to set SH-related roles. We will now demonstrate the capabilities of Oracle RAS using a Java-based approach.

Lightweight Session Management in Java

We first examine the Java class oracle.security.xs.XSSessionManager, which is the Oracle RAS Application Session Manager. The following key methods are found in this class:

■ **createSession** This method allows you to create a new Oracle RAS lightweight session in the context of a database connection using an application username, a cookie, and zero or more default namespace values.

- **attachSession** This method allows you to reattach to an existing Oracle RAS lightweight session within the context of a database connection using a session identifier or a cookie value. You can also assert the roles and namespace values that are active before a session is detached.

- **detachSession** This method detaches a currently attached Oracle RAS lightweight session from the database connection.

- **destroySession** This method destroys an Oracle RAS lightweight session by removing it from both the client session cache and the database server.

- **saveSession** This method saves the state (roles, namespace values, and so on) of an Oracle RAS lightweight session such that the next time the session is attached, the current state of the session is preserved.

NOTE
The XSSessionManager class is documented in detail at http://docs
.oracle.com/cd/E16655_01/security.121/e10480/oracle/security/xs/
XSSessionManager.html.

The XSSessionManager class operates on the Java object oracle.xs.Session within the Oracle RAS Java APIs. This class has methods that allow you to retrieve the session's username, cookies, enabled roles, and namespace values.

NOTE
The Session class is documented in detail at http://docs.oracle.com/
cd/E16655_01/security.121/e10480/oracle/security/xs/Session.html.

Let's now take a quick look at how we create, reattach, and destroy sessions using the RAS APIs. Refer to Chapter6/TestRASSession.java in the examples that accompany this book for a complete listing of this Java class.

The first step in the class is to create an instance of oracle.security.xs.XSSessionManager based on a connection to our DLAU dispatcher account SEC_DISPATCHER:

```
private XSSessionManager xsManager = null;
private Connection managerConnection = null;
...

// First, create a JDBC database connection to SEC_DISPATCHER
log.info("Connecting to " + url + " as SEC_DISPATCHER");
managerConnection =
    DriverManager.getConnection(url,"SEC_DISPATCHER",password);
...

// Second, create a RAS session manager using our dispatcher
// connection. The session manager controls
// lightweight session for our application connections.
// The second parameter specifies cache idle time in minutes
// and the third parameter specifies the max cache size in bytes.
xsManager = XSSessionManager.getSessionManager(
    managerConnection, 30, 8000000);
log.info("XSSessionManager created");
```

Next we use oracle.security.xs.Session to create two RAS lightweight sessions—one for MARY and one for ANTHONY—using a time-based cookie that is unique for executions of these examples. When used within a J2EE-based application server, we would use the JSESSIONID cookie maintained by the application server. The lightweight sessions are created using separate application-based connections that connect to the database using the DLAU account SH_DIRECT.

```
private final static String COOKIE_MARY =
    "MARY" + System.currentTimeMillis();
private final static String COOKIE_ANTHONY =
    "ANTHONY" + System.currentTimeMillis();
private Session sessionAnthony = null;
private Session sessionMary = null;
private Connection applicationConnection = null;
...

log.info("Connecting to " + url + " as SH_DIRECT");
applicationConnection =
    DriverManager.getConnection(url, "SH_DIRECT", password);
// Verify SH_DIRECT's default session roles
showSQLSelect("SELECT * FROM session_roles ORDER BY 1");
...
// Create lightweight sessions for MARY and ANTHONY
// providing a simple "cookie" that allows for "re-attaching" to
// a specific session later in the lifecycle
// of the Java application. The third parameter defines
// any namespaces values we want to set for the session.
// In our example we have no values so the parameter is null.
sessionMary = xsManager.createSession(applicationConnection,
    "MARY", COOKIE_MARY, null);
sessionAnthony = xsManager.createSession(applicationConnection,
    "ANTHONY", COOKIE_ANTHONY, null);
```

After the sessions are created, we can reattach to a lightweight session using XSSessionManager and the cookie defined for the session as follows:

```
// The null-ed parameters below allow you to
// enable or disable roles and update namespace values
log.info("Re-attaching to session with cookie: " + cookie);
Session lws = xsManager.attachSessionByCookie( applicationConnection,
    cookie, null, null, null, null, null);

// Display the enabled XS roles for the session
if (lws.getEnabledRoles() != null)
    for (Role role : lws.getEnabledRoles())
        log.info( "Application Roles enabled:" + role.getName());
// Verify that the application user roles took effect
showSQLSelect("SELECT * FROM session_roles ORDER BY 1");
// Demonstrate that the application user roles took effect
showSQLSelect("SELECT COUNT(*) SH_COUNT FROM sh.sales_history");
```

When we are done with the lightweight session, we must detach from it so that the connection is available for reattaching at a later time. When our application terminates, either normally or by exception, we must make sure to destroy all lightweight sessions in the same manner we would clean up JDBC ResultSet, Statement, or Connection objects. The following code snippets demonstrate these steps:

```
// We can now detach from the session as we are done using it.
log.info("Detaching from session for " + lws.getUser());
xsManager.detachSession(lws);
...

if ((xsManager != null) && (applicationConnection != null)) {
    // We should always destroy
    // lightweight sessions that are created, regardless
    // of whether an exception was generated or not.
    if (sessionMary != null) {
        log.info("Destroying session for MARY");
        xsManager.destroySession( applicationConnection,
        sessionMary);
    }
    if (sessionAnthony != null) {
        log.info("Destroying session for ANTHONY");
        xsManager.destroySession(applicationConnection,
            sessionAnthony);
    }
}
if (applicationConnection != null)
    applicationConnection.close();
if (managerConnection != null)
    managerConnection.close()

    // After the LSW sessions are closed then
// set the object to null for garbage cleanup
sessionAnthony = null;
    sessionMary = null;
```

We can run the example to see the program output as follows.

```
java -classpath ./xs.jar:./ojdbc6.jar:../classes ESBD.TestRASSession
"jdbc:oracle:thin:@nsgdc2:1521/sales" welcome1

Jan 30, 2014 3:04:09 PM ESBD.TestRASSession createSessionManager
INFO: Connecting to jdbc:oracle:thin:@nsgdc2:1521/sales as SEC_DISPATCHER
Jan 30, 2014 3:04:10 PM ESBD.TestRASSession showSQLSelect
INFO: Issuing SQL:SELECT * FROM session_roles ORDER BY 1
-------------------------------------------------
ROLE

no rows selected
Jan 30, 2014 3:04:12 PM ESBD.TestRASSession createSessionManager
INFO: Connecting to jdbc:oracle:thin:@nsgdc2:1521/sales as SH_DIRECT
Jan 30, 2014 3:04:14 PM ESBD.TestRASSession createSessionManager
INFO: XSSessionManager created
Jan 30, 2014 3:04:15 PM ESBD.TestRASSession createSessions
Jan 30, 2014 3:04:15 PM ESBD.TestRASSession showSession
INFO: Re-attaching to session with cookie: MARY1391115849335
Jan 30, 2014 3:04:15 PM ESBD.TestRASSession showSession
INFO: Application Roles enabled:XSPUBLIC
Jan 30, 2014 3:04:15 PM ESBD.TestRASSession showSession
```

```
INFO: Application Roles enabled:XS_SH_WRITE
Jan 30, 2014 3:04:15 PM ESBD.TestRASSession showSQLSelect
INFO: Issuing SQL:SELECT * FROM session_roles ORDER BY 1
-------------------------------------------------
ROLE
DB_SH_WRITE
1 rows selected.
-------------------------------------------------
Jan 30, 2014 3:04:16 PM ESBD.TestRASSession showSQLSelect
INFO: Issuing SQL:SELECT COUNT(*) SH_COUNT FROM sh.sales_history
-------------------------------------------------
SH_COUNT
7
1 rows selected.
-------------------------------------------------
Jan 30, 2014 3:04:16 PM ESBD.TestRASSession showSession
INFO: Detaching from session for MARY
Jan 30, 2014 3:04:16 PM ESBD.TestRASSession showSession
INFO: Re-attaching to session with cookie: ANTHONY1391115849335
Jan 30, 2014 3:04:16 PM ESBD.TestRASSession showSession
INFO: Application Roles enabled:XSPUBLIC
Jan 30, 2014 3:04:16 PM ESBD.TestRASSession showSession
INFO: Application Roles enabled:XS_SH_READ
Jan 30, 2014 3:04:16 PM ESBD.TestRASSession showSQLSelect
INFO: Issuing SQL:SELECT * FROM session_roles ORDER BY 1
-------------------------------------------------
ROLE
DB_SH_READ
1 rows selected.
-------------------------------------------------
Jan 30, 2014 3:04:16 PM ESBD.TestRASSession showSQLSelect
INFO: Issuing SQL:SELECT COUNT(*) SH_COUNT FROM sh.sales_history
-------------------------------------------------
SH_COUNT
7
1 rows selected.
-------------------------------------------------
Jan 30, 2014 3:04:16 PM ESBD.TestRASSession showSession
INFO: Detaching from session for ANTHONY
Jan 30, 2014 3:04:17 PM ESBD.TestRASSession runTest
INFO: Destroying session for MARY
Jan 30, 2014 3:04:17 PM ESBD.TestRASSession runTest
INFO: Destroying session for ANTHONY
```

Notice that once we attached to MARY's or ANTHONY's lightweight session, the authorized roles were appropriately enabled, DB_SH_WRITE or DB_SH_READ, respectively. Also notice that the DLAU (SH_DIRECT) account's roles were not enabled. The lightweight session will enable the DB_SH_% roles only while a RAS application session is active and attached.

Namespaces in Oracle RAS

An Oracle RAS namespace is conceptually analogous to a database session's application context that was presented in Chapter 5, except that the RAS namespace values apply to an individual lightweight session as opposed to the entire database session. Note that both session application contexts and global application contexts can be accessed from within an Oracle RAS lightweight session, so issuing the following SQL from within an attached session is valid:

```
SELECT SYS_CONTEXT('SALES_STATUS_CTX','SALES_STATUS') ,
    SYS_CONTEXT('USERENV','CON_NAME')
FROM DUAL;
```

There are two major differences between RAS namespaces and standard database namespaces. First, Oracle RAS must have all attributes defined ahead of time or defined by an account that has been granted the XS_NAMESPACE_ADMIN role. Standard database contexts can dynamically create attributes. Second, Oracle RAS offers a namespace value validation capability so you can enforce rules on the values.

Setting RAS Namespace Attribute Values from the Database Client

To demonstrate Oracle RAS namespaces, we must first grant SEC_MGR the ability to create RAS namespaces using the XS_NAMESPACE_ADMIN role. Note that this grant must be done using a database account with the SYSDBA privilege.

```
sys@db12cr[sales]> GRANT xs_namespace_admin TO sec_mgr;

Grant succeeded.
```

Next we extend our previous Java example and create a namespace to show how values can be set from both the client and the server:

```
sys@db12cr[sales]> CONNECT sec_mgr@sales
Enter password:
Connected.
sec_mgr@db12cr[sales]> -- create a namespace to hold
sec_mgr@db12cr[sales]> -- attributes about the Java client
sec_mgr@db12cr[sales]> BEGIN
  2   XS_NAMESPACE.CREATE_TEMPLATE (
  3    name => 'JAVA_CLIENT_CONTEXT');
  4   END;
  5   /

PL/SQL procedure successfully completed.

sec_mgr@db12cr[sales]> -- we track the version of Java
sec_mgr@db12cr[sales]> -- used by the client
sec_mgr@db12cr[sales]> BEGIN
  2   XS_NAMESPACE.ADD_ATTRIBUTES (
  3     template       => 'JAVA_CLIENT_CONTEXT'
  4     , attribute     => 'JAVA_VERSION'
  5     , default_value => '?');
  6   END;
  7   /

PL/SQL procedure successfully completed.

sec_mgr@db12cr[sales]> -- we add an attribute (SALES_STATUS) to
sec_mgr@db12cr[sales]> -- indicate the status of Sales: open or closed
sec_mgr@db12cr[sales]> -- from Chapter 5
```

```
sec_mgr@db12cr[sales]> BEGIN
  2   XS_NAMESPACE.ADD_ATTRIBUTES (
  3      template      => 'JAVA_CLIENT_CONTEXT'
  4      , attribute    => 'SALES_STATUS'
  5      , default_value => '?');
  6   END;
  7   /

PL/SQL procedure successfully completed.
```

Once the namespace and attribute have been defined, we can set the attribute's value when we create or attach to a lightweight session, as shown in the following code snippet:

```
private final static String MY_NAMESPACE = "JAVA_CLIENT_CONTEXT";
ArrayList<AttributeValue> attrList =
    new ArrayList<AttributeValue>();
// Set the namespace attribute's value to the value
// returned by getProperty call
attrList.add(new AttributeValue("JAVA_VERSION",
    System.getProperty("java.version")));
ArrayList<NamespaceValue> nsAttrList =
    new ArrayList<NamespaceValue>();
NamespaceValue nsValue = new NamespaceValue(MY_NAMESPACE, attrList);
nsAttrList.add(nsValue);
sessionMary = xsManager.createSession( applicationConnection
    , "MARY", COOKIE_MARY, nsAttrList);
```

Once the namespace values are set, we can subsequently access them from the lightweight session on the client, as shown in the following code snippet:

```
SessionNamespace ns = lws.getNamespace(MY_NAMESPACE);
if ( ns != null ) {
    if ( ns.getAttributes() != null ) {
        for ( SessionNamespaceAttribute nsAttr: ns.getAttributes() ) {
                log.info("attribute:" + nsAttr.toString());
        }
    } else {
            log.warning("Namespace attributes are null");
    }
}
```

The following output is displayed when we run the example:

```
Jan 30, 2014 4:08:54 PM ESBD.TestRASSession showSession
INFO: attribute:(JAVA_VERSION, 1.6.0_45, null)
```

The namespace values can also be retrieved on the server, as we will show later in the chapter. A word of caution is necessary at this point about accepting namespace values from a database client. These values should always be treated with caution, because these values can be set by the database client as desired. The use of these values in your security policies for Database Vault, VPD, or data redaction is not without risk. However, we can leverage the namespace validation capability in Oracle RAS to enforce rules on the values that are set.

Validating Namespace Attribute Values on the Database Server

To validate namespace attribute values on the database server, we must first create a PL/SQL package that performs the validation. In the following example, the PL/SQL validation routine in the SEC_POL schema will check that the JAVA_VERSION attribute value in the JAVA_CLIENT_CONTEXT namespace is either version 1.6 or version 1.7:

```
sec_mgr@db12cr[sales]> CONNECT sec_pol@sales
Enter password:
Connected.
sec_pol@db12cr[sales]> -- create a RAS namespace (ns) handler
sec_pol@db12cr[sales]> CREATE OR REPLACE PACKAGE ras_ns_handler AS
  2    FUNCTION handle_ns_event (
  3                      sessionID IN RAW
  4                    , namespace IN VARCHAR2
  5                    , attribute IN VARCHAR2
  6                    , oldValue  IN VARCHAR2
  7                    , newValue  IN VARCHAR2
  8                    , eventCode IN PLS_INTEGER)
  9                    RETURN PLS_INTEGER;
 10    END;
 11  /

Package created.

sec_pol@db12cr[sales]> CREATE OR REPLACE PACKAGE BODY
  2    ras_ns_handler AS
  3    FUNCTION handle_ns_event (
  4                      sessionID IN RAW
  5                    , namespace IN VARCHAR2
  6                    , attribute IN VARCHAR2
  7                    , oldValue  IN VARCHAR2
  8                    , newValue  IN VARCHAR2
  9                    , eventCode IN PLS_INTEGER)
 10                    RETURN PLS_INTEGER IS
 11    BEGIN
 12         -- Return if the attribute is being read
 13         IF eventCode =
 14             DBMS_XS_SESSIONS.ATTRIBUTE_FIRST_READ_EVENT THEN
 15           RETURN
 16             DBMS_XS_SESSIONS.EVENT_HANDLING_SUCCEEDED;
 17         ELSIF eventCode =
 18           DBMS_XS_SESSIONS.MODIFY_ATTRIBUTE_EVENT THEN
 19             -- Validate the value for JAVA_VERSION when
 20             -- it is being modified
 21           IF namespace = 'JAVA_CLIENT_CONTEXT'
 22           AND attribute = 'JAVA_VERSION' THEN
 23               IF newValue IS NULL OR
 24                 SUBSTR(newValue,1,3) NOT IN ('1.6','1.7')
 25               THEN
 26                 RETURN DBMS_XS_SESSIONS.EVENT_HANDLING_FAILED;
 27               END IF;
 28             END IF;
 29           RETURN
 30             DBMS_XS_SESSIONS.EVENT_HANDLING_SUCCEEDED;
 31         ELSE
 32           RETURN
```

```
33                    DBMS_XS_SESSIONS.EVENT_HANDLING_SUCCEEDED;
34            END IF;
35    END;
36  END;
37  /
```

Package body created.

We must now use the SEC_MGR account that has the XS_NAMESPACE_ADMIN role to re-create our namespace template JAVA_CLIENT_CONTEXT. The namespace template must be re-created to configure Oracle RAS to notify our handler with updates to attributes values in the namespace. The following code shows how to re-create the context:

```
sec_pol@db12cr[sales]> CONNECT sec_mgr@sales
Enter password:
Connected.
sec_mgr@db12cr[sales]> -- Delete the existing namespace.
sec_mgr@db12cr[sales]> BEGIN
  2    XS_NAMESPACE.DELETE_TEMPLATE (
  3      template       => 'JAVA_CLIENT_CONTEXT'
  4    , delete_option => XS_ADMIN_UTIL.DEFAULT_OPTION);
  5    END;
  6  /

PL/SQL procedure successfully completed.

sec_mgr@db12cr[sales]> -- Re-create the namespace to hold
sec_mgr@db12cr[sales]> -- attributes about Java clients,
sec_mgr@db12cr[sales]> -- adding our validation handler
sec_mgr@db12cr[sales]> -- for JAVA_VERSION
sec_mgr@db12cr[sales]>
sec_mgr@db12cr[sales]> DECLARE
  2      attrList XS$NS_ATTRIBUTE_LIST := XS$NS_ATTRIBUTE_LIST();
  3  BEGIN
  4      attrList.EXTEND(2);
  5      -- Register the JAVA_VERSION attribute
  6      -- as being in need of validation.
  7      attrList(1) := XS$NS_ATTRIBUTE(
  8        name             => 'JAVA_VERSION'
  9      , default_value   => '?'
 10      , attribute_events => XS_NAMESPACE.UPDATE_EVENT);
 11
 12      -- Register the SALES_STATUS attribute
 13      -- as being in need of validation.
 14      attrList(2) := XS$NS_ATTRIBUTE(
 15        name             => 'SALES_STATUS'
 16      , default_value   => '?'
 17      , attribute_events => XS_NAMESPACE.UPDATE_EVENT);
 18
 19      -- Re-create our namespace template
 20      XS_NAMESPACE.CREATE_TEMPLATE (
 21        name       => 'JAVA_CLIENT_CONTEXT'
 22      , attr_list => attrList
 23      , schema     => 'SEC_POL'
 24      , package   => 'ras_ns_handler'
 25      , function   => 'handle_ns_event'
```

```
26      , acl        => 'SYS.NS_UNRESTRICTED_ACL');
27  END;
28  /
```

PL/SQL procedure successfully completed.

In this example, we used the XS$NS_ATTRIBUTE object type to indicate that we want to be alerted on any updates (XS_NAMESPACE.UPDATE_EVENT) to the two attributes in our namespace template. You will notice that some additional parameters are used in the call to XS_NAMEPSPACE .CREATE_TEMPLATE to identify the namespace validation package owner, package name, and function. Finally, note that each namespace template can have an associated ACL to control the permissible operations. By default, the predefined ACL SYS.NS_UNRESTRICTED_ACL is assigned to namespace templates. As the name indicates, this ACL allows unrestricted operations on the namespaces created from the template. In practice, you will want to create ACLs on namespace templates that restrict the ability to modify the values of namespace attributes. We will demonstrate this technique later in this chapter.

Now that our server-side namespace validation is in place, we change our TestRASSesion.java example code to pass a hard-coded value of 1.5 for JAVA_VERSION:

```
private final static String MY_NAMESPACE = "JAVA_CLIENT_CONTEXT";
ArrayList<AttributeValue> attrList =
    new ArrayList<AttributeValue>();
// Comment out the old code that sets the value to 1.6
// attrList.add(new AttributeValue("JAVA_VERSION",
//    System.getProperty("java.version")));

// Add code to set JAVA_VERSION to the invalid value of 1.5
attrList.add(new AttributeValue("JAVA_VERSION","1.5"));
ArrayList<NamespaceValue> nsAttrList =
    new ArrayList<NamespaceValue>();
NamespaceValue nsValue = new NamespaceValue(MY_NAMESPACE, attrList);
nsAttrList.add(nsValue);
sessionMary = xsManager.createSession( applicationConnection
    , "MARY", COOKIE_MARY, nsAttrList);
```

When we run this example code, we find that the namespace value from the client does not generate an exception; instead, the value is not accepted and is set to null:

```
Jan 31, 2014 11:09:24 AM ESBD.TestRASSession showSession
INFO: attribute:(JAVA_VERSION, null, null,  MODIFY)
```

Server-Side Event Handling and Namespaces in Oracle RAS

In the last section we described how to define Oracle RAS namespace attributes and use them from lightweight sessions on the client. The next natural question is, how do we get or set these namespace attribute values from the database server? The answer lies in the DBMS_XS_SESSIONS PL/SQL package with the procedures GET_ATTRIBUTE and SET_ATTRIBUTE. The package also has a procedure ADD_GLOBAL_CALLBACK to register PL/SQL-based callback handlers that are called in response to lightweight session events that are fired as part of the lightweight session lifecycle. These events include create session, attach session, detach session, destroy session, enable/disable role, and DLAU account login. The DBMS_XS_SESSIONS package also has procedures DELETE_GLOBAL_CALLBACK, DISABLE_GLOBAL_CALLBACK, and ENABLE_GLOBAL_CALLBACK to delete, disable, and enable callback handlers.

Defining the Lightweight Session Event Handler in PL/SQL

To demonstrate the DBMS_XS_SESSIONS package capabilities, we first create a simple table and procedure in the SEC_POL schema to log the lightweight session events as they occur and to log the namespace attribute values:

```
sec_mgr@db12cr[sales]> CONNECT sec_pol@sales
Enter password:
Connected.
sec_pol@db12cr[sales]> CREATE TABLE ras_events (
  2              event_date DATE DEFAULT SYSDATE NOT NULL
  3            , event_data VARCHAR2(4000) NOT NULL
  4  ) TABLESPACE SALES;

Table created.
```

Next we create a package that will be used as the event callback handler for the lightweight session events, log attribute values, and set server-side namespace values.

```
sec_pol@db12cr[sales]> -- create a package to call when session events occur
sec_pol@db12cr[sales]> CREATE OR replace PACKAGE ras_event_handler AS
  2      PROCEDURE create_session(
  3        sess_id    IN VARCHAR2,
  4        username   IN VARCHAR2,
  5        event_code IN VARCHAR2);
  6      PROCEDURE attach_session(
  7        sess_id    IN VARCHAR2,
  8        event_code IN VARCHAR2);
  9  END;
 10  /

Package created.

sec_pol@db12cr[sales]> CREATE OR REPLACE PACKAGE BODY ras_event_handler AS
  2      PROCEDURE log_event(message IN VARCHAR2)
  3      IS
  4        PRAGMA AUTONOMOUS_TRANSACTION;
  5      BEGIN
  6         INSERT INTO ras_events(event_data)
  7         VALUES( message);
  8         COMMIT;
  9      END;
 10      PROCEDURE create_session( sess_id    IN VARCHAR2,
 11                                username   IN VARCHAR2,
 12                                event_code IN VARCHAR2) IS
 13        l_cookie VARCHAR2(1024);
 14      BEGIN
 15         DBMS_XS_SESSIONS.GET_ATTRIBUTE('XS$SESSION'
 16                , 'COOKIE', l_cookie);
 17         log_event ('ras_event_handler.create_session, session:'
 18                || sess_id
 19                || ',code:'   || event_code
 20                || ',user:'   || username
 21                || ',cookie:' || l_cookie
 22                );
 23      EXCEPTION
 24          WHEN OTHERS THEN
```

```
25         log_event ('ras_event_handler.attach_session'
26                 || ' error:'     || sqlerrm
27                 || ', session:'  || sess_id
28                 || ',code:'      || event_code
29                 || ',user:'      || username
30                 || ',db user:'   ||
31                              SYS_CONTEXT('USERENV','SESSION_USER')
32                 || ',cookie:'    || l_cookie
33                 );
34     END;
35     PROCEDURE attach_session(sess_id    IN VARCHAR2,
36                            event_code IN VARCHAR2) IS
37       l_user    VARCHAR2(1024);
38       l_cookie VARCHAR2(1024);
39       l_java    VARCHAR2(1024);
40     BEGIN
41         -- we grab the default namespace attribute values
42         -- exposed by RAS
43         DBMS_XS_SESSIONS.GET_ATTRIBUTE('XS$SESSION', 'USERNAME'
44                   , l_user);
45         DBMS_XS_SESSIONS.GET_ATTRIBUTE('XS$SESSION', 'COOKIE'
46                   , l_cookie);
47         -- we grab the Java version set by the client
48         DBMS_XS_SESSIONS.GET_ATTRIBUTE('JAVA_CLIENT_CONTEXT'
49                   , 'JAVA_VERSION', l_java);
50         -- we set the status of the Sales
51         -- status using the value from the database session context
52         -- from our example in Chapter 5
53         DBMS_XS_SESSIONS.SET_ATTRIBUTE('JAVA_CLIENT_CONTEXT'
54                 , 'SALES_STATUS'
55                     , SYS_CONTEXT('SALES_STATUS_CTX','SALES_STATUS'));
56         log_event ('ras_event_handler.attach_session, session:'
57                 || sess_id
58                 || ',code:'    || event_code
59                 || ',user:'    || l_user
60                 || ',cookie:' || l_cookie
61                 || ',java:'    || l_java
62                 );
63     EXCEPTION
64         WHEN OTHERS THEN
65         log_event ('ras_event_handler.attach_session'
66                 || ' error:'     || sqlerrm
67                 || ', session:'  || sess_id
68                 || ',code:'      || event_code
69                 || ',user:'      || l_user
70                 || ',db user:'   ||
71                              SYS_CONTEXT('USERENV','SESSION_USER')
72                 || ',cookie:'    || l_cookie
73                 || ',java:'      || l_java
74                 );
75     END;
76 END;
77 /
```

Package body created.

Configuring Session Event Handler Callbacks

Finally we use the procedure ADD_GLOBAL_CALLBACK to associate the handler package created in the SEC_POL schema to all create session and attach session events. To perform this association, we must first grant SEC_MGR the PROVISIONER role using an account with SYSDBA privilege:

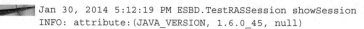

```
sec_pol@db12cr[sales]> CONNECT sys@sales as sysdba
Enter password:
Connected.
sys@db12cr[sales]> GRANT provisioner TO sec_mgr;

Grant succeeded.

sys@db12cr[sales]> CONNECT sec_mgr@sales
Enter password:
Connected.
sec_mgr@db12cr[sales]> BEGIN
  2    DBMS_XS_SESSIONS.ADD_GLOBAL_CALLBACK(
  3      event_type            => DBMS_XS_SESSIONS.CREATE_SESSION_EVENT
  4     ,callback_schema     => 'SEC_POL'
  5     ,callback_package    => 'RAS_EVENT_HANDLER'
  6     ,callback_procedure  => 'CREATE_SESSION');
  7  END;
  8  /

PL/SQL procedure successfully completed.

sec_mgr@db12cr[sales]> BEGIN
  2    DBMS_XS_SESSIONS.ADD_GLOBAL_CALLBACK(
  3      event_type            => DBMS_XS_SESSIONS.ATTACH_SESSION_EVENT
  4     ,callback_schema     => 'SEC_POL'
  5     ,callback_package    => 'RAS_EVENT_HANDLER'
  6     ,callback_procedure  => 'ATTACH_SESSION');
  7  END;
  8  /

PL/SQL procedure successfully completed.

sec_mgr@db12cr[sales]> -- Set the Sales cycle status to OPEN
sec_mgr@db12cr[sales]> CONNECT sh@sales
Enter password:
Connected.
sh@db12cr[sales]> BEGIN
  2      sales_status_pkg.set_status (
  3          sales_status_pkg.OPEN );
  4  END;
  5  /

PL/SQL procedure successfully completed.
```

Once the callback handler is in place, we can re-execute our Java application and observe the value returned from the call to Session.getNamespace (JAVA_CLIENT_CONTEXT) and the value returned from getting the SALES_STATUS attribute, which was set in the server-side database handler listed previously.

```
Jan 30, 2014 5:12:19 PM ESBD.TestRASSession showSession
INFO: attribute:(JAVA_VERSION, 1.6.0_45, null)
```

```
Jan 30, 2014 5:12:19 PM ESBD.TestRASSession showSession
INFO: attribute:(SALES_STATUS, OPEN, null)
```

If we query the SEC_POL.RAS_EVENTS table, we find the following entries that demonstrate that we can access namespace values set in our lightweight session from the database server. One of the important things to notice is that some namespace attributes (for example, the Oracle RAS cookie or the custom Java version attribute) are not available on the database server for the create session event but do become available in the first session attach event.

```
sh@db12cr[sales]> CONNECT sec_pol@sales
Enter password:
Connected.
sec_pol@db12cr[sales]> SELECT event_data
  2   FROM ras_events
  3   ORDER BY event_date;

EVENT_DATA
-------------------------------------------------------------------------
ras_event_handler.create_session, session:F1390D5EB75A2FFCE043EB42920AB763,code:0,user:M
ARY,cookie:
ras_event_handler.create_session, session:F1390D5EB75B2FFCE043EB42920AB763,code:0,user:A
NTHONY,cookie
:
ras_event_handler.attach_session, session:F1390D5EB75A2FFCE043EB42920AB763,code:0,user:M
ARY,cookie:MARY1391123812911,java:1.6.0_45

ras_event_handler.attach_session, session:F1390D5EB75B2FFCE043EB42920AB763,code:0,user:A
NTHONY,cookie:ANTHONY1391123812911,java:1.6.0_45


4 rows selected.
```

This example begs the question, How do we prevent database clients from changing a namespace attribute value set on the database server? Previously we discussed the ability to set an ACL on the namespace template, but unfortunately the ACEs apply only to a principal, such as an application user or an application role. Oracle RAS does not offer the ability to create an ACE based on the context of the operation being performed. However, if we revisit our namespace validation handler package SEC_POL.RAS_NS_HANDLER, we can easily prevent a client from setting a namespace value by determining whether the value is set from the appropriate Oracle RAS session event callback handler. We modify SEC_POL.RAS_NS_HANDLER to determine if the session event callback handler SEC_POL.RAS_EVENT_HANDLER exists in the PL/SQL call stack using the Oracle Database's DBMS_UTILITY.FORMAT_CALL_STACK function. If SEC_POL.RAS_EVENT_HANDLER exists in the call stack, then the namespace value is being set from the server; if it does not exist, then the value is being set by the client.

The following example code demonstrates this approach:

```
sec_pol@db12cr[sales]> CREATE OR REPLACE PACKAGE BODY
  2   ras_ns_handler AS
  3   FUNCTION handle_ns_event (
  4                   sessionID IN RAW
  5              , namespace IN VARCHAR2
  6              , attribute IN VARCHAR2
```

```
 7                        , oldValue   IN VARCHAR2
 8                        , newValue   IN VARCHAR2
 9                        , eventCode IN PLS_INTEGER)
10                        RETURN PLS_INTEGER IS
11     BEGIN
12         IF eventCode =
13                 DBMS_XS_SESSIONS.ATTRIBUTE_FIRST_READ_EVENT THEN
14            RETURN
15                 DBMS_XS_SESSIONS.EVENT_HANDLING_SUCCEEDED;
16         ELSIF eventCode =
17           DBMS_XS_SESSIONS.MODIFY_ATTRIBUTE_EVENT THEN
18             -- Validate the java version when
19                -- it being modified
20            IF namespace = 'JAVA_CLIENT_CONTEXT'
21            AND attribute = 'JAVA_VERSION' THEN
22                IF newValue IS NULL OR
23                  SUBSTR(newValue,1,2) NOT IN ('1.6','1.7')
24                THEN
25                  RETURN DBMS_XS_SESSIONS.EVENT_HANDLING_FAILED;
26                END IF;
27              -- Validate the Sales Status is being
28              -- set from the appropriate PL/SQL package
29            ELSIF namespace = 'JAVA_CLIENT_CONTEXT'
30            AND attribute = 'SALES_STATUS' THEN
31                -- INSTR returns 0 if the string is not found
32                IF INSTR(DBMS_UTILITY.FORMAT_CALL_STACK
33                    ,'package body SEC_POL.RAS_EVENT_HANDLER') < 1
34                THEN
35                    -- The SEC_POL.RAS_EVENT_HANDLER was not found
36                    RAISE_APPLICATION_ERROR(
37                       -20002,'An error has occurred.');
38                END IF;
39            END IF;
40            RETURN
41                 DBMS_XS_SESSIONS.EVENT_HANDLING_SUCCEEDED;
42         ELSE
43            RETURN
44             DBMS_XS_SESSIONS.EVENT_HANDLING_SUCCEEDED;
45         END IF;
46     END;
47  END;
48  /

Package body created.
```

We modify our TestRASSession.java code to attempt to modify the now protected namespace value. As shown next, the system generates an error, because the client is trying to change the value—that is, the client is not using the authorized event handler to modify the namespace value.

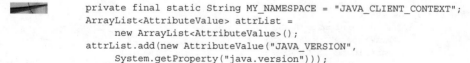

```
private final static String MY_NAMESPACE = "JAVA_CLIENT_CONTEXT";
ArrayList<AttributeValue> attrList =
    new ArrayList<AttributeValue>();
attrList.add(new AttributeValue("JAVA_VERSION",
    System.getProperty("java.version")));
```

```
attrList.add(new AttributeValue("SALES_STATUS", "CLOSED"));
ArrayList<NamespaceValue> nsAttrList =
    new ArrayList<NamespaceValue>();
NamespaceValue nsValue = new NamespaceValue(MY_NAMESPACE, attrList);
nsAttrList.add(nsValue);
sessionMary = xsManager.createSession( applicationConnection
    , "MARY", COOKIE_MARY, nsAttrList);
```

Here we can see the exception being generated from the RAS_NS_HANDLER (client event callback) when we run the example program. This verifies that we can adequately protect namespace values that are set on the database server.

```
oracle.security.xs.XSException: java.sql.SQLException: ORA-46071: Error occurred in
event handler "SEC_POL"."RAS_NS_HANDLER"."HANDLE_NS_EVENT"
ORA-20002: An error has occurred.
ORA-06512: at "SEC_POL.RAS_NS_HANDLER", line 34
ORA-06512: at line 1
        at oracle.security.xs.internal.XSSessionManagerImpl.createSessionInternal(
    XSSessionManagerImpl.java:392)
        at oracle.security.xs.internal.XSSessionManagerImpl.createSession(
    XSSessionManagerImpl.java:472)
```

Session Performance in Oracle RAS

The examples we have shown so far demonstrate that Oracle RAS is similar to the Oracle Proxy Authentication feature we presented in Chapter 3. Both technologies assert an application user's identity for the purpose of identity preservation to the database. The Oracle Database Security team designed and built Oracle RAS as an improvement to the proxy authentication model with consideration for application sessions context, fine-grained access control, end-user auditing, and performance. These requirements came from the Oracle Fusion Applications product teams. Consider the processing characteristics of Oracle Fusion Applications, where hundreds or thousands of end users must use business applications to access database objects through connection pools. With so many users sharing the same connection pool resource, any improvements in session switching and context initialization on behalf of an end user would be of great benefit to Oracle Fusion Applications.

Let's examine these performance improvements using some slight modifications to the Java-based example we created for proxy authentication in Chapter 3 and the example for Oracle RAS presented earlier. Refer to Chapter6/TestProxyAuthRAS.java and Chapter6/TestRASPerformance .java in the examples that accompany this book for a complete listing of these two Java classes. First let's modify the proxy authentication example to loop through the process of getting a proxied connection and then closing the proxied connection inside of a loop. The core part of this code is shown in the following listing:

```
// Set up proxy authentication properties for Wendy
java.util.Properties userNameProp = new java.util.Properties();
userNameProp.setProperty(
        OracleOCIConnectionPool.PROXY_USER_NAME
        ,"wendy");
// Loop a finite number of
// times and get a proxied connection
// then close the connection inside the loop
long startTime = System.currentTimeMillis();
for ( int i = 0; i < count; i++ ) {
    Connection connWendy = ods.getProxyConnection(
```

```
    OracleOCIConnectionPool.PROXYTYPE_USER_NAME
      , userNameProp);
    connWendy.close();
}
long endTime = System.currentTimeMillis();
System.out.println("Proxy Authentication stats for count:"
                + count
                + ",seconds:" + ((endTime-startTime)/1000L) );
```

If we run this example with a loop count of 100, we find it takes 35 seconds to perform 100 iterations of getting the proxied connection and then closing the proxied connection, even after we disabled the AFTER LOGON trigger we created in the last chapter.

Now let's modify our Oracle RAS example to perform a session attach and detach operation within a loop, as shown in the following code listing:

```
// Here we can use XSSessionManager to look up a
// session by its associated cookie value.
// We loop for a finite number and
// attach and detach the session inside the loop.
long startTime = System.currentTimeMillis();
for ( int i = 0 ; i < count ; i++ ) {
    Session lws =
          xsManager.attachSessionByCookie(
                    applicationConnection
                        , cookie, null, null, null, null);
    if (lws != null) {
          xsManager.detachSession(lws);
    }
} // for
long endTime = System.currentTimeMillis();
log.info("Re-attaching stats for count:"
            + count + ",seconds:"
            + ((endTime-startTime)/1000L));
```

If we run this example with a loop count of 100, we find it takes 14 seconds to perform 100 iterations of a session attach and detach operation. That is an improvement in session switching of around 60 percent, which is quite an improvement for applications that leverage the connection pool model.

Privilege Management and Data Security in Oracle RAS

Oracle RAS includes support for creating a fine-grained access control model for SQL DML (SELECT, INSERT, UPDATE, and DELETE) against database tables and views. This model is based on two core components:

- **Access control lists** ACLS are a set of application privileges associated to an Oracle RAS application role or application user (principal) that govern what actions can be performed on an associated set of elements. The set of associated elements are called access control entries (ACEs). ACLs are "scoped" by a component called a security class for strong typing. ACLs and Security classes support inheritance.

- **Data security policies** DSPs are row-level and column-level access constraint policies that can be applied to database tables or views. Row-level constraints are parameterized SQL expressions that can be based on table data or namespace values. Row-level constraints are known as *data realms* and they are authorized by ACLs. DSPs can also include privilege-based restrictions on column-level access, where the privilege name is user-defined and the authorization is resolved via ACLs from the associated user-defined privilege. DSPs are an extension of the Oracle Virtual Private Database feature and DSPs leverage the materialized views performance feature.

The objects involved in the access control model are depicted in Figure 6-3.

Let's examine each of these concepts and demonstrate Oracle RAS fine-grained access controls using our Sales History data model. In order to help you better understand the concepts of DSP and ACL, we first lay out the requirements of a notional (theoretical) scenario. First, let's take a look at the table SH.SALES_HISTORY:

```
sec_mgr@db12cr[sales]> CONNECT sh@sales
Enter password:
Connected.
sh@db12cr[sales]> SELECT product, quantity, total_cost
  2  FROM sales_history
  3  ORDER by product;
```

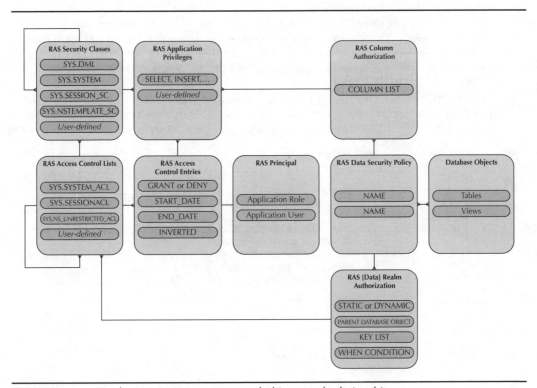

FIGURE 6-3. *Oracle RAS DML access control objects and relationships*

```
PRODUCT          QUANTITY TOTAL_COST
--------------- ---------- ----------
Cell Phone              2        300
LCD TV                  7       3500
LCD TV                 23      12500
Plasma TV               7      12000
Speakers                4        521
Stereo                  1        100
Walkman                 5        250

7 rows selected.
```

In our notional scenario, we want to allow principals (MARY) who have the XS_SH_WRITE role to be able to read and update all data rows and all columns in this table. For principals (ANTHONY) who have the XS_SH_READ role, we want to restrict them from reading any records where the product is LCD TV or Plasma TV, and we want to prevent them from viewing the TOTAL_COST column. Now that the scenario has been laid out, let's discuss the ACLs that are required to support this scenario.

Security Classes, Application Privileges, and ACLs

ACLs are constructed using a set of primitives called access control entries (ACEs) that grant (or deny) a privilege to an Oracle RAS principal (application user or application role). Application privileges are fundamentally different from database object privileges, such as SELECT, because application privileges don't convey the SQL operator-to-database object mapping. Rather, application privileges control the use of the database object privilege. Considering our example for access to the SALES_HISTORY table, we still need the standard database roles DB_SH_READ and DB_SH_WRITE granted to our two Oracle RAS application roles XS_SH_READ and XS_SH_WRITE.

Configuring Security Classes

The first step in constructing the ACLs required for our scenario is to define a custom security class that will be used to group and scope the privileges. The procedure XS_SECURITY_CLASS. CREATE_SECURITY_CLASS is used to create a security class, as shown in the following example:

```
sh@db12cr[sales]> CONNECT sec_mgr@sales
Enter password:
Connected.
sec_mgr@db12cr[sales]> -- Create a security class to group ACLs
sec_mgr@db12cr[sales]> -- related to Sales History
sec_mgr@db12cr[sales]> BEGIN
  2         XS_SECURITY_CLASS.CREATE_SECURITY_CLASS(
  3                 name => 'SH_SECURITY_CLASS'
  4                 , parent_list => XS$NAME_LIST('SYS.DML')
  5                 , priv_list => XS$PRIVILEGE_LIST(
  6                 XS$PRIVILEGE('ACCESS_TOTAL_COST')
  7                 )
  8                 );
  9  END;
 10  /

PL/SQL procedure successfully completed.
```

In this example, we define a security class named SH_SECURITY_CLASS that inherits privileges (names) from a security class named SYS.DML that is provided with Oracle RAS. SYS.DML contains four privileges: SELECT, INSERT, UPDATE, and DELETE. What's interesting in the example is that we've defined a security class that inherits from another security class. In the future, we could easily define a new security class that inherits from SH_SECURITY_CLASS.

```
parent_list => XS$NAME_LIST('SH_SECURITY_CLASS')
```

In our security class example, we have defined a custom privilege named ACCESS_TOTAL_COST that will be used to support our scenario's requirement to restrict access to the SH.SALES_HISTORY.TOTAL_COST column.

Configuring ACEs and ACLs

Next we define a set of ACEs that contain the grant (or deny) privileges to a principal along with time constraints around when the ACEs are in effect. ACEs are constructed using the object type SYS.XS$ACE_TYPE, whose constructor is shown here:

```
FINAL CONSTRUCTOR FUNCTION XS$ACE_TYPE RETURNS SELF AS RESULT
 Argument Name                Type                      In/Out Default?
 ---------------------------- ------------------------- ------ --------
 PRIVILEGE_LIST               XS$NAME_LIST              IN
 GRANTED                      BOOLEAN                   IN     DEFAULT
 INVERTED                     BOOLEAN                   IN     DEFAULT
 PRINCIPAL_NAME               VARCHAR2                  IN
 PRINCIPAL_TYPE               PLS_INTEGER               IN     DEFAULT
 START_DATE                   TIMESTAMP WITH TIME ZONE  IN     DEFAULT
 END_DATE                     TIMESTAMP WITH TIME ZONE  IN     DEFAULT
```

The PRIVILEGE_LIST parameter in the constructor contains a list of privilege names (SELECT, UPDATE, and so on) for which the ACE applies, or the parameter contains custom-defined privilege names such as the ACCESS_TOTAL_COST privilege in our example. The GRANTED parameter is a BOOLEAN data type, which can be set to TRUE or FALSE for grant or deny respectively. The PRINCIPAL_NAME parameter defines the user or role that is being granted or denied the ability to use the privileges defined by the PRIVILEGE_LIST parameter. The INVERTED parameter is a handy mechanism to meet conditions where you grant access to all principals except for the one specified in the PRINCIPAL_NAME parameter. ACEs also have a temporal aspect as to when they are in effect, by using the START_DATE and END_DATE parameters.

Once the ACEs have been defined, you can begin creating ACLs and associating them with one or more security classes. The following example demonstrates this process for our notional scenario:

```
sec_mgr@db12cr[sales]> -- Create our ACLs
sec_mgr@db12cr[sales]> DECLARE
  2         l_access_control_entries XS$ACE_LIST := XS$ACE_LIST();
  3  BEGIN
  4         l_access_control_entries.EXTEND(1);
  5         -- Create an access control entry (ACE) for
  6         -- the XS_SH_WRITE application role
  7         -- to perform SELECT, UPDATE
  8         -- and view on the TOTAL_COST column.
  9         l_access_control_entries(1) := XS$ACE_TYPE(
 10               privilege_list => XS$NAME_LIST( 'SELECT'
 11                          ,'UPDATE','ACCESS_TOTAL_COST')
 12              , principal_name => 'XS_SH_WRITE'
```

```
13                          );
14              -- Create an ACL with this ACE and associate
15              -- the ACL to the SH security class.
16              XS_ACL.CREATE_ACL(
17                      name     => 'ACL_SH_WRITE'
18                      , ace_list => l_access_control_entries
19                      , sec_class => 'SH_SECURITY_CLASS'
20                      );
21
22              -- Create an access control entry (ACE) for
23              -- the XS_SH_READ application role
24              -- to perform SELECT.
25              l_access_control_entries(1) := XS$ACE_TYPE(
26                      privilege_list => XS$NAME_LIST('SELECT')
27                      , principal_name => 'XS_SH_READ'
28                      );
29
30              -- Create an ACL with this ACE and associate
31              -- the ACL to the SH security class.
32              XS_ACL.CREATE_ACL(
33                      name     => 'ACL_SH_READ'
34                      , ace_list => l_access_control_entries
35                      , sec_class => 'SH_SECURITY_CLASS'
36                      );
37      END;
38      /

PL/SQL procedure successfully completed.
```

In this example, we first created an ACE list, l_access_control_entries, that grants the privileges SELECT, UPDATE, and ACCESS_TOTAL_COST to the principal XS_SH_WRITE, which is the Oracle RAS application role granted to the application user MARY. Oracle RAS defines a special privilege named ALL that denotes all privileges that are defined for a security class.

We then created an ACL named ACL_SH_WRITE that associates the ACE list to the security class SH_SECURITY_CLASS using the XS_ACL.CREATE_ACL procedure. Note that the XS_ACL .CREATE_ACL procedure also has a parameter named PARENT that allows you to inherit ACEs from another ACL. There is also a parameter named INHERIT_MODE that allows you to specify that the ACL inheritance extends from or is constrained by the inheritance based on the conditions of the session—for example, the active principal. The firewall example in Chapter 4 of the *Oracle RAS Developer's Guide* is enlightening on a constrained condition. In that example, if you access an application outside of the corporate firewall, you would be operating as a less-privileged principal, but if you access the application inside of the corporate firewall, you would be operating as a more privileged principal. Oracle RAS allows a set of ACE objects to be shared among ACLs.

Finally, we created an ACE list that grants the privilege SELECT to the principal XS_SH_READ, which is the Oracle RAS application role we granted to the application user ANTHONY. We then created an ACL named ACL_SH_READ that associates the ACE list to the security class SH_ SECURITY_CLASS using the XS_ACL.CREATE_ACL procedure.

Now that we have our ACLs defined, we can define the data security policies that leverage these ACLs. The data security policies provide the row-level and column-level access controls we need for our notional scenario.

Data Security Policies

To provide row-level security in our data security policies, we must first define RAS objects called *data realms*. A data realm is a filter-like SQL expression (that is, the WHERE clause from a SELECT statement) that filters records and is active when the associated ACL is active. To define a data realm, we use the object type XS$REALM_CONSTRAINT_TYPE to associate filter expressions to ACLs. In our notional scenario, we want to associate the filter expression 1=1 to the ACL ACL_SH_WRITE and the filter expression, product NOT IN ('LCD TV', 'Plasma TV'), to the ACL ACL_SH_READ.

You can use Oracle's built-in SQL functions, references to session or global application context values, and references to PL/SQL functions in your filter expressions. For example, suppose we have a PL/SQL function, defined as follows, that returns the numeric value 1 if a product is a TV:

```
CREATE OR REPLACE FUNCTION sh.is_tv ( product VARCHAR2 ) RETURN NUMBER;
```

We can easily incorporate this function and a global application context value in a filter, as shown in the following example:

```
l_realms(2) := XS$REALM_CONSTRAINT_TYPE(
        realm => 'SYS_CONTEXT (''sales_status_ctx''
        , ''sales_status'') = ''OPEN'' AND (sh.is_tv(product) = 0)'
        , acl_list => XS$NAME_LIST('ACL_SH_READ')
        );
```

In Chapter 5, we discussed the performance of view filters based on PL/SQL functions compared to filters based on Oracle SQL built-in functions or application context values. The same performance considerations should be applied to data realm filters. If you can set up the appropriate namespace values and application context values, and use these and Oracle SQL built-in functions in your filters, you will improve the overall performance of RAS-protected table access.

To provide column-level security, we use the object type XS$COLUMN_CONSTRAINT_TYPE to associate a list of columns with a privilege. To support our scenario's restriction of allowing the XS_SH_WRITE application role to view only the TOTAL_COST column, we use the object type to associate the TOTAL_COST column to our custom ACCESS_TOTAL_COST privilege that we grant to the XS_SH_WRITE principal during the creation of the ACL ACL_SH_WRITE.

Once the data realms and column constraints have been defined, we use the XS_DATA_SECURITY.CREATE_POLICY PL/SQL procedure to associate the constraints to a named policy. The following code listing shows how we construct these two constraints for our notional scenario to create a policy that leverages them:

```
sec_mgr@db12cr[sales]> DECLARE
  2             l_realms XS$REALM_CONSTRAINT_LIST
  3                   := XS$REALM_CONSTRAINT_LIST();
  4             l_columns XS$COLUMN_CONSTRAINT_LIST
  5                   := XS$COLUMN_CONSTRAINT_LIST();
  6   BEGIN
  7             l_realms.EXTEND(2);
  8             -- Create a data realm for the ACL ACL_SH_WRITE
  9             -- which is associated to the XS_SH_WRITE
 10             -- application role to see all rows
 11             -- in the Sales History.
 12             l_realms(1) := XS$REALM_CONSTRAINT_TYPE(
 13                     realm    => '1 = 1'
```

```
14                         , acl_list => XS$NAME_LIST('ACL_SH_WRITE')
15                         );
16                  -- Create a data realm for the ACL ACL_SH_READ
17                  -- which is associated to the XS_SH_READ
18                  -- application role to only see
19                  -- Sales History rows where the
20                  -- products are not TVs.
21                  l_realms(2) := XS$REALM_CONSTRAINT_TYPE(
22                         realm => 'product NOT IN (''LCD TV'',''Plasma TV'')'
23                         , acl_list => XS$NAME_LIST('ACL_SH_READ')
24                         );
25
26                  -- Create a constraint on the TOTAL_COST
27                  -- column based on the ACCESS_TOTAL_COST privilege.
28                  l_columns.extend(1);
29                  l_columns(1) := XS$COLUMN_CONSTRAINT_TYPE(
30                         column_list => XS$LIST('TOTAL_COST')
31                         , privilege   => 'ACCESS_TOTAL_COST'
32                         );
33            XS_DATA_SECURITY.CREATE_POLICY(
34                   name                  => 'SH_DATA_SECURITY_POLICY'
35                 , realm_constraint_list => l_realms
36                 , column_constraint_list => l_columns
37                 );
38  END;
39  /
```

PL/SQL procedure successfully completed.

Static and Dynamic Data Realms

The XS$REALM_CONSTRAINT_TYPE object type's constructor includes a parameter IS_STATIC that allows you to control the overall evaluation performance of the policy based on the update profile of the tables being protected. Oracle RAS leverages Oracle materialized views to bind the rows in these base tables with the ACLs that protect them. If your base tables are updated frequently, you will want to set the IS_STATIC parameter to FALSE (which is the default). If the tables being protected are not updated, set the parameter to TRUE, which will dramatically increase the performance for queries against the protected tables.

Parameterized Data Realms

Data realm filter expressions can be parameterized to support multiple use cases. If you consider our notional scenario, we could have defined a data realm that was specific to one product, with separate ACLs required for each product. For this type of use case, we could define a data realm without an associated ACL:

```
XS$REALM_CONSTRAINT_TYPE(
  realm => 'product = &PRODUCT)'
);
```

We then call the XS_DATA_SECURITY.CREATE_ACL_PARAMETER procedure with the following parameters:

```
XS_DATA_SECURITY.CREATE_ACL_PARAMETER(
  policy => 'SH_DATA_SECURITY_POLICY'
```

```
, parameter => PRODUCT,
, param_type => XS_ACL.TYPE_VARCHAR
);
```

Finally, we use the XS_ACL.ADD_ACL_PARAMETER to create ACLs for each product and identify specific values as follows:

```
XS_ACL.ADD_ACL_PARAMETER(
      acl        => 'XS_SH_WRITE_PLASMA_TV'
    , policy     => 'SH_DATA_SECURITY_POLICY'
    , parameter => 'PRODUCT'
    , value      => 'Plasma TV');
XS_ACL.ADD_ACL_PARAMETER(
      acl        => 'XS_SH_WRITE_LCD_TV'
    , policy     => 'SH_DATA_SECURITY_POLICY'
    , parameter => 'PRODUCT'
    , value      => 'LCD TV');
```

Parameterized data realms offer the flexibility to meet your access control requirements without your having to maintain multiple policies that are only slightly different in structure.

Master-Detail Relationships

Anyone who has used Oracle VPD or Oracle Label Security knows that modeling row-level access control can be cumbersome the first time you have to configure policies for tables that are involved in a master-detail relationship. Data realms have a feature that supports this scenario. If a principal is authorized to view the master table's record, then the user is authorized to see all of the detail records. For example, the EMP_ID column of SH.SALES_HISTORY is a foreign key to the EMPLOYEE_ID column in the HR.EMPLOYEES table. We could use a different constructor for the XS$REALM_CONSTRAINT_TYPE to define a policy on SH.SALES_HISTORY as shown in the following example:

```
XS$REALM_CONSTRAINT_TYPE(
        parent_schema  => 'HR'
      , parent_object  => 'EMPLOYEES'
      , key_list       =>
            XS$KEY_LIST(
                 XS$KEY_TYPE(
                   primary_key => 'EMPLOYEE_ID'
                 , foreign_key => 'EMP_ID'
                 , foreign_key_type => 1
                 )
            )
      , when_condition => 'SALES_DATE > (SYSDATE - 365)');
```

The XS$KEY_TYPE constructor's foreign_key_type parameter has two valid values: 1 or 2. A value of 1 indicates that the foreign_key parameter is a column name. A value of 2 indicates that the foreign_key parameter is a column value. The second option allows you to specify specific row(s) in the detail table that you are authorizing through the master-detail relationship.

The XS$KEY_LIST constructor accepts a list of XS$KEY_TYPE object types, so you have the control to define a set of authorized EMP_ID records by creating multiple XS$KEY_TYPE objects. Note that this constructor includes an optional WHEN_CONDITION parameter, which allows you to define a WHERE clause filter to further restrict the visibility of rows in the detail table. In this example, we are allowing only SALES_HISTORY detail records for the past year.

Applying Data Security Policies

Once your DSP is in place, you must use the XS_DATA_SECURITY.APPLY_OBJECT_POLICY procedure to activate the DSP. The following listing demonstrates this step:

```
sec_mgr@db12cr[sales]> -- Activate the data security policy we just
sec_mgr@db12cr[sales]> -- created on the SALES_HISTORY table
sec_mgr@db12cr[sales]> BEGIN
  2          XS_DATA_SECURITY.APPLY_OBJECT_POLICY(
  3            policy => 'SH_DATA_SECURITY_POLICY'
  4          , schema => 'SH'
  5          , object =>'SALES_HISTORY'
  6          );
  7  END;
  8  /
PL/SQL procedure successfully completed.
```

The XS_DATA_SECURITY.APPLY_OBJECT_POLICY procedure includes a parameter named OWNER_BYPASS that allows the object owner to bypass the policy's access controls. This parameter is FALSE by default. You can also use the STATEMENT_TYPES parameter to define separate policies for SELECT, INSERT, UPDATE, and DELETE, or some combination thereof, to meet complex requirements, where one must be able to UPDATE rows yet still preserve column-level restrictions on SELECT. The REMOVE_OBJECT_POLICY procedure can be used to remove the policy from the table; the DISABLE_OBJECT_POLICY can be used to disable a policy; and the ENABLE_OBJECT_POLICY procedure can be used to re-enable a disabled table policy.

Validating Data Security Policies

After you have applied your policies, you should run the XS_DIAG.VALIDATE_WORKSPACE procedure to ensure that there are no configuration errors in your policies:

```
sec_mgr@db12cr[sales]> SET SERVEROUTPUT ON;
sec_mgr@db12cr[sales]> BEGIN
  2      IF (XS_DIAG.VALIDATE_WORKSPACE()) THEN
  3          DBMS_OUTPUT.PUT_LINE('All configurations are correct.');
  4      ELSE
  5          DBMS_OUTPUT.PUT_LINE('Some configurations are incorrect.');
  6      END IF;
  7  END;
  8  /
All configurations are correct.
```

There are no issues in this example; however, during the course of writing up this example, I mistyped the ACCESS_TOTAL_COST privilege and the validation code reported that I had an incorrect configuration. To determine the problem area, I had to issue the following SELECT statement:

```
sec_mgr@db12cr[sales]> SELECT *
  2  FROM xs$validation_table
  3  ORDER BY 1, 2, 3, 4;
CODE
DESCRIPTION
```

```
-------------------------------------------------------------------OBJECT
------------------------------------------------------------------------
NOTE
------------------------------------------------------------------------
    -1002
Reference does not exist
[Data Security "SEC_MGR"."SH_DATA_SECURITY_POLICY"]-->[Privilege "SYS"."XACCESS_TOTAL_COST"]
```

Testing Data Security Policies

We are now ready to test our ACLs and the DSP on the SH.SALES_HISTORY table. We use a slightly modified version of our example Java programs. Refer to Chapter6/TestRASACL.java in the examples that accompany this book for a complete listing of the two Java programs. The program performs a SQL query **SELECT product,quantity,total_cost FROM SH.sales_history**. As you can see in the next listing, the application user MARY, who has the XS_SH_WRITE application role, can view all seven records and can view the TOTAL_COST column. The application user ANTHONY, who has the XS_SH_READ role, can view only four records (no TV!) and cannot see the TOTAL_COST column.

```
INFO: Re-attached to session with cookie: MARY1391153255518, user is MARY
Jan 31, 2014 1:27:39 AM ESBD.TestRASACL showSession
INFO: Application Roles enabled:XSPUBLIC
Jan 31, 2014 1:27:39 AM ESBD.TestRASACL showSession
INFO: Application Roles enabled:XS_SH_WRITE
Jan 31, 2014 1:27:39 AM ESBD.TestRASACL showSQLSelect
INFO: Issuing SQL:SELECT product,quantity,total_cost FROM SH.sales_history
--------------------------------------------------
PRODUCT      QUANTITY     SH_COUNT
Stereo       1            100
Walkman      5            250
LCD TV       23           12500
Plasma TV    7            12000
Cell Phone   2            300
LCD TV       7            3500
Speakers     4            521
7 rows selected.
--------------------------------------------------
...
INFO: Re-attached to session with cookie: ANTHONY1391153255518, user is ANTHONY
Jan 31, 2014 1:27:39 AM ESBD.TestRASACL showSession
INFO: Application Roles enabled:XSPUBLIC
Jan 31, 2014 1:27:39 AM ESBD.TestRASACL showSession
INFO: Application Roles enabled:XS_SH_READ
Jan 31, 2014 1:27:39 AM ESBD.TestRASACL showSQLSelect
INFO: Issuing SQL:SELECT product,quantity,total_cost FROM SG.sales_history
--------------------------------------------------
PRODUCT      QUANTITY     SH_COUNT
Stereo       1            null
Walkman      5            null
Cell Phone   2            null
Speakers     4            null
4 rows selected.
--------------------------------------------------
Jan 31, 2014 1:27:39 AM ESBD.TestRASACL showSession
INFO: Detaching from session for ANTHONY
```

Protecting Namespaces with ACLs

As we mentioned earlier, ACLs can and should be used to protect namespaces, particularly if you consider supporting more than one application or organization in a multitenant database. You will recall that we created two variations of a custom namespace template named JAVA_CLIENT_ CONTEXT. In the second form, we pointed out that namespace was essentially unprotected by having the ACL SYS.NS_UNRESTRICTED_ACL associated to it. We now want to demonstrate the steps of how we can protect this namespace with an ACL.

We will first create a new security class for purpose of protecting the namespace, and we also have to declare the two privileges that the ACL will use: MODIFY_NAMESPACE and MODIFY_ ATTRIBUTE.

```
sec_mgr@db12cr[sales]> BEGIN
  2     XS_SECURITY_CLASS.CREATE_SECURITY_CLASS(
  3            name => 'SH_NAMESPACE_CLASS'
  4          , parent_list => NULL
  5          , priv_list => XS$PRIVILEGE_LIST(
  6                           XS$PRIVILEGE('MODIFY_NAMESPACE')
  7                         , XS$PRIVILEGE('MODIFY_ATTRIBUTE')
  8                         )
  9           );
 10     END;
 11     /

PL/SQL procedure successfully completed.
```

Next we create an ACL that grants the DLAU account SEC_DISPATCHER and standard database account SEC_POL the privileges required to perform all namespace usages we have demonstrated so far.

```
sec_mgr@db12cr[sales]> DECLARE
  2     l_access_control_entries XS$ACE_LIST;
  3   BEGIN
  4     -- First create an ACE to allow the SEC_DISPATCHER
  5     -- to create session namespaces and
  6     -- to modify namespace attributes.
  7     -- We also allow a standard database account
  8     -- SEC_POL to set attributes like SALES_STATUS.
  9     l_access_control_entries := XS$ACE_LIST(
 10          XS$ACE_TYPE(
 11                 privilege_list => XS$NAME_LIST('MODIFY_NAMESPACE')
 12               , principal_name => 'SEC_DISPATCHER' )
 13          ,
 14          XS$ACE_TYPE(
 15                 privilege_list => XS$NAME_LIST('MODIFY_ATTRIBUTE')
 16               , principal_name => 'SEC_DISPATCHER' )
 17          ,
 18          XS$ACE_TYPE(
 19                 privilege_list => XS$NAME_LIST('MODIFY_ATTRIBUTE')
 20               , principal_name => 'SEC_POL'
 21               , principal_type => XS_ACL.PTYPE_DB )
 22
 23          );
 24     -- Next create an ACL with this ACE
```

```
25     -- associated to in the database defined
26     -- security class SH_NAMESPACE_CLASS.
27     -- Note the ACL must be prefixed with SYS
28     -- to be used in the namespace template.
29     XS_ACL.CREATE_ACL(
30                 name => 'SYS.ACL_JAVA_NAMESPACE'
31               , ace_list => l_access_control_entries
32               , sec_class => 'SH_NAMESPACE_CLASS'
33               );
34   END;
35   /

PL/SQL procedure successfully completed.
```

Finally we re-create the namespace template using the newly created ACL:

```
sec_mgr@db12cr[sales]> DECLARE
  2       attrList XS$NS_ATTRIBUTE_LIST
  3                   := XS$NS_ATTRIBUTE_LIST();
  4   BEGIN
  5       attrList.EXTEND(2);
  6           -- Register the JAVA_VERSION attribute
  7           -- as being in need of validation.
  8       attrList(1) := XS$NS_ATTRIBUTE(
  9                 name=>'JAVA_VERSION'
 10               , default_value=> '?'
 11               , attribute_events=>
 12                       XS_NAMESPACE.UPDATE_EVENT
 13               );
 14
 15           -- Register the SALES_STATUS attribute
 16           -- as being in need of validation.
 17       attrList(2) := XS$NS_ATTRIBUTE(
 18                 name=>'SALES_STATUS'
 19               , default_value=> '?'
 20               , attribute_events=>
 21                       XS_NAMESPACE.UPDATE_EVENT
 22               );
 23           -- Re-create our namespace template
 24       XS_NAMESPACE.CREATE_TEMPLATE (
 25                 name       => 'JAVA_CLIENT_CONTEXT'
 26               , attr_list => attrList
 27               , schema    => 'SEC_POL'
 28               , package   => 'ras_ns_handler'
 29               , function  => 'handle_ns_event'
 30               , acl       => 'SYS.ACL_JAVA_NAMESPACE'
 31               );
 32   END;
 33   /

PL/SQL procedure successfully completed.
```

At this point, you can run the TestRASSession.java or the TestRASACL.java example code to verify that it still works. You can create a new dispatcher account in the same way we created SEC_DISPATCHER, granting the account XSSESSIONADMIN and XSCACHEADMIN. If you change the example Java programs to use this new dispatcher account, these examples will fail on createSession() invocation with the following error.

```
oracle.security.xs.XSException: java.sql.SQLException: ORA-46070: insufficient privileges
```

If you were to grant the new dispatcher account the XSDISPATCHER or XSNAMESPACEADMIN roles, you will find the examples allow the new account to make changes to the namespace. The lesson learned here is that you do not want to grant the XSDISPATCHER or XSNAMESPACEADMIN roles to any DLAU accounts or standard database accounts used for connection pools or XSSessionManager operations. Always protect namespaces with ACLs.

Auditing in Oracle RAS

One of the most important aspects of database security is auditing. Auditing has traditionally been used to record who performed what actions on which objects with the context of when and where those actions took place. In today's computing world, "auditing" is also a term used in the process of proving regulatory compliance for legal reasons. Software-based auditing is a key technology enabler for meeting regulatory compliance requirements. Auditing is also a key technology in understanding and defending against cyber security attacks that can result in data loss or a compromised system.

The Oracle Database Security development team has made great strides in Oracle Database 12*c* in creating a unified audit trail. Doing so allows you to correlate database activity from all of the security-related feature sets of the product. The team has also created a dynamic auditing policy feature that allows you to fine-tune audit policies to capture audit events with a great deal of precision. In the process of creating these audit capabilities, the team was careful not only to account for Oracle RAS but to create very well thought out default audit policies for Oracle RAS. Chapter 12 is dedicated to auditing in Oracle Database 12*c*, but here we'll mention a few aspects of this topic as they relate to Oracle RAS.

Default Audit Policies for Oracle RAS

Oracle RAS comes with two unified audit policies:

- **ORA_RAS_POLICY_MGMT** This audit policy audits all Oracle RAS configuration operations that a RAS administrator performs, such as managing application users, DLAU account passwords, application roles, namespace templates, session event callbacks, security classes, ACLs, and data security policies.

- **ORA_RAS_SESSION_MGMT** This audit policy audits all Oracle RAS session lifecycle events such as create, destroy, role enablement, setting namespace attributes, and so on.

As you can see, these two audit policies are comprehensive and can be used as a starting point for defining your audit policies. They address the typical event types we need to audit in our implementations, such as session management, account management, role management, privilege management, and generally any security-related configuration. For more information on RAS auditing, review Chapter 22 in the *Oracle Database Security Guide 12c Release* to understand other events available for auditing.

You may find that some audit events, such as setting namespace attributes or session attachments, generate too many events. You can tune or filter out the audit events by trial and observation. You should also verify that you are auditing the use of the standard AUDIT and NOAUDIT statements to capture the event where someone tries to modify or disable your Oracle RAS audit policies.

You can enabled these policies for specific accounts in your applications. For our example scenario, the following **AUDIT** command enables auditing of activities performed by the SEC_MGR account:

```
sec_mgr@db12cr[sales]> AUDIT POLICY ora_ras_policy_mgmt BY sec_mgr;

Audit succeeded.
```

For session-based auditing, we recommend enabling the ORA_RAS_SESSION_MGMT policy for all potential database sessions as follows:

```
sec_mgr@db12cr[sales]> AUDIT POLICY ora_ras_session_mgmt;

Audit succeeded.
```

Reporting on Audit Events and Audit Policies in RAS

As we mentioned, the Oracle unified audit trail includes coverage for Oracle RAS audit events. The database view UNIFIED_AUDIT_TRAIL includes several columns prefixed with "XS_" that are related to Oracle RAS. You can correlate audit events that occur within Oracle RAS with audit events that occur within other security areas of Oracle Database 12c, such as standard Oracle Database auditing, Database Vault, and fine-grained auditing.

Oracle RAS also includes a database view named DBA_XS_AUDIT_TRAIL that focuses on audit events specifically related to Oracle RAS policy configuration activity. The database view DBA_XS_AUDIT_POLICY_OPTIONS lists the specifics of audit policies that were created for Oracle RAS using the **CREATE AUDIT POLICY** command with the XS component type. The view DBA_XS_ENB_AUDIT_POLICIES lists the Oracle RAS audit policies that are enabled for individual accounts.

Validating Policies and Tracing in Oracle RAS

Oracle RAS includes a number of facilities for troubleshooting issues you might encounter during your application development.

Validating Policy Components

Earlier in this chapter we demonstrated the use of the XS_DIAG PL/SQL package to validate our data security policy. The package determined whether our policy contained erroneous configuration data. This package also contains functions to validate ACLs (VALIDATE_ACL), namespace templates (VALIDATE_NAMESPACE_TEMPLATE), principals (VALIDATE_PRINCIPAL), and security classes (VALIDATE_SECURITY_CLASS). If you find yourself wondering why some of your RAS configuration is not working as expected, make sure to validate your configuration using the XS_DIAG package. Using this package will save you considerable time troubleshooting your code.

Tracing Sessions and Data Security Policies

You can trace your Oracle RAS lightweight sessions and data security policies using the standard Oracle Database session and system SET EVENTS feature. To enable RAS session tracing from SQL*Plus, issue the following commands:

```
ALTER SESSION SET EVENTS 'TRACE[XSXDS] disk=high';
ALTER SESSION SET EVENTS 'TRACE[XSVPD] disk=high';
ALTER SESSION SET EVENTS 'TRACE[XSSESSION)] disk=high';
```

To enable system-level tracing for your Java programs, issue the following commands:

```
ALTER SYSTEM SET EVENTS 'TRACE[XSXDS] disk=high';
ALTER SYSTEM SET EVENTS 'TRACE[XSVPD] disk=high';
ALTER SYSTEM SET EVENTS 'TRACE[XSSESSION] disk=high';
```

Once tracing is enabled, you can view the trace files in the user dump (for ALTER SESSION) or system dump (for ALTER SYSTEM) directory.

The session-based trace files (XSSESSION) will show information about all DLAU and SAU accounts that create standard or lightweight sessions in the database. This information includes session cookies, namespace values, and roles, as shown in the following listing:

```
kzxs_createSession():
1 : username = SH_DIRECT
    sessionID = F160E05B615F6B98E043EB42920AF458
2 : userID = 2147493728
    userGUID = 00000000000000000000000000000000
    CreateTime = 01-FEB-14 10.33.15.115 PM +00:00
    AccessTime = 01-FEB-14 10.33.15.115 PM +00:00
    AuthenticationTime = 01-FEB-14 10.33.15.115 PM +00:00
2.1 : scversionID = 257
    scinstanceID = 1
4 :   cookie = (null)
kzxs_attach():
1 : username = SH_DIRECT
    sessionID = F160E05B615F6B98E043EB42920AF458
2 : All Enabled Roles
        Role UID = 2147484637, Role Name = XSPUBLIC, Role Flag = 1
2 : Explicitly Enabled Roles
2 : Explicitly Disabled Roles
3 : Application Namespace with Attribute Values
4 : Security Context
        scversionID = 258
        scinstanceID = 1


*** 2014-02-01 17:33:15.485
kzxsidpKeyHashGetKey: DB Instance id: 1
kzxsidpKeyHashGetKey: MT Dispatcher id: F160E057F02E6B96E043EB42920AA4E9
kzxs_set_nsattrvalues():
2 : Namespace = JAVA_CLIENT_CONTEXT; Attribute = JAVA_VERSION; Old-Value = ?; New-Value
= 1.6.0_45CC2C13C72C5801D1FC012A946E6A37C074745CE09FAE55F818A36344AUTH_PROGRAM_NM
kzxs_createSession():
1 : username = MARY
    sessionID = F160E05B61606B98E043EB42920AF458
2 : userID = 2147493908
    userGUID = 00000000000000000000000000000000
```

```
    CreateTime = 01-FEB-14 10.33.15.488 PM +00:00
    AccessTime = 01-FEB-14 10.33.15.488 PM +00:00
    AuthenticationTime = 01-FEB-14 10.33.15.488 PM +00:00
2.1 : scversionID = 259
    scinstanceID = 1
4 :   cookie = MARY1391294924198
```

The trace files that show details on data security policy events (XSXDS and XSVPD) include information about the data tables involved, the security policy involved, and how the SQL was transformed from its original form to its final form after merging all data realm WHERE expressions and ACLs. An example portion of one DSP trace file is shown next:

```
Logon user      : XS$NULL
Table/View      : SH.SALES_HISTORY
VPD Policy name      : SH_DATA_SECURITY_POLICY
Triton Policy Name : SH
Triton Policy Owner : SEC_MGR
RLS view :
SELECT   "PRODUCT","SALES_DATE","QUANTITY",DECODE (ADC76A9BC5F2624D7_4,1,ADC76A9BC
5F2624D74,NULL) "TOTAL_COST","DEPT_ID","COMMISSION","EMP_ID", ADC76A9BC5F2624D74,
ADC76A9BC5F2624D7_4 FROM "SH"."SALES_HISTORY"    "SALES_HISTORY"

...

XDS - Privilege Name = ACCESS_TOTAL_COST, ID = 2147494509
XDS - Virtual column for ORA_GET_ACLIDS(SALES_HISTORY) = ACL_F297B390F2979980
Privilege List =
 'ACCESS_TOTAL_COST'
2147494509
...

-- XDS merged privileges --
 -2147483647
XDS cursor loading of the Triton policy:
XDS enabled object = SH.SALES_HISTORY
XDS Static ACL rewrite:
XDS USER SPECIFIC rewrite =
SELECT   "PRODUCT","SALES_DATE","QUANTITY","TOTAL_COST","DEPT_ID","COMMISSION","EMP_
ID", (select '0000000080002A6E' from dual where sys_filter_acls('0000000080002A
6E',2147494509) is not null and (1 = 1))||(select '0000000080002A72' from dual where
sys_filter_acls('0000000080002A72',2147494509) is not null and (product NOT IN ('LCD
TV','Plasma TV')))||(select SYS_XSID_TO_RAW(2147483664) from dual) ACL_F297B390F2979980
FROM "SH"."SALES_HISTORY"    "SALES_HISTORY" WHERE ((((1 = 1)))
```

When you have completed your tracing, make sure to disable tracing using one of the following command sets:

```
ALTER SESSION SET EVENTS 'TRACE[XSXDS] off';
ALTER SESSION SET EVENTS 'TRACE[XSVPD] off';
ALTER SESSION SET EVENTS 'TRACE[XSSESSION] off';
-- OR
ALTER SYSTEM SET EVENTS 'TRACE[XSXDS] off';
ALTER SYSTEM SET EVENTS 'TRACE[XSVPD] off';
ALTER SYSTEM SET EVENTS 'TRACE[XSSESSION] off';
```

Summary

In this chapter, we presented a series of detailed examples that exercised the new Oracle Real Application Security feature in Oracle Database 12c. Oracle RAS can be used to provide comprehensive and declarative security policies that can be shared among all enterprise applications in your organization.

Oracle RAS enables you to define application users and application roles as a basis for building a lightweight database session model. This lightweight database session model is similar to Oracle Proxy Authentication, yet as we have demonstrated, Oracle RAS performs context switching of user sessions much faster. Oracle RAS also has integrated capabilities for the resolution of application roles and privileges within this lightweight session model. The lightweight session model also provides a namespace that is similar to the standard Oracle session application context, yet Oracle RAS supports validation of attribute values and provides ACL-based security to protect namespace access.

Oracle RAS also introduces a new declarative fine-grained access control model for DML against database table and views. This model also supports row-level and column-level filtering. This access control model is based on static or dynamic SQL expressions that can leverage business data or business rules. This security model enforces the use of database object privileges using ACLs that are tied to the Oracle RAS application users and roles.

Oracle RAS has been fully incorporated into the Oracle unified auditing capabilities that were added to Oracle Database 12c. Oracle RAS offers very well-designed and comprehensive audit policies out of the box. Oracle RAS is also integrated into the standard Oracle diagnostic event tracing subsystem, making it easy to troubleshoot and correct issues with your Oracle RAS policies.

If you are building new applications for Oracle Database 12c that require connection pooling in the middle-tier and row-level or column-level access controls, we recommend that you leverage Oracle RAS versus the traditional security approach of using Oracle Proxy Authentication, application context, and Oracle VPD. In the next chapter we will demonstrate how to use Oracle VPD to provide row-level or column-level access controls for database versions prior to Oracle Database 12c.

PART
II

Advanced
Database Security

CHAPTER
7

Controlled Data Access
with Virtual Private
Database

A s we indicated in the last chapter, Oracle Real Application Security (RAS) with its support for access control entries (ACEs) and access control lists (ACLs) is the most current and feature-rich method of controlling access to data in Oracle Database. The value of using a declarative security model versus writing custom security code should be apparent from reading Chapter 6. However, if you are using a version of Oracle Database prior to 12*c* (11*g*, 10*g*, 9*i*, or 8*i*), then it is important that you have a working understanding of the fundamental security framework provided by Oracle Virtual Private Database (VPD). As explained in Chapter 6, VPD is the foundation of RAS data realms and policy enforcement.

Introduction to Virtual Private Database

VPD is a database security feature that is implemented using Oracle's Row-Level Security (RLS) package DBMS_RLS. The feature restricts rows or columns of data from objects accessible via SQL SELECT or DML statements. The restriction is based on security criteria defined in a *policy function*, PL/SQL code that you write to enforce your security policy. It contains the programming logic that implements your rules for governing access to data (row or column) in a table.

The scope of VPD in Oracle Database 12*c* is limited to the current database. If you are in the root container and create a VPD policy, only objects in the root container are affected. If you are in a pluggable database and create a VPD policy, only objects within the pluggable database are affected. You cannot create a single policy in the root container that can be enforced in all the pluggable databases.

How VPD Works

VPD works by registering a table (or schema) with a policy function and the type of SQL statement VPD will protect. You typically create VPD policies for SELECT statements, but VPD also supports INSERT, UPDATE, DELETE, and INDEX SQL statements. VPD does not support DDL statements (except CREATE INDEX) because, in general, DDL statements do not read or write data in protected tables. After a table is registered or is "under policy control," when a SQL statement is issued against the table, Oracle executes the associated policy function. The policy function returns a VARCHAR2 predicate that is more or less appended to the original SQL statement's WHERE clause in the case of SELECT, UPDATE, and DELETE statements. VPD also enables you to configure INSERT statements to honor the filter condition. We describe in detail later in the chapter how Oracle handles INSERT statements against a VPD-controlled table.

You should understand that Oracle does not parse and execute the original query and then filter the results during the fetch phase of SQL statement processing. The three broad phases of SQL statement processing are parse, execute, and fetch. Oracle executes the policy function, modifies the original query, parses the modified query, executes the modified query, and returns the results. The policy execution happens during the parse phase and, as you will see later in this chapter, the policy function is also executed during the execute phase of SQL statement processing.

Figure 7-1 illustrates three users accessing SH's SALES_HISTORY table. This example shows a simple policy function that appends the filter EMP_ID=<*user's employee ID*>. With this example, the policy function allows each user to view only his or her sales history records. This RLS function is simple in nature for illustration purposes, but your policy functions can be as complex as needed to support your security policy.

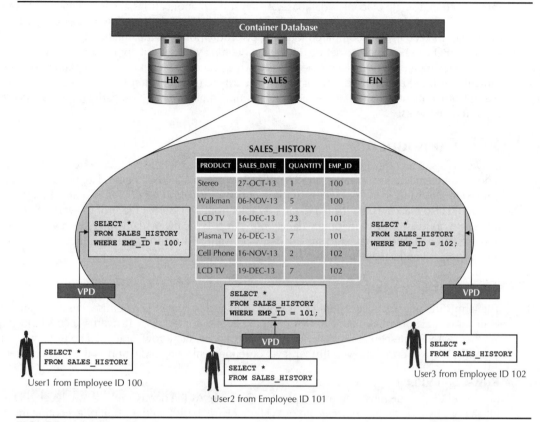

FIGURE 7-1. *VPD overview*

VPD supports multiple policies and a variety of policy types for tables, views, or synonyms. Being able to support multiple policies on a single object is an important feature when it comes to implementing security policies to satisfy complex security requirements.

You should create the VPD policy with definer's rights for obvious reasons (such as policy function object resolution, object privileges, least privileges, and so on). Furthermore, the VPD policy does not need to be granted to users/roles to work properly.

Benefits

A key benefit of VPD is that end users, application accounts, and even certain types of database administrators don't realize or need to know that a security policy is in effect. Another benefit is that because most applications handle NULL or "no rows selected" results, application modification is typically not required.

Put security close to data: Building data access security in applications is a bad idea because it can be easily circumvented by someone using SQL*Plus and connecting to the database directly. So regardless of how a user may try to access the data via SQL*Plus, a J2EE application, or SQL Developer, your VPD security policy will be effective when the security policy is created and maintained in a single place: the database. As a result, all applications accessing the database benefit by saving time and money in not developing redundant data security procedures, which are harder to keep in-sync compared to a single security policy in the database.

Yes, VPD can be simple to set up. However, defining your security policy or requirements may not be that simple. We have seen several cases where security practitioners complain about how difficult it is to set up VPD security (or Oracle security in general); after talking through the issues, we've learned that the hard part was actually defining their company's security policy or access rights requirements.

VPD Components

VPD consists of a policy function and an RLS policy. You can implement VPD by simply creating a policy function and then creating an RLS policy. You can, but are not required to, use an application context to store and speed up access to the security information used in your policy function. You could also read the data from a database table, from an external file, from a web service call, and so on, to assist in security policy decision-making. Typically, when you create a VPD policy, you use an application context to store security relevant information regarding the session user or the context of the database session.

Types of Control

The term "fine-grained access control" is often used to describe VPD, because you can control the granularity table or column access. Discretionary access control (DAC) governs access to the table via the GRANT statement, but if you want to control access to a row, or even a column, you must use VPD. We will cover an even further level of refinement using redaction in the next chapter.

Row-Level VPD

Row-level VPD is the most common type of VPD in use. As the name implies, row-level VPD filters rows by modifying the predicate or WHERE clause based on the result of executing the policy function. The policy function executes or is triggered by a SELECT, DML, or INDEX SQL statement issued against a protected table. The result of executing the policy function is a modified predicate that is appended to the statement to filter rows.

Column-Level VPD

Column-level VPD policy executes when the SQL statement references a column listed in the security policy. If a policy column is listed in the projection (SELECT clause) or predicate (WHERE clause) of a protected table, then the policy function executes. For example, if we configured the COMMISSION column from the SALES_HISTORY table as a policy column, then the policy function would only fire/execute when the COMMISSION column or "*" was listed in the SELECT clause of the SELECT statement (**SELECT commission FROM sales_history;** or **SELECT * FROM sales_history;**).

Column-level VPD can filter data either at the row or column level. Column-level VPD with row filtering operates the same as row-level VPD, except that the policy function fires only when a policy column is referenced. Column-level VPD with column-level filtering filters only a column's value from the returned row. The filtered column's value is replaced with a NULL and the other columns being returned are not affected.

How to Use VPD

The first question you need to ask when setting up VPD is, "What do I need to protect and why?" Take some time to examine this statement. If the existence of a record is what you are protecting, you need to implement a table-level access VPD with row filtering. If you are protecting only one or a couple of columns, you might implement column-level access VPD with a row or column filter.

We often see overly protective VPD security policies implemented with table-level access VPD and row-level filtering. The downside of implementing an incorrect security policy or a policy that is overly protective is that the security policy will be turned off (disabled) or, to allow a user to accomplish a work assignment, an over-privileged account will be created for the user.

For example, consider the policy on the SALES_HISTORY table shown earlier, where the session user's employee ID is added to the predicate as the filter (EMP_ID=<*User's employee ID*>). How do we count the total number of sales or sales transactions by user? That is, how do we perform basic business reporting and analytics on this table if the user's employee ID is always added to the predicate for SELECT statements? We would invariably end up creating a SALES_REPORT account and grant EXEMPT ACCESS POLICY, or in some other way make the SALES_REPORT account exempt from the security policy. We have just created an over-privileged account that bypasses our security policy, which is never a good practice.

A smarter approach is to examine the columns that make up a SALES_HISTORY record and determine which column(s) we are really trying to protect. In our example, we are trying to protect the COMMISSION column. We do not want our sales associates to access the amount of commissions earned by other sales associates. So the existence of the SALES_HISTORY record is not what we are protecting. Rather, we are protecting the value of the COMMISSION column.

For this example, we might consider implementing a "column fire" VPD policy with a column filter on the COMMISSION column as a more efficient and secure way of protecting our data. This new approach would suit our security and business reporting needs better than a "table fire" VPD with a row filter, because we would not have to create an over-privileged account to perform our routine business reporting.

If the account we set up to perform our reporting was to issue the following query, then the results would be accurate:

```
SELECT emp_id, sum(total_cost)
FROM sales_history;
```

Which Type of VPD Is Right for Me?

Figure 7-2 illustrates a simple state diagram to assist you in deciding which type of VPD policy to create. For example, if the existence of a record or transaction is what you are protecting, then a table fire VPD with row filter might be appropriate. If the relationship between column values is what you are protecting or the policy function performance is of concern, then you might need policy enforcement only when certain columns are used in a SQL statement. Column fire VPD policy with row filter might be appropriate. If you are trying to hide the column value from a group of users (that is, you can see COMMISSION values from only your department or a user can see only his or her commission) per row, then column fire VPD policy with column filter might be appropriate.

We will show examples of each of these types of VPD policies in the next few sections.

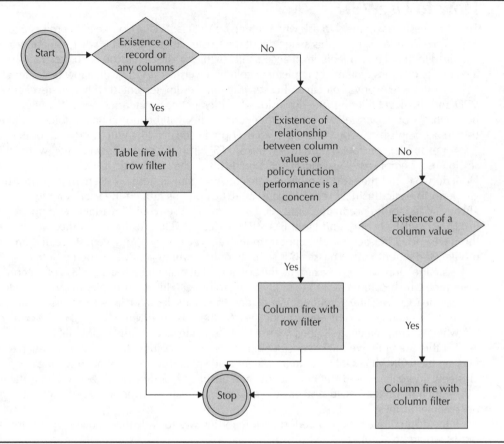

FIGURE 7-2. *VPD type decision state diagram*

Row-Level Security

RLS is a type of VPD that filters data at the row level based on a security policy. The security policy is triggered or fired when accessing the table under policy control. We refer to this type of RLS as *table fire with row filter* (TFRF).

RLS offers an additional level of refinement to apply when the policy function executes. Adding columns to the policy definitions tells Oracle to execute the policy function only if the corresponding columns are referenced in the SQL statement. We refer to this type of RLS as *column fire with row filter* (CFRF).

Table Fire with Row Filter

Table fire with row filter is a type of VPD that fires the policy function when a policy table is accessed, and it filters data at the row level. That means that regardless of columns being selected, functions being used, and so on, the policy function will execute. As the creator of the policy function, you do not have a perspective on which columns are in the projection, filter, and so on.

All you know is that the schema and table name of the protected object are being accessed. You create a policy function that returns a VARCHAR2 (default length is 4000 bytes but can be extended to 32K), which is used to augment the original SQL statement.

Let's create an example security policy that allows sales personnel to access only their records. In this example, we are protecting the existence of rows in the SALES_HISTORY table, so it is a good candidate for table fire with row filter. Creating an RLS policy is a two-step process: first, create the policy function, and then create the RLS policy. For reference, we query from the SH.SALES_HISTORY table to show all records.

```
sec_mgr@db12cr[sales]> CONNECT sh@sales
Enter password:
Connected.
sh@db12cr[sales]> -- All 8 records from SALES_HISTORY
sh@db12cr[sales]> SELECT *
  2  FROM sales_history;

PRODUCT     SALES_DAT  QUANTITY TOTAL_COST   DEPT_ID COMMISSION     EMP_ID
----------  ---------  -------- ----------  -------- ----------  ----------
Stereo      27-OCT-13         1        100       100         23         100
Walkman     06-NOV-13         5        250       100         23         102
LCD TV      16-DEC-13        23      12500       200         23         101
Plasma TV   26-DEC-13         7      12000       200         23         103
Cell Phone  16-NOV-13         2        300       300         23         102
LCD TV      19-DEC-13         7       3500       300         23         101
LCD TV      23-FEB-14        23      12500       100         23         100
Speakers    22-JAN-14         4        521       300         23         101

8 rows selected.
```

Create the Policy Function

We create the policy function in our security policy schema SEC_POL that retrieves the EMP_ID for the connected user from the HR.EMPLOYEES table. If the user's information is found, then the function will return the predicate EMP_ID=<*User's employee ID*>. If the user's information (that is, EMP_ID) is not found, then the function will raise an application error, thus alerting the end user of an issue, and because of the call to RAISE_APPLICATION_ERROR, no data will be returned.

```
sec_mgr@db12cr[sales]> CONNECT sec_pol@sales
Enter password:
Connected.
sec_pol@db12cr[sales]> CREATE OR REPLACE FUNCTION sales_history_emp_id_rls (
  2         p_schema  IN  VARCHAR2,
  3         p_object  IN  VARCHAR2) RETURN VARCHAR2 AS
  4     v_emp_id NUMBER := -1;
  5  BEGIN
  6
  7     -- Get the EMP_ID from HR.EMPLOYEES
  8     SELECT employee_id
  9     INTO v_emp_id
 10     FROM hr.employees
 11     WHERE ename=USER;
 12
 13     RETURN 'EMP_ID='||v_emp_id;
 14  EXCEPTION
```

```
15      -- If we have an issue then don't
16      -- allow access to any records and raise an error
17      WHEN NO_DATA_FOUND THEN
18          RAISE_APPLICATION_ERROR(-20001, 'Invalid user: '||USER);
19      WHEN OTHERS THEN
20          RAISE_APPLICATION_ERROR(-20002, 'An error occurred in the '||
21              'VPD policy function.');
22  END;
23  /

Function created.
```

RAISE_APPLICATION_ERROR is an Oracle procedure that you use to raise or notify the connected user or application of an error. The procedure has three parameters: a NUMBER with range of values from -20000 to -29999 that you can use to uniquely identify the error; a VARCHAR2 with a length of up to 2048 bytes for a custom message that you can associate with your error number; and an optional BOOLEAN value that can either be FALSE (default), which indicates that Oracle is to overwrite call stack errors (that is, the originating error—DAC GRANT on a table, HR.EMPLOYEES doesn't exist, and so on) or TRUE, which indicates that Oracle is to include the entire call stack. We recommend keeping track of error codes and being consistent with their use in your code. We also recommend using FALSE (the default) for the last value for security reasons, because you most likely do not want the end user/application to know the origin of the error.

Create the RLS Policy

Next we create an RLS policy and put the SH.SALES_HISTORY table under policy control using the ADD_POLICY procedure from the DBMS_RLS package. Most of the parameters in the ADD_POLICY procedure are intuitive; however, a couple parameters need further explanation and are listed and explained in Table 7-1. Parameters showing a default value of NULL are optional.

Parameter	Datatype	Default	Description
object_schema	VARCHAR2	NULL	The schema that contains the object to protect.
object_name	VARCHAR2		The object name to protect. Object types include table, view, and synonym.
policy_name	VARCHAR2		A policy name defined by the developer or security administrator.
function_schema	VARCHAR2	NULL	The schema that contains the policy function.
policy_function	VARCHAR2		The policy function name that returns the policy predicate.

TABLE 7-1. *Parameters in the ADD_POLICY Procedure* (continued)

Parameter	Datatype	Default	Description
statement_types	VARCHAR2	NULL	A comma-delimited list of the types of SQL statement to which the policy applies: INDEX, SELECT, INSERT, UPDATE, or DELETE. NULL means all these statement types except INDEX are under policy enforcement.
update_check	BOOLEAN	FALSE	TRUE checks the value after an INSERT or UPDATE statement. This parameter is explained in more detail in the section "VPD and INSERT Statements."
enable	BOOLEAN	TRUE	FALSE if you want to create the policy and enable it later.
static_policy	BOOLEAN	FALSE	TRUE if every user gets the same resultant predicate.
policy_type	BINARY_INTEGER	NULL	NULL, STATIC, SHARED_STATIC, CONTEXT_SENSITIVE, SHARED_CONTEXT_SENSITIVE, DYNAMIC; these values are explained in detail later in the chapter.
long_predicate	BOOLEAN	FALSE	FALSE limits predicate size to 4K. TRUE limits predicate size to 32K.
sec_relevant_cols	VARCHAR2	NULL	This column sensitive policy parameter is explained in more detail with the column fire with row filter and column fire with column filter examples later in the chapter.
sec_relevant_cols_opt	BINARY_INTEGER	NULL	NULL: If the value of NULL or no value is provided for this parameter, the VPD policy will filter at the row level. DBMS_RLS.ALL_ROWS: If the value of ALL_ROWS is provided, the VPD filters or masks values (returns NULL) at the column level.
namespace	VARCHAR2	NULL	The namespace to associate with the policy.
attribute	VARCHAR2	NULL	The attribute within the namespace to associate with the policy.

TABLE 7-1. *Parameters in the ADD_POLICY Procedure*

The function SH_EMP_ID_TFRF is referred to as the *policy function*, and it is executed to generate the policy predicate, which is added to the SALES_HISTORY table. The policy function resides in the SEC_POL schema.

```
sec_pol@db12cr[sales]> CONNECT sec_mgr@sales
Enter password:
Connected.
sec_mgr@db12cr[sales]> BEGIN
  2      DBMS_RLS.add_policy
  3          (object_schema   => 'SH',
  4           object_name     => 'SALES_HISTORY',
  5           function_schema => 'SEC_POL',
  6           policy_name     => 'SH_EMP_ID_TFRF',
  7           policy_function => 'SALES_HISTORY_EMP_ID_RLS',
  8           statement_types => 'SELECT,INSERT,UPDATE,DELETE,INDEX');
  9  END;
 10  /

PL/SQL procedure successfully completed.
```

Verify the RLS Policy and Function Status

We can now verify that the RLS policy is valid and enabled by querying the DBA_POLICIES view:

```
sec_mgr@db12cr[sales]> -- Verify RLS Policy
sec_mgr@db12cr[sales]> SELECT policy_name, sel, ins, upd, del,
  2     idx, policy_type, enable
  3  FROM dba_policies
  4  WHERE policy_name = 'SH_EMP_ID_TFRF';

POLICY_NAME          SEL INS UPD DEL IDX POLICY_TYPE   ENABLE
-------------------- --- --- --- --- --- ------------- ------
SH_EMP_ID_TFRF       YES YES YES YES YES DYNAMIC       YES

1 row selected.
```

As you can see from the output, VPD is enabled for SELECT, INSERT, UPDATE, DELETE, and INDEX statements. Also notice that the POLICY_TYPE is DYNAMIC, which means the policy function will execute for each of the statements issued against the table.

Multiple VPD Policies

Multiple VPD policies can be used to protect the same table. Each VPD policy must have a different policy name, statement types, and/or policy function. For example, you could have one VPD policy that controls read access (such as SH_EMP_ID_TFRF_READ) and one VPD policy that controls write/update access (such as SH_EMP_ID_TFRF_WRITE), and both VPD policies can be applied to the same table. Oracle will execute either function based on which statement is issued against the table. The following example demonstrates multiple VPD policies on the SH.SALES_HISTORY table:

```
sec_mgr@db12cr[sales]> BEGIN
  2      DBMS_RLS.add_policy
  3          (object_schema   => 'SH',
  4           object_name     => 'SALES_HISTORY',
```

```
     5          function_schema => 'SEC_POL',
     6          policy_name     => 'SH_EMP_ID_TFRF_READ',
     7          policy_function => 'SALES_HISTORY_EMP_ID_RLS_READ',
     8          statement_types => 'SELECT,INDEX');
     9  END;
    10  /

PL/SQL procedure successfully completed.

sec_mgr@db12cr[sales]> BEGIN
  2 DBMS_RLS.add_policy
  3         (object_schema   => 'SH',
  4          object_name     => 'SALES_HISTORY',
  5          function_schema => 'SEC_POL',
  6          policy_name     => 'SH_EMP_ID_TFRF_WRITE',
  7          policy_function => 'SALES_HISTORY_EMP_ID_RLS_WRITE',
  8          statement_types => 'INSERT,UPDATE,DELETE');
  9  END;
 10  /

PL/SQL procedure successfully completed.
```

This multiple-policy capability can also be applied to the same type of SQL statement—for example, a SELECT statement—to create a compounding VPD policy. So, for example, the first policy could filter for SALES_HISTORY records per region, and the second VPD policy could filter for SALES_HISTORY records per department.

VPD Policy Groups

VPD can also group VPD policies together. If you have multiple tables and policies to manage, creating VPD policy groups helps you administer and manage VPD. For example, if you have three different read VPD policies and two different write policies, you could have a total of six different group policies that could be active against a table or a set of tables at any given time. By creating VPD policies, you can enable or disable based on the connected user, the operating environment, the application, the user role, and similar factors. The DBMS_RLS.CREATE_POLICY_ GROUP procedure creates a VPD policy group and the DBMS_RLS.ADD_GROUPED_POLICY procedure adds VPD policies to the group.

Enable and Disable the VPD Policy or Policy Groups

DBMS_RLS has procedures to enable and disable VPD policies: DBMS_RLS.ENABLE_POLICY and DBMS_RLS.ENABLE_POLICY_GROUP. By default, when you create a VPD policy, it is enabled. For troubleshooting or result validation, you may need to disable a VPD policy. To disable a policy, then, we could issue a command similar to the following:

```
sec_mgr@db12cr[sales]>  -- Disable the SH_EMP_ID_TFRF policy
sec_mgr@db12cr[sales]>  BEGIN
  2     DBMS_RLS.ENABLE_POLICY (
  3         object_schema => 'SH',
  4         object_name   => 'SALES_HISTORY',
  5         policy_name   => 'SH_EMP_ID_TFRF',
  6         enable        => FALSE);
  7  END;
  8  /
```

```
PL/SQL procedure successfully completed.

sec_mgr@db12cr[sales] >  -- Enable the SH_EMP_ID_TFRF policy
sec_mgr@db12cr[sales] >  BEGIN
  2      DBMS_RLS.ENABLE_POLICY (
  3          object_schema => 'SH',
  4          object_name   => 'SALES_HISTORY',
  5          policy_name   => 'SH_EMP_ID_TFRF',
  6          enable        => TRUE);
  7  END;
  8  /

PL/SQL procedure successfully completed.
```

Test the VPD

At this point, we can test our new RLS policy and function. We connect as user WMAROULIS with employee ID 102 (EMP_ID=102) and query the protected table:

```
sec_mgr@db12cr[sales] > CONNECT wmaroulis@sales
Enter password:
Connected.
wmaroulis@db12cr[sales] > SELECT *
  2  FROM sh.sales_history;
```

PRODUCT	SALES_DAT	QUANTITY	TOTAL_COST	DEPT_ID	COMMISSION	EMP_ID
Walkman	06-NOV-13	5	250	100	23	**102**
Cell Phone	16-NOV-13	2	300	300	23	**102**

```
2 rows selected.
```

We see only records for WMAROULIS. We can then connect as SGAETJEN, whose employee ID is 101 (EMP_ID=101), and query the protected table. We see records only for SGAETJEN.

```
wmaroulis@db12cr[sales] > CONNECT sgaetjen@sales
Enter password:
Connected.
sgaetjen@db12cr[sales] > SELECT *
  2  FROM sh.sales_history;
```

PRODUCT	SALES_DAT	QUANTITY	TOTAL_COST	DEPT_ID	COMMISSION	EMP_ID
LCD TV	16-DEC-13	23	12500	200	23	**101**
LCD TV	19-DEC-13	7	3500	300	23	**101**
Speakers	22-JAN-14	4	521	300	23	**101**

```
3 rows selected.
```

Verify the VPD Predicate

It is clear from the preceding query results that user SGAETJEN viewed only records where EMP_ID=101 and that user WMAROULIS viewed only records where EMP_ID=102. But what if the policy function was complex, and verifying the results of the policy function wasn't as simple as shown here? The question then becomes, "How do we verify the returned predicate value from the policy function?" Oracle has a view for that named V$VPD_POLICY, which shows the first 4000 characters of the generated predicate. You will learn other techniques later in the chapter to view all 32K of the predicate.

```
sgaetjen@db12cr[sales]> CONNECT sec_mgr@sales
Enter password:
Connected.
sec_mgr@db12cr[sales]> SELECT object_owner, object_name, policy, predicate
  2  FROM  v$vpd_policy;

OBJECT_OWNER    OBJECT_NAME     POLICY          PREDICATE
--------------- --------------- --------------- --------------------
SH              SALES_HISTORY   SH_EMP_ID_TFRF  EMP_ID=102
SH              SALES_HISTORY   SH_EMP_ID_TFRF  EMP_ID=101

2 rows selected.
```

You can see that the "first" predicate returned was EMP_ID=102 and the second predicate was MP_ID=101, corresponding to users WMAROULIS and SGAETJEN, respectively, querying the SALES_HISTORY table.

The V$VPD_POLICY is a dynamic view that shows all connected session predicates for cursors currently in the library cache; once the SQL cursor ages from the library cache, the predicate information is no longer available. Also, if you are running in an RAC environment, you should use the view GV$VPD_POLICY to access predicates generated across all nodes in the cluster. We will illustrate other ways of logging and troubleshooting predicates later in the chapter.

Column Fire with Row Filter

Column fire with row filter (CFRF) is a type of VPD that fires the policy function only when a table and column under policy control are accessed. CFRF filters data at the row level. This type of VPD is similar to table fire with row filter (TFRF) in that the RLS filtering is done at the row level. However, a difference occurs when the policy function is executed or fired. CFRF executes only when a policy column is accessed. Otherwise, there is no reason to execute the policy, because the SQL statement is not accessing a protected column.

So we can adapt the preceding example by adding the COMMISSION column to this policy. First, we remove the TFRF policy by using the DROP_POLICY procedure in the DBMS_RLS package:

```
sec_mgr@db12cr[sales]> BEGIN
  2     DBMS_RLS.DROP_POLICY
  3        (object_schema  => 'SH',
  4         object_name    => 'SALES_HISTORY',
  5         policy_name    => 'SH_EMP_ID_TFRF');
  6  END;
  7  /

PL/SQL procedure successfully completed.
```

Next we modify the RLS policy to include the security-relevant columns parameter. When we add a value for this parameter, the policy function will execute only when a SQL statement uses the COMMISSION column. Otherwise, the policy function will not fire and the connected user's query will not be modified.

```
sec_mgr@db12cr[sales]> BEGIN
  2     DBMS_RLS.add_policy
  3        (object_schema    => 'SH',
  4         object_name      => 'SALES_HISTORY',
  5         function_schema  => 'SEC_POL',
  6         policy_name      => 'SH_EMP_ID_CFRF',
  7         policy_function  => 'SALES_HISTORY_EMP_ID_RLS',
  8         statement_types  => 'SELECT,INSERT,UPDATE,DELETE,INDEX');
  9         sec_relevant_cols => 'COMMISSION');
 10  END;
 11  /

PL/SQL procedure successfully completed.
```

Verify the RLS Policy and Function Status

We can now verify that the RLS policy is valid and enabled by querying the DBA_POLICIES view:

```
sec_mgr@db12cr[sales]> -- Verify RLS Policy
sec_mgr@db12cr[sales]> SELECT policy_name, sel, ins, upd, del,
  2     idx, policy_type, enable
  3  FROM dba_policies
  4  WHERE policy_name = 'SH_EMP_ID_CFRF';

POLICY_NAME            SEL INS UPD DEL IDX POLICY_TYPE    ENABLE
-------------------    --- --- --- --- --- -------------- ------
SH_EMP_ID_CFRF         YES YES YES YES YES DYNAMIC        YES

1 row selected.
```

Test the VPD

We are ready to test our new RLS policy and function. We connect as WMAROULIS (EMP_ID=102) and query the protected table. Note that we are using "*" for the projection so all columns are being returned, which has the effect of firing our policy function:

```
sec_mgr@db12cr[sales]> CONNECT wmaroulis@sales
Enter password:
Connected.
wmaroulis@db12cr[sales]> SELECT *
  2  FROM sh.sales_history;

PRODUCT      SALES_DAT   QUANTITY TOTAL_COST    DEPT_ID COMMISSION     EMP_ID
-----------  ---------  --------- ----------  --------- ----------  ---------
Walkman      06-NOV-13          5        250        100         23        102
Cell Phone   16-NOV-13          2        300        300         23        102

2 rows selected.
```

In the preceding listing, we see records only for WMAROULIS, as we did previously, because we indirectly accessed the policy column (COMMISSION). However, if we select all columns except the POLICY column, all rows will be returned, because we did not cause the policy function to fire:

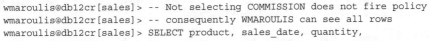

```
wmaroulis@db12cr[sales]> -- Not selecting COMMISSION does not fire policy
wmaroulis@db12cr[sales]> -- consequently WMAROULIS can see all rows
wmaroulis@db12cr[sales]> SELECT product, sales_date, quantity,
  2     total_cost, dept_id, emp_id
  3  FROM sh.sales_history;

PRODUCT          SALES_DAT  QUANTITY  TOTAL_COST   DEPT_ID     EMP_ID
---------------  ---------  --------  ----------  ----------  ----------
Stereo           27-OCT-13         1         100         100         100
Walkman          06-NOV-13         5         250         100         102
LCD TV           16-DEC-13        23       12500         200         101
Plasma TV        26-DEC-13         7       12000         200         103
Cell Phone       16-NOV-13         2         300         300         102
LCD TV           19-DEC-13         7        3500         300         101
LCD TV           23-FEB-14        23       12500         100         100
Speakers         22-JAN-14         4         521         300         101

8 rows selected.
```

For completeness, we connect as SGAETJEN and perform the same queries:

```
wmaroulis@db12cr[sales]> CONNECT sgaetjen@sales
Enter password:
Connected.
sgaetjen@db12cr[sales]> -- Fires policy because we use "*" which includes
sgaetjen@db12cr[sales]> -- the COMMISSION column
sgaetjen@db12cr[sales]> SELECT *
  2  FROM sh.sales_history;

PRODUCT       SALES_DAT   QUANTITY TOTAL_COST    DEPT_ID COMMISSION      EMP_ID
-----------   ---------   -------- ----------  ---------- ---------- ----------
LCD TV        16-DEC-13         23      12500         200         23         101
LCD TV        19-DEC-13          7       3500         300         23         101
Speakers      22-JAN-14          4        521         300         23         101

3 rows selected.
sgaetjen@db12cr[sales]> -- Not selecting COMMISSION doesn't fire policy
sgaetjen@db12cr[sales]> -- consequently SGAETJEN can see all rows
sgaetjen@db12cr[sales]> SELECT product, sales_date, quantity,
  2     total_cost, dept_id, emp_id
  3  FROM sh.sales_history;

PRODUCT          SALES_DAT  QUANTITY  TOTAL_COST   DEPT_ID     EMP_ID
---------------  ---------  --------  ----------  ----------  ----------
Stereo           27-OCT-13         1         100         100         100
Walkman          06-NOV-13         5         250         100         102
LCD TV           16-DEC-13        23       12500         200         101
Plasma TV        26-DEC-13         7       12000         200         103
Cell Phone       16-NOV-13         2         300         300         102
LCD TV           19-DEC-13         7        3500         300         101
LCD TV           23-FEB-14        23       12500         100         100
Speakers         22-JAN-14         4         521         300         101

8 rows selected.
```

Verify the VPD Predicate

We can now check the V$VPD_POLICY view to see that the "first" predicate returned was EMP_ID=102 and the second predicate was EMP_ID=101, corresponding to users WMAROULIS and SGAETJEN, respectively, querying the SALES_HISTORY table.

```
sgaetjen@db12cr[sales]> CONNECT sec_mgr@sales
Enter password:
Connected.
sec_mgr@db12cr[sales]> SELECT object_owner, object_name, policy, predicate
  2  FROM  v$vpd_policy;

OBJECT_OWNER    OBJECT_NAME     POLICY          PREDICATE
--------------- --------------- --------------- ------------
SH              SALES_HISTORY   SH_EMP_ID_CFRF  EMP_ID=102
SH              SALES_HISTORY   SH_EMP_ID_CFRF  EMP_ID=101

2 rows selected.
```

VPD and INSERT Statements

SELECT (INDEX recursively uses SELECT), UPDATE, and DELETE statements all have WHERE clauses, but what about INSERT? INSERT does not have a WHERE clause, so how does VPD work for INSERT statements?

A little background on how INSERT works in VPD is needed first. By default, you can INSERT into a table protected with VPD using values that you do not have access to. That is, if a policy function returned a predicate of EMP_ID=200 and you are inserting the value of 100 for EMP_ID, then the INSERT statement will succeed. Here's an example:

```
sh@db12cr[sales]> -- We can only access records where EMP_ID=200
sh@db12cr[sales]> select * from sales_history;

PRODUCT      SALES_DAT  QUANTITY TOTAL_COST  DEPT_ID COMMISSION    EMP_ID
------------ ---------- --------- ----------- --------- ----------- ----------
LCD TV       16-DEC-13        23       12500      200          23       200
Plasma TV    26-DEC-13         7       12000      200          23       200

2 rows selected.

sh@db12cr[sales]> -- INSERT with EMP_ID=100 will succeed
sh@db12cr[sales]> INSERT INTO SALES_HISTORY (product, sales_date, quantity,
  2  total_cost, dept_id, commission, emp_id)
  3  VALUES ('LCD WIDE SCREEN TV', sysdate, 23, 12500, 100, 20, 100);

1 row created.

sh@db12cr[sales]> -- However, the user can't access the record
sh@db12cr[sales]> SELECT *
  2  FROM sales_history;

PRODUCT      SALES_DAT QUANTITY  TOTAL_COST  DEPT_ID COMMISSION    EMP_ID
------------ --------- --------- ----------- --------- ----------- ----------
LCD TV       16-DEC-13       23       12500      200          23       200
Plasma TV    26-DEC-13        7       12000      200          23       200

2 rows selected.
```

If you don't want to allow the inserting of records that are outside the scope of what you are protecting (that is, where EMP_ID=100), then you have to set the UPDATE_CHECK parameter to TRUE. Doing so forces Oracle to query the table after inserting (or updating) the values. If Oracle can't query the values it just inserted, it will rollback the INSERT statement and raise an "ORA-28115 error – policy with check option violation."

```
sh@db12cr[sales] > CONNECT sec_mgr@sales
Enter password:
Connected.
sec_mgr@db12cr[sales] > BEGIN
  2     DBMS_RLS.DROP_POLICY
  3          (object_schema     => 'SH',
  4           object_name       => 'SALES_HISTORY',
  5           policy_name       => 'SH_EMP_ID_CFRF');
  6    END;
  7   /

PL/SQL procedure successfully completed.

sec_mgr@db12cr[sales] > -- Add back our CFRF policy for the COMMISSION column
sec_mgr@db12cr[sales] > BEGIN
  2     DBMS_RLS.add_policy
  3          (object_schema     => 'SH',
  4           object_name       => 'SALES_HISTORY',
  5           function_schema   => 'SEC_POL',
  6           policy_name       => 'SH_EMP_ID_CFRF',
  7           policy_function   => 'SALES_HISTORY_EMP_ID_RLS',
  8           statement_types   => 'SELECT,INSERT,UPDATE,DELETE,INDEX',
  9           sec_relevant_cols => 'COMMISSION',
 10           update_check      => TRUE);
 11    END;
 12   /

PL/SQL procedure successfully completed.
```

For example, if the VPD policy function returns a predicate of EMP_ID=200 and we attempt to insert a record as employee ID 100, then the policy function will fail, because Oracle cannot query the record that it just inserted. The following example demonstrates this point:

```
sec_mgr@db12cr[sales] > CONNECT sh@sales
Enter password:
Connected.
sh@db12cr[sales] > -- Connected user has EMP_ID=200, so INSERT will fail
sh@db12cr[sales] > INSERT INTO SALES_HISTORY (PRODUCT, SALES_DATE, QUANTITY,
  2   TOTAL_COST, DEPT_ID, COMMISSION, EMP_ID)
  3   VALUES ('LCD TV', sysdate, 23, 12500, 100, 20, 100);
INSERT INTO SALES_HISTORY (PRODUCT, SALES_DATE, QUANTITY, TOTAL_COST, DEPT_ID,
COMMISSION, EMP_ID)
             *
ERROR at line 1:
ORA-28115: policy with check option violation
```

```
sh@db12cr[sales]> -- Connected user has EMP_ID=200, so INSERT will succeed
sh@db12cr[sales]> INSERT INTO SALES_HISTORY (PRODUCT, SALES_DATE, QUANTITY,
  2  TOTAL_COST, DEPT_ID, COMMISSION, EMP_ID)
  3  VALUES ('LCD TV', sysdate, 23, 12500, 200, 20, 200);

1 row created.

sh@db12cr[sales]> -- We don't need this record for our purposes.
sh@db12cr[sales]> ROLLBACK;

Rollback complete.
```

VPD and INDEX Statements

The INDEX statement (CREATE INDEX) must be protected, similarly to SELECT. If a user has the CREATE INDEX privilege on a table that is under TFRF or CFRF VPD policy control, the user could create an index, dump or query the index values, and thereby circumvent the security policy. Consequently, we typically create VPD policies with at a minimum SELECT, INSERT, UPDATE, DELETE, and INDEX enforcement.

Column-Level Security

Column-level Security (CLS) is a type of VPD security that filters data at the column level; it is also referred to as cell-level security or column masking.

CLS is different from RLS VPD types in several ways:

- It applies only to SELECT statements.
- The CLS policy function must return a simple Boolean expression.
- The CLS column's value is NULL in both the SELECT clause or result, and the CLS column's value is NULL in the query's predicate, the WHERE clause. Consequently, CLS can give the appearance of row filtering. For example, if we had a CFCF policy on the SH.SALES_ HISTORY table using the COMMISSION column, and we issued the following query, we might have rows (not just columns) filtered from the result:

```
sh@db12cr[sales]> CONNECT sgaetjen@sales
Enter password:
Connected.
sgaetjen@db12cr[sales]> SELECT *
  2  FROM sales_history
  3  WHERE COMMISSION > 50;

no rows selected
```

Column Fire with Column Filter

Column fire with column filter (CFCF) is fired when accessing the policy table's column, as with CFRF; however, filtering happens at the column level. Oracle NULLs out the columns value if the simple Boolean expression returned from the policy function evaluates to FALSE.

Create a CLS Policy

We can create the new CFCF policy by first dropping the old CFRF policy:

```
sgaetjen@db12cr[sales]> CONNECT sec_mgr@sales
Enter password:
Connected.
sec_mgr@db12cr[sales]> BEGIN
  2    DBMS_RLS.DROP_POLICY
  3       (object_schema   => 'SH',
  4        object_name     => 'SALES_HISTORY',
  5        policy_name     => 'SH_EMP_ID_CFRF');
  6  END;
  7  /

PL/SQL procedure successfully completed.
```

Next we add the CFCF policy by including the parameter SEC_RELEVANT_COLS_OPT. We set the value of the new parameter to DBMS_RLS.ALL_ROWS, which means that we want "all rows" returned, but we want the policy to filter or mask values at the column level. The columns listed in the SEC_RELEVANT_COLS parameter might be filtered depending on the value returned by the policy function.

For example, let's create a CFCF policy on the COMMISSION column. We want to display the COMMISSION value for records that are owned by the connected user and return NULL for all other COMMISSION values. That is, unlike the preceding CFRF or TFRF policies that displayed only SH.SALES_HISTORY records for the connected user, we want our policy to show all records and return NULL for the COMMISSION column for those records the connected user does not own.

We first create a CFCF policy listing populating the parameter SEC_RELEVANT_COLS_OPT as follows:

```
sec_mgr@db12cr[sales]> -- We add the CFCF policy to the SALES_HISTORY table
sec_mgr@db12cr[sales]> BEGIN
  2     DBMS_RLS.add_policy
  3        (object_schema          => 'SH',
  4         object_name            => 'SALES_HISTORY',
  5         function_schema        => 'SEC_POL',
  6         policy_name            => 'SH_EMP_ID_CFCF',
  7         policy_function        => 'SALES_HISTORY_EMP_ID_RLS',
  8         sec_relevant_cols      => 'COMMISSION',
  9         statement_types        => 'SELECT,INSERT,UPDATE,DELETE,INDEX',
 10         sec_relevant_cols_opt  => DBMS_RLS.ALL_ROWS);
 11  END;
 12  /

PL/SQL procedure successfully completed.
```

Verify the CLS Policy and Function Status

Next we verify that the CLS policy is valid and enabled by querying the DBA_POLICIES view:

```
sec_mgr@db12cr[sales]> -- Verify CLS Policy
sec_mgr@db12cr[sales]> SELECT policy_name, sel, ins, upd, del,
  2     idx, policy_type, enable
  3  FROM dba_policies
  4  WHERE policy_name = 'SH_EMP_ID_CFCF';
```

```
POLICY_NAME           SEL INS UPD DEL IDX POLICY_TYPE   ENABLE
--------------------  --- --- --- --- --- ------------  ------
SH_EMP_ID_CFCF        YES YES YES YES YES DYNAMIC       YES

1 row selected.
```

Test the VPD

Notice that for the CFCF policy output, we see all records of the SH.SALES_HISTORY table. However, we see the COMMISSION values only for records that were created by the connected user WMAROULIS (EMP_ID=102).

```
sec_mgr@db12cr[sales]> CONNECT wmaroulis@sales
Enter password:
Connected.
wmaroulis@db12cr[sales]> -- With CFCF all rows are returned
wmaroulis@db12cr[sales]> SELECT *
  2  FROM sh.sales_history;
```

PRODUCT	SALES_DAT	QUANTITY	TOTAL_COST	DEPT_ID	COMMISSION	EMP_ID
Stereo	27-OCT-13	1	100	100		100
Walkman	06-NOV-13	5	250	100	23	102
LCD TV	16-DEC-13	23	12500	200		101
Plasma TV	26-DEC-13	7	12000	200		103
Cell Phone	16-NOV-13	2	300	300	23	102
LCD TV	19-DEC-13	7	3500	300		101
LCD TV	23-FEB-14	23	12500	100		100
Speakers	22-JAN-14	4	521	300		101

```
8 rows selected.
```

We also connect as SGAETJEN (EMP_ID=101) and query the table. Again, we see all records in the table, but COMMISSION values only for records that were created by SGAETJEN.

```
wmaroulis@db12cr[sales]> CONNECT sgaetjen@sales
Enter password:
Connected.
sgaetjen@db12cr[sales]> -- With CLS all rows are returned
sgaetjen@db12cr[sales]> SELECT *
  2  FROM sh.sales_history;
```

PRODUCT	SALES_DAT	QUANTITY	TOTAL_COST	DEPT_ID	COMMISSION	EMP_ID
Stereo	27-OCT-13	1	100	100		100
Walkman	06-NOV-13	5	250	100		102
LCD TV	16-DEC-13	23	12500	200	23	101
Plasma TV	26-DEC-13	7	12000	200		103
Cell Phone	16-NOV-13	2	300	300		102
LCD TV	19-DEC-13	7	3500	300	23	101
LCD TV	23-FEB-14	23	12500	100		100
Speakers	22-JAN-14	4	521	300	23	101

```
8 rows selected.
```

Verify the VPD Predicate

Similar to the preceding output, we see the "first" predicate returned was EMP_ID=102 and the second predicate was EMP_ID=101, corresponding to users WMAROULIS and SGAETJEN, respectively, querying the SALES_HISTORY table:

```
sgaetjen@db12cr[sales]> CONNECT sec_mgr@sales
Enter password:
Connected.
sec_mgr@db12cr[sales]> SELECT object_owner, object_name, policy, predicate
  2  FROM  v$vpd_policy;

OBJECT_OWNER    OBJECT_NAME      POLICY           PREDICATE
--------------- ---------------- ---------------- ------------
SH              SALES_HISTORY    SH_EMP_ID_CFCF   EMP_ID=102
SH              SALES_HISTORY    SH_EMP_ID_CFCF   EMP_ID=101

2 rows selected.
```

You might be thinking, "Column-level filter returning a predicate? But I am filtering at the column level, not the row level. I am not tracking this example!" We learned that in TFRF and CFRF VPD policies, the policy function returned a value that added to the predicate (WHERE clause) of the SQL statement. But for column- or cell-level filtering, the policy function's value isn't added to the predicate; instead, you can think of it like this: for each row, the policy function is executed to determine if the column's value should be displayed or if a NULL should be returned. In this case, Oracle Database is checking (hence the need for a simple Boolean expression) to determine if the column's value should be returned or not.

VPD Exemptions

VPD was introduced in Oracle 8*i* and has been working since the mid-1990s. However, sometimes it can be problematic or get in the way when you're performing administrative tasks such as exporting data or developing an application against a complex security model. Sometimes you want or need to remove all VPD policies from a table to export its data or verify its contents. Oracle has an EXEMPT ACCESS POLICY privilege that allows the grantee to be exempt from VPD policy enforcement. The security implications of granting this privilege should be obvious, so use extreme caution. If you think you need to grant this privilege, we recommend that you audit its use and review your audit records regularly. You can also use fine-grained auditing to alert you in real-time when the privileged has been used. Refer to Chapter 13 for more information.

We will now demonstrate the use of the EXEMPT ACCESS POLICY privilege.

Audit EXEMPT ACCESS POLICY Privilege

We start by auditing the EXEMPT ACCESS POLICY by access. The following statement enables auditing on this privilege:

```
sec_mgr@db12cr[sales]> -- Audit the use of the
sec_mgr@db12cr[sales]> -- EXEMPT ACCESS POLICY privilege
sec_mgr@db12cr[sales]> AUDIT EXEMPT ACCESS POLICY BY ACCESS;

Audit succeeded.
```

Verify EXEMPT ACCESS POLICY Privilege

Next we connect as SYS, who has the EXEMPT ACCESS POLICY privilege by default, and can SELECT from the SH.SALES_HISTORY table:

```
sec_mgr@db12cr[sales]> -- SYS is exempt from VPD policy because the account
sec_mgr@db12cr[sales]> -- has EXEMPT ACCESS POLICY
sec_mgr@db12cr[sales]> connect SYS@sales as sysdba
Enter password:
Connected.
sys@db12cr[sales]>  SELECT *
  2  FROM session_privs
  3  WHERE privilege in ('EXEMPT ACCESS POLICY','SELECT ANY TABLE');

PRIVILEGE
----------------------------
SELECT ANY TABLE
EXEMPT ACCESS POLICY

2 rows selected.

sys@db12cr[sales]> -- The above two privileges give SYS the ability
sys@db12cr[sales]> -- to select from the table and be exempt from VPD policy
sys@db12cr[sales]> SELECT *
  2  FROM sh.sales_history;

PRODUCT     SALES_DAT  QUANTITY TOTAL_COST    DEPT_ID COMMISSION     EMP_ID
----------- ---------- -------- ---------- ---------- ---------- ----------
Stereo      27-OCT-13         1        100        100         23        100
Walkman     06-NOV-13         5        250        100         23        102
LCD TV      16-DEC-13        23      12500        200         23        101
Plasma TV   26-DEC-13         7      12000        200         23        103
Cell Phone  16-NOV-13         2        300        300         23        102
LCD TV      19-DEC-13         7       3500        300         23        101
LCD TV      23-FEB-14        23      12500        100         23        100
Speakers    22-JAN-14         4        521        300         23        101

8 rows selected.
```

Note that if we were to grant the EXEMPT ACCESS POLICY privilege to any database account, the account could bypass the VPD policies on any table the account has the privileges to access—for example SELECT, INSERT, SELECT ANY, and so on.

```
sec_mgr@db12cr[sales]> GRANT exempt access policy TO wmaroulis;

Grant succeeded.
```

EXEMPT ACCESS POLICY is a very powerful privilege because it applies to all schemas and all policies. By default, users acting as SYSDBA are exempt from VPD policies. You can determine who has been granted this privilege by querying DBA_SYS_PRIVS:

```
wmaroulis@db12cr[sales]> CONNECT sec_mgr@sales
Enter password:
Connected.
sec_mgr@db12cr[sales]> SELECT grantee
  2  FROM dba_sys_privs
  3  WHERE privilege = 'EXEMPT ACCESS POLICY';
```

```
GRANTEE
------------------------------
WMAROULIS

1 row selected.
```

Verify Audit Trail

Next we query the audit tail to verify that the audit event was recorded:

```
sec_mgr@db12cr[sales]> BEGIN
  2      FOR row IN (SELECT *
  3                    FROM dba_audit_trail
  4                    WHERE obj_name = 'SALES_HISTORY' and
  5                       priv_used is not null
  6                    ORDER by timestamp) LOOP
  7         DBMS_OUTPUT.put_line ('-------------------------');
  8         DBMS_OUTPUT.put_line ('Who:    '|| row.username);
  9         DBMS_OUTPUT.put_line ('What:   '|| row.action_name
 10            || ' on '|| row.owner|| '.'|| row.obj_name);
 11         DBMS_OUTPUT.put_line ('When:   '|| TO_CHAR
 12            (row.TIMESTAMP, 'MM/DD HH24:MI'));
 13         DBMS_OUTPUT.put_line ('How:    "'|| row.sql_text || '"');
 14         DBMS_OUTPUT.put_line ('Using: '|| row.priv_used);
 15      END LOOP;
 16    END;
 17  /
-------------------------
Who:   WMAROULIS
What:  SELECT on SH.SALES_HISTORY
When:  03/08 22:41
How:   ""
Using: EXEMPT ACCESS POLICY

PL/SQL procedure successfully completed.
```

The audit trail shows the privilege EXEMPT ACCESS POLICY was used by WMAROULIS to access the SH.SALES_HISTORY table.

Debugging and Troubleshooting VPD Policies

There are generally two reasons for troubleshooting VPD: the policy function is invalid or is raising an error, or the security policy is sufficiently complex that the results of the policy function (predicate) are nontrivial. That means that at some point you will be asked to validate the results from your VPD security policy. The question invariably is, "Are these query results correct for this user?"

First, let's examine some ways to troubleshoot VPD policy functions. For the following examples we use the table fire with row filter (TFRF) VPD policy.

Invalid Policy Functions

If the policy function has a dependency on a table or other object and the table is dropped, the policy function will be marked with an INVALID status. Oracle attempts to recompile the policy function automatically to get its status to VALID; however, if the policy function is dependent on a table or an object that no longer exists, you will have to update your policy function or restore the dependent object. Also, be sensitive to whether or not your table is in a DBV-protected realm; if so, Oracle (SYS) might not be able to recompile the function automatically even though the dependent object was restored. We cover DBV in Chapter 10.

The first indication that something is wrong with VPD typically happens when you try to query a policy table and receive an error message. For example, if we drop the HR.EMPLOYEES table, which is a dependency for our policy function, and then try to query the SH.SALES_HISTORY table, we will receive an error message.

```
sec_mgr@db12cr[sales]> BEGIN
  2     DBMS_RLS.DROP_POLICY
  3        (object_schema    => 'SH',
  4         object_name      => 'SALES_HISTORY',
  5         policy_name      => 'SH_EMP_ID_CFRF');
  6   END;
  7   /

PL/SQL procedure successfully completed.

sec_mgr@db12cr[sales]> -- Add TFRF policy for remaining examples
sec_mgr@db12cr[sales]> BEGIN
  2     DBMS_RLS.add_policy
  3        (object_schema    => 'SH',
  4         object_name      => 'SALES_HISTORY',
  5         function_schema  => 'SEC_POL',
  6         policy_name      => 'SH_EMP_ID_TFRF',
  7         policy_function  => 'SALES_HISTORY_EMP_ID_RLS',
  8         statement_types  => 'SELECT,INSERT,UPDATE,DELETE,INDEX',
  9         update_check     => TRUE);
 10   END;
 11   /

PL/SQL procedure successfully completed.

sec_mgr@db12cr[sales]> -- First - we show the dependencies on
sec_mgr@db12cr[sales]> -- the policy function
sec_mgr@db12cr[sales]> SELECT name, referenced_owner, referenced_name
  2   FROM all_dependencies
  3   WHERE owner = 'SEC_POL' and
  4      name = 'SALES_HISTORY_EMP_ID_RLS'
  5   ORDER by 1;

NAME                            REFERENCED_OWNER   REFERENCED_NAME
------------------------------  -----------------  ------------------------
SALES_HISTORY_EMP_ID_RLS        SYS                STANDARD
SALES_HISTORY_EMP_ID_RLS        SYS                SYS_STUB_FOR_PURITY_ANALYSIS
SALES_HISTORY_EMP_ID_RLS        HR                 EMPLOYEES

3 rows selected.
```

Be sensitive to the fact that Oracle not only drops the objects, but it also removes the object from dependency lists and removes object privileges granted to users or roles.

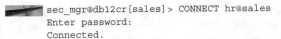

```
sec_mgr@db12cr[sales]> CONNECT hr@sales
Enter password:
Connected.
```

```
hr@db12cr[sales]> -- CTAS EMP for backup
hr@db12cr[sales]> CREATE TABLE emp as SELECT * FROM employees;

Table created.

hr@db12cr[sales]>  DROP TABLE employees PURGE;

Table dropped.

hr@db12cr[sales]> CONNECT sec_mgr@sales
Enter password:
Connected.
sec_mgr@db12cr[sales]> -- Re-verify dependencies
sec_mgr@db12cr[sales]> -- notice EMPLOYEES is not listed
sec_mgr@db12cr[sales]> SELECT name, referenced_owner, referenced_name
  2  FROM all_dependencies
  3  WHERE owner = 'SEC_POL' and
  4    name = 'SALES_HISTORY_EMP_ID_RLS'
  5  ORDER by 1;

NAME                          REFERENCED_OWNER  REFERENCED_NAME
----------------------------- ----------------- -----------------------
SALES_HISTORY_EMP_ID_RLS      SYS               STANDARD
SALES_HISTORY_EMP_ID_RLS      SYS               SYS_STUB_FOR_PURITY_ANALYSIS

2 rows selected.

sec_mgr@db12cr[sales]> -- Verify that the policy function is INVALID
sec_mgr@db12cr[sales]> SELECT object_name, status
  2  FROM all_objects
  3  WHERE owner= 'SH' and
  4    object_name = 'SALES_HISTORY_EMP_ID_RLS';

OBJECT_NAME               STATUS
------------------------- -------
SALES_HISTORY_EMP_ID_RLS  INVALID

1 row selected.

sec_mgr@db12cr[sales]> -- Attempt a query even though the policy
sec_mgr@db12cr[sales]> -- function is invalid
sec_mgr@db12cr[sales]> CONNECT wmaroulis@sales
Enter password:
Connected.
wmaroulis@db12cr[sales]> SELECT *
  2  FROM sh.sales_history;
FROM sh.sales_history
     *
ERROR at line 2:
ORA-28110: policy function or package SEC_POL.SALES_HISTORY_EMP_ID_RLS has error
```

Simply re-creating the HR.EMPLOYEES table is not good enough to fix our problem. We have to regrant the privileges as well:

```
wmaroulis@db12cr[sales]> CONNECT hr@sales
Enter password:
Connected.
```

```
hr@db12cr[sales]> -- Re-create the EMPLOYEES table
hr@db12cr[sales]> create table employees as select * from emp;

Table created.

hr@db12cr[sales]> CONNECT sec_pol@sales
Enter password:
Connected.
sec_pol@db12cr[sales]> -- Will not work because SEC_POL is missing
sec_pol@db12cr[sales]> -- the SELECT GRANT on HR.EMPLOYEES
sec_pol@db12cr[sales]> ALTER FUNCTION sales_history_emp_id_rls COMPILE;

Warning: Function altered with compilation errors.

sec_pol@db12cr[sales]> SHOW ERRORS
Errors for FUNCTION SALES_HISTORY_EMP_ID_RLS:

LINE/COL ERROR
-------- ------------------------------------------------------
8/4      PL/SQL: SQL Statement ignored
10/12    PL/SQL: ORA-00942: table or view does not exist

sec_pol@db12cr[sales]> -- We would check row 10 of the function
sec_pol@db12cr[sales]> -- and determine that HR.EMPLOYEES
sec_pol@db12cr[sales]> CONNECT hr@sales
Enter password:
Connected.
hr@db12cr[sales]> GRANT SELECT ON employees TO SEC_POL;

Grant succeeded.
```

At this point, we have the dependencies and privileges resolved. We could either connect as SEC_POL and manually recompile the policy function or we could connect as WMAROULIS and query the SH.SALES_HISTORY table, which forces the database to recompile the policy function automatically, returning its status to VALID. Let's try the automatic route by logging in as WMAROULIS and querying the table. If we receive results from querying the table, then the compilation worked.

```
hr@db12cr[sales]> CONNECT wmaroulis@sales
Enter password:
Connected.
wmaroulis@db12cr[sales]> -- Oracle attempts to recompile the policy function
wmaroulis@db12cr[sales]> SELECT *
  2  FROM sh.sales_history;

PRODUCT      SALES_DAT  QUANTITY TOTAL_COST   DEPT_ID COMMISSION     EMP_ID
-----------  ---------  -------- ----------   ------- ----------  ---------
Walkman      06-NOV-13         5        250       100         23        102
Cell Phone   16-NOV-13         2        300       300         23        102

2 rows selected.
```

Auto-recompilation worked. Let's now verify the restoration of object dependencies and verify the status of the policy function:

```
wmaroulis@db12cr[sales]> CONNECT sec_mgr@sales
Enter password:
Connected.
sec_mgr@db12cr[sales]> -- Verify dependencies
sec_mgr@db12cr[sales]> SELECT name, referenced_owner, referenced_name
  2  FROM all_dependencies
  3  WHERE owner='SEC_POL' and
  4     name = 'SALES_HISTORY_EMP_ID_RLS'
  5  ORDER by 1;

NAME                           REFERENCED_OWNER  REFERENCED_NAME
------------------------------ ----------------- -------------------------
SALES_HISTORY_EMP_ID_RLS       SYS               STANDARD
SALES_HISTORY_EMP_ID_RLS       SYS               SYS_STUB_FOR_PURITY_ANALYSIS
SALES_HISTORY_EMP_ID_RLS       HR                EMPLOYEES

3 rows selected.

sec_mgr@db12cr[sales]> -- Verify that the policy function is VALID
sec_mgr@db12cr[sales]> SELECT object_name, status
  2  FROM all_objects
  3  WHERE owner= 'SH' and
  4     object_name = 'SALES_HISTORY_EMP_ID_RLS';

OBJECT_NAME              STATUS
------------------------ -------
SALES_HISTORY_EMP_ID_RLS VALID

1 row selected.
```

Verifying and Validating Predicates

We just demonstrated that we can see the generated predicate by querying the Oracle view V$VPD_PREDICATE (or GV$VPD_PREDICATE for RAC environments). However, this view truncates the generated predicate to 4000 characters, which might be adequate for your security policy. But what if you have a lengthy predicate or don't have access to the V$VPD_POLICY view? How can you access or see the generated value?

There are several ways of resolving this issue, and we will demonstrate three:

- You could add a DBMS_OUTPUT.PUT_LINE in the policy function and print the resulting predicate before it is returned. This approach is useful in a development environment or in a situation where the connected user is using SQL*Plus and the connected user is simply trying to determine the resulting predicate.

- You could create a logging table and invoke a PRAGMA AUTONOMOUS_ TRANSACTION function to INSERT and COMMIT the predicate into a logging table. This is helpful in a multi-user or multithreaded environment or in situations where you want to collect and save session context values or other external values from standard/ extended auditing. The logging table can be used as part of the "audit" of the system or to determine who is getting access to what data.

■ You could turn on tracing and review the predicate in a trace file. This approach is useful for a database or security administrator who has access to the trace directory on the database server and only requires tracing select database sessions.

Each of these approaches has pros and cons. Where you are in your development cycle, what access you have to the database server, or what security personnel will allow will dictate which approach to use.

DBMS_OUTPUT Approach

This approach works well for developers who simply need a quick way to determine whether the generated policy is correct (syntactically and/or semantically). We modify the policy function SALES_HISTORY_EMP_ID_RLS to print the predicate before it is returned using the DBMS_OUTPUT procedure in the script named 07.logging.dbms_output.sql in the example scripts that are available with this book:

```
sec_pol@db12cr[sales]> CONNECT wmaroulis@sales
Enter password:
Connected.
wmaroulis@db12cr[sales]> -- By default SERVEROUTPUT is OFF
wmaroulis@db12cr[sales]> -- so you will not see the output
wmaroulis@db12cr[sales]> SELECT *
  2  FROM sh.sales_history;

PRODUCT      SALES_DAT   QUANTITY TOTAL_COST    DEPT_ID COMMISSION    EMP_ID
-----------  ---------  ---------- ----------  ---------- ----------  ----------
Walkman      06-NOV-13          5        250        100         23         102
Cell Phone   16-NOV-13          2        300        300         23         102

2 rows selected.

wmaroulis@db12cr[sales]> -- Try it again with the output on
wmaroulis@db12cr[sales]> SET SERVEROUTPUT ON
wmaroulis@db12cr[sales]> SELECT *
  2  FROM sh.sales_history;

PRODUCT      SALES_DAT   QUANTITY TOTAL_COST    DEPT_ID COMMISSION    EMP_ID
-----------  ---------  ---------- ----------  ---------- ----------  ----------
Walkman      06-NOV-13          5        250        100         23         102
Cell Phone   16-NOV-13          2        300        300         23         102

2 rows selected.

PREDICATE RTN: EMP_ID=102
PREDICATE RTN: EMP_ID=102
```

Two prints are present because the policy function actually is called twice during SQL statement processing—once during the parse phase and once during the execute phase.

Table Logging Approach

Next we demonstrate the table logging approach by creating a logging table and logging function with a PRAGMA AUTONOMOUS_TRANSACTION declaration. We then update the SALES_HISTORY_EMP_ID_RLS policy function to call the logging function in the script named 07.logging.table.sql in the example scripts that are available with this book.

We connect as WMAROULIS and query the table to generate a record in the VPD_LOGGING table:

```
sec_pol@db12cr[sales]> CONNECT wmaroulis@sales
Enter password:
Connected.
wmaroulis@db12cr[sales]> SELECT *
  2  FROM sh.sales_history;

PRODUCT      SALES_DAT  QUANTITY TOTAL_COST   DEPT_ID COMMISSION     EMP_ID
-----------  ---------  ---------- ----------  ---------- ---------- ----------
Walkman      06-NOV-13         5        250        100         23        102
Cell Phone   16-NOV-13         2        300        300         23        102

2 rows selected.

wmaroulis@db12cr[sales]> CONNECT sec_pol@sales
Enter password:
Connected.
sec_pol@db12cr[sales]> -- Again, two records for PARSE and EXECUTE
sec_pol@db12cr[sales]> SELECT *
  2  FROM VPD_LOGGING;

AUSER      CTIME      PREDICATE          CODE MESSAGE
---------- ---------  ---------- ---------- ----------
WMAROULIS  09-MAR-14  EMP_ID=102
WMAROULIS  09-MAR-14  EMP_ID=102

2 rows selected.
```

Again, use this approach with caution, because it is meant for troubleshooting. It should be obvious that this approach could fill up the logging table, depending on the number of users, amount of use, and so on. You could add an enable/disable flag to the policy function to turn on/off logging based on a value from the session context or a query from a configuration table, or, depending on how often or when you want to recompile your code, you could add compilation directives around the logging part of the PL/SQL block for which you would enable or disable printing.

For example, we use the session variable DEBUG_OUTPUT with value of "0" to indicate no debug output and value "1" to indicate output as the following listing demonstrates. The SALES_HISTORY_EMP_ID_RLS policy function is created with this approach in the script named 07.logging.condcomp.sql in the example scripts that are available with this book.

We could simply change the session variable to DEBUG_OUTPUT:1 and recompile the PL/SQL function to turn on debugging output:

```
sec_pol@db12cr[sales]> -- To Enable DEBUG output
sec_pol@db12cr[sales]> ALTER SESSION SET PLSQL_CCFlags = 'DEBUG_OUTPUT:1';

Session altered.

sec_pol@db12cr[sales]> ALTER FUNCTION sales_history_emp_id_rls COMPILE;

Function altered.
```

You can rerun the test shown above for the DBMS_OUTPUT approach to view the same results that were previously shown.

Trace File Approach

We enable database session tracking and review the resulting OS trace file after a query. First we create a database view (based on a contribution from Tom Kyte @ "Ask Tom" http://asktom.oracle .com) that is used to determine the trace file name and use the original policy function. This approach is found in the script named 07.logging.event.sql in the example scripts that are available with this book.

Next we connect as WMAROULIS and run the query to generate the trace file:

```
sec_mgr@db12cr[sales]> connect wmaroulis@sales
Enter password:
Connected.
wmaroulis@db12cr[sales]> ALTER SESSION SET EVENTS
  2  '10730 trace name context forever, level 12';

Session altered.

wmaroulis@db12cr[sales]> -- Query the table to generate a trace file
wmaroulis@db12cr[sales]> SELECT *
  2  FROM sh.sales_history;

PRODUCT       SALES_DAT   QUANTITY TOTAL_COST    DEPT_ID COMMISSION     EMP_ID
-----------   ---------  --------- ---------- ---------- ---------- ----------
Walkman       06-NOV-13          5        250        100         23        102
Cell Phone    16-NOV-13          2        300        300         23        102

2 rows selected.

wmaroulis@db12cr[sales]> SELECT *
  2  FROM get_trace_filename;

FILENAME
----------------------------------------------------------------------
/u01/app/oracle/diag/rdbms/db12cr/db12cr_1/trace/db12cr_1_ora_14241.trc

1 row selected.

wmaroulis@db12cr[sales]>  -- Most of the contents of the file
wmaroulis@db12cr[sales]>  -- are omitted for brevity
wmaroulis@db12cr[sales]> host
[oracle@nsgdc2 ~]$ cat /u01/app/oracle/diag/rdbms/db12cr/db12cr_1/trace/db12cr_1_
ora_14241.trc
...
-------------------------------------------------------------
Logon user       : WMAROULIS
Table/View       : SH.SALES_HISTORY
VPD Policy name  : SH_EMP_ID_CFCF
Policy function  : SEC_POL.SALES_HISTORY_EMP_ID_RLS
RLS view :
SELECT  "PRODUCT","SALES_DATE","QUANTITY","TOTAL_COST", "DEPT_ID","COMMISSION","EMP_ID"
FROM "SH"."SALES_HISTORY" "SALES_HISTORY"
WHERE (EMP_ID=102)
-------------------------------------------------------------
...
```

We see the SQL statement and predicate are displayed in the file. Obviously, our example has a simple predicate, but you can realize the value of this approach if the predicate were complex and lengthy.

All of these approaches should be used with caution, as each has pros and cons regarding troubleshooting value versus opening up the possibility of denial-of-service. You should monitor your approach carefully and enable or use it only where appropriate.

VPD Performance

A seemingly ubiquitous concern when implementing any type of security is performance. VPD performance is based on how well you write PL/SQL code. Obviously, if you have multiple cursors or have to make LDAP calls per policy function execution, then the overall performance is going to suffer.

As you have seen in the previous section, we can trace a session or query from V$VPD_POLICY to determine the returned predicate. We can then use the SQL statements to determine an optimal execution plan by adding indexes, implement a partition strategy, enable parallelism on the table, and so on. In other words, after we understand what is being executed, we can determine how to optimize its performance. The task becomes a SQL statement tuning issue.

Application Context and Logon Trigger

The examples presented so far demonstrated a simple policy function that looked up the EMP_ID from a table. However, the majority of work we do in VPD involves using an application context to cache values in the session context for quicker retrieval. Refer back to Chapter 5 with regard to VIEW performance with application contexts. The same performance advantages apply to VPD.

We demonstrate how to create a VPD policy with an application context and logon trigger in the following code:

```
wmaroulis@db12cr[sales]> CONNECT sec_mgr@sales
Enter password:
Connected.
sec_mgr@db12cr[sales]> -- Create the context
sec_mgr@db12cr[sales]> CREATE CONTEXT sales_ctx USING sales_ctx_pkg;

Context created.

sec_mgr@db12cr[sales]> CREATE OR REPLACE PACKAGE sales_ctx_pkg AS
  2      PROCEDURE set_emp_id;
  3      PROCEDURE clear_emp_id;
  4  END;
  5  /

Package created.

sec_mgr@db12cr[sales]> CREATE OR REPLACE PACKAGE BODY sales_ctx_pkg AS
  2
  3  PROCEDURE set_emp_id IS
  4        v_emp_id NUMBER := -1;
  5  BEGIN
  6
  7     -- Get the EMP_ID from HR.EMPLOYEES
  8     SELECT employee_id
```

```
 9      INTO v_emp_id
10      FROM hr.employees
11      WHERE ename= sys_context('userenv','session_user');
12
13      DBMS_SESSION.SET_CONTEXT('sales_ctx', 'emp_id', v_emp_id);
14  EXCEPTION
15      WHEN OTHERS THEN
16          NULL;
17  END;
18
19  PROCEDURE clear_emp_id IS
20      BEGIN
21      DBMS_SESSION.CLEAR_ALL_CONTEXT('sales_ctx');
22  END;
23
24  END;
25  /

Package body created.

sec_mgr@db12cr[sales]> -- Create the logon trigger
sec_mgr@db12cr[sales]> CREATE OR REPLACE TRIGGER set_emp_id
  2      AFTER LOGON ON DATABASE
  3  BEGIN
  4      sec_mgr.sales_ctx_pkg.set_emp_id;
  5  EXCEPTION
  6      WHEN NO_DATA_FOUND THEN
  7          NULL;
  8  END;
  9  /

Trigger created.

sec_mgr@db12cr[sales]> -- Update the policy function to use
sec_mgr@db12cr[sales]> -- the context value
sec_mgr@db12cr[sales]> CONNECT sec_pol@sales
Enter password:
Connected.
sec_pol@db12cr[sales]> CREATE OR REPLACE FUNCTION sh_emp_id_rls_func (
  2      p_schema   IN   VARCHAR2,
  3      p_object   IN   VARCHAR2) RETURN VARCHAR2 AS
  4  BEGIN
  5      RETURN 'EMP_ID=SYS_CONTEXT(''sales_ctx'',''emp_id''))';
  6  EXCEPTION
  7      -- If we have an issue then don't
  8      -- allow access to any records and raise an error
  9      WHEN OTHERS THEN
 10        RAISE_APPLICATION_ERROR(-20002,
 11            'An error occurred in the VPD policy function.');
 12  END;
 13  /

Function created.

sec_pol@db12cr[sales]> SHOW ERRORS
No errors.
```

Bind Variables

Bind variables help to ensure better performance in SQL statement processing, allowing the database to save time by reusing execution plans and reusing SQL statement parsing results. The database can share an execution plan if bind variables are used. We can apply the bind variable concept to VPD to assist with performance. For example, if you have a choice of resolving SYS_CONTEXT values (that is, execute the SYS_CONTEXT function in a policy function and append the results) or returning the predicate with an embedded SYS_CONTEXT function, you can achieve better performance by leaving the SYS_CONTEXT function in the predicate.

Our previous examples demonstrate querying EMP_ID from the EMPLOYEES table. However, if we used a logon trigger and an application context, the resulting predicate should perform better if we returned EMP_ID=SYS_CONTEXT('SALES_CTX','EMP_ID') instead of EMP_ID=101.

The number of rows returned from using either of the preceding predicates in a SELECT statement is equivalent. However, the predicates are not equivalent in performance, because Oracle treats the SYS_CONTEXT function as a bind variable. Oracle will generate an execution plan, and then simply replace the bind variable value with a new value based on the connected user. Oracle is forced to generate a new execution plan for the predicate EMP_ID=101 or EMP_ID=102.

VPD Caching

Oracle offers several types of predicate caching. Caching can significantly improve performance by limiting the number of times the system calls your policy function. However, if the policy function looks up dynamic values from a table, checks different session context attributes depending on the session/system state, makes external REST calls, and so on, then caching might not be appropriate for your implementation.

VPD Policy Types

Oracle offers five VPD policy types, depending on your security and performance requirements. By default, Oracle does not cache predicates, which is policy type DYNAMIC. Table 7-2 lists the policy types with a short description.

Previous examples in this chapter have demonstrated DYNAMIC VPD policy types, so we will show examples using STATIC, SHARED_STATIC, and SHARED_CONTEXT_SENSITIVE.

STATIC Caching Example

We demonstrate how the STATIC caching policy type works by introducing a 5-second pause during policy function execution. We introduce this arbitrary 5-second pause to prove that Oracle is retrieving the predicate from cache and not calling the policy function. So if the time it takes to execute the query is greater than 5 seconds, we know that Oracle did not retrieve the predicate from cache. If the query takes less than 5 seconds, we know that Oracle did reuse an execution plan from cache.

First we modify the policy function to pause 5 seconds, using the DBMS_LOCK.SLEEP procedure:

```
sec_pol@db12cr[sales]> CONNECT sec_mgr@sales
Enter password:
Connected.
sec_mgr@db12cr[sales]> GRANT EXECUTE ON dbms_lock TO sec_pol;

Grant succeeded.
```

Policy Type	Description
STATIC	This policy type assumes the predicate returned by the policy function does not change from execution to execution. The policy function is executed once per object and cached in the SGA. The predicate can still contain SYS_CONTEXT function references that access session context values, and the session context values can change. STATIC simply means the returned predicate stays the same and that the policy function isn't executed for each access.
SHARED_STATIC	This policy type is the same as STATIC, except the cached predicate can be shared across multiple database objects. For example, if two tables have the same enforcement column (EMP_ID), then system could reuse the predicate for both tables.
CONTEXT_SENSITIVE	This policy type executes only if Oracle determines changes to the context since the last time a cursor was executed within a database session. This policy type applies only to one object and is typically used during session switching with pooled connections. That is, if a connection pool is switching from end user to end user, the application is responsible for resetting the session context and re-executing a cursor (SELECT), which will trigger Oracle to re-execute the policy function, generating a new predicate.
SHARED_CONTEXT_SENSITIVE	This policy type is the same as CONTEXT_SENSITIVE, except that it can be shared across multiple database objects.
DYNAMIC	The policy function is invoked each time the SQL statement is parsed or executed. This is the default policy type.

TABLE 7-2. *Oracle VPD Policy Types*

```
sec_mgr@db12cr[sales]> connect sec_pol@sales
Enter password:
Connected.
sec_pol@db12cr[sales]> CREATE OR REPLACE FUNCTION sales_history_emp_id_rls (
  2        p_schema  IN  VARCHAR2,
  3        p_object  IN  VARCHAR2) RETURN VARCHAR2 AS
  4  BEGIN
  5     -- Wait for 5 seconds
  6     DBMS_LOCK.sleep (5);
  7     RETURN 'EMP_ID=sys_context(''sales_ctx'',''emp_id'')';
  8  EXCEPTION
  9     -- if we have an issue then don't
 10     -- allow access
```

```
11 WHEN OTHERS THEN
12        RETURN '1=2';
13 END;
14 /

Function created.
```

Next we connect as WMAROULIS and query the SALES_HISTORY table:

```
sec_pol@db12cr[sales]> connect wmaroulis@sales
Enter password:
Connected.
wmaroulis@db12cr[sales]> SELECT *
  2 FROM sh.sales_history
  3 WHERE EMP_ID = 102;

PRODUCT      SALES_DAT  QUANTITY TOTAL_COST  DEPT_ID COMMISSION   EMP_ID
----------- ---------- ---------- ---------- ---------- ---------- ----------
Walkman      06-NOV-13         5        250        100         23        102
Cell Phone   16-NOV-13         2        300        300         23        102

2 rows selected.

Elapsed: 00:00:10.04
```

There was a 10-second pause because of the new call to the DBMS_LOCK.SLEEP procedure in the policy function. Recall that the policy function is actually called twice during SQL statement processing: once during the parse phase (first 5-second pause) and second time during the execute phase (second 5-second pause). Also remember that the existing VPD policy has a policy type of DYNAMIC, which means the policy function is called for every access.

Next we drop and re-create the VPD policy with policy type STATIC:

```
sec_mgr@db12cr[sales]> BEGIN
  2   DBMS_RLS.DROP_POLICY
  3        (object_schema  => 'SH',
  4         object_name    => 'SALES_HISTORY',
  5         policy_name    => 'SH_EMP_ID_TFRF');
  6 END;
  7 /

PL/SQL procedure successfully completed.

sec_mgr@db12cr[sales]> BEGIN
  2   DBMS_RLS.add_policy
  3        (object_schema   => 'SH',
  4         object_name     => 'SALES_HISTORY',
  5         function_schema => 'SEC_POL',
  6         policy_name     => 'SH_EMP_ID_TFRF',
  7         policy_function => 'SALES_HISTORY_EMP_ID_RLS',
  8         policy_type     => DBMS_RLS.static);
  9 END;
 10 /

PL/SQL procedure successfully completed.
```

We now determine if Oracle is calling the policy function or retrieving the predicate from cache:

```
sec_mgr@db12cr[sales]> CONNECT wmaroulis@sales
Enter password:
Connected.
wmaroulis@db12cr[sales]> set timing on
wmaroulis@db12cr[sales]> SELECT *
  2  FROM sh.sales_history;

PRODUCT      SALES_DAT  QUANTITY TOTAL_COST    DEPT_ID COMMISSION     EMP_ID
-----------  ---------  -------- ---------- ---------- ---------- ----------
Walkman      06-NOV-13         5        250        100         23        102
Cell Phone   16-NOV-13         2        300        300         23        102

2 rows selected.

Elapsed: 00:00:05.05
```

So, why do we have a 5-second pause and not a 10-second pause? Oracle started processing the SQL statement and called the policy function during the parse phase, which caused the 5-second pause. Then during the execute phase, Oracle retrieved the predicate from cache and didn't re-execute the policy function.

If we execute the query again, we will see that Oracle didn't call the policy function. Instead, Oracle retrieved the predicate from cache during both the parse and execute phases.

```
wmaroulis@db12cr[sales]> SELECT *
  2  FROM sh.sales_history;

PRODUCT      SALES_DAT  QUANTITY TOTAL_COST    DEPT_ID COMMISSION     EMP_ID
-----------  ---------  -------- ---------- ---------- ---------- ----------
Walkman      06-NOV-13         5        250        100         23        102
Cell Phone   16-NOV-13         2        300        300         23        102

2 rows selected.

Elapsed: 00:00:00.01
```

As a positive side effect of using the SYS_CONTEXT function in the predicate, Oracle treats the SYS_CONTEXT function as a bind variable (recall from earlier). Oracle doesn't require a unique execution plan for each access. Also, recall the policy function returns **'EMP_ID=sys_context ("sales_ctx","emp_id")'**, which acts more like **EMP_ID=:B1**, where :B1 is a bind variable reference of the SYS_CONTEXT function.

How can we prove our SYS_CONTEXT bind variable hypotheses? We can connect as a different user and time the query. If the query happens in 5 or 10 seconds, we know that Oracle is regenerating an execution plan. If the query happens in 0.0X seconds, then we know Oracle is retrieving the predicate from cache and recalculating the value for the bind variable.

```
wmaroulis@db12cr[sales]> connect sgaetjen@sales
Enter password:
Connected.
sgaetjen@db12cr[sales]> set timing on
sgaetjen@db12cr[sales]> SELECT *
  2  FROM sh.sales_history;
```

```
PRODUCT      SALES_DAT  QUANTITY TOTAL_COST   DEPT_ID COMMISSION     EMP_ID
-----------  ---------- ---------- ---------- ---------- ---------- ----------
LCD TV       16-DEC-13         23      12500        200         23        101
LCD TV       19-DEC-13          7       3500        300         23        101
Speakers     22-JAN-14          4        521        300         23        101

3 rows selected.

Elapsed: 00:00:00.03
```

The query ran in 0.03 seconds and returned the correct values for SGAETJEN. So, Oracle retrieved the predicate from cache, updated the :B1 bind variable with 101, and fetched the corresponding rows.

SHARED_STATIC Caching

The next cache example uses the SHARED_STATIC setting, which allows the cached predicate to be used for multiple objects. This type of VPD policy is practically useful as you will likely be using the same policy function and column for multiple object enforcement. For illustration purposes, we create a backup of SH.SALES_HISTORY and add it to our policy enforcement.

The following is an example of SHARED_STATIC policy using multiple objects:

```
sgaetjen@db12cr[sales] > connect sec_mgr@sales
Enter password:
Connected.
sec_mgr@db12cr[sales] >  BEGIN
  2   DBMS_RLS.DROP_POLICY
  3     (object_schema    => 'SH',
  4      object_name      => 'SALES_HISTORY',
  5      policy_name      => 'SH_EMP_ID_TFRF');
  6   END;
  7   /

PL/SQL procedure successfully completed.

sec_mgr@db12cr[sales] > CONNECT sh@sales
Enter password:
Connected.
sh@db12cr[sales] > CREATE TABLE sales_history_bkp AS
  2    SELECT * FROM sales_history;

Table created.

sh@db12cr[sales] > GRANT select ON sales_history_bkp TO wmaroulis, sgaetjen;

Grant succeeded.

sh@db12cr[sales] > CONNECT sec_mgr@sales
Enter password:
Connected.
sec_mgr@db12cr[sales] > BEGIN
  2    DBMS_RLS.add_policy
  3       (object_schema        => 'SH',
  4        object_name          => 'SALES_HISTORY',
  5        function_schema      => 'SEC_POL',
  6        policy_name          => 'SH_EMP_ID_TFRF',
```

```
   7          policy_function      => 'SALES_HISTORY_EMP_ID_RLS',
   8          policy_type          => DBMS_RLS.shared_static);
   9   END;
  10   /

PL/SQL procedure successfully completed.

sec_mgr@db12cr[sales]> BEGIN
   2     DBMS_RLS.add_policy
   3        (object_schema       => 'SH',
   4         object_name         => 'SALES_HISTORY_BKP',
   5         function_schema     => 'SEC_POL',
   6         policy_name         => 'SH_EMP_ID_TFRF',
   7         policy_function     => 'SALES_HISTORY_EMP_ID_RLS',
   8         policy_type         => DBMS_RLS.shared_static);
   9   END;
  10   /

PL/SQL procedure successfully completed.
```

We now verify the SHARED_STATIC policy. We are expecting to see the same types of query performance results that we achieved with the above SHARED policy, except this time across multiple objects:

```
sec_mgr@db12cr[sales]> CONNECT wmaroulis@sales
Enter password:
Connected.
wmaroulis@db12cr[sales]> SET timing on
wmaroulis@db12cr[sales]> SELECT *
  2  FROM SH.SALES_HISTORY;

PRODUCT      SALES_DAT   QUANTITY TOTAL_COST   DEPT_ID COMMISSION     EMP_ID
----------   ---------  ---------- ----------  ---------- ---------- ----------
Walkman      06-NOV-13          5        250        100         23        102
Cell Phone   16-NOV-13          2        300        300         23        102

2 rows selected.

Elapsed: 00:00:05.06
```

Again, Oracle calls the policy function during the parse phase of the SQL statement; then it receives the predicate from cache during the execute phase.

```
wmaroulis@db12cr[sales]> SELECT *
  2  FROM SH.SALES_HISTORY;

PRODUCT      SALES_DAT   QUANTITY TOTAL_COST   DEPT_ID COMMISSION     EMP_ID
-----------  ---------  ---------- ----------  ---------- ---------- ----------
Walkman      06-NOV-13          5        250        100         23        102
Cell Phone   16-NOV-13          2        300        300         23        102

2 rows selected.

Elapsed: 00:00:00.02
```

The 0.02 time indicates that Oracle retrieved the predicate from cache and did not call the policy function for SALES_HISTORY.

Likewise, when we query the SALES_HISTORY_BKP table, Oracle retrieves the predicate from cache and does not call the policy function. This proves that the SHARED part of the SHARED_STATIC policy is working properly.

```
wmaroulis@db12cr[sales]> SELECT *
  2  FROM SH.SALES_HISTORY_BKP;

PRODUCT      SALES_DAT   QUANTITY TOTAL_COST    DEPT_ID COMMISSION     EMP_ID
-----------  ---------  --------- ----------  --------- ----------  ----------
Walkman      06-NOV-13          5        250        100         23         102
Cell Phone   16-NOV-13          2        300        300         23         102

2 rows selected.
```

Elapsed: 00:00:00.05

How about the STATIC part of the SHARED_STATIC policy? We now connect as SGAETJEN to verify that the bind variable aspect (STATIC) of the policy is working properly:

```
wmaroulis@db12cr[sales]> CONNECT sgaetjen@sales
Enter password:
Connected.
sgaetjen@db12cr[sales]> SET timing on
sgaetjen@db12cr[sales]> SELECT *
  2  FROM SH.SALES_HISTORY;

PRODUCT      SALES_DAT   QUANTITY TOTAL_COST    DEPT_ID COMMISSION     EMP_ID
-----------  ---------  --------- ----------  --------- ----------  ----------
LCD TV       16-DEC-13         23      12500        200         23         101
LCD TV       19-DEC-13          7       3500        300         23         101
Speakers     22-JAN-14          4        521        300         23         101

3 rows selected.
```

Elapsed: 00:00:00.02

```
sgaetjen@db12cr[sales]> SELECT *
  2  FROM SH.SALES_HISTORY_BKP;

PRODUCT      SALES_DAT   QUANTITY TOTAL_COST    DEPT_ID COMMISSION     EMP_ID
-----------  ---------  --------- ----------  --------- ----------  ----------
LCD TV       16-DEC-13         23      12500        200         23         101
LCD TV       19-DEC-13          7       3500        300         23         101
Speakers     22-JAN-14          4        521        300         23         101

3 rows selected.
```

Elapsed: 00:00:00.03

The performance results are similar to the bind variable example in the STATIC policy. So we can conclude that the SHARED_STATIC policy is reusing the predicate for multiple objects, and because we are using the SYS_CONTEXT function, we can also conclude that the policy function isn't being called for different users.

If you want to use the SHARED_STATIC policy type, but you have a need to refresh the cached statements, consider using the DBMS_RLS procedure REFRESH_POLICY, which will reparse all cached statements associated with a policy. For example, if you had a SHARED_STATIC policy, and every morning at 8:00 A.M. you needed to check whether the sales quarter was OPEN or CLOSED, you could create a database job using DBMS_SCHEDULER to refresh the VPD policy, checking for the status of the sales quarter.

SHARED_CONTEXT_SENSITIVE

The final example demonstrates the SHARED_CONTEXT_SENSITIVE policy type. This policy type enables the policy function not to be executed until the associated namespace attribute value has changed. In our example, the EMP_ID is cached in session context during a logon trigger. In theory, an end user's employee identification probably isn't going to change during the course of a database session. However, we will arbitrarily change the value of EMP_ID to illustrate the caching/parsing effect on the policy function.

```
sgaetjen@db12cr[sales] > connect sec_mgr@sales
Enter password:
Connected.
sec_mgr@db12cr[sales] > -- We drop the old policy
sec_mgr@db12cr[sales] > BEGIN
  2   DBMS_RLS.DROP_POLICY
  3     (object_schema   => 'SH',
  4      object_name     => 'SALES_HISTORY',
  5      policy_name     => 'SH_EMP_ID_TFRF');
  6   END;
  7  /

PL/SQL procedure successfully completed.

sec_mgr@db12cr[sales] > BEGIN
  2   DBMS_RLS.DROP_POLICY
  3     (object_schema   => 'SH',
  4      object_name     => 'SALES_HISTORY_BKP',
  5      policy_name     => 'SH_EMP_ID_TFRF');
  6   END;
  7  /

PL/SQL procedure successfully completed.

sec_mgr@db12cr[sales] > -- We update the package to add a new
sec_mgr@db12cr[sales] > -- procedure to change the EMP_ID
sec_mgr@db12cr[sales] > CREATE OR REPLACE PACKAGE sales_ctx_pkg AS
  2      PROCEDURE set_emp_id;
  3      PROCEDURE set_emp_id(p_emp_id in number);
  4      PROCEDURE clear_emp_id;
  5   END;
  6  /

Package created.

sec_mgr@db12cr[sales] > CREATE OR REPLACE PACKAGE BODY sales_ctx_pkg AS
  2      PROCEDURE set_emp_id IS
  3          v_emp_id NUMBER := -1;
  4      BEGIN
  5          -- Get the EMP_ID from HR.EMPLOYEES
  6          SELECT employee_id
  7          INTO v_emp_id
  8          FROM hr.employees
```

```
 9        WHERE ename= sys_context('userenv','session_user');
10        DBMS_SESSION.SET_CONTEXT('sales_ctx', 'emp_id', v_emp_id);
11    EXCEPTION
12      WHEN OTHERS THEN
13          NULL;
14    END;
15    PROCEDURE set_emp_id (p_emp_id in number) IS
16      BEGIN
17          DBMS_SESSION.SET_CONTEXT('sales_ctx', 'emp_id', p_emp_id);
18      END;
19    PROCEDURE clear_emp_id IS
20      BEGIN
21          DBMS_SESSION.CLEAR_ALL_CONTEXT('sales_ctx');
22      END;
23  END;
24  /

Package body created.

sec_mgr@db12cr[sales]> GRANT EXECUTE ON sales_ctx_pkg TO
  2    wmaroulis, sgaetjen;

Grant succeeded.
```

We grant users WMAROULIS and SGAETJEN execute privileges to allow these accounts to manipulate the application context directly. This is done only to illustrate how caching works, and you would not typically grant users privileges to execute on this namespace package if the context values are used for security purposes.

We now add a VPD policy to the SALES_HISTORY_BKP and SALES_HISTORY tables. We also add the context name SALES_CTX and attribute EMP_ID to the VPD policy:

```
sec_mgr@db12cr[sales]> BEGIN
  2      DBMS_RLS.add_policy
  3          (object_schema    => 'SH',
  4           object_name      => 'SALES_HISTORY_BKP',
  5           function_schema  => 'SEC_POL',
  6           policy_name      => 'SH_EMP_ID_TFRF',
  7           policy_function  => 'SALES_HISTORY_EMP_ID_RLS',
  8           policy_type      => DBMS_RLS.shared_context_sensitive);
  9  END;
 10  /

PL/SQL procedure successfully completed.

sec_mgr@db12cr[sales]> BEGIN
  2    DBMS_RLS.add_policy
  3          (object_schema    => 'SH',
  4           object_name      => 'SALES_HISTORY',
  5           function_schema  => 'SEC_POL',
  6           policy_name      => 'SH_EMP_ID_TFRF',
  7           policy_function  => 'SALES_HISTORY_EMP_ID_RLS',
  8           policy_type      => DBMS_RLS.shared_context_sensitive);
  9  END;
 10  /

PL/SQL procedure successfully completed.
```

```
sec_mgr@db12cr[sales]> BEGIN
  2  DBMS_RLS.add_policy_context
  3    (object_schema   => 'SH',
  4     object_name     => 'SALES_HISTORY',
  5     namespace       => 'SALES_CTX',
  6     attribute       => 'EMP_ID');
  7  END;
  8  /

PL/SQL procedure successfully completed.

sec_mgr@db12cr[sales]> BEGIN
  2  DBMS_RLS.add_policy_context
  3    (object_schema   => 'SH',
  4     object_name     => 'SALES_HISTORY_BKP',
  5     namespace       => 'SALES_CTX',
  6     attribute       => 'EMP_ID');
  7  END;
  8  /

PL/SQL procedure successfully completed.
```

At this point, we are ready to try our new VPD policy. We start by connecting as WMAROULIS and querying the SH.SALES_HISTORY table:

```
sec_mgr@db12cr[sales]> CONNECT wmaroulis@sales
Enter password:
Connected.
wmaroulis@db12cr[sales]> SET timing on
wmaroulis@db12cr[sales]> SELECT *
  2  FROM sh.sales_history;

PRODUCT      SALES_DAT   QUANTITY  TOTAL_COST    DEPT_ID  COMMISSION     EMP_ID
-----------  ---------  ---------  ----------  ---------  ----------  ---------
Walkman      06-NOV-13          5         250        100          23        102
Cell Phone   16-NOV-13          2         300        300          23        102

2 rows selected.

Elapsed: 00:00:05.06

wmaroulis@db12cr[sales]> SELECT *
  2  FROM sh.sales_history;

PRODUCT      SALES_DAT   QUANTITY  TOTAL_COST    DEPT_ID  COMMISSION     EMP_ID
-----------  ---------  ---------  ----------  ---------  ----------  ---------
Walkman      06-NOV-13          5         250        100          23        102
Cell Phone   16-NOV-13          2         300        300          23        102

2 rows selected.

Elapsed: 00:00:00.01
```

Next we cause Oracle to re-execute the policy function by changing the value of the policy context variable:

```
wmaroulis@db12cr[sales]> SET timing off
wmaroulis@db12cr[sales]> EXEC sec_mgr.sales_ctx_pkg.set_emp_id(100);
```

```
PL/SQL procedure successfully completed.

wmaroulis@db12cr[sales]> SET timing on
wmaroulis@db12cr[sales]> SELECT *
  2  FROM sh.sales_history;

PRODUCT      SALES_DAT  QUANTITY TOTAL_COST    DEPT_ID COMMISSION     EMP_ID
-----------  ---------  -------- ----------  --------- ----------  ----------
Stereo       27-OCT-13         1        100        100         23         100

1 row selected.

Elapsed: 00:00:05.04

wmaroulis@db12cr[sales]> SELECT *
  2  FROM sh.sales_history;

PRODUCT      SALES_DAT  QUANTITY TOTAL_COST    DEPT_ID COMMISSION     EMP_ID
-----------  ---------  -------- ----------  --------- ----------  ----------
Stereo       27-OCT-13         1        100        100         23         100

1 row selected.

Elapsed: 00:00:00.00
```

We can see from the preceding output that Oracle called the policy function, because the elapsed time was 5.04.

We now connect as SGAETJEN to verify the "shared" aspect of the application context:

```
wmaroulis@db12cr[sales]> CONNECT sgaetjen@sales
Enter password:
Connected.
sgaetjen@db12cr[sales]> SET timing on
sgaetjen@db12cr[sales]> SELECT *
  2  FROM sh.sales_history;

PRODUCT      SALES_DAT  QUANTITY TOTAL_COST    DEPT_ID COMMISSION     EMP_ID
-----------  ---------  -------- ----------  --------- ----------  ----------
LCD TV       16-DEC-13        23      12500        200         23         101
LCD TV       19-DEC-13         7       3500        300         23         101
Speakers     22-JAN-14         4        521        300         23         101

3 rows selected.

Elapsed: 00:00:05.03

sgaetjen@db12cr[sales]> SELECT *
  2  FROM sh.sales_history;

PRODUCT      SALES_DAT  QUANTITY TOTAL_COST    DEPT_ID COMMISSION     EMP_ID
-----------  ---------  -------- ----------  --------- ----------  ----------
LCD TV       16-DEC-13        23      12500        200         23         101
LCD TV       19-DEC-13         7       3500        300         23         101
Speakers     22-JAN-14         4        521        300         23         101

3 rows selected.
```

```
Elapsed: 00:00:00.02

sgaetjen@db12cr[sales]> SET timing off
sgaetjen@db12cr[sales]> EXEC sec_mgr.sales_ctx_pkg.set_emp_id(100);

PL/SQL procedure successfully completed.

sgaetjen@db12cr[sales]> SET timing on
sgaetjen@db12cr[sales]> SELECT *
  2  FROM sh.sales_history;

PRODUCT     SALES_DAT   QUANTITY TOTAL_COST   DEPT_ID COMMISSION     EMP_ID
----------- ---------  ---------- ----------  ---------- ---------- ----------
Stereo      27-OCT-13          1        100         100         23        100

1 row selected.

Elapsed: 00:00:05.03

sgaetjen@db12cr[sales]> SELECT *
  2  FROM sh.sales_history;

PRODUCT     SALES_DAT   QUANTITY TOTAL_COST   DEPT_ID COMMISSION     EMP_ID
----------- ---------  ---------- ----------  ---------- ---------- ----------
Stereo      27-OCT-13          1        100         100         23        100

1 row selected.

Elapsed: 00:00:00.01
```

User SGAETJEN received the same results as WMAROULIS, which validates that this type of VPD is working properly. The policy-caching capabilities can increase performance by bypassing the policy function invocation.

Summary

VPD provides a powerful and flexible way to filter data at both the row and column levels. A VPD policy is defined as a mapping of a PL/SQL function to a policy object (table, view, or synonym). The PL/SQL policy implementation can be based on an IP address, employee ID, location of client access, context values, and other factors that are required to satisfy your security policy. VPD policies are transparent to administrators, legacy applications, and end users.

VPD also supports column-sensitive policies, which allow for a more selective invocation of the policy function. This is very practical and allows you to more easily store data with different sensitivities within the same table. We demonstrated three different debugging or troubleshooting methods, which come in handy when you're trying to determine root cause or when you're trying to determine whether a resulting query is returning the correct results.

To ensure high performance, VPD has been written to modify SQL statements before being parsed and executed. This allows the database to use indexes and optimization plans to ensure fast access to data. The use of bind variables, application contexts, and enabling policy caching can significantly improve performance.

In the next chapter, we explore how to identify and control your company's sensitive data.

CHAPTER
8

Essential Elements of
Sensitive Data Control

In the past two chapters we demonstrated how the Oracle Real Application Security (RAS) and Oracle Virtual Private Database (VPD) features could be used to prevent a column from being visible in a result set. This technique is commonly referred to as "redaction" in the information technology field. The redaction technique is not a new concept in the area of information release. You may remember (or have at least seen in a movie) how information in a courtroom proceeding was redacted using a black magic marker on the original information release technology—paper.

In the modern age, many applications redact a portion of a data attribute that is displayed. You can probably recall a time when you were asked for the last four digits of your Social Security number so that the party can validate that you are who you say you are. Or, if you've ordered products online, you may recall seeing the last four digits of your credit card number displayed before you check out. These modern examples are commonly referred to as partial or dynamic redaction, while the examples in previous chapters are static or full redaction. This type of redaction is often driven by compliance regulations such as the following:

- Primary account number (PAN) for Payment Card Information Data Security Standard (PCI DSS) (www.pcisecuritystandards.org/documents/PCI_DSS_v3.pdf)

- Personal identifiable information (PII) (csrc.nist.gov/publications/nistpubs/800-122/ sp800-122.pdf) compliance for Social Security numbers, e-addresses, and phone numbers

With the release of Oracle Database 12c, you can now implement full or partial redaction on result sets that are generated from database queries using a technology called Oracle Data Redaction (DR). DR is available as a feature of the Oracle Advanced Security option and has been back-ported to Oracle Database 11g R2. The initial implementation of DR can be used to mask information in an application, but we recommend that you use RAS or VPD if you truly want to protect sensitive data.

Oracle Database 12c also includes a new feature called Transparent Sensitive Data Protection (TSDP) that enables you to discover sensitive data in your databases, define categories of sensitive information types, and define policies that will automatically apply DR or VPD policies to your sensitive data tables. The Quality Management Data Discovery (QMDD) feature of Oracle Enterprise Manager Cloud Control (OEMCC) will analyze databases in your enterprise to detect sensitive information. QMDD will then send the findings to TSDP in your Oracle Database to finalize your DR or VPD policies.

Consider sensitive data discovery findings when developing policies for Oracle RAS or Oracle VPD. You can also use the findings to assist with the development of policies for Oracle Label Security (OLS), Transparent Data Encryption (TDE), Database Vault (DBV), and Oracle Database Auditing, which we will cover in subsequent chapters.

In this chapter we will examine how to leverage TSDP and VPD together.

Sensitive Data Protection Challenges

Following are some of the challenges you face in trying to meet compliance regulations or determine how to go about identifying and protecting sensitive data:

- **Understanding what sensitive data exists in your company's databases** For example, do you know whether your company is storing PII or PCI data? Is there a formal policy on what data is considered sensitive? Although you may not have PII or PCI data, your company may be storing IP addresses or contact information that are sensitive to your business or business partners. That may sound scary, but no single person in a large company can know for sure what is in every database in the organization. There may be older, forgotten databases; new databases set up without proper approvals or certification; or databases acquired through acquisitions. You should also understand the specifics of any compliance regulations your company is subject to, as this will often help you at least understand what you should be concerned about protecting.

■ **Understanding where sensitive data resides**   Once you have identified that your database is storing sensitive data or you have formalized what data your company considers sensitive, your next task is to identify where sensitive data is stored in your company's databases. For example, do you have an accurate inventory of all the active databases in your company? For each database, do you have a data dictionary of all of the columns in each table? We will demonstrate for you later how to use the Quality Management, Data Discovery feature of OEMCC to aid in this sensitive data discovery process.

■ **Understanding when and how to protect sensitive data**   You will need to analyze each of the applications in use by your organization and how they use sensitive data. You will need to analyze transactional systems, reporting systems, and batch programs to consider whether they need full access to sensitive information or some form of redacted access. The analysis should include coverage for database authentication methods, the machines, and the networks involved to gain a complete understanding of the context in which the access occurs so you can use that information in your policies. This access could also include chronological or time-based factors such as time of day or day of the month. Performing this analysis in addition to understanding the compliance regulations your company is subject to will aid you in understanding how to protect sensitive information.

Oracle Database 12c Transparent Sensitive Data Protection

Two of the challenges discussed are knowing what sensitive data your organization has and knowing where the sensitive data resides. Knowing when to protect sensitive data is largely driven by regulatory compliance requirements. You need a strategy to identify what sensitive data exists in your company and where it resides.

Transparent Sensitive Data Protection (TSDP) is a new feature in Oracle Database 12c that allows you to discover sensitive data in your databases, to define categories of sensitive information types, and to define policies that will automatically apply DR or VPD policies to tables that contain sensitive information. You can also configure TSDP to protect sensitive data used in SQL bind variables, because their values are written to the database audit trail.

You manage TSDP using the following two PL/SQL packages:

■ **DBMS_TSDP_MANAGE**   This package enables you to define sensitive types by logical name and associate table columns to the sensitive type. The package also enables you to import sensitive column information from analyses performed in OEMCC.

■ **DBMS_TSDP_PROTECT**   This package enables you to define policies that will define the DR or VPD configurations. The package will also associate these policies to the sensitive types that were created using the DBMS_TSDP_MANAGE package. With this package, you can also enable or disable these policies by directly calling the appropriate DBMS_ REDACT or DBMS_RLS package procedures.

You can use the QMDD feature of OEMCC to analyze all of the databases in your Enterprise to detect sensitive information, import the findings, and then define TSDP policies in order to *redact* the sensitive information with DR or to *protect* the sensitive information with VPD.

Discover Sensitive Information with Enterprise Manager

The QMDD feature of OEMCC was initially built to discover application data models. Once an application data model was discovered, it was then easy for you to create masked data subsets of sensitive data that could be transferred to a target system such as a test, development, or partner environment. A data subset copies a fraction of the actual production data to the target environment. Data masking uses Oracle Data Masking (ODM) to permanently redact sensitive data being copied to the target environment. Unlike DR, which redacts information only in the SQL result sets, ODM permanently redacts the data in the target environment's database storage (that is, on disk) using some of the same type of redaction methods that DR supports. TSDP has been integrated into the application data model steps of the OEMCC process flow that supports data subsets and data masking. This process flow is depicted in Figure 8-1.

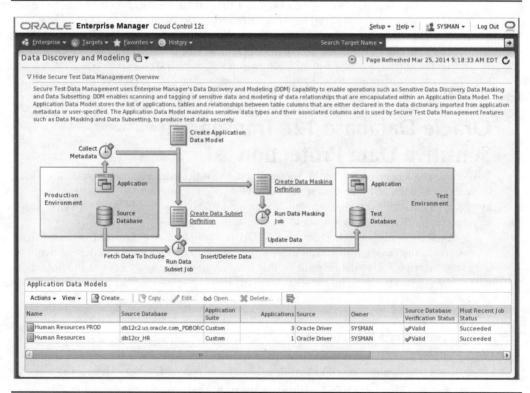

FIGURE 8-1. *Data subset and masking flow in Enterprise Manager*

Following are the high-level steps to discover your sensitive information:

1. *Create the application data model.* Select the source database and the schemas that you want to analyze. The analysis checks tables, views, and relationships among these types of database objects. Oracle has built-in support for Oracle E-Business Suite and Oracle Fusion Applications, as well as your own custom application databases. As a result of this step, an OEMCC job is created to connect to the source database to perform data model or object discovery.

2. *Discover sensitive columns.* This step allows you to review iteratively the discovery job's results created from the first step. You can select or define the types of sensitive information in the tables or views that you are interested in discovering. An OEMCC job is then created to connect to the source database to perform the discovery by sampling data from the selected tables or views.

3. *Mark discovered columns as sensitive.* In this step, you review the sensitive column discovery job results from the previous step to designate individual columns as containing sensitive data. Designating columns as sensitive makes them candidates for TSDP policies.

4. *Export sensitive column findings to TSDP.* In this last step, you export the sensitive column findings from the previous step into the source database to finalize the TSDP policies.

Let's take a closer look at this flow using the example data table HR.EMPLOYEES we created in Chapter 5.

Creating an Application Data Model

Let's create a copy of the example HR.EMPLOYEES table from Chapter 5 so that we can use the table for our application data model discovery.

First, modify the table to include a Social Security Number (SSN) column as follows:

```
sys@db12cr[hr]> CONNECT hr@hr
Enter password:
Connected.
hr@db12cr[hr]> -- Create a new table to demonstrate the
hr@db12cr[hr]> -- chapter's coverage for
hr@db12cr[hr]> -- sensitive data protection
hr@db12cr[hr]> ALTER TABLE hr.employees
  2    ADD ssn VARCHAR2(11);

Table altered.
```

Now populate the SSN column for a couple records to demonstrate the effect of various protection policies:

```
hr@db12cr[hr]> -- Update a couple records for demonstration
hr@db12cr[hr]> UPDATE employees SET ssn = '888-98-7654'
  2    WHERE ename = 'sgaetjen';
  3  ,
1 row updated.
```

```
hr@db12cr[hr]> UPDATE employees SET ssn = '777-45-6789'
  2    WHERE ename = 'wmaroulis';
  3    ,
1 row updated.

hr@db12cr[hr]> COMMIT;


Commit complete.

hr@db12cr[hr]> -- Create the copy of the EMPLOYEES table
hr@db12cr[hr]> CREATE TABLE employees_tsdp AS
  2    SELECT * FROM employees;

Table created.

hr@db12cr[hr]> -- Enable audit on the table for demonstrating redaction
hr@db12cr[hr]> -- of audit bind variables
hr@db12cr[hr]> AUDIT SELECT, INSERT, UPDATE, DELETE ON employees_tsdp
  2    BY ACCESS;

Audit succeeded.

hr@db12cr[hr]> -- Grant read access on the test account
hr@db12cr[hr]> GRANT SELECT, INSERT ON employees_tsdp
  2    TO sgaetjen;
Grant succeeded.
```

Now log into the OEMCC and select Enterprise | Quality Management | Data Discovery and Modeling from the top-level menu. The Data Discovery and Modeling screen shown in Figure 8-1 is displayed.

From the Data Discovery and Modeling screen, choose Sensitive Column Types from the Actions menu to manage the sensitive column type names and their associated regular expression patterns that will be used to discover sensitive data in our application tables or views. The OEMCC provides a number of prebuilt patterns for credit cards, national identifiers such as SSN, phone numbers, and so on—or you can create your own patterns. The prebuilt patterns are owned by the SYSMAN database account, as you will see in the XML output.

Next, click Create, provide a name for the application suite, select the database of interest, and finally select the Create Custom Application Suite. Then provide a login credential and select one or more of the database schemas of interest, as shown in Figure 8-2.

Once the schemas are selected, submit the job to perform the data model discovery.

Searching for Sensitive Information

Once the application data model discovery job successfully completes, you can edit the application suite from the main page under Enterprise | Quality Management | Data Discovery and Modeling. In edit mode, you can navigate to the Sensitive Columns tab and choose Create Sensitive Column Discovery Job from the Actions menu. You can then select the database schema(s) and sensitive column type(s) you want to search, as shown in Figure 8-3.

Once the schema(s) and sensitive type(s) are selected, submit the job to perform the sensitive data discovery.

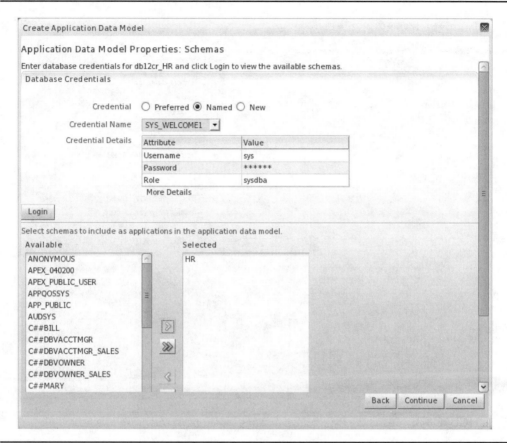

FIGURE 8-2.   *Discover application data model in Enterprise Manager*

Marking for Sensitive Columns

After the Sensitive Column Discovery Job successfully completes, you can edit the application suite from the main page under Enterprise | Quality Management | Data Discovery and Modeling. In edit mode, navigate to the Sensitive Columns tab and choose Sensitive Column Discovery Results from the Actions menu. Mark or approve each column that was identified in the discovery job as Sensitive or Not Sensitive, or leave it as Undefined based on your knowledge of the data. The management screen for this approval process is shown in Figure 8-4.

When the approval process is complete, save your work by clicking OK and then Save And Return.

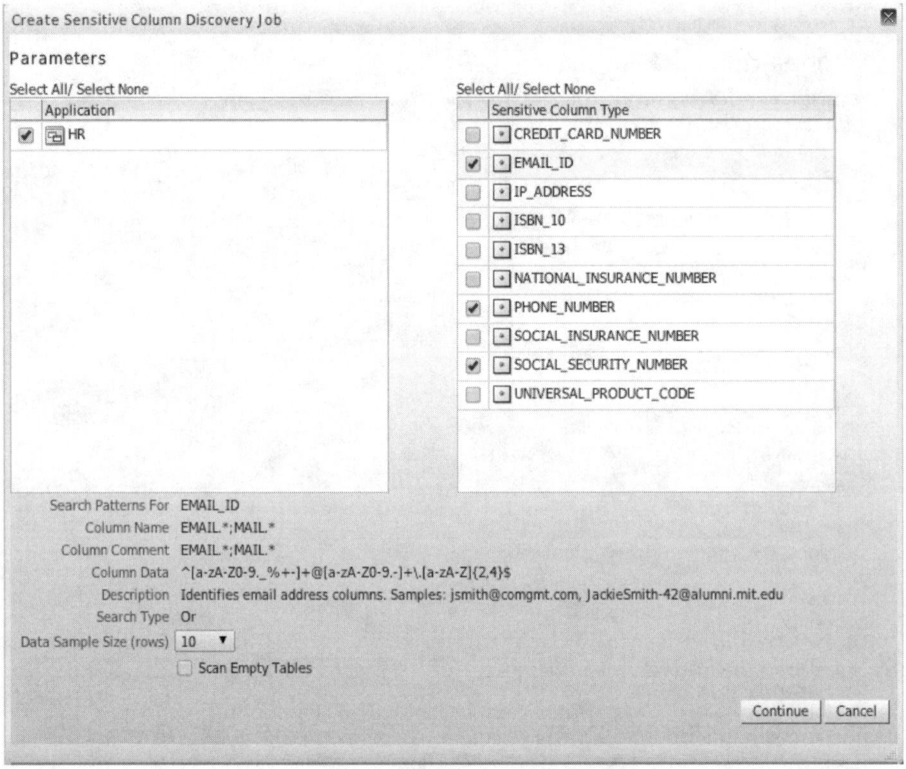

FIGURE 8-3. *Searching for sensitive database columns in Enterprise Manager*

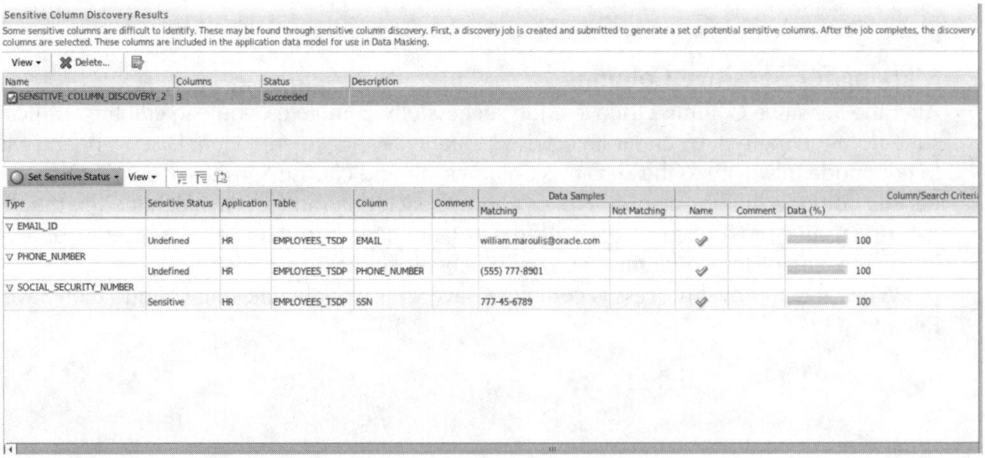

FIGURE 8-4. *Approving sensitive database columns in Enterprise Manager*

Exporting the Sensitive Columns to TSDP

Now let's export our findings from the target to the source database from the Data Discovery and Modeling screen by selecting an Application Data Model and choosing Export | Export to TSDP Catalog from the Actions menu. This step will prompt you for login credentials for the target database and will call the PL/SQL package procedure DBMS_TSDP_MANAGE.IMPORT_DISCOVERY_RESULTS to create the associated sensitive types and physical column mappings to these types in the target database. A portion of the report OEMCC would export (and then import using the package) is shown here:

```
<!DOCTYPE DDRM SYSTEM "DDRM.dtd" >
<DDRM META_VER="1.0" PROD_VER="12.1.0.4.0">
<NAME>Human Resources</NAME>
<APP_SUITE_NAME>GENERIC</APP_SUITE_NAME>
<VERSION_INFO>1.0</VERSION_INFO>
<SOURCE>ORACLE_DRIVER</SOURCE>
...
<SENSITIVE_TYPE IS_SYS_DEFINED="Y">
  <NAME>SOCIAL_SECURITY_NUMBER</NAME>
  <OWNER>SYSMAN</OWNER>
  <COL_NAME_PATTERN>SOCIAL.*;SSN.*;SOCIAL_SEC.*</COL_NAME_PATTERN>
  <COL_COMMENT_PATTERN>SOCIAL.*;SSN.*;SOCIAL_SEC.*
                </COL_COMMENT_PATTERN>
  <DATA_REGEX>^[0-9]{3}[- ]?[0-9]{2}[- ]?[0-9]{4}$</DATA_REGEX>
  <DESCRIPTION>Identifies Social Security number columns. Samples: 123-45-6789,
123456789</DESCRIPTION>
  <OPERATOR>OR</OPERATOR>
</SENSITIVE_TYPE>
...
<APPLICATION>
  <NAME>HR</NAME>
  <SHORT_NAME>HR</SHORT_NAME>
  <SCHEMA_NAME>HR</SCHEMA_NAME>
  <SOURCE>DATA_DICTIONARY</SOURCE>
  <TABLE_INFO>
    <NAME>EMPLOYEES_TSDP</NAME>
    <TYPE>Transaction Data</TYPE>
    <SOURCE>DATA_DICTIONARY</SOURCE>
  </TABLE_INFO>
  <SENSITIVE_INFO>
    <SHORT_NAME>HR</SHORT_NAME>
    <COMMENT/>
    <TABLE_NAME>EMPLOYEES_TSDP</TABLE_NAME>
    <COLUMN>SSN</COLUMN>
    <STATUS>1</STATUS>
    <REF_REL_TYPE/>
    <SOURCE>SENSITIVE_COLUMN_DISCOVERY</SOURCE>
    <TYPE>SOCIAL_SECURITY_NUMBER</TYPE>
  </SENSITIVE_INFO>
</APPLICATION>
</DDRM>\
```

Once these sensitive types and physical column mappings to these types exist in the target database, you can use the DBMS_TSDP_PROTECT PL/SQL package to define policies for those sensitive types. In the remainder of this chapter, we will show you how to use the DBMS_TSDP_

MANAGE and DBMS_TSDP_PROTECT PL/SQL packages from start to finish so you get a sense for what OEMCC has done up to this point in the example and how to finish up.

Configuring a TSDP Administrator

To allow the security administrator account, SEC_MGR, to manage TSDP policies, we have to grant execute on the DBMS_TSDP_MANAGE and DBMS_TSDP_PROTECT PL/SQL packages as shown in the following example:

```
hr@db12cr[hr]> CONNECT sys@hr AS SYSDBA
Enter password:
Connected.
sys@db12cr[hr]> GRANT EXECUTE ON dbms_rls TO sec_mgr;

Grant succeeded.

sys@db12cr[hr]> GRANT EXECUTE ON dbms_tsdp_manage TO sec_mgr;

Grant succeeded.

sys@db12cr[hr]> GRANT EXECUTE ON dbms_tsdp_protect TO sec_mgr;

Grant succeeded.
```

Defining Sensitive Information Types

The most fundamental concept of TSDP policies is a sensitive type that is simply defined with a name and comment using the procedure DBMS_TSDP_MANAGE.ADD_SENSITIVE_TYPE, as shown in the example for a sensitive DATE. Sensitive types are used to mark specific table columns as being sensitive, while simultaneously giving your company an indicator as to what makes it sensitive. You can also enable and disable TSDP policies for all columns associated to a specific sensitive type.

```
sys@db12cr[hr]> CONNECT sec_mgr@hr
Enter password:
Connected.
sec_mgr@db12cr[hr]> -- Declare a sensitive type for SSNs
sec_mgr@db12cr[hr]> BEGIN
  2      DBMS_TSDP_MANAGE.ADD_SENSITIVE_TYPE (
  3           sensitive_type => 'SENSITIVE_SSN'
  4         , user_comment   => 'Type for sensitive SSN columns');
  5  END;
  6  /

PL/SQL procedure successfully completed.
```

In this OEMCC output is a sensitive type named SOCIAL_SECURITY_NUMBER that was created during the export/import process that we could use, but we want to demonstrate the process of creating your own. If your company is subject to PCI DSS compliance, then every database administrator and compliance auditor understands why the column HR.EMPLOYEES_TSDP.SSN was marked as sensitive. You can drop sensitive types using the procedure DBMS_TSDP_MANAGE.DROP_SENSITIVE_TYPE.

Mapping Sensitive Information Types to Columns

Once our sensitive types are defined, we can start to associate table columns to the sensitive type using the procedure DBMS_TSDP_MANAGE.ADD_SENSITIVE_COLUMN as shown in the following example:

```
sec_mgr@db12cr[hr]> -- Identify the physical columns
sec_mgr@db12cr[hr]> -- that are associated to this
sec_mgr@db12cr[hr]> -- sensitive type
sec_mgr@db12cr[hr]> BEGIN
  2      DBMS_TSDP_MANAGE.ADD_SENSITIVE_COLUMN(
  3          schema_name    => 'HR'
  4          , table_name     => 'EMPLOYEES_TSDP'
  5          , column_name     => 'SSN'
  6          , sensitive_type => 'SENSITIVE_SSN'
  7          , user_comment   =>
  8              'Associate type SENSITIVE_SSN to a column'
  9      );
 10  END;
 11  /

PL/SQL procedure successfully completed.
```

TSDP includes two important dictionary views that you can use in your compliance reporting: DBA_SENSITIVE_COLUMN_TYPES and DBA_SENSITIVE_DATA. DBA_SENSITIVE_COLUMN_TYPES shows all the sensitive types you have defined. DBA_SENSITIVE_DATA lists the columns you have associated to sensitive types as shown in the following example:

```
sec_mgr@db12cr[hr]> -- We can query the data dictionary
sec_mgr@db12cr[hr]> -- to see the association of
sec_mgr@db12cr[hr]> -- sensitive types to columns.
sec_mgr@db12cr[hr]> SELECT schema_name, table_name
  2    , column_name, sensitive_type
  3    , source_name
  4  FROM dba_sensitive_data
  5  WHERE column_name = 'SSN';

SCHEMA_NAME TABLE_NAME      COLUMN_NAME  SENSITIVE_TYPE     SOURCE_NAME
----------- --------------- ------------ ------------------ -----------
HR          EMPLOYEES_TSDP  SSN          SENSITIVE_SSN      SEC_MGR

1 row selected.
```

You can change a column's sensitive type by using the procedure DBMS_TSDP_MANAGE .ALTER_SENSITIVE_COLUMN, or drop the association using the procedure DBMS_TSDP_ MANAGE.DROP_SENSITIVE_COLUMN.

Creating Sensitive Information Policies

Creating TSDP policies gives you the choice to define either collections of parameters to DR's DBMS_REDACT PL/SQL package for redaction on columns or collections of parameters to VPD's DBMS_RLS PL/SQL package for defining policies for security-relevant columns.

To demonstrate VPD, let's create the VPD policy function using the SEC_POL account:

```
sec_mgr@db12cr[hr] > CONNECT sec_pol@hr
Password:
Connected.
sec_pol@db12cr[hr] > CREATE OR REPLACE FUNCTION hr_user_only (
  2         in_schema IN VARCHAR2
  3       , in_objname IN VARCHAR2) RETURN VARCHAR2 AS
  4   BEGIN
  5     IF SYS_CONTEXT('USERENV','SESSION_USER')
  6       = 'HR' THEN
  7         RETURN '1=1';
  8     ELSE
  9         RETURN '1=0';
 10     END IF;
 11   END;
 12   /

Function created.
```

Next use the procedure DBMS_TSDP_PROTECT.ADD_POLICY to define a TSDP policy named PROTECT_SENSITIVE_SSN that will protect the column SSN in the HR.EMPLOYEES_TSDP table using a VPD policy:

```
sec_mgr@db12cr[hr] > CONNECT sec_mgr1@hr
Password:
Connected.
sec_mgr@db12cr[hr] > -- Next we define the VPD policy that will be
sec_mgr@db12cr[hr] > -- used to protect the sensitive type we have defined.
sec_mgr@db12cr[hr] > DECLARE
  2         l_options DBMS_TSDP_PROTECT.FEATURE_OPTIONS;
  3         l_policy  DBMS_TSDP_PROTECT.POLICY_CONDITIONS;
  4   BEGIN
  5         l_options ('FUNCTION_SCHEMA') := 'SEC_POL';
  6         l_options ('POLICY_FUNCTION') := 'HR_USER_ONLY';
  7         l_options ('SEC_RELEVANT_COLS_OPT') := DBMS_RLS.ALL_ROWS;
  8         DBMS_TSDP_PROTECT.ADD_POLICY(
  9             policy_name        =>
 10               'PROTECT_SENSITIVE_SSN'
 11           , security_feature     =>
 12               DBMS_TSDP_PROTECT.VPD
 13           , policy_enable_options  => l_options
 14           , policy_apply_condition => l_policy
 15         );
 16   END;
 17   /

PL/SQL procedure successfully completed.
```

The security_feature parameter dictates whether DR or VPD is to be used. The variable (l_options) of type DBMS_TSDP_PROTECT.FEATURE_OPTIONS used for the parameters defines the actual parameters to the DBMS_REDACT or DBMS_RLS policy management APIs. The variable (l_policy) of type DBMS_TSDP_PROTECT.POLICY_CONDITIONS used for the policy_apply_ condition parameter defines the criteria, such as schema name, table name, column data type, and/or column length. The criteria must be met for the policy to be applied to a column. This later variable comes into play when we attempt to enable a TSDP policy.

You can view the details about your policy definitions for TSDP using the views DBA_TSDP_POLICY_FEATURE, DBA_TSDP_POLICY_PARAMETER, and DBA_TSDP_POLICY_CONDITION. You can use the procedure DBMS_TSDP_PROTECT.DROP_POLICY to remove a TSDP policy.

Mapping Sensitive Information Policies to Sensitive Types

Once you have defined your TSDP policy parameters and policy conditions, you need to configure TSDP to associate the policy for one or more sensitive types using the procedure DBMS_TSDP_PROTECT.ASSOCIATE_POLICY. The step enables you to associate sensitive types and their related table columns to the methods in which they are redacted with DR or protected with VPD.

```
sec_mgr@db12cr[hr]> -- We then associate the policy to the sensitive type.
sec_mgr@db12cr[hr]> BEGIN
  2       DBMS_TSDP_PROTECT.ASSOCIATE_POLICY(
  3           policy_name      => 'PROTECT_SENSITIVE_SSN'
  4         , sensitive_type => 'SENSITIVE_SSN'
  5         , associate      => TRUE
  6       );
  7  END;
  8  /

PL/SQL procedure successfully completed.
```

Associations can be queried from the DBA_TSDP_POLICY_TYPE view. Associations can be removed by passing the value FALSE to the associate parameter of the procedure DBMS_TSDP_PROTECT.ASSOCIATE_POLICY.

Enabling Sensitive Information Redaction

The last step in configuring TSDP is to enable the policies you have created. You can use three procedures in the DBMS_TSDP_PROTECT package to do this:

- **ENABLE_PROTECTION_TYPE** Enables policies for an individual sensitive type, so it has the potential to affect more than one column.

- **ENABLE_PROTECTION_COLUMN** Provides great flexibility for controlling which policies are enabled, because it takes optional parameters for policy name, schema name, table name, and column name with standard Oracle wildcard support. At a fine-grained level, you could enable a specific policy for a specific table column. At a coarse-grained level, you could enable all policies for a specific schema.

- **ENABLE_PROTECTION_SOURCE** Allows you to enable policies for a specific source that was used to import or define the policy. If your sensitive type(s) were exported and then imported from OEMCC, you can use this source name. If the policies were defined using the DBMS_TSDP PL/SQL packages, the source will be the name of the user that defined the policies, such as SEC_MGR. This option also has the potential to affect more than one column.

In the following example, we enable policies for the sensitive type SENSITIVE_SSN that we created manually as part of our examples.

```
sec_mgr@db12cr[hr]> -- Finally we enable our protections
sec_mgr@db12cr[hr]> -- for the sensitive type which will
sec_mgr@db12cr[hr]> -- create the VPD policy
sec_mgr@db12cr[hr]> BEGIN
  2    DBMS_TSDP_PROTECT.ENABLE_PROTECTION_TYPE(
  3         sensitive_type => 'SENSITIVE_SSN'
  4    );
  5    END;
  6    /

PL/SQL procedure successfully completed.
```

You can use the view DBA_TSDP_POLICY_PROTECTION to examine the enabled TSDP policies. The DBMS_TSDP_PROTECT package also includes a separate DISABLE_PROTECTION_TYPE procedure that corresponds to the enable options in the preceding example, which allow you to disable the TSDP policies. If you disable the protection for TDSP you will still need to use DBMS_REDACT.DROP_POLICY or DBMS_REDACT.ALTER_POLICY to remove run-time DR policy on the affected columns. Any associated VPD policies are in fact removed when the DISABLE_PROTECTION_TYPE procedure is called.

We can validate that our VPD policy was enabled by querying the DBA_POLICIES view as shown in the next example. Note that the POLICY_NAME is auto-generated by TSDP.

```
sec_mgr@db12cr[hr]> SELECT object_owner, object_name, policy_name
  2  , pf_owner, function
  3  FROM dba_policies
  4  WHERE object_name = 'EMPLOYEES_TSDP'
  5  ORDER BY 1,2,3;

OBJECT_OWNER OBJECT_NAME     POLICY_NAME           PF_OWNER    FUNCTION
------------ --------------- --------------------- ----------- ---------------
HR           EMPLOYEES_TSDP  ORA$VPD_MYJXDMFCV0DP  SEC_POL     HR_USER_ONLY
                             LLI3O1QEDQ

1 row selected.
```

We can also validate that the run-time effect of our TSDP policy is consistent with the expectations of the VPD policy, where the HR account can view the SSN but other accounts cannot:

```
sec_mgr@db12cr[hr]> CONNECT hr/welcome1@hr
Connected.
hr@db12cr[hr]> column ssn format a15
hr@db12cr[hr]> SELECT ename, ssn
  2  FROM hr.employees_tsdp
  3  ORDER BY ename;

ENAME       SSN
----------  ---------------
sgaetjen    888-98-7654
wmaroulis   777-45-6789
```

```
2 rows selected.

hr@db12cr[hr]> CONNECT sgaetjen/welcome1@hr
Connected.
sgaetjen@db12cr[hr]> column ssn format a15
sgaetjen@db12cr[hr]> SELECT ename, ssn
  2   FROM hr.employees_tsdp
  3   ORDER BY ename;


ENAME        SSN
----------  ---------------
sgaetjen
wmaroulis

2 rows selected.
```

Redacting Sensitive Information in the Database Audit Trail

As mentioned earlier, TSDP can also be used to ensure that our redaction policies carry over to bind variables that are displayed in the database audit trail. If you are not familiar with bind variables, review Chapter 15 of the *Oracle Database SQL Tuning Guide*. The guide defines bind variables as follows: "A bind variable is a placeholder in a SQL statement that must be replaced with a valid value or value address for the statement to execute successfully."

Bind variables are not only beneficial for performance (SQL parsing, cursor sharing, JDBC statement batching), but they also help reduce the risk of security exploits such as SQL injection. TSDP is preconfigured with a policy named REDACT_AUDIT that you can use to enable the redaction of bind variables in the audit trail. Once you've defined the sensitive type, the related physical columns, and a TSDP policy on the column, you can use the DBMS_TSDP_PROTECT .ENABLE_PROTECTION_COLUMN procedure to enable audit redaction. The example that follows depicts the configuration for the SSN column in the HR.EMPLOYEES_TSDP table:

```
sgaetjen@db12cr[hr]> CONNECT sec_mgr@hr
Enter password:
Connected.
sec_mgr@db12cr[hr]>
sec_mgr@db12cr[hr]> BEGIN
  2       DBMS_TSDP_PROTECT.ENABLE_PROTECTION_COLUMN(
  3         schema_name => 'HR'
  4       , table_name => 'EMPLOYEES_TSDP'
  5       , column_name => 'SSN'
  6       , policy => 'REDACT_AUDIT'
  7           );
  8   END;
  9   /
```

We can now log in as our EUS user and perform a SQL INSERT statement on the HR.EMPLOYEES_TSDP table that uses a bind variable for the HIRE_DATE column to trigger the audit redaction to occur. The bind variable marker is denoted with ":p1" in the SQL INSERT statement and the USING l_ssn clause binds the l_ssn variable to this placeholder.

```
sec_mgr@db12cr[hr]> CONNECT hr@hr
Enter password:
Connected.
```

```
hr@db12cr[hr] > DECLARE
  2    l_ssn VARCHAR2(11) := '123-45-6789'
  3  BEGIN
  4    EXECUTE IMMEDIATE 'INSERT INTO hr.employees_tsdp('
  5       || 'employee_id,ename,ssn
  6       || ') VALUES ('
  7       || '200,''dknox'',:p1)'
  8          USING l_ssn;
  9  END;
 10  /

PL/SQL procedure successfully completed.

hr@db12cr[hr] > COMMIT;

Commit complete.
```

We now log in to the database as SEC_MGR and query the audit trail via the DBA_AUDIT_TRAIL view. We validate that the SSN value was redacted from the SQL_BIND column in the following example:

```
hr@db12cr[hr] > CONNECT sec_mgr@hr
Enter password:
Connected.
sec_mgr@db12cr[hr] > SELECT sql_text, sql_bind
  2  FROM dba_audit_trail
  3  WHERE action_name = 'INSERT';

SQL_TEXT
-------------------------------------------------------------------------

SQL_BIND
-------------------------------------------------------------------------
INSERT INTO hr.employees_tsdp(employee_id,ename,ssn) VALUES (200,'dknox',:p1)

 #1(1):*

1 row selected.
```

As you can see, the single bind variable (#1) for the SSN column is not the actual value we provided, 123-45-6789, but it was replaced by the text #1(1):*. The format for SQL_BIND value is *position*(*value length*):*value*, which can be repeated for more than one bind variable. This audit redaction feature helps to cover redaction of sensitive data in the audit trail. This is very important, because SQL_BIND values can show up in the audit trail during compliance reviews.

Summary
The redaction and protection of sensitive data is very commonplace in today's computing world. We encounter redaction in our everyday lives when we order goods and services online or have to interact with vendors over the phone. Protections such as the encryption of sensitive data on disk or over the network are standard practices in most production environments. As a supplier of these types of services, redaction and protection of sensitive data is usually mandated by compliance regulations for the industry in which those services are provided. Failure to comply with these regulations can result in legal troubles as well as troubles with the public reputation of your company.

The challenges of becoming compliant include knowing what data is sensitive, where the sensitive data resides, when to redact or protect the sensitive data, and how redact or protect the sensitive data.

In this chapter we examined how the OEMCC's Quality Management, Data Discovery feature can be used to automate the discovery of what types of sensitive data your databases contain based on standard compliance needs or custom-sensitive data definitions. This is a powerful feature that also reveals where the sensitive data resides, not only in production, but in test and development environments. You will need to analyze the applications that use these databases as well as the compliance regulations you are subject to in order to determine when the data should be redacted or protected. The context of the sensitive data's usage can be leveraged in your redaction or protection policies. The Transparent Sensitive Data Protection (TSDP) feature of Oracle Database 12c is integrated with this OEMCC discovery feature. This integration makes it easy to convert your findings from OEMCC into redaction policies in DR or column protection polices in VPD. The findings from OEMCC can also be used to define policies for other security technologies in Oracle Database such as auditing, TDE, and DBV.

CHAPTER
9

Access Controls with
Oracle Label Security

O racle Label Security (OLS) controls row-level access to data in a protected table. The foundation of OLS is Virtual Private Database (VPD), implemented using the row-level security package DBMS_RLS. OLS is another example of table fire with row filter (TFRF) as we saw with VPD in Chapter 7 and RAS in Chapter 4.

About Oracle Label Security

OLS is uniquely different from VPD and RAS because OLS offers a declarative policy with constructs for its components. OLS does not require the deep technical programming know-how that RAS and VPD require. Also, VPD, RAS, and OLS can be used as separate security components, or they can be used together to address your specific security requirements.

History

As with most new and innovative ideas at Oracle, necessity is the mother of all invention. Oracle customers needed finer grained access control of data than what was available using GRANT statements. GRANT authorizes a user to access an object; however, GRANT cannot authorize the user to access individual records within a table.

Secure Access (SA) was the Oracle consulting solution that was created to provide TFRF before VPD/OLS existed. Patrick Sack was the creator of SA, and it was sold by the Oracle consulting group (APG/NSG) for several years before Oracle Corporation created the label-based access control (LBAC) framework that integrated the SA functionality into the database. You can still see some the original SA packages/procedures in OLS. In some of the examples in this chapter, you will see package and function names with the prefix "SA".

OLS Functional Overview

OLS does not supplant discretionary access control (DAC). Instead, OLS is used in conjunction with DAC. That is, to achieve finer grained access control on/in an object (that is, a table or view), you must first have been given access to the object via the GRANT statement. Consider the example statement, **GRANT select ON sh.sales_history TO wmaroulis**. This GRANT statement authorizes user WMAROULIS to issue SELECT statements against the SH.SALES_HISTORY table. Basic Oracle security controls mediate user access to objects based on privileges granted to or inherited by the user.

OLS mediates access to each record in the table based on what the connected user has been authorized to access. User access is established at database connection time and saved in the session context. User access can be changed during the course of the database session; however, this rarely happens. As queries are issued against an OLS-protected table, OLS mediates access to each record based on the user's label versus the data label (a numeric form of a character label known as a "tag value") stored on each record. Consequently, OLS offers much finer grained access control to the contents of the table than what can be achieved with the GRANT statement.

Figure 9-1 illustrates a user accessing data in the SH.SALES_HISTORY table.

OLS vs. VPD

Invariably OLS gets compared to VPD. We are constantly asked, "Can't I just use VPD to do table fire with row filter (TFRF)? Why do I need OLS?" The answer is a simple matter of *buy* versus *build*. Is it cheaper to buy OLS or build a custom security solution using VPD?

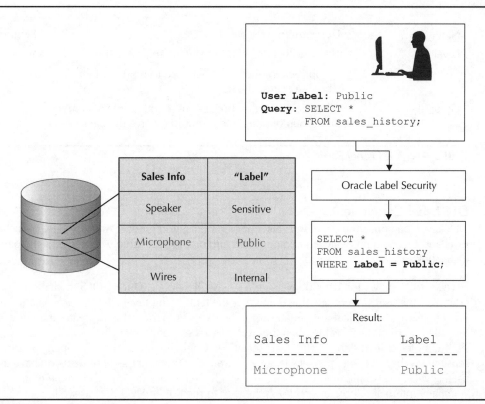

FIGURE 9-1.   *OLS mediation and access control*

OLS has all of the supporting tables, functions, procedures, packages, synonyms, views, and other tools that have been built, tested, and documented for your security implementation. Furthermore, OLS has been Evaluation Assurance Level (EAL) 4+ evaluated by the National Information Assurance Partnership (NIAP), has been used as the security foundation on numerous system accreditations, has a Oracle development/testing staff behind it, and has a worldwide user base that is constantly testing, verifying, and refining the product. You don't get this with VPD, because you have to maintain the code, updates, bug fixes, and so on. In addition, if you use VPD as the basis for accreditation, you might be faced with additional documentation, code review, third-party pen testing, and so on. It has been our experience that, in the long run, you are better off purchasing a proven product that has a history of more than 20 years in the marketplace than trying to write it from scratch.

Label-Based Access Control

OLS is a form of label-based access control (LBAC). LBAC is the mediation between an object and subject. The object in OLS is a user's label and the subject is the record's data label (numeric version is the tag). A user is given access to the record if he or she passes the mediation evaluation between these two labels. So, depending on how the OLS policy is established, typically if the user's label dominates the record's data label, then the user gets access to the record.

Name	Description	Required
Level	The sensitivity level of what you are protecting	Yes
Compartment	An optional part of the label used to refine further who can access the data	No
Group	An optional part of the label used to include a team or a group of people that should receive the data	No

TABLE 9-1. *OLS Label Parts*

OLS Label Components

OLS labels comprise three parts: levels, compartments, and groups. An OLS label must contain a level and can optionally have a compartment and/or a group. Table 9-1 describes the parts of the OLS label.

Levels   OLS allows for 10,000 levels for a single OLS policy. During OLS mediation, Oracle compares the user's numeric value (known as the tag) for the level against each data record's numeric value. For typical configurations, if the user's numeric value is greater than or equal to the data record numeric value, then the user gets access to the record.

Examples of levels are Public (least sensitive), Company Internal, or Company Sensitive (most sensitive). When you set the user's level, you are indicating what level of trust you have in this user. Levels are also hierarchical in nature, which means for our simple example that giving a user Company Internal authorization allows the user to see Public level data as well.

Compartments   OLS allows for 10,000 compartments for a single OLS policy. OLS compares the user's compartments to the data record compartments. For typical configurations, if the user possesses the same compartments or more as the data record (and the level check passes), the user gets access to the record.

For example, if the data level is set to Company Internal and the compartment is set to Legal, then only members of the Legal department with their levels set to Company Internal can see the data. If your level is Company Sensitive, but you are in the Accounting department, you would not have access to this data.

Groups   OLS allows for 10,000 groups in a single OLS policy. For a typical installation, OLS checks to see if the user possesses at least one of the groups listed on the data record. If you have at least one and you pass the compartment and level checks, then you get access to the record.

For example, a company might have partners or service providers that need access to company information. These users are different from an internal group of users such as the accounting team, and thus require a different access/labeling model.

Groups also support a hierarchical structure. You can have a parent group (SALES_DIRECTOR) that has several children groups (SALES_MANAGER_EAST, SALES_MANAGER_WEST), and SALES_MANAGER_EAST has children groups (SALES_EMPLOYEE and SALES_SUPPORT).

Oracle propagates access down the group hierarchal structure. So if a user is part of the SALES_MANAGER_EAST group, then OLS grants authorization down the hierarchical structure (the user also gets access to SALES_EMPLOYEE and SALES_SUPPORT). The hierarchical structure of groups is stored in OLS and is not reflected in the numeric value for the group.

Inverse Groups OLS supports the concept of inverse groups, which require that the user have all groups listed on the data label to access the record. For example, if a data label's inverse groups were Board of Directors and Supplier, then the user would have to have both inverse groups to access the record.

Labels and Tags

As stated, the label comprises three parts: levels, compartments, and groups as shown in Figure 9-2. Each of the three parts of the label is separated by a colon (:). Two types of labels are used in OLS: data and user labels. From the preceding descriptions, the long version of a label might look like this: Company Internal :<no compartment>: Board of Directors or Company Sensitive:Accounting:<no group>. The level component is the only part of the label that is required.

Oracle does not store the character representation of the label on the data record. Oracle creates a numeric value for the label called a "tag." The tag is stored on the data record in the security policy column that is added to the table when it is put under OLS control.

OLS Mediation

OLS uses dominance (by default) access mediation between user's label and data label to determine if a user is authorized to access data. With dominance, each component of the user's label and the data label is compared. If the user's label does not dominate the data label, then the user doesn't get access to the data. The user's level must be greater than or equal to the data label's level, *and* the user's compartment list must contain all of the compartments of the data label, *and* the user's group list must contain at least one of the groups listed on the data label.

```
wmaroulis@db12cr[sales]> SELECT product,
  2     LABEL_TO_CHAR(sh_com_pol_col) DATA_LABEL
  3  FROM sh.sales_history;

PRODUCT          DATA_LABEL
---------------  -----------------------------
Stereo           PUB:EXE,LEG,ACC:BOD,STATP,SUP
Walkman          PUB:EXE
LCD TV           CS::BOD
Plasma TV        CI:LEG,ACC:BOD
```

Level : Compartment : Group

FIGURE 9-2. *OLS components*

OLS Label Types

In this section we discuss how to create OLS labels to assign fine-grained access control of data records and to authorize end user accounts or application schemas to access those data records.

User's Session Label

The user's *session label*, sometimes referred to as the effective session label, indicates what the user is authorized to access in the database session. The session label comprises several parts, as shown in the following example:

```
wmaroulis@db12cr[sales]> SELECT *
  2   FROM session_context
  3   WHERE namespace like 'LBAC%'
  4   ORDER BY namespace, attribute;


NAMESPACE                         ATTRIBUTE                       VALUE
-------------------------------   -----------------------------   ----------
LBAC$0_LAB                        LBAC$AUDIT_TAG                  30400
LBAC$0_LAB                        LBAC$BYPASS                     0
LBAC$0_LAB                        LBAC$DEFAULT_ROW_TAG            30400
LBAC$0_LAB                        LBAC$LABELCOUNT                 7
LBAC$0_LAB                        LBAC$MAXLABEL                   30400
LBAC$0_LAB                        LBAC$MINLABEL                   10000
LBAC$LABELS                       10000                           21
LBAC$LABELS                       10100                           21
LBAC$LABELS                       10400                           21
LBAC$LABELS                       20000                           21
LBAC$LABELS                       30000                           21
LBAC$LABELS                       30100                           21
LBAC$LABELS                       30400                           21
LBAC$LABELS                       LBAC$LASTSEQ                    -1

14 rows selected.
```

Oracle uses these session "labels," which are actually the numeric tag values, during access mediation. The numeric tag values are discussed in the section "Create OLS USER/DATA Labels" later in the chapter.

User Labels

OLS user labels (along with OLS privileges, discussed later in the section "OLS Privileges") define what data a user can access from an OLS protected table. A user label includes several parts: a minimum and maximum level, a default level, and a row level. Table 9-2 describes the different OLS session labels.

Data Labels

OLS data labels are typically used to tag data records. As you will see, Oracle actually creates data/user labels, which indicates that the label either can be given to a user or can be used on a data record.

User Label Component	Description
Minimum level	The minimum level at which the connected user/application can *write* data. This setting can be used to control what label the connected user uses to write data. The setting can be used to ensure that the connected user is not "writing down" data or setting the label on the record lower than it should be for the connected network.
Maximum level	The maximum level at which the connected user/application can *read* data.
Default level	The default level for the connected user/application's session for query access—that is, the user can set the default level lower than the maximum level and higher than the minimum level.
Row level	The default level for the connected user/application for write access. If a user/application inserts a record into an OLS-protected table and doesn't provide a data label, Oracle will use this label as the default value for the associated tag.
Read compartments	The compartments the connected user has access to.
Write compartments	The compartments the connected user is authorized to use for writing or updating records.
Read groups	The groups the connected user is authorized to have access to or to read (SELECT) from.
Write groups	The groups the connected user/application is authorized to use for writing or updating records.

TABLE 9-2. *User Data Labels*

OLS Installation

OLS is a licensed database option available from the Oracle Corporation, which requires that you purchase a license before using the option; however, OLS is installed by default in Oracle Database version 12c. OLS is not automatically registered and enabled.

Installing OLS

If you are running a version of Oracle Database prior to 12c, you must first determine if OLS is installed by querying V$OPTION (see the next section). If OLS is not installed, use the OUI installer and DBCA to install it. If you are running Oracle 12c, OLS is already installed and needs to be registered in the root container and then registered and enabled in each pluggable database (PDB).

Verify OLS Installation

First, check the database registry to see if OLS has been installed. The V$OPTION dynamic view displays which options and/or features are installed in the database. Options are typically installed by default and may require separate licenses. Features pertain to the type of database you are running—Enterprise versus Standard edition, for example.

```
sec_mgr@db12cr[sales]> CONNECT sys@sales AS SYSDBA
Enter password:
Connected.
sec_mgr@db12cr[sales]> -- Check V$OPTION for the status of OLS in your DB
sec_mgr@db12cr[sales]> SELECT parameter, value
  2  FROM v$option
  3  WHERE parameter = 'Oracle Label Security';

PARAMETER                         VALUE
------------------------------    ----------
Oracle Label Security             TRUE

1 row selected.
```

If you receive FALSE as a result, or depending on the version of the Oracle Database you are running, you might see "no rows selected," then you must install OLS. We describe the process of installing OLS in the next section.

If OLS is installed, check its status from the DBA_REGISTRY. Components, like OLS, can have a variety of statuses in the database. OLS could be in any one of the following states: INVALID, VALID, LOADING, LOADED, UPGRADING, UPGRADED, DOWNGRADING, DOWNGRADED, REMOVING, and REMOVED. We need to be certain that the OLS component is VALID.

```
sys@db12cr[sales]> -- Check DBA_REGISTRY for the status of OLS
sys@db12cr[sales]> SELECT comp_name, status
  2  FROM dba_registry
  3  where comp_name = 'Oracle Label Security';

COMP_NAME                         STATUS
------------------------------    -------
Oracle Label Security             VALID

1 row selected.
```

If you receive any status other than VALID, then you must address the issue or install OLS before proceeding.

Use Database Configuration Assistant (DBCA) to Install OLS

For versions prior to 12c, start DBCA from the $ORACLE_HOME/bin directory, and then select the database in question and check to see if OLS is installed. Figure 9-3 illustrates the OLS check in the Database Configuration Assistant (DBCA).

Manually Install OLS

For versions prior to 12c, alternatively to using DBCA, you can manually install OLS in a database using the OLS admin script catols.sql located in the $ORACLE_HOME/rdbms/admin folder. You must connect to the database as SYS using AS SYSDBA and then run the catols.sql script. Oracle will restart the database once the installation is complete, so make sure that you have exclusive access to the database or you have coordinated an outage with your team before starting.

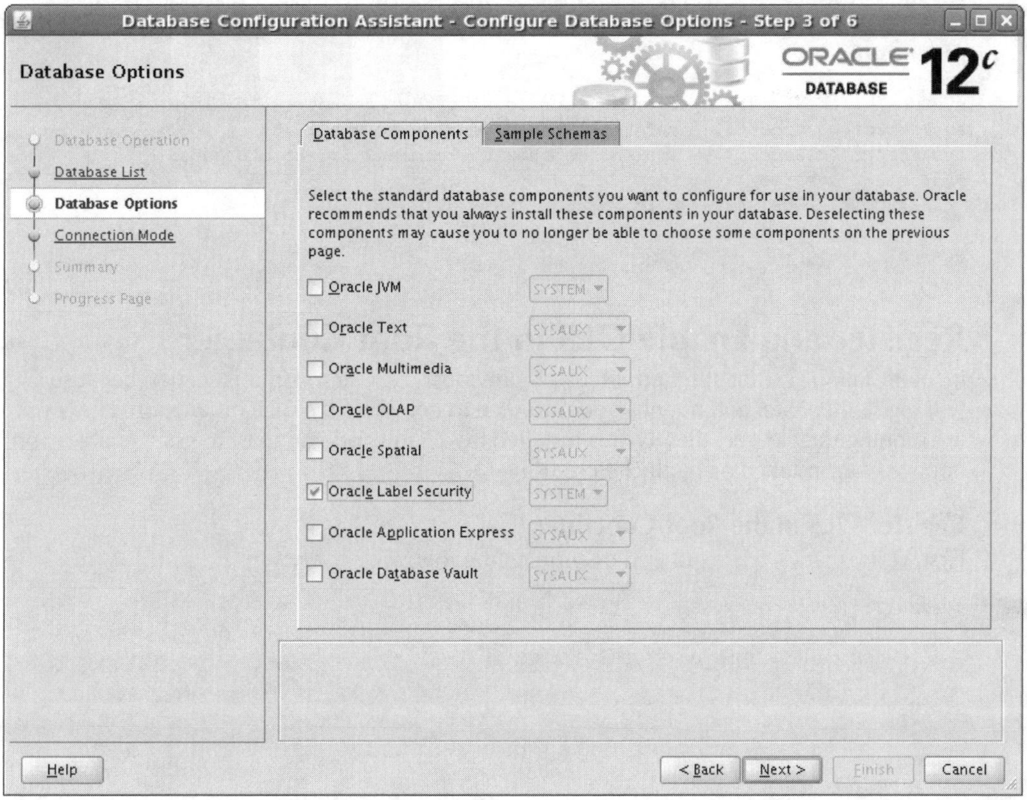

FIGURE 9-3. *DBCA OLS database security options*

Installing OLS creates the LBACSYS user and LBAC_DBA database roles. The default password for LBACSYS is *LBACSYS* and you should change it after Oracle has completed the install, and then lock and expire the account. In the following example, we install OLS in the root container of our pluggable database:

```
sec_mgr@db12cr[sales]> -- Connect to the root container
sec_mgr@db12cr[sales]> CONNECT / AS SYSDBA
Enter password:
Connected.
sys@db12cr[cdb$root]> -- Oracle will install then reboot the database
sys@db12cr[cdb$root]> -- Output cropped for brevity
sys@db12cr[cdb$root]> $ORACLE_HOME/rdbms/admin/catols.sql

...

sys@db12cr[cdb$root]> -- Depending on how far you take separation of duties
sys@db12cr[cdb$root]> -- you may want to set the password to something
sys@db12cr[cdb$root]> -- other than the default LBACSYS before locking the
```

```
sys@db12cr[cdb$root]> -- account.  This is an optional step.
sys@db12cr[cdb$root]> ALTER USER lbacsys IDENTIFIED BY <your password here>;

User altered.

sys@db12cr[cdb$root]> -- We recommend locking the account (which is done by
sys@db12cr[cdb$root]> -- default), but depending on the state of your
sys@db12cr[cdb$root]> -- system, we show the command for completeness.
sys@db12cr[cdb$root]> ALTER USER lbacsys
  2  ACCOUNT LOCK PASSWORD EXPIRE CONTAINER=all;

User altered.
```

Register and Enable OLS in the Root Container

If you install OLS using the step discussed previously, you can skip this section because Oracle will register, enable, and bounce your instance to complete the OLS installation. However, if you are running Oracle 12*c*, then OLS is installed by default and you must register, enable, and bounce your instance manually before using OLS.

Register OLS in the Root Container

First, verify that OLS is registered by running the following query:

```
sys@db12cr[cdb$root]> SELECT status
  2  FROM dba_ols_status
  3  WHERE name = 'OLS_CONFIGURE_STATUS';

STATUS
----------
FALSE

1 row selected.
```

If the result of the query is FALSE, then you must register OLS in the root container by issuing the following statement:

```
sys@db12cr[cdb$root]> EXEC lbacsys.configure_ols;

PL/SQL procedure successfully completed.
```

Enable OLS in the Root Container

Now verify that OLS is enabled by running the following query:

```
sys@db12cr[cdb$root]> SELECT value
  2  FROM v$option
  3  WHERE parameter = 'Oracle Label Security';

VALUE
---------------------
FALSE

1 row selected.
```

If the result of preceding query returns FALSE, then you must enable OLS in the root container by issuing the following statement:

```
sys@db12cr[cdb$root]> EXEC lbacsys.ols_enforcement.enable_ols;

PL/SQL procedure successfully completed.
```

Restart the Database, if Necessary

If from the preceding steps you either registered or enabled OLS, then you must stop and restart the database. If you are running in a RAC database configuration, use the server control utility (srvctl) to stop and restart the database.

If you are running in a single instance configuration, you can issue the SHUTDOWN and STARTUP statements. Remember to use the ALTER PLUGGABLE DATABASE <pdb_name> OPEN statement to open all PDBs.

Register and Enable OLS in a Pluggable Database

Once you have installed, registered, and enabled OLS in the root container, you can move on to each PDB in which you plan on using OLS. You must register and enable OLS in each PDB after you have installed OLS in the root container. Again, OLS is a licensed product and you are required to have proper licensing for OLS in each pluggable database you intend to use.

Let's proceed to registering and enabling OLS in the PDB.

Register OLS in the PDB

The following example registers and enables OLS in the SALES PDB:

```
sys@db12cr[cdb$root]> CONNECT sys@sales AS SYSDBA
Enter password:
Connected.
sys@db12cr[sales]> -- Register OLS in the PDB
sys@db12cr[sales]> EXEC LBACSYS.CONFIGURE_OLS

PL/SQL procedure successfully completed.

sys@db12cr[sales]> -- Verify that OLS is registered in the PDB
sys@db12cr[sales]>  SELECT status
  2  FROM dba_ols_status
  3  WHERE name = 'OLS_CONFIGURE_STATUS';

STATUS
------
TRUE

1 row selected.
```

Enable OLS in the PDB

Now you must enable OLS in the PDB. You can disable and then re-enable OLS later if you need to. Being able to enable and disable OLS is helpful in troubleshooting and performance testing.

```
sys@db12cr[sales]> -- Enable OLS in the PDB
sys@db12cr[sales]> EXEC LBACSYS.OLS_ENFORCEMENT.ENABLE_OLS

PL/SQL procedure successfully completed.
```

```
sys@db12cr[sales]> -- Verify that OLS is enabled in the PDB
sys@db12cr[sales]> SELECT value
  2  FROM v$option
  3  WHERE parameter = 'Oracle Label Security';

VALUE
-----
TRUE

1 row selected.
```

Restart the PDB

Similar to the root container, you must restart the PDB for OLS to take effect:

```
sys@db12cr[sales]> SHUTDOWN IMMEDIATE
Pluggable Database closed.
sys@db12cr[sales]> STARTUP
Pluggable Database opened.
```

You are now set to start using OLS. The next section covers the administration of OLS policies and components.

Administering OLS

After OLS is installed and configured properly, you should configure a database account for the administration of OLS. For security purposes, you should not use the LBACSYS account to administer OLS, and we suggest locking the account and expiring the password, as described. The administration of OLS is done via the LBAC_DBA role.

OLS Role LBAC_DBA

The LBAC_DBA role contains the privileges necessary to create and modify policies, components, and so on, for OLS. The role should be granted to your security manager database account (SEC_MGR in our examples).

Grant LBAC_DBA Role

Let's grant LBAC_DBA to SEC_MGR and verify that the role is available:

```
sys@db12cr[cdb$root]> CONNECT sys@sales AS SYSDBA
Enter password:
Connected.
sys@db12cr[sales]> GRANT lbac_dba TO sec_mgr;

Grant succeeded.

sys@db12cr[sales]> -- Connect as SEC_MGR and verify granted role
sys@db12cr[sales]> CONNECT sec_mgr@sales
Enter password:
Connected.
```

```
sec_mgr@db12cr[sales]> SELECT role
  2  FROM session_roles
  3  WHERE role like 'LBAC%';

ROLE
----------
LBAC_DBA

1 row selected.
```

OLS Administration Packages

OLS has several PL/SQL packages you can use to assist in administration. Table 9-3 lists the OLS packages and describes their uses.

The following section demonstrates using several of the OLS PL/SQL packages during the course of creating and administering our example OLS policy.

OLS Administration Using OEMCC

Oracle also supports administering OLS using Oracle Enterprise Manager (OEM), shown in Figure 9-4. Refer to the OEM administration documentation for more information.

OLS Package	Description
SA_SYSDBA	Contains procedures to create, alter, and drop OLS policies.
SA_COMPONENTS	Contains procedures to create, alter, and drop the individual components (levels, compartments, and groups) of an OLS label.
SA_LABEL_ADMIN	Contains procedures to create, alter, and drop OLS labels.
SA_POLICY_ADMIN	Contains procedures to add, remove, and enable/disable OLS policy control on database tables or database schema. The package can also be used to control the synchronization of OLS policies stored in LDAP.
SA_USER_ADMIN	Contains procedures to add, modify, and set user labels.
SA_AUDIT_ADMIN	Contains functions and procedures to establish and enable/disable auditing on OLS objects.
SA_SESSION	Contains procedures and functions to retrieve OLS labels and label components from the connected session. You can also set the label for the connected session using this package.
SA_UTL	Contains general utility functions for OLS.

TABLE 9-3.   *OLS Packages*

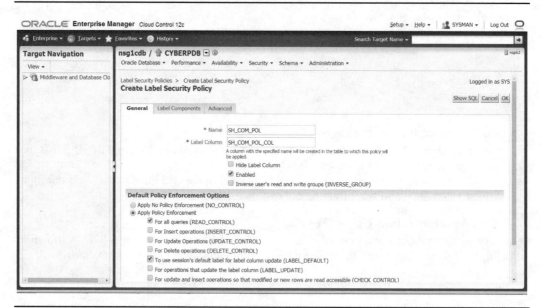

FIGURE 9-4. *OLS administration using OEM*

OLS Example

You can use OLS and create a policy against the SALES_HISTORY table from the SH schema. The OLS policy we create in the following example is equivalent to the TFRF VPD policy from Chapter 7. You can create a VPD policy and an OLS policy on the same table to achieve the same effect.

Create a Policy

You cannot create OLS policies or OLS enforcement in the root container. Furthermore, you cannot share OLS policies across pluggable databases—that is, each PDB's implementation or use of OLS is exclusively contained in that PDB. You can duplicate the OLS policy name and components in multiple PDBs without unique name constraint violations. To create an OLS policy, we use the SA_SYSDBA package and specifically the CREATE_POLICY procedure. The procedure takes three parameters, but only the first parameter, POLICY_NAME, is required; this is an arbitrary name that must be unique to the PDB. The second parameter, COLUMN_NAME, indicates the column name that Oracle will add to the protected table(s) and will use to store the numeric OLS data label (tag) for the record. The default value for COLUMN_NAME is <policy_name>_COL. Note that, similar to the policy name, the column name must be unique, as two OLS policies cannot share the same column name. OLS also creates a database role named <policy_name>_DBA to administer the OLS policy. The role aids in the separation of security administrative duties, as you are not required to grant the LBAC_DBA role to each OLS policy administrator.

Here is how you grant the policy specific role <policy_name>_DBA:

```
sec_mgr@db12cr[sales]> DESCRIBE sa_sysdba
...
PROCEDURE CREATE_POLICY
 Argument Name                  Type                    In/Out Default?
 ------------------------------ ----------------------- ------ --------
 POLICY_NAME                    VARCHAR2                IN
 COLUMN_NAME                    VARCHAR2                IN     DEFAULT
 DEFAULT_OPTIONS                VARCHAR2                IN     DEFAULT
...
```

The final parameter, DEFAULT_OPTIONS, describes how Oracle enforces the OLS policy for objects under policy control. At this point, you have two choices: You can set the enforcement option for the policy and, as you add tables to the policy, the table will inherit the policies' default enforcement control. Or you can leave this value NULL (the default value) and set policy enforcement specific to each object (table) you add later. The following section describes the enforcement options.

OLS Policy Enforcement Options

OLS has several policy enforcement types, which can be applied individually or aggregated together based on the desired level of security for your system. Table 9-4 describes the different OLS policy enforcement types.

Typically, we use the ALL_CONTROL policy type, unless there is a security relevant reason. At this point, we can create our OLS policy as demonstrated in the following example. We create an OLS policy name SH_COM_POL for the sales history commission policy, and because we did not indicate a value for the COLUMN_NAME parameter, Oracle will added a security policy column to the table named SH_COM_POL_COL.

```
sec_mgr@db12cr[sales]> BEGIN
  2   sa_sysdba.create_policy (
  3      policy_name => 'SH_COM_POL');
  4   END;
  5   /

PL/SQL procedure successfully completed.

sec_mgr@db12cr[sales]>  -- Verify the status of the OLS policy
sec_mgr@db12cr[sales]>  SELECT policy_name, column_name, status
  2   FROM dba_sa_policies;

POLICY_NAME   COLUMN_NAME       STATUS
------------  ----------------  --------
SH_COM_POL    SH_COM_POL_COL    ENABLED

1 row selected.
```

You can think of the OLS policy as a folder that keeps track of several components of the OLS policy: labels, label components, and so on.

Create Label Components

The next step in our example is to create the label components necessary for our policy—or, stated differently, the components that are necessary to implement our company's security policy.

Enforcement Type	Description
READ_CONTROL	Enforce OLS policy during SELECT, UPDATE, and DELETE statement processing. Read on UPDATE and DELETE might not seem obvious at first, but to update or remove data, you first must be able to query or access the data.
WRITE_CONTROL	Enforce OLS policy during INSERT, UPDATE, and DELETE statement processing. This is a shortcut for using INSERT_CONTROL, UPDATE_CONTROL, and DELETE_CONTROL together.
INSERT_CONTROL	Enforce OLS policy during INSERT statement processing. Typically used when WRITE_CONTROL is not specified and you want statement-level control.
UPDATE_CONTROL	Enforce OLS policy during UPDATE statement processing. Typically used when WRITE_CONTROL is not specified and you want statement-level control.
DELETE_CONTROL	Enforce OLS policy during DELETE statement processing. Typically used when WRITE_CONTROL is not specified and you want statement-level control.
LABEL_DEFAULT	Insert the user's default ROW LEVEL label during an INSERT, if the user does not explicitly set the label for the record.
LABEL_UPDATE	Insert the user's default ROW LEVEL label during an UPDATE, if the user does not explicitly set the label for the record.
LABEL_CHECK	Enforce/verify that when the user issues an INSERT or UPDATE statement, the user can access the record after the statement completes. Depending on your security policy, you may want the connected user to be able to read the record(s) after an INSERT or UPDATE statement. This type of enforcement protects against a user inserting or updating data outside of his or her security or authorization realm.
INVERSE_GROUP	Sets the policy for inverse group enforcement.
ALL_CONTROL	Applies all enforcement control options.
NO_CONTROL	Does not enforce an OLS policy

TABLE 9-4.   *OLS Policy Enforcement Types*

Create OLS Levels

Levels are required, and they constitute the sensitivity of the data being protected. In our example, we will create three levels: PUBLIC, COMPANY INTERNAL, and COMPANY SENSITIVE. OLS uses a hierarchical approach to the way it processes levels. You can think of PUBLIC as the lowest level or least significant in our policy, with COMPANY INTERNAL being the next, and COMPANY SENSITIVE being the highest level. We set the numeric values for the levels correspondingly. This allows Oracle to compare the user's level numerically to the data level to determine if we get access to the record or not.

We use the CREATE_LEVEL procedure from the SA_COMPONENTS package to create the components:

```
sec_mgr@db12cr[sales]> DESCRIBE sa_components
...
PROCEDURE CREATE_LEVEL
 Argument Name                  Type                    In/Out Default?
 ------------------------------ ----------------------- ------ --------
 POLICY_NAME                    VARCHAR2                IN
 LEVEL_NUM                      NUMBER(38)              IN
 SHORT_NAME                     VARCHAR2                IN
 LONG_NAME                      VARCHAR2                IN
...
```

The policy name is the name we previously created. The LEVEL_NUM parameter indicates the numeric value used in mediation, as we described earlier. The SHORT_NAME (used in assigning, creating users, data labels) and LONG_NAMES (mainly used for display purposes only) are the names we give the label. The following example creates our labels based on our hierarchical and security policy needs:

```
sec_mgr@db12cr[sales]>  BEGIN
  2      -- Most sensitive level
  3      sa_components.create_level
  4               (policy_name    => 'SH_COM_POL',
  5                long_name      => 'COMPANY SENSITIVE',
  6                short_name     => 'CS',
  7                level_num      => 9000);
  8   END;
  9   /

PL/SQL procedure successfully completed.

sec_mgr@db12cr[sales]> BEGIN
  2      -- Company sensitive level
  3      sa_components.create_level
  4               (policy_name    => 'SH_COM_POL',
  5                long_name      => 'COMPANY INTERNAL',
  6                short_name     => 'CI',
  7                level_num      => 8000);
  8   END;
  9   /

PL/SQL procedure successfully completed.

sec_mgr@db12cr[sales]>  BEGIN
  2      -- Least sensitive level
  3      sa_components.create_level
  4               (policy_name    => 'SH_COM_POL',
  5                long_name      => 'PUBLIC',
  6                short_name     => 'PUB',
  7                level_num      => 7000);
  8   END;
  9   /

PL/SQL procedure successfully completed.
```

```
sec_mgr@db12cr[sales] > -- Verify the levels
sec_mgr@db12cr[sales] > SELECT *
  2  FROM dba_sa_levels
  3  WHERE policy_name = 'SH_COM_POL'
  3  ORDER BY level_num DESC;

POLICY_NAME   LEVEL_NUM SHORT_NAME LONG_NAME
------------  --------- ---------- ----------------
SH_COM_POL         9000 CS         COMPANY SENSITIVE
SH_COM_POL         8000 CI         COMPANY INTERNAL
SH_COM_POL         7000 PUB        PUBLIC

3 rows selected.
```

Levels are all that are required to create OLS labels; however, we demonstrate OLS compartments and groups for completeness. Whether or not you need to create compartments and groups depends on the complexity and extensiveness of your security policy and requirements.

Create OLS Compartments

Compartments are optional, and they indicate special or refined access or privileges needed to access the data. For our example, we create three compartments, ACCOUNTING, EXECUTIVE, and LEGAL, which represent a further refinement of who can access what data.

We use the CREATE_COMPARTMENT procedure from the SA_COMPARTMENTS package to create our compartments:

```
sec_mgr@db12cr[sales] > DESCRIBE sa_compartments
...
PROCEDURE CREATE_COMPARTMENT
 Argument Name                 Type                   In/Out Default?
 ----------------------------- ---------------------- ------ --------
 POLICY_NAME                   VARCHAR2               IN
 COMP_NUM                      NUMBER(38)             IN
 SHORT_NAME                    VARCHAR2               IN
 LONG_NAME                     VARCHAR2               IN
...
```

This procedure has the same parameter signature (except for the name COMP_NUM versus LEVEL_NUM) as CREATE_LEVEL shown previously. However, COMP_NUM simply indicates the notional order of the compartment and not a comparative order as with levels. As you recall, in non-inverse configurations, Oracle requires that you have been granted all compartments that exist on the record's data label to access the record.

We create our compartments in the following example:

```
sec_mgr@db12cr[sales] > BEGIN
  2      sa_components.create_compartment
  3              (policy_name => 'SH_COM_POL',
  4               long_name   => 'EXECUTIVE',
  5               short_name  => 'EXE',
  6               comp_num    => 1000);
  7  END;
  8  /

PL/SQL procedure successfully completed.
```

```
sec_mgr@db12cr[sales]> BEGIN
  2     sa_components.create_compartment
  3              (policy_name => 'SH_COM_POL',
  4               long_name   => 'LEGAL',
  5               short_name  => 'LEG',
  6               comp_num    => 2000);
  7  END;
  8  /

PL/SQL procedure successfully completed.

sec_mgr@db12cr[sales]> BEGIN
  2     sa_components.create_compartment
  3              (policy_name => 'SH_COM_POL',
  4               long_name   => 'ACCOUNTING',
  5               short_name  => 'ACC',
  6               comp_num    => 3000);
  7  END;
  8  /

PL/SQL procedure successfully completed.

sec_mgr@db12cr[sales]> -- Verify the compartments
sec_mgr@db12cr[sales]> SELECT *
  2  FROM dba_sa_compartments
  3  WHERE policy_name = 'SH_COM_POL'
  4  ORDER BY comp_num;

POLICY_NAME      COMP_NUM SHORT_NAME LONG_NAME
------------ ---------- ---------- --------------------
SH_COM_POL       1000 EXE        EXECUTIVE
SH_COM_POL       2000 LEG        LEGAL
SH_COM_POL       3000 ACC        ACCOUNTING

3 rows selected.
```

Create Groups

Groups are optional, and they indicate additional entities that the data can be shared with. We create three groups, BOARD OF DIRECTORS, STRATEGIC PARTNER, and SUPPLIER, to indicate types of B2B interactions with groups outside the company (not PUBLIC), but who need access to company information or with whom the company needs to interact. Group interactions tend to be less sensitive in nature than compartment interactions. As seen in our example, the company acquisitions and legal team will have access to more data than a strategic partner or company supplier of goods and services.

We use the CREATE_GROUP procedure from the SA_COMPONENTS package to create our groups.

```
sec_mgr@db12cr[sales]> DESCRIBE sa_components
...
PROCEDURE CREATE_GROUP
 Argument Name                     Type                    In/Out Default?
 --------------------------------- ----------------------- ------ --------
 POLICY_NAME                       VARCHAR2                IN
 GROUP_NUM                         NUMBER(38)              IN
 SHORT_NAME                        VARCHAR2                IN
```

```
LONG_NAME                     VARCHAR2              IN
PARENT_NAME                   VARCHAR2              IN      DEFAULT
...
```

The signature for the CREATE_GROUP procedure is similar to that of CREATE_LEVEL and CREATE_COMPARTMENT, except for PARENT_NAME. PARENT_NAME indicates that groups can have a hierarchy or parent/child relationship with another group. If the PARENT_NAME is NULL, then the group is considered a parent. If you indicate a value for the PARENT_NAME, then the group must exist and the group being created is the child to the existing parent. The GROUP_NUM is an arbitrary value that only affects the order in which the group names are displayed.

We create our groups in the following example:

```
sec_mgr@db12cr[sales]> BEGIN
  2   sa_components.create_group
  3              (policy_name => 'SH_COM_POL',
  4               long_name   => 'BOARD OF DIRECTORS',
  5               short_name  => 'BOD',
  6               group_num   => 1000);
  7   END;
  8   /

PL/SQL procedure successfully completed.

sec_mgr@db12cr[sales]> BEGIN
  2      sa_components.create_group
  3              (policy_name => 'SH_COM_POL',
  4               long_name   => 'STRATEGIC PARTNER',
  5               short_name  => 'STATP',
  6               group_num   => 2000);
  7   END;
  8   /

PL/SQL procedure successfully completed.

sec_mgr@db12cr[sales]> BEGIN
  2      sa_components.create_group
  3              (policy_name => 'SH_COM_POL',
  4               long_name   => 'SUPPLIER',
  5               short_name  => 'SUP',
  6               group_num   => 3000);
  7   END;
  8   /

PL/SQL procedure successfully completed.

sec_mgr@db12cr[sales]> -- Verify the OLS Groups
sec_mgr@db12cr[sales]> SELECT *
  2   FROM DBA_SA_GROUPS
  3   ORDER BY group_num;
```

POLICY_NAME	GROUP_NUM	SHORT_NAME	LONG_NAME	PARENT_NUM	PARENT_NAME
SH_COM_POL	1000	BOD	BOARD OF DIRECTORS		
SH_COM_POL	2000	STATP	STRATEGIC PARTNER		
SH_COM_POL	3000	SUP	SUPPLIER		

```
3 rows selected.
```

Inverse Groups

You use the CREATE_POLICY procedure in the SA_SYSDBA package to create inverse groups. You cannot modify or remove inverse groups from the policy after the policy is created. You must drop and re-create the policy without indicating inverse groups. Also, you cannot elect to use inverse groups or not use inverse groups when you apply the policy to the table. Inverse groups are different from other policy options in that, if the policy is set to use inverse groups, then all tables automatically inherit the inverse groups setting when added to the policy.

The following example demonstrates how to create an inverse group:

```
sec_mgr@db12cr[sales]> BEGIN
  2  sa_sysdba.create_policy (
  3    policy_name      => 'SH_COM_POL_IG',
  4    default_options => 'INVERSE_GROUP');
  5  END;
  6  /

PL/SQL procedure successfully completed.
```

At this point we are ready to create OLS labels.

Create OLS Labels

OLS labels can be of type user or type data. There are two types of labels because of the semantic interpretation of the label or your business rules regarding the use of the label. For example, suppose we have a level of PUBLIC and a compartment of LEGAL; however, our business rules state that the label PUBLIC:LEGAL level/compartment combination is invalid. So our company does not permit a publicly released document to contain sensitive legal information. We recommend spending time evaluating which combinations level/compartments/groups are valid for your security policy before you start creating arbitrary labels.

Create OLS USER/DATA Labels

We create labels by using the CREATE_LABEL procedure from the SA_LABEL_ADMIN package:

```
sec_mgr@db12cr[sales]> DESCRIBE sa_label_admin
...
PROCEDURE CREATE_LABEL
 Argument Name                   Type                     In/Out Default?
 ------------------------------- ------------------------ ------ --------
 POLICY_NAME                     VARCHAR2                 IN
 LABEL_TAG                       BINARY_INTEGER           IN
 LABEL_VALUE                     VARCHAR2                 IN
 DATA_LABEL                      BOOLEAN                  IN     DEFAULT
...
```

The POLICY_NAME parameter is the same policy name that we created for the levels, compartments, and groups. The LABEL_TAG parameter must be a unique value that identifies the label. Oracle supports 10 numeric digits (9,999,999,999) for the label tag value, or approximately 10 billion labels. Be sensitive to the fact that lots of labels with lots of users may impact performance. The LABEL_VALUE parameter is an amalgam of the level and/or compartment and/or group short names separated by a colon(s). The DATA_LABEL parameter indicates whether the label can be used to label a record (the default value is TRUE) or whether it can only be assigned to a user.

We now create our OLS labels for the SH_COM_POL policy. Notice that we are using a number convention for the LABEL_VALUE: 10000 for PUB, 20000 for CI, and 30000 for CS. The numbers with the corresponding levels represent a label series. As we add more labels to our system, we will then associate the label number to the appropriate label series. For example, if we add PUB::SUP, the corresponding LABEL_VALUE will start with 3 (such as 300010). Consequently, if we are querying the security column directly or are interacting with the data, then we can tell which series the label is from by looking at the first digit.

The following example is very simple, and you should spend time thinking about the LABEL_VALUE with respect to the growth in the number of labels for your company/system:

```
sec_mgr@db12cr[sales]> -- For Public information
sec_mgr@db12cr[sales]> BEGIN
  2     sa_label_admin.create_label
  3        (policy_name => 'SH_COM_POL',
  4         label_tag   => 10000,
  5         label_value => 'PUB::',
  6         data_label  => TRUE);
  7  END;
  8  /

PL/SQL procedure successfully completed.

sec_mgr@db12cr[sales]> -- For Company Internal information
sec_mgr@db12cr[sales]> BEGIN
  2     sa_label_admin.create_label
  3        (policy_name => 'SH_COM_POL',
  4         label_tag   => 20000,
  5         label_value => 'CI::',
  6         data_label  => TRUE);
  7  END;
  8  /

PL/SQL procedure successfully completed.

sec_mgr@db12cr[sales]> -- For Company Sensitive information
sec_mgr@db12cr[sales]> BEGIN
  2     sa_label_admin.create_label
  3        (policy_name => 'SH_COM_POL',
  4         label_tag   => 30000,
  5         label_value => 'CS::',
  6         data_label  => TRUE);
  7  END;
  8  /

PL/SQL procedure successfully completed.

sec_mgr@db12cr[sales]> -- For Public Board of Directors
sec_mgr@db12cr[sales]> BEGIN
  2     sa_label_admin.create_label
  3        (policy_name => 'SH_COM_POL',
  4         label_tag   => 10100,
  5         label_value => 'PUB::BOD',
  6         data_label  => TRUE);
```

```
  7  END;
  8  /

PL/SQL procedure successfully completed.

sec_mgr@db12cr[sales]> -- For Public Strategic Partners
sec_mgr@db12cr[sales]> BEGIN
  2      sa_label_admin.create_label
  3          (policy_name => 'SH_COM_POL',
  4           label_tag   => 10200,
  5           label_value => 'PUB::STATP',
  6           data_label  => TRUE);
  7  END;
  8  /

PL/SQL procedure successfully completed.

sec_mgr@db12cr[sales]> -- For Public Suppliers
sec_mgr@db12cr[sales]> BEGIN
  2      sa_label_admin.create_label
  3          (policy_name => 'SH_COM_POL',
  4           label_tag   => 10300,
  5           label_value => 'PUB::SUP',
  6           data_label  => TRUE);
  7  END;
  8  /

PL/SQL procedure successfully completed.

sec_mgr@db12cr[sales]> -- For Public Board of Directors, Strategic Partners,
sec_mgr@db12cr[sales]> -- or Suppliers
sec_mgr@db12cr[sales]> BEGIN
  2      sa_label_admin.create_label
  3          (policy_name => 'SH_COM_POL',
  4           label_tag   => 10400,
  5           label_value => 'PUB::BOD,STATP,SUP',
  6           data_label  => TRUE);
  7  END;
  8  /

PL/SQL procedure successfully completed.

sec_mgr@db12cr[sales]> -- For Company Sensitive Executive Staff
sec_mgr@db12cr[sales]> BEGIN
  2      sa_label_admin.create_label
  3          (policy_name => 'SH_COM_POL',
  4           label_tag   => 30100,
  5           label_value => 'CS:EXE:',
  6           data_label  => TRUE);
  7  END;
  8  /

PL/SQL procedure successfully completed.

sec_mgr@db12cr[sales]> -- For Company Sensitive Legal and Executive Staff
```

```
sec_mgr@db12cr[sales]> BEGIN
  2    sa_label_admin.create_label
  3       (policy_name => 'SH_COM_POL',
  4        label_tag   => 30200,
  5        label_value => 'CS:LEG,EXE:',
  6        data_label  => TRUE);
  7  END;
  8  /

PL/SQL procedure successfully completed.

sec_mgr@db12cr[sales]> -- For Company Sensitive Accounting
sec_mgr@db12cr[sales]> BEGIN
  2    sa_label_admin.create_label
  3       (policy_name => 'SH_COM_POL',
  4        label_tag   => 30300,
  5        label_value => 'CS:ACC:',
  6        data_label  => TRUE);
  7  END;
  8  /

PL/SQL procedure successfully completed.

sec_mgr@db12cr[sales]> -- Notice that Oracle stripped the trailing ":"
sec_mgr@db12cr[sales]> -- from some of the labels
sec_mgr@db12cr[sales]> SELECT *
  2  FROM dba_sa_labels
  3  WHERE policy_name = 'SH_COM_POL'
  3  ORDER BY label_tag;

POLICY_NAME   LABEL                 LABEL_TAG LABEL_TYPE
-----------   ------------------    --------- ---------------
SH_COM_POL    PUB                       10000 USER/DATA LABEL
SH_COM_POL    PUB::BOD                  10100 USER/DATA LABEL
SH_COM_POL    PUB::STATP                10200 USER/DATA LABEL
SH_COM_POL    PUB::SUP                  10300 USER/DATA LABEL
SH_COM_POL    PUB::BOD,STATP,SUP        10400 USER/DATA LABEL
SH_COM_POL    CI                        20000 USER/DATA LABEL
SH_COM_POL    CS                        30000 USER/DATA LABEL
SH_COM_POL    CS:EXE                    30100 USER/DATA LABEL
SH_COM_POL    CS:EXE,LEG                30200 USER/DATA LABEL
SH_COM_POL    CS:ACC                    30300 USER/DATA LABEL

10 rows selected.
```

As you can see from the LABEL_TYPE column, these labels can be assigned to a user or used on a data record.

Noncomparable Labels

OLS includes the concept of noncomparable labels if neither label dominates the other. For example, if CS:EXE and CS:ACC are noncomparable because they do not dominate each other.

Dominance Functions

You can use several functions to compare labels. Table 9-5 lists the functions found in the SA_UTL package and describes their use.

OLS Function	Description
STRICTLY_DOMINATES (L1, L2)	L1 label dominates L2 label and L1 is not equal to L2
DOMINATES (L1, L2)	L1 label dominates L2 label or L1 is equal to L2
DOMINATED_BY (L1, L2)	L1 label is dominated by L2
STRICTLY_DOMINATED_BY (L1, L2)	L1 label is dominated by L2 and L1 is not equal to L2

TABLE 9-5.   *OLS Dominance Functions*

Assign OLS Labels to Users

We use the SET_USER_LABELS procedure from the SA_USER_ADMIN package to set the user's label. The SA_USER_ADMIN package has several procedures you can use to assign components of the OLS label to the user.

```
sec_mgr@db12cr[sales]> DESCRIBE sa_user_admin
...
PROCEDURE SET_USER_LABELS
 Argument Name                 Type                     In/Out Default?
 ----------------------------- ------------------------ ------ --------
 POLICY_NAME                   VARCHAR2                 IN
 USER_NAME                     VARCHAR2                 IN
 MAX_READ_LABEL                VARCHAR2                 IN
 MAX_WRITE_LABEL               VARCHAR2                 IN     DEFAULT
 MIN_WRITE_LABEL               VARCHAR2                 IN     DEFAULT
 DEF_LABEL                     VARCHAR2                 IN     DEFAULT
 ROW_LABEL                     VARCHAR2                 IN     DEFAULT
...
```

The MAX_READ_LABEL is the user's maximum authorized access label. The MAX_WRITE_LABEL is the user's maximum write label, and if you do not specify a value, then the MAX_READ_LABEL is used. The MIN_WRITE_LABEL is the user's minimum authorized write label, and if no value is specified, then the lowest level with no compartment or group is used. The DEF_LABEL is the user's database session default label, and if no value is used, then the MAX_READ_LABEL is used. The ROW_LABEL is the user's default write label for newly created rows.

```
sec_mgr@db12cr[sales]> -- WMAROULIS can access Company Internal, Legal, and
sec_mgr@db12cr[sales]> -- Board of Director information
sec_mgr@db12cr[sales]> BEGIN
  2     sa_user_admin.set_user_labels (
  3        policy_name     => 'SH_COM_POL',
  4        user_name       => 'wmaroulis',
  5        max_read_label  => 'CI:LEG:BOD');
  6  END;
  7  /

PL/SQL procedure successfully completed.

sec_mgr@db12cr[sales]> -- SGAETJEN can access Company Sensitive, Executive, and
sec_mgr@db12cr[sales]> -- Board of Director information
sec_mgr@db12cr[sales]>  BEGIN
  2     sa_user_admin.set_user_labels (
```

```
3           policy_name    => 'SH_COM_POL',
4           user_name      => 'sgaetjen',
5           max_read_label => 'CS:EXE:BOD');
6  END;
7  /

PL/SQL procedure successfully completed.

sec_mgr@db12cr[sales]> -- SH can access Company Sensitive, (Executive,
sec_mgr@db12cr[sales]> -- Legal, and Accounting) and
sec_mgr@db12cr[sales]> -- Board of Director information
sec_mgr@db12cr[sales]>  BEGIN
2       sa_user_admin.set_user_labels (
3           policy_name    => 'SH_COM_POL',
4           user_name      => 'SH',
5           max_read_label => 'CS:EXE,LEG,ACC:BOD');
6  END;
7  /

PL/SQL procedure successfully completed.

sec_mgr@db12cr[sales]> -- Verify user's labels
sec_mgr@db12cr[sales]> SELECT user_name, policy_name, max_read_label,
2       default_write_label
3 FROM dba_sa_users;

USER_NAME   POLICY_NAME   MAX_READ_LABEL        DEFAULT_WRITE_LABEL
----------  ------------  --------------------  --------------------
SGAETJEN    SH_COM_POL    CS:EXE:BOD            CS:EXE:BOD
WMAROULIS   SH_COM_POL    CI:LEG:BOD            CI:LEG:BOD
SH          SH_COM_POL    CS:EXE,LEG,ACC:BOD    CS:EXE,LEG,ACC:BOD

3 rows selected.
```

Let's go back and look at the labels now that we've assigned MAX_READ_LABEL procedures to the database accounts:

```
sec_mgr@db12cr[sales]> -- Oracle creates new labels
sec_mgr@db12cr[sales]> -- and assigns them the label type of
sec_mgr@db12cr[sales]> -- "USER LABEL"
sec_mgr@db12cr[sales]> SELECT *
2  FROM dba_sa_labels
3  WHERE policy_name = 'SH_COM_POL'
4  ORDER BY label_tag;

POLICY_NAME   LABEL                LABEL_TAG  LABEL_TYPE
------------  -------------------  ---------- ---------------
SH_COM_POL    PUB                      10000  USER/DATA LABEL
SH_COM_POL    PUB::BOD                 10100  USER/DATA LABEL
SH_COM_POL    PUB::STATP               10200  USER/DATA LABEL
SH_COM_POL    PUB::SUP                 10300  USER/DATA LABEL
SH_COM_POL    PUB::BOD,STATP,SUP       10400  USER/DATA LABEL
SH_COM_POL    CI                       20000  USER/DATA LABEL
SH_COM_POL    CS                       30000  USER/DATA LABEL
SH_COM_POL    CS:EXE                   30100  USER/DATA LABEL
SH_COM_POL    CS:EXE,LEG               30200  USER/DATA LABEL
SH_COM_POL    CS:ACC                   30300  USER/DATA LABEL
```

```
SH_COM_POL    CS:EXE:BOD           1000000000 USER LABEL
SH_COM_POL    CI:LEG:BOD           1000000001 USER LABEL
SH_COM_POL    CS:EXE,LEG,ACC:BOD   1000000020 USER LABEL
13 rows selected.
```

Verify User's Labels

We use the MAX_READ_LABEL procedure from the SA_SESSION package to verify the user's session label. This label is sometimes referred to as the "effective session label."

```
sec_mgr@db12cr[sales]> CONNECT sgaetjen@sales
Enter password:
Connected.
sgaetjen@db12cr[sales]> -- Use the SA_SESSION package to view label
sgaetjen@db12cr[sales]> SELECT sa_session.max_read_label ('SH_COM_POL')
  2      "Read Label"
  3  FROM DUAL;

Read Label
-------------------
CS:EXE:BOD

1 row selected.

sgaetjen@db12cr[sales]> -- Or, query from session context to retrieve
sgaetjen@db12cr[sales]> -- the session label
sgaetjen@db12cr[sales]> SELECT *
  2  FROM session_context
  3  WHERE attribute = 'SH_COM_POL'
  4  ORDER BY namespace, attribute;

NAMESPACE                   ATTRIBUTE               VALUE
-----------------------     --------------------    -------------------
ORA_OLS_SESSION_LABELS      SH_COM_POL              CS:EXE:BOD

1 row selected.
```

We now demonstrate a couple more commonly used OLS functions, because there are many. The first function determines the greatest lower bound, or the "lesser" of the two labels. The second function determines the greatest upper bound, or the "greater" of the two labels. These functions and others from SA_UTL come in handy when you're trying to determine whether a user or an object dominates another user or object.

```
sgaetjen@db12cr[sales]> -- CI:EXE is the Greatest Lower Bound
sgaetjen@db12cr[sales]> SELECT OLS_GREATEST_LBOUND(
  2      char_to_label('SH_COM_POL','CS:EXE'),
  3      char_to_label('SH_COM_POL','CI:EXE')) GREATEST_LOWER_BOUND
  4  FROM dual;

GREATEST_LOWER_BOUND
-------------------
CI:EXE

1 row selected.

sgaetjen@db12cr[sales]> -- CS:EXE is the Greatest Upper Bound
sgaetjen@db12cr[sales]> SELECT OLS_LEAST_UBOUND(
```

```
   2       char_to_label('SH_COM_POL','CS:EXE'),
   3       char_to_label('SH_COM_POL','CI:EXE')) LEAST_UPPER_BOUND
   4   FROM dual;

LEAST_UPPER_BOUND
-----------------
CS:EXE

1 row selected.
```

The next function we demonstrate is the MERGE_LABEL function from the SA_UTL package. It merges two OLS labels based on the rule or format that you provide. In the next example, we are telling OLS to merge based on least (level), intersection (compartments), and least (groups) of the two labels. See Chapter 6 of the *Oracle Label Security Administrator's Guide* for more information on the format model.

```
sgaetjen@db12cr[sales]> SELECT label_to_char(sa_utl.merge_label(
   2       char_to_label('SH_COM_POL','CI:ACC,EXE'),
   3       char_to_label('SH_COM_POL','CS:ACC,LEG'), 'LII'))
   4       LEAST_INTERSECT_INTERSECT
   5   FROM dual;

LEAST_INTERSECT_INTERSECT
-------------------------
CI:ACC

1 row selected.
```

Apply OLS Policy to a Table

We use the APPLY_TABLE_POLICY procedure from the SA_POLICY_ADMIN package to put a table under OLS policy control:

```
sgaetjen@db12cr[sales]> CONNECT sec_mgr@sales
Enter password:
Connected.
sec_mgr@db12cr[sales]> DESCRIBE sa_policy_admin
...
PROCEDURE APPLY_TABLE_POLICY
 Argument Name                   Type                          In/Out Default?
 ------------------------------  ----------------------------  ------ --------
 POLICY_NAME                     VARCHAR2                      IN
 SCHEMA_NAME                     VARCHAR2                      IN
 TABLE_NAME                      VARCHAR2                      IN
 TABLE_OPTIONS                   VARCHAR2                      IN     DEFAULT
 LABEL_FUNCTION                  VARCHAR2                      IN     DEFAULT
 PREDICATE                       VARCHAR2                      IN     DEFAULT
...
```

The value for TABLE_OPTIONS is a list of OLS enforcements. If none are given, then the OLS policy's default enforcements that were created with sa_sysdba.create_policy are used. The LABEL_FUNCTION parameter takes a function name and/or parameters as its value. This function dynamically computes the default label for the table. The PREDICATE parameter is used for ALL_CONTROL (READ_CONTROL) mediation to extend the functionality of OLS and include a VPD-like capability that appends a Boolean predicate condition to the query (that is, **AND my_func(commission)=23**).

We can add the SH.SALES_HISTORY table to the SH_COM_POL OLS policy.

NOTE
Before you apply the OLS policy to this table, you should remove the VPD policy that was created in Chapter 7. The script named 09.drop .vpd.pol.sql that comes with the examples for this book can be used for this purpose.

```
sec_mgr@db12cr[sales] > DESCRIBE sh.sales_history
  Name                                      Null?     Type
  ----------------------------------------- --------- ---------------------------
  PRODUCT                                              VARCHAR2(30)
  ...
  EMP_ID                                               NUMBER

sec_mgr@db12cr[sales] > -- Apply label policy to table
sec_mgr@db12cr[sales] > -- The table is now "Under OLS Control"
sec_mgr@db12cr[sales] > BEGIN
  2      sa_policy_admin.apply_table_policy
  3          (policy_name   => 'SH_COM_POL',
  4           schema_name   => 'SH',
  5           table_name    => 'SALES_HISTORY',
  6           table_options => 'ALL_CONTROL');
  7    END;
  8    /

PL/SQL procedure successfully completed.

sec_mgr@db12cr[sales] > DESCRIBE sh.sales_history
  Name                                      Null?     Type
  ----------------------------------------- --------- ---------------------------
  PRODUCT                                              VARCHAR2(30)
  ...
  EMP_ID                                               NUMBER
  SH_COM_POL_COL                                       NUMBER(10)
```

Recall that the pattern of the policy column added to the table is <OLS Security Policy Name>_COL as shown here (that is, SH_COM_POL_COL).

Create Optional WHERE Function

OLS provides an optional capability to include a PL/SQL call to a function for even further refinement or custom security during OLS mediation. This capability is very similar to the VPD capability using the trusted VPD package. However, with OLS you do not need to create the package and can simply create a function that returns a VARCHAR2 predicate addition. So if your specific security requirements dictate a custom security addition to the OLS policy, you would create a function.

This feature can be used, for example, if you want to add time-based release of information (such as after 30 days of receipt or only during working business hours) or pull application context attributes/values to be used during OLS mediation. This feature is like having the best of VPD coupled with the best of OLS and allows for a more flexible security policy. You can use AND and OR Boolean logic in the PREDICATE to create complex extensions.

Hide Security Column

OLS does offer the capability to add a table into OLS policy control and hide the policy label column. This is helpful when you are integrating legacy applications that dynamically retrieve the structure of the table from the data dictionary or expect the structure of a table to be a certain way and are not able to handle an added column.

```
sec_mgr@db12cr[sales] > -- Remove the OLS policy and drop the policy column
sec_mgr@db12cr[sales] > BEGIN
  2     sa_policy_admin.REMOVE_TABLE_POLICY
  3        (policy_name   => 'SH_COM_POL',
  4         schema_name   => 'SH',
  5         table_name    => 'SALES_HISTORY',
  6         DROP_COLUMN   => TRUE);
  7  END;
  8  /

PL/SQL procedure successfully completed.

sec_mgr@db12cr[sales] > -- Re-apply the policy this time hiding the
sec_mgr@db12cr[sales] > -- policy column
sec_mgr@db12cr[sales] > BEGIN
  2     sa_policy_admin.apply_table_policy
  3        (policy_name   => 'SH_COM_POL',
  4         schema_name   => 'SH',
  5         table_name    => 'SALES_HISTORY',
  6         table_options => 'ALL_CONTROL, HIDE');
  7  END;
  8  /

PL/SQL procedure successfully completed.

sec_mgr@db12cr[sales] > DESCRIBE sh.sales_history
 Name                                     Null?    Type
 ---------------------------------------- -------- --------------------------
 PRODUCT                                            VARCHAR2(30)
 ...
 EMP_ID                                             NUMBER
```

As you can see from the description of the SALES_HISTORY table, the SH_COM_POL_COL column does not appear to the user/application.

Authorize OLS Access

Oracle allows user access to an object (table) via DAC controls. GRANT/REVOKE statements are the mechanism for authorized users to grant access to objects. GRANT/REVOKE statements are a part of the basic Oracle security. OLS does not authorize a user to access an object. OLS authorizes users to access individual records. That said, OLS does have the ability to grant special privileges to users so that they can access more information than what their user label will allow.

The OLS privileges are not needed in typical OLS use cases. A typical database user needs only an OLS user label assigned using the SET_USER_LABELS procedure, as shown earlier.

OLS Privilege	Description
READ	This privilege authorizes the grantee to bypass read (SELECT) access mediation. That is, if a table is under OLS policy control and a user with READ privilege queries the table, then Oracle will bypass the OLS policy mediation and allow the user to query the table accessing all data. However, if enabled, OLS mediation is still in effect for INSERT, UPDATE, and DELETE statements.
FULL	This privilege effectively turns off for all OLS processing against an OLS protected table. This is the most powerful OLS privilege and should be rarely, if ever, granted. As you will see in Chapter 13, you should check for FULL privilege grants to database users, like a Linux security admin should check for setuid attributes on OS files.
WRITEDOWN	This privilege authorizes the user to change the level component of a data label to lower or less than its existing value. For example, from the preceding example, if the level was set to COMPANY SENSITIVE, then a user with this privilege could set the level to PUBLIC. This privilege is applicable only to policies that use LABEL_UPDATE enforcement.
WRITEUP	This privilege authorizes the user to change the level component of a data label to higher or greater than its existing value. For example, from the preceding example, if the level was set to PUBLIC, then a user with this privilege could set the level to COMPANY SENSITIVE. This privilege is applicable only to policies that use LABEL_UPDATE enforcement.
WRITEACROSS	This privilege authorizes the user to modify the label compartment and/ or group values to any valid value. That is, the user can add or remove compartments or groups to the label. This privilege is applicable only to policies that use LABEL_UPDATE enforcement.
PROFILEACCESS	This privilege authorizes the user to assume the authorization from another user.

TABLE 9-6. *OLS Privileges*

OLS Privileges

OLS has additional privileges that can be granted based on need or specific security policy requirements. These privileges extend or authorize a user to access more information than what he or she would be able to access simply using user labels. Table 9-6 lists and describes OLS privileges.

The following example grants user PSACK the WRITEDOWN privilege using the SA_USER_ ADMIN package and SET_USER_PRIVS procedure.

```
sec_mgr@db12cr[sales]>  BEGIN
  2     SA_USER_ADMIN.SET_USER_PRIVS(
  3        policy_name => 'SH_COM_POL',
  4        user_name   => 'PSACK',
  5        privileges  => 'WRITEDOWN');
  6   END;
  7   /
```

```
PL/SQL procedure successfully completed.

sec_mgr@db12cr[sales]> -- Verify privs for policy
sec_mgr@db12cr[sales]> SELECT user_name, policy_name, user_privileges
  2  FROM dba_sa_user_privs
  3  WHERE policy_name = 'SH_COM_POL';

USER_NAME                             POLICY_NAME            USER_PRIVILEGES
-----------------------------------   --------------------   -----------------
PSACK                                 SH_COM_POL             WRITEDOWN

1 row selected.
```

Insert Data Using OLS Functions

OLS provides several ways to insert data into an OLS table. Before we start inserting data, however, we remove the OLS policy and add it back without hiding the policy column:

```
sec_mgr@db12cr[sales]> BEGIN
  2   sa_policy_admin.remove_table_policy
  3     (policy_name   => 'SH_COM_POL',
  4      schema_name   => 'SH',
  5      table_name    => 'SALES_HISTORY',
  6      drop_column   => TRUE);
  7  END;
  8  /

PL/SQL procedure successfully completed.

sec_mgr@db12cr[sales]> -- Apply label policy to table
sec_mgr@db12cr[sales]> -- The table is now "Under OLS Control"
sec_mgr@db12cr[sales]> BEGIN
  2      sa_policy_admin.apply_table_policy
  3        (policy_name   => 'SH_COM_POL',
  4         schema_name   => 'SH',
  5         table_name    => 'SALES_HISTORY',
  6         table_options => 'READ_CONTROL, WRITE_CONTROL, LABEL_DEFAULT');
  7  END;
  8  /

PL/SQL procedure successfully completed.
```

INSERT with Default Label

If you are using LABEL_DEFAULT enforcement, then Oracle will use the connected user's DEFAULT_ROW_TAG value (ROW_LABEL in this case) as the policy column value. The following INSERT statement will implicitly use the CS label (actually the corresponding numeric tag value) as the default policy column value:

```
sec_mgr@db12cr[sales]> CONNECT sh@sales
Enter password:
Connected.
sh@db12cr[sales]>  SELECT sa_session.ROW_LABEL('SH_COM_POL') "Default Row Label"
  2  FROM DUAL;
```

```
Default Row Label
-----------------------------------
CS

1 row selected.

sh@db12cr[sales]> INSERT INTO sales_history (PRODUCT, SALES_DATE,
  2        QUANTITY, TOTAL_COST, DEPT_ID, COMMISSION, EMP_ID)
  3  VALUES ('Headphones', sysdate,
  4        1, 100.23, 10, 23, 101);

1 row created.

sh@db12cr[sales]> commit;

Commit complete.

sh@db12cr[sales]> -- Verify policy label
sh@db12cr[sales]> SELECT product, sh_com_pol_col,
  2        label_to_char(sh_com_pol_col) POLICY_DATA_LABEL
  3  FROM sh.sales_history
  4  WHERE PRODUCT = 'Headphones';

PRODUCT          SH_COM_POL_COL POLICY_DATA_LABEL
---------------  -------------- --------------------
Headphones                30000 CS

1 row selected.
```

INSERT Using CHAR_TO_LABEL Function

You can use the function CHAR_TO_LABEL to set the policy column label explicitly as we demonstrate in the following example:

```
sh@db12cr[sales]> INSERT INTO sales_history (PRODUCT, SALES_DATE,
  2        QUANTITY, TOTAL_COST, DEPT_ID, COMMISSION, EMP_ID, SH_COM_POL_COL)
  3  VALUES ('Microphones', sysdate,
  4        101, 10000, 10, 23, 101,
  5        char_to_label ('SH_COM_POL', 'CS:EXE,LEG,ACC'));

1 row created.

sh@db12cr[sales]> commit;

Commit complete.

sh@db12cr[sales]> -- INSERT with an invalid label we produce the following error
sh@db12cr[sales]> INSERT INTO sales_history (PRODUCT, SALES_DATE,
  2        QUANTITY, TOTAL_COST, DEPT_ID, COMMISSION, EMP_ID, SH_COM_POL_COL)
  3  VALUES ('Microphones2', sysdate,
  4        101, 10000, 10, 23, 101,
  5        char_to_label ('SH_COM_POL', 'CS:EXE,LEG,ACC:BOD'));

INSERT INTO sales_history (PRODUCT, SALES_DATE,
*
ERROR at line 1:
ORA-12406: unauthorized SQL statement for policy SH_COM_POL
```

The label CS:EXE,LEG,ACC:BOD does not exist, so Oracle responds with an error. However, the side effect of using the CHAR_TO_LABEL function on an invalid label or previously nonexistent label is that a new USER label is created. The label cannot be used on a data record; however, it can be assigned to a user.

```
sh@db12cr[sales]> CONNECT sec_mgr@sales
Enter password:
Connected.
sec_mgr@db12cr[sales]> SELECT *
  2  FROM dba_sa_labels
  3  WHERE label = 'CS:EXE,LEG,ACC:BOD';

POLICY_NAME                LABEL                 LABEL_TAG    LABEL_TYPE
------------------------   -------------------   ----------   ----------
SH_COM_POL                 CS:EXE,LEG,ACC:BOD    1000000043   USER LABEL

1 row selected.
```

INSERT Using the Numeric Value
You can also use the numeric value for the policy column without using an OLS function. After all, Oracle stores the numeric value for the column.

```
sec_mgr@db12cr[sales]> CONNECT sh@sales
Enter password:
Connected.
sh@db12cr[sales]> -- Insert CI/20000 for SH_COM_POL_COL value
sh@db12cr[sales]> INSERT INTO sales_history (PRODUCT, SALES_DATE,
  2      QUANTITY, TOTAL_COST, DEPT_ID, COMMISSION, EMP_ID, SH_COM_POL_COL)
  3  VALUES ('Microphones3', sysdate,
  4      101, 10000, 10, 23, 101, 20000);

1 row created.
```

INSERT Using TO_DATA_LABEL Function
OLS provides another function, TO_DATA_LABEL, to assist during INSERT. The purpose of the function is to create a new data label and then use its numeric value for the policy column value. The TO_DATA_LABEL function should be used with caution, however, because you typically do not want to create new data labels after you have set up your security policy. We do not recommend using this function; it is shown here for completeness.

```
sh@db12cr[sales]> CONNECT sec_mgr@sales
Enter password:
Connected.
sec_mgr@db12cr[sales]> GRANT execute ON to_data_label TO sh;

Grant succeeded.

sec_mgr@db12cr[sales]> CONNECT sh@sales
Enter password:
Connected.
sh@db12cr[sales]> -- We create and use the data label, which failed above
sh@db12cr[sales]> INSERT INTO sales_history (PRODUCT, SALES_DATE,
```

```
    2     QUANTITY, TOTAL_COST, DEPT_ID, COMMISSION, EMP_ID, SH_COM_POL_COL)
    3  VALUES ('Microphones', sysdate,
    4        101, 10000, 10, 23, 101,
    5        to_data_label ('SH_COM_POL', 'CS:EXE,LEG,ACC:BOD'));

1 row created.

sh@db12cr[sales]> CONNECT sec_mgr@sales
Enter password:
Connected.
sec_mgr@db12cr[sales]> SELECT *
  2   FROM dba_sa_labels
  3   WHERE label = 'CS:EXE,LEG,ACC:BOD';

POLICY_NAME               LABEL                  LABEL_TAG    LABEL_TYPE
------------------------  ---------------------  -----------  ----------------
SH_COM_POL                CS:EXE,LEG,ACC:BOD     1000000043   USER/DATA LABEL

1 row selected.
```

As illustrated from the result of the query, the label was converted from a USER LABEL type to a USER/DATA LABEL type by using the TO_DATA_LABEL function during INSERT.

Querying Data from an OLS Protected Table

We can now connect to the database as two users and query the data. You will see that the user's security session is different for each user, and as a result, different data is returned.

```
sgaetjen@db12cr[sales]> CONNECT sgaetjen@sales
Enter password:
Connected.
sec_mgr@db12cr[sales]> SELECT sa_session.LABEL ('SH_COM_POL')
  2       "Read Label"
  3   FROM dual;

Read Label
-----------------------------
CS:EXE:BOD

1 row selected.

sgaetjen@db12cr[sales]> SELECT PRODUCT, SALES_DATE, SH_COM_POL_COL,
  2       label_to_char(sh_com_pol_col) OLS_LABEL
  3   FROM sales_history;

PRODUCT         SALES_DAT SH_COM_POL_COL OLS_LABEL
--------------- --------- -------------- --------------------
Stereo          27-OCT-13         10000 PUB
Walkman         06-NOV-13         10000 PUB
LCD TV          16-DEC-13         10000 PUB
Plasma TV       26-DEC-13         10000 PUB
Cell Phone      16-NOV-13         10000 PUB
LCD TV          19-DEC-13         10000 PUB
LCD TV          23-FEB-14         10000 PUB
Headphones      03-MAY-14         30000 CS
Microphones     03-MAY-14         20000 CI
```

```
Speakers         22-JAN-14           10000 PUB

10 rows selected.

sgaetjen@db12cr[sales]> SELECT PRODUCT, SALES_DATE, SH_COM_POL_COL,
  2     label_to_char(sh_com_pol_col) OLS_LABEL
  3  FROM sh.sales_history
  4  WHERE label_to_char (SH_COM_POL_COL) like 'PUB%';

PRODUCT          SALES_DAT SH_COM_POL_COL OLS_LABEL
---------------  --------- -------------- --------------------
Stereo           27-OCT-13          10000 PUB
Walkman          06-NOV-13          10000 PUB
LCD TV           16-DEC-13          10000 PUB
Plasma TV        26-DEC-13          10000 PUB
Cell Phone       16-NOV-13          10000 PUB
LCD TV           19-DEC-13          10000 PUB
LCD TV           23-FEB-14          10000 PUB
Speakers         22-JAN-14          10000 PUB

8 rows selected.

sgaetjen@db12cr[sales]> CONNECT wmaroulis@sales
Enter password:
Connected.
wmaroulis@db12cr[sales]> SELECT sa_session.LABEL ('SH_COM_POL')
  2     "Read Label"
  3  FROM dual;

Read Label
----------------------------
CI:LEG:BOD

wmaroulis@db12cr[sales]> SELECT PRODUCT, SALES_DATE, SH_COM_POL_COL,
  2     label_to_char(sh_com_pol_col) OLS_LABEL
  3  FROM sh.sales_history;

PRODUCT          SALES_DAT SH_COM_POL_COL OLS_LABEL
---------------  --------- -------------- --------------------
Stereo           27-OCT-13          10000 PUB
Walkman          06-NOV-13          10000 PUB
LCD TV           16-DEC-13          10000 PUB
Plasma TV        26-DEC-13          10000 PUB
Cell Phone       16-NOV-13          10000 PUB
LCD TV           19-DEC-13          10000 PUB
LCD TV           23-FEB-14          10000 PUB
Microphones      03-MAY-14          20000 CI
Speakers         22-JAN-14          10000 PUB

9 rows selected.
```

OLS and the Connection Pool

OLS includes several functions to assist with the integration of connections pools using OLS security. As a developer, you can set, change, and restore the connection pool labels using functions and procedures found in the SA_SESSION package. The following example demonstrates setting user SGAETJEN's session label lower than what he is authorized for, and then restoring the session back to its original security state:

```
sgaetjen@db12cr[sales]> -- Default access
sgaetjen@db12cr[sales]> SELECT sa_session.label('SH_COM_POL') SESSION_LABEL
  2 FROM dual;

SESSION_LABEL
--------------
CS:EXE:BOD

1 row selected.

sgaetjen@db12cr[sales]> -- Set SGAETJEN's access to PUBLIC (PUB)
sgaetjen@db12cr[sales]> BEGIN
  2 SA_SESSION.SET_LABEL (
  3    policy_name => 'SH_COM_POL',
  4    label       => 'PUB');
  5 END;
  6 /

PL/SQL procedure successfully completed.

sgaetjen@db12cr[sales]> SELECT sa_session.label('SH_COM_POL') SESSION_LABEL
  2 FROM dual;

SESSION_LABEL
-------------
PUB

1 row selected.

sgaetjen@db12cr[sales]> -- Restore SGAETJEN's access to the default
sgaetjen@db12cr[sales]> EXEC SA_SESSION.RESTORE_DEFAULT_LABELS('SH_COM_POL')

PL/SQL procedure successfully completed.

sgaetjen@db12cr[sales]> SELECT sa_session.label('SH_COM_POL') SESSION_LABEL
  2 FROM dual;

SESSION_LABEL
-------------
CS:EXE:BOD

1 row selected.
```

Auditing OLS Privileges and Use

You can audit OLS specific events using the AUDIT procedure from the SA_USER_ADMIN package. You can also use the AUDIT procedure from the SA_AUDIT_ADMIN package for policy-specific auditing. If you want to use unified auditing, see Chapter 23 of the *Oracle Database Security Guide* for information about configuring unified auditing. Table 9-7 describes auditable OLS options.

OLS Audit Option	Description
APPLY	Generates an audit record when an OLS policy is applied to tables or schemas.
PRIVILEGES	Generates an audit record when an OLS privilege is used in the execution of a SQL statement (for example, FULL was used to query the SH.SALES_HISTORY table).
REMOVE	Generates an audit record when an OLS policy is removed from tables or schemas.
SET	Generates an audit record when user authorizations or privileges are set (for example, setting the session label different from the default).

TABLE 9-7.   *Auditable OLS Options*

Now let's start auditing for the OLS policy SH_COM_POL and generate an audit event. The following example demonstrates OLS auditing:

```
sgaetjen@db12cr[sales]> CONNECT sec_mgr@sales
Enter password:
Connected.
sec_mgr@db12cr[sales]> EXEC sa_audit_admin.audit ('SH_COM_POL')

PL/SQL procedure successfully completed.

sec_mgr@db12cr[sales]> -- We create a view with default name
sec_mgr@db12cr[sales]> -- DBA_SH_COM_POL_AUDIT_TRAIL
sec_mgr@db12cr[sales]> EXEC sa_audit_admin.create_view (policy_name => 'SH_COM_POL')

PL/SQL procedure successfully completed.

sec_mgr@db12cr[sales]> SELECT *
  2  FROM LBACSYS.DBA_SH_COM_POL_AUDIT_TRAIL;

no rows selected

sec_mgr@db12cr[sales]> -- Generate an OLS audit event
sec_mgr@db12cr[sales]> BEGIN
  2 sa_policy_admin.REMOVE_TABLE_POLICY
  3    (policy_name   => 'SH_COM_POL',
  4     schema_name   => 'SH',
  5     table_name    => 'SALES_HISTORY',
  6     DROP_COLUMN   => TRUE);
  7  END;
  8  /

PL/SQL procedure successfully completed.

sec_mgr@db12cr[sales]> -- Query the policy specific view for the event
```

```
sec_mgr@db12cr[sales]> SELECT username, action_name, timestamp
  2  FROM LBACSYS.DBA_SH_COM_POL_AUDIT_TRAIL;

USERNAME    ACTION_NAME                               TIMESTAMP
----------  ----------------------------------------  ---------
SEC_MGR     REMOVE TABLE OR SCHEMA POLICY             17-MAY-14

1 row selected.
```

Trusted Stored Procedures

From time to time, you might find the need to over-privilege a user account to accomplish a business analytic or report. That is, you might find yourself needing to create a database account that has "all" privileges or is exempt from OLS policy so that a report can be generated that accesses all the data (such as quarterly sales report, number of incidents of a particular type, and so on) in an OLS-protected table.

OLS offers a better way of solving this problem without over-privileging or exempting a database account (which are less secure ways of solving this problem). OLS allows for granting OLS exempt access (FULL) and read access (READ) to trusted procedures. This enables you to have a "regular" database account with limited OLS access call the trusted stored procedure to access data necessary to run the report or complete the business analytic. During the course of the trusted procedure executing, it has access to all data in the protected table. We use the SET_PROG_PRIVS procedure in the SA_USER_ADMIN package to set a procedure as trusted:

```
sec_mgr@db12cr[sales]> DESCRIBE sa_user_admin
...
PROCEDURE SET_PROG_PRIVS
  Argument Name                    Type                      In/Out Default?
  -------------------------------- ------------------------- ------ --------
  POLICY_NAME                      VARCHAR2                  IN
  SCHEMA_NAME                      VARCHAR2                  IN
  PROGRAM_UNIT_NAME                VARCHAR2                  IN
  PRIVILEGES                       VARCHAR2                  IN
...
```

Refer back to Table 9-6 for a list of applicable privileges. The following example demonstrates granting READ access to the trusted procedure QUARTERLY_REPORT_PROC. So no matter who is connected at the time the procedure executes, the procedure will have access to all records in the table regardless of the data label.

```
sec_mgr@db12cr[sales]> BEGIN
  2      SA_USER_ADMIN.SET_PROG_PRIVS (
  3          policy_name       => 'SH_COM_POL',
  4          schema_name       => 'SH',
  5          program_unit_name => 'QUARTERLY_REPORT_PROC',
  6          privileges        => 'READ');
  7  END;
  8  /

PL/SQL procedure successfully completed.
```

Integrating OLS and Oracle Internet Directory

OLS can be integrated with Oracle Internet Directory (OID) to gain significant efficiencies of label administration. Policies and user authorization profiles can be created and managed directly in the directory by means of the commands described in Appendix C of the *Oracle Label Security Administrator's Guide*. Changes are automatically propagated to the associated directories and to the user's session at the next connection.

Performance with OLS

Partitioning is a performance feature of Oracle Database that, in simple terms, splits the table into smaller tables or partitions. Oracle evaluates the SELECT statement to determine which of the smaller partitions it can eliminate to execute the query. Partitioning is most effective when the partition column is always used in the predicate or WHERE clause of the SELECT statement.

OLS, unless the user is exempt from policy enforcement with the FULL privilege, always puts the security policy column in the predicate for evaluation. Consequently, if you are concerned about performance, you should take a look at using partitioning. Furthermore, you should consider making the security policy column the first column in the partition key (and consequently partition index). Also, if you are able, consider creating a local index with the security column prefixed or first in the key. Depending on the number of labels and the structure of your tables, you may consider subpartitioning the security label.

Summary

There are many benefits to using OLS, but the main benefit of OLS is that it's simple to implement and does not require coding. It's easy to integrate OLS transparently into existing applications, especially given the fact that you can hide the numeric data label in tables and use default labels, thereby avoiding having to refactor the application code to incorporate OLS. It can be incorporated into an enterprise labeling strategy with OID. But the more pragmatic reason to purchase and use OLS versus building your security using VPD comes down to the simple buy versus build comparison. Sure, you could write enough VPD code to implement an OLS feature, but do you have the time, money, and testing team to surpass the more than 20 years of testing and refinement put into OLS?

OLS, VPD, and other security products sometimes get a bad rap as being "too complicated" to use. What we find in unraveling the substance behind this stigma is that the problem isn't the complexity of OLS as much as the complexity of the security policy being implemented. With OLS and VPD, Oracle provides powerful, flexible, and scalable security tools to implement most all complex security policies; you just have to take the time to define what your policies are.

You have seen how OLS is installed in the CDB and how to register and enable OLS in a specific PDB or multiple PDBs. The basis of OLS is the label and its corresponding tag value. The label is made up of three parts: level, compartment, and group. The user's session label controls what the connected user can read, write, and update from tables that are protected with OLS.

CHAPTER
10

Oracle Database Vault: Securing for
the Compliance Regulations,
Cybersecurity, and Insider Threats

I n the early 2000s, the need to address compliance regulations and cybersecurity threats, and the risks of insider threats, became common challenges for large enterprises. Compliance regulations were created for every major industry, threatening legal and/or financial ramifications for failure to comply. In addition, hackers were probing the Internet looking for holes in corporate systems that they could exploit. Also, internal employees were stealing corporate information assets in hopes of reaping huge rewards. Every significant IT vendor was eager to provide solutions that could address these challenges. At the core of the challenge was protecting sensitive data so that it would be accessed or manipulated only as it was intended.

Oracle Database Vault (DBV) was introduced in 2005 to address these challenges with additional layers of security, resulting in a fundamental change in how security is enforced. Unlike many features of the database, DBV radically changes what you do as a DBA and how you do it.

In this chapter we will discuss the reasons why DBV came into existence. Your understanding the design and intent of a product is important to having a complete understanding of why you should use it, when you should use it, and how you should use it.

History of Privileged Accounts

In an Oracle Database, the SYS account owns the metadata tables that make up the database engine (data dictionary). The Oracle Database uses these tables to perform nearly all operations. The fact that SYS owns these tables has strong security implications, because SYS is perceived to be as powerful as the root user in a Linux operating system. Recall the security implications for object owners: they have all privileges on objects they own. So for SYS, this translates to full rights on many of the core database objects and even the objects owned by accounts other than SYS. An Oracle Database also contains the SYSTEM account, which also has DBA privileges. Administrators often use this account to create users and tablespaces, and to perform day-to-day DBA functions. Both the SYS and SYSTEM accounts have access to all data in the database because the accounts have the DBA role, which has the SELECT ANY TABLE privilege.

The outrage surrounding unlimited administrator access reached its peak in the early 2000s due in part to the sensitivity of data such as financial/commerce records (PCI), medical records (PHI), and personally identifiable information (PII). Unlimited administrator access came to the forefront of discussion due to governance and compliance issues and concepts such as separation of duty (SoD). The concern revolves around the fact that there exists a database user (SYS) with complete and unregulated capability to do absolutely anything and everything in the database. And unlike SYSTEM, SYS doesn't need additional administrative privileges to perform these operations. The privileges are available to SYS because of the object owner principle and, quite frankly, because they are required for the database to function properly.

The insider threat concerns from a security perspective were not only about the ability to grant privileges to accounts, create accounts, or delete data, but were also about other misguided use, such as the ability to disable security policies (such as VPD or OLS policies) and delete records from the audit trail. These translate into the ability not only to do bad things, but to do them without a trace. In fact, the last issue of deleting from the audit tables drove the requirement for external audit logging in the OS for actions SYS performs in the database. So, although we cannot stop what SYS does in the database, we have the ability to audit SYS without the risk of SYS deleting or changing the audit logs.

SYS as SYSDBA (Super User 0)

As you know, SYS is a unique schema, and it was never intended to be a user. This can be confusing, because you can log in to the SYS account with a password in the same way that you would log in to the database with any database user account. Therefore, it's hard to discuss "SYS is not a database user" with someone unfamiliar with Oracle but familiar with compliance initiatives. It turns out that in addition to owning many of the objects that run the database, much of the database code checks to see if the user is SYS. If you query SYS.USER$, you will notice a column USER# and that the value for SYS is zero. What makes SYS a "super-user" with unyielding rights has a lot to do with this fact. There are two important points to be made here:

■ First, we need SYS. We need to have a container for the core database objects. Furthermore, we need to be able to log on as SYS to install patches, perform upgrades, conduct backup/recovery, and so forth. The point is that removal of the SYS account is not an option.

■ The second point is that the SYS account is a huge security risk, because database security is intentionally bypassed. This is not optimal for many security architects. It is also undesirable if you are trying to conform to compliance guidelines around SoD.

Therefore, one of the fundamental objectives of DBV was to ensure that the SYS account could be controlled and that SYS could not bypass the new security layers introduced by DBV. The primary risk of using the SYS account is not necessarily when an actual person has connected to the database as SYSDBA, but instead when the code underneath the user's session is operating as SYS. The concern is around techniques, such as privilege escalation or SQL injection. If these techniques are successful, then someone could tamper with the database security controls and/or gain access to sensitive data. You can significantly reduce these risks, however, by upgrading to DBV and adding a few DBV policies for your applications.

Security Should Haves

In building security in the database over the years, you have probably come across a few techniques and methods that you found extremely useful and effective. As avid security practitioners, we, too, have found successful security patterns both inside and outside of the database. In this section, we'll review a few of these methods as they, too, found their way into DBV.

Multifactored Security

You are probably familiar with the notion of *multifactor authentication*. Multifactor authentication is defined as "using more than one thing to authenticate a user (or entity)." Multifactor authentication is usually considered in striking contrast to password authentication. A password is knowledge of a single thing, as are many other types of authentication. With multifactor authentication, it is much more difficult to compromise or spoof multiple things that are required to authenticate than any single thing. Therefore, multifactor authentication is considered more secure than single-factor.

An objective of DBV was to take the notion of multifactor authentication and bring it to privilege enablement. The multifactor philosophy was the basis for the most used privilege enablement techniques in the database: secure application roles (SARs). SARs are enabled from within secure and well-defined procedural code that can check other factors before enabling the role. DBV works on the same principle, but DBV uses DBV rule sets to examine other factors.

Conditional Security

Conditional security extends the basic privilege execution model built into the Oracle kernel by requiring that additional declarative conditions be met. A description of the conditional security categories follows:

- **Context-based security** The system's recognition that a privilege can be used only when it is part of a specific configuration, function, or business flow. If one of these situations does not exist, then there is an incongruity in the transaction and therefore the privilege cannot be enabled. For example, the privilege can be enabled only at a certain time of day or on a certain day of the week—a conditional GRANT if you will. Alternatively, it may check how the user authenticated, where the user is coming from, and which application the user is using.

- **Adaptive security** The security posture of a system changes in near real time. Procedural code can detect the current state of the system and loosen or tighten privileges accordingly. For example, if an intrusion detection system (IDS) detects an attack and raises a signal, the procedure could read the signal and potentially deny the execution of an otherwise authorized statement.

- **Separation of Duty (SoD)** SoD separates administrator privileges such that no single person is authorized to perform all actions to complete an administrative task. For example, administrator account A is capable of creating (via the CREATE USER statement) a database account, and administrator account B is capable of provisioning (via the GRANT statement) a database account. Just as a single factor is less secure than multiple factors, a single person is less secure than multiple people.

- **Conditional auditing** Auditing is part of the security lifecycle, but it suffers many of the problems similar to the privilege enablement requirements. Auditing is generally on or off. The invention of fine-grained auditing was a major step forward in achieving the desired objective: We want to audit only when we want to audit. The "when" is based on the contextual basis and adaptive security objectives stated earlier.

Some of the examples and requirements you derive will probably land in multiple categories. This discussion is meant to serve as a new way of thinking about security. The commonality is that security can be conditional; it is not rigid like a role with its static set of privileges. It should not be either on or off. The answer to deciding whether a user may perform an action is often, "It depends on the context of use."

DBV Components

Now that we have identified a few areas to improve, let's look at how DBV addresses these requirements. The objective of DBV is to impart a natural and intuitive architecture. DBV provides an architecture that doesn't allow for unfettered access to company data just because an administrator is a DBA. Having this fundamental understanding of the DBV components—why they are what they are—will help you better employ DBV in an effective manner.

DBV is built largely around a declarative framework that transparently evaluates all SQL statements submitted to the Oracle Database to determine if the statement should be allowed to execute. It consists of tables owned by an account named DVSYS. The security policy can be configured using either a set web-based user interface that runs within Oracle Enterprise Manager Cloud Control 12c (OEMCC) or a set of API calls that exist in the PL/SQL package DBMS_MACADM. In addition, under the Oracle multitenant architecture, the DBV security policies are specific to and isolated in the container (root or PDB) in which they are defined.

One of the key design principles of DBV was to provide a framework for higher levels of assurance through additional security mechanisms separate and distinct from the existing database security. Recall that security risks are not always associated with an actual user's session privileges, but rather when the code underneath a user's session is operating in the context of a powerful privilege that could be exploited for malicious use.

We want to introduce a new security concept that helps you increase the assurance level of your system. The *High Assurance Principle (HAP)* defines a basic security axiom: the use of multiple security mechanisms from different sources provides a higher level of assurance than using multiple security mechanisms from a single source.

NOTE
HAP for database security = 1 DB mechanism + 1 DBV mechanism

To achieve HAP for database security, you must separate security mechanisms into two sources: core database security and DBV security. Examples of core database security mechanisms are accounts, privileges, roles, VPD, views, PL/SQL, and triggers. Examples of DBV security mechanisms are factors, rules, realms, and command rules, which are described in the following sections.

Aside from making a robust security implementation possible, the declarative nature of DBV helps others—auditors in particular—verify and validate security policies. When security is buried inside code, it is more difficult to understand, modify, and reuse. Furthermore, it is extremely hard for a certifier to verify and validate.

Factors

We'll start first at the most elementary DBV component, the *factor*, which is a declared item that can be used to make security decisions. Think back to the previous discussion about multifactored and conditional security. Conditional security says that we are not simply making security decisions on whether or not a person has the "privilege" to do something. Security is more dynamic and may involve multiple points of input or condition.

You know that you often need to consider multiple factors when deciding whether or not to enable a privilege or allow an action: time of day, day of the week, how the user authenticated, whether the request was part of a specific transaction, and so forth. Each of these elements can be a factor in the overall security decision-making process. Therefore, you can think of the individual elements as security factors. Factors are discrete security-related attributes that resolve to a specific value (known as an *identity*). As you might guess, factors are generally resolved using PL/SQL expressions.

Protecting the Security Mechanisms

If you have ever used SARs or written VPD policies with application context variables, you should be familiar with the use of factors. Everything from the user's identity, to a client identifier, to an IP address are factors commonly used to ensure that the security policies are being upheld. DBV factors are declared, named, and stored in tables, and this enables reuse, factor validation, and enhanced security.

We make this last point about factor security because the entire DBV infrastructure is secured (with itself). One of the biggest risks to any security implementation is an attack on the logical implementation itself. For example, if we use a PL/SQL procedure to protect our data either as part of a SAR or VPD policy, then what protects the PL/SQL procedure? The answer is nothing without using DBV—that is, there is no protection against SYS or system ANY privileges.

Put another way, DBV protects the security that is being used to secure the database. This is an important point, because it significantly strengthens any security implementation. Furthermore, because DBV is written into the Oracle kernel, it cannot be replicated using any other database mechanism.

Rules

If you have written security code, you may be familiar with the implementation of security policies. You understand that within your implementation, you generally construct a set of logical statements to meet your security requirements. These statements are used to determine whether an action should take place. Many of these decision points take the form of Boolean logic using logical AND's and OR's, nested inside of IF-THEN-ELSE statements. You usually write code that says something analogous to this: "If this condition AND that condition OR the user is an administrator then do choice one, else do choice two." One way to describe this logic is to say it is the security *rule* that determines which choice will occur.

For example, you can ask questions similar to the following to decide whether a user can SELECT from the SH.SALES_HISTORY table:

- Did the user authenticated using SSL?
- Is the user's request coming from the application server's known IP address?
- Is the request day between Monday and Friday?
- Is the time sometime other than between the hours of midnight and 6:00 A.M.?
- Is the user a member of the SALES_DEPARTMENT database role?

What you know about each of these checks is that they are individual inputs into the security decision process. In DBV, each check will be represented as a factor. A factor returns a value in a secure way when it is called. Essentially, what we are doing is taking security factors and combining them with a series of logical AND's and OR's to create our security rule. This leads us naturally to DBV rules.

DBV Rule

A *DBV rule* is a sequence of factors used to make a security decision. For example, you could take the five checks, convert them into factors, and combine them into a rule that determines whether access to the data is permitted or not. If all five factors are satisfied, then the user can query the table.

As with factors, rules are stored in the DBV declarative framework. The security code reads the security metadata from the tables and executes the enforcement. The declarative framework makes it very easy to add or modify security factors or rules.

DBV Rule Sets

As DBV was being designed, it became clear that rules had high reusability. Therefore, DBV supports the notion of a library of rule groupings known as *rule sets*. Aggregating the rules together into a rule set allows for a much simpler and more maintainable security model, and at the same time, rule sets allow for the implementation of complex security policies.

Realms

A DBV *realm* is a security layer that eliminates inadvertent or malicious accesses to realm objects based on system privileges (ANY privileges). Realms are the collection of application-relevant objects that are grouped together for security reasons. When you create a realm, you are simply marking a set of objects (tables, views, roles, PL/SQL) that you want to protect, regardless of who owns the objects. Once the objects are placed in a DBV realm, they are instantly protected from users with system ANY privileges.

You can consider each application set of objects stored in a realm as being in its own security sandbox. System ANY privileges no longer give the DBA access to items protected within a realm. Therefore, putting application objects in the same protected sandbox, or realm, enables you to limit specifically who gets access to what.

Our definition used the natural grouping of objects that generally is associated with applications only as a way to help explain why you would group objects. There is, however, no restriction in DBV for realm objects to be bound to an application or anything else in particular. Realms are logical groupings that you arbitrarily define.

Realm Deep Dive

In Oracle Database 10*g* and 11*g*, DBV realms were enforced only for SQL statements when the privilege to run the statement was gained through a system ANY privilege. The object owner account and users that had direct object privileges to the object were not subject to the realm boundary protection. This fact led to a lot of confusion in how a realm should work. It also resulted in complex and difficult to maintain DBV command rules used to protect sensitive data from object owner accounts and users with direct object privileges. Oracle Database 12*c* introduced an option of defining a realm as a *mandatory realm*. A mandatory realm is a realm in which even the object owner and users with direct object privileges are subject to the realm boundary protection. This new feature provides for more intuitive security policies.

Realms can also have associated users and roles. The ability to map users to realms supports most security policies that define specific application administrators and SoD requirements. Users are either realm administrators or realm participants. The difference between an administrator and a participant is that an administrator can execute privilege management commands (GRANT and REVOKE) on objects and roles that are protected by the realm, while a participant cannot.

DBV protects the security infrastructure—that is, it secures the components that enforce the security for the database.

In practice, realms are flexible and transparent. External applications require no changes or knowledge of realms. When implemented correctly, the standard security and application capabilities remain functioning. You'll recall that transparency is essential to an effective implementation such that applications aren't negatively affected after the security capabilities are enabled.

Command Rules

Command rules offer a context-based or rules-based mechanism for additional security for the execution of SQL statements. With DBV command rules, you can control the execution of statements for which the user has been granted direct object privileges or for statements that require system privileges (such as CREATE USER). DBV command rules are similar to the conditional security checks that you would programmatically implement for something such as SARs; however, DBV command rules can be applied to any SQL statement.

Command rules are a new security layer that allows the authorization of a database statement based on custom-defined rules. The command rules often use the rules and factors we just described. The result is that you derive the same conditional security capabilities that you might otherwise get from enabling a role with SARs. The decision to allow a command to execute is based on the existence of the required privilege and passing a command rule.

An important differentiation exists between SARs and command rules. With SARs, the user does not have the privileges to perform the action. Instead, the privileges are granted to the role, and when the role is enabled, the user can perform the action. The conditional security check was performed to enable the role, thus giving the user the privileges. With command rules, the user must already have the requisite privileges to execute a command. DBV acts as an additional security control mechanism that takes place after the basic database privileges have been verified.

NOTE
DBV adds a layer of security, which executes at run-time to mediate actions and access: Access = Privilege + DBV rule.

DBV is transparent and works with existing applications. So if the existing application security model prevents a user from performing an action, then DBV cannot override the existing security model to allow the user to perform the action.

DBV Secure Application Roles

You will recall that Oracle provides SARs, which are database roles that can be enabled from within a PL/SQL program. The PL/SQL program typically performs a series of checks to determine whether the applicable conditions are met for the role to be enabled. DBV provides an integration SAR that enables you to define the applicable conditions using a DBV rule set. With DBV SARs, you can control the enablement of sensitive privilege sets using business or application rules defined by your organization.

Configuring and Enabling DBV

Now that you have an understanding of the core DBV components, it's time to get started. In this section, we'll review the initial configuration and enablement process of DBV.

In Oracle Database 12c, DBV is installed by default in the same way that OLS is installed. Before you configure and enable DBV, you must enable OLS in the database, as introduced in the last chapter. Next, you must configure DBV in the database either by running a PL/SQL API procedure or by using the Oracle Database Configuration (DBCA) tool.

We demonstrate DBCA by using the Advanced Mode option of DBCA to create a new multitenant database named DB12CR, with one pluggable database (PDB) named SALES. We configure DBV for the root container under the Database Options parameter screen, as shown in Figure 10-1.

DBV Administration Using Common Accounts

From the Database Options screen, we can choose either to create one account to manage DBV security policies and database accounts, or to create two separate accounts—one for each

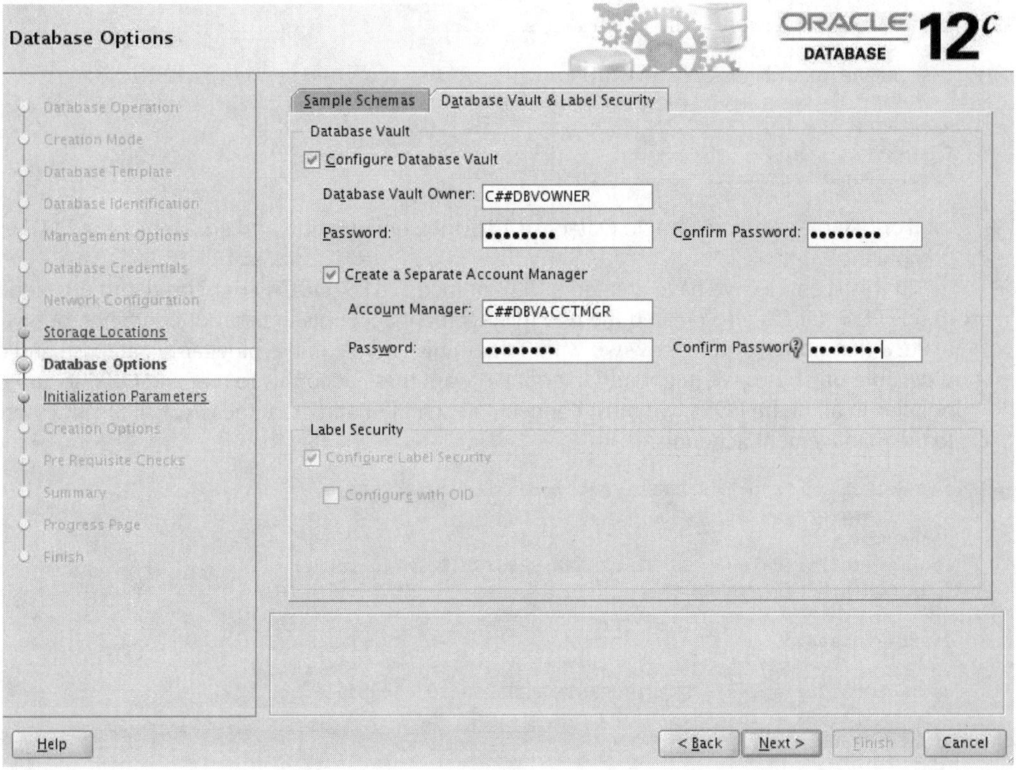

FIGURE 10-1.   *DBV configuration in the DBCA*

management role. Both options provide for SoD, but we recommend that you create two accounts in environments that require more stringent two-person controls. In our scenario, we create separate accounts in the root container for each management role. The account C##DBVOWNER will manage DBV security policies, and the account C##DBVACCTMGR will manage database accounts in the root container.

```
sec_mgr@db12cr[sales]> CONNECT sys AS sysdba
Enter Password:
Connected.
sys@db12cr[cdb$root]> SELECT username
  2    FROM dba_users
  3    WHERE username LIKE 'C##%';

USERNAME
------------------------------
C##DBVACCTMGR
C##DBVOWNER
```

We verify that DBCA has enabled DBV in the root container with the following query:

```
sys@db12cr[cdb$root]> SELECT parameter, value
  2  FROM v$option
  3  WHERE parameter LIKE '%Vault%';

PARAMETER                       VALUE
------------------------------- -------------------------------
Oracle Database Vault           TRUE
```

For databases before Oracle Database 12*c*, the configuration and enablement of DBV is complete.

In this scenario, we have created a PDB named SALES. DBCA configured and enabled DBV in this PDB. DBCA also created the two management accounts in the root container, but we must make a decision regarding how we want to administer DBV in the pluggable database and other pluggable databases we might add later. If we want these accounts to manage DBV security policies in all of the PDBs, we must connect to each PDB and grant the CREATE SESSION privilege to the management accounts:

```
sys@db12cr[cdb$root]> CONNECT sec_mgr@sales AS SYSDBA
Enter password:
Connected.
sec_mgr@db12cr[sales]> GRANT CREATE SESSION TO c##dbvowner
  2  CONTAINER = CURRENT;

Grant succeeded.

sec_mgr@db12cr[sales]> GRANT CREATE SESSION TO c##dbvacctmgr
  2  CONTAINER = CURRENT;
Grant succeeded.
```

However, we might have a requirement for delegated administration accounts that are local to each PDB.

DBV Administration Using Delegated Accounts

To create delegated DBV administrators in a PDB, we must first log on to the PDB as the DBV account administrator (C##DBVACCTMGR) and create the two container administrative accounts as follows:

```
sys@db12cr[sales]> CONNECT c##dbvacctmgr@sales
Enter password:
Connected.
c##dbvacctmgr@db12cr[sales]> CREATE USER dbvowner IDENTIFIED BY welcome1
  2  CONTAINER = CURRENT;

User created.

c##dbvacctmgr@db12cr[sales]> CREATE USER dbvacctmgr IDENTIFIED BY welcome1
  2  CONTAINER = CURRENT;

User created.
```

We then grant the DV_ACCTMGR role (discussion to follow) to the new DBVACCTMGR account:

```
c##dbvacctmgr@db12cr[sales]> GRANT dv_acctmgr to dbvacctmgr WITH ADMIN OPTION;

Grant succeeded.
```

Next, we grant the DV_OWNER role (discussion to follow) to the new DBVOWNER account:

```
c##dbvacctmgr@db12cr[sales]> CONNECT c##dbvowner@sales
Enter password:
Connected.
c##dbvowner@db12cr[sales]> GRANT dv_owner TO dbvowner WITH ADMIN OPTION
  2  CONTAINER = CURRENT;

Grant succeeded.
```

Finally, we grant the CREATE SESSION privilege to the two new administrator accounts to allow them to log in to the PDB:

```
c##dbvowner@db12cr[sales]> CONNECT sys@sales AS SYSDBA
Enter password:
Connected.
sys@db12cr[sales]> GRANT CREATE SESSION TO dbvowner
  2  CONTAINER = CURRENT;

Grant succeeded.

sys@db12cr[sales]> GRANT CREATE SESSION TO dbvacctmgr
  2  CONTAINER = CURRENT;

Grant succeeded.
```

Manually Configuring DBV in a PDB

Another approach for configuring DBV in a PDB is to create the local accounts manually and use the DVSYS.CONFIGURE_DV PL/SQL procedure to configure DBV in the PDB. In the following example we create a PDB named HR:

```
sys@db12cr[sales]> CONNECT / AS SYSDBA
Enter password:
Connected.
sys@db12cr[cdb$root]> CREATE PLUGGABLE DATABASE hr
  2    ADMIN USER hradmin IDENTIFIED BY welcome1
  3    ROLES = (DBA)
  4    FILE_NAME_CONVERT = ('/pdbseed/','/hr/');

Pluggable database created.

sys@db12cr[cdb$root]> ALTER PLUGGABLE DATABASE hr OPEN;

Pluggable database altered.
```

We can use the script from Chapter 2 to create the SEC_MGR account for this new PDB at this point. We then use the SEC_MGR account to create two DBV administration accounts and enable session access to the PDB for the accounts:

```
sys@db12cr[cdb$root]> CONNECT sec_mgr@hr AS SYSDBA
Enter password:
Connected.
sec_mgr@db12cr[hr]> CREATE USER dbvowner IDENTIFIED BY welcome1;

User created.

sec_mgr@db12cr[hr]> CREATE USER dbvacctmgr IDENTIFIED BY welcome1;

User created.

sec_mgr@db12cr[hr]> GRANT CREATE SESSION TO dbvowner;

Grant succeeded.

sec_mgr@db12cr[hr]> GRANT CREATE SESSION TO dbvacctmgr;

Grant succeeded.
```

Finally, we use the SYS account to configure the two accounts as our DBV administrators. Note that the dvacctmgr_uname parameter is optional and defaults to dvowner_uname if not specified.

```
sec_mgr@db12cr[cdb$root]> CONNECT sys@hr AS SYSDBA
Enter password:
Connected.
sys@db12cr[hr]> BEGIN dvsys.configure_dv (
  2      dvowner_uname    => 'dbvowner'
  3      ,dvacctmgr_uname => 'dbvacctmgr'
  4      );
  5  END;
  6  /

PL/SQL procedure successfully completed.
```

We can then log in to the PDB as the DBV owner account to enable DBV in the PDB:

```
sys@db12cr[hr]> CONNECT dbvowner@hr
Enter password:
Connected.
dbvowner@db12cr[hr]> EXECUTE DBMS_MACADM.ENABLE_DV;

PL/SQL procedure successfully completed.
```

The last part of this example demonstrates an important new feature of DBV in Oracle Database 12*c*. You must log in to the PDB to completely enable (EXECUTE DBMS_MACADM .ENABLE_DV) or disable (EXECUTE DBMS_MACADM.DISABLE_DV) DBV. You might recall that in Oracle Database versions 10*g* and 11*g*, you were required to run the OS make utility to link/ unlink DBV into the Oracle kernel to enable or disable DBV. Another important requirement is that DBV must be configured and enabled in the root container before DBV can be configured and enabled in a PDB.

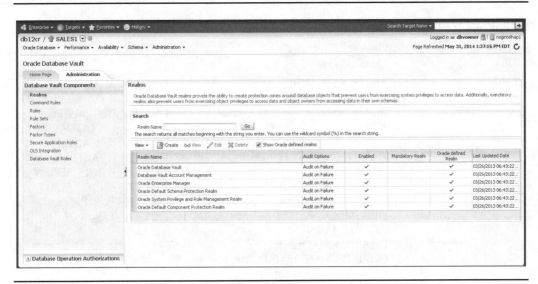

FIGURE 10-2. *DBV Administration page in OEMCC*

Managing DBV Configuration

You can configure DBV policy either by using the DBV API (DVSYS.DBMS_MACADM) or by using OEMCC. PL/SQL scripts that leverage the PL/SQL package. DBV administration pages in OEMCC manage policies local to a database, report on DBV policy violations (audit events), report on DBV policy configuration, and can be used to propagate policy components between databases. The DBV Administration page in OEMCC is shown in Figure 10-2.

In Oracle Database 10*g* and 11*g*, you can use the Database Vault Administration (DVA) web application to manage policies local to a database, report on DBV policy violations (audit events), and report on DBV policy configuration. You can use the DVSYS.DBMS_MACADM PL/SQL package to administer DBV configuration, but the account being used to administer DBV must be granted either the DV_ADMIN role or DV_OWNER role. Most of the DBV policy configuration examples in this book use the DVSYS.DBMS_MACADM PL/SQL package and the DBVOWNER account.

DBV Administration PL/SQL Package and Configuration Views

The DVSYS.DBMS_MACADM PL/SQL package enables you to script the DBV configuration using a database client tool such as SQL*Plus. DBV also includes a number of database views that are owned by the DVSYS account that you can use to query configuration information. Table 10-1 depicts the configuration procedures in the DBMS_MACADM package and associated configuration views organized by their intended configuration usage.

Configuration Usage	DBMS_MACADM Procedure(s)	DVSYS View(s)
Enable and disable DBV	DISABLE_DV ENABLE_DV	V$OPTION
General DBV configuration	AUTHORIZE_DDL AUTHORIZE_PROXY_USER AUTHORIZE_SCHEDULER_USER AUTHORIZE_TTS_USER ENABLE_DV_DICTIONARY_ACCTS ENABLE_DV_PATCH_ADMIN_AUDIT ENABLE_EVENT ENABLE_ORADEBUG DISABLE_DV_DICTIONARY_ACCTS DISABLE_DV_PATCH_ADMIN_AUDIT DISABLE_EVENT DISABLE_ORADEBUG UNAUTHORIZE_DATAPUMP_USER UNAUTHORIZE_DDL UNAUTHORIZE_PROXY_USER UNAUTHORIZE_SCHEDULER_USER UNAUTHORIZE_TTS_USER	DBA_DV_AUTH DBA_DV_DATAPUMP_AUTH DBA_DV_DDL_AUTH DBA_DV_DICTIONARY_ACCTS DBA_DV_JOB_AUTH DBA_DV_ORADEBUG DBA_DV_PATCH_ADMIN_AUDIT DBA_DV_PROXY_AUTH DBA_DV_PUB_PRIVS DBA_DV_TTS_AUTH
Configure DBV realm name, description, enabled status, and default auditing options	CREATE_REALM RENAME_REALM UPDATE_REALM UPDATE_REALM_AUTH DELETE_REALM DELETE_REALM_CASCADE	DBA_DV_REALM
Configure DBV realm secured objects and roles	ADD_OBJECT_TO_REALM DELETE_OBJECT_FROM_REALM	DBA_DV_REALM_OBJECT
Configure DBV realm authorization grantee and authorization rule set	ADD_AUTH_TO_REALM DELETE_AUTH_FROM_REALM	DBA_DV_REALM_AUTH
Configure DBV command rule command, object owner, object name, rule set, and enabled status	CREATE_COMMAND_RULE UPDATE_COMMAND_RULE DELETE_COMMAND_RULE	DBA_DV_COMMAND_RULE
Configure DBV rule names and logical expressions	CREATE_RULE RENAME_RULE UPDATE_RULE DELETE_RULE	DBA_DV_RULE

TABLE 10-1. *DBV Administration PL/SQL Packages and Associated Configuration Views* (continued)

Configuration Usage	DBMS_MACADM Procedure(s)	DVSYS View(s)
Configure DBV rule set name, description, enabled status, evaluation option, audit options, failure processing options, and custom handler	CREATE_RULE_SET DELETE_RULE_SET RENAME_RULE_SET UPDATE_RULE_SET	DBA_DV_RULE_SET
Configure association of DBV rules to DBV rule sets	ADD_RULE_TO_RULE_SET DELETE_RULE_FROM_RULE_SET	DBA_DV_RULE_SET_RULE
Configure DBV factor types	CREATE_FACTOR_TYPE RENAME_FACTOR_TYPE UPDATE_FACTOR_TYPE DELETE_FACTOR_TYPE	DBA_DV_FACTOR_TYPE
Configure DBV factor name, description, factor type, identification options, retrieval method, audit options, validation expression assignment, DBV rule set, and failure options	CREATE_FACTOR RENAME_FACTOR UPDATE_FACTOR DELETE_FACTOR	DBA_DV_FACTOR
Configure DBV identity value and trust level	CREATE_IDENTITY UPDATE_IDENTITY DELETE_IDENTITY CHANGE_IDENTITY_FACTOR CHANGE_IDENTITY_VALUE CREATE_DOMAIN_IDENTITY DROP_DOMAIN_IDENTITY	DBA_DV_IDENTITY
Configure DBV identity maps	CREATE_IDENTITY_MAP DELETE_IDENTITY_MAP ADD_FACTOR_LINK DELETE_FACTOR_LINK	DBA_DV_IDENTITY_MAP DBA_DV_FACTOR_LINK
Configure DBV SAR name, enable DBV rule set and enabled status	CREATE_ROLE RENAME_ROLE UPDATE_ROLE DELETE_ROLE	DBA_DV_ROLE
Configure OLS policy as policy integrated with DBV factors	CREATE_MAC_POLICY UPDATE_MAC_POLICY DELETE_MAC_POLICY_CASCADE	DBA_DV_MAC_POLICY

TABLE 10-1. *DBV Administration PL/SQL Packages and Associated Configuration Views* (continued)

Configuration Usage	DBMS_MACADM Procedure(s)	DVSYS View(s)
Configure DBV factor as linked to OLS policy	ADD_POLICY_FACTOR DELETE_POLICY_FACTOR	DBA_DV_MAC_POLICY_FACTOR
Configure OLS label for DBV identity	CREATE_POLICY_LABEL DELETE_POLICY_LABEL	DBA_DV_POLICY_LABEL

TABLE 10-1.   *DBV Administration PL/SQL Packages and Associated Configuration Views*

DBV Security Policies in Action

Once DBV is configured and enabled, security policy administration differs in a number of ways when compared to administering a standard Oracle Database without DBV enabled. These differences are intentional and designed to provide a more secure database environment. In this section, we highlight these differences so that you understand how the database security posture has changed. These changes result in a database that is in a better position to meet compliance regulations and to ward off external and internal threats. We also demonstrate how you can customize the default DBV policy to extend these protections to support custom-built applications.

Refer to Chapter 1 of the *Oracle Database Vault Administrator's Guide* for specific compliance regulations that DBV can help address. If you are using packaged applications such as Oracle Siebel, Oracle PeopleSoft, Oracle JD Edwards, or Oracle WebCenter Content, refer to Oracle Support Note 1623425.1 to obtain DBV policy templates that help jumpstart your efforts to secure these products.

Installed DBV Roles

In Oracle Database 12c, database roles have been added to allow the database to be patched, replicated, and backed up by administrators without having to provide access to data protected by DBV or, worse, having to disable DBV. These DBV roles can be categorized as follows.

DBV Administration and Reporting

These roles are related to DBV policy reporting and administration:

- **DV_SECANALYST**   This role has the privileges needed to read DBV configuration and audit information. This role can also access the read-only DBV administration pages in OEMCC.

- **DV_ADMIN**   This role has the privilege to execute the DVSYS.DBMS_MACADM administration PL/SQL package. This role is also authorized to administer DBV using OEMCC. The DV_ADMIN role is granted the DV_SECANALYST role, so it inherits the configuration read privileges.

- **DV_OWNER**   This role can grant the DV_SECANALYST, DV_ADMIN, and DV_OWNER roles to other accounts. This role is granted the DV_ADMIN role, so it inherits the ability to manage security configuration and the ability to read the DBV configuration.

- **DV_AUDIT_CLEANUP** This role is responsible for archiving and purging the DBV audit trail. This role has the SELECT and DELETE privileges on the DBV audit trail table DVSYS .AUDIT_TRAIL$ and two views built upon this table named DVSYS.DV$ENFORCEMENT_ AUDIT and DVSYS.DV$CONFIGURATION_AUDIT. By default this role is granted to the role DV_OWNER (using the WITH ADMIN option) and would be useful when you want further SoD and protection of the DBV audit trail (from DV_OWNER).

- **DV_MONITOR** This role is granted to the DV_OWNER role and the DBSNMP account, which is used by OEMCC to monitor databases. This role allows for DBV policy violations to be reported to OEMCC and for DBV policies to be propagated between databases. This role also has SELECT access to a subset of the configuration tables owned by DVSYS.

DBV Account Administration

The DV_ACCTMGR role is created for account administration. This role has the system privileges and the exclusive ability to CREATE, ALTER, and DROP database accounts (Oracle USER object types) as well as database profiles (Oracle PROFILE object types). Note that database accounts can still change their own password.

Operational DBV Roles

The following roles allow the database to be patched, replicated, and backed up by administrators without having to provide access to the data protected by DBV or disabling DBV:

- **DV_PATCH_ADMIN** This role is intended to be temporarily granted by DV_OWNER to an account to perform patching activity. Use the DBV procedure named DVSYS .DBMS_MACADM.ENABLE_DV_PATCH_ADMIN_AUDIT to ensure that all activity by the account using the DV_PATCH_ADMIN role is audited.

- **DV_DATAPUMP_NETWORK_LINK** This role must be granted by DV_OWNER to an account to perform Data Pump imports using the NETWORK_LINK Data Pump option. Note that in order to authorize an account to perform any Data Pump operations on a DBV-enabled database, you must use the PL/SQL procedure DBMS_MACADM .AUTHORIZE_DATAPUMP_USER.

- **DV_GOLDENGATE_ADMIN** and **DV_GOLDENGATE_REDO_ACCESS** These roles must be granted by DV_OWNER to accounts to configure database replication using Oracle GoldenGate on a DBV-enabled database. In order for GoldenGate to modify data protected by a DBV realm, you must authorize the account in the appropriate realms using the PL/SQL procedure DBMS_MACADM.ADD_AUTH_TO_REALM.

- **DV_STREAMS_ADMIN** This role must be granted by DV_OWNER to accounts that will configure database replication using Oracle Streams on a DBV-enabled database.

- **DV_XSTREAM_ADMIN** This role must be granted by DV_OWNER to accounts that will configure database inbound or outbound data change communications with the Oracle Database 12c XStream feature on a DBV-enabled database. To modify data protected by a DBV realm, you need to authorize the XStream account in the appropriate realms using the PL/SQL procedure DBMS_MACADM.ADD_AUTH_TO_REALM.

Template Roles
DBV enablement also creates two template roles used for realm administrators and realm object owner accounts: DV_REALM_OWNER and DV_REALM_RESOURCE, respectively.

> **NOTE**
> *The DV_PUBLIC role that was used to grant access to DVSYS objects to all users (PUBLIC) in DBV versions prior to Oracle Database 12c has been deprecated and no longer has associated grants.*

SoD with Roles, Realms, and Command Rules
DBV enablement also creates a default DBV security configuration using DBV realms and command rules, which is based on SoD principles that provide the following responsibilities:

- Database Account Administrator (DAA)
- Operational Database Administrator (ODBA)
- Security Administrator (SA)

With the security design concept of this SoD management model, the DAA can create accounts, the ODBA is responsible for granting privileges to the account to execute nonpublic commands, and the SA is responsible for defining policies to protect objects owned by the account.

Database Account Administrator
DBV also includes a DBV realm named Database Vault Account Management that you can use to help enforce the concept of a DAA responsibility. This realm protects the DV_ACCTMGR role and the CONNECT role. The DV_ACCTMGR role is the realm owner, and consequently only accounts that have been granted the DV_ACCTMGR role can manage the delegation of this role to other accounts. The account DBVACCTMGR was granted the DV_ACCTMGR role during DBV enablement and is therefore the default DAA. The default DBV policy that is installed includes a collection of DBV command rules to restrict commands related to database account management and enforce the concept of DAA. DBV command rules restrict the use of the CREATE/ALTER/DROP USER and CREATE/ALTER/DROP PROFILE SQL statements and the **PASSWORD** SQL*Plus command.

The realm Database Vault Account Management and the seven DBV command rules enforce the DAA concept. The DAA is responsible for managing not only the initial provisioning of named user accounts, but also the locking and unlocking of user accounts and shared accounts. With this default DBV policy in place, we can see in the following example that user SYSDBA is prevented from escalating his privileges to become the SA or DAA:

```
dbvowner@db12cr[hr]> CONNECT sys@sales AS SYSDBA
Enter password:
Connected.
sys@db12cr[sales]> -- SYSDBA cannot change the password for others
sys@db12cr[sales]> ALTER USER dbvowner IDENTIFIED BY welcome1;
ALTER USER dbvowner IDENTIFIED BY welcome1
                  *
```

```
ERROR at line 1:
ORA-01031: insufficient privileges


sys@db12cr[sales]> -- SYSDBA cannot grant DBV account management roles
sys@db12cr[sales]> GRANT dv_acctmgr TO sys;
GRANT dv_acctmgr TO sys
*
ERROR at line 1:
ORA-47410: Realm violation for GRANT on DV_ACCTMGR
```

In this example, the DBV command rule for ALTER USER prevented the password change for the DBVOWNER account, and the realm Database Vault Account Management prevented the GRANT of the DV_ACCTMGR role. Privilege escalation attacks that come from SQL injection often make use of account creation, privilege granting, or account manipulation techniques. As you can see, the default DBV policy considers these techniques in its defenses.

Operational Database Administrator

In the SoD model created by DBV, the DAA creates the database account, but the ODBA is responsible for granting the account the following:

■   Standard Oracle Database roles such as DBA or RESOURCE

■   System privileges such as CREATE TABLE or CREATE PROCEDURE

■   System ANY privileges such as CREATE ANY TABLE or SELECT ANY TABLE

The control over the granting of these roles and system privileges is dependent on the default DBV realm, Oracle System Privilege and Role Management Realm, in Oracle Database 12*c*. When system privileges are being granted, the DBV kernel code determines if the end user performing the grant is the owner of the realm. The realm owner is the only account authorized to grant privileges and roles. The SYS account is the only account authorized in this realm after DBV is configured, but you can customize this configuration, as we will demonstrate later in this chapter. This realm also protects 24 database roles that include DBA, RESOURCE, DBV_REALM_RESOURCE, DBV_REALM_OWNER, EXP_FULL_DATABASE, IMP_FULL_DATABASE, SCHEDULER_ADMIN, and AQ_ADMINISTRATOR_ROLE. When these roles are being granted, DBV verifies that the user granting the role is the owner of the realm and otherwise rejects the grant. In Oracle Database 10*g* and 11*g* the realm Oracle Data Dictionary serves the same purpose as the realm Oracle System Privilege and Role Management Realm in Oracle Database 12*c*.

Pluggable Database and Storage Management   The ODBA is not entirely focused on privilege management. The design concept for the ODBA extends into such areas as PDB management (CREATE/ALTER/DROP PLUGGABLE DATABASE), storage management (CREATE/ALTER/DROP TABLESPACE), and backup/recovery management (such as redo log maintenance with ALTER DATABASE). In the default DBV configuration, there are no protections around these types of management commands because they are not considered security-relevant commands. The ODBA requires these privileges to perform day-to-day management of the database. We will re-examine this default policy later in the chapter in the section "Protections for Audit Configuration, Dump Directories, and Secure Initialization Parameters" to use DBV to protect the integrity of your database's security-related initialization parameters.

Protections for Database Option Accounts   The default DBV configuration also creates a realm Oracle Default Schema Protection Realm to protect the standard object owner accounts such as MDDATA (Spatial), MDSYS (Spatial), and CTXSYS (Text) and the roles CTXAPP, OLAP_DBA, OLAP_USER, and EJBCLIENT. The ODBA is responsible for maintaining the objects and data in these object owner accounts for such operational procedures as index maintenance, patching, and upgrades. The only accounts that are authorized participants in this realm are CTXSYS, MDDATA, MDSYS, and SYS.

Protections for Log Miner, Replication, Materialized View Objects, and Optimizer Plans
Use Oracle LogMiner, Oracle Streams, and materialized views to create several database objects that are owned by the SYSTEM account. Oracle Database also provides a plan stability performance feature to store query optimizer plans in a schema account named OUTLN. The default DBV configuration includes a realm named Oracle Default Component Protection Realm that protects the objects in the SYSTEM and OUTLN schemas. By default, SYSTEM and SYS are the only authorized accounts in this realm. This realm is very important if you use these features because it prevents accounts with the DBA role or similar privileges from manipulating the objects in an unauthorized manner.

Protections for the Enterprise Manager Cloud Control Performance Data   The default DBV configuration also includes a realm named Oracle Enterprise Manager Realm that protects performance statistics collected under the DBSMP account as well as the PL/SQL statistics management collection APIs from unauthorized access by accounts with system ANY privileges. This realm also protects the OEM_MONITOR role. By default, SYSTEM and DBSNMP are the only authorized accounts in this realm.

Protections for Audit Configuration, Dump Directories, and Secure Initialization Parameters
The DBV includes a DBV command rule for the ALTER SYSTEM statement that prevents the ODBA from modifying security-sensitive database initialization parameters, such as disabling the auditing of commands executed by the SYS account, enabling OS authentication, or changing the database dump destinations. The complete list of protected database initialization parameters is listed in the "Default Rules" section of Chapter 6 in the *Oracle Database Vault Administrator's Guide*.

This default command rule for ALTER SYSTEM is important because it prevents SYSDBA from disabling the audit configuration. For example, this command rule protects against changing the AUDIT_SYS_OPERATIONS parameter that audits SYSDBA, or changing the standard "secure-by-default" database privilege settings such as 07_DICTIONARY_ACCESSIBILITY and SQL92_SECURITY. The following example demonstrates this DBV command rule:

```
sys@db12cr[sales]> CONNECT / AS SYSDBA
Connected.
sys@db12cr[cdb$root]> SHOW PARAMETER audit_sys_operations

NAME                                 TYPE         VALUE
------------------------------------ ----------- ---------------------------
audit_sys_operations                 boolean      TRUE

sys@db12cr[cdb$root]> ALTER SYSTEM SET audit_sys_operations = FALSE
  2  SCOPE = SPFILE;

ALTER SYSTEM SET audit_sys_operations = FALSE SCOPE = SPFILE
*
ERROR at line 1:
ORA-01031: insufficient privileges
```

Note that in Oracle Database 12*c*, a number of accounts support optional database features that are not protected in a realm by default. These accounts include the following:

- **APEX040200, APEX_PUBLIC_USER and FLOWS_FILES**   Used by Oracle Application Express (APEX)
- **OLAPSYS**   Used by Oracle Online Analytical Processing (OLAP)
- **ORDSYS, ORDATA and ORDPLUGINS**   Used by Oracle interMedia
- **XDB**   Used by Oracle XML Database
- **WMSYS**   Used by Oracle Workspace Manager

We recommend that you create a new realm for each of the features you intend to use and protecting the schemas in the realm. You can then authorize the schema(s) and SYS as the default realm owners. You can augment the realm ownership configuration based on the policies you create for ODBAs and any application data administrators that use these features.

Security Administrator

DBV stores configuration data for realms, command rules, rule sets, and factors in tables owned by an object owner account named DVSYS. Direct DML (INSERT, UPDATE, and DELETE) against these configuration tables can be done only by the DVSYS account or definer's rights PL/SQL code owned by the DVSYS account. The DVSYS.DBMS_MACADM package is the only means to manipulate these tables—even the DBV Administration pages in OEMCC use this package. The ability to execute this package is granted to the DV_ADMIN role (and indirectly to DV_OWNER role), so that when DBV is installed, the account granted the DV_OWNER role is created in your SA. The default DBV configuration includes a realm named Database Vault Realm to enforce the concept of an SA responsibility and as a protection for the DBV configuration data. This realm protects the following database objects:

- Objects owned by the DVSYS, including the DBV configuration tables, the PL/SQL administration package DBMS_MACADM, and the DBV audit trail (DVSYS.AUDIT_TRAIL$)
- Objects owned by the DVF object owner account that stores DBV factor PL/SQL functions
- The DBV roles that were described earlier
- Objects owned by the OLS object owner account (LBACSYS)
- The OLS administration role LBAC_DBA
- The Oracle VPD administration package DBMS_RLS

As you can see, security-relevant configuration data for statement-level security (SLS), such as DBV, and row-level security (RLS), such as VPD and OLS, are protected by this realm. The realm is "owned" by the DV_OWNER role. Only accounts with the DV_OWNER role can manage the roles protected by this realm. This realm capability offers a secure mechanism to provision and delegate the SA responsibility to other accounts using DV_OWNER or DV_ADMIN. The realm named Database Vault Realm enforces the SA concept and is responsible for security-relevant configuration data and managing the provisioning of additional SAs. Further, **GRANT** and **REVOKE** commands on the VPD administration package (DBMS_RLS) and the OLS role (LBAC_DATA) can be performed only by the DV_OWNER role.

As you can see in the following example, even SYSDBA is blocked from using the DVSYS
.DBMS_MACADM package, granting DBV roles, granting roles protected by DBV, and reading
DBV configuration data.

```
sys@db12cr[cdb$root]> CONNECT sys@sales AS SYSDBA
Enter password:
Connected.
sys@db12cr[sales]> -- SYSDBA cannot manipulate the DBV policy
sys@db12cr[sales]> BEGIN
  2      DVSYS.DBMS_MACADM.ADD_AUTH_TO_REALM(
  3        realm_name => 'Database Vault Realm'
  4        , grantee => 'SYS'
  5        , auth_options => 1);
  6   END;
  7  /
    DVSYS.DBMS_MACADM.ADD_AUTH_TO_REALM(
        *
ERROR at line 2:
ORA-06550: line 2, column 9:
PLS-00904: insufficient privilege to access object DVSYS.DBMS_MACADM
ORA-06550: line 2, column 3:
PL/SQL: Statement ignored

sys@db12cr[sales]> -- SYSDBA cannot grant DBV administrator roles
sys@db12cr[sales]> GRANT dv_owner TO sys;
GRANT dv_owner TO sys
*
ERROR at line 1:
ORA-47410: Realm violation for GRANT on DV_OWNER
sys@db12cr[sales]> -- SYSDBA cannot even see the DBV policy
sys@db12cr[sales]> SELECT name FROM dvsys.dba_dv_realm;
SELECT name FROM dvsys.dba_dv_realm
                        *
ERROR at line 1:
ORA-01031: insufficient privileges

sys@db12cr[sales]> -- SYSDBA cannot grant privileges to use VPD
sys@db12cr[sales]> GRANT EXECUTE ON dbms_rls TO system;
GRANT EXECUTE ON dbms_rls TO system
                    *
ERROR at line 1:
ORA-47401: Realm violation for GRANT on SYS.DBMS_RLS


sys@db12cr[sales]> -- SYSDBA cannot grant the OLS DBA role
sys@db12cr[sales]> GRANT lbac_dba TO system;
GRANT lbac_dba TO system
*
ERROR at line 1:
ORA-47410: Realm violation for GRANT on LBAC_DBA
```

This default protection extends to your use of OLS and the associated policy configuration data.
With this triad of database administrators (DAA, ODBA, and SA) and the SoD model that is
created with the default DBV policy, your enterprise can immediately operate in a posture of checks
and balances to help achieve whatever compliance regulations your organization is trying to meet.

Default Audit Policies

The auditing of DBV policy enforcement is a standard feature of DBV. In the discussion so far, we have introduced a number of default DBV realms and command rules that are provided with DBV. DBV realms and command rules generate audit records based on the underlying configuration of the DBV rule sets that control their enforcement. When you create custom DBV rules sets that control realms, command rules, DBV secure application roles, and DBV factors, you also have the option to control how they are audited. Figure 10-3 shows audit information generated for this type of DBV enforcement (the Attempted Violations Report is available in OEMCC). In this figure, you see the audit record that was generated as a result of the **ALTER SYSTEM** command we attempted earlier.

Default DBV Audit Policy

DBV includes a comprehensive standard database audit policy designed to audit commands and activity related to the DBV product's DVSYS and DVF accounts and the OLS product account LBACSYS. This policy ensures that changes to (or attempts to change) the configuration data for these two products is captured. Any subversive commands such as **NOAUDIT**, **REVOKE**, or **RENAME** against these object-owning accounts are also captured by this audit policy. The DBV default audit policy also includes a comprehensive audit policy for the database that audits the following categories of database activity:

- **Session login and logoff**   For example, when accounts with the SYSDBA privilege, the DV_OWNER role, or your own custom database applications access the database
- **Privilege management**   For example, when **GRANT** and **REVOKE** commands are issued

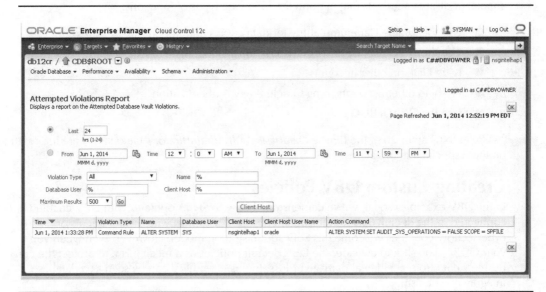

FIGURE 10-3.   *DBV Attempted Violations Report in OEMCC*

■ **Database account management** For example when **CREATE**, **ALTER**, or **DROP USER** commands are issued

■ **Audit policy management** For example, when **AUDIT** and **NOAUDIT** commands are issued

■ **Structural changes** For example, when tablespace management commands or object management commands with syntax like **CREATE** <object>, **ALTER** <object>, and **DROP** <object> are issued

■ **Privileged administrator changes** For example, use of restricted sessions, system ANY privileges, privileged statements such as ALTER SYSTEM, BECOME USER, and TRUNCATE TABLE

NOTE
This audit policy was developed from research conducted by leading commercial and government authorities on computer security that continuously publish up-to-date recommendations on this subject. The protection of the DBV and OLS configuration was added to this policy to audit these security-relevant features. For a complete listing of the statements that are audited, refer to Appendix A-2 of the Oracle Database Vault Administrator's Guide.

General Database Maintenance and Operations Authorizations

A DBV-enabled database requires special authorizations for general database maintenance and operations. You must use the DBMS_MACADM package AUTHORIZE% API calls to authorize, enable, or disable accounts that perform the following types of functions:

■ Use the Oracle DataPump utility for data export and import

■ Use the Oracle Scheduler for database job scheduling

■ Issue DDL on other accounts

■ Proxy to other accounts using Oracle Proxy Authentication

■ Use the ORADEBUG utility

Refer to Chapter 20 of the *Oracle Database Vault Administrator's Guide* for more information on these special authorizations.

Creating Custom DBV Policies

In the DBV examples so far, we've demonstrated how SYSDBA operates with DBV enabled and configured in the default SoD administration model. Customers with insider threats or cybersecurity concerns welcome this SoD administration model. However, even when you trust your ODBA, you should consider the DBV default policies as a mechanism to protect the core business data from accidental damage or loss. In this case, DBV can be seen as a database integrity mechanism.

In this section, we demonstrate how to create custom DBV policies within the context of a simple scenario, in which we will protect the Sales History (SH) and Human Resources (HR) schemas.

An organization's IT and security policy should have controls on the types of database administration that can occur when critical systems are being used by the general user population. An organization's IT department will typically create system maintenance windows in which to make changes to a system in addition to the configuration management procedures for validating these changes before they are deployed.

In our scenario, we will allow upgrades, patching, and general database maintenance on the SH and HR schemas during a maintenance window that occurs on Fridays from 7 P.M. until 12 A.M. (midnight). With this simple scenario, we can demonstrate how to create custom DBV policies that leverage all of DBV components such as realms, factors, rule sets, secure application roles, and command rules.

Creating Realms

Creating a realm for the SH or HR schemas removes access to the Sales History data from accounts such as SYS and SYSTEM, and from roles such as DBA. First we log in to the database using the SA account named DBVOWNER and create the realm:

```
sys@db12cr[sales]> CONNECT dbvowner@sales
Enter password:
Connected.
dbvowner@db12cr[sales]> -- Create a REGULAR realm for Sales History (SH)
dbvowner@db12cr[sales]> BEGIN
  2      dbms_macadm.create_realm(
  3            realm_name     => 'Sales History'
  4          , description    => 'Realm for protection of SH objects and roles'
  5          , enabled        =>  dbms_macutl.g_yes
  6          , audit_options  =>  dbms_macutl.g_realm_audit_fail
  7          , realm_type     =>  0 );
  8   END;
  9   /

PL/SQL procedure successfully completed.

dbvowner@db12cr[sales]> -- Create a MANDATORY realm for Human Resources (HR)
dbvowner@db12cr[sales]> BEGIN
  2      dbms_macadm.create_realm(
  3            realm_name     => Human Resources'
  4          , description    => 'Realm for protection of HR objects and roles'
  5          , enabled        =>  dbms_macutl.g_yes
  6          , audit_options  =>  dbms_macutl.g_realm_audit_fail
  7          , realm_type     =>  1 );
  8   END;
  9   /

PL/SQL procedure successfully completed.

dbvowner@db12cr[sales]> SELECT name, realm_type
  2   FROM dvsys.dba_dv_realm
  3   ORDER BY name;

NAME                                                             REALM_TYPE
---------------------------------------------------------------- ---------------
Database Vault Account Management                                REGULAR
Human Resources                                                  MANDATORY
Oracle Database Vault                                            REGULAR
```

```
Oracle Default Component Protection Realm                    REGULAR
Oracle Default Schema Protection Realm                       REGULAR
Oracle Enterprise Manager                                    REGULAR
Oracle System Privilege and Role Management Realm            REGULAR
Sales History                                                REGULAR

8 rows selected.
```

In this example, we defined a name and description for our realms. We also declared that the realm be enabled. We chose to audit when a realm violation occurs with the audit parameter value of G_AUDIT_REALM_FAIL. You could configure DBV to audit each realm access evaluation with G_AUDIT_REALM_SUCCESS, or you could combine the parameters by simply adding them together. As mentioned, in Oracle Database 12c you can define a realm as a mandatory realm by specifying the value of parameter REALM_TYPE equal to 1. This requires that the object owner account (HR) and users with direct object privileges on the objects protected by the realm be authorized in the realm. Specifying a REALM_TYPE of 0 (regular) allows the object owner account (SH) and users with direct object privileges access to the objects protected by the realm. As you can see from the preceding listing, the default DBV realms are of type REGULAR.

The PL/SQL package DVSYS.DBMS_MACUTL contains constants and utility functions used throughout the DBV administration. The constants are also beneficial when using DVSYS.DBMS_MACADM package for administration, because they avoid the need to remember character or numeric values for DBV components.

Realm Objects   We have not identified the actual objects in the SH schema that will be protected by the realm, but we can do this with the DBMS_MACADM.ADD_OBJECT_TO_REALM procedure as follows:

```
dbvowner@db12cr[sales]> BEGIN
  2       dbms_macadm.add_object_to_realm (
  3            realm_name     => 'Sales History'
  4          , object_owner => 'SH'
  5          , object_type   => '%'
  6          , object_name   => '%');
  7    END;
  8    /

PL/SQL procedure successfully completed.
```

The configuration of a realm can be defined at the schema level as we demonstrated in the SH example, such that all objects regardless of type are protected. However, it is also possible to configure the realm to protect specific objects by type or name. For example, it's possible to protect just the tables in the HR schema as follows:

```
dbvowner@db12cr[sales]> BEGIN
  2       dbms_macadm.add_object_to_realm (
  3            realm_name     => 'Human Resources'
  4          , object_owner => 'HR'
  5          , object_type   => 'TABLE'
  6          , object_name   => '%');
  7    END;
  8    /

PL/SQL procedure successfully completed.
```

It is also possible to configure the realm to protect individual objects by specifying an object name in the OBJECT_NAME parameter.

Objects in this MANDATORY realm are immediately protected after the configuration step has executed. In the following example, we see that when SYSTEM tries to query the HR. EMPLOYEES table using the SELECT ANY privilege, or even when HR tries to query its own tables, they are unauthorized! HR is not authorized to query its tables because the realm is of type MANDATORY and HR has not been added to the realm authorizations (described next).

```
dbvowner@db12cr[sales]> CONNECT system@sales
Enter password:
Connected.
system@db12cr[sales]> SELECT COUNT(*) FROM hr.employees;
SELECT COUNT(*) FROM hr.employees
                          *
ERROR at line 1:
ORA-01031: insufficient privileges

system@db12cr[sales]> CONNECT hr@sales
Enter password:
Connected.
hr@db12cr[sales]> SELECT COUNT(*) FROM hr.employees;
SELECT COUNT(*) FROM hr.employees
                          *
ERROR at line 1:
ORA-01031: insufficient privileges
```

Note that schemas or schema objects can belong to multiple realms. The session user must be authorized in at least one of the realms protecting the object for a command to be executed.

Realm Authorizations Realm authorizations define the accounts and roles that are authorized to use system ANY privileges against realm-protected objects. Realm authorizations can be declared as either a realm participant or a realm owner. Both realm participants and realm owners can leverage system ANY privileges. The difference is that a realm owner can do the following:

- GRANT or REVOKE object privileges on objects protected by the realm
- GRANT or REVOKE database roles that are protected in the realm

Realm authorizations can be configured by accounts with the DV_ADMIN or DV_OWNER role, such as our DBVOWNER account. Note that realm authorizations do not GRANT system privileges or even object privileges. Realm authorizations allow the use of system ANY privileges on objects that are protected by the realm or allow the use of direct object privileges in the case of a mandatory realm. The underlying system ANY privileges or direct object privileges still need to be granted to the account or role. In other words, a realm participant needs to be explicitly granted the SELECT ANY TABLE privilege or SELECT on the object to use a realm authorization, and a realm owner needs to be granted the GRANT ANY OBJECT or GRANT ANY ROLE privilege to use a realm authorization. To grant or revoke a role that is protected by a DBV realm, the session user must be authorized in the realm and have the system privilege GRANT ANY ROLE.

NOTE
Realm authorizations do not implicitly or explicitly grant privileges.
They simply authorize the use of system ANY privileges or direct
object privileges.

As mentioned, the ability to grant privileges is restricted after DBV is enabled because of the default DBV realm named Oracle System Privilege and Role Management Realm.

We can authorize the HR object owner account as the realm owner using the DBMS_MACADM.ADD_AUTH_TO_REALM procedure:

```
hr@db12cr[sales]> CONNECT dbvowner@sales
Enter password:
Connected.
dbvowner@db12cr[sales]> -- Authorize a schema account to use
dbvowner@db12cr[sales]> -- directory object privileges in the MANDATORY
dbvowner@db12cr[sales]> -- realm on objects protected by the realm
dbvowner@db12cr[sales]> BEGIN
  2    dbms_macadm.add_auth_to_realm (
  3      realm_name    => 'Human Resources'
  4    , grantee       => 'HR'
  5    , rule_set_name => NULL
  6    , auth_options  => dbms_macutl.g_realm_auth_owner );
  7  END;
  8  /

PL/SQL procedure successfully completed.

dbvowner@db12cr[sales]> -- we will also authorize a schema account
dbvowner@db12cr[sales]> -- as the realm owner in the REGULAR
dbvowner@db12cr[sales]> -- realm so that the account can perform
dbvowner@db12cr[sales]> -- grants to objects protected by the realm
dbvowner@db12cr[sales]> BEGIN
  2    dbms_macadm.add_auth_to_realm (
  3      realm_name    => 'Sales History'
  4    , grantee       => 'SH'
  5    , rule_set_name => NULL
  6    , auth_options  => dbms_macutl.g_realm_auth_owner );
  7  END;
  8  /

PL/SQL procedure successfully completed.
```

The grantee parameter can be an account or a role. In our example, we authorized the HR schema to use the direct object privileges (SELECT, INSERT, and so on) on objects the account owns within the MANDATORY realm. You should lock and expire object owner accounts whenever possible. Database access should be based on named user accounts as we recommended in the first few chapters of this book. In practice, this is not always possible. Consider Oracle Fusion Middleware products, where the object owner account is also the account used by the WebLogic Server JDBC data sources.

As mentioned earlier in this book, you should strive to define roles for your database applications to simplify overall privilege management. In keeping with this recommendation, you should use roles whenever possible for realm authorizations. We recommend that you create roles based on the concept of an application DBA when hosting more than one application in a single database.

This approach provides a flexible and secure SoD model for your applications that are protected with DBV. With the application DBA roles in place, you can then grant roles to named user accounts to achieve the appropriate level attribution in your audit trails.

In the preceding example, you will also notice that a DBV rule set can be configured to control when and how a realm authorization is permissible. A value of NULL for the RULE_SET_NAME parameter implies that the authorization is always permissible. We will examine DBV rule sets in the section "Creating Rules and Rule Sets" later in this chapter.

For security reasons, the DBV roles DV_OWNER, DV_ADMIN, DV_SECANALYST, and DV_ ACCTMGR cannot be authorized in user-defined realms. If this were allowed, then the SA could authorize himself in the Sales History realm, grant himself the realm-protected roles, and gain access to all realm-protected data.

Creating Factors

DBV factors are security-relevant attributes that help establish the security context for a session to authorize commands or actions, such as the following:

- Connecting to the database when used as part of a DBV CONNECT command rule
- Executing a (SQL) statement against a database object, or a statement-level authorization when used as part of a DBV command rule or realm authorization
- Filtering data in the WHERE clause of a SELECT and DML statement
- Row-level security (RLS) authorization, when used in Oracle Virtual Private Database (VPD) policy or the DBV Oracle Label Security (OLS) integration
- Branching in application code, or logic authorizations, when used with the DBV factor function (DVF.<FACTOR_NAME>) or the DVSYS.GET_FACTOR function in PL/SQL logic

These types of DBV factor usage scenarios are depicted in Figure 10-4.

DBV factors are typically defined and maintained outside of database applications. Factors can use information that may be internal or external to the information stored in the database. DBV factors are primarily used to establish the context of the "subject" (who) in your security policy and the "conditions" (when, how, where) in your security policy. The context of the subject may include session information on roles granted, group/organizational membership, privileges granted, or even identity management-related attributes such as job title. Conditional attributes may include information such as time of day or month, authentication method used, client location, or access path (recall the trusted package example). The Oracle Database 12c default DBV configuration includes 17 factors that may be useful for your organization's security policy.

The fundamental configuration of a DBV factor is the factor name and the PL/SQL expression used to retrieve the factor's value, or the *identity*, as it is called. One factor that is installed by DBV is Client IP, which is the client's IP address. The factor uses the PL/SQL expression UPPER(SYS_CONTEXT('USERENV','IP_ADDRESS')) to retrieve its identity. To define a custom factor, you should follow these steps:

1. Define the factor's retrieval method using a PL/SQL function if the factor cannot be expressed in a simple PL/SQL expression.
2. Grant EXECUTE privileges on the PL/SQL function to the DVSYS account.
3. Create the DBV factor using the SA (DBVOWNER) account.

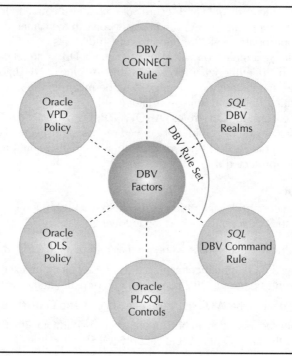

FIGURE 10-4. *DBV factor usage scenarios*

Factor Retrieval Method The factor retrieval method is a PL/SQL expression or SQL SELECT statement that returns a VARCHAR2 value. PL/SQL expressions can be based on a SQL built-in function or they can be based on a custom PL/SQL function. The important point is the function must return a VARCHAR2 value, even if it is NULL, or some other data type that can be cast to a VARCHAR2. The function's signature can be defined as follows:

```
FUNCTION some_factor RETURN VARCHAR2;
```

or

```
FUNCTION another_factor(param1 IN data_type1 … paramN IN data_typeN)
     RETURN VARCHAR2;
```

Notice in the latter signature that it is possible to pass parameters to your function if you need information. When user-developed PL/SQL functions are used as the retrieval method for DBV factors, the functions are typically defined with definer's rights versus invoker's rights.

Returning to our scenario, we use DBV factors to define a maintenance window by creating two factors: one for the day of the week and another for the hour of the day:

```
dbvowner@db12cr[sales]> -- Create a factor for the day of the week
dbvowner@db12cr[sales]> BEGIN
  2     dbms_macadm.create_factor(
```

```
 3            factor_name      => 'Current_Day',
 4            factor_type_name => 'Time',
 5            description      => 'The current day of the week',
 6            rule_set_name => NULL ,
 7            get_expr         => 'TO_CHAR(SYSDATE,''DY'')',
 8            validate_expr => NULL,
 9            identify_by      => dbms_macutl.g_identify_by_method,
10            labeled_by       => dbms_macutl.g_labeled_by_self,
11            eval_options     => dbms_macutl.g_eval_on_access,
12            audit_options => dbms_macutl.g_audit_on_get_error,
13            fail_options     => dbms_macutl.g_fail_with_message);
14   END;
15   /

PL/SQL procedure successfully completed.

dbvowner@db12cr[sales]> -- Create a factor for the hour of the day
dbvowner@db12cr[sales]> BEGIN
 2      dbms_macadm.create_factor(
 3            factor_name      => 'Current_Hour',
 4            factor_type_name => 'Time',
 5            description      => 'The current hour of the day',
 6            rule_set_name => NULL ,
 7            get_expr         => 'TO_CHAR(SYSDATE,''HH24'')',
 8            validate_expr => NULL,
 9            identify_by      => dbms_macutl.g_identify_by_method,
10            labeled_by       => dbms_macutl.g_labeled_by_self,
11            eval_options     => dbms_macutl.g_eval_on_access,
12            audit_options => dbms_macutl.g_audit_on_get_error,
13            fail_options     => dbms_macutl.g_fail_with_message);
14   END;
15   /

PL/SQL procedure successfully completed.

dbvowner@db12cr[sales]> COMMIT;

Commit complete.

dbvowner@db12cr[sales]> -- Show the factor runtime evaluation
dbvowner@db12cr[sales]> -- using both the GET_FACTOR
dbvowner@db12cr[sales]> -- and DVF factor functions
dbvowner@db12cr[sales]> CONNECT sh@sales
Enter password:
Connected.
sh@db12cr[sales]> SELECT get_factor('CURRENT_DAY') DAY_OF_WEEK
 2   , DVF.F$CURRENT_HOUR HOUR_OF_DAY
 3   FROM dual;

DAY_OF_WEEK          HOUR_OF_DAY
-------------------- --------------------
MON                  17

1 row selected.
```

In this example, we are using the SQL built-in function (GET_FACTOR) that serves as input into the DBV rule set examples to follow. Note that you can also use a SQL statement in the GET_ EXPR parameter, as shown in the following code snippet:

```
get_expr        => '(SELECT platform_name FROM v$database)',
```

When using SQL SELECT statements, you must embed the SELECT statement in parentheses and the DVSYS account must be granted SELECT privileges on the table or view being queried.

TIP
It is important that you name your factors with identifiers that convey the attribute retrieved to improve the readability of your DBV policy. In other words, using factor names such as Current_Hour or Database_Platform, compared to CURHR or DBPLTFRM, greatly improves readability of the security policy.

Factor Evaluation   The EVAL_OPTIONS parameter in the DBMS_MACADM.CREATE_FACTOR procedure controls when the identity (i.e. the value) of the factor should be resolved. A factor's identity can be resolved just once, at the time the database session is started, using the constant dbms_macutl.g_eval_on_SESSION. With this constant, the factor's identity is cached in the database session namespace MAC$FACTOR. Subsequent calls to resolve the factor's identity are read from this namespace to improve performance. If the constant dbms_macutl.g_eval_on_ ACCESS is used for this parameter, then each call to resolve the factor's identity will call the factor's retrieval method. For example, the value of the database platform would not change over the course of a database session, so the factor's identity resolution dbms_macutl.g_eval_on_ SESSION would be used. Factors such as Current_Day and Current_Hour will change during the course of a database session, so their identity resolution is set to dbms_macutl.g_eval_on_ACCESS.

Factor Auditing   It is possible that the PL/SQL function used in the factors retrieval method (the GET_EXPR parameter) could encounter an error or return a NULL value. DBV factors can be configured to audit these outcomes using the AUDIT_OPTIONS parameter in the DBMS_ MACADM.CREATE_FACTOR procedure. The DBV Administration pages of OEMCC provide the ability for the SA to query these audit records.

Factor Functions   When a factor is created, the DBV creates a PL/SQL function of the form, DVF.F$<Factor Name>, that can be used in DBV rule set expressions or your PL/SQL code. When we created the factor Current_Hour, a function named DVF.F$CURRENT_HOUR was created and an EXECUTE on the function was granted to PUBLIC, making this function available to all database sessions. If the name of the factor is dynamically resolved, then the DBV rule set or your PL/SQL application logic can use the function DVSYS.GET_FACTOR('<Factor Name>') to get the value of the factor. The use of these two factor function forms are shown at the end of the preceding code example.

Factor Identities   The term "identity" is used in identity management systems as the unique identifier of a user. In DBV, the term "identity" means the value of a factor. DBV can be configured with several security-relevant attributes other than the connected user. We can have identities for client IP addresses, client machines, the time of day, user departments, and so on. As we have discussed, DBV factor configuration supports the use of a simple PL/SQL expressions, such as

SYS_CONTEXT or TO_CHAR(SYSDATE), and it supports the use of custom PL/SQL code. Creating a DBV factor this way requires the value DBMS_MACUTL.G_IDENTIFY_BY_METHOD for the parameter IDENTIFY_BY. It also requires us to put the PL/SQL expression in the GET_EXPR parameter in the call to the DBMS_MACADM.CREATE_FACTOR procedure.

Factor Identity as a Constant   The PL/SQL expression used to establish the factor's identity can also be a constant value. We specify a constant identity using the constant DBMS_MACUTL.G_IDENTIFY_BY_CONSTANT for the parameter IDENTIFY_BY and place the constant value in the GET_EXPR parameter in the call to the procedure DBMS_MACADM.CREATE_FACTOR. A factor with a constant identity can be useful in security policies with IF/THEN/ELSE or CASE/SWITCH logic. For example, you may have a highly restrictive policy in a production database and a less restrictive policy in a development database. You could define a factor such as IS_PRODUCTION to return 0 or 1 based on the current database. You could have a factor such as ENVIRONMENT_NAME that returns a value such as DEV, TEST, or PROD to handle this type of scenario.

Factors Identified by Other Factors   We can also identify a factor based on the identity of another factor. With this method, we can assert the identity of a factor using a declarative DBV construct called "identity maps." Identity maps allow for a multifactored security capability to be defined and do not require special PL/SQL code. This method of factor resolution requires the use of the constant DBMS_MACUTL.G_IDENTIFY_BY_FACTOR for the parameter IDENTIFY_BY when creating the factor using DBMS_MACADM.CREATE_FACTOR. Multifactored security is one of the most interesting and powerful security features of the DBV product.

Creating factors based on the identity of other factors requires the following steps:

1. Define the parent factor to be used by other factors.
2. Define factor links between the parent and contributing factors. The DBV Administration pages in OEMCC automatically define links using the underlying DBMS_MACADM APIs.
3. Define the identities for the parent factor.
4. Define child factors and the identities for the parent factor.
5. Define the identity map to connect child factor identities to the parent factor.

Creating Rules and Rule Sets
A DBV rule is an elementary DBV logic component that is written as an Oracle PL/SQL expression that returns a Boolean result. An example of a simple rule would be USER != 'SYS'. This rule uses the standard Oracle PL/SQL function USER, which returns the name of the connected database account. The expression returns TRUE or FALSE based on whether or not the connected user is SYS. A DBV rule can be associated with more than one DBV rule set. You can develop a library of DBV rules that can be used throughout your DBV security policy.

TIP
Create DBV rules as reusable security policy controls applicable to more than one application.

DBV rule sets can be used in DBV realm authorizations or DBV command rules. DBV rule sets can also control the assignment of a DBV factor's identity and the ability to enable DBV SARs. Auditing of these components is controlled by the audit settings of the DBV rule set. DBV rule sets can be configured to execute custom PL/SQL procedures so that if a DBV command rule is violated, this information could be passed to a monitoring system or could alert the SA in real time.

Rule Set Evaluation Mode   The configuration of DBV rule sets allows for the association of multiple DBV rules. DBV rule sets have an evaluation mode that can be configured to require that ALL associated rules return TRUE, or at least one rule (ANY) returns TRUE.

The DBV rule set configuration allows for a DBV rule set to be disabled. The effect of disabling a DBV rule set is that the DBV rules engine will return TRUE during rule evaluation. In the following example, we create DBV rules and a DBV rule set to model the maintenance window concept of our scenario to help clarify the evaluation mode:

```
sh@db12cr[sales]> CONNECT dbvowner@sales
Enter password:
Connected.
dbvowner@db12cr[sales]> BEGIN
  2       dbms_macadm.create_rule(
  3          rule_name => 'Is Maintenance Day of Week'
  4        , rule_expr => 'GET_FACTOR(''Current_Day'') = ''FRI'''
  5       );
  6  END;
  7  /

PL/SQL procedure successfully completed.

dbvowner@db12cr[sales]> BEGIN
  2       dbms_macadm.create_rule(
  3          rule_name => 'Within Maintenance Hours'
  4        , rule_expr => 'TO_NUMBER(GET_FACTOR(''Current_HOUR''))
  5             BETWEEN 19 AND 23');
  6  END;
  7  /

PL/SQL procedure successfully completed.

dbvowner@db12cr[sales]> -- Create the Maintenance Window DBV Rule Set
dbvowner@db12cr[sales]> -- requiring all rules to be true
dbvowner@db12cr[sales]> BEGIN
  2       dbms_macadm.create_rule_set(
  3          rule_set_name   => 'Inside Maintenance Window',
  4          description     => 'Checks to see if maintenance and
  5             patch activity can be executed.',
  6          enabled         => dbms_macutl.g_yes,
  7          eval_options    => dbms_macutl.g_ruleset_eval_all,
  8          audit_options   => dbms_macutl.g_ruleset_audit_fail,
  9          fail_options    => dbms_macutl.g_ruleset_fail_show,
 10          fail_message    => NULL,
 11          fail_code       => NULL,
 12          handler_options => dbms_macutl.g_ruleset_handler_off,
 13          handler         => NULL);
 14  END;
 15  /

PL/SQL procedure successfully completed.
```

```
dbvowner@db12cr[sales]> -- Associate the DBV Rules to the DBV Rule Set
dbvowner@db12cr[sales]> BEGIN
  2      dbms_macadm.add_rule_to_rule_set (
  3        rule_set_name => 'Inside Maintenance Window'
  4        , rule_name     => 'Is Maintenance Day of Week'
  5      );
  6  END;
  7  /

PL/SQL procedure successfully completed.

dbvowner@db12cr[sales]> BEGIN
  2      dbms_macadm.add_rule_to_rule_set (
  3        rule_set_name => 'Inside Maintenance Window'
  4        , rule_name     => 'Within Maintenance Hours'
  5      );
  6  END;
  7  /

PL/SQL procedure successfully completed.
```

In Oracle Database 12c, the DBMS_MACADM.CREATE_RULE_SET procedure includes a new parameter named IS_STATIC that enables you to evaluate and cache a rule set once for a session.

Rule Set Auditing   When we configured the preceding DBV rule set, we used the constant DBMS_MACUTL.G_RULESET_AUDIT_FAIL, which means "audit on failure only" or "audit when the DBV rule set evaluation is FALSE." Auditing on a failed access attempt is typically a minimum requirement for all DBV rule sets; however, some regulatory requirements may mandate auditing on any data access—in other words, you should create an audit record regardless of the evaluation result of the DBV rule set. You should consider the performance and storage impacts of this level of auditing given the frequency of evaluation in your production system.

Custom Event Handlers   The DBV rule set standard auditing component can be extended using the custom event handlers feature. This feature enables you to integrate DBV with external alerting, systems management, and monitoring systems. Like DBV rule set auditing, this feature can be configured to audit on success, failure, or both. Follow these steps to enable this feature:

1. Define a procedure that will be called when the DBV rule set is evaluated.

2. Grant EXECUTE on the procedure to DVSYS. The DVSYS account executes the DBV rules engine and calls the procedure.

3. Configure the DBV rule set to use the custom event handling procedure.

Chapter 6 of the *Oracle Database Vault Administrator's Guide* includes a nice example of generating an e-mail message from a DBV rule set event handler. This opens up many possibilities to use electronic messaging or integrate DBV with existing monitoring and management tools.

Rule Configuration   The rule expression used in a DBV rule set must be a valid PL/SQL expression that evaluates to TRUE or FALSE. This does not mean that the expression needs to return a PL/SQL BOOLEAN data type, but rather that you must construct the rule as a PL/SQL expression that can be used in a SQL statement WHERE clause. The way to test your rule is to append it to a SELECT statement in SQL*Plus or SQL Developer using this syntax:

```
SELECT COUNT(*) FROM SYS.DUAL WHERE <rule expression>;
```

If the rule expression passes this check, meaning that the SQL executes without an error, then the rule expression is safe to use.

We recommended using PL/SQL package functions (or standalone PL/SQL functions) if your rule expression logic is large or complex, or requires PL/SQL components not normally available in SQL expressions. Using this approach helps in the following ways:

- Helps performance as the code is compiled and does not need to be parsed at runtime
- Improves maintenance of the security policy as the code can be changed and tuned as testing for both security and performance begin
- Improves readability of the security policy for auditors, especially if the functions names are indicative of their purpose
- Leverages predefined DBV rule set event functions as parameters to this function

The process for creating a rule expression involves defining PL/SQL functions that simply return 0 or 1 for failure and success, respectively, and then granting EXECUTE on the function to DVSYS. In your rule expression, you can then yield a TRUE evaluation result for the rule using the following syntax:

```
rule_expr => 'mypackage.myfunction = 1'
```

If the result of the package function mypackage.myfunction returns 0, the evaluation result for the rule will be FALSE.

Creating DBV Secure Application Roles

DBV allows for Oracle SAR to be enabled according to the evaluation of a DBV rule set. To help illustrate how SARs work, consider the DBV rule set named Inside Maintenance Window that we created in the preceding code example. We can use this rule set to control when a privileged role is enabled. Privileges that allow for the update or deletion of data are typically considered security-sensitive operations and are perfect candidates for SARs.

TIP
Use DBV SARs for security-sensitive privilege sets.

The first step to create this type of security capability requires the SA (DBVOWNER) to create the SAR using the DBMS_MACADM.CREATE_ROLE PL/SQL procedure:

```
dbvowner@db12cr[sales]> BEGIN
  2      dbms_macadm.create_role(
  3        role_name      => 'SH_DELETE_ROLE'
  4      , enabled        => 'Y'
  5      , rule_set_name => 'Inside Maintenance Window'
  6      );
  7  END;
  8  /
```

```
PL/SQL procedure successfully completed.

dbvowner@db12cr[sales]> -- Grant the role to the sgaetjen account for testing
dbvowner@db12cr[sales]> GRANT sh_delete_role TO sgaetjen;

Grant succeeded.
```

The role that is created is a SAR, and it is visible from the DBA_APPLICATION_ROLES view, but the PL/SQL procedure that can enable the role is defined by DBV:

```
dbvowner@db12cr[sales]> CONNECT sys@sales AS SYSDBA
Enter password:
Connected.
sys@db12cr[sales]> -- We can see that a database role has been created
sys@db12cr[sales]> SELECT *
  2  FROM dba_application_roles
  3  WHERE role = 'SH_DELETE_ROLE';

ROLE             SCHEMA           PACKAGE
---------------  ---------------  --------------------
SH_DELETE_ROLE   DVSYS            DBMS_MACSEC_ROLES

1 row selected.
```

DBV provides a single PL/SQL procedure named DVSYS.DBMS_MACSEC_ROLES.SET_ROLE that is used to enable the SAR. This procedure has an invoker's rights definition required for SAR and will perform the DBV rule set evaluation to determine if the role should be set. This procedure eliminates the need to create a separate PL/SQL procedure for each SAR required by your application and offers an increased level of reuse of the DBV rule sets you develop.

The next step is to grant the required privileges to the SAR that are required to serve its intended purpose. In our simple example, the SH_DELETE_ROLE requires DELETE privileges on the SALES_HISTORY table owned by the SH account:

```
sys@db12cr[sales]> -- Grant DELETE privilege on the SH table
sys@db12cr[sales]> CONNECT sh@sales
Enter password:
Connected.
sh@db12cr[sales]> GRANT DELETE ON sh.sales_history TO sh_delete_role;

Grant succeeded.
```

We now test the use of these privileges and the SAR as the SGAETJEN user to demonstrate how the configuration works when operating outside of the authorized system maintenance window:

```
sh@db12cr[sales]> CONNECT sgaetjen@sales
Enter password:
Connected.
sgaetjen@db12cr[sales]> -- Show the default session roles for sgaetjen
sgaetjen@db12cr[sales]> SELECT * FROM session_roles;

no rows selected
```

```
sgaetjen@db12cr[sales]> -- sgaetjen cannot access sh.sales_history by default
sgaetjen@db12cr[sales]> DELETE sh.sales_history;
DELETE sh.sales_history
               *
ERROR at line 1:
ORA-00942: table or view does not exist


sgaetjen@db12cr[sales]> -- What day and time is it according to our factors ?
sgaetjen@db12cr[sales]> SELECT get_factor('CURRENT_DAY') DAY_OF_WEEK
  2  , DVF.F$CURRENT_HOUR HOUR_OF_DAY
  3  FROM dual;

DAY_OF_WEEK          HOUR_OF_DAY
-------------------- --------------------
TUE                  14

1 row selected.

sgaetjen@db12cr[sales]> -- Attempt to enable the DBV SAR SH_DELETE_ROLE;
sgaetjen@db12cr[sales]> EXEC dvsys.dbms_macsec_roles.set_role('SH_DELETE_ROLE');
BEGIN dvsys.dbms_macsec_roles.set_role('SH_DELETE_ROLE'); END;

*
ERROR at line 1:
ORA-47305: Rule Set violation on SET ROLE (Inside Maintenance Window)
ORA-06512: at "DVSYS.DBMS_MACUTL", line 38
ORA-06512: at "DVSYS.DBMS_MACUTL", line 387
ORA-06512: at "DVSYS.DBMS_MACSEC", line 306
ORA-06512: at "DVSYS.ROLE_IS_ENABLED", line 4
ORA-06512: at "DVSYS.DBMS_MACSEC_ROLES", line 58
ORA-06512: at line 1
```

As you can see, the SGAETJEN account cannot enable the SAR due to the day of the week and the hour of the day. If we fast forward to Friday at 7 P.M. we can demonstrate the success scenario for enabling the SAR and leveraging the privileges the role provides:

```
sgaetjen@db12cr[sales]> CONNECT sgaetjen@sales
Enter password:
Connected.
sgaetjen@db12cr[sales]> -- What day and time is it according to our factors ?
sgaetjen@db12cr[sales]> SELECT get_factor('CURRENT_DAY') DAY_OF_WEEK
  2  , DVF.F$CURRENT_HOUR HOUR_OF_DAY
  3  FROM dual;

DAY_OF_WEEK          HOUR_OF_DAY
-------------------- --------------------
FRI                  19

1 row selected.

sgaetjen@db12cr[sales]> -- Attempt to enable the DBV SAR SH_DELETE_ROLE;
sgaetjen@db12cr[sales]> EXEC dvsys.dbms_macsec_roles.set_role('SH_DELETE_ROLE');

PL/SQL procedure successfully completed.
```

```
sgaetjen@db12cr[sales]> -- Show the newly enabled session role for sgaetjen
sgaetjen@db12cr[sales]> SELECT * FROM session_roles;

ROLE
------------------
SH_DELETE_ROLE

1 row selected.

sgaetjen@db12cr[sales]> -- sgaetjen can now delete sh.sales_history
sgaetjen@db12cr[sales]> DELETE sh.sales_history;

13 rows deleted.
```

As you can see, SARs provide a very secure and flexible way to safeguard your sensitive data from potentially damaging privileges and commands. The integration of DBV rules sets with SARs enables you to create and reuse security logic that complies with your business rules and your organization's regulatory compliance requirements.

Creating Command Rules

DBV command rules are part of the same enforcement process flow in which DBV realms exist; command rules provide another layer of security within DBV. DBV command rules are examined and enforced immediately after the realm protections are evaluated. DBV command rules do not take into consideration whether system ANY privileges or even direct object privileges are used, but focus on the command being issued and the object being acted upon. DBV command rules are like database triggers and were designed as a separate DBV security mechanism where declarative rules can be applied to the execution of SQL statements and PL/SQL procedures. The user must have the required privileges to execute the statement before a DBV command rule will be enforced.

This implies that a realm authorization that would allow for a command to be executed can be overruled by a command rule. Furthermore, a database object does not need to be protected by a realm in order for a command rule to be evaluated. A fundamental difference in the behavior of command rules and realms is that command rules apply to both the use of system ANY privileges and the use of direct object privileges. Table 10-2 compares the differences between these two controls.

Let's look at an example that demonstrates the relationship between DBV realms and command rules. Building on the DBV realms and DBV rule set examples from earlier, we use DBV command rules to establish controls based on a business rule, such as a system maintenance window for the activities of the database administrators who manage the objects protected by the Sales History realm or even the SH schema account.

DBV Control	Direct Object Privileges	System ANY Privileges or Mandatory Realms
DBV realm	Implicitly allowed for REGULAR realms	Requires realm authorization and realm authorization rule set to be TRUE (if defined)
DBV command rule	Rule set must be TRUE	Rule set must be TRUE

TABLE 10-2. *DBV Realm and Command Rule by Privilege Type Authorization Decision Matrix*

A DBV command rule is particularly well-suited for a potentially dangerous SQL statement like DROP TABLE. We can be define a DBV rule set to protect the tables in the SH object owner account. We can use the rule set to define a DBV command rule for this scenario using the DBMS_MACADM.CREATE_COMMAND_RULE procedure as follows:

```
sgaetjen@db12cr[sales]> CONNECT dbvowner@sales
Enter password:
Connected.
dbvowner@db12cr[sales]> BEGIN
  2        dbms_macadm.create_command_rule (
  3            command        =>  'DROP TABLE'
  4          , rule_set_name => 'Inside Maintenance Window'
  5          , object_owner  => 'SH'
  6          , object_name   => '%'
  7          , enabled       => 'Y'
  8      );
  9   END;
 10   /

PL/SQL procedure successfully completed.

dbvowner@db12cr[sales]> CONNECT sh@sales
Enter password:
Connected.
```

To demonstrate the effect of protecting the use of the SQL statement DROP TABLE outside of the maintenance window, we will issue the command as the SH account owner:

```
dbvowner@db12cr[sales]> CONNECT sh@sales
Enter password:
Connected.
sh@db12cr[sales]> -- What day and time is it according to our factors ?
sh@db12cr[sales]> SELECT get_factor('CURRENT_DAY') DAY_OF_WEEK
  2   , DVF.F$CURRENT_HOUR HOUR_OF_DAY
  3   FROM dual;

DAY_OF_WEEK          HOUR_OF_DAY
-------------------- --------------------
TUE                  14

1 row selected.

sh@db12cr[sales]> -- Attempt to drop the table
sh@db12cr[sales]> DROP TABLE sh.sales_history;
DROP TABLE sh.sales_history
*
ERROR at line 1:
ORA-47400: Command Rule violation for DROP TABLE on SH.SALES_HISTORY
```

The takeaway from this example is that DBV realms enable you to meet compliance regulations for SoD, and DBV command rules enable you to layer on to your organization's business rules.

Command Rule Components   A DBV command rule is configured for a specific database command being controlled by a DBV rule set. The SA will define the policy to state the following:

"When this command is attempted, evaluate this rule set to determine whether or not to allow the command to execute."

You cannot define a DBV command rule for a group of database commands. For example, you cannot create a single DBV command rule for a group of DDL commands such as **CREATE TABLE**, **ALTER TABLE**, and **DROP TABLE**. Each database command must have a separate DBV command rule similar to the DROP TABLE example shown earlier. Command rules can be enabled and disabled by the SA in the same way that realms can. Command rules can be further qualified by configuring an object owner and/or an object name according to the following options:

■ If the object owner and object name are not specified, the DBV command rule applies to all object owners and object names when the command is issued. An alternative form of the DROP TABLE example could have specified the OBJECT_OWNER parameter as '%'.

   If a command rule is configured for a specific object owner and any object name ('%'), then if the rule set evaluates to TRUE the command is allowed.

■ If a DBV command rule is configured with both an object owner and object name, the DBV command rule evaluation applies only to the object name.

It is possible to define multiple DBV command rules for the same command. One or more DBV command rules can be defined for a *specific* owner's object and one DBV command rule can be defined for *all* objects. For example, the SA could define multiple DBV command rules for the **DROP TABLE** database command as shown in the following notional example:

```
-- DROP TABLE for all SH tables from above example
BEGIN
    dbms_macadm.create_command_rule (
        command       =>  'DROP TABLE'
      , rule_set_name => 'Inside Maintenance Window'
      , object_owner  => 'SH'
      , object_name   => '%'
      , enabled       => 'Y'
    );
END;
/
-- DROP TABLE for objects owned by any account
BEGIN
    dbms_macadm.create_command_rule (
        command       =>  'DROP TABLE'
      , rule_set_name => 'System Backup Complete'
      , object_owner  => '%'
      , object_name   => '%'
      , enabled       => 'Y'
    );
END;
/
```

In this example, the SA defined the first DROP TABLE DBV command rule to check the system maintenance timeframe when the objects are owned by the SH account. The second DROP TABLE DBV command rule checks to see if the system backup has completed when the objects are owned by any account. When multiple DBV command rules apply to a database command, all of the DBV command rules must be authorized for the command to be allowed.

Certain commands, such as **CREATE TABLESPACE** or **ALTER SYSTEM**, can be defined only with the first option, because these objects are not defined within an object-owner schema; so the concept of an owner does not apply in the Oracle Database. In these cases, you can simply use the percent ('%') parameter for both the OBJECT_OWNER and OBJECT_NAME parameters.

The ability to specify more than one DBV command rule for a given object is an important point, because it allows the SA to define specific-to-general statement-level protections.

Commands Supported in Command Rule   Database commands within Oracle Database can be categorized as follows:

- **SELECT**   A read only query against a table or view.

- **Data Manipulation Language (DML)**   Write actions such as INSERT, UPDATE, or DELETE against a table or view, or EXECUTE actions on PL/SQL code.

- **Data Definition Language (DDL)**   Database structure–related commands that typically have the form CREATE <object type>, ALTER <object type>, and DROP <object type>. This category also includes privilege-related commands such as **GRANT** and **REVOKE**, auditing commands such as **AUDIT** and **NOAUDIT**, and table administration commands such as **ANALYZE**, **COMMENT**, **FLASHBACK**, **PURGE**, **RENAME**, and **TRUNCATE**.

- **System control**   Commands such as **ALTER SYSTEM** and **ALTER DATABASE**.

- **Session control**   Commands such as **ALTER SESSION** and **SET ROLE**.

- **Transaction control**   Commands such as **COMMIT** and **ROLLBACK**.

SELECT and DML commands cannot use '%' for both the object owner and object name. Also, you cannot apply command rules for the SYS and DVSYS accounts. DBV does not offer command rules for transaction control commands, because these commands are not considered security relevant nor do they operate on database objects. By *security relevant*, we mean the commands do not change the session user, change the current user, or give the session user additional system or object privileges. Command rules cannot be defined for the **ALTER DATABASE** or **ALTER SESSION** command. The **SET ROLE** command is not directly supported but the SAR feature discussed earlier offers a mechanism to control the activation of a database role with a DBV rule set. There are more than 100 additional commands that the SA can control with DBV command rules.

To maintain a database's integrity, we recommend you create a collection of DBV command rules around ALTER <object> and DROP <object> for database objects such as pluggable databases and tables. Protecting application code from CREATE, ALTER, and DROP type commands is also important from an integrity perspective. We also recommend you augment the default DBV security policies with DBV commands for GRANT, REVOKE, AUDIT, and NOAUDIT to protect the integrity of your database security policies.

DBV CONNECT Command Rule   One of the most powerful DBV command rules is used to control when accounts can establish connections to the database. The DBV command rule named Connect uses a special DBV database operation named CONNECT to authorize a connection once the standard authentication processing has completed. With this DBV command rule, we can offer higher levels of assurance around when and how an account is able to connect to the database. It is important that you keep a database session open in SQL*Plus that has the DV_OWNER or DV_ADMIN role while you are developing your CONNECT DBV command rule so that you do not inadvertently lock out all accounts from the database.

TIP
*Keep a separate session open with the DV_ADMIN or DV_OWNER
role while developing your DBV command rule for CONNECT to
avoid locking out all users.*

Suppose, for example, the IT department wants to tighten the controls around database administrators connecting to the company's database. The data and applications they are working with are very sensitive. The first step is to decide under what conditions DBAs are allowed to perform their administration tasks. If the IT department allows VPN access to the corporate network, doesn't that mean that an administrator can be sitting in a coffee shop with a laptop viewing sensitive financial data? VPN access is typically considered less secure than sitting in the company's office, as the external networks are more prone to snooping and the environment is less secure from a physical security perspective. Who else has access to the administrator laptop if the administrator walks away from her computer to take a break? Would the employees stored in the HR.EMPLOYEES table approve of this access? With DBV command rules, we can simply define a rule set that resolves whether the database session is being established from a machine that is physically located within the company's building(s).

The examples presented so far for DBV realms demonstrated the SoD for privileged administrators. With DBV command rules, we can add a layer of control that considers the business rules and IT policies an organization must support. The access controls provided by DBV realms and DBV command rules are configured in a protected account (DVSYS) with an enforcement mechanism integrated directly into the database kernel's SQL engine. Application logic that issues SQL statements to an Oracle Database does not need to change to leverage DBV access controls. The main benefit of this external enforcement point model is that DBV can help cover the gaps in your application's security model so that you can meet compliance regulations without needing to recode or redesign the application. In summary, DBV enables you to add security to applications that weren't built with adequate security controls or to add security controls that your organization now requires.

Summary

As they did with some security capabilities in the past, people often believe that they have a security approach that is equal or equivalent to DBV, which is implemented through a clever set of (database) technologies. It's important that you understand that they are misguided so that you, too, aren't inclined to try to build your own version of DBV. They would argue that DBV is a buy versus build decision. To be very clear, however, *you cannot build an equivalent DBV*.

Oracle DBV features such as DBV realms, DBV command rules, and SARs are critical for addressing many of the issues we face today around consolidation, compliance, and separation of duties. These DBV features serve as effective defensive measure for cybersecurity by limiting the extent to which statements and privileges can be exploited by an attacker. In this chapter, we demonstrated how these DBV features reduce the threat that the privilege set is used outside of the context in which the usage was intended.

DBV has a declarative framework at its core. The invaluable security validation and verification capability has been made possible through the use of this framework. The result is that you can almost always enable DBV for an application and get things working in a more secure manner than ever before. Simply add your objects of interest to a realm, add the right users as participants or administrators, and you are off and running.

Perhaps the most impressive statement about DBV is that it addresses security by taking an innovative approach to governing who gets access to what, where, when, and how. Conditional security that is based on factors chained together in reusable rule set format enables you to create a myriad of realistic and useful security controls.

We have provided a compelling argument to show why database administrators should consider updating their production databases to DBV to meet security threats and challenges. The declarative policy configuration of the product's security rules, based on multiple factors, helps to ensure the appropriateness of an organization's defense against these threats and challenges as they change over time.

CHAPTER
11

Oracle Transparent Data
Encryption: Securing for the
Compliance Regulations,
Cybersecurity, and Insider Threats

Transparent Data Encryption (TDE) is a transparent way to encrypt data in a database. The encryption is transparent because it occurs below the Structured Query Language (SQL) layer. The database engine automatically encrypts and decrypts data as it reads and writes it from the file system. In this chapter, we'll explore how to use TDE and discuss some of the advantages of using it. First, we'll put TDE in perspective with the various other Oracle encryption mechanisms.

Oracle has offered some level of cryptographic support for data stored inside a database for many years. Oracle developed the DBMS_OBFUSCATION_TOOLKIT for release 8i, which gave developers a set of PL/SQL libraries for encrypting data, hashing data, and generating keys in the database. The DBMS_OBFUSCATION_TOOLKIT, however, suffered from several shortcomings, it was difficult to use, and it required significant application design changes.

In Oracle 10g, the second generation of encryption technology came with many improvements over its predecessor, and the encryption package was renamed DBMS_CRYPTO. Over nearly a decade, these packages served as the primary method of encrypting data within the database. DBMS_CRYPTO uses, caveats, and many useful examples are detailed in *Effective Oracle Database 10g Security by Design*. Suffice it to say that although DBMS_CRYPTO offered improved algorithms, key generation, and better datatype support over the DBMS_OBFUSCATION_TOOLKIT, it still did not manage keys and required a programming interface to use. So if you wanted to encrypt and decrypt data, you had to write encrypt and decrypt PL/SQL functions. As with many programmatic approaches, this approach to using the technology tends be unsupported and difficult to use with many commercial off-the-shelf (COTS) applications.

Oracle introduced TDE in Oracle Database 10gR2 as the third generation of encryption technology. TDE is significantly different from DBMS_CRYPTO. The first difference is that TDE is licensed as part of the Oracle Advanced Security Option (ASO). DBMS_OBFUSCATION_TOOLKIT and DBMS_CRYPTO were features of the database. TDE is not simply another way to encrypt data; the integration with the database engine and ability to implement encryption through SQL Data Definition Language (DDL) make it unique. Another difference between DBMS_CRYPTO and TDE is that TDE doesn't require application changes or extensive development effort to implement. Instead, TDE provides a declarative SQL syntax to change the way columns or tablespaces store data. TDE is a convenient and practical way to implement encryption inside the database.

In this chapter, we highlight TDE capabilities. You will read about several practical uses of TDE, learn details on the mechanics, and see examples of how to get it working for your applications.

Encryption 101

Before we dive head-first into TDE, let's review the basics of cryptography. If you are familiar with the concepts of encryption, such as public and private keys, key management, encryption algorithms, and most importantly when to use encryption and what problems it solves and does not solve, then you can skip to the next section.

Goal of Encryption

Encryption has an interesting history. It dates back thousands of years and can even be traced to the Roman Empire. At that time, it was common for Julius Caesar, who was acting president and CEO of the Roman Empire, to send messages to his generals in the field. These sensitive messages gave orders on how to proceed regarding new military objectives.

The messages were sent by way of a messenger at great risk of capture before the messages could be delivered, which would seriously jeopardize the military strategy. Because of this, a simple encryption algorithm was devised and used to encrypt Caesar's missives. Only the generals and Caesar knew how to encrypt and decrypt them. If the messenger was captured, bribery, persuasive arguments, or torture were ineffective in divulging the contents.

To put the use of encryption into proper perspective, it's important that you understand the basic problem that encryption was designed to solve. Encryption provides protection of sensitive data for an *unprotected* medium. The messages represented sensitive data, and the messengers had to cross unprotected media (land, mountains, water, and so on).

In today's interconnected world, encryption is widely used because it clearly meets the criteria for which it was designed: encryption protects sensitive data passing through the unprotected Internet. Many security professionals have extensive experience in network security and a strong understanding of cryptography. This is one reason why encryption is so popular today.

Databases and database security are significantly different from networks and network security. This is an important principle to understand, because the value of encryption differs when applied to problems outside its original problem definition. This will be your guiding principle for understanding when to use and when not to use encryption within the database.

Today, encryption sits behind every Transport Layer Security (TLS) or Secure Sockets Layer (SSL) connection and practically every Internet login page and e-commerce site. Many people use it without even knowing it. That's good, and it's called *transparency*. You will recall that we posited that transparency was one of the key principles to achieving successful security. The fact that TLS or SSL are transparently securing user interactions is a major part of what makes it a successful security technology.

The Basics

Encryption is the process of converting plaintext data into an undecipherable form. The decryption (the act of unencrypting) of data returns the ciphertext to its original plaintext form. The study of these two processes is called *cryptography*.

A plethora of books is available on the market discussing cryptography, and we recommend Bruce Schneier's *Applied Cryptography: Protocols, Algorithms, and Source Code in C* (Wiley, 1996). The mathematics involved and the issues and nuances of cryptography are staggering in number and complexity and well beyond the scope of this book. Fortunately, you don't need to understand all aspects of encryption. This chapter defines only what you need to know to make the critical decisions about how and when to use encryption within the database.

Encryption Choices

Although data can be encrypted in many ways, there are fewer ways to do it effectively. Many people are inclined to write their own encryption, just as Julius Caesar did. However, unless they are geniuses or very lucky, chances are their encryption will be poor. Today, effective encryption implies the use of standard and proven encryption algorithms. The proven part is important because it ensures that the encryption doesn't have some fatal flaw that would allow an unauthorized person to determine the contents of the sensitive data. Since you want to use standard encryption algorithms, you have quite a few from which to choose. Before you start picking algorithms to use in the database, you need to understand a little more about how encryption works.

The Algorithm and the Key

To encrypt data, two things are required: an encryption algorithm and an encryption key. The high-level description of encrypting data is quite simple: plaintext data is fed into the encryption algorithm. An encryption key is also provided. The algorithm uses the key and very sophisticated logic to encrypt the data. The process of decryption is analogous. It also requires a key and an algorithm.

Figure 11-1 illustrates how basic symmetric key encryption works. A plaintext message, "Oracle Database 12c", is encrypted using an algorithm and a key. To recover the original message, you must use the same key (because it is symmetric key encryption) and algorithm.

The overall strength of the encryption is not determined by just the choice of algorithm or the key size. The strength is determined by the combination of the two. A common misconception is that larger keys for one algorithm mean that the algorithm is stronger than another algorithm that uses a smaller key size. Some algorithms demand larger keys to make them as strong as other algorithms that actually use smaller key sizes. However, in some cases, larger keys used within the same algorithm do make the encryption stronger.

By studying Figure 11-1, you may see a challenge to effective encryption. If Caesar is sending General Mark Antony an encrypted message, then Mark Antony needs to know both the algorithm and the key that were used to encrypt the message. Studies of cryptography have shown that with today's algorithms, the only thing that needs to remain a secret is the key. Public knowledge of the algorithm doesn't aid the attacker in recovering the sensitive data. Obscuring the algorithm may seem like good security, but it's only a nuisance to a determined attacker.

Symmetric Key Encryption

Two categories of encryption are used today: *symmetric key encryption* and *asymmetric key encryption, or public key encryption (PKE)*. The algorithms for symmetric key encryption use the same key for both the encryption and decryption processes. A message encrypted with one key can be decrypted only with the same key.

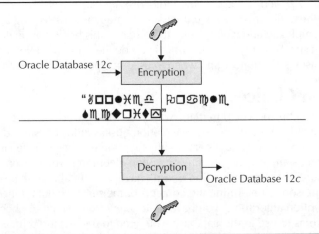

FIGURE 11-1. *Symmetric key encryption requires the use of the same key for both the encryption and decryption processes.*

Symmetric key algorithms are very secure and efficient at encrypting and decrypting data. Some popular examples are RC4, RC5, Data Encryption Standard (DES), triple-DES (3DES), and Advanced Encryption Standard (AES). Because of their strength and efficiency, these algorithms are used for "bulk encryption"—they encrypt large amounts of data.

When two people want to use symmetric key encryption, they need to have either a pre-established key or a secure way to transport the key. When two parties already know each other, it's possible that they will both already know the encryption key. For two parties that have never met and that want to share data securely, the problem of getting the key between the two parties becomes the major challenge. You can't leave the key in plaintext because an attacker could see it. If you encrypt the key, you have to do so with another key, which simply moves the problem elsewhere. This motivated the development of the second variation of encryption.

Public Key Encryption

With PKE, two keys act in a complementary manner. The PKE algorithms are mathematical inverses: whatever one key does, the other key undoes. Furthermore, knowing the algorithm and having one of the keys doesn't give the attacker an advantage in determining the other key or in recovering the encrypted data. The two PKE keys are called the *private key* and the *public key*. Data encrypted with the private key can be decrypted only with the public key, and vice versa. *Private* and *public* are used to describe the keys because it is typical for the public key to be accessible to many people. The private key remains a secret known only to the owner.

PKE solves the key distribution problem. For two parties to communicate, they need access to each other's public keys. Figure 11-2 illustrates how PKE can be used to send a secret message between two parties. To ensure that the recipient is the only one who receives the message, the message is encrypted with the recipient's public key. As such, only the recipient (Mark Antony) will be able to decrypt the message, because the only key that can be used is his private key (which only he has). Trying to decrypt the message with an incorrect key yields gibberish. A man-in-the-middle

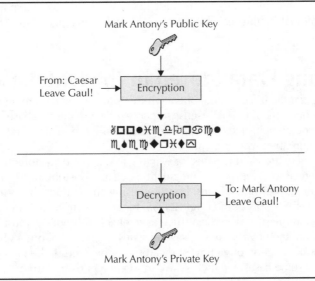

FIGURE 11-2.   *PKE uses two complementary keys to pass sensitive data securely.*

attack will be unsuccessful in decrypting the message because the potential attacker will not have the private key. Note that the private key can't be used to decrypt the message that was also encrypted with the private key.

PKE provides another complementary capability. The private key can be used as an authentication method from the sender. As Figure 11-2 illustrates, a sender can encrypt a message with his or her private key. The recipient can use the sender's public key to decrypt the message. If the message decrypts, the sender's identity is authenticated, because only the sender has access to his private key, so only he could have encrypted the message. Because Mark Antony was able to decrypt Caesar's message using Caesar's public key (turned out to be a simple three-character shift of the alphabet), then he is assured that the message was sent by Caesar (provided he is keeping his private key private!).

Symmetric Key and Public Key

Unfortunately, the public key algorithms require larger keys to achieve the same strength received from their symmetric key counterparts. Consequently, the public key algorithms perform more slowly and are more computationally expensive.

Today, public key and symmetric key encryption are used together as a part of the standard TLS and SSL network protocols. TLS is the de facto standard encryption mechanism for data on the Internet. Due to its superior performance characteristics, symmetric key encryption is used within TLS for bulk data encryption. To transport the symmetric keys securely between the two parties, PKE is used to encrypt the symmetric keys. In Figures 11-2 and 11-3, the secret message is actually the symmetric encryption key.

Public key technology gets more than its fair share of the attention considering that proportionately it actually encrypts a lot less data than symmetric key encryption. This is because the administrators and users have to interface directly with the public key technology. The symmetric key algorithms are neatly concealed and hidden from view.

Understanding and acknowledging the use of public key and symmetric key encryption is important to the Oracle Database because the database supports only symmetric key algorithms. The performance and efficiency of symmetric key algorithms make them a natural choice for the database. Unfortunately, this leaves open the issue of key management, which is addressed later in this chapter.

Encrypting Data Stored in the Database

Understanding that the primary goal of encryption is to protect data in an unprotected medium, you might be wondering if it makes sense to encrypt data in the database at all. As you probably expected, this book emphasizes making the database a *more* secure medium. So, if the database is inherently secure then why encrypt?

It turns out there *are* valid reasons for wanting to encrypt data stored in the database. First, you might be forced to comply with a regulation (legal, industrial, or organizational directive) that states that certain classes of data *must* be stored using encryption. This is the case with Payment Card Industry Data Security Standard (PCI DSS) for credit card data, and many companies have developed internal rules for what data (such as intellectual property) must be encrypted when stored. In addition, the privacy laws of several states, such as California's SB 1386, remove the requirement for notification of victims of data privacy breaches if the data in question was encrypted. So in some cases, we are told we must encrypt data, and in others it may be in our best interest in protecting company trade secrets, corporate reputation, brand value, and customer relationships.

A second requirement for encryption is assurance that data can be protected throughout its life cycle. Think about data storage as a life cycle: Data over time is created, stored, modified, moved, backed up, and deleted. At some points in the life cycle, data can be found outside of the protected medium of the database, as data is moved from the database to tape or another system for backup or disaster recovery purposes. Employing encryption in the database provides a level of security that can be maintained throughout the entire storage life cycle. Again, we must think of encryption as one "layer" in a defense-in-depth strategy that has multiple layers of defense. By storing sensitive data in the clear, we have missed a critical part of a comprehensive security strategy.

For example, historically, it might be the case that policy dictates that database administrators (DBAs) must not have access to sensitive data. This is often a requirement when trying to protect privacy-related data and is a valid security concern. Before Oracle Database 10gR2, encryption was the only way to keep data protected from DBAs. Their privileges allowed them to select data from any table and could be controlled only with the use of auditing (a compensation, rather than proactive control). Many organizations used DBMS_CRYPTO to selectively encrypt and store highly sensitive data in the database, protecting the contents of the encrypted data from the DBA. This was a difficult and costly method, in terms of application development and maintenance, to protect data. Protection of data from DBAs can now be addressed with the release of Oracle Database Vault, which separates the administrative functions data into access realms, as you learned about in Chapter 10.

In summary, the two driving requirements for storing data in the database are regulatory mandates and life-cycle protection. Next, you will see the technical vulnerability that's at the root of both requirements.

Where the Data "Rests"

To understand why encrypting data stored in the database is important, let's look at the SH.SALES_HISTORY example that we have been using in this book. We will modify this table as follows to store a credit card number that was used to make a purchase so that we can protect the table according to PCI DSS regulations.

```
sh@db12cr[sales]> ALTER TABLE sales_history
2  ADD cust_credit_card_no VARCHAR2(19);


Table altered.
```

We populate the table with a set of randomly generated test credit card numbers (see www .paypalobjects.com/en_US/vhelp/paypalmanager_help/credit_card_numbers.htm) as follows:

```
sh@db12cr[sales]> UPDATE sales_history
   2  SET cust_credit_card_no =
   3  DECODE ( product, 'Cell Phone', '378282246310005'
   4  , 'Headphones', '5610591081018250'
   5  , 'LCD TV', '5555555555554444'
   6  , 'Microphones', '4111111111111111'
   7  , 'Plasma TV', '378734493671000'
   8  , 'Speakers', '4012888888881881'
   9  , 'Stereo', '6011111111111117'
  10  , '4222222222222');
```

```
13 rows updated.

sh@db12cr[sales]> COMMIT;

Commit complete.
```

Data housed within the Oracle Database is stored using a proprietary format that makes efficient, high-performance data access possible. Data is stored in *datafiles* that contain header information, extent details, and offset information, and the actual columns of data as they were inserted. Datafiles are made available to the database to use in a logical storage construct called *tablespaces*, which can store tables as implied by the name. We can see the tablespace used by the SH.SALES_HISTORY table is named SALES with the following query:

```
sh@db12cr[sales]> SELECT tablespace_name
  2  FROM user_tables
  3  WHERE table_name = 'SALES_HISTORY';

TABLESPACE_NAME
------------------------------
SALES

1 row selected.
```

We can then examine the DBA_DATA_FILES view to determine which datafile(s) is used for the SALES tablespace:

```
sh@db12cr[sales]> CONNECT sys@sales AS SYSDBA
Enter password:
Connected.
sys@db12cr[sales]> SELECT file_name
  2  FROM dba_data_files
  3  WHERE tablespace_name = 'SALES';

FILE_NAME
----------------------------------------------------------------
/u01/app/oracle/oradata/db12cr/sales/sales_plaintext.dbf

1 row selected.
```

Note that VARCHAR and VARCHAR2 are stored in human-readable format within the datafile. Until the release of TDE, no protection mechanism was available from the database to protect the contents of these data structures without your having to write and maintain cryptographic code, often wreaking havoc on existing applications.

Protecting the Data

Another challenge arises for backup files. Backups of large mission-critical databases are often performed using backup software that writes data from systems over the network to tapes. The centralization of the backup function can increase reliability and reduce the cost of performing backups with economies of scale. As a result, you may find that your database's backup copies of datafiles are on tapes being handled by operators who may not fully understand (or worse yet, do understand) the value of data such as credit card numbers passing over the network.

As the number of individuals with access to these backup media increases, and as we move these tapes off site for greater disaster recoverability, our ability to control access to this media is reduced.

Simple Example of the Technical Requirement for Encryption

Let's illustrate the point by looking at an example. First we will query a single record from the SALES_HISTORY table as follows:

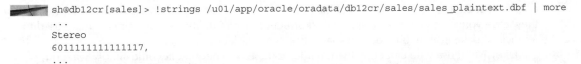

```
sys@db12cr[sales] > CONNECT sh@sales
Enter password:
Connected.
sh@db12cr[sales] > SELECT product, cust_credit_card_no
  2  FROM sales_history
  3  WHERE product = 'Stereo';

PRODUCT                         CUST_CREDIT_CARD_NO
------------------------------  -------------------
Stereo                          6011111111111117
```

The credit card number and product data are clearly visible within the context of the database (as they should be through SQL), so we know exactly what we are looking for in the datafile. We can use commonly available editors or operating system tools such as grep or strings, to find the information in the datafile, as follows:

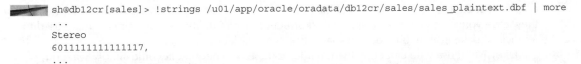

```
sh@db12cr[sales] > !strings /u01/app/oracle/oradata/db12cr/sales/sales_plaintext.dbf | more
...
Stereo
6011111111111117,
...
```

Using **strings**, you can filter out all the readable ASCII characters and see the data. Unlike opening the datafile in an editor (some editors will not open files that are locked), this technique can also be used against open datafiles without disrupting database operations, making it a handy tool for hackers as well.

NOTE
Although this looks all too easy to accomplish, remember that such access to a datafile requires access to the operating system and read permissions on the datafile.

Using the **strings** command, you won't see control characters or many "structural" components of the datafile, only ASCII data. If a backup tape with company data, such as credit card numbers, were to fall into the hands of someone who shouldn't have it, a simple shell script that parsed through datafiles looking for clear text data would expose credit card data. In addition, with the help of regular expressions and utilities included with most operating systems, it would be trivial to script the process of looking for patterns matching, such as credit cards, Social Security numbers, or other interesting data.

It is also important to note that viewing the data is not operating system–specific. Windows datafiles are susceptible to the same type of file-level reads.

Data stored in a tablespace's underlying datafile is readable and potentially exploitable. This is a security risk that must be managed like any other risk, based on the value of the data, the likelihood of someone gaining unauthorized access to the data, and the amount of risk that you and your organization are willing to accept. Although your first layer of defense in ensuring that the database's datafiles are well protected and that backup media is maintained using established policies, it becomes apparent that additional controls should be applied to any and all high-value data. It is important that you use the Oracle Database standard network encryption feature to encrypt data between the database client and database server or between database servers.

Applied Example

Imagine that your example datafile exists on a physical disk drive in a production system, perhaps in a disk array. Disk arrays provide a great deal of value to organizations by making certain that data is highly available. To do this, disk arrays generally employ RAID (Redundant Arrays of Inexpensive Disks) technology, which allows a single datafile to exist on several physical devices at one time for redundancy. If one copy of the data were lost or corrupt, the overall data availability would be maintained using the duplicate copies. With many such data storage devices, it is conceivable that a drive could be removed, making data on the drive vulnerable without the database ever being shut down. Another possibility with many of these storage arrays is the hardware sensing that a drive is close to failure (showing errors, and so on). Often, technicians will replace these failing drives with new ones, making it important for security administrators to know the disposition of the replaced drives since they contain potentially sensitive data. Your corporate security policies should include procedures to delete data on disks securely before they leave your data center for disposal or destruction. UNIX utilities such as shred can be used to remove all data, even in unallocated space, from your disk devices.

Likewise, those who can copy the datafiles to tape or other media could simply walk out of a data center with usable data. As the good custodians of data, we create backup copies of this data in the event of disaster or loss of the data center, often shipping copies of data to remote locations. This means that local and offsite backup media are also potential targets for would-be data thieves. Disaster recovery locations are required by many customers, yet these locations often maintain more copies of your sensitive data that must also be protected by some combination of technology, policy, and procedure.

As has been determined, a database's datafile may sometimes be outside of your security controls, and it may occasionally exist in the unprotected medium that could easily be secured by encryption.

Encrypting in the Database

We have demonstrated and discussed valid reasons for requiring data stored in a database to be encrypted. Now let's look at three approaches to remedy clear text data being stored in the database's datafiles and in subsequent copies used for redundancy or copied to backup media. The approach customers choose is influenced by complexity, cost, performance, openness, and portability of the solution(s). You might choose to use an encrypted file system, building a custom encryption strategy, or making use of a feature that is built into the database.

In an encrypted file system, everything that is written to disk undergoes encryption to protect it from unauthorized viewing. This approach deals with the problem of clear text appearing on disk and backup media by taking a blanket approach—that is, everything gets encrypted. While this approach does work in many situations, encrypted file systems are generally considered to be expensive, proprietary implementations, and you rely completely on the operating system of the host machine to make access control decisions. In fact, the PCI DSS (as we will discuss later in this chapter) calls out disk encryption specifically, requiring that logical access "be managed independently of native operating system access control mechanisms," which effectively takes most file-system encryption out of the possible solution set.

Another potential solution is to encrypt your data before inserting it into the database (perhaps by using the DBMS_CRYPTO package or by writing our own encryption algorithm). You must decrypt the data to make it available to other applications and users when reading the data from the database. Programmatic encryption can provide selective encryption at relatively little to moderate costs (for development and testing), but it requires specialized skills and good design. In *Effective Oracle Database 10g Security by Design*, Knox offers some great examples of using DBMS_CRYPTO. With some development effort and use of function-based views, you can make DBMS_CRYPTO fairly transparent to developers, thus making this an attractive short-term solution. However, let's look at the longer term impacts of such a solution—issues of character set conversions, potential required use of the RAW datatype, long-term code maintenance, and the lack of a native key management solution make the programmatic encryption approach potentially complex and expensive.

The Transparent Data Encryption Solution

What is needed is a straightforward, no-code solution to protect data throughout the full data life cycle. If you are planning to store the data in Oracle 10gR2 or later, you should choose TDE. TDE provides declarative encryption within the DDL SQL syntax, is a key management framework, and is supported with all of the Oracle Database native features. TDE is an implementation of standards-based encryption algorithms built into the database engine. Data stored in the database is encrypted upon write (INSERT/UPDATE) and decrypted upon read (SELECT).

The focus of the remainder of this chapter will be on TDE within the context of Oracle Database 12c. This incarnation of TDE represents the most feature-rich and mature cryptography offering from Oracle. You can find a mapping of the Oracle Database 12c key management command syntax used in previous database releases in Chapter 5 of the *Oracle Database Advanced Security Guide for Oracle Database 12c*.

TDE provides a no-code solution to this "clear text on disk" vulnerability by allowing data architects or DBAs to choose individual columns (introduced in 10gR2) or entire tablespaces (introduced in 11g) to be encrypted.

TDE proves to be a straightforward and simple solution, because it manages the keys and the implementation of the encryption/decryption rather than putting the burden on the developer. The key management problem is important, because when you want to turn plaintext into ciphertext, you need to use a key. Similarly, when you want to decrypt ciphertext into plaintext, you must have the key available. *How and where* this key is stored is part of the challenge in developing a programmatic approach to using the DBMS_CRYPTO solution. In addition, you are challenged with issues of key rotation, backup, and recoverability.

Key storage is particularly challenging, because if the key were stored in the database, it might be vulnerable on the file system or in backups. In an attempt to remedy this vulnerability, you could encrypt the key, but then you are left with the same question: Where do I securely store this key? TDE provides the answer to this question by using the Oracle keystore (an Oracle wallet) to store the encryption key.

Key Management Facilities

The cryptographic key that makes TDE possible (master key) is stored in a keystore. The Oracle keystore can be securely opened or closed, thus making it possible to control the decryption of data by essentially flipping a switch. The keys for all encrypted tablespaces and encrypted columns are encrypted using the database's master key. In the multitenant architecture of Oracle Database 12*c*, a single Oracle keystore is created for all pluggable databases (PDBs) and you create a separate encryption key for each PDB. You can configure the Oracle keystore technology in one of three ways:

- **Password-based**   In this configuration you must supply a custom password that is used to open the keystore manually before the encryption keys can be used. A DBA must be present to enter the wallet password when the database is starting up (such as the middle of the night or on weekends).

- **Auto-login**   In this configuration the Oracle Database will auto-generate a password and auto-open the keystore at the time it is required and can be used on any system. These types of keystores are ideal for systems that have stringent up-time requirements and must be available as much as possible.

- **Local auto-login**   Auto-login wallets can be used only on the system (server) on which they were created. A local auto-login wallet is also used in systems that require high availability.

TDE also enables you to integrate with PKCS#11 standard-compliant hardware security modules (HSMs), which are hardware devices that store encryption keys and can offload encryption and decryption processing for secure and optimized performance. We will discuss HSMs later in this chapter.

To prepare our database to use Oracle's key management framework, we must first create a directory for the keystore:.

```
mkdir /u01/app/oracle/admin/db12cr/wallet
```

We will then edit the file $ORACLE_HOME/network/admin/sqlnet.ora to declare the location for our keystore using the ENCRYPTION_WALLET_LOCATION parameter section. The parameter section looks similar to the following:

```
ENCRYPTION_WALLET_LOCATION =
    (SOURCE=(METHOD=FILE)
    (METHOD_DATA=(DIRECTORY=/u01/app/oracle/admin/db12cr/wallet))
    )
```

For databases that use ASM, you can also specify that the wallet be kept inside ASM with a DIRECTORY specification similar to the following:

```
DIRECTORY=+DATA01/db12cr/wallet
```

When integrating with HSM devices, the METHOD specification will be HSM versus FILE and no METHOD_DATA section is used:

```
ENCRYPTION_WALLET_LOCATION=
    (SOURCE=(METHOD=HSM))
```

You must also obtain and copy the vendor's PKCS#11 standard–compliant library to a directory that the Oracle Database can access in order to use HSM. The details of this process will be dependent on your HSM vendor and the platform. Refer to Chapter 3 of the *Oracle Advanced Security Guide* for details on HSM integration with TDE.

After configuring sqlnet.ora and any dependencies, you must stop and restart your database and any associated PDBs.

Key Management Roles

As we described in Chapter 2, Oracle Database 12*c* provides the special SYSKM privilege that allows you to enable a separation of duty model around key management for the entire database. The ADMINISTER KEY MANAGEMENT privilege allows you to create key managers that are specific to an individual pluggable database. In the following example, we are granting the SYSKM privilege to the security manager account (C##SEC_MGR) for the root container:

```
sh@db12cr[sales]> CONNECT sys AS SYSDBA
Enter password:
Connected.
sys@db12cr[cdb$root]> GRANT syskm TO c##sec_mgr;

Grant succeeded.
```

C##SEC_MGR can now be used to manage the creation, opening, and closing of the keystore for the entire CDB and associated PDBs.

In the following example, we grant the ADMINISTER KEY MANAGEMENT privilege to the security manager role SEC_MGR_ROLE for the SALES and HR PDBs. Accounts that have this role are responsible for managing the PDB's master keys. We will also grant SELECT on a few database views to help determine the status of the wallet (open or closed) and the master key information.

```
sys@db12cr[cdb$root]> CONNECT sys@sales AS SYSDBA
Enter password:
Connected.
sys@db12cr[sales]> GRANT administer key management TO sec_mgr_role;

Grant succeeded.

sys@db12cr[sales]> GRANT SELECT ON gv_$encryption_wallet
  2  TO sec_mgr_role;

Grant succeeded.

sys@db12cr[sales]> GRANT SELECT ON gv_$encryption_keys
  2  TO sec_mgr_role;

Grant succeeded.

sys@db12cr[sales]> GRANT SELECT ON gv_$encrypted_tablespaces
  2  TO sec_mgr_role;

Grant succeeded.

sys@db12cr[sales]> CONNECT sys@hr AS SYSDBA
Enter password:
Connected.
```

```
sys@db12cr[hr]> GRANT administer key management
  2  TO sec_mgr;

Grant succeeded.

sys@db12cr[hr]> GRANT SELECT ON gv_$encryption_wallet
  2  TO sec_mgr_role;

Grant succeeded.

sys@db12cr[hr]> GRANT SELECT ON gv_$encryption_keys
  2  TO sec_mgr_role;

Grant succeeded.

sys@db12cr[hr]> GRANT SELECT ON gv_$encrypted_tablespaces
  2  TO sec_mgr_role;

Grant succeeded.
```

Creating Keystores and a Master Key in the Root Container

Once our TDE management accounts are configured, we create the keystore that TDE will use. The Oracle multitenant option requires that the keystore be created from the root container, as demonstrated in the following example:

```
sys@db12cr[hr]> CONNECT c##sec_mgr AS SYSKM
Enter password:
Connected.
syskm@db12cr[cdb$root]> ADMINISTER KEY MANAGEMENT
  2  CREATE KEYSTORE '/u01/app/oracle/admin/db12cr/wallet'
  3  IDENTIFIED BY welcome1;

keystore altered.
```

This command creates the password-based keystore file to hold the master keys used by TDE, as you can see:

```
syskm@db12cr[cdb$root]> !ls -ltr /u01/app/oracle/admin/db12cr/wallet
total 4
-rw-r--r-- 1 oracle dba 2408 Jun 14 16:32 ewallet.p12
```

The keystore is based on the PKCS #12 standard, which is a standard key-storage type under Public Key Cryptography standards. The default filename is ewallet.p12. The file itself is encrypted and must be protected by operating system permissions. In the preceding directory listing, you will notice that the ewallet.p12 file has global or world read access, which means that anyone with session access to the database server can read the file. We recommend that you remove the world read access with the following command:

```
chmod 640 /u01/app/oracle/admin/db12cr/wallet/ewallet.p12
```

Chapter 6 of the *Oracle Database Advanced Security Guide* documentation for Oracle Database 12c includes a discussion of the considerations around the file system storage for the keystore when using Oracle Real Application Clusters (RAC). We encourage you to review this documentation if you are using or intend to use RAC so that you understand the process for keystore create, open, and close operations in this type of environment.

Create Auto-Login Keystore

With the major emphasis on security and protecting the wallet file and password, you may be surprised to learn that an auto-login feature is supported. This allows the keystore to remain open—that is, after a reboot of the database or host operating system, the keystore is automatically accessible to the database, thus not requiring a DBA to type in the password manually to start the database.

There are good reasons for using auto-login. Having a security administrator and the separation of duties provided by a separate keystore password is often *not* a requirement in development, testing, and other nonproduction environments. In these situations, auto-login is an easy way to mirror the production security environment, but still allow for easy restarting of the database and not requiring manual password entry for keystore access at startup.

CAUTION
Auto-login is a relatively insecure method of wallet management and its use should be reserved for nonproduction environments. Auto-login creates a wallet that requires no password to open (since it's always open); you should take extra care when using this feature.

In the following example, we create a local auto-login keystore from the password-based keystore:

```
syskm@db12cr[cdb$root] > ADMINISTER KEY MANAGEMENT
  2   CREATE LOCAL AUTO_LOGIN KEYSTORE
  3   FROM KEYSTORE '/u01/app/oracle/admin/db12cr/wallet'
  4   IDENTIFIED BY welcome1;

keystore altered.
```

An auto-login keystore is always open, and this feature can be recognized by a second file (cwallet.sso) in the keystore directory. When a keystore has been set to auto-login, the directory appears as follows:

```
syskm@db12cr[cdb$root] > !ls -ltr  /u01/app/oracle/admin/db12cr/wallet
total 8
-rw-r----- 1 oracle dba 2408 Jun 14 16:32 ewallet.p12
-rw-r--r-- 1 oracle dba 2461 Jun 14 16:34 cwallet.sso
```

We recommend that you remove the world read access to the auto-login file with the following command:

```
chmod 640 /u01/app/oracle/admin/db12cr/wallet/cwallet.sso
```

Opening the Keystore

The keystore itself can be in one of two states: open or closed. The open state means the keystore is accessible to the database and encryption and decryption can be performed. The closed state means that the credentials are locked in the keystore. The keystore file in the operating system also needs to be protected.

After the creation of a keystore, it is left in an open state until it is closed or the database is restarted. The following example opens the wallet in the root container and all associated PDBs:

```
syskm@db12cr[cdb$root]> ADMINISTER KEY MANAGEMENT SET KEYSTORE
  2  OPEN IDENTIFIED BY welcome1
  3  CONTAINER = ALL;

keystore altered.
```

The SYSKM privilege can also be used to verify the state of the wallet with the following query on GV_$ENCRYPTION_WALLET:

```
syskm@db12cr[cdb$root]> SELECT wrl_parameter, wallet_type, status
  2  FROM sys.gv_$encryption_wallet;

WRL_PARAMETER                      WALLET_TYPE STATUS
---------------------------------- ----------- -------------------
/u01/app/oracle/admin/db12cr/wallet PASSWORD    OPEN

1 row selected.
```

An administrator can close the keystore using the command **ADMINISTER KEY MANAGEMENT SET KEYSTORE CLOSE**. If a person closes the keystore intentionally or unintentionally, all encryption and decryption halts.

Create Master Keys in the Root Container

Oracle Database 12c allows for each PDB to have its own master key. To create master keys in our PDBs, we must first CREATE a master key in the root container and then USE the key as follows:

```
syskm@db12cr[cdb$root]> ADMINISTER KEY MANAGEMENT
  2  CREATE KEY
  3  USING TAG 'root'
  4  IDENTIFIED BY welcome1
  5  WITH BACKUP USING 'root_create';

keystore altered.

syskm@db12cr[cdb$root]> SELECT key_id
  2  FROM sys.gv_$encryption_keys
  3  WHERE tag = 'root';

KEY_ID
---------------------------------------------------
AeU89QMfa0/uv+epyiNWsTAAAAAAAAAAAAAAAAAAAAAAAAAAAAA

1 row selected.

syskm@db12cr[cdb$root]> ADMINISTER KEY MANAGEMENT
  2  USE KEY 'AeU89QMfa0/uv+epyiNWsTAAAAAAAAAAAAAAAAAAAAAAAAAAAAA'
  3  USING TAG 'root'
  4  IDENTIFIED BY welcome1
  5  WITH BACKUP USING 'root_use';

keystore altered.
```

Within the root container you also have the option of specifying CONTAINER = ALL with the **CREATE KEY** command syntax, which would make a key that is available to all PDBs. If your organization is using PDBs for many internal databases, this shared master key option can be convenient. If your organization is hosting databases for different organizations, a separate master key per PDB makes more sense from a security perspective, as you are ensuring separation of concerns.

The TAG clause allows the administrator to associate a human-readable label for the key. All master key management operations within the ADMINISTER KEY MANAGEMENT statement syntax require the use of the WITH BACKUP USING clause to preserve the last master key (and keystore) in case the administrator did not intend to change the key. There are also BACKUP KEYSTORE, EXPORT, and IMPORT statement options that allow you to back up and recover from mistakes. Another important role these command syntax options serve is for keystore escrow and protection. You need to make sure to keep a backup copy of your keystores in a safe place, preferably in an offsite remote location from the data center where your key is in use and not with the same datafile backups that the keystore encrypts. There are third-party software companies that offer escrow services to ensure your keystores are kept in a safe and secure location. If you accidentally lose or delete the keystore, there is no TDE recovery option. Your data will be permanently encrypted inside the Oracle datafiles.

CAUTION
Always back up and store your keystores in a remote and secure location different from the datafiles. There are no back doors in TDE to recover encrypted data without the original key.

There are also other key management options within the ADMINISTER KEY MANAGEMENT statement, including the following:

- **SET**   This option is used to rekey your data with a new master key.

- **MERGE**   This option is used to merge two keystores.

- **MIGRATE**   This option is used to move from the Oracle keystore to HSM or vice versa.

- **PASSWORD**   This option is used to change the keystore.

We can query the GV_$ENCRYPTION_KEYS view to examine additional details of the key. This view acts as a master key history table when sorted by the CREATION_TIME column.

```
syskm@db12cr[cdb$root]> SELECT tag,creator,key_use
  2  ,to_char(creation_time,'DD-MON-YYYY HH24:MI:SS') creation_time
  3  FROM sys.gv_$encryption_keys
  4  ORDER BY creation_time;

TAG        CREATOR     KEY_USE    CREATION_TIME
---------- ----------- ---------- ----------------------------
root       SYSKM       TDE IN PDB 16-JUN-2014 15:52:23

1 row selected.
```

Creating Master Keys in Pluggable Databases

Now that our keystore is open in all of our container databases and we have created a master key in the root container, the TDE management account can create and use a TDE master key within the SALES PDB as follows:

```
syskm@db12cr[cdb$root]> CONNECT sec_mgr@sales
Enter password:
Connected.
sec_mgr@db12cr[sales]> ADMINISTER KEY MANAGEMENT
  2   CREATE KEY
  3   USING TAG 'sales'
  4   IDENTIFIED BY welcome1
  5   WITH BACKUP USING 'sales_create';

keystore altered.

sec_mgr@db12cr[sales]> SELECT tag,key_id
  2   FROM sys.gv_$encryption_keys;

TAG        KEY_ID
---------- --------------------------------------------------------
sales      AZ3h/RRLpk8Ov/mT6XuUYVcAAAAAAAAAAAAAAAAAAAAAAAAAAAAAAA

1 row selected.
```

In the same manner, we will now use the master key which activates the key for use in all subsequent TDE encryption operations in the SALES PDB:

```
sec_mgr@db12cr[sales]> ADMINISTER KEY MANAGEMENT
  2   USE KEY 'AZ3h/RRLpk8Ov/mT6XuUYVcAAAAAAAAAAAAAAAAAAAAAAAAAAAAAAA'
  3   USING TAG 'sales'
  4   IDENTIFIED BY welcome1
  5   WITH BACKUP USING 'sales_use';

keystore altered.
```

We can also create a TDE master key in the HR PDB in the same way we did for the SALES PDB. Notice that a query on GV_$ENCRYPTION_KEYS view returns master keys that are available to the PDB, and Oracle Database12c restricts master keys from being shared among PDBs.

```
sec_mgr@db12cr[sales]> CONNECT sec_mgr@hr
Enter password:
Connected.
sec_mgr@db12cr[hr]> ADMINISTER KEY MANAGEMENT
  2   CREATE KEY
  3   USING TAG 'hr'
  4   IDENTIFIED BY welcome1
  5   WITH BACKUP USING 'hr_create';

keystore altered.

sec_mgr@db12cr[hr]> SELECT tag,key_id
  2   FROM sys.gv_$encryption_keys;

TAG        KEY_ID
---------- --------------------------------------------------------
```

```
hr          AV+bpjpVYU+Yv5NsTz6Og70AAAAAAAAAAAAAAAAAAAAAAAAAAAAA

1 row selected.

sec_mgr@db12cr[hr] > ADMINISTER KEY MANAGEMENT
   2  USE KEY 'AV+bpjpVYU+Yv5NsTz6Og70AAAAAAAAAAAAAAAAAAAAAAAAAAAAA'
   3  USING TAG 'hr'
   4  IDENTIFIED BY welcome1
   5  WITH BACKUP USING 'hr_use';

keystore altered.
```

You can also see that all of our WITH BACKUP USING parameters result in physical copies of the keystore file being created:

```
sec_mgr@db12cr[hr] > !ls   /u01/app/oracle/admin/db12cr/wallet
cwallet.sso
ewallet_2014061616241200_root_create.p12
ewallet_2014061616241212_root_use.p12
ewallet_2014061616294642_sales_create.p12
ewallet_2014061616311375_sales_use.p12
ewallet_2014061616361014_hr_create.p12
ewallet_2014061616361427_hr_use.p12
ewallet_2014061616442970.p12
ewallet.p12
```

TDE Key Management in Oracle Enterprise Manager

Support for TDE key management is built into OEM Database Control and Grid Control for Oracle Database 11*g*. Oracle has also integrated TDE key management into OEM Cloud Control (OEMCC) for Oracle Database 12*c* and 11*g*. The OEMCC interface for TDE key management is shown in Figure 11-3.

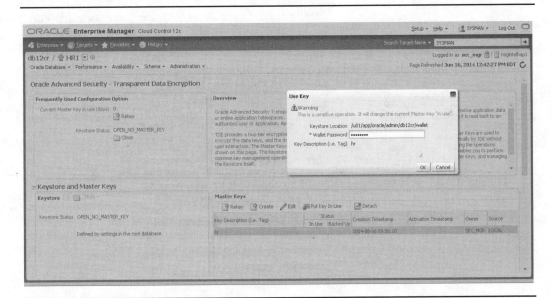

FIGURE 11-3. *TDE key management for PDBs in OEMCC*

In the example in Figure 11-3, we show the use of OEMCC key management interface to perform the equivalent of calling the ADMINISTER KEY MANAGEMENT statement with the USE option for the HR PDB keystore. The management of the keystore is presented with a more intuitive GUI in OEMCC. From a central location and for all databases in your enterprise, OEMCC enables you to open and close the keystore, as well as create, use, and regenerate the TDE master keys.

The SYSKM privilege can access all master keys that have been created for all containers using the TDE view in OEMCC from the root container, as shown in Figure 11-4.

OEMCC also allows for keystore import and export operations from this root container view.

Creating an Encrypted Column in a New Table

Let's start with basic column-level encryption. This capability was introduced in the Oracle Database 10*g*R2 release and encrypts the contents of a specific column. The general form of SQL to create a new table with an encrypted column is as follows:

```
SQL> CREATE TABLE <table_name> (<column_name> <date_type> ENCRYPT [algorithm] [nomac]
[no salt]);
```

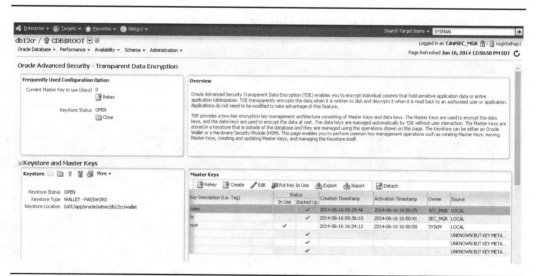

FIGURE 11-4. *TDE key management for CDB in OEMCC*

Three elements relating to TDE are relevant to this statement. First, ENCRYPT [algorithm] tells the database which algorithm to use to encrypt the column data. The following encryption algorithms are available:

- **3DES168**   The 168-bit key length implementation of the Digital Encryption Standard (DES)
- **AES128**   The 128-bit key length implementation of the Advanced Encryption Standard (AES)
- **AES192**   The 192-bit key length implementation of the AES (the default if not specified)
- **AES256**   The 256-bit key length implementation of the AES

Second, the NOMAC directive/parameter was introduced in 10.2.0.4 and is not available in the original Oracle Database 10gR2 (10.2.0.3) release. A message authentication code (MAC) is generated by default when encrypting a column. The MAC requires an additional 20 bytes of storage for each encrypted value. The MAC's purpose is to provide an integrity check for the encrypted data. A performance penalty is paid when building the integrity check, as it requires additional CPU cycles to build for each encrypted column's value inserted into a table. A storage penalty also results, and although 20 bytes may not seem like much, depending on the volume of data stored in the encrypted table, it could become significant. As is often seen in matters of security, a trade-off exists between performance and security/integrity of stored data. If the NOMAC directive is not specified, then Oracle defaults the MAC algorithm to SHA-1.

Salt

Salt is a cryptographic tool that effectively makes any encryption algorithm stronger by introducing a random value (16 bytes in TDE) that is concatenated with the plaintext to stop brute-force attacks on encrypted data. Although valuable for additional security, adding salt in your definition also somewhat limits the ability to create meaningful indexes on encrypted columns by essentially removing the relationship between values. The use of salt is required when data is sufficiently sensitive to necessitate the strongest protections possible. Doing so may require data architects to build surrogate keys on tables with naturally occurring keys, making it time-consuming, costly, and detrimental to project schedules.

The DDL for creating a new table with an encrypted column in its most basic form is performed by adding the ENCRYPT directive to a CREATE TABLE statement:

```
CREATE TABLE foo (columnA datatype, columnB datatype ENCRYPT);
```

This statement defaults to the AES encryption algorithm, with a key length of 192 bits, a salt value, and a MAC of 20 bytes.

Any column that you might consider a candidate for an index should use the NO SALT directive:

```
CREATE TABLE foo (columnA datatype, columnB datatype ENCRYPT NO SALT);
```

Chapter 3 of the *Oracle Database Advanced Security Guide for Oracle Database 12c* includes a listing of all of the datatypes for columns that can be encrypted. The support covers the basic datatypes for character, numeric, and date/time data. In Chapter 6 of the same documentation, you can find information about how to encrypt binary and character large objects (LOBs) with TDE when using Oracle SecureFiles.

Column Encryption Example

You create a table with an encrypted column by adding the directive ENCRYPT to the CREATE TABLE statement. This generates a new table key that's stored in the data dictionary after being encrypted by the database master key. Oracle then uses the new table key to encrypt data written to that column. Here is an example used to encrypt the Social Security number column in the HR.EMPLOYEES table:

```
sec_mgr@db12cr[hr]> CONNECT hr@hr
Enter password:
Connected.
hr@db12cr[hr]> CREATE TABLE employees (
  2       EMPLOYEE_ID     NUMBER NOT NULL
  3     , ENAME           VARCHAR2(10)
  4     , SSN             VARCHAR2(11)
  5                       ENCRYPT USING 'AES256'
  6     , FIRST_NAME      VARCHAR2(10)
  7     , LAST_NAME       VARCHAR2(15)
  8     , EMAIL           VARCHAR2(30)
  9     , PHONE_NUMBER    VARCHAR2(14)
 10     , HIRE_DATE       DATE
 11     , HIRE_YEAR       VARCHAR2(75)
 12     , LAB_BADGE_NO    VARCHAR2(5)
 13     );

Table created.
```

This column will be encrypted using AES with a 256-bit key length. You can validate that the Social Security numbers are protected by inserting data, querying it back:

```
hr@db12cr[hr]> INSERT INTO employees (
  2       employee_id
  3     , ename
  4     , ssn
  5     , first_name
  6     , last_name
  7     , email
  8     , phone_number
  9     , hire_date
 10     , lab_badge_no
 11     )
 12     VALUES (
 13       101
 14     , 'sgaetjen'
 15     , '888-98-7654'    -- plaintext SSN
 16     , 'Scott'
 17     , 'Gaetjen'
 18     , 'scott.gaetjen@oracle.com'
 19     , '(555) 888-4567'
 20     , TO_DATE('11-10-1996','MM-DD-YYYY')
 21     , NULL
 22     );

1 row created.

hr@db12cr[hr]> COMMIT;

Commit complete.
```

If you use the UNIX command strings against the datafile, you'll see that the Social Security number doesn't appear in plaintext:

```
$ strings   /u01/app/oracle/oradata/db12cr/hr/hr.dbf | more
@AV+bpjpVYU+Yv5NsTz6Og70AAAAAAAAAAAAAAAAAAAAAAAAAAAAAA
1AwAAAAAAAAAAAAAAAAAAABAPUtnhlGHNIO5SwA68ImWavF3JuCmzo9FoQF0p1fKnV33MO5j8xOzKGfJo3zj8Fmm
16ePvTA9C6AepxxqQK99
sgaetjen4
hg%V
Scott
Gaetjen
scott.gaetjen@oracle.com
(555) 888-4567
```

TDE's protection renders the encrypted column's data unreadable from a file system.

Determining TDE Encrypted Columns

The database dictionary enables administrators and schema owners to determine which columns from which tables are encrypted. The database dictionary also provides information regarding the encryption algorithm and other directives set on the table's column. This data is stored in the DBA_ENCRYPTED_COLUMNS view (for administrators). Similarly, the USER_ENCRYPTED_COLUMNS view allows a schema owner access to the details of encrypted columns in their schema.

```
hr@db12cr[hr]> CONNECT sec_mgr@hr
Enter password:
Connected.
sec_mgr@db12cr[hr]> SELECT owner, table_name, column_name
  2  , encryption_alg, salt
  3  FROM dba_encrypted_columns;

OWNER       TABLE_NAME      COLUMN_NAME      ENCRYPTION_ALG      SALT
---------   -------------   --------------   ------------------  -----
HR          EMPLOYEES       SSN              AES 256 bits key    YES

1 row selected.
```

You can also use OEMCC to view information regarding encrypted columns. OEMCC enables you to encrypt columns in a new table or an existing table.

TDE generates a separate encryption key for each table rather than using the same encryption key for every table. TDE uses symmetric key technology to encrypt and decrypt the data using the same key. Symmetric key is the standard approach to performing bulk encryption because of its optimal performance characteristics. Table encryption keys are stored in the Oracle data dictionary after first being encrypted using the master key.

This two-key mechanism for storing keys used in TDE provides the additional benefit of allowing for rekeying of data (as is often specified in security guidelines and mandates) without having to first decrypt/re-encrypt each column in each row. When only the master key is rekeyed, only the table's key is decrypted and then encrypted with the new master key. This dramatically reduces the number of reads and writes required to rekey.

Encrypting an Existing Column

In many organizations, applications have been running for many years, having been built on an Oracle Database or perhaps built on another database subsystem and later migrated to Oracle Database. It certainly makes sense to look at these legacy applications with a critical eye with regard to security and compliance initiatives. It is easy to make some minor changes to the underlying schemas of these legacy applications to make them more secure in their handling and use of sensitive data.

TDE allows for the modification of existing tables to encrypt columns at rest. The general form for changing an existing column in a table from plaintext to ciphertext is as follows:

```
ALTER TABLE <table_name> MODIFY
    (<column_name> ENCRYPT ['nomac'] [no salt]);
```

You should consider both storage and performance impacts when encrypting an existing column. We mentioned that adding a MAC to an encrypted column requires 20 additional bytes of space, including salt adds a few more bytes, and the encryption algorithm itself adds a few bytes per column as it "pads" data to create evenly sized chunks of data to encrypt. As a result of this extra space being added to your plaintext, it may not fit into the blocks it occupied before encryption.

If there is not enough free space on the block, the database handles this additional requirement for more space by row-chaining or storing it out of line in a new block/extent. Row-chaining will not be noticed in many situations, especially with tables that have a small number of rows (less than 10,000). When the number of rows chained is greater than 10,000, the row-chaining created by the encryption process will increase the load on the database's I/O subsystem by potentially doubling the number of read operations. Oracle first reads the row of data and then it reads the encrypted column in a separate read.

Knowing that the encryption operation can lead to a slightly greater load on the CPU and storage subsystem gives you some specific areas for preproduction testing. Often, a simple reorganization of the table can be the easiest solution to the performance impact of row-chaining. In very highly available environments with mission-critical applications, online redefinition should be considered, because it takes the affected table offline for only an instant.

Manually Reorganizing a Table

DBAs often reorganize a table by first exporting the data (exp or datapump) to pull data out of the existing table, then dropping the old cleartext table, and then creating a new table with the sensitive columns encrypted (usually in a newly created tablespace). Reloading the contents into the newly created table resolves the row-chaining problem. This technique also takes care of any unencrypted "artifacts" (unencrypted data left in their original data block while newly encrypted blocks are stored in a new data block/extent) that may remain in datafiles. The caveat to this approach is that it requires a significant amount of time to convert large tables, and the table is unavailable while the conversion process is being carried out.

NOTE
It is a best practice to reorganize a table that has been modified to include an encrypted column.

Automating Table Reorganization

Another technique to remove row-chaining is to use online redefinition. First introduced with Oracle Database 9*i*, online redefinition allows for reorganization to take place. But instead of the database administrator doing the work of creating the new structure, loading data from the old table into the new, and dropping the old and reloading the data into the new table, row-chaining instructs the database to handle the whole process and doesn't require a manual process.

To perform an online redefinition of our example, you would follow these steps:

1. `EXECUTE dbms_redefinition.can_redef_table ('HR', 'EMPLOYEES');`

2. `CREATE TABLE hr.employees_stage as SELECT * FROM hr.employees;`

3. `ALTER TABLE hr.employees_stage MODIFY (ssn ENCRYPT);`

4. `EXECUTE dbms_redefinition.start_redef_table ('HR', 'EMPLOYEES', 'EMPLOYEES_STAGE');`

5. `EXECUTE dbms_redefinition.finish_redef_table ('HR', 'EMPLOYEES', 'EMPLOYEES_STAGE');`

Caveats to Column-Level TDE

Column-level TDE encrypts and decrypts data between the SQL level and kernel level, which makes it transparent to the end user. As a result, several database features that access data at the kernel level are incompatible with column-level TDE. Using change data capture (both synchronous and asynchronous), streams (in Oracle Database 10*g*), materialized views, transportable tablespaces, and LOBs are not supported with encrypted columns. These limitations were removed with tablespace encryption, available in Oracle Database 11*g*, as you will see in the next section.

Another potential drawback in TDE's column-based encryption is that it cannot be used in certain types of indexes or in the definition of a primary key/foreign key (PK/FK) relationship. Indexes built on encrypted columns are created using the encrypted values stored in the column. As a result, use of an index is possible for an equality match provided that the encryption was defined using the NO SALT option. The index will not be used in queries that perform range scans. In fact, you cannot create an index on a column that is encrypted using salt. Oracle will fail the attempt with the error message "ORA-28338: cannot encrypt indexed column[s] with salt."

In the case of PK/FK relationships, since each table is encrypted using its own table-level key, the keys are different among tables and, therefore, the encrypted values for related columns are different. The relationship that existed between the data/columns is lost without first decrypting the column.

Although many will argue that natural keys (those that are managed outside of the application, such as SSNs, employee IDs, or credit card numbers) are not good candidates as primary keys for establishing uniqueness, the fact is they are and have been used as primary keys and are often found in legacy applications. Furthermore, applications have also been ported from other database environments. As such, dealing with PK/FK relationships in applications that require the protection offered by TDE presents challenges with column-level TDE. This limitation and others (LOBs, streams, and so on) are addressed in Oracle Database 11*g* and beyond with the introduction of *tablespace encryption*.

Tablespace Encryption

Column-level encryption addresses several real-world business problems. However, column-level encryption has limitations that can make it challenging to encrypt individual data elements to achieve the desired outcome and balance security with performance.

For instance, you might find that an existing application was built to use the most sensitive information as a primary key. Enterprise resource planning (ERP) or customer relationship management (CRM) applications trying to remain database-agnostic often present this problem. Also, legacy applications for which you have little control or limited knowledge of the data relationships present this as a similar problem. To compound this issue, you might also be faced with the challenges of the PCI DSS or with new privacy legislation (California's SB 1386) that requires healthcare providers to make substantial investments in cataloging, analyzing, and remedying potential leaks of PCI, personally identifiable health information (PHI), or personally identifiable information (PII).

Beginning with Oracle Database 11g, the tablespace encryption feature makes it possible for you to move all sensitive data into an encrypted tablespace without needing to redesign the application. Additionally, features such as Oracle Streams and Change Data Capture are not excluded as they were for column-level encryption. Tablespace encryption is a better choice for use in a wider variety of applications than column-level encryption.

Creating a tablespace with encryption turned on automatically encrypts objects stored in the tablespace using the encryption algorithm specified at definition time. In the following examples we demonstrate how to encrypt the SH.SALES_HISTORY table by creating an encrypted tablespace and then moving the table to this tablespace:

```
sec_mgr@db12cr[hr]> CONNECT sys@sales AS SYSDBA
Enter password:
Connected.
sys@db12cr[sales]> CREATE TABLESPACE sales_encrypt
  2   DATAFILE '/u01/app/oracle/oradata/db12cr/sales/sales_encrypt.dbf'
  3   SIZE 500M
  4   ENCRYPTION USING 'AES256'
  5   DEFAULT STORAGE (ENCRYPT);

Tablespace created.

sys@db12cr[sales]> ALTER USER sh QUOTA UNLIMITED ON sales_encrypt;

User altered.
```

In this example, we created a tablespace with AES 256-bit encryption. If we omit the ENCRYPTION USING parameter and keep the DEFAULT STORAGE (ENCRYPT) parameter, then the tablespace defaults to AES-128 encryption. The Oracle data dictionary keeps track of the algorithm used to encrypt the tablespace in the V$ENCRYPTED_TABLESPACES view:

```
sys@db12cr[sales]> SELECT ts.name, et.encryptedts, et.encryptionalg
  2   FROM v$tablespace ts, v$encrypted_tablespaces et
  3   WHERE ts.ts# = et.ts#;

NAME                             ENC ENCRYPT
-------------------------------- --- -------
SALES_ENCRYPT                    YES AES256

1 row selected.
```

You can use the OEMCC interface to the ASO to view the encrypted tablespaces. OEMCC also allows you to specify encryption options while creating new tablespaces.

With the encrypted tablespace set up, you can move tables into the new encrypted tablespace, which causes Oracle to encrypt the data automatically:

```
sys@db12cr[sales] > CONNECT sh@sales
Enter password:
Connected.
sh@db12cr[sales] > ALTER TABLE sales_history
  2  MOVE TABLESPACE sales_encrypt;

Table altered.
```

We can once again use the UNIX strings utility to see that (after the plaintext tablespace header information) table data stored in the tablespace is encrypted:

```
$ strings /u01/app/oracle/oradata/db12cr/sales/sales_encrypt.dbf | head
}|{z
DB12CR
SALES_ENCRYPT
$wK87
Trl%
qdZ|d
gTrp
||m{2g
B>      n
bW70
```

Oracle stores the tablespace key in the data dictionary after encrypting the tablespace key using the master key.

TDE and Oracle Database Tools Interoperability

TDE protects data at rest with a high level of assurance. However, your company's data doesn't rest. Organizations move data from production to preproduction/test environments, data is loaded into data warehouses, data is replicated to offsite disaster recovery locations, data is moved temporarily to make administrative changes to systems, or data is moved as a result of hardware changes. Any or all of these possible scenarios require that your data be moved.

When moving data is a requirement, you cannot simply discard the security mechanisms you've used to protect your data at rest; instead, you must extend the security mechanisms to these new processes, procedures, and locations. To accomplish the move in a secure fashion, you must think about data security (Is the data in clear text or ciphertext?) and communication channel (network, file, and so on). The *Oracle Database Advanced Security Guide* documentation includes a number of well-written and detailed discussions on how TDE interoperates with data migration tools such as Oracle GoldenGate (Chapter 4), Oracle Active Data Guard (Chapter 6), and Oracle Data Pump (Chapter 6). We encourage you to review these sections of the documentation to understand the technical details of interoperating with these tools once TDE is in place. Tools such as Oracle SQL*Loader and general applications built upon the Oracle Call Interface (OCI) interoperate with TDE in a transparent way.

Performance

The second question asked after "How does TDE work?" is typically "What effect will encryption have on the performance of my system?" Everyone is trying to maximize their resources and get the most out of their hardware while keeping their user community and security officials satisfied. So they are disappointed to hear that although the first question is easy to answer (you've already got a pretty good idea of the mechanics), the answer to the second question usually starts with, "It depends…" followed by a less than satisfying conversation.

The truth is that the answer depends on a number of factors—index participation for candidate columns, current system performance, the number of tables having encrypted columns, the number of rows in the average transaction having encrypted columns, and so on. Once you understand these factors, the performance impact becomes apparent and typically falls into one of two categories: minimal effects or drastic effects. Most applications fall into the first category, especially if tablespace encryption is used.

Encryption and decryption use arithmetic operations that slow system actions by taking processing power from other tasks. Oracle cannot state a guaranteed maximum percent performance impact regarding query performance but does offer examples for reference.

Be sure to test applications and the overall system thoroughly after encrypting a column to gauge the impact of encryption adequately. If an outage is permissible during the implementation of column-level encryption, then the following course of action helps to minimize the risk of improper implementation:

1. Identify candidate columns and corresponding datatypes for encryption (credit card numbers, national identifiers, and so on). We recommend using the OEMCC Quality Management features for sensitive data discovery that were discussed in Chapter 8.

2. Ensure that these are TDE-supported datatypes.

3. Ensure that the column doesn't participate in an index.

4. Ensure that the column is not part of a PK/FK relationship.

5. Alter the table and encrypt the column(s).

6. Reorganize the table.

7. Rebuild your indexes.

If an outage is not permissible during the implementation, follow these steps:

1. Identify candidate columns and corresponding datatypes for encryption (credit card numbers, national identifiers, and so on). We recommend using the OEMCC Quality Management features for sensitive data discovery that were discussed in Chapter 8.

2. Ensure that these are TDE-supported datatypes.

3. Ensure that the column doesn't participate in an index,

4. Ensure that the column is not part of a PK/FK relationship.

5. Use online reorganization to modify the table as shown in the "Encrypting an Existing Column" section earlier in this chapter. This will lock both the old and new tables for a short period of time while you rename the tables.

6. Rebuild your indexes.

Because column-level encryption has limitations, not every application is a good fit for its use. This can result from the need for index range scans, PK/FK relationships, or unsupported datatypes. In these cases, tablespace encryption provides a good alternative by removing these restrictions and encrypting data at coarser granularity. The other area of performance to consider is storage. Column-level TDE requires more space for each encrypted column (17–51 bytes per column per row). This additional space requirement is the result of three things: padding required by the algorithm, message authentication code (20 bytes), and salt (16 bytes). To minimize the amount of additional storage consumed by using TDE, consider using the NO SALT and NOMAC directives when encrypting columns. When dealing with relatively minor size impacts (36 bytes), it's easy to forget that with large data volumes, these additional bytes add up quickly. For example, a table with one encrypted column and 2 million rows requires 68 MB of additional storage for encryption overhead. However, a customer with 7 billion rows requires an additional 240 GB of storage for encryption overhead. It is important that you account for this storage impact during planning and testing.

The process for migrating to tablespace encryption in an Oracle 11*g* or later environment can be best described as follows:

1.   Identify table(s) containing sensitive columns.

2.   Create a new encrypted tablespace.

3.   Move the table(s) from the unencrypted tablespace to the encrypted tablespace using either **ALTER TABLE <table> MOVE TABLESPACE <encrypted_tablespace>** or **CREATE TABLE AS SELECT**.

If you have a lot of schemas (and tables) to migrate, organized into one or more separate tablespaces, you should use the following approach:

1.   Use DBMS_METADATA.GET_DDL to generate the tablespace definitions.

2.   Export the data from the tablespaces by schema (account) using Oracle Data Pump export (expdp).

3.   Drop the old tablespaces including the datafiles.

4.   Modify the output from the DBMS_METADATA.GET_DDL step 1 to include TDE encryption settings.

5.   Create new TDE-enabled tablespaces from the modified script in step 4.

6.   Grant quotas on the new TDE-enabled tablespaces to the schema accounts.

7.   Import the data for the schema accounts using Oracle Data Pump import (impdp).

8.   Use the $ORACLE_HOME/rdbms/admin/utlrp.sql script to resolve any invalid objects.

With tablespace encryption in effect, you may want to increase the size of your SGA buffer cache as TDE will use more buffer cache to improve performance.

With either column-level or tablespace encryption, the use of Oracle partitioning (with the appropriate queries) can improve performance by avoiding full table scans (FTS), which would increase the number of decryption operations.

Finally, take advantage of servers that have cryptographic acceleration built into the CPUs, such as Intel AES-NI and Oracle SPARC T4/T5. Cryptographic processing on the Oracle Exadata platform with Intel AES-NI CPU has shown 5x acceleration. We encourage you to read the Oracle Support note, *1365021.1 – How to Benefit from Hardware Acceleration for Tablespace Encryption* to see platform-specific and version-specific recommendations to get the best results from the cryptographic acceleration built into the CPUs.

Advanced Encryption Protection Support

One of the important new capabilities in Oracle Database 12*c*'s encryption capabilities is compliance with Level 2, the Federal Information Processing Standard (FIPS) 140 Publication, known as FIPS 140-2. FIPS 140-2 is a U.S. government computer security standard published by the National Institute of Standards and Technology (NIST). Level 2 compliance implies that the Oracle Database 12*c*'s encryption capabilities meet the basic production-grade requirements of Level 1, such as using approved algorithms (i.e., AES), and also show evidence of tampering of encrypted data or access plaintext cryptographic keys.

You must use the 12.1.0.2 version of the Oracle Database to take advantage of the FIPS 140-2 support. When you enable FIPS 140-2 support in the Oracle Database or Oracle Client, the software will leverage software libraries from third parties that is included and supported with your Oracle software license(s). These software libraries have been formally evaluated to be compliant with the FIPS 140-2 standard. These libraries can also take advantage of native cryptographic acceleration capabilities that may exist on your server or client machine's CPUs to offer performance improvements for cryptographic operations used to meet the FIPS 140-2 standard's requirements.

Configuring FIPS 140-2 Support

You can enable support for FIPS 140-2 in three core areas of the Oracle Database and Database Client:

- Encryption of data at rest with TDE
- Encryption of data used in procedures of the DBMS_CRYPTO PL/SQL package
- Encryption of network communications to and from the Oracle Database

To enable FIPS 140-2 support for TDE and the DBMS_CRYPTO PL/SQL package, you simply need to issue the following statement as SYSDBA and then restart your database:

```
ALTER SYSTEM SET dbfips_140 = TRUE;
```

Configuring this advanced encryption support for network communications to and from the Oracle Database will depend on whether you are using the SSL or native encryption methods supported by Oracle Database 12*c*, but it is as simple as adding a single setting in a configuration file. Please refer to Appendix E of the *Oracle Database Security Guide* for specific details on these configuration steps.

We encourage you to research your compliance or certification requirements to determine if you must be compliant with FIPS 140-2 standards so you can take advantage of these capabilities that are included.

Summary

Encryption is quickly moving from the wish list to the must-have list as organizations are faced with tighter internal and external security standards such as PCI DSS. The ability for organizations to prove that they are doing enough to protect personal and company data is enhanced with the addition of encryption. TDE provides greater security for sensitive data throughout the data life cycle by encrypting data as it is written to disk and decrypting it as needed. The master key needed to perform encryption/decryption operations can be controlled by a non-DBA user, such as a security officer/administrator. Having this separation of duty is important as it helps meet regulatory compliance mandates.

The use of column-level TDE available in Oracle Database 10gR2 and later, provides strong encryption of data stored in sensitive columns, but column-level encryption has limitations regarding datatypes and is not supported with additional database capabilities. (See Chapter 7 of the *Oracle Database Advanced Security Guide for Oracle Database 12c* for a list of specific limitations by version.)

Oracle Database 11g introduced tablespace encryption, which makes it possible to protect all objects stored in a tablespace. Tablespace encryption also removes many of the restrictions levied by column-level encryption. Tablespace encryption provides the most transparent mechanism for protecting data in both new and existing applications. The performance impact of either column-level or tablespace encryption is minimal (average impact is single digits in most test scenarios for non-indexed encrypted values). Implementing encryption can be accomplished as databases are upgraded and tested in Oracle Database 11g or 12c environments.

TDE can also take advantage of an HSM device to secure the master key with a minimal performance impact. HSM provides both encryption capabilities for performance and separates the administrative duties for encryption key management to a centralized location.

PART
III

Security and Auditing
for the Cloud

CHAPTER
12

Audit for Accountability

Auditing is one of those not-so-exciting areas of security that everyone knows they should do, but rarely do. There are many reasons for this. Some don't know what to audit, some don't know how to audit, some don't know what to do with the audit records once they have audited, and some believe the audit performance overhead is a penalty that does not justify the process.

In this chapter, we will respond to each of these issues. You will see why auditing is not only possible, but also invaluable in the modern IT era. Auditing allows you to meet compliance regulations and helps defend against cybersecurity attacks. We will explore ways to audit in the database and look at standard database auditing, fine-grained auditing, and the new Oracle Unified Audit Trail (OUA) technology available in Oracle Database 12*c*.

We will start with a bit of philosophy on how auditing fits into your architecture and why it is important to your enterprise security posture. Then we'll dive into examples that show various methods and aspects of auditing. You will see that auditing is a complementary process of the security cycle, and how, when performed effectively, it can act as an invaluable tool in your security toolbox.

The Security Cycle

Before we begin discussing *how* and *what* to audit, you need to understand *why* we audit. The security cycle associated with security begins with prevention, moves to detection, and finishes with response.

Prevention, which includes access control, is the first process in the cycle. Prevention describes all of the measures put in place to control who can do what and how they can do it. In the preceding chapters, we explained a number of preventative measures for securing a database system, such as locking unused database accounts, encrypting datafiles, implementing role-based access to privileges and objects, as well as fine-grained access controls to database records and columns. IT professionals typically discuss all of the preventative measures they use when they describe their security policies. Although this may seem intuitive, it is an incomplete story.

The interesting part is that access control mechanisms cannot guarantee unauthorized access. Several things could occur to inadvertently allow access, such as the following:

- The design of the security policy may have been incomplete.
- The security implementation may have been insufficiently tested.
- Someone may have inadvertently left a security policy disabled after a system maintenance cycle.

It is a simple fact that humans make mistakes. Consequently, you need to take the time to develop and document detailed security policies, test plans, and create operational procedures. The policy development process should identify gaps and risks in your system. Detection is the next step, and it can easily occur if people are watching when the attack or theft happens. An attack that occurs to a corporate database during the midmorning hours might be detected by end users or applications using the database. If the attack happens at night or a set of datafiles are simply stolen, detection may be more subtle. Auditing is a detection mechanism that often tells you the who, what, when, and how of an attack. However, auditing cannot prevent an attack.

Once an attack or theft is detected, a response is usually desired. Typically the first step in the response is to notify someone of authority. You could also use the advanced security capabilities in Oracle Database to disable system access until the cause and impact are assessed.

Auditing for Accountability

Many IT professionals use auditing to provide detection capabilities to support their overall database security efforts. Others audit to satisfy compliance regulations, corporate or organizational policies, or contractual agreements. Generally, the common thread among all of these is user accountability. You want to ensure that users are doing only what they are supposed to do. You want to capture privilege abuse and misuse. Auditing allows you to hold users responsible for their actions by tracking their behavior.

Auditing Provides the Feedback Loop

The only thing worse than having your data stolen is not knowing about the theft. If you are actively monitoring audit records and you see something happen, then you can quickly respond. Your response may result in readjusting your access control mechanisms, removing the user from your system, or possibly alerting the authorities.

Two important things have to happen for effective auditing. First, you have to be auditing on the correct thing. Second, you have to read and interpret the audit records.

Audit records act as a feedback mechanism into your prevention and access control systems. Audit records also play an important role in any investigative activities that occur as a result of either a breach or suspicious activity. Without auditing, you may have no way of knowing whether your security is sound or whether your data has been read or modified by an unauthorized user.

Auditing Is Not Overhead

Some IT professionals believe that auditing introduces excessive overhead and is not worth the effort when compared to their actionable value. This philosophy is flawed for several reasons.

Clearly, auditing all actions by all users on all data is not useful, and doing so *will* make a system perform miserably. Auditing must target the correct data, processes, and users. The audit records also have to be reviewed and acted upon when necessary. This means that you must have a regular process of reviewing, archiving, and deleting unneeded records as appropriate. Chances are this is not happening if the performance overhead issue is raised.

People who are unfamiliar with how and when to audit may in fact end up with a slower performing system. A system full of audit records makes it hard to distinguish users doing legitimate work from people with malevolent intentions.

The truth about auditing is that it does not add unnecessary overhead when it is performed for compliance reasons, cybersecurity concerns, or to complete the security cycle.

Audit Methods

Auditing takes many forms in today's applications. In the following sections, we consider some of the popular methods and the benefits and drawbacks of each. We discuss server logs, application auditing, and Oracle Database auditing.

Note that these auditing techniques are not mutually exclusive. They should be combined to build complementary layers of defense within the auditing realm. We will explain how each layer possesses certain advantages and disadvantages.

Infrastructure and Application Server Logs

Network switch logs, firewall logs, intrusion detection system (IDS) logs, and application server access logs are considered basic forms of auditing. These files vary in the amount of information they contain. In the general sense, they list the resources that have been accessed, when and how the access occurred, and the result by way of a status code—such as success, failure, unknown, and so on.

Benefits

This class of logs is very useful. The records contained in the log files are often direct indicators of the actions the user performed. For example, an update posted from a web page would have a distinct URL signature, and network-based logs might indicate from which workstation, mobile device, or virtual private network (VPN) the access originated. As such, the user (or rather the user's IP address) can be audited as having invoked some program.

These logs are very useful in determining suspicious behavior. For example, denial-of-service (DoS) attacks or failed authentication attempts may be evident. Many administrators actually use the logs to track abnormal network activity or a user's behavior as they navigate a web site.

Simply stated, including this class of logs in your audit provides a more complete picture of the network and machine access activity that may have led to a data loss incident or a database breach. You can correlate these logs with other audit trails by time, server, or sometimes even the end user to better understand what occurred.

Drawbacks

The challenge with using this class of log files is that the information can be indirect. It is useful only when combined with other data that links a message authentication code (MAC) address or an IP address to a user, the URLs with actual programs, and what data was accessed. For this reason, application or database auditing is usually performed in addition to auditing infrastructure and application server log files.

Application Auditing

One of the most frequently used auditing techniques is application auditing. This class of auditing refers to the built-in auditing services that are sometimes part of a larger application. Regardless of the implementation, application auditing can be transparent to the developer, and this type of auditing can meet most auditing requirements. It can achieve this lofty goal because the auditing is extensible and is manually programmed into the application.

Application auditing is often used when the developers do not understand or cannot take advantage of database auditing. It may also be the choice when the application wants to remain database agnostic and usually involves code that simply inserts the desired audit data into a table every time a transaction occurs.

As users perform actions, the application code selectively audits. Various aspects of auditing are generally seen, including user logins, data manipulations, and administration tasks. In mature applications, this class of auditing may be implemented as a service.

Benefits

One of the greatest benefits of application auditing is that it is inherently extensible, and if implemented properly it can be transparent to the developer. As security and auditing requirements evolve, application auditing can often be modified to meet new and ever-changing requirements.

Not only can application auditing support many requirements, but it also controls *how* the auditing is performed. This has benefits as applications in the application server may elect to audit to a file on the application server or audit to a separate database, which protects audit records from the production database administrators. An auditing implementation based on database tables provides the structure needed to make audit reporting useful. It is generally considered simple to create SQL-based reports on the audit data. Questions such as, "What has the user SCOTT accessed in the last three days?" can be easily answered when the audit records are stored in database tables.

Another benefit of application auditing is that all aspects of the application can be audited, not just the data access. If the application interfaces with multiple databases, flat files, and a web service, then all of that can be audited in a consistent way.

Application auditing may also be done to help ensure database independence. To do this effectively, a service layer would be implemented that would separate the auditing interface calls from the actual audit implementation. Although this may seem noble at first, the reality is that to get the most use of your investment, your applications should be exploiting as much database technology as possible. Why reinvent the wheel?

Finally, application auditing requires no knowledge of database auditing. Even if knowledge is not the issue, the database auditing may provide little value if the application architecture does not support it. Consider an application that does not propagate the user's identity to the database. Database auditing would not add much value, at least for user-level auditing.

Drawbacks

You might be tempted to rush right out and build in application auditing. Before you do, consider some of the following issues.

First, the programmatic nature of application auditing can be a drawback as well as a benefit. The audit code is just that—code. It is therefore subject to all the challenges that plague code, such as logic errors, bugs, and the additional cost of maintaining the code over time.

From the security angle, the most important drawback occurs when the application is bypassed. If a user or even a database administrator conducts a direct update on the table using SQL*Plus, then the application auditing will not be done because the application has been circumvented.

This type of auditing also hints at another challenge in application auditing. The application has to know that it is supposed to call the auditing programs. One possible way to enforce this is to have the audit program set a value in a user-defined application context. You could then create a row-level security policy using views or a VPD that checks for this value. The point is, without a way to enforce the auditing, auditing may not occur.

Trigger Auditing

Within the database, a very popular technique for auditing is to use database triggers. We will specifically be looking at Data Manipulation Language (DML) triggers: Oracle supports triggers for INSERT, UPDATE, and DELETE statements. Oracle does not support SELECT statement triggers, but similar functionality can be achieved using fine-grained auditing—details on how to do this are in the "Fine-Grained Auditing" section later in this chapter. Trigger auditing provides transparency, allowing you to enable auditing without requiring application modifications.

Auditing via triggers usually consists of writing to an auxiliary auditing table. Generally, the new and old data, along with some other useful information, is captured.

Benefits

One major benefit to trigger auditing is that the auditing can be transparent to the application. If you have purchased an application in which the code cannot be modified, then trigger auditing may provide a robust mechanism for adding or augmenting what is already provided.

Additionally, the triggers can be enabled only when specific columns are being manipulated. This allows selectivity in auditing and reduces the number of unnecessary audit records.

As with application auditing, trigger auditing is code stored in the database. From the benefits angle, this gives you many of the extensibility virtues that were discussed earlier.

Drawbacks

Triggers, while effective, are not guaranteed. They do not fire for certain actions, such as TRUNCATE statements, and are bypassed during direct path loads using Oracle's import utility.

Triggers do not allow applications to pass additional parameters. They are constrained to the table columns. Outside of the new and old values of the data, the only other information the trigger can use are application contexts and environmental data such as the user's name, connecting IP address, and so on.

Finally, just like application auditing, triggers have to be created and defined for every object. Calling procedures from within triggers can help if the procedures can be shared across several triggers.

Database Auditing

From a native database perspective, auditing comes in four flavors: mandatory SYS auditing (MSA), traditional auditing (TA), fine-grained auditing (FGA), and Oracle unified auditing (OUA).

MSA audits three important database events: database startup, database shutdown, and users authenticating with the SYSDBA, SYSOPER, SYSADM, SYSKM, SYSBACKUP, or SYSBACKUP privilege (referred to as "SYS privileges" in this chapter). This mandatory auditing allows you to determine whether an administrator has disabled auditing (set the AUDIT_TRAIL initialization parameter to NONE) and is now restarting the database. These audit records have to be stored on the operating system because the database is not available (it's being started or stopped). As of Oracle Database 9*i*R, MSA allows for the auditing of all actions performed by users authenticating with SYS privileges, not just database startup and shutdown.

TA in the Oracle Database allows auditing for session login and logoff, database object access, the use of specific commands, the use of system privileges, and the execution of PL/SQL. With TA you have one implicit policy that can audit controls on events such as any that use the UPDATE ANY or CREATE SESSION privilege, all actions by a specific user, or the use of a specific statement such as DELETE or UPDATE against a specific table. TA is the only option available in Oracle Database 11*g*R2 and earlier. TA is still comprehensive and sufficient to meet stringent certifications such as the Common Criteria for Information Technology Security Evaluation (CC). TA has also been used in countless compliance regulation evaluations for Oracle customers. Over time, however, customers have asked for even more control of what is audited, when audit records are created, and how much audit data is generated. In Oracle Database 11*g*R2 and earlier, audit records for options such as Oracle Database Vault (DBV) and the FGA feature are stored in separate tables from the audit records for TA.

Oracle Database 9*i*R introduced another level of auditing with FGA. FGA allows you to create a VPD-like policy for SELECT, INSERT, UPDATE, and DELETE statements based on information in application session contexts or the values of the record being accessed. For example, you could define an FGA policy for SELECT on the HR.EMPLOYEES table when the SALARY is greater than $100,000. This policy-based auditing with conditional controls was extremely useful, but it did not offer conditional controls over all auditable events.

OUA is a new feature in Oracle Database 12*c* that is driven by named policies that can be organized and enabled (or disabled) separately. OUA policies can be used to control auditing based on privileges, statements, objects, and roles that were found in TA. OUA also supports policies based on components such as Oracle Database Real Application Security (RAS), FGA,

DBV, Oracle Label Security (OLS), Oracle Data Mining, Oracle Data Pump, and Oracle SQL*Loader. Oracle Recovery Manager (RMAN) operations are automatically audited by OUA. OUA will also store the audit records for these components in a single protected table for ease of reporting and audit management.

One of the best features of OUA is its ability to define the conditions in which auditing occurs, which includes support for standard and custom application context namespaces. This conditional auditing feature allows you to fine-tune your audit activity for reporting without extraneous audit records (referred to as "noise"), which also reduces the performance overhead for auditing and reduces your overall storage requirement for auditing.

Benefits

The primary benefit of database auditing is that it applies to all applications that access your information assets as well as the administrators who maintain this information. Unlike the application auditing approach, the audit policy cannot be bypassed. Unlike the database trigger approach, the audit records can be created for all SQL statements.

Drawbacks

Database auditing is not a complete standalone solution. You should combine application server logging and operating system auditing with database auditing to provide a comprehensive audit trail that can be correlated by dimensions such as time and username. Database auditing does not capture data related to an end user's workstation IP for a web application that was used to DELETE a database, for example. Leveraging all of the appropriate audit trails at your disposal and a centralized audit retention and reporting tool, such as Oracle Audit Vault (AV), is a recommend strategy for large enterprise systems.

Enabling Auditing in the Database

If you are using Oracle Database 12c, we recommend that you use the OUA and MSA features, because they provide the most flexible and comprehensive auditing capability for the database. If you are using Oracle Database 11gR2 or earlier, we recommend using the TA and MSA features, because they are the most complete approach to auditing for these databases.

Regardless of your database versions, there are some cases for which you may need to leverage FGA, such as for operations on potentially sensitive data (such as salaries or PII data), where the conditions of the auditing can only be controlled based on the context of record data.

Audit Destination for Standard Auditing and FGA

If you are using Oracle Database 11gR2 or earlier, or if you do not plan to use OUA in Oracle Database 12c, your first decision is how and where you want to store the audit records for TA and FGA. You can specify that TA and FGA audit records are stored in XML files on the database server, in tables in the database (DB), or in a syslog facility (OS). The syslog option is controlled using the AUDIT_TRAIL database initialization parameter. For the XML and DB options, you can include the optional EXTENDED clause to capture the SQL text and any SQL bind variables associated the audited statement.

From a performance perspective, OS syslog has the least amount of overhead, but the syslog records are not complete with respect to the amount of information that is available in the audit record. XML is the second best performing storage option, having the most overhead from a performance perspective. For TA and FGA, we recommend using the XML option if you are concerned about the performance overhead and plan to report from a centralized audit repository like AV. If you plan to report from each database, it makes sense to use the DB option if the performance overhead for auditing does not impact your applications in a negative manner.

For XML files and MSA audit files, the audit location varies depending on OS platform—for example, on Windows, the records are written to the Event Log. On Linux and UNIX platforms, the audit records are found in files with the .aud extension (MSA) or .xml extension (XML) located in the $ORACLE_BASE/admin/<SID>/adump directory. The location of these files is controlled by the AUDIT_FILE_DEST database initialization parameter.

When the DB option is selected, MSA audit records are written to the location defined by the AUDIT_FILE_DEST database initialization parameter. TA audit records are written to the table SYS.AUD$ or SYSTEM.AUD$ if the Oracle Label Security (OLS) option is enabled. FGA audit records are written to the SYS.FGA$ table. We recommend that you use the DBMS_AUDIT_MGMT .MOVE_DBAUDIT_TABLES PL/SQL procedure to move the system audit tables to a user-defined tablespace that has been sized for your expected audit storage needs. As you perform development and testing of your system, you can gather statistics on storage usage from views such as DBA_SEGMENTS to determine your expected space requirements.

In Oracle Database 12*c*, audit-related database parameters must be set in the root container, because the parameters are shared by all PDBs. The following example demonstrates how to set the AUDIT_TRAIL database parameter:

```
sys@db12cr[cdb$root]> ALTER SYSTEM SET audit_trail = XML,EXTENDED
  2  SCOPE = SPFILE;

System altered.
```

We also recommend that you audit all SYS operations by setting the AUDIT_SYS_OPERATIONS database parameter to TRUE, as follows:

```
sys@db12cr[cdb$root]> ALTER SYSTEM SET audit_sys_operations = TRUE
  2  SCOPE = SPFILE;

System altered.
```

Any of the audit-related database parameter changes have to be written to the database initialization file (SPFILE) first; then the database has to be restarted. Trying to change these parameters at runtime (SCOPE=BOTH or SCOPE=MEMORY) results in the error, "ORA-02095: specified initialization parameter cannot be modified." This is a security feature. If the database could be modified at run-time, then a SYSDBA privileged user could turn off auditing, do something bad, and then re-enable auditing, thus hiding his tracks. By forcing a restart, you know that you have captured the event of both the disabling of the auditing as well as the restart.

Enable Oracle Unified Auditing in Oracle Database 12*c*

You have the option to run OUA in Oracle Database 12*c* using the mixed-mode auditing option where the TA, MSA, and FGA audit records are written to the traditional locations. Locations are defined by the AUDIT_TRAIL and AUDIT_FILE_DEST database initialization parameters, as well as the OUA audit trail. This option might be warranted if you need to migrate to OUA over time, but we do not recommend this approach for general use. You would observe a greater impact to performance and your storage needs would increase if you ran in a mixed-mode configuration.

If you are upgrading your database from Oracle Database 11*g*R2 or earlier to Oracle Database 12*c*, you can archive and optionally purge your existing TA, MSA, and FGA audit records (DB, XML, or .aud) using the procedures defined in Chapter 23, "Administering the Audit Trail," of the *Oracle Database Security Guide*.

OUA offers improved performance in auditing by queuing auditing records in a cache area of the System Global Area (SGA) and then flushing those audit records to disk when the cache is full. The size of this cache defaults to 1 MB and can be set as high as 30 MB using the database initialization parameter UNIFIED_AUDIT_SGA_QUEUE_SIZE. This queued-write mode is the default behavior of OUA. You also have the option to run OUA in immediate-write mode if you must have immediate access to audit records, but this option does not offer the same performance characteristics as queued-write mode. To modify OUA to use immediate-write mode, you would issue the following command:

```
EXECUTE DBMS_AUDIT_MGMT.SET_AUDIT_TRAIL_PROPERTY(
   DBMS_AUDIT_MGMT.AUDIT_TRAIL_UNIFIED
 , DBMS_AUDIT_MGMT.AUDIT_TRAIL_WRITE_MODE
 , DBMS_AUDIT_MGMT.AUDIT_TRAIL_IMMEDIATE_WRITE);
```

To operate OUA without mixed-mode, you set the AUDIT_TRAIL database parameter to NONE as shown in this example:

```
sys@db12cr[cdb$root]> ALTER SYSTEM SET audit_trail = NONE
  2  SCOPE = SPFILE;

System altered.
```

To enable OUA in the default queued-write mode, you shut down the database, link the OUA execution code into the database executable, and restart the database as follows:

```
sys@db12cr[cdb$root]> SHUTDOWN IMMEDIATE
Database closed.
Database dismounted.
ORACLE instance shut down.
sys@db12cr[cdb$root]> exit
Disconnected from Oracle Database 12c Enterprise Edition Release 12.1.0.2.0 - 64bit
Production
With the Partitioning, Oracle Label Security, OLAP, Advanced Analytics,
Oracle Database Vault and Real Application Testing options

$ cd $ORACLE_HOME/rdbms/lib
$ make -f ins_rdbms.mk uniaud_on ioracle
... output omitted for brevity ...
$ sqlplus / as sysdba
SQL*Plus: Release 12.1.0.2.0 Production on Sun Jul 20 16:58:09 2014
Copyright (c) 1982, 2013, Oracle.  All rights reserved.
Connected to an idle instance.
sys@db12cr[cdb$root]> STARTUP
ORACLE instance started.
Total System Global Area 1202556928 bytes
Fixed Size                  2288576 bytes
Variable Size             603980864 bytes
Database Buffers          587202560 bytes
Redo Buffers                9084928 bytes
Database mounted.
Database opened.
sys@db12cr[cdb$root]> -- verify OUA is enabled
```

```
sys@db12cr[cdb$root]> SELECT parameter, value
  2  FROM v$option
  3  WHERE parameter LIKE '%Unified%';


PARAMETER                                VALUE
---------------------------------------- --------------------
Unified Auditing                         TRUE
```

At this point you are ready to configure OUA policies.

Who Conducts the Audit Policy and Audit Reporting?

In keeping with the spirit of the separation of duty (SoD) principle, you should create a separate class of users who can control audit policies and conduct audit reporting. In Chapter 10, we discussed the SoD model that includes a Database Account Administrator (DAA), an Operational DBA (ODBA), and a Security Administrator (SA). You can quickly enable the SA user class to be responsible for creating and maintaining audit policies. This can be achieved by granting database accounts in this class the AUDIT_ADMIN role that comes with Oracle Database 12c, along with optional security roles such as the DV_OWNER that was discussed in Chapter 10. Depending on the requirements for the compliance regulations you are subject to or the security certifications you must achieve, you may have to create a separate class of administrators known as an Audit Administrator (AA) for audit policy administration. You may also be required to create a class of database users for Audit Reporting (AR, or simply Auditor) for read-only verification of policies and audit records using the AUDIT_VIEWER role.

Audit Administrator Role

The AUDIT_ADMIN role includes two system privileges, AUDIT ANY and AUDIT SYSTEM. The AUDIT ANY privilege allows the user granted this role to execute AUDIT statements on objects in any schema, except SYS, for TA policies. The AUDIT SYSTEM privilege allows the user to execute CREATE AUDIT POLICY, ALTER AUDIT POLICY, and DROP AUDIT POLICY statements for OUA policies and AUDIT statements for system privileges or non-object statements in TA policies. In TA, a database account can define auditing criteria (using AUDIT) on objects owned by the account.

The AUDIT_ADMIN role also includes grants to EXECUTE the audit trail maintenance PL/SQL package DBMS_AUDIT_MGMT as well as grants to EXECUTE the FGA policy administration package DBMS_FGA.

Finally, the AUDIT_ADMIN role includes grants to SELECT on a number of views related to auditing, as described next:

- **OUA Configuration Views** The views that start with AUDIT_UNIFIED%, such as AUDIT_UNIFIED_POLICIES, which contains the details of the defined OUA policies, and the AUDIT_UNIFIED_ENABLED_POLICIES view that shows the details of the enabled OUA policies.

- **RAS Audit Configuration Views** The views DBA_XS_AUDIT_POLICY_OPTIONS and DBA_XS_ENB_AUDIT_POLICIES.

- **Standard Audit Configuration Views** The views DBA_OBJ_AUDIT_OPTS (object audit), DBA_PRIV_AUDIT_OPTS (privilege audit), and DBA_STMT_AUDIT_OPTS (statement audit).

- **FGA Audit Configuration Views** The views DBA_AUDIT_POLICIES and DBA_AUDIT_POLICY_COLUMNS.

- **Historical Audit Trail Views** The views such as UNIFIED_AUDIT_TRAIL and CDB_UNIFIED_AUDIT_TRAIL for the OUA audit trail; views such as DBA_AUDIT_TRAIL and DBA_FGA_AUDIT_TRAIL that show TA audit trails for standard and FGA audit records; and views such as DV$CONFIGURATION_AUDIT and DV$ENFORCEMENT_AUDIT that show audit records created by Database Vault (DBV) configuration and run-time audit policies.

- **Audit Trail Management Views** The views such as DBA_AUDIT_MGMT_CONFIG_PARAMS that store audit trail configuration settings and DBA_AUDIT_MGMT_CLEANUP_JOBS that store information on audit trail archival/purge activity.

The only gap we see in the AUDIT_AMDIN role is the ability to SELECT from the OLS audit configuration views DBA_OLS_AUDIT_OPTIONS and DBA_SA_AUDIT_OPTIONS. If you are using OLS, you should create a new role (for example, AUDIT_OLS_VIEWER) and grant SELECT on these views to the new role. You can then grant SELECT on OLS audit trail views (see Chapter 9). Refer to the SQL script audit.ols.viewer.sql in the examples collection for this book.

Audit Reporting Role

The AUDIT_VIEWER role is for read-only access to audit configuration views and audit trail data. The role is granted the same SELECT access to audit-related views as the AUDIT_ADMIN role described earlier. This role does not have the AUDIT ANY or AUDIT SYSTEM privileges granted to it or EXECUTE privileges on the DBMS_AUDIT_MGMT or DBMS_FGA PL/SQL packages.

Figure 12-1 depicts the similarities and differences between the AUDIT_VIEWER and AUDIT_ADMIN roles as far as the use cases they can participate in.

In Oracle Database 11gR2 and earlier versions, the AUDIT_ADMIN and AUDIT_VIEWER roles do not exist, but you can easily create two similar roles in these versions of the database by studying how they are constructed in Oracle Database 12c.

For the purposes of this chapter, we will grant the AUDIT_ADMIN role that comes with Oracle Database 12c to our SA account SEC_MGR in both the SALES and HR PDBs, as shown next:

```
sys@db12cr[cdb$root]> CONNECT sys@sales AS SYSDBA
Enter password:
Connected.
sys@db12cr[sales]> GRANT audit_admin TO sec_mgr;


Grant succeeded.

sys@db12cr[sales]> CONNECT sys@hr AS SYSDBA
Enter password:
Connected.
sys@db12cr[hr]> GRANT audit_admin TO sec_mgr;

Grant succeeded.
```

If you are using Oracle DBV, we recommend that you create a realm to protect the AUDIT_ADMIN and AUDIT_VIEWER roles from being granted and revoked by a database administrator. You can create named user accounts that are authorized as the owner of the realm to manage the provisioning of these roles.

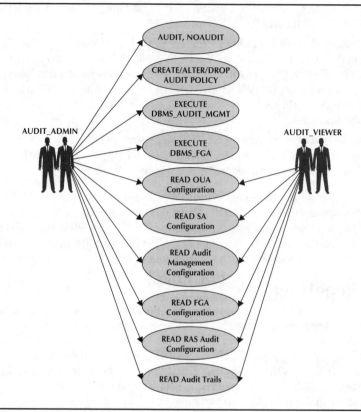

FIGURE 12-1. *Use case participation for Oracle Database 12c audit roles*

What Should be Audited? Creating the Audit Policy

As mentioned, effective auditing can be done successfully only after you have a clear idea of why you are auditing and what you are auditing. If you audit too much, the system could suffer performance degradation, and equally important you could generate excessive and potentially useless audit records. Culling through thousands of audit records is ineffective, especially when most of the audit records were generated for users who were merely performing daily tasks. The greater the fidelity in the auditing capability, the greater your chances of focusing auditing to the right level on the right things.

Auditing can help you identify gaps in your security policies if you cannot use the DBV privilege analysis in Oracle Database 12c. From reviewing the audit records, you may notice that authorized users don't have the necessary privileges to perform a task or, on the other extreme, that they are over-privileged. You may even identify contradictions within your security policy. For example, it is typical to have one requirement to support database backups, which allows a user to gain access to the entire database, and another requirement to protect data based on "need to know" may require that users are allowed access only to certain records based on their affiliation. These two requirements may be in conflict.

This highlights an important point to auditing. In cases where administrators require super privileges, *auditing may be the only thing you can do to ensure privileges are not abused and misused*. This is exactly why the database conducts mandatory audits for SYS privileges.

Best Practices for Audit Policies

Following is a collection of best practices that will serve as a guideline helping you develop your own audit policies. These best practices have been developed from decades of experience in preparing Oracle Database for regulatory compliance and advanced system certifications across many industries. As you will soon see, when OUA is enabled in an Oracle Database 12*c* database, the Oracle Database Security team has taken great strides to provide out-of-the-box policies that adhere to these best practices.

Audit All Activities of Privileged Administrators

As already mentioned and explained, the Oracle Database includes mandatory auditing for operations executed using the SYS privileges. Accounts with these privileges, especially SYSDBA, typically have full rights to access or change the data in your database. Privileges such as SYSKM can make changes to your data encryption policies. Technologies such as DBV can restrict the use of these privileges during normal operations. There are normal operations such as maintenance windows, when DBV policies might be relaxed, and you need to ensure that you have a complete audit trail of SYS privilege usage during these times.

Audit on Database Session Creation and Termination

Auditing when users log on and log off of the database is a good thing to do. You should also know who has been in your database(s) and when. If something happens to the database and you know about when the incident occurred, then it's invaluable to be able to correlate who was working in the database when the incident happened.

However, two things have to be done to ensure that this type of auditing is effective. Most importantly, you have to be able to distinguish between users. Auditing on applications that conceal the end user's identity may be pointless—after all, you really cannot distinguish the "who," only that it was a person running the application. For applications that use connection pools, this type of auditing may be ineffective. In the previous chapters, we discussed how to use Oracle technologies such as Proxy Authentication and Real Application Security to achieve this type of identity preservation, coupled with the PL/SQL procedure DBMS_SESSION.SET_IDENTIFIER.

Second, and this applies to all auditing, you have to come up with a life-cycle management of the audit records. You need to have a plan to archive and/or delete the old records depending on compliance regulations. This is where the DBMS_AUDIT_MGMT PL/SQL package can help.

Audit on Account, Privilege, and Audit Management Commands

Your database's discretionary access control (DAC) security policy is based on a finite set of database accounts, roles, and privileges that were created at some point to lead you through functional testing and system certification. Some scenarios occur during normal operations, such as employee on-boarding or deprovisioning, where you would expect to encounter CREATE USER, DROP USER, GRANT, and/or REVOKE statements. However, privilege escalation is one of the most common approaches to attacking a system or database, so it is important always to audit CREATE USER, ALTER USER, DROP USER, CREATE ROLE, ALTER ROLE, DROP ROLE, GRANT, and REVOKE (system or object privileges) statements that occur.

In Chapter 2 of this book, we discussed the use of database profiles as a means to enforce secure password policies and governing system resource usage to reduce the risk of system overload. The creation or modification of these database profiles using the **CREATE PROFILE**, **ALTER PROFILE**, and **DROP PROFILE** commands should be audited to ensure that the policy changes are detectable.

Your database's audit policy should also be based on a finite set of AUDIT, CREATE AUDIT POLICY, and ALTER AUDIT POLICY statements. During normal operations, you would not expect to encounter a NOAUDIT statement or a DROP AUDIT POLICY statement execution, so it is important to audit the execution of these statements.

Audit Whenever Commands Are Unsuccessful

Auditing unsuccessful actions represents your ability to detect possible break-in attempts from external sources or insiders attempting to access information they are not authorized to access. This is especially important with SQL statements such as SELECT or UPDATE on tables that contain sensitive data, such as privacy-related data. Also, audit powerful system privileges such as ALTER USER, where someone might be attempting to change a password or unlock an account and the attempt fails.

Many of the remaining best practices audit the use of system ANY privileges. You can develop policies that capture the failed use of system ANY privileges using the native capabilities in Oracle auditing.

Audit on Data Access and Data Modification Commands

In previous chapters, we discussed how to use the quality management, data discovery, and modeling tools in Oracle Enterprise Manager Cloud Control (OEMCC) to identify tables with sensitive data in order to develop information protection policies. The analysis conducted for the purpose of information protection can feed into the audit policy development. Performance reports, such as the Automated Workload Repository (AWR) report, also available within OEMCC or in the script $ORACLE_HOME/rdbms/admin/awrrpt.sql, can help you identify frequently accessed tables in your database. Frequently accessed tables can also represent the list of critical information assets to your organization.

At a minimum you will want to audit all modifications (INSERT, UPDATE, MERGE, DELETE, TRUNCATE, RENAME, and COMMENT) on tables containing sensitive data or tables that represent critical information assets. Some compliance regulations may require you to audit all read access (SELECT) to these tables; however, you should make sure this is a requirement before implementing it, as it can result in a significant increase in audit storage requirements. As suggested earlier, you should audit failed SELECT attempts on tables that contain sensitive data.

In addition to auditing object access to sensitive or mission-critical tables, the audit trails maintained by the database need to be audited for INSERT, UPDATE, and DELETE statements.

Audit on Object Management Commands

In most cases, your database was set up using finite set of CREATE <object> and ALTER <object> statements to prepare the system for functional testing and system certification. Some applications dynamically create tables to store information (temporary or for historical backup) and you would expect to encounter CREATE TABLE statements, but you may not expect to see CREATE TABLE AS SELECT, DROP TABLE, or CREATE PROCEDURE statements, especially on sensitive data tables. These types of statements can represent attempts to steal information, disable system functionality, or deploy unauthorized system modifications. To this end, it is a best practice to audit all Data Definition Language (DDL) commands in your database.

Audit on System Management Commands

The system management command **ALTER SYSTEM** is used to modify database initialization parameters (including security-related parameters) and to manage wallets in Transparent Data Encryption (TDE) in Oracle Database 11gR2 and earlier. It should be obvious to you that you should always audit the use of the **ALTER SYSTEM** command.

The **ALTER DATABASE** command can be used to control database backup parameters (ARCHIVELOGMODE and FLASHBACK), to perform point-in-time database recovery, and to control the standby features used by Oracle Active Data Guard. Auditing these types of operations is important because you should be able to detect if someone has modified the parameters that control the integrity of your data and your ability to provide continuous operations.

Audit on Security Policy Management Commands and Configuration Tables

In previous chapters we discussed the technologies available to provide row-level and column-level protections on database objects (RAS, VPD, OLS, TSDP, and Data Redaction), statement level controls (DBV), and encryption of data at rest (TDE). We will discuss FGA later in this chapter. As you recall, technologies such as DBV, OLS, and RAS include built-in mechanisms for auditing, and that is important but not necessarily sufficient, because they may audit only run-time enforcement. Auditing of policy-related changes is important because the configuration tables used by these technologies are subject to direct access using standard SQL. We recommend that you enable auditing of the EXECUTE statement on all PL/SQL APIs used to administer these technologies, specifically the following:

- **RAS** The DBMS_XS_SESSIONS, XS_ACL, XS_ADMIN_UTIL, XS_DATA_SECURITY, XS_DATA_SECURITY_UTIL, XS_NAMESPACE_UTIL, XS_PRINCIPAL, and XS_SECURITY_CLASS packages
- **VPD** The DBMS_RLS package
- **OLS** The SA_AUDIT_ADMIN, SA_COMPONENTS, SA_LABEL_ADMIN, SA_SYSDBA, and SA_USER_ADMIN packages
- **Data Redaction** The DBMS_REDACT package
- **TSDP** The DBMS_TSDP_MANAGE and DBMS_TSDP_PROTECT packages
- **DBV** The DBMS_MACADM and DBMS_MACSEC_ROLE_ADMIN packages
- **TDE** The **ADMINISTER KEY** command
- **FGA** The DBMS_FGA package

For more stringent security certifications or compliance regulations, you may be required to audit failed SELECT and DML statements against the underlying tables that are managed by these packages using the best practice described for data access and data modification commands. For example, you might audit on INSERT, UPDATE, DELETE, and failed SELECT statements on the SYS.RLS$ table used by VPD.

OUA Audit Policy Configuration

In Oracle Database 12c, OUA comes with a collection of default policies that were built to meet many of the best practices that we've discussed in this chapter. You can also create your own audit policies based on custom application schemas and audit-based conditions that are unique to your own database environment. In this section we review these default policies and explain how to create and activate your own policies.

Default Policies

The following query the AUDIT_UNIFIED_POLICIES view to show the names of the default OUA policies that are defined in the SALES PDB:

```
sys@db12cr[hr]> CONNECT sec_mgr@sales
Enter password:
Connected.
sec_mgr@db12cr[sales]> -- show the unique policy names
sec_mgr@db12cr[sales]> SELECT DISTINCT policy_name
  2  FROM audit_unified_policies
  3  ORDER BY policy_name;

POLICY_NAME
-------------------------
ORA_ACCOUNT_MGMT
ORA_DATABASE_PARAMETER
ORA_RAS_POLICY_MGMT
ORA_RAS_SESSION_MGMT
ORA_SECURECONFIG

5 rows selected.
```

These policies were created using the **CREATE AUDIT POLICY** command (discussed shortly), and you can see how some of these policies were created in Chapter 22 of the *Oracle Database Security Guide*. You can obtain a full list of details for each policy by running the SQL script oua .poldetail.sql that is included with the examples for this book. We have included an abbreviated listing of the default OUA policies in the following example to give you a sense of what is included in these policies:

```
sec_mgr@db12cr[sales]> SELECT policy_name, audit_option_type
  2  , audit_option
  3  FROM audit_unified_policies
  4  ORDER BY policy_name, audit_option_type, audit_option
  5  ;

POLICY_NAME             AUDIT_OPTION_TYPE  AUDIT_OPTION
----------------------- ------------------ ------------------
ORA_ACCOUNT_MGMT        STANDARD ACTION    ALTER ROLE
ORA_ACCOUNT_MGMT        STANDARD ACTION    ALTER USER
ORA_ACCOUNT_MGMT        STANDARD ACTION    GRANT
ORA_ACCOUNT_MGMT        STANDARD ACTION    REVOKE
...
ORA_DATABASE_PARAMETER  STANDARD ACTION    ALTER DATABASE
ORA_DATABASE_PARAMETER  STANDARD ACTION    ALTER SYSTEM
...
ORA_RAS_POLICY_MGMT     XS ACTION          ADD GLOBAL CALLBACK
ORA_RAS_POLICY_MGMT     XS ACTION          ADD PROXY
...
ORA_RAS_SESSION_MGMT    XS ACTION          ASSIGN USER
ORA_RAS_SESSION_MGMT    XS ACTION          CREATE SESSION
...
ORA_SECURECONFIG        OBJECT ACTION      EXECUTE [SYS.DBMS_RLS]
ORA_SECURECONFIG        STANDARD ACTION    LOGOFF
ORA_SECURECONFIG        STANDARD ACTION    LOGON
ORA_SECURECONFIG        STANDARD ACTION    SET ROLE
```

```
ORA_SECURECONFIG          SYSTEM PRIVILEGE   ADMINISTER KEY MANAGEMENT
ORA_SECURECONFIG          SYSTEM PRIVILEGE   ALTER ANY TABLE
...
106 rows selected.
```

Table 12-1 demonstrates how the OUA and MSA policies map to the best practices we have discussed.

As you can see from Table 12-1, the combination of the ORA_SECURECONFIG policy and standard MSA auditing covers a wide range of the best practices. The ORA_SECURECONFIG policy audits a number of object management commands that leverage system ANY privileges such as CREATE ANY TABLE. This policy even audits VPD and TDE administration commands.

We recommend enabling the ORA_ACCOUNT_MGMT and ORA_DATABASE_PARAMETER policies to provide a more complete coverage for the "audit on account, privilege, and audit management commands" and "audit on system management commands" best practices. If you are using Oracle RAS, you should enable the ORA_RAS_POLICY_MGMT and ORA_RAS_SESSION_MGMT policies.

You will notice a gap for the best practice "audit on data access and data modification commands." The intent here is that auditing on SELECT and DML statements is typically reserved

Audit	ORA_ACCOUNT_MGMT	ORA_DATABASE_PARAMETER	ORA_RAS_POLICY_MGMT	ORA_RAS_SESSION_MGMT	ORA_SECURECONFIG	MSA
All activities of privileged administrators					✓	✓
Database session creation and termination				✓	✓	✓
Account, privilege, and audit management commands	✓		✓		✓	✓
Unsuccessful commands	✓	✓	✓	✓	✓	✓
Data access and data modification commands						✓
Object management commands			✓		✓	✓
System management commands		✓			✓	✓
Security policy management commands and configuration tables			✓		✓	✓

TABLE 12-1. *Mapping OUA and MSA Policies to Best Practices*

for customer data, your data, as you can determine what data is sensitive and therefore appropriate to audit. The ORA_SECURECONFIG policy is the only policy that is enabled by default, as shown in the following query on the AUDIT_UNIFIED_ENABLED_POLICIES view:

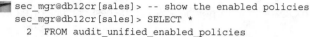

```
sec_mgr@db12cr[sales]> -- show the enabled policies
sec_mgr@db12cr[sales]> SELECT *
  2  FROM audit_unified_enabled_policies
  3  ORDER BY policy_name, user_name;

USER_NAME   POLICY_NAME                ENABLED_OPT SUCCESS    FAILURE
----------  -------------------------- ----------- ---------- ----------
ALL USERS   ORA_SECURECONFIG           BY          YES        YES

1 row selected.
```

Notice that the policy is enabled for all users and will audit on both success and failure for the policy's audit criteria. This example brings up a few important aspects of OUA. First, you create policies that define the types of commands, privileges, or objects you want audited and the conditions in which they are audited using the CREATE AUDIT POLICY statement. Second, a policy is not active until it is enabled, specifying the users to which the policy applies (or does not apply), and whether to audit for success and/or failure of the commands that are covered by the policy. Let's take a look at the policy enablement process.

Enabling OUA Policies

In the preceding section we recommended that you enable both the ORA_ACCOUNT_MGMT and the ORA_DATABASE_PARAMETER policies to provide the most complete coverage and for the best practices in auditing. You can achieve this using new clauses available for the AUDIT statement in Oracle Database 12c, as shown in the following example:

```
sec_mgr@db12cr[sales]> -- enable the policies
sec_mgr@db12cr[sales]> AUDIT POLICY ora_account_mgmt;

Audit succeeded.

sec_mgr@db12cr[sales]> AUDIT POLICY ora_database_parameter;

Audit succeeded.

sec_mgr@db12cr[sales]> -- show the enabled policies
sec_mgr@db12cr[sales]> SELECT *
  2  FROM audit_unified_enabled_policies
  3  ORDER BY policy_name, user_name;

USER_NAME   POLICY_NAME                ENABLED_ SUCCESS    FAILURE
----------  -------------------------- -------- ---------- ----------
ALL USERS   ORA_ACCOUNT_MGMT           BY       YES        YES
ALL USERS   ORA_DATABASE_PARAMETER     BY       YES        YES
ALL USERS   ORA_SECURECONFIG           BY       YES        YES

3 rows selected.
```

The AUDIT POLICY syntax supports one of two optional parameters, WHENEVER SUCCESSFUL and WHENEVER NOT SUCCESSFUL, which control when audit records are logged based on the outcome of the command. If omitted, both success and failure statements are audited as the example shows.

The syntax for the AUDIT POLICY statement also supports one of two optional, multivalued parameters, BY <user1,user2,...,userN> and EXCEPT < user1,user2,...,userN>, which allow you to control the session users subject to policy auditing. In the preceding example, we enabled two policies for all users. The rules around using these clauses is a little tricky to understand, but the basic concept is that if a policy is enabled for a specific user, it will be chosen so that you can control when (WHENEVER) the audit record is created:

```
sec_mgr@db12cr[sales]> -- Audit when commands for SYS fail for the policy
sec_mgr@db12cr[sales]> AUDIT POLICY ora_account_mgmt BY sys
  2  WHENEVER NOT SUCCESSFUL;

Audit succeeded.

sec_mgr@db12cr[sales]> -- Audit commands from SEC_MGR succeed
sec_mgr@db12cr[sales]> -- for the policy
sec_mgr@db12cr[sales]> AUDIT POLICY ora_account_mgmt BY sec_mgr
  2  WHENEVER SUCCESSFUL;

Audit succeeded.

sec_mgr@db12cr[sales]> -- show the enabled policies
sec_mgr@db12cr[sales]> SELECT * FROM audit_unified_enabled_policies;
```

USER_NAME	POLICY_NAME	ENABLED_	SUCCESS	FAILURE
SYS	ORA_ACCOUNT_MGMT	BY	NO	YES
SEC_MGR	ORA_ACCOUNT_MGMT	BY	YES	NO
ALL USERS	ORA_SECURECONFIG	BY	YES	YES
ALL USERS	ORA_ACCOUNT_MGMT	BY	YES	YES
ALL USERS	ORA_DATABASE_PARAMETER	BY	YES	YES

```
5 rows selected.
```

In this example, we have explicit conditions for when the ORA_ACCOUNT_MGMT policy applies to SYS and SEC_MGR and an implicit policy for all other users. Note that you can have only one of the following:

- a collection of BY <user list> conditions with the ALL USERS as the default condition, or
- a single EXCEPT <user list> condition without the ALL USERS as the default condition.

If we try to use the EXCEPT <user list> syntax it will fail, because we have to remove the BY <user list> conditions and the ALL USERS default condition first using the **NOAUDIT POLICY** command:

```
sec_mgr@db12cr[sales]> -- try an EXCEPT form of the command for SYS
sec_mgr@db12cr[sales]> AUDIT POLICY ora_account_mgmt EXCEPT sys
  2  WHENEVER SUCCESSFUL;
AUDIT POLICY ora_account_mgmt EXCEPT sys
*
ERROR at line 1:
ORA-46350: Audit policy ORA_ACCOUNT_MGMT already applied with the BY clause.
```

```
sec_mgr@db12cr[sales]> -- remove the ALL_USERS condition sec_mgr@db12cr[sales]> -- in
order to add EXCEPT
sec_mgr@db12cr[sales]> NOAUDIT POLICY ora_account_mgmt;

Noaudit succeeded.

sec_mgr@db12cr[sales]> -- retry an EXCEPT form of the command for SYS
sec_mgr@db12cr[sales]> AUDIT POLICY ora_account_mgmt EXCEPT sys
  2  WHENEVER SUCCESSFUL;

Audit succeeded.

sec_mgr@db12cr[sales]> -- retry an EXCEPT form of the command for SEC_MGR
sec_mgr@db12cr[sales]> AUDIT POLICY ora_account_mgmt EXCEPT sec_mgr
  2  WHENEVER NOT SUCCESSFUL;

Audit succeeded.

sec_mgr@db12cr[sales]> -- as you can see the last EXCEPT effectively
sec_mgr@db12cr[sales]> -- overwrites the last EXCEPT for the policy
sec_mgr@db12cr[sales]> SELECT * FROM audit_unified_enabled_policies ;

USER_NAME   POLICY_NAME               ENABLED_  SUCCESS     FAILURE
----------  ------------------------  --------  ----------  ----------
SEC_MGR     ORA_ACCOUNT_MGMT          EXCEPT    NO          YES
ALL USERS   ORA_SECURECONFIG          BY        YES         YES
ALL USERS   ORA_DATABASE_PARAMETER    BY        YES         YES

3 rows selected.

sec_mgr@db12cr[sales]> -- restore our recommendation
sec_mgr@db12cr[sales]> NOAUDIT POLICY ora_account_mgmt;

Noaudit succeeded.

sec_mgr@db12cr[sales]> AUDIT POLICY ora_account_mgmt;

Audit succeeded.
```

As you can see in this example, you must specify every user for which the policy is EXCEPT-ed because only one condition can be active at any given time.

Auditing with Session Context

In previous chapters we discussed and demonstrated how to use the DBMS_SESSION.SET_ IDENTIFIER PL/SQL procedure to associate a named end user to each TA audit trail record. OUA has extended this concept to offer support for associating any application context value to each audit trail record. Here's an example:

```
sec_mgr@db12cr[sales]> -- Audit a few of the interesting session context
sec_mgr@db12cr[sales]> -- attributes that are not found in the default
sec_mgr@db12cr[sales]> -- OUA audit trail
sec_mgr@db12cr[sales]> AUDIT CONTEXT
  2  NAMESPACE userenv
```

```
   3   ATTRIBUTES authenticated_identity
   4   ,authentication_method
   5   ,client_identifier
   6   ,client_info
   7   ,ip_address;

Audit succeeded.

sec_mgr@db12cr[sales]> -- We can verify the audit context configuration
sec_mgr@db12cr[sales]> -- in the AUDIT_UNIFIED_CONTEXTS view
sec_mgr@db12cr[sales]> SELECT * FROM audit_unified_contexts
   2   ORDER BY namespace, attribute, user_name;

NAMESPACE        ATTRIBUTE                                  USER_NAME
---------------  -----------------------------------------  ---------------
USERENV          AUTHENTICATED_IDENTITY                     ALL USERS
USERENV          AUTHENTICATION_METHOD                      ALL USERS
USERENV          CLIENT_IDENTIFIER                          ALL USERS
USERENV          CLIENT_INFO                                ALL USERS
USERENV          IP_ADDRESS                                 ALL USERS

5 rows selected.
```

One of the best features of application context auditing is that you can also audit your own custom namespaces, which makes this OUA feature extensible to a number of compliance regulations and certification requirements. The **AUDIT CONTEXT** command also includes an optional clause to specify BY <user list> that works in the same manner as the **AUDIT POLICY** command. Like **AUDIT POLICY**, you would use **NOAUDIT CONTEXT** to disable the capture of the application context attributes.

As we mentioned, we are using the queued-mode of OUA so we must use the DBMS_AUDIT_MGMT.FLUSH_UNIFIED_AUDIT_TRAIL PL/SQL procedure to make audit trail records available for reporting:

```
sec_mgr@db12cr[sales]> EXECUTE DBMS_AUDIT_MGMT.FLUSH_UNIFIED_AUDIT_TRAIL;

PL/SQL procedure successfully completed.
```

We can then see the effect of our application context auditing by issuing the following query:

```
SELECT audit_type, unified_audit_policies, event_timestamp,
    dbusername, application_contexts
FROM unified_audit_trail
WHERE action_name = 'LOGOFF'
AND application_contexts IS NOT NULL
ORDER BY event_timestamp DESC;
```

Figure 12-2 shows the output of the query using SQL Developer.

Creating a Custom Policy for Actions on Customer Data

In discussing the default OUA policies earlier in the chapter, we recommended auditing SELECT and DML statements for critical or sensitive customer data as part of the "audit on data access and

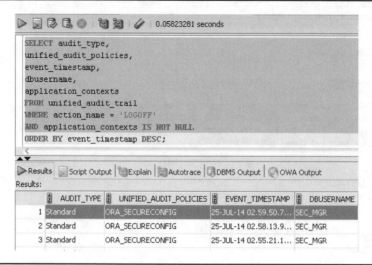

FIGURE 12-2. *OUA audit trail with application context data*

data modification commands" best practice. The following example demonstrates how to create a policy that covers the DML aspect of this best practice for the SH.SALES_HISTORY table:

```
sec_mgr@db12cr[sales]> -- Audit all data modifications to
sec_mgr@db12cr[sales]> -- a critical data table like the
sec_mgr@db12cr[sales]> -- SALES_HISTORY table in our examples
sec_mgr@db12cr[sales]> CREATE AUDIT POLICY sales_history_modification
  2   ACTIONS
  3      ALTER      ON sh.sales_history,
  4      AUDIT      ON sh.sales_history,
  5      COMMENT    ON sh.sales_history,
  6      DELETE     ON sh.sales_history,
  7      FLASHBACK  ON sh.sales_history,
  8      GRANT      ON sh.sales_history,
  9      INDEX      ON sh.sales_history,
 10      INSERT     ON sh.sales_history,
 11      RENAME     ON sh.sales_history,
 12      UPDATE     ON sh.sales_history;

Audit policy created.

sec_mgr@db12cr[sales]> -- Enable the policy
sec_mgr@db12cr[sales]> AUDIT POLICY sales_history_modification;
```

As you can see, a number of statements on the table are available to audit. The list of auditable statements depends on the database object type. Refer to Table 14-1 in the *Oracle SQL Reference* for a list of the statements by database object type. The statements can also be queried from the database using the follow SQL statement:

```
SELECT name
FROM auditable_system_actions
WHERE component = 'Standard'
ORDER BY name;
```

The keyword ALL is available as a shorthand to indicate that you want to audit all commands available for the database object type. If you want to audit READ and WRITE operations on Oracle Database directory objects, you must specify the DIRECTORY keyword as follows:

```
ACTIONS READ, WRITE ON DIRECTORY mydir
```

In many cases, you may have a PL/SQL package that performs DML for one or more of your application tables. We would also recommend that you audit all executions of these packages (**EXECUTE ON owner.plsql_package**) in addition to the direct DML statements against application tables so that you can determine when data is modified outside of the PL/SQL package.

As we mentioned, it is important that you understand the requirements for the "audit on data access" (SELECT) part of the best practice so you can plan for the increased database storage. We recommend that you audit failed SELECT statements for the core tables in your database application, as shown in the next example, though you may be required to audit all SELECT statements:

```
sec_mgr@db12cr[sales]> -- Audit failed data access to
sec_mgr@db12cr[sales]> -- the same table
sec_mgr@db12cr[sales]> CREATE AUDIT POLICY sales_history_read
  2  ACTIONS
  3    SELECT    ON sh.sales_history;

Audit policy created.

sec_mgr@db12cr[sales]> -- Enable the policy
sec_mgr@db12cr[sales]> AUDIT POLICY sales_history_read
  2  WHENEVER NOT SUCCESSFUL;

Audit succeeded.
```

You drop audit policies using the DROP AUDIT POLICY <policy_name> statement. If the policy is enabled, you must first issue the NOAUDIT POLICY <policy name> statement before dropping the policy.

We've included a policy named recommended_actions in a script named oua.policy.sql in the examples that accompany this book. This policy audits additional statements related to the best practice for "data access and data modification." In this policy you will find auditing for statements such as TRUNCATE TABLE and PURGE TABLE.

Creating a Custom Policy Based on System Privileges

OUA also supports creating policies based on the use of system privileges. In the following example, we create a policy that audits the failed use of system ANY privileges for SELECT, DML, and EXECUTE statements, which is related to the best practice for "audit on data access and data modification."

```
sec_mgr@db12cr[sales]> -- Audit the use of system ANY SELECT,
sec_mgr@db12cr[sales]> -- DML, or EXECUTE statements to track
sec_mgr@db12cr[sales]> -- DBA's modifying critical or sensitive data
sec_mgr@db12cr[sales]> CREATE AUDIT POLICY system_any_priv_fail
  2  PRIVILEGES SELECT ANY TABLE,
  3    INSERT ANY TABLE,
  4    UPDATE ANY TABLE,
  5    DELETE ANY TABLE,
  6    EXECUTE ANY PROCEDURE;
```

```
Audit policy created.

sec_mgr@db12cr[sales]> -- Enable the policy
sec_mgr@db12cr[sales]> AUDIT POLICY system_any_priv_fail
  2  WHENEVER NOT SUCCESSFUL;

Audit succeeded.
```

You can issue a query to obtain a list of system privileges that are available to audit upon with the following SQL statement:

```
SELECT name FROM system_privilege_map ORDER BY name;
```

Conditional Auditing

The **CREATE AUDIT POLICY** and **ALTER AUDIT POLICY** commands include a WHEN clause to define the conditions (SQL Boolean expressions) under which the auditing should occur. These conditional expressions are intended to be used when the BY <user list> or EXCEPT <user list> clauses in the **AUDIT** command are not granular or specific enough to support your auditing needs.

The SQL Boolean expression can leverage application contexts using the SYS_CONTEXT function. The expressions also support many of the SQL built-in functions for character, date, time, and numeric data manipulation.

The WHEN clause includes an EVALUATE syntax to specify the condition when the expression is to be evaluated, such as for each statement, once for each session, or once for the lifetime of the instance (that is, once after the database is started).

The following example demonstrates how to create a conditional policy that audits database session logons using a variety of mechanisms in which you may be authorized to connect to a database. The condition of this policy states that we want to audit logons for every user except DBSNMP, when DBSNMP is coming from an Oracle Enterprise Manager Cloud Control (OEMCC) server named cloud12c.nsg.net.

```
sec_mgr@db12cr[sales]> CREATE AUDIT POLICY conditional_session
  2  PRIVILEGES CREATE SESSION
  3  ACTIONS LOGON
  4  ROLES connect
  5  WHEN
  6    'NOT (SYS_CONTEXT(''USERENV'',
               ''SESSION_USER'') = ''DBSNMP''
          AND SYS_CONTEXT(''USERENV'',
               ''HOST'') = ''cloud12c.nsg.net'')'
  7  EVALUATE PER STATEMENT;

Audit policy created.

sec_mgr@db12cr[sales]> AUDIT POLICY conditional_session;

Audit succeeded.
```

Notice in this example that we are able to combine the use of the criteria for PRIVILEGES, ACTIONS, and ROLES in a single **CREATE AUDIT POLICY** command.

This is the first example that includes the use of the ROLES clause. The ROLES clause supports a comma-delimited list of database roles, which indicates that you want to audit the use of all privileges granted to the role(s). The default OUA policy named ORA_SECURECONFIG audits any time a role is assumed for a session (SET ROLE).

Unconditional Auditing

Conditional auditing is the norm; however, there are times when you are trying to meet strict compliance or jurisdictional requirements and it is simpler to enable auditing of all activities by certain users in specific scenarios, such as named developers accessing a production database. This approach can be easily implementing by creating a policy with ACTIONS ALL in your CREATE AUDIT POLICY statement and specifying the required conditional criteria in the WHEN clause.

Creating a Custom Policy for Components

As mentioned previously, you can develop OUA policies for components such as RAS, DBV, OLS, Oracle Data Pump, and Oracle SQL*Loader. You must use a special syntax in the form of ACTIONS COMPONENT = <component> to create policies for these components.

Also mentioned earlier, Oracle Database 12c includes default policies for RAS. If you are using RAS, we recommend that you leverage these default policies as a starting point. You can then add to them to satisfy your auditing requirements.

You can also create policies for Oracle data mining models in which you use a special syntax in the form of ACTIONS <action> ON MINING MODEL schema.model. Supported action values include AUDIT, COMMENT, GRANT, RENAME, and SELECT.

The Oracle RMAN utility used to back up and recover your database is audited by default by an OUA audit policy. The UNIFIED_AUDIT_TRAIL view has five columns related to RMAN activities that include session information, the type of operation (such as BACKUP, RECOVERY, and so on), the object type (such as database, datafile), and the device used for the operation. Refer to Chapter 22 in the *Oracle Advanced Security Guide* for details on the type of information that is audited for this component.

The following example demonstrates how to create a single OUA audit policy for Oracle Data Pump, Oracle SQL*Loader, and OLS:

```
sec_mgr@db12cr[sales]> -- Audit all Datapump exports and imports
sec_mgr@db12cr[sales]> -- and all Direct Path Load activity
sec_mgr@db12cr[sales]> CREATE AUDIT POLICY component_common_all
  2  ACTIONS COMPONENT = DATAPUMP EXPORT, IMPORT
  3  ACTIONS COMPONENT = DIRECT_LOAD LOAD;

Audit policy created.

sec_mgr@db12cr[sales]> -- Audit on all configuration
sec_mgr@db12cr[sales]> -- changes to OLS
sec_mgr@db12cr[sales]> ALTER AUDIT POLICY component_common_all
  2  ADD ACTIONS COMPONENT = OLS ALL;

Audit policy altered.

sec_mgr@db12cr[sales]> -- Enable the policy
sec_mgr@db12cr[sales]> AUDIT POLICY component_common_all;

Audit succeeded.
```

This example demonstrates how to use multiple criteria in the **CREATE AUDIT POLICY** command as well as the use of the **ALTER AUDIT POLICY** command to ADD new auditing criteria to an existing policy. The **ALTER AUDIT POLICY** also supports a DROP clause to drop an existing auditing criteria as well as a DROP CONDITION clause to drop the condition associated with the policy.

You can view the actions that are available for each component with the following SQL statement:

```
SELECT component,name
FROM auditable_system_actions
ORDER BY component,name;
```

When creating an audit policy for DBV, you must specify an action related to a specific realm, rule set, or factor. The following example creates an OUA audit policy for the Sales History DBV realm and a DBV rule set that is used to control the GRANT of EXECUTE (via a DBV command rule) on the PL/SQL package DBMS_RLS that is used to managed VPD policies:

```
sec_mgr@db12cr[sales]> -- Audit Database Vault violations on
sec_mgr@db12cr[sales]> -- realms and rule sets used for command rules,
sec_mgr@db12cr[sales]> -- realm authorizations, DBV roles
sec_mgr@db12cr[sales]> CREATE AUDIT POLICY component_dv_example
  2  ACTIONS COMPONENT=DV REALM VIOLATION ON "Sales History"
  3  , RULE SET FAILURE ON "Can Grant VPD Administration";

Audit policy created.

sec_mgr@db12cr[sales]> -- Enable the policy
sec_mgr@db12cr[sales]> AUDIT POLICY component_dv_example
  2  WHENEVER NOT SUCCESSFUL;

Audit succeeded.
```

If you run the script named oua.demo.sql that is included with the examples for this book, you will create audit events based on the audit criteria we created or enabled in the preceding example. Figure 12-3 demonstrates the database audit correlation reporting capability that is enabled by OUA. We show the output from the following SQL statement run in the SQL Developer tool:

```
SELECT event_timestamp,audit_type,unified_audit_policies,
    dbusername,action_name, sql_text
FROM unified_audit_trail
ORDER BY event_timestamp DESC;
```

From the output, you can see audit records from TA actions, components such as DBV, Data Pump, and FGA in chronological order, annotated with which OUA policy caused the audit event record to be generated.

Traditional Audit Policy Configuration

If you are using a version prior to Oracle Database 12c, then you have one implicit audit policy that is created using a collection of **AUDIT** commands. You can disable audit criteria only by issuing the **NOAUDIT** command for the audit criteria that you want to disable.

Results: Script Output | Explain | Autotrace | DBMS Output | OWA Output
Results:

	EVENT_TIMESTAMP	AUDIT_TYPE	UNIFIED_AUDIT_POLICIES	DBUSERNAME	ACTION_NAME	SQL_TEXT
1	26-JUL-14 02.29.37.683938000 PM	Standard	(null)	SYS	EXECUTE	(CLOB) BEGIN DBM
2	26-JUL-14 02.29.36.793825000 PM	Standard	ORA_SECURECONFIG, CONDITIONAL_SESSION, ORA_SECURECO...	SYS	LOGON	(null)
3	26-JUL-14 02.29.36.654227000 PM	Standard	ORA_SECURECONFIG, ORA_SECURECONFIG	SYS	LOGOFF	(null)
4	26-JUL-14 02.29.36.121195000 PM	Standard	ORA_SECURECONFIG, CONDITIONAL_SESSION, ORA_SECURECO...	SYS	LOGON	(null)
5	26-JUL-14 02.28.58.056236000 PM	Standard	ORA_SECURECONFIG	TESTAUDIT2	LOGOFF	(null)
6	26-JUL-14 02.28.51.427525000 PM	Standard	RECOMMENDED_ACTIONS	TESTAUDIT2	TRUNCATE TABLE	(CLOB) truncate ta
7	26-JUL-14 02.28.45.821862000 PM	Standard	RECOMMENDED_ACTIONS	TESTAUDIT2	TRUNCATE TABLE	(CLOB) truncate ta
8	26-JUL-14 02.28.19.087936000 PM	Datapump	(null)	TESTAUDIT2	EXPORT	(CLOB) BEGIN SY
9	26-JUL-14 02.28.11.608745000 PM	Standard	ORA_SECURECONFIG, CONDITIONAL_SESSION, CONDITIONAL_S...	TESTAUDIT2	LOGON	(null)
10	26-JUL-14 02.27.49.308245000 PM	Standard	ORA_SECURECONFIG, ORA_SECURECONFIG	SYS	LOGOFF	(null)
11	26-JUL-14 02.26.52.216953000 PM	Standard	ORA_SECURECONFIG, CONDITIONAL_SESSION, ORA_SECURECO...	SYS	LOGON	(null)
12	26-JUL-14 02.26.39.507848000 PM	Database Vault	(null)	SYS	REALM ACCESS	(CLOB) SELECT CO
13	26-JUL-14 02.26.39.293258000 PM	Standard	ORA_DATABASE_PARAMETER, ORA_SECURECONFIG, ORA_SECU...	SYS	ALTER SYSTEM	(CLOB) ALTER SYS
14	26-JUL-14 02.26.39.275914000 PM	Standard	ORA_ACCOUNT_MGMT, ORA_ACCOUNT_MGMT	SYS	GRANT	(CLOB) GRANT REA
15	26-JUL-14 02.26.39.169166000 PM	Standard	ORA_SECURECONFIG, CONDITIONAL_SESSION, ORA_SECURECO...	SYS	LOGON	(null)
16	26-JUL-14 02.26.39.042325000 PM	Standard	ORA_SECURECONFIG	DBVOWNER	LOGOFF	(null)
17	26-JUL-14 02.26.38.764869000 PM	Standard	ORA_SECURECONFIG, CONDITIONAL_SESSION, CONDITIONAL_S...	DBVOWNER	LOGON	(null)
18	26-JUL-14 02.26.38.725113000 PM	Standard	ORA_SECURECONFIG	SH	LOGOFF	(null)
19	26-JUL-14 02.26.38.724226000 PM	FineGrainedAudit	(null)	SH	SELECT	(CLOB) SELECT pro
20	26-JUL-14 02.26.38.722166000 PM	Standard	SALES_HISTORY_MODIFICATION	SH	UPDATE	(CLOB) update sale

FIGURE 12-3. *Correlated audit trails from multiple OUA policies*

Auditing in versions prior to Oracle Database 12*c* does allow for auditing all supported SQL statements. The following types of auditing are supported in these database versions:

- Audit on session creation and deletion
- Audit account management, privilege management, and audit management commands
- Audit on successful actions, unsuccessful actions, or both
- Audit on specific objects such as tables and views—for example, every time someone issues an INSERT statement against the SH.SALES_HISTORY table, an audit will be recorded
- Audit on PL/SQL program unit executions
- Audit on Oracle Database directory objects, data mining models, and SQL direct path loading operations
- Audit when someone exercises a system privilege such as disabling a trigger or uses one of the ANY privileges
- Audit on system management commands such as **ALTER DATABASE** or **ALTER SYSTEM**
- Restrict your audit criteria to be applicable to specific database users

With all of the preceding, you can audit every time someone performs the action, or audit only once per session regardless of the number of times they perform the action.

Auditing in versions prior to Oracle Database 12*c* does not allow you to use conditional Boolean logic, and it does not allow for arbitrary namespace attributes to be associated to the audit records.

For components such as DBV, OLS, and FGA, you must rely on the native audit management in these components as well as their native audit trail.

Despite some differences, TA is an extensive capability that enables you to create an auditing plan that supports auditing best practices. This fidelity is what makes auditing a real asset in these versions, and it has been successfully used in thousands of system certifications over the years to ensure regulatory compliance.

Configuring Statement, Privilege, and Role Auditing

Traditional TA enables you to define audit criteria for the use of specific statements, the use of system privileges, or the use of privileges associated to a role with the **AUDIT** command, as shown in the following example:

```
sec_mgr@db12cr[sales]> -- Audit session logins using the
sec_mgr@db12cr[sales]> -- CREATE SESSION privilege
sec_mgr@db12cr[sales]> AUDIT CREATE SESSION;

Audit succeeded.

sec_mgr@db12cr[sales]> -- Audit session logins using the
sec_mgr@db12cr[sales]> -- CONNECT role which is granted the
sec_mgr@db12cr[sales]> -- CREATE SESSION privilege
sec_mgr@db12cr[sales]> AUDIT CONNECT;

Audit succeeded.

sec_mgr@db12cr[sales]> -- Audit any time a table is created,
sec_mgr@db12cr[sales]> -- dropped, or truncated
sec_mgr@db12cr[sales]> AUDIT TABLE;

Audit succeeded.

sec_mgr@db12cr[sales]> -- Audit the failed use of the
sec_mgr@db12cr[sales]> -- system DELETE ANY privilege
sec_mgr@db12cr[sales]> AUDIT DELETE ANY TABLE WHENEVER NOT SUCCESSFUL;

Audit succeeded.
```

Notice the rather cryptic statement, AUDIT TABLE. TA supports the use of several shortcuts to specify the auditing of two or more SQL statements—in this case, CREATE TABLE, DROP TABLE, and ALTER TABLE. TA also supports a single SQL statement on two or more object types. Refer to Tables 13-1 and 13-2 in the *Oracle SQL Reference* for a detailed list of these shortcuts. You can use the SYSTEM_PRIVILEGE_MAP view to determine the list of system privileges that can be audited.

The previous AUDIT statement demonstrates use of the WHENEVER clause that enables you to define whether the audit criteria is active for success, failure, or both (if the clause is omitted). The AUDIT statement also includes a clause IN SESSION CURRENT that allows you to dynamically define audit criteria that are active only for the current database session.

You can specify the BY <user_list> clause to configure audit criteria to be applicable to specific database users in much the same way you observed with OUA.

You can disable specific audit criteria using the NOAUDIT statement, as shown in the following example:

```
sec_mgr@db12cr[sales]> -- Disable a specific audit criteria
sec_mgr@db12cr[sales]> NOAUDIT TABLE;

Noaudit succeeded.
```

Configuring Object Auditing

TA allows you to define audit criteria for specific SQL statements on specific objects using the **AUDIT** command with the ON clause, as shown in the following example:

```
sec_mgr@db12cr[sales]> -- Audit all DML on the
sec_mgr@db12cr[sales]> -- table SH.SALES_HISTORY
sec_mgr@db12cr[sales]> AUDIT INSERT, UPDATE, DELETE ON sh.sales_history;

Audit succeeded.

sec_mgr@db12cr[sales]> -- Audit failed selects on the
sec_mgr@db12cr[sales]> -- table SH.SALES_HISTORY
sec_mgr@db12cr[sales]> AUDIT SELECT ON sh.sales_history
  2  WHENEVER NOT SUCCESSFUL;

Audit succeeded.
```

Notice that you can specify multiple SQL statements, such as INSERT, UPDATE, and DELETE, on a single object like SH.SALES_HISTORY.

Determining Audit Status

Evaluating the current audit status is important for proving compliance with a security policy. When you want to inspect the audit status of your objects, you can query the DBA_OBJ_AUDIT_OPTS or the USER_OBJ_AUDIT_OPTS view. These views show the audit status of every audited object even if auditing is not enabled. You should therefore qualify your query to target an object or statement of interest:

```
sec_mgr@db12cr[sales]> SELECT sel "select option"
  2  FROM dba_obj_audit_opts
  3  WHERE owner = 'SH'
  4  AND object_name = 'SALES_HISTORY';

select op
---------
-/A

1 row selected.
```

The format is a bit cryptic, but it is easy to decipher once you understand the code. The view lists all the options that can be performed on an object. In this query, we are looking at the select option. There are two values represented for each option. The first field, shown with a hyphen value in the preceding output, holds the value that controls when auditing should occur after the user is successful in performing the action. The second field, shown with an "A" in the output, holds the value that controls whether auditing should occur for unsuccessful actions. A hyphen or a blank means no auditing will occur. An "A" means auditing will occur for every access (the default), and an "S" means auditing will occur once for each session.

If we enable auditing by session on the table, we can verify the preceding rules:

```
sec_mgr@db12cr[sales]> -- Audit failed selects on the
sec_mgr@db12cr[sales]> -- table SH.SALES_HISTORY
sec_mgr@db12cr[sales]> AUDIT SELECT ON sh.sales_history BY SESSION
  2  WHENEVER SUCCESSFUL;

Audit succeeded.

sec_mgr@db12cr[sales]> SELECT sel "select option"
  2  FROM dba_obj_audit_opts
  3  WHERE owner = 'SH'
  4  AND object_name = 'SALES_HISTORY';

select op
---------
S/A

1 row selected.
```

We recommend you use the default of BY ACCESS for object auditing versus BY SESSION. The BY ACCESS option results in a more accurate audit trail used in reporting. The audit trail's integrity is less likely to be challenged when you're trying to achieve regulatory compliance.

The DBA_STMT_AUDIT_OPTS view shows system-wide auditing. You can view auditing that was enabled to track user logons by using this query:

```
sec_mgr@db12cr[sales]> SELECT audit_option, success, failure
  2  FROM dba_stmt_audit_opts
  3  WHERE audit_option = 'CREATE SESSION';

AUDIT_OPTION         SUCCESS     FAILURE
-------------------- ----------- -----------
CREATE SESSION       BY ACCESS   BY ACCESS

1 row selected.
```

The last essential audit view is DBA_PRIV_AUDIT_OPTS. This view enables you to check the auditing status of system privileges. For example, we enabled auditing for users exercising the DELETE ANY TABLE privilege, and you can check the status of auditing the privilege as follows:

```
sec_mgr@db12cr[sales]> SELECT privilege, success, failure
  2  FROM dba_priv_audit_opts
  3  WHERE privilege = 'DELETE ANY TABLE';

PRIVILEGE            SUCCESS     FAILURE
-------------------- ----------- -----------
DELETE ANY TABLE     NOT SET     BY ACCESS

1 row selected.
```

Fine-Grained Auditing

TA's auditing fidelity is good, but it may not be adequate for some requirements. For example, if you want to capture audits on specific table columns or when specific conditions arise in the data, then TA would be ineffective.

When FGA was originally introduced, it offered four major advantages over TA. The first advantage is that it allows for auditing to occur when a specific condition is met. In other words, the audit policy tests a Boolean condition during SQL statement execution. If the audit condition is met, then the transaction is audited.

This has enormous advantages over TA, because the Boolean condition can be anything specified in SQL. Another advantage over TA is that FGA conditional auditing helps to eliminate unnecessary audits.

TA enables you to audit any time someone queried a table. However, you cannot specify exemptions to the audit based on specific conditions. Perhaps you are more concerned with sensitive data access issues, and you want to set up access control to prevent certain users from seeing sensitive records. In TA, there is no inherent way to create an audit policy for this scenario. You could set up auditing for SELECT statements on your table. However, the problem is that the audit records would indicate only that a user SELECT-ed from the table and the audit records would not indicate whether the user was able to access sensitive records. You might be able to derive the result set of the query by looking at the captured SQL statement, but this would prove cumbersome and unreliable. Assuming users are supposed to access the table to see their records, auditing SELECT statements to meet this requirement is ineffective.

With FGA, you can complement the security policy by auditing only when a user is accessing sensitive data records or sensitive columns. The database allows you to specify a condition on the table's data, as well as application context values, that when met will generate an audit record.

Enabling FGA

Enabling FGA is completely different from enabling TA. The FGA administer uses the DBMS_FGA package. We'll use the ADD_POLICY procedure from this package to add a policy on the SH.SALES_HISTORY table. We want to audit only when the TOTAL_COST column has a value greater than $10,000. Therefore, we specify the condition as shown in this example:

```
sec_mgr@db12cr[sales]> BEGIN
  2    DBMS_FGA.ADD_POLICY(
  3        object_schema => 'SH'
  4      , object_name => 'SALES_HISTORY'
  5      , policy_name => 'FGA_LARGE_ORDER'
  6      , audit_condition => 'TOTAL_COST > 10000'
  7      , audit_column => NULL
  8      , handler_schema => NULL
  9      , handler_module => NULL
 10      , enable => TRUE
 11      , statement_types => 'INSERT,UPDATE,DELETE,SELECT'
 12    );
 13  END;
 14  /

PL/SQL procedure successfully completed.
```

If we set the audit_condition parameter to NULL, then the audit will always occur. As with many of the conditional examples we've seen so far, you can use application context namespace attributes, Oracle SQL built-in functions on the column values in the data record, as well as your own custom PL/SQL program units.

The statement_types parameter allows you to control the activation of the policy for specific SELECT or DML statements. The audit_column parameter is a comma-delimited list of the table's columns that are considered sensitive. This option allows you to specify that auditing occurs when both the sensitive column(s) are queried and the Boolean condition is met. If no condition is specified, the auditing occurs only when the sensitive column is queried or manipulated. In our example, the TOTAL_COST column contains sensitive data. In our human resources examples, we might only be concerned about the SSN column from the HR.EMPLOYEES table. The point is you can define FGA policies that do not fire if the user is querying or updating nonsensitive columns.

In the preceding example, if you query the SALES_HISTORY table as shown in the following example, you can observe the audit record that is generated on line 19 in Figure 12-3.

```
sec_mgr@db12cr[sales]> CONNECT sh@sales
Enter password:
Connected.
sh@db12cr[sales> SELECT product, total_cost
  2  FROM sales_history
  3  WHERE total_cost > 10000;

PRODUCT                         TOTAL_COST
------------------------------- ----------
LCD TV                               12500
Plasma TV                            12000
LCD TV                               12500

3 rows selected.
```

Acting on the Audit

FGA enables you to invoke an event handler using the handler_schema and handler_module parameters. In TA, the records are written as they occur, but there is no guarantee that they will be viewed and subsequently acted upon in a timely fashion. Suppose, for example, that the DBA leaves at 6:00 P.M. Friday night and a hacker begins to poke around the system 10 minutes later. Finally, on Sunday afternoon the hacker has gathered enough information to do something destructive. The audit records were being generated while the hacker was updating the system, but unfortunately no one was around to monitor the audit trail. This is like having a burglar alarm for a remote cabin in the woods that no one hears. The DBA returned Monday to a compromised database. It would have been nice if the DBA was alerted when the hacker was compromising the system.

With FGA, you do have the ability to invoke an event handler. In this manner, you can see FGA as analogous to a SELECT trigger. The event handler can do anything you like, because you write the code. One thing the event handler should not do is to write (redundant) audit data to a private audit table. We have seen this countless times, as people fail to realize that the audit data is already being written. A variation of the theme is a good idea: you may find it useful to write the audit data to another database or to the file system in hopes of protecting the data from a malicious and privileged database administrator.

The event handler is a PL/SQL procedure that has the following signature:

```
PROCEDURE handle_proc (
, object_schema VARCHAR2 -- the schema of the object being audited
, object_name VARCHAR2   -- the name of the object being audited
, policy_name VARCHAR2   -- the name of the auditing policy
) AS ...
```

Within the procedure, you can easily access any application context as well as the SQL that caused the audit event to occur. You can obtain the SQL by referencing the USERENV attribute named CURRENT_SQL. You could then use standard Oracle PL/SQL network communication packages such as UTL_TCP, UTL_HTTP, or UTL_SMTP to send an alert message to an external system that will route the message to the appropriate person(s). Refer the script named fga_alert.sql in the examples that are included with this book for a simple example.

Although the audit provides a wealth of information, it does not tell you what the user received as a result from the query. You only know that they successfully issued the query. In addition, note that audits don't occur when no query records are returned.

Audit Storage, Audit Retention, and Reporting

Once you have defined your audit policies, you have to decide how long to retain your audit trails, a concept called "retention." Audit retention policies are usually driven by compliance regulations and laws that govern states, provinces, and countries in which you may conduct business. Most entities require that multiple years of audit data be available electronically.

You also need to consider how you will provide audit reporting on your databases to corporate security officers and compliance auditors. Audit reporting requirements will be impacted by your audit retention requirements, and vice versa.

Oracle Audit Vault

If you run a large enterprise with many databases, the best approach is to use Oracle Audit Vault (AV) to centralize the collection of audit trails for both reporting and retention. You push audit trails to AV on a scheduled basis so that they can be removed from the source system as soon as possible.

AV is not limited to Oracle Database audit trails. AV includes a REDO LOG Collector component that allows you to capture and report on old and new values for columns in your tables. AV can also collect audit trails from third-party databases and operating systems, and includes a software development kit (SDK) that enables you to collect and report on any audit or log data.

AV performs audit reporting and retention from a central location. This approach has many advantages, including the following:

■ AV reduces the management complexity and resource consumption compared to reporting from individual servers.

■ AV frees up space required for audit retention processing on individual servers.

■ AV allows you to perform audit reporting and alerting on the combined view of your enterprise, which might uncover abnormal behaviors of employees or system intrusions across the enterprise.

■ AV is built as a data warehouse so it is optimized for reporting and alerting.

This combined view can include database audit trails, operating system audit trails, and the audit trails from a number of additional audit sources supported by AV. AV provides audit reduction reporting with comprehensive data summarization, filtering, and drill-down features. Audit reduction enables you to look at summarizations of audit data, generally based on dimensions such as time, user, or source, so that you can quickly locate audit data of interest and drill down to great levels of detail when required. AV can also perform alerting and notifications based on audit reduction. There is no native audit reporting and alerting feature in Oracle Database.

If you do not plan to use AV, it is important that you determine where the audit data resides within both the OUA and TA in your databases. In addition, you must determine the capabilities available to manage the life cycle audit trails under both options to manage audit retention and meet regulatory compliance. You will also need to develop a custom strategy for reporting and alerting if you choose not to use a product like AV. For smaller organizations, you can get by with tools such as SQL Developer using custom SQL scripts to conduct this type of reporting. At some point, you should consider the rationale and costs associated with building and maintaining a custom audit solution compared to the cost savings and value you achieve by purchasing AV, because AV provides audit collection, retention, reporting, and alerting.

Audit Trail Retention Under OUA

The OUA audit trail is maintained in a schema named AUDSYS. This schema is protected by the database kernel in a number of ways. First, no one, not even accounts with SYSDBA, can directly query data or modify data in the tables owned by this schema. You cannot even DESCRIBE the tables in this schema. The read-only view named UNIFIED_AUDIT_TRAIL is the only way to view the audit data. Second, you cannot log in to the AUDSYS account, even if the account is unlocked.

MSA occurs in OUA when the database is being started or when the database is mounted but not open. OUA will write auditable events under these conditions to operating system files in the $ORACLE_BASE/audit/$ORACLE_SID directory. This file-based audit trail will be loaded into the OUA audit trail when the database is opened or when the PL/SQL procedure DBMS_AUDIT_MGMT.LOAD_UNIFIED_AUDIT_FILES is called.

To archive audit data under OUA, you need to have a process to archive and then delete the data in the UNIFIED_AUDIT_TRAIL view on a scheduled basis. First, you must create an archive table based on a simple example policy of archiving anything older than the last two days:

```
sh@db12cr[sales]> CONNECT sec_mgr@sales
Enter password:
Connected.
sec_mgr@db12cr[sales]> -- How many records in the audit trail
sec_mgr@db12cr[sales]> SELECT COUNT(*) FROM unified_audit_trail;

  COUNT(*)
----------
       758

1 row selected.

sec_mgr@db12cr[sales]> -- How many records in the audit
sec_mgr@db12cr[sales]> -- trail from before 2 days ago
sec_mgr@db12cr[sales]> SELECT COUNT(*) FROM unified_audit_trail
  2  WHERE event_timestamp < TRUNC(SYSDATE-2);
```

```
  COUNT(*)
----------
       116

1 row selected.

sec_mgr@db12cr[sales]> -- Create a table with audit trail
sec_mgr@db12cr[sales]> -- records that are older than 2 days
sec_mgr@db12cr[sales]> SET SERVEROUT ON
sec_mgr@db12cr[sales]> DECLARE
  2          l_save_before DATE := TRUNC(SYSDATE-2);
  3          l_suffix      VARCHAR2(10) ;
  4   BEGIN
  5     l_suffix := TO_CHAR(l_save_before,'YYYY_MM_DD');
  6     EXECUTE IMMEDIATE
  7       'CREATE TABLE unified_audit_trail_' || l_suffix
  8       || ' AS SELECT * FROM unified_audit_trail'
  9       || ' WHERE event_timestamp < '
 10       || ' TO_DATE(''' || l_suffix || ''',''YYYY_MM_DD'' )';
 11     DBMS_OUTPUT.PUT_LINE('Create table unified_audit_trail_' || l_suffix);
 12   END;
 13   /
Create table unified_audit_trail_2014_07_25

PL/SQL procedure successfully completed.

sec_mgr@db12cr[sales]> -- Verify we've created the right number of records
sec_mgr@db12cr[sales]> SELECT COUNT(*) FROM unified_audit_trail_2014_07_25;

  COUNT(*)
----------
       116

1 row selected.
```

At this point, you could use Oracle Data Pump to export the table unified_audit_trail_2014_07_25 to disk and transfer it to your archive location. Next, you use the DBMS_AUDIT_MGMT.SET_LAST_ARCHIVE_TIMESTAMP PL/SQL procedure to set the last archive timestamp, and then use the DBMS_AUDIT_MGMT.CLEAN_AUDIT_TRAIL PL/SQL procedure to delete audit records from the OUA audit trail that are older than the archive timestamp:

```
sec_mgr@db12cr[sales]> BEGIN
  2     DBMS_AUDIT_MGMT.SET_LAST_ARCHIVE_TIMESTAMP(
  3         audit_trail_type  => DBMS_AUDIT_MGMT.AUDIT_TRAIL_UNIFIED
  4       , last_archive_time => TRUNC(SYSTIMESTAMP - 2)
  5       , container         => DBMS_AUDIT_MGMT.CONTAINER_CURRENT
  6     );
  7   END;
  8   /

PL/SQL procedure successfully completed.

sec_mgr@db12cr[sales]> SELECT COUNT(*) FROM unified_audit_trail;
```

```
   COUNT(*)
----------
       760

1 row selected.

sec_mgr@db12cr[sales] > BEGIN
   2     DBMS_AUDIT_MGMT.CLEAN_AUDIT_TRAIL(
   3         audit_trail_type          => DBMS_AUDIT_MGMT.AUDIT_TRAIL_UNIFIED
   4       , use_last_arch_timestamp => TRUE
   5       , container               => DBMS_AUDIT_MGMT.CONTAINER_CURRENT
   6       );
   7   END;
   8   /

PL/SQL procedure successfully completed.

sec_mgr@db12cr[sales] > SELECT COUNT(*) FROM unified_audit_trail;

   COUNT(*)
----------
       647

1 row selected.

sec_mgr@db12cr[sales] > SELECT TO_CHAR(MIN(event_timestamp),'YYYY-MM-DD')
   2     FIRST_DATE
   3   FROM unified_audit_trail;

FIRST_DATE
----------
2014-07-25

1 row selected.
```

At this point, audit trail records that are more than two days old have been deleted. You can use the DBMS_AUDIT_MGMT.CREATE_PURGE_JOB PL/SQL procedure to automate the execution of the DBMS_AUDIT_MGMT.CLEAN_AUDIT_TRAIL procedure based on a number of hours to rerun the cleanup. Refer to Chapter 29 of the *Oracle Database PL/SQL Packages and Types Reference* documentation for more information on creating, dropping, enabling, and disabling this purge process.

Audit Trail Retention Under Traditional Auditing

With TA, the complete audit trail will be composed of text files (.xml, .aud) on the operating system under the $ORACLE_BASE/admin/<SID>/adump directory and tables in the database. If the AUDIT_TRAIL parameter is set to some form of database audit retention, you will find audit data in the SYS.AUD$ or SYSTEM.AUD$ table for TA and OLS audit records, SYS.FGA$ for FGA audit records, and DVSYS.AUDIT_TRAIL$ for DBV audit records.

The example to archive and clean the OUA applies to TA as well. The DBMS_AUDIT_MGMT PL/SQL package supports setting the last archive timestamp and clean routine for audit trails such as SYS.AUD$, SYS.FGA$, XML audit files, and .aud audit files for MSA.

You must write routines to schedule the collection of operating system audit records under the $ORACLE_BASE/admin/<SID>/adump directory for transfer to your archive location (a feature is provided by AV). The PL/SQL procedure DBMS_AUDIT_MGMT.SET_AUDIT_TRAIL_PROPERTY has routines to set the maximum age of these files before a new one is created so that your files are rotated on a chronological basis, much like the UNIX syslog facility. Harvesting audit files on the operating system and transferring them to an archive location is important to avoid system administrators tampering with these files. If you are using TA, we recommend that you leverage Oracle DBV to protect the database-resident audit trails from unauthorized access or modification, because it can provide similar protections to the way that the AUDSYS schema is protected under OUA.

Reporting on Database History

One question that is often raised after a security incident is, "Can we determine what information a person may have seen at a certain date and time?" The answer to this question is easily provided with the use of the Oracle Flashback Data Archive (FDA) feature, also known as Oracle Total Recall (OTR) in earlier versions of Oracle Database. With FDA, you simply create a FLASHBACK ARCHIVE with the appropriate tablespace storage and retention policy parameters. Then you specify the FLASHBACK ARCHIVE clause in the CREATE TABLE or ALTER TABLE statement for your sensitive tables, as shown in the following example:

```
sec_mgr@db12cr[sales]> CONNECT sys@sales AS SYSDBA
Enter password:
Connected.
sys@db12cr[sales]> -- Create the Flashback Archive
sys@db12cr[sales]> CREATE FLASHBACK ARCHIVE
  2   DEFAULT sales_archive TABLESPACE sales
  3   QUOTA 1G RETENTION 5 YEAR;

Flashback archive created.

sys@db12cr[sales]> -- Enable the use of FBA
sys@db12cr[sales]> -- on the SALES_HISTORY table
sys@db12cr[sales]> ALTER TABLE sh.sales_history
  2   FLASHBACK ARCHIVE sales_archive;

Table altered.
```

Once your tables are set up to use FDA, you can query them at any time by adding the AS OF clause to the SELECT statement, as shown in the following example:

```
SELECT * FROM sales_history
AS OF TIMESTAMP TO_TIMESTAMP('2014-06-15 16:00:00'
                 ,'YYYY-MM-DD HH24:MI:SS');
```

You can also flashback the table's data to the state of the table before it was modified by an **ALTER TABLE** command (column modifications for example) or **TRUNCATE TABLE** command. FDA also provides a convenient mechanism to DELETE and restore specific records in a table using the SELECT.. AS OF syntax.

You can purge FDA using the **ALTER FLASHBACK ARCHIVE** command with either the PURGE BEFORE TIMESTAMP or PURGE BEFORE SCN clause. Refer to Chapter 16 in the *Oracle Database Development Guide* for more details on how to configure FDA and tables that use FDA.

Summary

Auditing is not prevention; it is detection. Auditing is a complementary part of the security process. Prevention and access control will always be important in security. However, auditing should not be overlooked. Providing the detection and response capabilities can be equally, if not more, important. Effective auditing is critical to ensuring that performance and the value received from auditing are balanced.

OUA, TA, and FGA provide a powerful and secure way to ensure user accountability. Both OUA and TA allow for auditing to occur in many different ways to meet many different requirements. FGA augments this and allows for a higher fidelity in auditing, which reduces the number of extraneous audit records. The FGA event handler can be used to incorporate real-time alerts and notifications for customers that are concerned about cybersecurity attacks. The overall auditing capability in Oracle Database acts as both the detection and response system.

Database auditing provides high auditing assurance, because the auditing process cannot be circumvented or bypassed. Auditing is consistent regardless of application, query, user, and protocols being used to access the data. When done correctly, auditing can provide valuable information about users and their interactions with the database. Oracle has a declarative auditing capability that does not require you to write code to have a comprehensive audit policy.

We recommend you leverage Oracle Audit Vault in your enterprise, versus trying to build and maintain a custom system with similar features. AV provides centralized collection, retention, reporting, and alerting for a variety of existing and custom audit trail formats. Attempting to reproduce this capability to comply with regulations or laws would simply not make good business sense.

CHAPTER
13

An Applied Approach to Multitenancy and Cloud Security

I n this chapter we pull together all of the concepts and technologies included in this book. We give you a pragmatic approach to building a secure database system in a multitenant architecture. This approach can also be used for a standalone database system storing your company's important information.

We realize that not all systems need all security capabilities described in this chapter or in this book. The important thing to keep in mind is that you must apply as much security as required by the compliance or regulation standard that you are trying to achieve. This might sound obvious at first, but there is no reason to apply all security features described here or additional security features if they are not required. Doing so may give you a false sense of security and may make the overall system unnecessarily harder to manage, which might cause an administrator to remove security features or weaken the system.

For example, if the standards you are trying to meet do not require complex 15-character passwords, don't use them. Using them on a system where they are not required can make it difficult for an administrator to remember passwords, tempting him or her to write down the passwords and store them in an unsafe location. This type of policy impact clearly makes the system more vulnerable than using a password length and complexity that the administrator can remember.

You should also keep in mind that the approach to database security is often a matter of implementing multiples layers of security, similar to a multilayered bulletproof vest with an iron backing plate—the projectile might penetrate a couple layers of the vest, but the projectile will ultimately be stopped and doesn't make its way through to the intended target. Some people think of this multilayered approach to security as the "security onion," in which an intruder may peel back one layer but will find another layer preventing his advance. The point is that not one layer of security is good enough, but all the layers of security have a compounding effect that make the overall system security extremely strong and resilient.

System Baseline and Configuration

Getting into the details of facilities, infrastructure, and personnel are above and beyond the scope of this book. However, these topics do have a direct impact on the overall security posture of your system and they must be addressed. These areas should receive the same amount of due diligence and scrutiny applied to them as you apply to securing your database system. We present the following information to get you thinking about security from a holistic perspective.

Facility and Infrastructure Security

The first part of building a secure system is ensuring that the foundational elements of your system are secure. You must determine how secure the facilities are where your system will operate.

Facility Security

You must use physical security controls for the campus, building, and datacenter where the system will run and require that redundant power and cooling systems are in place to ensure the availability of your system.

As the security architect, you should ask questions such as the following:

- How are people granted access to the campus or site where your computers are located? For example, is there a badging system or security officer controlling access to the site?

- Are campus visitors required to show identification? Is the visit audited, and is there an approval process for campus visits?

- Are there physical security controls to the buildings in which the computers are running? For example, is there a badging system or security officer controlling access to the building?

- Will the servers be located in a server room with limited access? Does the room require badge access or require a second person to gain access?

- Are procedures in place to remove site, room, and system access when employees leave or are terminated?

- Will the servers reside in a locked rack cage, or will other projects' equipment be co-located in your rack?

- Are controls in place to audit who has keys or who was given keys to access the rack cage?

- Are protocols in place to inventory and track all computer equipment that enters and leaves the facility?

- Will the systems run on building power or a redundant uninterruptible power supply (UPS) system?

The security concern with facilities is the unauthorized physical access to your servers. Unauthorized physical access could allow an unauthorized person to take a data drive and walk out of the datacenter undetected, or a person could reboot your server with a bootable device (such as a USB or CD-ROM) and gain access to the server's contents. The focus of facility security is on identifying and securing the physical or industrial dependencies that you require to operate your system in a secure manner.

The following National Institute of Standards and Technology (NIST) documents can help you understand and implement a number of physical and environment security controls:

- *Guide to General Server Security*, http://csrc.nist.gov/publications/nistpubs/800-123/ SP800-123.pdf

- *A Recommendation for the Use of Personal Identity Verification (PIV) Credentials in Physical Access Control Systems (PACS)*, http://csrc.nist.gov/publications/ nistpubs/800-116/SP800-116.pdf

Additional documents on a number of security-related topics are available from NIST and can be accessed from the following web site: http://csrc.nist.gov/publications/PubsSPs.html. These documents provide guidance on how to create and organize plans to implement some of the recommendations we make in this chapter.

Infrastructure Security

Infrastructure is the next area that you should baseline—that is, you should know what services are being provided to you that your system requires. What services do you depend on to operate your system and in a secure manner? As the security architect you should ask questions like the following:

- How are Domain Name System (DNS) and Network Time Protocol (NTP) services configured for availability, scale, and accuracy?
- What is the capacity and availability of the network?
- What type of firewall and/or intrusion detection system (IDS) protects your system, and/or will your system be connected directly to the Internet?
- Are backup and recovery services provided in the datacenter? How are backups protected? Who has access to the backups?
- What is your continuity of operation plan (COOP)?

The focus of infrastructure security is on identifying and securing the dependent services that are required to operate your system in a secure manner and ensuring that you have an understanding of the service level agreement (SLA) between each service and your company/project.

Personnel Security

Hiring or working with the right personnel is a complicated area of security. We realize that in an idyllic work environment you would get along perfectly with all of your colleagues and there would be no politics or job security concerns. However, this rarely is the case, and because of this, we suggest a process of background checks, security awareness training, and audit monitoring of all personnel. You may also develop security-specific questions to ask during the interview: "Is it OK to allow other users to use your account?" or "Do you grant access to administrative accounts without going through the formal process?"

The phrase "if he was hit by a bus" used to get a lot of play when managers would ask "Who else can administer the system…?" The focus of personnel security is on identifying and delegating administrative knowledge required for operating your system in a secure manner.

No single person on the team should have *exclusive* and intimate knowledge of the system so that if that one person did not work on the project, the overall security of the system would be in jeopardy—that is, no single person should own all network switches or hardware boot passwords, and so on. In addition, we recommend writing down passwords only if the passwords are in a log book stored in a secure container with controlled access.

It is also important to develop a secure termination process. You should be concerned with issues like the following:

- Have the dismissed employee's assets been returned?
- What is the process to clean and reuse his equipment?
- Have the employee's accounts been removed?
- Have the employee's badges, keys, and similar items been returned and deactivated from the perimeter access control system?
- If the employee had administrator accounts, have the administrator account passwords been updated?

Configuration Management

Configuration management (CM) is an important and relevant security topic, but to cover this subject with sufficient depth and focus is beyond the scope of this book. We do recommend having a formal CM plan or step-by-step procedures for security-relevant actions such as the following:

- Adding or removing hardware to or from your system
- Installing and patching software
- Adding or removing users to or from your system
- Changing security policy configuration

The important point here is that you have a documented process that all administrators are required to follow for any action on or to your system that has the potential to make a security-relevant change. The process should be vetted with your administrative and information assurance teams. To help develop and organize your CM plan, we recommend using the *Guide for Security-Focused Configuration Management of Information Systems,* at http://csrc.nist.gov/publications/nistpubs/800-128/sp800-128.pdf.

Equipment

As part of your CM process, you should develop a secure process to connect hardware to your network/system. The process should resemble something like this:

- Ensure that the latest firmware is installed and tested on the hardware.
- Install the operating system and immediately patch it with the latest patches.
- Encrypt all disk drives during operating system installation.
- Lock down the system to secure it from unauthorized access. (We will describe this process later in the chapter in the section "Locking Down Your System.")
- Install/update virus protection.
- Install an IDS.
- Collect a checksum listing the security-relevant configuration files on each machine in the system. (We will describe this process later in the chapter in the section "Monitoring and Alerting.")

You should follow these procedures for all equipment added to your network. Furthermore, we recommend that you follow the current trends in cybersecurity with regard to vulnerabilities and misconfigurations using the following resources (this is not a complete list):

- **Oracle's Critical Patch Updates, Security Alerts, and Third Party Bulletin Security Alerts** www.oracle.com/technetwork/topics/security/alerts-086861.html
- **MITRE's Common Vulnerabilities and Exposures (CVE) Database** http://cve.mitre.org/index.html
- **National Vulnerability Database (NVD)** http://nvd.nist.gov
- **Symantec Security Response** www.symantec.com/security_response

Hardware Address	IP Address	Interface	Server	Location
00:21:28:45:05:B2	10.196.212.13	eth0	proddb01	Rack 1/23u
00:21:28:44:D6:1E	10.196.212.15	eth0	proddb02	Rack 1/29u
50:3D:E5:DB:21:3F	10.196.212.45	eth0	prodsw01	Rack 7/40u
...	...	...	...	...

TABLE 13-1. *Datacenter Hardware Inventory*

The point of periodically monitoring these types of sites is to keep you aware of security-related issues that may affect your system's security posture and to help you understand how to mediate the risks associated with these issues.

Hardware Inventory

As part of your CM process, we suggest keeping track (via Oracle table, text file, CSV, and so on) of all hardware that is connected to or that interacts with your system. Keeping track of hardware is an important function in a secure system—you should know about each piece of hardware on your network or connected to your system. When issues arise, you are often presented only with a MAC address of an offending system or, if you are lucky, a machine name, which is enough information to start a forensic analysis of the issue.

Table 13-1 illustrates the minimal components of an inventory database.

If you observe abnormal behavior coming from a server on your network, the inventory database will become invaluable to help you locate the server in question and take further action.

Secure Virtualization

As much as consolidation and virtualization have consumed the marketing in the IT profession recently, secure operating system virtualization has somewhat trailed behind. Issues concerning security in a virtualized environment have been published in resources such as the CVE database we mentioned. Vendors are quick to respond to these CVEs, but you should still research the virtualization technologies that you are considering against some of the vulnerability databases we introduced earlier.

In a virtualized environment, the hypervisor is the software that runs a virtual machine (guest). If you are going to use virtualization, you must first determine if you are going to use one of the following types of hypervisors:

- Type 1, which runs on bare metal as the operating system on the server. Oracle VM Server for SPARC or Oracle VM Server for x86 are examples of Type 1 hypervisors.

- Type 2, which runs on top of the host operating system. Oracle VM VirtualBox is an example of a Type 2 hypervisor.

If you need to virtualize your system's environment, you should consider other security and operational factors such as these:

- Is the hypervisor compatible and supported with Oracle Grid Infrastructure Services and Oracle Real Application Clusters?

■ Will the hypervisor provide the same database performance characteristics as other hypervisors available or running the database on an operating system that is running on bare metal?

■ Does the hypervisor allow the guest virtual machine access to the Trusted Platform Module (TPM), if required for hardware authentication? Some hypervisors do not allow guests to access all underlying hardware features because either the hypervisor does not have the kernel/driver code to support the feature or the hypervisor considers the feature a security threat.

Oracle recommends and supports using Oracle VM Server for Oracle Database.

Operating System

The next security area you must address is the operating system. Choosing an operating system can involve evaluating multiples of variables such as these:

■ Is the database software compatible with the operating system? The following Oracle support site provides a list of operating systems to Oracle product certifications: https://support .oracle.com/epmos/faces/ui/certify/CertifyHome.jspx.

■ Can you find trained administrative staff for the operating system?

■ Is your operating system choice being dictated to you by your customer?

Oracle Database is most commonly used on the Linux, Solaris, and Windows operating systems. You can secure these operating systems using a number of lockdown procedures in the standards we discuss later in this chapter in the section "Locking Down Your System." Oracle Enterprise Manager Cloud Control (OEMCC) includes a number of operating system security checks in the Compliance Management feature that we describe in the section "Monitoring and Alerting."

Consider the following when locking down the operation system:

■ User and administrative accounts: Some operating systems allow for the conversion of an account to a group or role, and we recommend you do this for common accounts such as oracle and root.

■ Password policies

■ Pluggable Authentication Module (PAM) and console authentication policies

■ Networking configuration and who can change this configuration

■ File permissions, especially any setuid file permission sets

■ Kernel parameters

■ OS auditing

For more information regarding the operating system lockdown checklist, see http://docs.oracle .com/cd/E37670_01/E36387/html/ol_checklist_sec.html.

Oracle Solaris

Oracle Solaris 11 is considered the standard for secure operating systems. There has been much written about Oracle Solaris, and it has proven itself time and time again during compliance evaluations. Oracle Solaris 11 is certified under the Canadian Common Criteria Scheme at Evaluation Assurance Level 4 (EAL4). EAL4 is the highest level of evaluation recognized by 26 countries under the Common Criteria Recognition Arrangement (CCRA) (www.commoncriteriaportal.org).

Oracle Solaris natively supports a fine-grained role-based access control (RBAC) model and fine-grained privilege profiles that can be used to protect your database installation and provide separation of duty (SoD) for the administration of the installation. Refer to *Oracle Solaris 11 Security Guidelines* (http://docs.oracle.com/cd/E23824_01/html/819-3195/index.html) for more information regarding securing Oracle Solaris. The following is a good reference for how Solaris provides security in a multitenant environment: *Secure Database Consolidation Using the SPARC SuperCluster T4-4 Platform* at www.oracle.com/technetwork/server-storage/sun-sparc-enterprise/documentation/o12-087-1878511.pdf.

Oracle Linux
Oracle Linux with Unbreakable Enterprise Kernel (UEK) is the most reliable and secure Linux operating system for Oracle products. At first glance, that statement might sound like a couple of Oracle employees (authors) making a superlative argument for Oracle Linux. Although that might be true, it is also true that UEK is part of Oracle's contribution to the open source community.

As you may know, Oracle takes the Red Hat Linux distribution and updates/fixes issues found while testing against Oracle software. These updates/fixes are known as the Unbreakable Enterprise Kernel (UEK), which helps to ensure that Oracle software runs as reliably and securely as possible. See the *Oracle Linux Security Guide for Release 6* (http://docs.oracle.com/cd/E37670_01/E36387/html/index.html) for more information regarding configuring Linux security policies.

Jobs, Users, Groups/Roles, and Privileges
We espouse some general guidelines regarding securing administrative accounts that are applicable to the operating system and to the database. Typically, you are not creating end user OS or DB accounts; rather, you are creating and managing privileged OS and DB administrative accounts. You should apply several security-related concepts while designing and implementing a secure strategy for managing these accounts. Least privilege, separation of duties, and maintaining the integrity of the audit trail should be at the forefront of your design considerations.

Jobs
You should decouple the concept of functional job from role. Jobs allow you to abstract the duties of an administrator from the privileges needed to complete his or her job. For example, for databases administration, we often fall victim to granting roles and not the specific privileges to complete a job, such as GRANT CONNECT, RESOURCE to SGAETJEN so that SGAETJEN can complete his work.

You should also think in terms of the temporal, or time-related, aspects of a job. For example, does SGAETJEN need only the role RESOURCE to set up his schema objects? Can you remove this role after his schema is set up?

You should take the time to identify jobs and the associated privilege(s) or tool(s) needed to complete each job as we have done in Table 13-2. This effort requires you to think, and in some cases rethink, how each privilege is being used. From a security perspective, your goal is to determine how each job can be accomplished with the fewest number of privileges.

Job	Role/Function	Tool/Privilege
Backup administrator	Backup and recover	Oracle Recovery Manager (RMAN)
Database administrator	Create database account	CREATE USER
Operating system administrator	Create OS account	/usr/sbin/useradd
…	…	…

TABLE 13-2. *Job Breakout Worksheet*

Oracle Database 12*c* now has a READ object privilege and READ ANY TABLE system privilege for SELECT statements. The difference between SELECT and READ object privileges is that the SELECT object privileges allow for querying the table and for SELECT…FOR UPDATE. The READ object privilege allows only querying the table. Granting the READ object privilege allows you to guard against malicious and accidental DoS attacks by users or applications accidently locking the table and disrupting operations.

User Accounts

An important security-related aspect of OS and database administration is that each administrator should have an account—that is, you should not allow shared accounts. Although this might seem obvious at first, in reality this is almost never implemented or enforced. For example, you should not allow multiple administrators to access or use a shared account such as the oracle account. The security issue here is that if a user knows that multiple administrators are using a shared account such as oracle, then an administrator can feel a certain amount of anonymity when using the account. Furthermore, it may be impossible to reconcile audit entries and changes to the system to a specific user because the user's identity is not maintained with the use of the shared account. You should strive for an audit trail that identifies a specific user per audit event.

If the operating system provides the capability to convert user accounts to groups/roles, we recommend removing the ability to connect to the server as a shared account such as the oracle account. A more secure and better audited system requires an administrator to "SSH" to a server with his or her credentials, and then SSH to the server using a shared account such as oracle and perform actions. It is harder to determine "who did what" if you allow a shared account.

Managing multiples of named end users on multiples of systems is susceptible to misconfiguration, over-privilege, and human error. Depending on the size of your architecture and the number of systems you have to manage, you might consider a centralized account management system that can save time and money of administrative tasks, eliminates misconfigurations, and in general makes the system more secure by eliminating human error. The operating systems on which Oracle Database runs all support external authentication from a LDAP directory server, and we recommend you use this feature for all named end user accounts.

Nonrepudiation

To further understand the importance of the "one user to one account" principle, you must understand the implications and effect of being about to tie actions to users. Repudiation is a legal term that means "someone is trying to deny the truth," as in "I didn't remove data from the audit trail."

Nonrepudiation means that you have system in place with proper authentication, integrity, and proof of the origin of data so that you can assert that "User Frank removed data from the audit trail." Clearly, if a situation occurs in which an insider is performing nefarious activities on your system, you should seek legal counsel; however, having a well-established one-user-to-one-account plan will aid in securing the integrity of the audit trail, and, moreover, it will aid in any legal action that ensues.

The use of properly configured Network Time Protocol (NTP) services in your environment ensures that the audit trails will hold up in court. You must properly establish the date and time of all actions, with no discrepancies, if multiple audit trails will be used as evidence.

Privileges

As you review the jobs that need to be performed on the system, you should evaluate each privilege and ask yourself this question: "Does this user need this privilege to perform the duties of this job all the time or some of the time (for example, the privilege is only required during installation)?"

If the answer is all of the time, then the job must keep the privilege. However, if the answer is some of the time, then we recommend granting the privilege (i.e., CREATE TABLE) to the job/role to allow for installation, then revoking the privilege and verifying that the privilege has been revoked after installation is complete.

Unless your application requires it, there is no reason that a production account should have privileges (i.e., CREATE TABLE), which allows for the creation, removal, and modification of schema objects. Removing excess or unneeded privileges helps reduce if not eliminate certain types of DoS attacks.

Operating System Roles/Groups

Some operating systems allow changing an OS account to a role or group account—that is, you can change the OS account oracle from a user account to a group in Solaris. Doing so removes the ability to connect to the server as the oracle user, which offers security benefits. In addition, if you create named administrative accounts, then all actions taken on the system will be clearly identified as coming from a named user account.

Oracle Privileged Account Manager (OPAM)

Oracle Privileged Account Manager (OPAM) is a server-based password repository designed to generate and manage passwords for privileged or administrative accounts. OPAM is made up of an Oracle Fusion Middleware application running on an Oracle WebLogic Server. OPAM uses the Oracle Platform Security Services (OPSS) framework as a security foundation and Oracle Database as backend data storage. Oracle's Integrated Connector Framework (ICF) connectors link OPAM to external sources such as databases and operating systems.

OPAM is part of Oracle's integrated Identity Governance platform, which provides user provisioning, deprovisioning, self-service, approval workflow, risk-based, business user–friendly identity certification, and advanced role life-cycle management. OPAM enables you to escrow administrative passwords such that you can check them in and out of the OPAM database. Figure 13-1 illustrates, for example, that user DRING has checked out the password for the operating system account that owns the Oracle software.

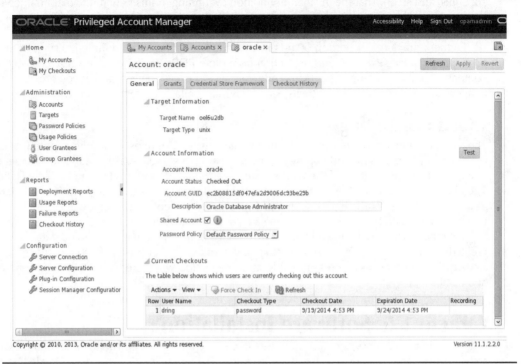

FIGURE 13-1. *OPAM privileged account checkout status*

Oracle Database 12c Multitenancy and Cloud Computing

Oracle Database 12c has hundreds of new features, and one new feature in particular, *consolidation*, has a significant impact on the current trends in IT industry. Oracle Database 12c *multitenancy* is a more secure and better performing consolidation approach than any existing consolidation or virtualization approach that exists today. Multitenancy offers a new architectural approach to consolidation that lessens the amount of redundant management overhead to operate multiples of database systems. One of the major axioms of consolidation is all about doing more with less. Multitenancy enables you to pack more databases running on the server with less resource consumption than existing consolidation strategies.

One of the first questions IT professionals ask when they are presented with new technology is, "What do I have to change in my existing application to use the new technology?" The great thing about the multitenant framework is that you don't have to change your application in order to use it.

The second question that is typically asked is, "How do you guarantee that other tenants of the multitenant database do not have access to my data?" There are multiple answers to this question, as you may have picked up on from previous chapters, but the best answer lies in the fact that each pluggable database (PDB) has its own master TDE key, OLS policy, DBV policy, user accounts, and so on. That means that, in addition to running in this new multitenant framework, you can apply the same security features to the PDB that you would have applied to databases prior to Oracle Database 12c.

Furthermore, a major portion of the Oracle kernel code has been modified to support the concept of instance isolation and protection from other PDBs. In a similar way, OLS protects the contents of a table by labeling data and allowing you to access only data that you are authorized to access, and the Oracle kernel treats each PDB in a similarly protected manner.

Cloud Computing

The *cloud computing* model can be defined in many ways. We refer to cloud computing as a dynamic way to provision and deploy an operating system and database to a machine or set of machines. The combination of the Oracle Enterprise Manager product stack and Oracle Database 12c allows you to provide Infrastructure as a Service (IAAS) for the operating system and Platform as a Service (PAAS) for the database in a private cloud. The deployment of the platform to the machine is either to bare metal or by using a type of virtualization.

We recommend deploying a locked-down image of the operating system and database created as an appliance. Doing so ensures that you maintain a consistent secure deployment strategy that removes, as much as possible, user interaction when creating the operating system and database.

Oracle 12c Software Installation

In this section we discuss how to install the Oracle software securely. The location of the Oracle software installation is known as the "Oracle Home." As with previous versions of Oracle Database, with version 12c you can create one or more databases from the Oracle Home. Oracle Database 12c also allows for each container database (CDB) to manage multiple PDBs.

Security-Related Installation Prerequisites and Installation Options

Following are security-related recommendations for database installation:

- Read all of Oracle's installation prerequisites.

- Identify the latest Patch Set Update (PSU) from the My Oracle Support (MOS) site before installation and plan to apply this patch set after installation. Security-related one-off patches may be available as well.

- Map SYS% privileges to OS groups (see Chapter 2) and create these groups for use in your installation.

- Establish strong passwords for system and feature accounts before installation.

- Configure the security notifications feature during the installation.

- Ensure that you have backup storage available (for database backup/recovery) before you begin the installation.

- Use GIS and RAC for high availability of your database.

- If you have OEMCC installed, configure the database to integrate with OEMCC for monitoring, patching, and so on.

Choosing the Number of Oracle Homes

Each Oracle home can have multiple CDBs, and each CDB can manage multiple PDBs (currently Oracle supports 256 PDBs per CDB). Typically, you should need only one Oracle Home. However, you may have multiple Oracle Homes if you have tenants that do not want to be affected by other tenants' outages. If you are using Oracle RAC, you may be able to apply patches in a rolling manner and not incur an outage (this is dependent on the type of patch). Keep in mind that all CDBs and corresponding PBDs running from Oracle Home are patched together. That is, if tenant A runs into an issue and needs a patch, then tenant B running from the same CDB/Oracle Home must take an outage while the Oracle Home binaries are patched.

The converse point to this argument is also true, in that having a single Oracle Home has the advantage of needing only one set of Oracle binaries, which outweighs the argument against a single Oracle Home.

Securing the Oracle Home

The oracle OS account typically owns the Oracle binaries, and we recommend keeping this convention. We also recommend locking the account so that administrators are not authorized to connect to the server as the account (ssh) or authorized to become the oracle user (su).

Oracle Home File Integrity

We also recommend using file integrity monitoring software such as AIDE (Advanced Intrusion Detection Environment; see http://aide.sourceforge.net) for Linux or BART (Basic Auditing and Reporting Tool) for Solaris to verify that files in the Oracle Home have not changed. If you don't use file integrity software, then at the very least, you should use a script such as the following to traverse the Oracle Home and generate an MD5 inventory of all files:

```
[oracle@nsgdc2 ~]$ cd $ORACLE_HOME
[oracle@nsgdc2 dbhome_1]$ for file in `find . -type f`
> do
>     echo `ls -al $file; md5sum $file | awk '{ print $1}'`
> done
. . .
-rwxr-x--x 1 oracle dba 629289 Jul 31 2014 wrcO 1acf02602bb6e9c8ba7b29923af11bbb
-rwsr-s--x 1 oracle dba 323762482 Jul 31 2014 oracle 0dc94a6fd69134c2798a84852b4095e7
-rwxr-x--- 1 oracle dba 0 Jul 31 2014 ctxlcO d41d8cd98f00b204e9800998ecf8427e
. . .
```

If you later find an issue or you want to verify that nothing has changed in your Oracle Home, you can reference the MD5 inventory for verification. Also, you can set up an OS scheduler job using crontab or similar to scan the files periodically in your Oracle Home and verify that the files haven't changed and still have integrity.

For Linux or Solaris systems, we recommend removing "other" or "world" access from Oracle files. If you have your ORACLE_BASE environment variable set, then you would issue the following command:

```
[oracle@nsgdc2 ~]$ cd $ORACLE_BASE
[oracle@nsgdc2 oracle]$ chmod -R o-rwx *
[oracle@nsgdc2 oracle]$
[oracle@nsgdc2 oracle]$ ## If you are not using OFA
[oracle@nsgdc2 oracle]$ ##   then also issue the following command
[oracle@nsgdc2 oracle]$ cd $ORACLE_HOME
[oracle@nsgdc2 dbhome_1]$ chmod -R o-rwx *
```

Are You Still Secure?

It is important that you develop an independent verification process and run it periodically to check the security integrity of your system. You should set up an OS cron job or an OEMCC scheduler job to run your security integrity scripts based on AIDE or BART to verify file and directory permissions and checksums. You can leverage the OEMCC compliance feature and configuration feature to verify that your database configuration is still locked down and maintains the same security posture that it did from the start.

Securing the Listener

Oracle Listener is the listener service that accepts client socket connections and instantiates or directs the connection to a server process. Consider the following when securing Oracle Listener.

- Change the default port from 1521 to an available port.
- Configure SSL for connections.
- Consider valid node checking (TCP_VALIDNODE_CHECKING).
- Consider using Oracle Connection Manager (CMAN) to multiplex database connections; access control through source, destination, and hostname filtering; and so on. You can find more information on CMAN at www.oracle.com/technetwork/database/enterprise-edition/cman-overview-084817.html.
- If you are using external procedures, you can now configure the extproc agent to run as a specific operating system user instead of using the privileges of the listener user or the Oracle server process by using the DBMS_CREDENTIAL package.

Managing Passwords

Storing passwords in unencrypted files or embedded in an application is not secure and should be avoided. Oracle provides a couple ways to manage accounts and passwords in a secure manner. Depending on the number of systems you are managing, you can use either an Oracle wallet or Oracle Key Vault.

NOTE
You can find an example that demonstrates this approach in the script named 13.password.mgmt.txt in the example scripts available with this book.

As we discussed in Chapter 12, you should use the Secure External Password Store feature of the Oracle wallet for applications running in the middle tier that connect to the database (such as connection pools, ingestion).

Secure Database Initialization Parameters

Oracle Database 12c comes with secure initialization parameters values; however, if you are using an earlier version, you might want to ensure that the initialization parameter values are as follows:

Parameter	Secure Default Setting
07_DICTIONARY_ACCESSIBILITY	FALSE
SEC_RETURN_SERVER_RELEASE_BANNER	FALSE
SEC_MAX_FAILED_LOGIN_ATTEMPTS	3
UTL_FILE_DIR	
REMOTE_LOGIN_PASSWORDFILE	SHARED
REMOTE_OS_AUTHENT	FALSE
REMOTE_OS_ROLES	FALSE
GLOBAL_NAMES	TRUE
SQL92_SECURITY	TRUE
RESOURCE_LIMIT	TRUE
OS_AUTHENT_PREFIX	
AUDIT_SYS_OPERATIONS	TRUE
OS_ROLES	FALSE
O7_DICTIONARY_ACCESSIBILITY	FALSE
AUDIT_TRAIL	XML,EXTENDED

This listing is not meant to be a complete listing. Use a complete checklist from the database lockdown information provided in the section "Standards for Lockdown."

Installing and Securing Your Application

At this point you are ready to install and secure your application in the database, which means that you need to create application-specific tablespaces, users/schemas, schema objects, and so on.

Sensitive Data Discovery

You must first determine where sensitive data exists in your database in order to define database security policies. If you have a small data model with a limited number of well-known and understood tables or you are absolutely sure you know where your company's sensitive data is stored in your data model, you can skip to the next section. If you are unsure where your company's sensitive data is stored or you are using a third-party application that has a complex or nonobvious data model, then we recommend running OEM Sensitive Data Discovery to locate sensitive data.

You can choose from multiples of existing data formats, such as 15- or 16-digit credit card numbers, 9-digit US formatted Social Security numbers, and so on. Refer to Chapter 8, where we discussed and demonstrated the identification of sensitive data. Note that OEM contains several formats of known sensitive data. However, your sensitive data might not match a known format. With OEM, you can create a new search format based on your sensitive data structure.

You can use the results of the OEM Sensitive Data Discovery tool to help scope the effort to define policies for account management, data access, encryption and auditing that we discuss in the remainder of this chapter.

Account Management

In Chapter 2 we discussed account management, and we expressed the importance of creating accounts, keeping in mind separation of duties (SoD) and least privilege. In Chapter 10 we expanded on the concept of a database administrator to maintain a secure SoD account model.

We discussed four general types of database accounts:

- Privileged Administrators/SYS% accounts
- Schema accounts
- Non-person entities (NPE) or batch program accounts
- Named user accounts

Each account created in your database should be categorized as one of these types of accounts and validated with Table 13-2. In other words, each account should be created with a specific, well-defined purpose. If an account exists in your system that doesn't get used or is never accessed, you should consider removing it.

Local Database Accounts vs. Enterprise Accounts

We recommend that you manage named end user accounts using a centralized LDAP directory, such as Oracle Unified Directory (OUD), and integrate the directory with the Enterprise User Security (EUS) feature of Oracle Database. This approach is discussed in detail in Chapter 3. We understand that if you are creating a system with one or two databases, then creating administrative accounts local to the database makes financial and administrative sense; however, if you have a system with tens or hundreds of databases and are managing them with tens or hundreds of administrative and end user accounts, then the investment in a centralized management system makes sense. Managing users in a centralized manner helps to ensure privilege and administrative consistency throughout your enterprise.

Database Profiles

Often an underused security feature of an Oracle Database is the database profile. As we discussed in Chapter 2, database profiles provide many security-relevant controls on user access and resource consumption. One specific aspect of the database profile is password management. We recommend not only using a complex password function (PASSWORD_VERIFY_FUNCTION), but also setting FAILED_LOGIN_ATTEMPTS, PASSWORD_LOCK_TIME, and so on, to be consistent with the operating system and the compliance or regulation standard that you are trying to achieve. (Note that user accounts are automatically assigned the profile DEFAULT unless otherwise indicated. Refer to Chapter 2 for more details on database profiles.)

We recommend creating profiles based on the different types of database accounts in your system. For example, you might have an administrative profile ADMIN_PROFILE that uses a strong password verify function (that is, this profile might require that passwords are fifteen characters long with multiple special characters and numbers), and a USER_PROFILE (which might require that passwords are eight characters long with one special character and one number), which might have IDLE_TIME (2 minutes) limits that differ from those of a CONN_POOL_PROFILE (1 hour).

Oracle Database 12*c* now uses a SHA-512 cryptographic hash to generate the 12*c* password verifier hash digests. Also, the DBMS_CRYPTO package now supports SHA-256, SHA-384, and SHA-512 hash digests.

Privilege Management

When creating a secure system, your focus on privilege management should be on least privilege and nonrepudiation. Not too many years ago, it was commonplace for database administrators to grant the CONNECT and RESOURCE database roles to a newly created database account. DBAs did not put much thought into the specific privileges contained in these roles, and, more importantly, DBAs did not put much thought into "What is the purpose of this new account?" and "What specific privileges are needed to accomplish the job?"

Least Privilege

CONNECT and RESOURCE database roles are examples of a top-down approach to privilege management. It's not that this approach is wrong, but we recommend using a bottom-up approach by creating your own database roles and scrutinizing each privilege added.

For example, if an account needs to connect to the database, we recommend creating an application-specific role (for example, SALES_CONN) and granting the single system privilege CREATE SESSION to the role, and then granting the role to the account. Furthermore, if you need to create tables, we recommend that you create a role SALES_DDL and grant the role the privilege CREATE TABLE.

Recall our discussion of the privilege analysis in Chapter 4. The point of this effort is to require you to evaluate every privilege granted to each user to determine if the user really requires the privilege to do his or her job.

Separation of Duties

Your next move is to protect your schema objects from the database administrator. Recall that SYS and other database administrator accounts that have the SELECT ANY TABLE privilege have access to your application tables. A secure way to protect your application data tables is to use DBV.

We recommend creating a DBV realm for your schema and a DBV realm for your custom database roles. The DBV schema realm should contain all of your schema objects (tables, views, and so on) and should have end user roles or end user accounts listed as participants of the realm. The DBV roles realm should contain all your application-specific roles, with an administrator of your choosing as the realm owner. The realm owner is the only account that is authorized to GRANT or REVOKE application roles.

Data Access Controls

As a result of running Sensitive Data Discovery, OEM has identified the tables that contain sensitive data. You must now determine how you are going to protect them. As you have read in previous chapters, Oracle provides several mechanisms for labeling and protecting your data. Your choices for protecting your data depend on the compliance or regulation standards that you are trying to achieve.

We recommend using statement-level DBV command rules, as we demonstrated in Chapter 10, to control specific commands. We also recommend using row- or column-level policies to protect sensitive data.

We recommend using RAS to protect data as discussed in Chapter 6. RAS provides a declarative security model that is intuitive to configure and manage. RAS also conforms to the strictest compliance standards and is based on the VPD security foundation that Oracle has included since Oracle Database 8*i*. We recommend using VPD for pre–Oracle Database 12*c* systems as discussed in Chapter 7.

Protecting Your Company Intellectual Property

You are now ready to secure your company's intellectual property, which means installing your data model and any proprietary code required to run your system. Oracle recommends using DBV for high assurance security to protect your intellectual property or proprietary PL/SQL. Oracle considers the PL/SQL OS command wrap a low assurance-security utility (see http://docs.oracle .com/database/121/LNPLS/wrap.htm#LNPLS016). However, the wrap utility will obfuscate PL/SQL code, making the code unreadable by an overly curious DBA querying text from DBA_SOURCE.

Oracle OS Wrap Utility

The Oracle OS wrap utility takes two parameters: iname or input file name, and oname or output file name. The following is an example of the wrap utility:

```
wrap iname=mySourceFile.sql oname=myWrappedFile.plb
```

After running the wrap utility, load the myWrappedFile.plb into the database in the same manner that you would load the original source file.

Oracle PL/SQL Wrap Utility

Oracle also provides the same obfuscation functionality in the DBMS_DDL PL/SQL package as the OS wrap utility. The following is an example of using DBMS_DDL to create a wrapped PL/SQL procedure. Note that GENERATE_PACKAGE_DDL is a procedure that you create to reconstruct the PL/SQL source you are interested in obfuscating.

```
DECLARE
    v_wrapped_text VARCHAR2(32767);
BEGIN
    v_wrapped_text := GENERATE_PACKAGE_DDL(...);
    DBMS_DDL.CREATE_WRAPPED(v_wrapped_text);
END;
/
```

We recommend using both the wrapping technique and DBV to protect the schema that stores the PL/SQL objects, with the understanding that there have been many attempts to "unwrap" Oracle's PL/SQL obfuscation capability. Consequently, you should not rely solely on the wrap utility as a way of protecting your company's intellectual property.

Network Access Control Policy

If you are using TCP-based callouts from the database (UTL_HTTP, UTL_TCP, UTL_FTP, and so on) you must define an access control list (ACL) policy. The DBMS_NETWORK_ACL_ADMIN PL/SQL package enables you to define a security ACL policy for TPC-based callouts. Refer to Chapter 10 in the *Oracle Database PL/SQL Packages and Types Reference* for a description of the DBMS_NETWORK_ACL_ADMIN PL/SQL package and for examples on configuring network access security policies.

Database Firewall

Oracle Database Firewall (DBFW) can be considered a first line of defense for your production database system. DBFW intercepts and parses the SQL grammar of issued commands before they are run against your production system. You can set up active or passive monitoring, alerting, and blocking of offensive commands (such as DROP TABLE, CREATE USER, and so on). DBFW has proven to be highly effective in stopping unauthorized SQL traffic before it reaches the database. Furthermore, a key factor of using DBFW is that it can be integrated into your system without requiring you to modify your application or augment your system data flow.

We recommend using DBFW in systems where you are integrating with legacy applications that weren't written to perform user input validation or processing. That is, if the application provides a "text edit box" or allows for URL rewrites and so on to be passed directly to the database, then the system might be susceptible to SQL ingestion attacks. Figure 13-2 illustrates setting up a DBFW policy to alert on unknown DML, DDL, PL/SQL, and so on, from affecting the SALES_HISTORY table.

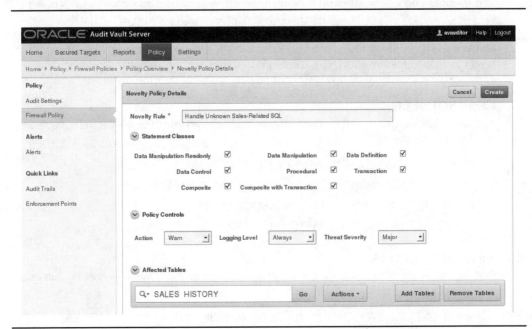

FIGURE 13-2. *DBFW alerting on unexpected SQL on the SALES_HISTORY table*

Data Encryption

Encryption is all about integrity and confidentiality. Integrity of data means that the data has not been changed by an unauthorized user in transit (over the network), while traversing up or down the OSI stack, in memory, or at rest (on disk). Confidentiality of data means that the data is not accessible by an unauthorized user. We recommend using encryption in transit and at rest whenever possible.

Oracle provides two types of encryption: network data encryption and integrity, and SSL encryption. Refer to Chapter 13, "Configuring Network Data Encryption and Integrity," and Chapter 18, "Configuring Secure Sockets Layer Authentication," in the *Oracle Database Security Guide 12c Release* documentation for more detail. We provide a synopsis of how to install and configure each in the following sections.

Network Data Encryption and Integrity

Oracle network data encryption and integrity was previously known as "native encryption." Oracle network data encryption and integrity is now part of Oracle Database and does not require an additional license to use. To use native encryption and integrity, however, you must update the $ORACLE_HOME/network/admin/sqlnet.ora file for both the client and server. You must restart the listener(s) on the server for these changes to take effect.

Prior to Oracle Database 12c, encrypting data in transit or "over the wire" required you to purchase the Oracle Advanced Security Option (ASO). Oracle Database 12c has included this option in its core database product, so you are no longer required to purchase ASO to encrypt data as it moves to and away from your database. We strongly recommend using encryption, from end user to application server, from application server to the backend database server, and, if applicable, to and from any system the application or database server communicates with. This includes encrypting data as it is being retrieved by your backup system, as it is being copied to your COOP system, or as any external system accesses data stored in the database.

The justification is in tools such as Wireshark (www.wireshark.org) and other packet capture and analysis tools. These tools have become more sophisticated in interpreting Oracle's native protocol (SQLNET, known as TNS packet in Wireshark) and the associated payload data. It is now a trivial task to capture and view unencrypted data traveling over the network.

Client SQLNET.ORA

Add the following entries to the client's sqlnet.ora file to enable Oracle's network data encryption and integrity checking:

- SQLNET.CRYPTO_CHECKSUM_CLIENT=REQUIRED
- SQLNET.CRYPTO_CHECKSUM_TYPES_CLIENT=(SHA256)
- SQLNET.ENCRYPTION_SERVER=REQUIRED
- SQLNET.ENCRYPTION_TYPES_SERVER=(AES256 and so on)

Server SQLNET.ORA

Add the following entries to the server's sqlnet.ora file to enable Oracle's network data encryption and integrity checking:

- SQLNET.CRYPTO_CHECKSUM_SERVER=REQUIRED
- SQLNET.CRYPTO_CHECKSUM_TYPES_SERVER=(SHA256)

- SQLNET.ENCRYPTION_SERVER=REQUIRED
- SQLNET.ENCRYPTION_TYPES_SERVER=(AES256, and so on)
- SEC_USER_AUDIT_ACTION_BANNER=auditWarning.txt
- SEC_USER_UNAUTHORIZED_ACCESS_BANNER=unauthorizedAccess.txt
- SQLNET.CLIENT_REGISTRATION=<unique client ID>

Encryption of Data at Rest

In Chapter 11 we demonstrated that by using simple operating system tools, such as the strings tool, and having access to the Oracle datafile, you can see text strings stored in the Oracle binary datafile. Although this works for character data, Oracle also publishes the technical specification on how it stores numbers, dates, and so on. You should therefore assume that all data can be retrieved by accessing the Oracle datafile.

Because TDE encrypts data after the SQL layer and before the data is written to disk, we strongly recommend installing TDE and encrypting all tablespaces. If your hardware uses a hardware security module (HSM), TDE can take advantage of the key management and accelerated cryptography such that the impact to performance is negligible.

Oracle Key Vault

The Oracle wallet works well with small-scale systems that do not require lots of keys; however, when your architecture requires multiple keys for multiple servers in a large-scale distributed architecture, you might consider using a tool that aids in key management.

Oracle Key Vault (OKV) manages keys similar to how OUD manages EUS users. You can manage users in a database, but then you have multiple databases running throughout your architecture. You are trying to keep administrative access in sync, and it is much easier to accomplish this with a centralized user manager tool such as OUD. Similarly, OKV manages keys from a centralized database, making provision, rotation, and expiration more controlled and consistent across the enterprise. For more on OKV, refer to the OKV section at the Oracle web site www.oracle.com/us/products/database/security/key-vault/overview/index.html.

OKV centralizes key management in a secure manner, and it can be not only integrated into applications connecting to the database, but it can enroll and provision server endpoints (such as operating systems, switches, and so on). OKV manages the key life cycle from creation and rotation to expiration. It also audits access to keys and key changes. The following are some of the capabilities of OKV:

- Centralizes key management in a secure manner for the enterprises
- Manages the key life cycle: creation, rotation, and expiration
- Easily enrolls and provisions endpoints
- Audits access to keys and key life cycle changes
- Provides a reporting and alerting system
- Separates administrator duties
- Supports primary and standby databases
- Supports the OASIS Key Management Interoperability Protocol (KMIP) standard

OKV is easy to install and use. Following is a summary of the steps for integrating PKV with TDE:

1. Define and register the endpoint under the Endpoints menu option. An endpoint is a name that you provide to describe the system you are registering with OKV (such as PROD_CDB, TEST_CDB, and so on). You provide the name, the type (Database, Wallet), and the platform (Linux, Solaris, and so on).

2. For Oracle Database type endpoints, create a wallet under the Keys And Wallets menu option.

3. Grant access to the endpoint to read, modify, and manage the wallet.

4. Enroll the endpoint and download the okvclient.jar file.

5. Transfer the ovkclient.jar file to the database server.

6. Install the OKV client and the OKV server-specific configuration file in ORACLE_BASE or ORACLE_HOME by running

   ```
   $ORACLE_HOME/jdk/bin/java -jar okvclient.jar -d /home/oracle/okvutil -v
   ```

7. Become root and run the root.sh file located at /home/oracle/okvutil/bin/root.sh. This will install the Oracle-supplied hardware security module (HSM) libraries to /opt/oracle so that TDE can use KMIP to communicate with OKV.

8. Update the sqlnet.ora with

   ```
   ENCRYPTION_WALLET_LOCATION=(SOURCE=(METHOD=HSM))
   ```

9. Connect to the DB as SYS and verify the registration is complete by issuing the following:

   ```
   select * from gv$encryption_wallet;
   ```

10. Follow the steps in Chapter 11 to open the wallet and create/use the master keys in the root container and the PDBs.

Figure 13-3 illustrates OKV managing encryption keys and wallets from the root CDB and the HR PDB.

Encryption of Backup Data

Backup files provide not only access to production data, but more importantly, to someone trying to gain access to unauthorized data, the files do not require the enforcement of security, auditing, and other protection mechanisms used on the active system. For this reason, we recommend encrypting your backups and storing them in a secure location.

RMAN supports encrypted backup sets, but the ASO is required. RMAN offers the following backup encryption modes:

- **Transparent Encryption** Uses the Oracle wallet for password and keys
- **Password Encryption** Requires a password to create and restore the backup
- **Dual Mode Encryption** Requires either the wallet or a password to create and restore the backup

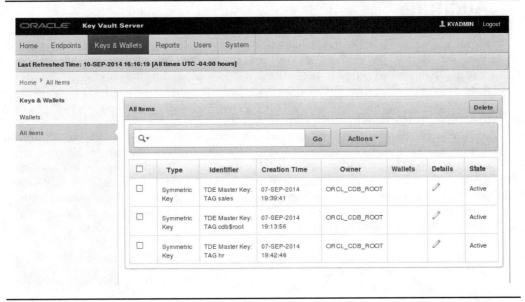

FIGURE 13-3. *OKV key and wallet management*

You can run the following query to determine which encryption algorithms are available for RMAN to encrypt your backups:

```
sys@db12cr[cdb$root]> SELECT algorithm_name
  2  FROM v$rman_encryption_algorithms;

ALGORITHM_NAME
----------------------
AES128
AES192
AES256

3 rows selected.
```

Wallet-based encryption is more secure than password-based encryption, because no user input of passwords is involved in wallet-based encryption; this means that you don't have to transmit the password to a remote location to use the encrypted backup. You do need to transmit wallets securely to your remote location and keep the wallets in a separate location from your backup sets, however. Also, keep in mind that if you are using TDE and your data is encrypted, you don't necessarily need to use RMAN encryption because the data is protected by TDE.

Auditing

Auditing often goes overlooked, not for its security significance, but for the relevance of securing the integrity of audit data or the audit trail. Security practitioners often indicate that an event needs to be audited (for example, audit all failed login attempts), but they overlook the importance of establishing limited access to audit data and strictly controlling the providence of audit data. After all, how do you prove that an event happened if there is no trace or audit record of the event? Attackers understand this principle and often perform action(s) against your system and then try to cover up their actions by removing audit trail data.

You should think of audit data as "read-only" data. That is, once the audit record is recorded, that information should never change. You need to establish a clear chain of custody. If an event occurs, the audit logs are often used in legal proceedings to prove or disprove the association of the action to a person or an account. Auditing is about detection. Every action undertaken by a user on your system should be associated to that user. You should not allow users to SSH to a server using a group account (such as oracle, root, and so on). The amount of auditing or the extent to which you audit will depend on the compliance or regulation standards that you are trying to achieve.

As we described in Chapter 12, we recommend using Oracle's Traditional Audit (TA) capability and, if SQL statement bind values are required, Oracle's Fine-Grained Audit (FGA) capability against your application tables. Also from Chapter 12, we recommend using Oracle's unified audit trail to aid in the management and reporting of audit data that originates from different database sources.

Oracle Auditing

We recommend that you audit your production tables, views, and other elements of your production schema. Keep in mind that auditing is only as good as the ability to tie the audit record to a specific user. So the audit trail must have the end user's identify stored in either the CLIENT_IDENTIFIER or the USER of the audit record.

Oracle Traditional Auditing (TA)

You shouldn't need to create, alter, or drop objects in your production schema, but if you find that your application needs these privileges because it dynamically creates and drops objects, then we recommend using the ON DEFAULT audit capability. The ON DEFAULT clause establishes the default audit options for objects that are subsequently created—one less thing the DBA has to worry about or remember.

For example, if we wanted our system always to audit on ALTER, AUDIT, FLASHBACK, GRANT, INDEX, LOCK, and RENAME of every object created, we could use the following AUDIT statement, setting them as the default audit options:

```
AUDIT ALTER, AUDIT, FLASHBACK, GRANT, INDEX, LOCK, RENAME ON DEFAULT;
```

Oracle Fine-Grained Auditing (FGA)

You may find that you need to use Oracle FGA if your compliance or regulation standards require its use. As we explained in Chapter 12, FGA enables you to refine the audit conditions, which helps reduce the number of superfluous audit trail records that do nothing more than to clog up the audit trail.

FGA also provides access to SQL statement bind variables. This is helpful if a well-designed application is trying to get the best performance from Oracle by preparing SQL statements and then adding the bind values during processing. The TA audit entry for this type of record will not show the bind values, and sometimes you need to know what the end user was looking for (that is, what is in the WHERE clause of the SELECT statement). If the application uses bind variables, this is not easily determined.

Oracle Audit Vault

Oracle Audit Vault (AV) offers the following features:

- Activity monitoring and blocking on the network combined with consolidation of audit data for Oracle, MySQL, Microsoft SQL Server, SAP Sybase, IBM DB2, and Oracle Big Data Appliance

- White list, black list, and exception list–based enforcement on the network

- Extensible audit collection framework with templates for XML and table-based audit data

- Dozens of built-in customizable compliance reports combined with proactive alerting and notification

- Interactive, PDF, and Excel reports

- Fine-grained source-based authorizations for auditors and administrators

- Highly scalable architecture to support a large number of databases with a high traffic volume

- Preconfigured software appliance for convenience and reliability

- External storage support for audit data repository and audit archives

We recommend using Oracle AV for medium- to large-scale audit systems where you are dealing with multiple systems with multiple audit trails. AV securely collects and stores the audit trail in a centralized database, which offers you a better analysis of what is going on in your entire system. You may need to review audit records from your RADIUS server or VPN server as well as logs from your network switching infrastructure to help determine how and where an unauthorized user accessed your system.

Figure 13-4 illustrates viewing AV audit trail reports for the HR and Sales PDBs. You can use the default AV policies or create your own based on your alerting requirements.

Figure 13-5 illustrates creating an AV policy alert. Again, you can see the flexibility and selectivity of AV as you choose the exact criteria in which you will be alerted.

Figure 13-6 illustrates the AV audit trail collection configurations.

Audit Life Cycle Management

Audit data takes up space (lots of space in a large enterprise system), and you need a way to manage all of that audit data. How long you need to keep audit data and the type of audit data you need to store depends on the governance and regulations that you are trying to achieve.

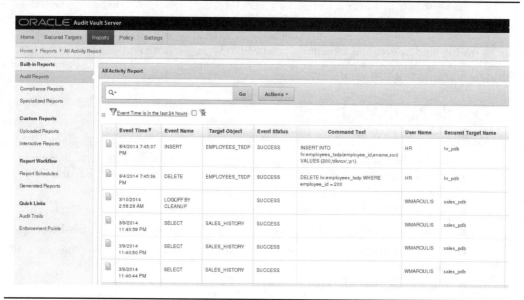

FIGURE 13-4. *AV audit reports from multiple audit trails*

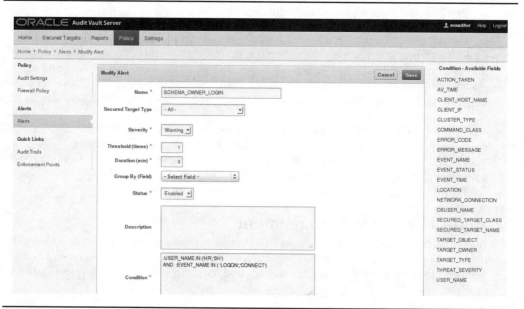

FIGURE 13-5. *AV policy alerts*

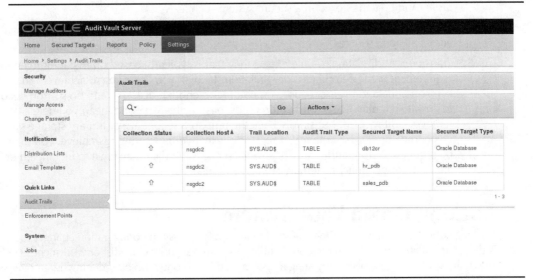

FIGURE 13-6. *AV audit trail collection configuration*

You must manage audit data, because it can consume your system resources if left unattended. It has been our experience that audit data progresses through the audit life cycle in the following five stages, also depicted in Figure 13-7:

1. *Create.* Audit sources are identified, and a mechanism is put in place to generate audit data.

2. *Collect.* A process is created to retrieve and, if necessary, parse and transform the raw audit data. You must identify the collection frequency from each audit source. Not all audit sources will collect audit data at the same frequency or at the same level of importance. For example, audit records collected on a badging system of employees entering and exiting a building might be collected and processed less frequently than attempted end user access to multiple applications on your system.

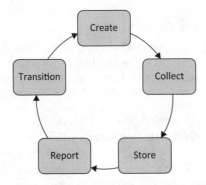

FIGURE 13-7. *Audit data life cycle*

3. *Store.* Audit data is stored in a secure system such as AV.

4. *Report.* Monitoring and alerting audit reports/queries are run to perform correlative analysis across all audit sources.

5. *Transition.* Audit data has a life expectancy that is typically based on the audit retention requirement of the compliance or regulation standard you are trying to achieve. You cannot keep audit data forever, because you don't have enough disk space to do so. You need to construct a plan to age off audit records/logs; by this we don't mean you delete or remove audit records, but simply back them up to a secondary or tertiary storage system. Depending on the governance or regulations that you are trying to achieve, you may be required to store audit data for several years. Audit data may have to be deleted or archived to secondary or tertiary storage and retained.

Locking Down Your System

Locking down a system is sometimes referred to as "applying system configuration changes to a default installation based on the recommendations from a security checklist or worksheet." Locking down the system is the process of getting a system ready for production by reducing or removing unnecessary packages and modules, accounts and privileges, network services, and so on that are not absolutely necessary to run the system. You should view every unnecessary account, package, module, or service as an opportunity for exploitation. The basic rule of thumb is "If you don't need it, remove it." Also consider, "If you need it, then who needs it and in what context do they need it?"

If you have not performed a lockdown process before, locking down the system will invariably "break" the system, or render it unusable for a number of scenarios. This is expected and is part of how you learn to lock down a system. In a lockdown, we assume the system has been previously operating with more privileges, packages, or processes than were necessary. We do not suggest locking down a development system, however, because development environments are typically very fluid in design and use. However, once you transition from development to a test system, we suggest you lock down the system so that you can verify that it still functions after being locked down.

Lockdown also introduces you to the world of separation of duties. For example, if you traditionally rely on the SYS database account to create and provision user accounts, then after lockdown, you should require two accounts to perform the function. One account is privileged enough to create the account but not provision it, and the other account is privileged enough to provision the account but not create it. As with using DBV for the first time, you'll find that it takes time to understand how standard operations are accomplished in a locked-down system.

Standards for Lockdown

How much you lock down a system will depend on the compliance or regulation standards that you are trying to achieve. You can either create your own standard or use an existing standard for locking down a system. We recommend using an existing standard, because several good documents and processes are in place to help you.

Defense Information Systems Agency (DISA)
Security Technical Implementation Guides (STIGs)

DISA has a good checklist for locking down your system (such as databases, servers, network, and so on). After you lock down your system, you run the DISA System Readiness Reviews (SRR) to determine whether your system complies with the lockdown standard. You can find more information on DISA STIG process at http://iase.disa.mil/stigs/Pages/index.aspx.

Oracle OEMCC STIG Standard

OEMCC contains more than 300 compliance standards for database and other related targets. You can choose to implement some or all of the standards. The following is a sample listing of a few select compliance standards, starting with Oracle Database standards:

- Basic Security Configuration for Oracle Database
- High Security Configuration for Oracle Database
- Patchable Configuration for Oracle Database
- Storage Best Practices for Oracle Database

And here are Oracle RAC standards:

- Basic Security Configuration for Oracle Cluster Database
- Configuration Best Practices for Oracle Real Application Cluster Database
- High Security Configuration for Oracle Cluster Database
- Patchable Configuration for Real Application Cluster Database
- Storage Best Practices for Oracle Real Application Cluster Database

For more information on the OEMCC compliance standards, visit the OEMCC site at http://docs.oracle.com/cd/E24628_01/doc.121/e36074/toc.htm.

If you are using OEMCC and have updated to OEMCC 12.1.0.5, Oracle now provides DISA STIG lockdown procedures and reporting capabilities. You can run reports from OEM to determine the security posture of your system, and, most importantly, you can take action as a result of the report. If you couple this capability with the OEMCC ability to schedule jobs and run them on an interval of your choosing, OEMCC can provide constant monitoring of your system.

Oracle Product Development is currently working closely with DISA to establish STIG detailed lockdown standards and reporting procedures specifically for Oracle Database 12c. DISA and Oracle are also working on similar efforts for Oracle operating systems (Linux and Solaris), Oracle middleware (WebLogic), and several hardware and software components that are used in Oracle Engineered Systems. We recommend you follow this activity in 2015 and beyond so you can take advantage of the combined DISA/Oracle research and development efforts to further secure your systems.

Oracle has a YouTube channel, "Oracle Learning Library," that walks through the process of using OEMCC to lock down a database using the DISA STIG process. You can find more information regarding the lockdown process at www.youtube.com/watch?v=E-RB-1G1EO8&feature=youtu.be.

Figure 13-8 illustrates OEMCC STIG security lockdown compliance status and reporting.

Other Lockdown Resources

The National Institutes of Standards and Technology (NIST) provides a good repository of security checklists and lockdown guides. You can find more information regarding NIST at http://web.nvd.nist.gov/view/ncp/repository.

The National Information Assurance Partnership (NIAP) Protection Profiles (PP) is a good resource for general purpose operating system and application-specific protection profiles. You can find more information regarding NIAP PP at www.niap-ccevs.org/pp/index.cfm.

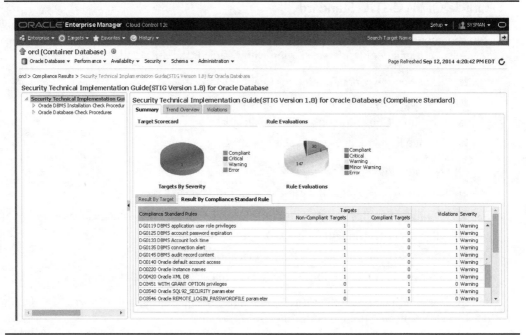

FIGURE 13-8. *OEMCC STIG security lockdown compliance status*

Secure Patching

Most malware operates on the premise that you (the administrator) are lazy or afraid of updating your system. Some malware works on the premise that you are not up-to-date on your patches. Malicious hackers love to find systems that are not patched, and there are treasure-troves of possibilities just waiting to be exploited. Tools such as Metasploit (www.metasploit.com/) assist malicious hackers in finding defects in software that is not patched or that is misconfigured.

Think about the following when you are applying patches:

- Where do you get your patches?
- If you apply patches annually or quarterly, what is your process to apply a one-off-patch?
- Did you get the SHA or MD5 checksum file and check the integrity of the file you downloaded?
- Are you running on a system that is not connected to the Internet?
- From which Internet site did you download your software? Did you check from which country the server is running?

These may seem like odd questions, but you might find that some compliance or regulation standards require a complete chain of custody for your software.

You are vulnerable during the patching process. You may or may not know or appreciate the extent to which a patch "unlocks" your system to be applied. To safeguard your system, you should create a process to apply a patch, which involves the following steps:

1. *Communicate that the system is being patched.* This not only notifies end users, but also tells system administrators that a new patch has been applied—this helps administrators add context to issues that might arise after the patch has been applied.

2. *Download the patch and associated checksum files.* The checksums of the patch files-based SHA or MD5 algorithms will be co-located with the patch on the web sites of reputable patch providers. Oracle Support provides a View Digest Details option for all downloads. The intent is to prevent man-in-the-middle attacks on your network that might modify the patch on download.

3. *Verify the checksum of the patch file.* Calculate the checksum of the downloaded patch file using utilities such as /usr/bin/sha1sum or /usr/bin/md5sum on Linux, and compare your results to the checksums reported by the patch's provider.

4. *Apply the patch to a test system.* Thoroughly test and verify that the system works as expected. You may be required to undo certain steps of your database or operating system lockdown procedures to apply a patch.

5. *Lock down the test system.* Reapply the lockdown procedures for the database and operating system. Use the OEMCC configuration comparison feature of the Lifecycle Management option to compare the new system configuration to a previously saved configuration. See http://docs.oracle.com/cd/E24628_01/em.121/e27046/config_mgmt.htm.

6. *Verify that the system works properly.* Do this before allowing users back on the system.

7. *Communicate that the production system will be patched.* If necessary, you should thoroughly communicate the fact that the system will be patched.

8. *Apply the patch to the production system.* As with the test system, the production system may need you to add privileges or unlock accounts to apply the patch. You may be required to undo certain steps of your database or operating system lockdown procedures to apply a patch.

9. *Lock down the production system.* Reapply the system lockdown and keep in mind that you should relock the DB and OS.

10. *Verify that the system works properly.* Do this before allowing users back on the system.

NOTE
It is common for IT professionals not to relock a system after a patch has been applied. They sometimes do not realize the extent to which a patch unlocks their system so that the patch can be applied.

Monitoring and Alerting

Monitoring and alerting are your "eyes" into what is happening on your system. The fact that an audit event happened loses significance if you are never made aware that the event occurred. For example, if you are auditing a Linux system for failed root SSH logins but you are not monitoring the /var/log/secure file, then you will not see the number of failed login attempts, the time of the events, and other information, which will prevent you from taking action to eliminate the threat.

If you do receive an alert, you can use the OEMCC configuration comparison feature of the Lifecycle Management option to investigate the details of any configuration changes that may have caused the alert to be raised. If you are not using Oracle AV, you could also use the Metric Extensions feature of OEMCC to create custom alerts based on database or operating system changes. The alerts that are raised offer a remediation workflow that enables you to track your alert investigation and resolution.

Monitoring Audit Events

We recommend setting up an alerting system such as Oracle AV to notify you of actionable audit events such as repeated failed login attempts, failed su or sudo attempts, failed connections to the database as SYS, and so on. Actionable audit events must be defined by your system and the type of attacks or security considerations you are monitoring. For example, you might not consider a failed root SSH login as an actionable audit event because you updated the /etc/ssh/sshd_config file and disallowed root from SSH-ing directly to the server (PermitRootLogin no).

If you receive an alert, you can use the OEMCC configuration comparison feature of the Lifecycle Management option to investigate the details of the change and determine why the alert was raised.

If you are not using Oracle AV, you can use the Metric Extensions feature of OEMCC to create custom alerts based on database or operating system changes. The alerts that are raised offer a remediation workflow that enables you to track your alert investigation and resolution.

We recommend that you review Chapter 11 of this book to determine what to audit. You should also review Chapter 10 to audit command rule violations and failed realm object access. We recommend that you secure and audit access to the init.ora parameters (ALTER SYSTEM) as we mentioned earlier. In addition, treat encryption key wallets, sqlnet.ora, Oracle password files, and other configuration files on the database servers with the same audit attention. In general, if your system depends on a DBV realm, OS file, and so on, for integrity, confidentiality, and availability, then you should audit actions against these components.

Abnormal Behavior and Tipoff Alerting

Abnormal behavior of a system is sometimes hard to quantify and often requires multiple data points to define. The goal of abnormal behavior is simple enough: "Tell me when someone or something is not using the system as intended." However, it may prove difficult to define normal behavior of your system depending on its size. The hard part is collecting enough information and, more importantly, the proper contextual information regarding an event to classify it as abnormal, especially if your system comprises many pieces of hardware, software, and services running in a distributed architecture.

System Monitoring Using OEMCC

OEMCC can create a report after monitoring the configuration and performance of the databases, operating systems, and other hardware and software components in your environment.

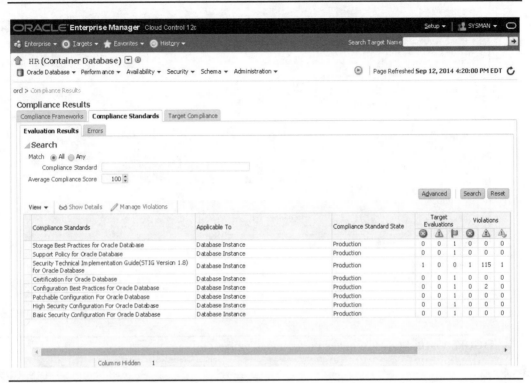

FIGURE 13-9. *OEMCC compliance monitoring*

Compliance Monitoring

OEMCC includes a number of configuration compliance frameworks and associated compliance standards, which can be used in the lockdown phase of your application release life cycle. Once you have applied these frameworks to an individual target (database, operating system, and so on), OEMCC will proactively alert you whenever the target violates a compliance standard. Figure 13-9 illustrates an OEMCC compliance report regarding the HR container database.

Performance Monitoring

Performance is important for many reasons, including system scale and growth and system responsiveness to meet service-level agreement (SLA) requirements. You should consider performance a part of security because it affects the system's overall availability. For example, if an attacker who wants to perform a DoS attack on your system realized that a five-table join without a valid join condition created a Cartesian product and effectively tied up all the system resources, he could successfully launch a DoS (see the next section for more on DoS). You can use technologies such as database resource profile groups, SQL*Net inbound and outbound connection timeout settings, connection limits and rate controls in the listener, and DBFW to help prevent these types of DoS attacks. You can use operating system profiling using SNMP traps/MIB information that feed information into a command and control system (such as OEMCC) to alert on the health and status of your database systems. Figure 13-10 illustrates OEMCC active performance monitor of the HR and SALES PDBs.

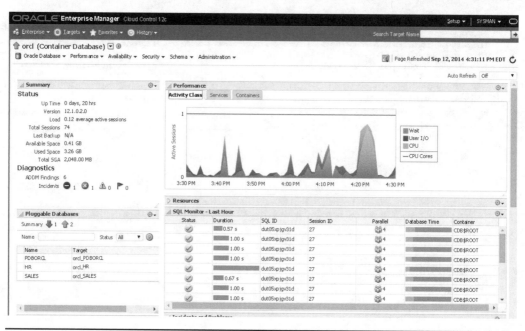

FIGURE 13-10.   *OEMCC active performance monitoring*

Availability, Backup and Recovery, and Continuity of Operations

Availability is an often overlooked area of security. Security practitioners get caught up in worrying about encrypting (protecting the integrity) and labeling (protecting the confidentiality) data, but they sometimes forget that availability is one of the three fundamental axioms of security (integrity, confidentiality, and availability).

Security practitioners also often neglect the importance of protecting backups. Backups are sometimes overlooked for having security value and are often not considered security relevant. However, nothing could be further from the truth. We will explain why in the following sections.

Availability is different from a Continuity of Operations (COOP) plan, which corresponds to your system's ability to recover from a catastrophic site or system failure. Also called Continuity of Government (COG), this topic may or may not be applicable to your organization, depending on the governance or regulations that you are trying to meet.

The necessity of a secondary site to maintain system availability should be justified by the costs that would be incurred by your company for being down or unable to perform normal business operations for a period of time. For example, if you are running a highly available RAC database system at your company's primary site in Chattanooga, Tennessee, and there is an outage to the power grid in Chattanooga, then your COOP procedures would be activated so that your system fails over to your secondary or backup site in Lake Tahoe, California.

A detailed discussion of the proper way to configure a COOP site is beyond the scope of this book; however, we recommend preparing your COOP site with as much security rigor as your primary site.

Availability

We typically think of availability as the amount of time the system can be used for normal operations. The system's availability is measured in the amount of usable uptime (that is, the system is 99.999% available). Conversely, there are many ways to make a system unavailable for use. One of the most common techniques is a DoS or distributed denial-of-service (DDoS) attack on your system. The goal of a DoS attack is to make the system unavailable for its intended use. Attackers often launch DoS attacks by trying to find the simplest way to make your system unavailable—by turning off the server, disrupting the DNS lookups your system requires, flooding your system with network traffic, and so on. Most basic DoS attacks should be addressed by your infrastructure and facilities teams, but having your database up and running is your responsibility.

Without having a plan to recover or continue operations after an attack, you might be particularly susceptible to DoS attacks. Depending on the amount of availability you are trying to achieve, you can choose from two approaches: active-passive or active-active system configuration.

Active-Passive Availability

We use the term "active-passive" to indicate that a single active system and a remote system are ready to become active at a moment's notice. There are many ways to achieve active-passive availability for a database system. It comes down to how much downtime you are willing to tolerate—or how much money your company is willing to lose while you are switching to the remote or failover system.

You might, for example, have a server running in a rack ready to go, or you might use Oracle Data Guard or Oracle GoldenGate to keep your remote system current. Depending on your budget and security requirements, you must decide which approach is right for your system. We recommend that the communication lines (to and from the remote site) and data (if it is stored on disk or transmitted over the network) always be encrypted.

NOTE
Explaining the variety of options and details of availability is beyond the scope of this book. For a good approach to building a highly available system using Oracle technology, we recommend the Oracle Database High Availability Overview documentation (http://docs .oracle.com/database/121/HAOVW/E49097-04.pdf). For more information on Oracle Data Guard, refer to the Oracle Data Guard Concepts documentation (http://docs.oracle.com/database/121/ SBYDB/E48552-05.pdf). For more information on GoldenGate, refer to the Oracle GoldenGate documentation (http://docs.oracle.com/cd/ E35209_01/doc.1121/e29397.pdf).

Active-Active Availability

Active-active availability addresses single instance failures, and as the name implies, it provides several systems that are running to sustain a single instance failure. We are not implying, however, that only two systems should be running with active-active availability. In fact, you can have multiple systems active by using Oracle RAC, which provides higher availability than active-passive systems with a standalone database. We therefore recommend RAC as part of your active system architecture and an active-passive configuration to provide COOP.

Backup and Recovery

Backups should be safeguarded with as much—if not more—protection as the active system, because an attacker can access data in a backup file without going through the system's authentication, authorization, and auditing control systems. Make sure that whichever backup and recovery tool you use has the ability to encrypt data at rest and data in transit.

Oracle Data Pump (Import/Export)

The Oracle Data Pump (ODP) utility provides a supplemental way to back up a schema or an entire database. We recommend using caution with Oracle Data Pump, however, because the extracted data sits in the OS with very little access or auditing controls, making it an easy target. If you find it absolutely necessary to use Oracle Data Pump, we recommend having a plan to address the proper handling and disposal of an export file; you should never leave it lingering unprotected in the OS. ODP can encrypt exports since version 11gR1, and we recommend using this feature if you are using ODP.

Oracle Recovery Manager (RMAN)

RMAN supports encrypted backups using encrypted communications. RMAN enables a full complement of backup options and recovery capabilities. We recommend setting up an RMAN recovery catalog, configuring and using encryption, and configuring your database system(s) to use RMAN as the backup system.

Backups of TDE tablespaces and columns are encrypted, so you should need to encrypt RMAN backups only if you are not using TDE.

NOTE
For more information on RMAN, refer to the Oracle Database Backup and Recovery User's Guide 12c Release 1 document, which can be found at http://docs.oracle.com/database/121/BRADV/E50658-04.pdf.

Summary

In this chapter we walked you through the process of creating a secure computing environment from a bottom-up approach. We have addressed everything from infrastructure to audit life cycle and have emphasized the application of security in a holistic manner. Although you may not be required to implement or use all of the ideas presented in this chapter, you should be aware of the security implications.

The most import aspect of security is to know your system's security requirements (such as PII, PCI, and so on), to ensure that they are incorporated into your design, development, and testing architecture from the start. It is common to see systems built in a vacuum without any applied security, only to fail when the system is secured and locked down.

We recommended starting with the foundation of the system—the infrastructure and facilities. You must understand what dependencies exist on external systems to provide system security. We explained that you have choices in how and where you install the Oracle software. You also have choices in how you consolidate your existing database systems.

We recommended spending time mapping all jobs that need to be performed to roles and privileges. This is an important effort not only for identifying the jobs for which your system requires privileges, but also for identifying the least amount of privileges required to perform those jobs. We also recommended securing your application with DBV realms and discovering and labeling your company's sensitive data. Furthermore, we recommended encrypting data in transit and at rest. Locking down and verifying the lockdown of the system is very important, because you should not rely on the system staying static.

And, most importantly, do not forget about auditing and availability with respect to securing your overall system. These two topics are the least addressed areas of security, and consequently they become the "low hanging fruit" for an attacker. Remember that the attacker's mindset is "How can I get the information that I am interested in with the least amount of effort, and how do I hide my tracks?"

Thank you for reading this book and we wish you secure computing.

APPENDIX

Sample Preparation Scripts

T his appendix describes the scripts that are used to set up the SALES and HR pluggable databases and security manager accounts (C##SEC_MGR, SEC_MGR) that are used in the examples contained in this book. These scripts can be downloaded from the Oracle Press web site at http://community.oraclepressbooks.com.

Sample Pluggable Databases

This section describes the creation of the SALES and HR pluggable databases. Once the pluggable databases have been created, you will want to update the file $ORACLE_HOME/network/admin/ tnsnames.ora to include an alias and address description for SALES, HR, and any other pluggable databases (PDBs) created in order to log in to these databases. If your connections fail with the following error, you are probably missing the required TNS alias:

```
ORA-12154: TNS:could not resolve the connect identifier specified
```

SALES Pluggable Database

Use the following scripts to create the PDB named SALES that is used in some of the samples contained in this book. Use the script Chapter2/appa.pdb.sales.asm.sql to create the PDB named SALES when using Oracle Automatic Storage Management (ASM) storage. The execution of this script is shown here:

```
sys@db12cr[cdb$root]> CREATE PLUGGABLE DATABASE sales
  2    ADMIN USER pdbadmin IDENTIFIED BY welcome1
  3    ROLES = (DBA)
  4    DEFAULT TABLESPACE sales;

Pluggable database created.
```

Use the script Chapter2/appa.pdb.sales.file.sql to create the PDB named SALES when using file system storage. Here's the execution of this script:

```
sys@db12cr[cdb$root]> CREATE PLUGGABLE DATABASE sales
  2    ADMIN USER pdbadmin IDENTIFIED BY welcome1
  3    ROLES = (DBA)
  4    FILE_NAME_CONVERT = ('/pdbseed/','/sales/')
  5    DEFAULT TABLESPACE sales;

Pluggable database created.
```

Human Resources (HR) Pluggable Database

Use the script Chapter2/appa.pdb.hr.asm.sql to create the PDB named HR when using Oracle ASM storage. The execution of this script is shown here:

```
sys@db12cr[cdb$root]> CREATE PLUGGABLE DATABASE hr
  2    ADMIN USER pdbadmin IDENTIFIED BY welcome1
  3    ROLES = (DBA)
  4    DEFAULT TABLESPACE hr;

Pluggable database created.
```

Use the script Chapter2/appa.pdb.hr.file.sql to create the PDB named HR when using file system storage. The execution of this script is shown here:

```
sys@db12cr[cdb$root]> CREATE PLUGGABLE DATABASE hr
   2    ADMIN USER pdbadmin IDENTIFIED BY welcome1
   3    ROLES = (DBA)
   4    FILE_NAME_CONVERT = ('/pdbseed/','/hr/')
   5    DEFAULT TABLESPACE hr;

Pluggable database created.
```

Sample Security Manager Account Creation

Use the following scripts to create the security manager accounts C##SEC_MGR and SEC_MGR used in some of the examples contained in this book.

Root Container

Use the script Chapter2/appa.cdb.secmgr.sql to create the C##SEC_MGR account used in the examples that execute in the root container. The execution of this script is shown here:

```
sys@db12cr[cdb$root]> CONNECT / as sysdba
Connected.
sys@db12cr[cdb$root]> -- drop the security manager role
sys@db12cr[cdb$root]> - and account if they exist
sys@db12cr[cdb$root]> DROP ROLE c##sec_mgr_role;

Role dropped.

sys@db12cr[cdb$root]> DROP USER c##sec_mgr CASCADE;

User dropped.

sys@db12cr[cdb$root]> -- create the security manager role and account
sys@db12cr[cdb$root]> CREATE ROLE c##sec_mgr_role ;

Role created.

sys@db12cr[cdb$root]> CREATE USER c##sec_mgr IDENTIFIED BY welcome1 ;

User created.

sys@db12cr[cdb$root]> -- grant security related privileges to the role
sys@db12cr[cdb$root]> GRANT c##sec_mgr_role to c##sec_mgr;

Grant succeeded.

sys@db12cr[cdb$root]> GRANT CREATE SESSION
   2 ,CREATE USER, ALTER USER, DROP USER
   3 ,CREATE ROLE
   4 ,GRANT ANY OBJECT PRIVILEGE, GRANT ANY PRIVILEGE, GRANT ANY ROLE
   5 ,AUDIT ANY
   6 ,CREATE ANY CONTEXT
   7 ,DROP ANY CONTEXT
   8 TO c##sec_mgr_role CONTAINER=CURRENT;
```

```
Grant succeeded.
-- for some of the SYS administrative privilege demos
sys@db12cr[cdb$root]> GRANT CREATE SESSION
  2  ,CREATE USER, ALTER USER, DROP USER
  3  ,SET OPERATOR, DBA
  4  TO c##sec_mgr CONTAINER=ALL;

Grant succeeded.
sys@db12cr[cdb$root]> GRANT SELECT ON sys.dba_objects TO c##sec_mgr_role
  2  CONTAINER=CURRENT;

Grant succeeded.

sys@db12cr[cdb$root]> GRANT SELECT ON sys.dba_tablespaces TO c##sec_mgr_role
  2  CONTAINER=CURRENT;

Grant succeeded.

sys@db12cr[cdb$root]> GRANT SELECT ON sys.dba_users TO c##sec_mgr_role
  2  CONTAINER=CURRENT;

Grant succeeded.

sys@db12cr[cdb$root]> GRANT SELECT ON sys.dba_profiles TO c##sec_mgr_role
  2  CONTAINER=CURRENT;

Grant succeeded.

sys@db12cr[cdb$root]> GRANT SELECT ON sys.dba_sys_privs TO c##sec_mgr_role
  2  CONTAINER=CURRENT;

Grant succeeded.

sys@db12cr[cdb$root]> GRANT SELECT ON sys.dba_role_privs TO c##sec_mgr_role
  2  CONTAINER=CURRENT;

Grant succeeded.

sys@db12cr[cdb$root]> GRANT SELECT ON sys.dba_tab_privs TO c##sec_mgr_role
  2  CONTAINER=CURRENT;

Grant succeeded.

sys@db12cr[cdb$root]> GRANT SELECT ON sys.dba_policies TO c##sec_mgr_role
  2  CONTAINER=CURRENT;

Grant succeeded.

sys@db12cr[cdb$root]> GRANT SELECT ON sys.cdb_users TO c##sec_mgr_role
  2  CONTAINER=CURRENT;

Grant succeeded.

sys@db12cr[cdb$root]> GRANT SELECT ON sys.cdb_pdbs TO c##sec_mgr_role
  2  CONTAINER=CURRENT;
```

```
Grant succeeded.

sys@db12cr[cdb$root]> GRANT SELECT ON sys.cdb_sys_privs TO c##sec_mgr_role
  2  CONTAINER=CURRENT;

Grant succeeded.

sys@db12cr[cdb$root]> GRANT EXECUTE ON dbms_rls TO c##sec_mgr
  2  WITH GRANT OPTION
  3  CONTAINER=ALL;

Grant succeeded.

sys@db12cr[cdb$root]> GRANT EXECUTE ON dbms_rls TO c##sec_mgr_role
  2  CONTAINER=CURRENT;

Grant succeeded.
```

Pluggable Databases

Use the script Chapter2/appa.pdb.secmgr.sql to create the SEC_MGR account used in the book examples that execute for the SALES and HR pluggable databases.

Index

A

abnormal behavior, 492
access, description, 6
access control, 94
access control entries (ACEs)
    ACLs, 224
    configuring, 227–228
    RAS, 205, 221
access control lists (ACLs)
    configuring, 227–228
    description, 94, 224–225
    namespace protection, 234–236
    network policies, 479
    security classes, 226–227
ACCESSED GLOBALLY clause, 157
Account lockout constraints controls, 42
account profiles, 42
    password management, 42–45
    resource limitations, 47–51
    working with, 45–47
accountability, auditing for, 425
accounts, 476
    auditing commands for, 435–436
    connection pool, 19–20
    in containers, 35–36
    creating, 34
    managing, 476–477
    multitenant architecture, 21–22
    passwords, 40–41
    in pluggable databases, 36–39

privileges, 24–33
profiles. *See* account profiles
in RAS, 197–201
types, 18–20
user, 19, 469–471
ACTIONS ALL clause, 447
active-active availability, 495–496
active-passive availability, 495
adaptive security in DBV, 348
ADD_ACL_PARAMETER procedure, 231
ADD_AUTH_TO_REALM procedure, 361, 372
ADD_GLOBAL_CALLBACK procedure, 217, 220
ADD_GROUPED_POLICY procedure, 253
ADD_OBJECT_TO_REALM procedure, 370
ADD_POLICY procedure, 250, 298, 453
ADD_SENSITIVE_COLUMN procedure, 297
ADD_SENSITIVE_TYPE procedure, 296
ADF (Application Development Framework),
    65, 196
ADMINISTER KEY MANAGEMENT privilege, 401
ADMINISTER KEY MANAGEMENT statement,
    405, 407
ADMINISTER KEY MANAGEMENT SET
    KEYSTORE CLOSE statement, 404
administrative privileges, 22–24, 97
Advanced Security Option (ASO), 125, 390, 480
AES128 algorithm, 409
AES192 algorithm, 409
AES256 algorithm, 409
algorithms, encryption, 392–394, 409
ALL_CONTROL enforcement, 320

S

Join the Largest Tech Community in the World

 Download the latest software, tools, and developer templates

 Get exclusive access to hands-on trainings and workshops

 Grow your professional network through the Oracle ACE Program

 Publish your technical articles – and get paid to share your expertise

Join the Oracle Technology Network
Membership is free. Visit oracle.com/technetwork

@OracleOTN   facebook.com/OracleTechnologyNetwork